BAD RAD
FOOTBALL NOMAD

Originator of
"Steel Curtain" Defensive Line;
Super Bowl IX, X, XIV Offensive Lines;
and Father of
Penn State's "Linebacker U"

by Dan Radakovich and Lou Prato

Copyright © 2012 by Dan Radakovich

All rights reserved, including the right to reproduce this book or portions thereof in any form whatsoever.

First printing: November 2012

revised edition 2016: Nimble Books LLC

www.badradfootballnomad.com

ISBN 978-1-60888-408-7

To my wife, Nancy, and my children, Danny, Lisa, Leslie and Lori who lived through my nomadic life, and to my best friends, Joe Moore, Bud Carson and Joe Paterno, who are no longer around to share all these memories.

Joe Moore　　　　**Bud Carson**　　　　**Joe Paterno**

PHOTO CREDITS: Thanks to several sources many photographs are being used in this book. Special thanks go to Art Rooney II, the president of the Pittsburgh Steelers, for permission to use all the photos of players, coaches, scouts and management of the Steelers, and team photographer Mike Fabus for providing those photographs.

The photographs of Pittsburgh Steelers receiver John Stallworth (on page 50) and Dallas Cowboys receiver Percy Howard (on page 74) are used with the permission of NFL Films and company representative Linda Endres.

Denver Bronco photographers Eric Bakke and Keith Bishop provided the following photographs: John Elway, John Hadl, Edgar Kaiser, Keith Bishop, Dave Studdard, Paul Howard, Tom Glassic, Ken Lanier, Bill Bryan, Keith Uecker and Mark Cooper.

San Francisco 49ers photographer Michael Zagaris provided the photos of Bill Walsh, Ed DeBartolo, Jr., Joe Montana and John Frank.

Cleveland Browns VP of Media Relations, Neal Gulkis provided the photos of Clay Matthews, Mike Johnson and Ernest Byner.

Buffalo Bills Media Manager Matt Heidt provided Nick Nicolau's photograph.

Photographs of Los Angeles Rams players Rich Saul, Dennis Harrah, Jackie Slater and Hacksaw Reynolds came from the private collection of retired sportswriter Jimmy Campbell, and Colorado University Sports Information Director David Plati provided the photographs of John Stearns, Cullen Bryant and Loren Richardson.

Certain Penn State photographs were provided by the Penn State Athletic Communications or the Penn State Patee-Paterno Library Archives.

Many photographs came from the private collection of Dan Radakovich. Other photographs came from the private collections of the following people mentioned in the book: Ray Alberigi, Dick Anderson, John Beake, Jay Huffman, Dave Joyner, Dennis Onkotz, Mike Reid, Steve Smear, Kevin Somerville and Augie Tammariello.

FOREWORD — By Jack Ham

There is no one like Dan Radakovich. He was by far the best technique coach I ever saw and I am indebted to him. He's also a character, a truly unique individual and sometimes a little wacky, as you will read in this book. I have more respect for Rad as a coach than anybody I've ever been around, and I've been around a lot of them. I don't think most people realize what a great coach he was, not just at Penn State and the Steelers but everywhere he went. He made every team better, from Penn State to Robert Morris and all the other college and pro teams in between.

Rad started this tradition at Penn State of Linebacker U and he started the Steel Curtain with the Steelers. These are two of the most famous nicknames in the history of football and Rad is the man behind both. Yet, that fact is hardly known by most football fans and the media. Others have been given credit but Rad really deserves the recognition, and I should know because I was there.

You'll never find Rad's name among the Hall of Fame coaches like Joe Paterno, Chuck Noll or Vince Lombardi. But, believe me, in his own special niche among all the assistant coaches in football who never were head coaches, Dan Radakovich is at the top. As to why he never became a head coach, I just don't think it was in his DNA. If you heard he was going to be a head coach, you're expecting a 10-car pileup on the turnpike. You know it's going to happen, you just don't know when. That's partly because of his personality, not just the crazy side but his honesty and bluntness. He was always one notch different than anyone else.

When Rad tells you something you never need to have a conversation afterwards and say, what did Rad really mean? You know exactly. Rad tells you straight forward and never minces words. There is no filter with him. You may not like it and you may even hate him for a while, but if you listen to him you're going to be a much better player, and maybe a great one.

Rad can watch a player for a few minutes or look at video tapes of players and know who can play, who can't play and who he can work with. If you're a secondary coach, you'd be hard pressed to be able to coach something else. It didn't matter to Rad. Tell him the next position you want him to coach next and he'll do that.

Look what he did when he joined the Steelers as defensive line coach in my rookie year, 1971. Here's the best linebacker coach I ever had and I watched him overhaul that defensive line and turn them into the Steel Curtain. Then he leaves but flips it around two years later when he comes back as the offensive line coach and turns what had been an average offensive line into a strength of the team.

Give him time and Rad could coach any position. Maybe not quarterbacks, but if you challenged him he'd probably be able to do that, too.

Rad simply loves the independence of being an assistant coach. He has his own little fiefdom as a position coach and that's when he's the happiest. All he's ever wanted to do was coach players in hands-on techniques and the on-field tactics and strategy that win games. That doesn't matter if the team is a Super Bowl champion, a small college or a five-man football team at a catholic grade school, he coaches them all the same way because that's what he loves to do—coach. He enjoys seeing guys getting better and better and better. And he never changed from the first day I met him at the Corner Room restaurant in State College.

It's pretty well known that I received the last scholarship at Penn State in 1967 thanks to my close friend from high school, Steve Smear. We had played football and basketball at Bishop McCort in Johnstown but I was hardly recruited. So in 1966 Steve got a scholarship to Penn State and I went to a military prep school to try improve my football skills. A year later Steve suggested they talk to me, and I met Rad on my recruiting trip. Rad tells the story in this book and I remember it well.

I paid my own way and went up to visit with Steve in the spring and we went to breakfast or lunch in the Corner Room, which is a typical popular restaurant in a college town. Steve had played tight end in high school and they had moved him to defensive tackle. He's just getting beat up there and he's crushed. So, we're sitting in the Corner Room and Steve's bitching to me about it and telling me he's going to transfer to IUP, and Rad pops in and sits down. Rad seems to think we had planned to meet but I don't remember it that way.

Rad starts talking right away and he's not very tactful. "You think you're going to play linebacker, huh? Well how quick are you? You look too small. Can you tackle anyone?" I mean I just met this guy who is going to be my linebacker coach if they gave me a scholarship and he's actually hassling me. No smooth talk. Just coming at me. I'm thinking why would I want to play for this guy. Rad leaves and I said to Steve, "What's with this guy? I just met him and he's attacking me." Steve said, "That's just Rad and you expect that from him." I'm wondering if I really want to play for this guy. In the end, I could have gone to the Virginia Military Institute but I was tired of the military regimen and I accepted the Penn State scholarship. Of course, Steve didn't transfer and became a two-time co-captain and great defensive tackle on our undefeated teams in 1968 and 1969.

I didn't have anything to do with Rad as a freshman, but in the winter, I'd see him playing basketball in Rec Hall with the younger guys and he was very physical, hitting people and bouncing them around and I thought this guy's crazy.

Now, it's my first day of spring practice; I'm working on a drill and Rad's my coach. We played some Cover-2 defense back then and the biggest thing you cannot do is let the tight end release inside on you up the field because the two safeties in the back are threatened too much and you can't let a guy be screaming down the middle at them. Our tight end was no chump. It was Ted Kwalick, who would become an All-American that season and the next.

So, Ted gets an inside release on me and goes up the field. Rad takes off his hat and throws it at me. He takes off his whistle and throws it at me. And he takes his clip board and throws it at me. I'm thinking, who is this guy? Who is this crazy man? That was Rad's style, and he just made you better. Every day in practice he made you better.

Rad left after my junior season and I became a consensus All-American as a senior, but, frankly that was not my best year. Maybe that's because I was moved to middle linebacker and I'm much more comfortable playing outside linebacker. But

I believe if Rad had continued to be my coach he would have made me better, even at a new position.

In fact, Rad tried to get Chuck Noll to move me from outside to inside linebacker in my rookie year with the Steelers. That's another story he tells in this book. If that had happened I am sure he would have spent some time helping me learn that position even though he was only responsible for the defensive line.

Although he was never my coach at Pittsburgh I had a comfort level with him while he was with the Steelers, and that's when I got to really know him. However, the players he coached on the defensive and offensive lines didn't like him initially. He worked them hard and he didn't care if they liked him or not. If he didn't think they were good enough to play, he told them up front in his usual blunt manner.

In Chapter One Rad writes in detail about the creation of the Steel Curtain line, and it is all true because I saw it happening. Before preseason practice started, he spent a lot of time watching film of the players he inherited. Then after seeing the linemen work out in the first couple of weeks of camp, he changed it all around, telling three of the starters they weren't good enough to play full time anymore. Of course, they didn't take it well.

One of those linemen was Lloyd Voss, a starting defensive end and seven year veteran. Rad moved Lloyd to tackle where he had to share the position. A year later Voss was playing in Denver and by 1973 was out of the NFL. Lloyd was a tough guy but a nice man and we had become friends. He was working in Pittsburgh after his playing days and I invited him to my wedding. That almost turned into a disaster for me and my wife Joanne when he and Rad almost got into a fight. They were drinking a lot and Lloyd was still teed off at Rad and they had words. I had to get them separated or Lloyd might have killed him.

Actually, when Rad came back in 1974 his offensive line players wanted to kill him because he was really tough on them and he had them doing so many things. I'll give you one example. In training camp at St. Vincent, Rad would have me come over after our formal practice and help him with his famous mirror dodge drill against some of the linemen.

I'd be positioned at the 10-yard line and Rad would have guys like Bruce Van Dyke, Gerry Mullin and Ray Mansfield try to keep me from scoring between two plastic traffic cones placed eight yards apart. Now that is hard to do for these big linemen and some of them were not very athletic. I could do any type of moves in a pretty wide area to get into the end zone. Rad figured if these guys could defend against a quick guy like me it would be easier in a game against a defensive end or tackle. This was a tough drill for those offensive linemen and they were frustrated because they were losing all the time. Sometimes a couple of other linebackers would come over and join us and the line was getting beat up. Remember this is after practice at camp when we're already having two-a-days. As I said, they were ready to kill him.

Then after the season began, I remember him having meetings with the offensive line at the airport before our plane left for a game. He'd have them come out an hour earlier than the rest of us and it used to drive those guys crazy. But that was Rad. At the end of the day, he made those players better. We won championships and our offensive line was a major reason why.

Now, I have written very little about Rad's eccentric nature and the many odd ball experiences he has had in his life. That's also part of what this autobiography is about. You can read them for yourself, and if you want a preview just look at his story titles in the table of contents. I've heard about a lot of them, such as the time he was going to law school and coaching in Cincinnati when he walked into the wrong house and started studying at the kitchen table before realizing it. Then there's that mirror dodge drill I just mentioned and the day Rad did the drill with the late actor Ray Bolger, Scarecrow from the *Wizard of Oz*, in the middle of a country club bar in Beverly Hills. One time he didn't show up for a game in Buffalo until nearly halftime, and at least twice—once when playing linebacker at Penn State and years later when coaching the Denver Broncos—his head coaches made him see a psychologist because of his off-beat personality. I think just about everyone who has met Rad has a zany story about him.

But, again, that's just Rad being Rad, whether it's on the field or off it. And when you say that's Rad being Rad, the guys who know him get it. We get this craziness. We get this weird personality that also makes him such a great coach. My dad understood it, too.

My father John was a quiet, unassuming guy who was a mechanic in the coal mines. If Rad said something to my dad, it was gospel. They were strange bedfellows. My dad never came into the locker room, and Paterno never saw him. My dad never said, "I want more playing time for my son," and some of the other stuff coaches have to put up with. But for some reason my dad felt that Rad was a stabilizing force and he just went to the wall with anything Rad said. I don't know if Rad realizes he and my dad had that kind of relationship, but if Rad said anything my dad would agree with him.

These days I still see Rad frequently. My office near the Pittsburgh International Airport is about a mile from Rad's home and neither I nor my office manager, Terrie Cook, are surprised when Rad pops in unexpectedly on one of his bike rides. He's been officially retired for five years from his last coaching job at Robert Morris, but Rad will never stop coaching and teaching. He is still doing coaching clinics around the country and he'll do that as long as he can. There is always one more player Rad believes he can make better, whether it is a veteran pro or a kid in high school. They might not like what he tells them and how he tells them but sooner or later they will be glad they listened to him.

He's Bad Rad, A Coaching Nomad, the man who created Linebacker U and the Steel Curtain, and I'm happy to call him my friend.

EDITOR'S NOTE – Jack Ham and Dave Robinson are the only Penn State football players enshrined in both the College Football Hall of Fame and the Pro Football Hall of Fame. After an All-American career at Penn State (1968-70) as a starter on back-to-back undefeated teams that finished No. 2 in the country, he was an All-Pro linebacker with the Pittsburgh Steelers (1971-82) and played on four Super Bowl champions. Ham is considered by most college football historians as the greatest linebacker ever at Penn State. After football he became a successful businessman, and since 2000 he also has been the game day analyst for the Penn State radio network.

INTRODUCTION

I never thought about writing an autobiography until a few years ago, and this is not your typical sports autobiography. I say that because this is written differently than most autobiographies. What I do is tell stories about my experiences in life and particularly in my career in football.

For decades I have been telling stories like the hundreds you will read, and after hearing my stories people have been telling me I should write a book. They said I was an innovative coach who was a "spacey character" and there was no one else like me in college and professional football. I'm not sure about that, but I know I have an unusual, quirky personality. I'm pretty sure that goes back to growing up around the famous Kennywood Amusement Park in suburban Pittsburgh. But I'm no kook. I have an undergraduate business degree, an MBA and have studied law. And I also have been pretty serious about playing football in high school, college and the NFL, and even more serious about coaching football—and coaching has been my profession for more than 50 years. In fact, even though I officially retired from coaching a team in 2008, I am still involved in football coaching clinics and football summer camps around the country. I love it and I'll continue doing it as long as I can.

Now, I'm not famous like a couple of the coaches I have worked with in my career, Joe Paterno and Chuck Noll. In fact, except for one day in Cincinnati, I have never been an official head coach—although I was an interim head coach for Robert Morris University for one week. It's not that I didn't have the ambition to be a head coach. Things just happened along the way, as you will read. Furthermore, I have pretty strong opinions about coaching and personal relationships. To use the cliché, I have been told I "march to my own drummer," and I guess that's right. It's one reason people say I've earned my nickname as "Bad Rad." You'll will have a better understanding of all that after reading this book.

However, I am well known within the football coaching fraternity. That goes back initially to my years at Penn State when I became the school's first linebacker coach and eventually became known as "The Father of Linebacker U." Then when I put together the defensive front line at the Pittsburgh Steelers that became "The Steel Curtain" and subsequently with the Steelers introduced a couple of innovations that changed the NFL rules in offensive line blocking, my reputation grew and was enhanced as an innovative assistant coach.

My co-author and friend, Lou Prato, says I epitomize the lifelong assistant coach who never became a head coach for one reason or another but was always a dedicated and loyal professional. He said it is "a capricious, insecure and itinerant way of life, with sudden job changes frequently predicated on the whim of a team owner or a beleaguered head coach rather than the quality of work of the assistant" and I have to agree with him. I was a coaching nomad. From 1957 through 2007 I coached at five universities and nine professional teams from coast to coast and in Europe—several times leaving a specific team and returning years later to coach for the same team. Lou says my resume "reads like a travel brochure—State College, Cincinnati, Pittsburgh, Boulder, Pittsburgh, San Francisco, Los Angeles, Raleigh, Denver,

Minneapolis, New York, Cleveland, Pittsburgh, Los Angeles, St. Louis, Pittsburgh, London in England and Pittsburgh."

I guess that's true, but it does include college teams that had three undefeated seasons and went to 10 bowl games. It also includes starting a college team from scratch at Robert Morris University in 1994 and taking that team to two consecutive national championships five and six years later in 1999 and 2000. Plus, I was a coach on NFL teams that were in 19 playoff games (including five conference championship games and three Super Bowls). I've coached dozens of college and professional players in my career, including three players in the College Football Hall of Fame—Jack Ham, Dennis Onkotz and Mike Reid—and four players in the Pro Football Hall of Fame—Ham, Mean Joe Greene, Jackie Slater and Mike Webster. I've also coached hundreds of high school kids like Bill Belichick and others you never heard of in summer football camps. It's been an interesting experience to say the least.

I've been asked if I have any regrets about my career or if I would have changed anything if I had a chance. Well, we all have some regrets but we don't live in the Hollywood world of Jimmy Stewart in the movie *It's A Wonderful Life*. We can't go back and do things differently. But there was one specific occasion I regret. That was when the Steelers wanted to hire me back for the third time in 1982, a few days after I had taken a job as offensive line coach at North Carolina State. Because of my loyalty to the kids I was coaching I turned down the offer and a few months later I was sandbagged by my head coach. You can read about it in the chapter entitled "The Fork in the Road."

Incidentally, I met Jimmy Stewart and other movie stars like Cary Grant, Ricardo Montalban and Jonathan Winters when I was coaching for the Los Angeles Rams. One of those actors, Ray Bolger, who played the Scarecrow in *The Wizard of Oz*, went one on one with me in a football drill in a country club bar and you'll read about that, too, in the story I call, "The Scarecrow."

It's stories like these that fill the pages in this book. I'll tell you about being sent to see a psychiatrist by my own college coach at Penn State because I looked like a Hippie and then 30 years later in the NFL I had to talk to another "shrink" because my head coach didn't like me showing up at the office wearing Bermuda shorts and flip flops. I'll tell you about the time I was going to law school and was so intent on my studies that I walked into the wrong house in my neighborhood and sat at the kitchen table with my books for several minutes before realizing it. And I'll tell you about the time I found myself at the bottom of my life, between coaching jobs, working in a warehouse near Disneyland with not enough money in my pocket to take a bus home. You can also read how I was involved in the Cleveland Browns' infamous Earnest Byner trade that helped the Washington Redskins reach the Super Bowl and win it.

You'll learn how Penn State came to be called Linebacker U and how Joe Paterno almost was fired in his first season as head coach. You'll also get the inside on a famous Pittsburgh Steelers quarterback controversy involving Terry Bradshaw and Jefferson Street Joe Gilliam. Then there is my story that hardly anyone remembers about a play that could have changed history in Super Bowl X—the game featured in the movie *Black Sunday*.

We all have our six degrees of separation with people we meet and I have my share. When I was growing up, the world famous Barnum & Baily circus clown Emmett Kelly frequently let me ride his midget bicycle around my neighborhood. Years later I would become friends with Billy Conn, one of the great boxers of all time. And who would have thought when Iowa coach Kirk Ferentz asked me to teach one of his graduated linemen how to coach linebackers a few years ago that the man would eventually became the head coach at Wisconsin, Bret Bielema?

Kirk's high school coach in suburban Pittsburgh was my best friend, Joe Moore, who may have been the greatest offensive line coach ever in college football. Joe is central to many of my stories, and a couple in particular about some linebacker drills I created at Penn State in the 1960s that were demonstrated in a court room 35 years later when Joe sued—and won—an age discrimination case against Notre Dame.

Yes, there's a lot about Penn State and the Pittsburgh Steelers in this book, but you'll also find much, much more as you read about my nomadic journey through college and professional football.

I hope you enjoy my book.

TABLE OF CONTENTS

Foreword [by Jack Ham]

CHAPTER ONE – The Steel Curtain — Page 1
A Future Lawyer, Calling Chuck Noll, Becoming a Steeler Coach, The Interview, B+ Post Card, Connoisseur Chuck Noll, Creating the Steel Curtain, Defensive Line-Quick as Linebackers, Defensive Hall of Fame Members, Not Good But Better, Jack Ham at Middle Linebacker, One Legged Cripple, Bad Rad's a Racist, Dwight White Visits Alma Mater, The Last Time I Saw Dwight, Cheering Coaches, Butkus is Hurt, Warfield's Greatest Game, Joe Greene Wants Traded, The Florida Everglades, Lionel Takes a Rookie Coach Under His Wing, Overnight Defensive Coordinator, Drafting Franco, The Chief

CHAPTER TWO – The Seven Dwarfs — Page 21
Hired as Offensive Line Coach, Building a Champion, 1974 Hall of Fame Draft, May Be Better Than Swann, Research Blocking Changes & Bending the Rules, Tailored Taped Jerseys A Crutch?, Pregame Ritual, The Seven Dwarfs, Please Don't Trade Jon Kolb, Kolb Does The Opposite, Don't Ever Do That To Me Again, High School Drills, A Lesson In Poise, 10 Worst Minutes Of My Life, Play Until You're 40, Spaz tells Bres, Lionel's Receiver Manual, Saga of Henry Davis, Strike During Training Camp

CHAPTER THREE – Bumpy Road to the Super Bowl — Page 39
The Quarterback Controversy, Crossing the Picket Line, Jefferson Street Joe, Marching to a Different Drummer, Wrong House, Bradshaw Becomes Starter Again, Joe Gilliam Fades Away, Earth to Rad...Earth to Rad, In a Football Haze, Back on the Sideline, First Playoff Game Dec. 22 1974, Fashion Show Christmas Present, Steeler Fever Joey Diven and Billy Conn, Art Thoms Lines up in the Steelers Backfield, Cousin Raymond Calls Howard Cosell, Worst Officials Call in History, Biggest Thrill of All, Ball Control And Defense, Bad Rad vs Jimmy Brown, Super Bowl IX Eve, Super Bowl IX Pregame Tension, The Surprise Kickoff

CHAPTER FOUR – Bad Rad Day — Page 55
Bad Rad Day, Unusual Coaching Experience, Bud Carson's Chauffeur, Bad Rad's Chauffeur, Bud's Dealer Car, Sleep Walking Bud, Lying to a Friend, Heard Footsteps, Early Bumpy Road, Curly Who?, The Play That Never Fails, Andy's Fumble, Recovery, Icy Snow-Swept Windy Playoff Game

CHAPTER FIVE – The Pass That Could Have Changed History — Page 69
The Pass That Changed History, Newsday Critique, Who's Percy Howard, Halftime of Super Bowl X, Nancy's Forever Ring, Not Entirely a Bed of Roses, Joe Had to Go, Good Idea Down the Drain, My Biggest Draft Mistakes, Blocking Defensive Coordinator, He's Going to be a Great Player, End of the Seven Dwarfs, 10 Game Winning Streak, Take a Miracle to Win, I'm Not Playing Right Tackle, Agent Orange, Late Surge Saves Season, I Beg Your Pardon, Last Game with the Steelers

CHAPTER SIX – The Roots of Linebacker U — Page 91
Kennywood Childhood, Put Back in 2nd Grade and Johnnie Saunders, 1st Athletic Experience, My Piano Stories, First Recruiting Experience, Football – A Man's Game, Camp Wintergreen, Make Him the Snapper, Cookie Becomes Bad Rad-Poor Coopuss, New Nickname, Recruiting was an Experience, Harvard, Ivy, Indiana, Boston U, Navy, Pitt, Penn State, Duquesne Serbs, Bad Rad Needs to See a Psychiatrist, Captain of the Freshmen Team, Pretty Freshman Girl, The Slide Block, Beetle Goes to Church, Knocking on the Door, Intramural Boxing Tournament, Bad Rad Sees a Psychiatrist, Stopping Jimmy Brown, Ubiquitous Penn State Party, Chasing Oscar, Sleeping Beauty, Bad Rad vs. Jimmy Brown, Summer School, A Historical Turning Point, Illegal Penalty for Legal Substitution, Playing Against Former Penn Staters, Getting Carried Away by a Victory, Blue Gray Game, The Wedding

CHAPTER SEVEN – The First Professor of Linebacker U — Page 119
Drafted by the Eagles, Preseason Games, My Last Game as a Player, Getting Cut, Coaching Freshman Football, The Father of Linebacker U, Becoming A Linebacker's Coach, Redskin Preseason Camp, Meeting Chuck Drazenovich, Redskin Drills, Getting Injured, Returning to Penn State, The First Liberty Bowl, In Bed with the Wrong Woman, The Tavern and The Hays in the Barn Party, Early Years Coaching Linebackers, Getting an MBA, Ralph Baker, Stuffing Glen Ressler in One-on-One Drill, The Intensity of Joe Blasenstein, The Creation of Mat Tackling & Mirror Dodge Drills, Mirror Dodge on Trial-In a Courtroom?

CHAPTER EIGHT – Rip's Last 5 Years   Page 141
My Cousin Raymond, Study Group with the Big Dumb Football Player, Meeting Dave Joyner's Father, Bowl Memories, Liberty Bowls, 1961 Gator Bowl, Blue and White Wins Because of Green, Back to St. Augustine with a Stop at the White House, Rocky Marciano and Al Davis, Eliminating Starting Blocks, Deaf Player Hears "Go", One of Woody Hayes' Worst Defeats of All Time, Last Player Bowl Vote, Con Job, Pioneer Ranch, Evolving the Multiple Defense That Helped Change Penn State Defensive Football, UCLA's Helmet Telephone, Rip's Last Year

CHAPTER NINE– Joe Paterno Era Begins   Page 157
New Head Coach, Fort Rad, Second Multiple Defense Presentation, Preseason Recruiting, Best Players Always Linebackers, Formation Change, Joe Paterno's 1st Game as Head Coach, Athletic Director's Threat to Fire Joe Paterno the First Year, The Moment Joe Paterno Started to Become a Great Coach, Do It Again, Defensive Spring Practice, Going with Experience, Crowd Cheering a Loss, When in Doubt, Punt!, Scissors in the Glove Compartment, Multiple Defense – Undefeated, Goal-Line Stand – 12 Man Defense, Athletic Grievance Board, 4 Point versus 3 Point Stance, Bill Belichick

CHAPTER TEN- The Phi Beta Kappa's of Linebacker U   Page 167
Blowing the National Championship, Mike Reid, Lineman and Linebacker, Mike Reid Meeting Dave Joyner, Beethoven, vs Gershwin, Reid and Smear Elected Co-Captains, Recruiting Smear and Jack Ham, Another Future NFL Linebacker, Playing the Unbeaten Former Penn Staters, Playboy All-American, Jack Ham and Fritz, Radgate, The Night Meeting, Coaching in Law School, Job Interview and Law School, Leaving Linebacker U, Linebacker U Continues, Nothing Succeeds Like Success

CHAPTER ELEVEN – My Marco Polo Journey Begins   Page 191
Book Room Bedroom, Benching a Two Year Starter, Coaching Dilemma, Player Quitting – Good or Bad, Better than Penn State, Reporting Weight, Deck of Cards Playbook, Legal Dribble, That's Not Sal Casola, My NCAA Record Throw, Never Help a Friend, Predictable Cradle of Coaches, No. 1 Draft Pick Bob Bell versus No. 2 Draft Pick Jack Ham, Missed Seeing Super Bowl V, Day Law School Rejection

CHAPTER TWELVE– Rocky Mountain High and the Dawn Patrol   Page 201
When You're Cool--the Sun Always Shines, Deck of Cards Again, Hale Learns Golf, Offensive Coaches Catch Hell, TV Show – Colorado Tomorrow, 1972- First Five Games, New and Different Experiences, The Spy and the FBI, Friday Night Defense, Bad Rad Coaches A Bad Dude, Radakovich Quits Undefeated, Always See an Ophthalmologist, Eddie Takes Control, Recruiting the Selmons, Disloyalty or Disagreement, Becoming a Receiver Coach, Hope to Finish the Season, Dawn Patrol

CHAPTER THIRTEEN – From the Steelers to the Golden Gate   Page 219
49er Organization, Take This Job and Shove It, Returning to the 49ers, Unique Penn Stater, Talking with Bill Walsh

CHAPTER FOURTEEN – Hooray for Hollywood   Page 227
Los Angeles Interview, Carroll Rosenbloom Funeral, The Scarecrow, Ram Mini-Camp and Tony Wise, Bed Check on Fred Dryer, Ram Equipment Men, The Party, 1979—The First Nine Games, Greatest Defensive Game in NFL History, Road to Super Bowl XIV, Family Ticket Deal, Super Bowl XIV, Mean Joe Greene and The 70s Steelers, The American Plan, No Wasted Motion, Offensive Line Coach Joe Moore, You've Got To Draft Grimm, John Frank Attends Rams Mini-Camp

CHAPTER FIFTEEN– "A Fork in the Road"   Page 251
Cowboys and Indians, Sleeping Beauty, Ray Malavasi's New Contract, Can He Recruit, Contract Trouble – On Strike, Congressman's Son, Drew Hill's Takeoff Pattern, Howard Cosell and Joe Montana, Escaping the Guillotine (For a Few Hours), American Express, Bill Walsh's Story, Working in the Warehouse, Wrong Bus, Singing Packer, Hot Line Rings, Chuck Noll Calls, Midseason Job Change, United States Football League

CHAPTER SIXTEEN - The Shrink   Page 267
Denver Interview, Like Father Like Son, Claudia Minor Retires, Trade for Elway, The Denver Offensive Line, Bad Rad Isn't Bad--Just Different, The Shrink Appears, Farewell Note to the Shrink

CHAPTER SEVENTEEN – From Siberia to Broadway   Page 281
Joining the Minnesota Vikings, The Old, The New, The Unusual, Please Draft Ed West, Lawyer Tim Irwin, The Seabees, A Tough Season, Below Zero, New York, New York, It's A Wonderful Town, Jets Linebacker Coach, The Honeymoon, Point Lookout a Unique Place, Crable's Corners, Jets Long-Snapping Coach, A New Defense, The 1985 Jets Season, Mark Gasteneau and the Sports Cars, Quick Hands, Cool Proposal

CHAPTER EIGHTEEN – Times Square to the Dog Pound Page 297

Players Union Sues Jets, No. 1 and No. 2 Draft Picks, Left Tackle – Right Handed Stance, Bad Rad Camp, Sports Illustrated Cover – Almost, High and Low Season, The Strike of 1987, After the Strike, The Vegetable, Buddy Ryan Keeps His Job, One and one Half Days of Royalty, Back on Defense, Coaching Linebackers for A Former Rival, Byner for Oliphant Trade, Plan B, Browns Defensive Staff, What About Me?, Buy or Build, Returning to Pittsburgh, Division Winners, Late for the Plane, You Were at the Same Game, The Interception and the Gloves, Third Time's A Charm, (Back on Offense), Offensive Line Coach Again, A Forgettable Season, Early Retirement

CHAPTER NINETEEN – Small College Football Page 317

Married for Better or For Worse, Filling 550 Beds, Great Deal on a Room, Turning a Night Job Into a Day Job, First Young Coach Hired, Prolific Phone Call, John Jay – An Easy Decision, Fired the Architect, Completing the First Football Staff, Corky Came Through in the Clutch, Joe Walton Celebrity Golf Tournament, Equipment Man Quits, First Football Meeting, First Injury in Team History, Generation Gap, He Looked Pretty Good, First Game Plan Meeting, Goal-Line Stand in First Game, Monday Night TV, Open Date Decision, Flunking Football, Winning Record, Ortmayer Calls- Returning to the Rams, Deke and I Are Roommates, Bidding War Nets Sweeney $600,000, Warren Sapp Worth the Risk, Preseason Camp in St. Louis, Where's Rad? Alternating Against Reggie White, How Bad Rad taught Reggie White "the Hump", First St. Louis Rams Home Game, Good Beginning-Bad Ending

CHAPTER TWENTY – The House That Bad Rad Built Page 359

Three Million to 17 Million, Can My Buddy Come, Too?, Freudian Slip, Not Outhit, But Outsmarted, I Love This Defense, NFL Europe Draft, Preseason NFL Europe, Move to London, Inexperienced Coach, 1997 NFL Europe Season, No Double Dipping, Political Poll for ECAC Bowl, Losing Season But Competitive, A New Look in '99, Last Piece of the Puzzle, Undefeated, Iowa Visitor, Bad Beginning-Good Ending, Quitting Smoking, Hindsight, Two Hail Mary's, Low Point at Robert Morris, The House That Rad Built, Getting even with R~owan & No. 1 on Defense, Head Coach for a Day, Saga of Mike Miller, Retirement & Offense-Defense Camps

LineBacker U. graphic

Index

Brown 93 diagram

Acknowledgements

Lou Prato and Wife

CHAPTER ONE – The Steel Curtain

I always wanted to play for the Pittsburgh Steelers, just like most kids who grow up in the Pittsburgh area. My hometown of Kennywood is famous for an amusement park that was practically in the middle of my neighborhood, and is about eight miles from the Oakland section of Pittsburgh, where the Steelers played in the 1940s and 1950s, either at Pitt Stadium or Forbes Field. Those old stadiums are gone now, but I remember seeing my first Steelers game in 1945 in Forbes Field.

My godfather, Dan Staisey, who was a close friend of Steelers owner Art Rooney Sr., gave me a gift of a reserve Steelers season ticket every Christmas from 1945 until I went to college in 1953. My Steelers heroes were Bullet Bill Dudley, an all around offensive and defensive back who is now in the Pro Football Hall of Fame, and middle linebacker Jerry Shipkey. I knew I could never be a running back because I lacked speed but I guess idolizing Jerry was my first inclination that I would someday be a linebacker.

Never in my dreams would I have thought my NFL playing career as a linebacker would come to a quick close at Forbes Field after being carried off the field near the end of a Steelers-Eagles preseason game in 1957. I'll tell you more about that in Chapter Seven. But I also never dreamed I would one day be standing on the sidelines at the Steelers home field, Three Rivers Stadium, as the team's newest assistant coach in 1971 in charge of the defensive line. It wasn't what I had dreamed about in Kennywood but it would turn out to be just as good—and probably better.

A Future Lawyer – I had never thought about being a football coach. But while finishing up my undergraduate business degree at Penn State in 1957-58, I was hired as an undergraduate assistant to help coach the freshman football team. As you will learn later, that ultimately led to me being Penn State's first full time linebackers coach from 1960 through 1969 when I decided I wanted to get a law degree.

So, at the end of Penn State's great undefeated 1968-69 football seasons, I resigned as the linebackers coach to become the defensive coordinator at the University of Cincinnati and attend Chase Law School at night. I loved Penn State and my job and I probably could have stayed coaching there the rest of my life, like most of my colleagues. Since I never envisioned coaching as a career, I had obtained an MBA at Penn State. Now, law school also appealed to me for many reasons. However, I couldn't afford to leave coaching and go to law school full time, but I knew I'd have to leave Penn State to do both. The nearest law school was in Carlisle or Pittsburgh and there was no way I could commute and coach at the same time. I had to find a place where I could coach during the day and go to law school at night. A lot of head coaches wouldn't even want an assistant spending much of his time attending law school and studying, but Ray Callahan at Cincinnati did. Sixteen months later, everything changed because of some political shenanigans involving the law school and not the team. My finances were draining, too, and I could no longer stay in Cincinnati.

Calling Chuck Noll – In the middle of May, 1971, I remembered that the Steelers defensive line coach, Walt Hackett, had died of a heart attack while watching practice at San Diego State University. On a whim I called the Steelers and got head coach Chuck Noll on the phone. Chuck didn't know who I was, but after I quickly informed him of my Penn State background, he was willing to talk to me. He said the Steelers hadn't hired anyone because the Rooney's, who owned the team, told him he couldn't do any interviews until six weeks after the funeral. I kept spouting off names of people that I knew that had coached with him, but he didn't seem interested at all. I hung up the phone and told my wife Nancy, "There's no job there. He doesn't know me from Adam."

Becoming A Steelers Coach – The next day, which was Thursday, the phone rang and it's Chuck Noll. He sounded like a different person. He was all enthused and wanted me to come for an interview. However, he was all booked up with interviews the next week and he wouldn't be able to see me until the week after. I said, "How about tomorrow?" It was already late Thursday afternoon. He said, "How can you do that?" I said I can get in the car in an hour, drive six or seven hours to Pittsburgh, stay at my parents' house and be there in the morning. He said, "Okay, be here at nine o'clock."

The Interview – I parked in front of the Steelers office at Three Rivers Stadium at 8:30 a.m., tried the front door and it was locked. At exactly one minute to 9 o'clock, Mrs. Duffy, the scouting department secretary, came by, opened the door, and invited me inside. In the next 15 minutes, everyone who worked in the football office came in—scouts, coaches, secretaries, etc. After having a cup of coffee, my interview started at exactly 9:30 with me standing in front of a blackboard talking to Noll, and Charlie Sumner, the secondary coach. They are both sitting in chairs. Without much chit-chat, Chuck said to tell them what I knew about defensive line play.

Now, if you are not a football coach, you might not completely understand what I was about to tell Chuck. I wanted to explain that I would coach the defensive linemen to be as aggressive as possible on both run and pass plays. For my readers who know the intricacies of football, this should be easy to understand. Here is what I actually told Chuck.

"Defensive lineman should squeeze the line of scrimmage as tight as possible without being offside. They should move on the snap of the ball, reading the offensive lineman in front of or to their inside as they charge. I don't like lineman reading before they move or being flexed back off the ball. The general rule is that they should close inside unless the offensive lineman goes to hook them outside or pulls outside. When being this aggressive, they will be caught many times (with the blocker between him and ball carrier). Then they must back door it (getting their arm over behind the blocker), give and go (jump back and go around the blocker) or rip (which is an uppercut) across blocker's face. On drop back passes, they should attack one side or the other of the blocker while staying in their pass rush lane using their hands and making as little contact as possible. The exception to this is a power rush, where the defensive lineman gets both hands inside the blocker's chest and drives him straight back, and then makes a rip (uppercut) or swim (arm over) move. They should get hands up whenever possible or reasonable. After the ball has been thrown, they should pursue full speed until the ball touches the ground, (use your eyes, don't rely on a whistle), and that's all I know about defensive line play."

I stopped. It was now 9:35. Chuck said, "Is that all?" I said, "Yep, but if you want to talk about coverage, I know a lot about that." Chuck said, "Okay, talk to us about coverage." Well, for the next 20 minutes I talked about cover two, cover two man, half coverage, and so on. They didn't even use most of it in pro ball yet. After 20 minutes (it's now 9:55), Chuck said, "That's enough," and he turned to Charlie Sumner and said, "Charlie, wouldn't it be great to have a defensive line coach that knows coverage." Charlie didn't answer, because I'm sure he knew, like I knew, that knowing coverage was not at all necessary to be a good defensive line coach.

Chuck Noll spent the rest of the day until 6:00 p.m. selling me on the Steelers, but said he couldn't offer me the job because it wouldn't be fair to the five people he was going to interview the next week. He said he would let me know at the end of that next week. At 3:05 on Friday of the next week the phone rang. It was Chuck Noll, and he offered me the job. The last interviewee must have just left the Steelers office. I said I'd take the job if I could go to law school nights at Duquesne University. We had talked about law school the day of my interview. He said fine. I hung up and went back to study for my last law exam in contracts.

B+ Postcard – I was to report to the Steelers soon after my final law exam in contracts. I left a postcard with the professor of my contracts class to mail me my grade. I addressed the card to the Steelers office because I thought by the time it was mailed that I would be there. My post card with a B+ grade in contracts on it preceded me by a couple of days. Noll, who had been a part-time law student when he played for the Cleveland Browns, spread the word that I had gotten a B+ on my contracts exam, and how tough a course that was. When I reported to the Steelers a few days after my postcard arrived, I could tell from comments that different people made that the word was out that I was really smart, and I tried not to do anything to discourage that view.

Connoisseur Chuck Noll – The month of June and the first week in July was vacation time in 1971 for most of the Steelers organization. However, Noll and Charlie Sumner spent the entire month of June tutoring me on the Steelers defenses. They really took me under their wing off the field as well. I had read in the newspaper that Chuck was a connoisseur of fine foods and wines. Every weekday during the month-long tutoring session, the three of us went to a different restaurant, diner, luncheonette, hotdog joint, or whatever for lunch. Chuck loved to go to different places to eat. After a month of eating lunch at every dive in Pittsburgh's North Side, I told him I knew what kind of connoisseur he was: "A connoisseur who loves to eat and drink anything and everything everywhere he goes." He laughed because he knew it was true.

Creating The Steel Curtain – During tutoring sessions on the Steelers defenses that June, I watched a lot of Steelers defensive film from the previous two years. At that time, the Steelers coaches and organization considered the defensive line the strongest part of the team. The defensive line starters were all experienced starters: Ben McGee and Lloyd Voss at defensive end and Joe Greene and Chuck Hinton at defensive tackle. They were all about 6-foot-3 or 4 and weighed between 260 and 280 pounds. Except for Joe Greene, they were all about 31 years old. At 25, Greene had the most ability, and was the fastest with a 5.1 in a 40-yard dash. He had been the Steelers' No. 1 draft choice in 1969 from North Texas State, the fourth player selected in the entire draft and an immediate starter. The others were very good technique players and hustlers who had been starters the previous two years. Voss, McGee and Hinton's times for the 40-yard dash were between 5.6 and 5.8.

While watching the films with Noll and Sumner, a skinny, tall player named L.C. Greenwood who was 6-foot-6, 235-pounds caught my attention as he ran like a deer in pursuit across the field. He had been clocked at a 4.7 in the 40-yard dash. L.C. had been drafted the same year as Greene out of little Arkansas-Pine Bluff but much later, in the 10th round and the 238th overall pick. He hardly played as a backup in two years with the Steelers, always late in games when the outcome had already been decided. The previous line coach, Walt Hackett, had thought that L.C. was both too light and inexperienced to play. Noll thought that L.C. had possibilities and that I should take a close look at him. On the first day of preseason camp at St. Vincent College, L.C. lapped the entire team—every single player—in the 12-minute run held at the end of the first day's practice. Needless to say, L.C. made a pretty good first impression on me early in camp.

Steel Curtain (left to right) – Dwight White, Ernie Holmes, Joe Greene, L.C. Greenwood

Two rookies also impressed me in camp. Dwight "Mad Dog" White was our fourth round draft pick from Texas A&M-Commerce and a 6-foot-4, 235-pound defensive end with a 4.7 in the 40 yard dash. And Ernie "Fats" Holmes was a 6-foot-2, 270-pound defensive tackle whom the Steelers drafted in the eighth round from Texas Southern. Ernie was still a little raw and unsure of himself but he had a 5.1 in the 40 and a body at that time that was not fat but was like a block of granite. I knew he had the potential to be a good one, but because he kept stopping his feet upon contact when rushing the passer, he wasn't quite ready.

After the first couple of weeks of preseason camp, I went to Chuck with a plan to change the defensive line. I wanted to replace both starting defensive ends, McGee and Voss, with Greenwood and White. I also wanted to put McGee and Voss at right defensive tackle, along with Hinton, and have the three of them compete for the starting right tackle position. I left Greene alone at the left tackle, and who wouldn't.

My reasoning for making these changes wasn't difficult to understand. Replacing two 5.7/40-yard dash ends with two 4.7/40-yard dash ends would increase our team pursuit and pass rush speed by at least two full seconds per play (in 40 yard dash language). Noll agreed, and immediately made the moves.

One of the assistant coaches, Lionel Taylor who coached the receivers, told me I was crazy to be messing with what he considered to be the strongest part of the team, the defensive line. Another assistant, our offensive line coach, Bob Fry, said, "How can you put Greenwood on the first team? Do you know what Butkus did to him?" "No," I said, "what did Butkus do?" Fry said, "Greenwood was running down under a kickoff against the Chicago Bears and Dick Butkus was on the Bears kickoff return team. Butkus hit Greenwood and knocked him out cold." I said, "Is that all? Butkus does that to everyone!" I had seen films of Butkus when he played in college. It was not unusual to get knocked around or down by Butkus.

After our second regular season game against the Bengals, we traded our right defensive tackle Chuck Hinton to the New York Jets for Dennis Onkotz, a linebacker I had coached at Penn State before we became known as Linebacker U who had been a two-time All-American. The trade left me with both the two former starting defensive ends to play the right tackle position. I didn't know which one would be a better right defensive tackle, so I decided to alternate them. Ben McGee had some injuries during the season, so Lloyd Voss ended up playing more than Ben. Ernie Holmes made the practice squad but for some reason which I don't remember, he took off for his home in Texas, right after he made the final cut. I told the Steelers front office to get him back because he was a great prospect. Art Rooney Jr. called Ernie in Texas and got Ernie to come back.

Ernie was only gone a few days. When Ernie was a rookie and rushed the passer, he could lift an offensive lineman off the ground and throw him out of his way. But he stopped his feet while doing this. He had to learn to keep his feet moving as he rushed the passer, which he eventually did. Ernie spent the 1971 season on the practice (taxi) squad. He practiced all year but was not activated to play in any league games. He was exceptionally quick laterally as a rookie. In 1972, when George Perles was the defensive line coach, Ernie alternated with Ben McGee at the right defensive tackle spot. In 1973, after McGee retired, Ernie became the full-time starter at right defensive tackle.

The revamped 1971 defensive line was so much better than the previous line that some fans wanted to give it a nickname. One of those fans wrote to the sports editor of the *Pittsburgh Post-Gazette*, Al Abrams, and Al mentioned it in his "Sideline on Sports" column on Oct. 9, 1971: "Richard D. Idler of Upper St. Clair thinks the Steelers great defensive line should be called the 'Iron Curtain.' That brief item stirred a lot interest, and a short time later sportscaster Tom Bender of WTAE radio and TV held a nickname contest.

The *Post-Gazette* published the results on November 12, 1971 in a brief, little obscure item buried at the bottom of a long story previewing our upcoming game at Miami, stating: "Tom Bender, sportscaster of WTAE has conducted a contest for the name of the Steelers front four on defense. Fred Kronz of Keiners Lane won with the name 'The Steel Curtain.'

"Runners up were 'The Mean Green Machine,' 'Noll Knockers,' 'The Bang Gang,' and 'God's Little Ackers.' The winner earned a trip to the game on Sunday in Miami."

The Noll Knockers? God's Little Ackers? And people think I have a weird sense of humor, eh? Anyway, who would've thought that three years later "The Steel Curtain" would become one of the most famous names in football history? Eventually, "The Steel Curtain" became the nickname for the entire Steelers defense, not just the defensive line.

For the record, here is Joe Greene's account. When Joe was enshrined into the Pro Football Hall of Fame on Aug. 8, 1987, Norm Vargo, sports editor of the *McKeesport Daily News*, wrote a story about Greene and the beginning of The Steel Curtain. The article, published the day before the Hall of Fame ceremonies in Canton, was entitled "Greene was the Heart of The Steel Curtain!" Here is an excerpt where he credits me for that original defensive line.

LATROBE—Joe Greene doesn't forget.

"How did The Steel Curtain get started?" Greene pondered an out-of-town writer's question. "Hmmm...."

"Well, I'd say it began in 1971 when Dan Radakovich, we called him 'Bad Rad,' took over the defensive line after Walt Hackett left," Greene recalled yesterday morning, just a few minutes before he departed for Canton, Ohio, to be inducted into the Pro Football Hall of Fame.

"Radakovich really shook things up. He moved L.C. (Greenwood) to the starting lineup and stationed him next to me. It was good chemistry right off...we came together and stayed together. That was the key move and the start of big things.

"Next, Rad put Dwight White on the other end and that made us even better. When Ernie (Fats) Holmes got here, it all happened. He was the missing ingredient.

"Rad left after that season. He pulled down The Steel Curtain but nobody noticed. George Perles came in and he was right for us. The rest is history..."

Radakovich is a Kennywood native who starred at Duquesne High and Penn State, and returned to the Steelers in 1974 as the offensive line coach. He watched The Steel Curtain come down in the teams' first two Super Bowl wins.

"I'm grateful Joe remembered how it started," Radakovich said from the New York Jets training camp at Hempstead, New York. "Especially during this special time for him."

Radakovich, who coaches the Jet's offensive line, laughed over the telephone as he learned of Greene's comments.

"Yeah, I really shook people up, I guess" Radakovich agreed. "I knew Joe Greene was going to be a great football player. What we needed to do was put people around him so he could do his thing.

"What I did, actually, was put the guys who were playing end at right tackle and put two younger and faster ends in the starting lineup. I took plenty of flak about L.C. 'Are you crazy? Putting a skinny guy out there?'

"People did think I was crazy...people always resist change even when it's for the better..."
The gregarious Perles took Radakovich's blueprint and forged what is reputed to be the best front four in National Football League history.

George Perles succeeded me as defensive line coach when I left the Steelers after the 1971 season and we became colleagues when I returned to Pittsburgh three years later as the offensive line coach. In 1974 George was the architect of the stunt 4-3 defensive alignment which became the primary Steelers defense in their march to four Super Bowls in six years. In 1982 George became the head football coach at Michigan State, which won the Big Ten title in 1987 and beat USC in the Rose Bowl, 20-17.

Defensive Line—Quick As Linebackers – As the Steelers defensive line coach in 1971, I had my linemen do a lateral movement drill every day that I had devised when I was the linebacker coach at Penn State. The drills (named Mirror Dodge) were my attempt to make my linebackers quicker laterally and better at changing directions. Simply, one defensive player tried to keep an opposing player from juking or dodging him and scoring between two traffic plastic cones five, six, seven or eight yards apart. The defender tries to stay in front of the juker (or dodger) by mirroring him like a basketball player does in man-for-man defense. I used to kid the defensive linemen that our goal was to have a defensive line that was quick as any group of linebackers. This was the same drill that I did eight years later with the Scarecrow in the Bell Air Country Club in Hollywood (see The Scarecrow story in Chapter 14).

You can imagine how I felt when, four years later, I saw the Pittsburgh defensive line pictured on the cover of the December 8, 1975 issue of *Time* magazine entitled "Pittsburgh's Front Four." George Perles was their defensive line coach at the time. In the cover story with the headline "Half a Ton of Trouble," Washington Redskins Head Coach George Allen was quoted as follows: "There are some great lines in the league, but the edge has to go to Pittsburgh. They put fear into the heart of a passer.... What impresses me is that they're all so quick. They move like linebackers." Enough to make a former linebacker coach smile.

Defensive Line Hall Of Fame Members – The Minnesota Vikings have two members of their famous defensive front four from the late 1960s and the 1970s deservedly in the Pro Football Hall of Fame—defensive end Carl Eller and defensive tackle Alan Page. They're known as The Purple People Eaters. They were all great players, but so were the Steelers of The Steel Curtain who are even more famous than that Minnesota front four. Yet there is only one member of The Steel Curtain in the Hall of Fame, defensive tackle Joe Greene. I sincerely believe that defensive end L.C. Greenwood, who became a starter in 1971 and led the line that year with 14 sacks in a 14-game season, deserves to be in the Hall of Fame as much as anyone.

Comparing statistics can give you some idea of how The Steel Curtain compared to The Purple People Eaters. Both defensive lines played in four Super Bowls, including Super Bowl IX when the Steelers played the Vikings. In Minnesota's four Super Bowls, their defense gave up a total of 862 rushing yards—151 in IV, 196 in VIII, 249 in IX and 266 in XI—and lost all four games. In Pittsburgh's four Super

Bowls, The Steel Curtain gave up a total of 386 rushing yards—17 in IX, 108 in X, 154 in XIII and 107 in XIV—and won all the games. The difference in rushing yards was 476. The Steelers also had more sacks than the Vikings, 13-5.

No wonder the Steelers won their four Super Bowls and the Vikings lost theirs.

Although the above statistics can't completely determine the value of an individual to a team, I believe they are pertinent to show how strong the Steelers front four was as a group. I only coached L.C. for one year, in '71 when they got their nickname, The Steel Curtain, but I believe he first showed me he was a future Hall of Famer when he lapped the entire Steelers team after that first day of practice in camp at St. Vincent's College in the summer of 1971.

In Super Bowl IX when The Purple People Eaters and The Steel Curtain faced each other, the Vikings gave up 249 yards rushing while the Steelers gave up only 17 yards rushing. That was also the first game that L.C. Greenwood wore his famous gold football shoes. Besides stopping the run, L.C. knocked down three of Fran Tarkenton's passes that day. And in Super Bowl X, when the Steelers beat the

Joe Greene (75) and L.C. Greenwood (68)

Dallas Cowboys, 21-17, and set a Super Bowl record by sacking quarterback Roger Staubach seven times, L.C. made three of those sacks.

L.C. started at left defensive end in all four of those Steelers Super Bowl championships, and he definitely is worthy of being inducted into the Pro Football Hall of Fame.

Not Good But Better – Even with The Steel Curtain, 1971 was not a very good year, but it was better than the previous two seasons. From Chuck's first year as the head coach in '69 when the only victory was against Detroit in the season opener, he was focused on turning the Steelers from a perennial also-ran into a consistent playoff contender. Since the Steelers started playing in 1933, they had only won one division title—and even had to share that in 1947 with Philadelphia Eagles, and then quickly lost to the Eagles, 21-0, in the division playoff. In fact, from 1933 through 1970 (when they had a 5-9 record), the Steelers had just seven winning seasons. So, Chuck had his work cut out for him. But with the support of owner Art Rooney's sons, Dan and Art Jr., who were now more deeply involved in running the franchise, Chuck was quickly trying to build a winning program.

Jack Ham At Middle Linebacker — Although I was in charge of the defensive line in 1971 and Noll handled the linebackers, I took a special interest in the linebackers and not just because of my extensive experience as the linebacker coach at Penn State. One of the Steelers linebackers was rookie Jack Ham. I helped recruit Jack at Penn State and coached him up until his senior year when I left for Cincinnati. I'll get more into all that in Chapter Ten when I tell more about how Penn State became Linebacker U. But of all the linebackers I had at Penn State—and many of them went on to play in the NFL—Jack was, without a doubt, one of the most talented with the most potential. I believe he was quite happy to see me on the Steelers coaching staff because he now had a counselor and a friend. I know Jack's dad was happy to see me on the Steelers staff. When Jack was at Penn State, Jack's dad would not let him join the Phi Delta Theta fraternity until I said it was all right, which I reluctantly did.

During the preseason games, Jack was backing up two veterans, Andy Russell and Henry Davis, at outside linebacker. The middle linebacker was Chuck Allen, a 10-year pro with San Diego whom the Steelers had picked in a trade in 1970. Jack played well during the preseason but I thought he should be starting, so the week before the last preseason game against the New York Giants, I asked Noll to move Jack to the middle as the starter.

Chuck said he didn't think Ham wanted to be a middle linebacker, but allowed me to try to convince him otherwise. On Monday, the players' day off, I had Ham to my house for dinner and tried to convince him to play middle linebacker. He hated the idea, but reluctantly agreed to try it. Before Wednesday's practice, Henry Davis turned up injured, and Ham's move to middle linebacker was delayed because he had to start in Henry's place at left outside linebacker. Ham intercepted three passes off of Fran Tarkenton in the preseason game against the Giants, which locked in the starting position at left outside linebacker ahead of poor Henry. This killed my idea of Jack playing middle linebacker and I went back to worrying about my defensive line—but only for a little while

Ham was not the only outstanding linebacker I had at Penn State. Three Penn Staters were playing linebacker for the New York Jets—Ralph Baker, John Ebersole, and Dennis Onkotz—and all of them helped Penn State eventually earn the reputation as Linebacker U. Dennis was as good as Jack at Penn State—maybe even better—and they had both been starters on the 1968 and 1969 Penn State teams that were one of the greatest in college football history. I thought both of them would someday be all-pros, and the Jets had made Onkotz their No. 3 draft choice in 1970. I heard he was doing a great job backing up Baker and two other veterans that season when he severely injured his leg in the ninth game of the year against the Los Angeles Rams. He was trying to make a comeback in training camp but in late August, about three weeks before the regular season, the Jets put Onkotz on their list of players "physically unable to play."

One-Legged Cripple – After Ham intercepted those three Tarkenton passes, Chuck Noll was ecstatic. He said he had never had a linebacker who could play pass defense like Ham. I told him that I knew of a linebacker, Dennis Onkotz, that was just as good who had broken his leg as a rookie the year before playing for the Jets. I said, if his leg was healed, he might be available. Chuck found out he was supposedly healed and available, and three days before our third game of the regular season against San Diego we traded our right defensive tackle Chuck Hinton to the Jets for Onkotz.

Ham was upset because he thought I was getting Onkotz to replace him. Now, I didn't think Jack was serious because he had just intercepted three passes in his first start. I told him we were getting Onkotz for middle linebacker, not outside. After Onkotz limped around the first practice with us, Ham, I, and the rest of the Steelers coaches knew that Dennis wasn't healed enough to play—and, sorry to say, he never did. He would have been a good middle linebacker. The first Jets game after we traded Chuck Hinton, he won some type of NFL Defensive Lineman of the Week award. I remember the assistant coaches putting a newspaper clipping on my desk along with a note saying, "You traded the NFL defensive lineman of the week for a one-legged cripple! Congratulations." A few years later, after his leg had completely healed, Dennis was the doubles racquetball champion for the state of Pennsylvania.

Bad Rad's A Racist – At one of our later 1971 preseason games, the fourth or fifth, Dwight White, our starting rookie defensive end, got a lot of ink in the paper about how well he had played in that particular game. When I graded his performance I gave him 17 pluses. I simply gave a plus whenever the defensive linemen did something positive—a tackle was a plus, an assisted tackle was a plus, a sack was a plus, a batted ball was a plus, recovering a fumble was a plus, and so on. Having 17 pluses for a defensive lineman is a very productive game. I also gave minuses. If you had an offside penalty, it was a minus. If you didn't go full speed until the ball touched the ground, it was a minus—I termed that a "loaf" minus—and so on. At the defensive meeting where I gave the defensive linemen their grades, I said to Dwight, "You had 17 pluses in this game, which is very, very impressive. I'm sorry to say that you also had 19 minuses or loafs and 19 from 17 is a minus two. And in my 15 years as a coach, you are the first starter I have ever coached that graded out with a minus average."

As soon as the meeting was over, Dwight went to see Lionel Taylor, our receivers coach, who was an African American like Dwight. Dwight told him, "Lionel, that Bad Rad Man is a racist. I didn't deserve that grade that he gave me. He's definitely a racist!" Lionel told me that he asked Dwight, "How many rookie defensive ends in the National Football League are starting for their teams? Only one, Dwight. That's you. Even that defensive lineman from Notre Dame [Mike McCoy], who was the second pick in the entire draft after Bradshaw last year, is not starting yet for Green Bay. Also, that 'racist' took a starting white veteran defensive right end [Lloyd Voss] and put him at tackle, so you could start at right defensive end. And you're calling him a racist. Get out of here."

Dwight White Visits Alma Mater –

Dwight and I rarely had a problem after that and he became one of my biggest supporters. Three years later when I was back with the Steelers as the offensive line coach, I did something for Dwight off the field that really affected him emotionally and was probably a turning point for his life after football.

It happened in the spring of '74, just a few months after I rejoined the Steelers. Each of the assistant coaches were assigned to a two-week scouting trip where we visited one college per

Dwight White

day, watched practice, and turned in a scouting report on each prospect we had seen. I was assigned all the colleges in the state of Texas. One of the main cities I visited was Houston, where a good friend of mine, Rod Paige, was the head football coach of Texas Southern. Rod and I had coached together at the University of Cincinnati in 1970 where Rod was the receivers coach. I should add that Rod later became the Secretary of Education under President George W. Bush. Another big city was Dallas where Joe Greene and Dwight White lived in the off season. I called Dwight and asked him if he would like to accompany me on my visit to his alma mater, East Texas State, which was about 65 miles north east of Dallas. I knew Dwight hadn't finished his degree and I told him he may want to go with me to see about what he had to do to get his degree. He said he wasn't interested in that. I then asked him to come along and just keep me company. He said okay, so we drove to East Texas State.

When we were in the football office, Dwight asked if he could work out in sweats with the team (they were in pads), and his former coaches said he could. After warm-ups and some drills, the East Texas coaches had a live one-on-one pass drill. The coaches invited Dwight to participate. Well, Dwight ran by those East Texas State offensive tackles like they weren't even there. He pass rushed from both the right and left sides, went inside and outside, and used all the pass rush techniques— arm over, rips, spin, club and so on. He used his entire repertoire of moves and put on an awesome display. When the drill was over after 30 minutes, Dwight was all smiles and strutting. He said, "Rad, do you mind if we leave now? I'd like to take a quick shower and go see some of my professors and the admissions office about finishing my degree," and that's what led Dwight to eventually getting his undergraduate degree in history from East Texas State, which is now known as Texas A&M-Commerce. After Dwight retired from football in 1981, he became a stockbroker and then one of the most successful and respected businessmen in the state of Pennsylvania.

The Last Time I Saw Dwight – In the late winter or early spring of 2008, I started to enter the Barnes and Noble bookstore in Robinson Township, near Pittsburgh, when I spied a bunch of books on sale in the store's entry way. As I was leafing through a very large book (approximately 16x11 inches) on football in the NFL (I can't remember the title), I saw a full page, colored 8x11 photo of Dwight White sacking Roger Staubach of Dallas in Super Bowl X. The retail price of the book was about $50, but was on sale for around $5.

I immediately went to my car, got my personal phone-address book and called Dwight at his home in Pittsburgh. I described the book and the photo to Dwight and asked him if he had ever seen it. He said no. I told him that I was going to buy it for him as a present, and wanted to know when I could meet him to give it to him. We made arrangements to meet at 11:30 the next morning at his stockbroker's office in downtown Pittsburgh and go to lunch together.

I met Dwight the next day at his office and we walked five or six blocks to the William Penn Hotel for lunch. After lunch and some general conversation, I gave him the book. Dwight said that although he had never seen or heard of the book before, he said he had seen that photo somewhere and that he had not sacked Roger on that play. Dwight said the photo didn't show it, but he said he had fallen off Roger a second or two after the photo was snapped. We both laughed about the fact that the photo didn't tell the true or whole story. Dwight said he really liked my present and that it was a perfect book to keep on a coffee table. We then walked back to his office and said our goodbyes.

That's the last time I saw Dwight. A few months later, I received call from Rocky Bleier informing me that Dwight had passed away suddenly from complications following a back operation. I'm sure glad we had that last time together.

Cheering Coaches – On a Monday or Tuesday morning after our last or next to last preseason game in 1971, I was in the Steelers kitchen in their offices in Three Rivers Stadium getting a cup of coffee, when I heard a lot of loud cheering from the other end of a long hallway where our coaches' offices were. I wondered what was going on, so I went quickly down the hall to find out. I hollered, "What's all the yelling about?" One of the assistant coaches yelled, "Houston just cut the best kicker in the league and we have first rights to pick him up." I hollered, "Who's that?" Someone else yelled, "Roy Gerela! We evaluated all the kickers in our conference and he's by far the best." I yelled, "If he's that good,

Roy Gerela

why did they put him on waivers?" One of the coaches hollered, "According to one of their coaches he didn't show any emotion when he missed a field goal in the last exhibition game and that upset the head coach (Ed Hughes) and he cut him."

Gerela had been the Oilers place kicker for two years, after they had picked him No. 4 in 1969 NFL draft from New Mexico State. He had kicked 19 field goals in 1969, 18 in 1970 and had not missed an extra point in 52 attempts. At the time we didn't have a decent kicker and our No. 1 need was kicking.

The Steelers immediately claimed Roy Gerela, and he reported to us a day or two later. When he showed up, I went out with him the first time he practiced his kicking. Besides being the defensive line coach, I also was the coach for the center snapper because I had been a snapper in high school and college. After I watched Roy kick about eight field goals from about 25, 30 and 35 yards, I said to him, "That's really good." Then, kiddingly, I said, "But can you kick it through left-footed?" To my surprise, Roy said, "Sure," and he told the holder to get on the other side because he was going to kick it with the left foot. Well, I watched him kick two 35-yard field goals left footed. Wow! Now I knew why the coaches were yelling so loud. The Oilers head coach, Ed Hughes, had just given us the best Christmas present we could ask for four months early.

Roy played 11 years in the NFL—1969-70 with Houston, 1971-78 with Pittsburgh and 1979 with San Diego—made two appearances in the Pro Bowl and has three Steelers Super Bowl rings. He didn't realize it at the time, but getting cut by Houston was one of the best breaks he ever had. He was so well-liked in Pittsburgh that the fans formed a "Gerela's Gorillas" fan club soon after he arrived in town, and for years, the fans would show up at the stadium wearing jerseys with his uniform number and displaying a large banner that was frequently shown on television. That was probably the best waiver pick up in Steeler history.

Butkus Is Hurt – I can remember my first official game as an NFL coach. It was on September 19, 1971 at Soldiers Field against the Chicago Bears. After our first offensive series I can vividly remember an offensive player running off the field and yelling, "Butkus is hurt! Butkus is hurt!" Dick Butkus, the Bears All-Everything middle linebacker was out there playing and limping around on basically one leg. He had started the game limping and continued playing the entire game on defense. He even intercepted a pass while limping around, and then near the end made the big play that changed the course of the game.

The Steelers completely dominated the game until the last two minutes. At that point, we were winning 15-3, had gained 352 total yards to their 133 total yards, 88 yards passing and 45 yards rushing, and we now had the ball with a first-and-10 on our own 36-yard line. Then disaster struck. The Bears blitzed and as Pat Livingston of the *Pittsburgh Press* reported,

> "Bradshaw handed off to fullback Warren Bankston. Defensive end Ed O'Bradovich sailed through, blasted Bankston, and separated the Steelers fullback from the ball. It bounced crazily into the arms of defensive lineman Ross Brubacker, who untouched, ran it 30 yards into the end zone for a touchdown. Two minutes later, on first down again, Butkus blasted into

Bankston, and there was O'Bradovich again falling on the ball at the Steelers 17. [Bears quarterback Kent] Nix (an ex-Steeler) threw an incomplete pass and then evading a rush, dashed madly all the way down to the Steelers three. Two plays later, Nix nailed George Farmer, a wide receiver, with a bull's-eye in the end zone."

The Bears kicked the extra point and won the game, 17-15 and we were stunned and angry. Pat Livingston summed up the game perfectly:

"The opening day defeat, no doubt cast a pall over the Steelers fans who watched the completely incredible ending on television but it infuriated tackle Joe Greene, who played perhaps his finest game as a Steeler. In his frustration at Chicago's game-winning score, Greene ripped off his helmet and fired it toward the distant stands. Even the hard hat missed its mark. It crashed into the goal post 20 yards away."

It's tough to lose your first NFL league game as a defensive line coach, when you hold the other team to less than 100 yards passing and less than 50 yards rushing.

After the game, I showered and dressed quickly and went outside to smoke a cigarette. After about 10 minutes, Lionel Taylor, [our receivers coach] came out and yelled, "I've been looking for you." I said, "What for?" He said, "Nobody saw you after the game, and Chuck was worried that maybe you were so disgusted with the way we lost the game that you quit." I laughed and said, "I just wanted to hurry up and go have a smoke. I never thought of quitting. Heck, they don't pay you if you quit." Especially if you quit after losing a game to a one-legged middle linebacker.

Warfield's Greatest Game — Besides that memorable loss to the Bears in the 1971 season opener, the other game I remember most was also a defeat to the eventual Super Bowl runner-up Miami Dolphins in the ninth game of the season. Dolphins quarterback Bob Griese did not start because he had spent Saturday night in the hospital with a stomach disorder. He did not come into the game until the last 15 seconds of the first quarter and after five plays into the second quarter, the Steelers led 21-3. Griese was warmed up. In seven plays he took Miami 80 yards for a touchdown. Payoff came on a 12-yard pass to Paul Warfield. The extra point conversion narrowed the margin to 21-10.

Shortly afterward, we had the Dolphins bottled up deep in their own territory when they ran a screen pass to the right. The Steelers defensive line reacted and covered the screen. Griese saw that the screen was covered and scrambled left. Our cornerback, who had the deep third on that side, came up to contain Griese. Noll and I were yelling, "No, no. Stay back." Warfield, who had seen the corner go up in front of him to contain the quarterback, started to wave for the ball. Griese spotted him and threw him a wide open, easy pass of 56 yards. Warfield stepped the remaining 30 yards for an 86-yard touchdown play, which, at the time, set a new Miami record for longest touchdown pass. A conversion made the score at halftime: Steelers 21– Miami 17.

The third quarter was scoreless, but on the first play of the last quarter, disaster struck again. Miami had the ball and we called "reverse 3-deep Zone" coverage. Miami ran a pass where both backs went strong (to the tight end side) and our weak side cornerback—second year man Mel Blount—was to cover the deep weak one-third zone (the open side away from the tight end). But Blount went up into the weak flat instead. Warfield, the Dolphins' All-Pro receiver, had run a hook pattern into the weak deep third area. He saw no one around and waved for the ball. Griese spotted him and threw him a 60-yard pass for the go ahead touchdown and Miami led 24-21. The rest of the game was scoreless with the Steelers' Roy Gerela trying a 51-yard field goal with six seconds left that was short. An offside Dolphins penalty gave Roy another try from 52 yards which was blocked.

Mel Blount

Warfield had scored all three Miami touchdowns on the only three passes he had caught in the game. It is considered one of his greatest games in the NFL, although on two of the touchdowns all he did, basically, was wave for the ball because no one was around him. I guess to be a great receiver you have to be lucky as well as good.

In an article the next day entitled "Steelers let Dolphins Off the Hook," Pat Livingston, the Sports Editor of the *Pittsburgh Press*, wrote that "Mel Blount (Steelers cornerback) played a pigeon to perfection, giving Paul Warfield two cheap touchdowns in the Miami Dolphins surprisingly close 24-21 win over the Steelers.

"Blount's performance had Coach Chuck Noll muttering to himself. 'Cheap touchdowns, why do we give up those cheap touchdowns?' asked Noll. 'We work like blazes and drill like blazes to avoid these mistakes, but every week we keep repeating them. Why would a guy who's playing the deep third of a zone come up to tackle somebody who's scrambling?' Noll was upset at Blount's reaction on Miami's second touchdown, the turning point in the game and the longest touchdown pass in the Dolphins' history...

"It was a misplay on Blount's part, the Steelers sophomore admitted. 'I saw the quarterback start to run and I reacted wrong,' said Blount sheepishly.

"Blount's second lapse was just as mental and just as costly. It came on the opening play of the fourth quarter when Warfield streaked downfield to take the game winning score, a 60-yard bomb that he captured in isolation far beyond the reach of the secondary.

"Blount misread his key, the flow of the Miami backs. Eye-balling and concentrating on Warfield, Blount missed the tell-tale moves in the Miami backfield which changed his defensive assignment. As a result, Blount covered Warfield only part of the way—expecting [Ocie] Austin (Steelers safety) to pick up the Miami receiver down the line.

"'That's exactly what I'm talking about,' said Noll. 'We're missing basic parts of our defense. We're not concentrating on keys. That's why we're getting beat. It's not that we can't cover these men.'

"While the Steelers defense must bear the onus of defeat, it is an unjustified rap. Aside from Blount's misplays, the Steelers put up a near-impregnable front against the high-geared Dolphin offense."

Blount and some of his teammates responded to the criticism in a sidebar story below Pat Livingston's article.

"Blount was a subdued Steeler afterward," the unknown Press reporter wrote. " 'Certainly you have to feel something about a day like this,' said Blount, referring to his frightful afternoon in the sun. 'But I'm not going to let it bother me.'

"Blount's teammates were quick to come to his defense. 'People only see the bad things you do,' said L.C. Greenwood. 'Mel did a lot of good things out there that nobody saw. That's the trouble with being a cornerback. Every mistake you make is out in the open—where there's nobody to cover up for you.'

"'I'm not worried about Blount,' said linebacker Andy Russell, captain of the defensive unit. 'I've seen the same thing happen to Lem Barney, Jimmy Marsalis, Erich Barnes. Anyone who plays that position is going to get beat and beat bad. Warfield's beaten a lot of great ones in his day—and he beat another great one today.' "

Mel Blount went on to have a 14-year career, earning four Super Bowl rings, making the Pro Bowl five times. He led the league in interceptions (11) in 1975, and had 61 interceptions (including playoffs) in his career. In 1989, Mel was inducted into the Pro Football Hall of Fame. There is an old saying in football that states: "Everybody makes mistakes. The difference between a great player and a poor player is that the great player learns from his mistakes while the poor player does not." Or, as the Chinese sage Confucius once said, "If you make a mistake and do not correct it, this is called a mistake." Mel certainly ended up in the great category.

Joe Greene Wants Traded – The 24-21 loss to the Dolphins and the way that the loss occurred, with two of their three comeback touchdowns being complete gifts, had a devastating effect on the morale of our players. One of the players most deeply affected was Joe Greene. I saw him go in Coach Noll's office to have a private conversation, and he must've been in there three hours. On the practice field, he started to loaf in my drills. I got on his case about it but it didn't seem to be having any effect on him, until finally I told him I wanted to see him in my office after practice on Thursday.

In my office, I went over how he was practicing and how he should be practicing. He replied that if I didn't like the way he was practicing, that I should trade him. I said, "Are you serious?" He said he was. I replied that regardless of how he acted, the Rooney's would never trade him. If he didn't perk up, he would be benched but never traded. I said, if he was not playing, fans would want to know why, and I would tell them that Joe Greene doesn't want to play for the Steelers. Until he does, he'll sit on the bench, but he'll never get traded. I told Joe that the Rooney's had drafted him No. 1 and fourth overall in 1969 to help make the Steelers a winner and that they would never allow him to play anywhere else ever! Joe replied, "Gee, I didn't know they thought that way about me," and I had no more practice problems with Joe Greene.

The Florida Everglades – We lost the last game of the '71 season at home to the Los Angeles Rams, 23-14, and that evening my phone rings at home in Mount Lebanon, and it's Chuck Noll. He wanted to know if I would like to go with him to scout the North-South All-Star game in southern Florida. Chuck said it would be a good opportunity for me to learn how to scout. Of course, I said I'd love to go, and the next day he and I flew to Florida.

The second day that we're there, Chuck told me that since both the North and South teams were practicing in the afternoon that he would like to get up early and go visit the Everglades and see the wildlife there. He said I was welcome to join him, but it wasn't necessary. I said I'd love to join him, and so the next morning we drove to the Everglades. For the next four hours, we walked on these paths for tourists, all through the Everglades. We hardly saw any wildlife. I remember an old alligator sleeping under a tree but that was about it. As were walking over a pedestrian bridge built over the swamp, I said, "Chuck, you look unhappy. What's wrong?" He said, "Oh I'm so disappointed. I was told that the best time to see the wildlife at the Everglades was in the winter when the water level was low and the wildlife congregated around the water holes. I was hoping to see some Gallinule and Anhinga birds, but we haven't seen anything." (I didn't know the actual names of the birds but I later looked them up. Gallinules are better known as swamp hens and Anhingas are known as water turkeys.) Just then, I spotted some big birds under a tree about 30 yards away from the bridge on which we were walking. I shouted, "Chuck, there's two of those birds over there." He said, "What birds? Where?" I said, "Those Anhinga birds. There's a couple of them over there under that tree." He looked and looked and finally saw the birds I was pointing at. Then he said, "Those are crows!" We left the Everglades and drove back to the hotel. Chuck has lived in Florida for a few years since retiring and I sure hope he's finally seen some of those birds we were looking for that day. Coaching with Chuck Noll certainly had some unique and some unusual moments.

Lionel Takes A Rookie Coach Under His Wing – After my scouting trip with coach Noll was over, Lionel Taylor, and I were selected by the scouting department to scout the All-American bowl in Tampa. Lionel told me that because I was new to pro football that he would take me under his wing and introduce me to all the people attending the American Bowl practices. We went to the hotel where the players of both teams were staying and I introduced Lionel to everyone instead of the other way around. Lionel didn't realize that the whole football world, especially the pro scouts and coaches, sooner or later visit the Penn State football office. Since I was the youngest Penn State coach for 10 years, I was in charge of taking care of all the pro scouts or college coaches visiting. So I spent the four days in Tampa introducing Lionel to everyone. You might say I took Lionel under my wing instead.

Lionel Taylor

Overnight Defensive Coordinator – During the Christmas vacation in 1971, Augie Tammariello, the offensive line coach at Colorado University, visited me. We had coached together at Penn State 10 years earlier when Augie was a graduate assistant. Augie informed me that Colorado had a defensive coordinator job open. At this point, I wasn't enamored with pro football and thought I would be better off for my future by coaching in college. I also liked the thought of living in Colorado. Augie set up an interview with head coach Eddie Crowder at the American Football Coaches Association convention. Eddie offered me $26,000 for 1972 and $31,000 for 1973. My contract with the Steelers was for $18,500, but with a $5,000 Christmas bonus, it amounted to $23,500. I decided to take the Colorado job. I told Chuck Noll, and he immediately offered me the job of defensive coordinator and linebacker coach at $24,000, which with a $5,000 Christmas bonus, would be $29,000. I turned it down, but he told me to think about it. He was in no hurry for a decision. I went home, talked to Nancy, and decided to take Chuck's offer. I called him, then went over to his house to talk about the coordinators' job. I then accepted the Steelers job as defensive coordinator and linebackers coach. The next morning, when I woke up, I changed my mind again and decided to go to Colorado. As soon as I got to the Steelers offices I told Chuck. Thus ended my overnight reign in January of 1972 as Steelers defensive coordinator and linebackers coach.

Drafting Franco – When I told Chuck Noll that I was definitely going to Colorado, he asked me if I would wait until after the NFL draft. He said that the Steelers were seriously thinking of drafting Franco Harris, the star fullback at Penn State, and that I was the only one in the organization that knew him personally. Also, he said since I had scouted the practices of a couple of the All-Star games and watched films of a lot of college players, I had knowledge that might be of use in the draft. I agreed to stay until the draft was over.

Franco Harris

Art Rooney Jr., who was in charge of the Steelers drafts, really pushed for Franco as the Steelers first round pick. He had tapes made of the opinions of every scout that he knew who had watched Franco practice. Everyone in the organization was sold on drafting Franco except Chuck and Bill Nunn. Chuck continued to have some reservations. Bill had scouted running back Robert Newhouse from the University of Houston and was pushing to draft him. Bill had not scouted Franco and did not know much about him. Dick Haley, our chief scout, had scouted both Franco and Newhouse and was pushing to draft Franco. I had no reservations because I had coached Franco in linebacker drills for two weeks the spring of his freshman year. Plus, I had watched him for his first two years in practice and games. One of my Penn State linebackers, Gary Gray, was Franco's roommate, and my wife even baked cupcakes for Gary and Franco.

I had played basketball against Franco in pickup games at Penn State. He was quick as a cat in my linebacker drills, and when carrying the football he could make a cut and get turned up field going full speed. Why Franco didn't tear up the field in his last two years at Penn State was beyond me. All I knew was that he was awesome as a sophomore. I also knew that he had been a great high school basketball player, averaging 30 points a game. And he was also a good student, smart and quiet.

Chuck finally yielded to Art Rooney Jr. and almost everyone else's opinion and agreed to draft Franco No.1 if he was there when our choice came up. I was standing in the doorway of our draft room at Three Rivers Stadium when the announcement came over the loudspeaker. "Steelers up. You have 15 minutes." Chuck turned in his chair and looked at me and said, "Well?" Remember, I was leaving the next day for Colorado as soon as the draft is over. I said, "Take him. We already decided!" We took Franco as planned and Chuck went to talk to Franco on the phone. After he came back, he said to me, "He sounds like a dead head." I said, "Chuck, he's just a shy quiet kid. Believe me. He's smart, you'll like him." I'd say that 'dead head' did okay for himself in the NFL. Bob Newhouse, the player Bill Nunn was promoting as an alternate choice to Franco, was Dallas' No. 1 pick and played 12 years for the Cowboys. He wasn't Franco but he also would have been a very good No. 1 draft choice.

The Chief – The second day of the 1972 draft was nearing its conclusion when I walked into the draft room and told Chuck I had to go and get ready to leave for Colorado. He said I could leave but to make sure I turned in my office keys to the business office before I left the building. I went down the hallway to the business office and gave my keys to Dennis Thimons the 20-year-old assistant business manager.

The Rooneys (left to right)–Dan Rooney, Art Rooney Sr., Art Rooney Jr.

Dennis gave me a check for $6,200. I said "What's that for?" He said it was for the remainder of my contract. I said, "There's some mistake. I started June 1 of last year. My contract still has four months to run. I haven't earned this money." Dennis said the Chief, Art Rooney Sr., told him to give me a check for the remainder of my contract, which was $6,200. I said, "Hold on. I'm going to see the Chief." I ran down the hall to the Chief's office and said to him, "Mr. Rooney, there's been a mistake. Dennis gave me a check for $6,200 for the remainder of my contract. I appreciate the $5,000 Christmas bonus that you gave me but I didn't earn this check for $6,200." He got up from behind his desk, walked over to me, and said, "Dan, I appreciate what you did for us this past year. Just take the money and come back and coach again for us some time." I thanked him and left the Steelers with $11,200 ($5,000 Christmas bonus and $6,200 unearned check) more than I had contracted for, and all that after a 6-8 season. With part of that extra money, Nancy and I bought a new station wagon to take our family to Colorado. We called it "the Rooney car."

By the way, that young Steelers assistant, Dennis Thimons, who handed me the check for $6,200 is currently the controller and vice president (chief financial officer) of St. Vincent College where the Steelers still hold their preseason camp.

I now knew why everyone in Pittsburgh had a love affair with the Steelers, despite all that mediocrity on the field. It was because of the Chief and his family. There never will be another owner like the Rooneys in the NFL. And I often wondered what my professional—and personal—life would have been if I had taken that defensive coordinator's job Chuck offered in January of 1972. Would I still have had the same nomadic coaching career? At least, he was willing to hire me back two years later to coach, not the defense but the offensive line, which was not my idea but Chuck's.

Three Penn Staters as Steelers: Bad Rad, Franco Harris, Dick Hoak

1974-1975 Super Bowls IX & X Steelers Coaching Staff
Back Row: Lionel Taylor, Dan Radakovich, Chuck Noll, Woody Widenhofer, George Perles
Front Row: Dick Hoak, Lou Riecke, Bud Carson, Paul Uram

CHAPTER TWO – The Seven Dwarfs

When I returned to the Steelers in 1974, the Chief was one of the first people in the organization to welcome me back. He didn't say a word that I should have never left, but I could sort of see that in the twinkle of his eyes. For a lot of the folks in the organization and most of the players, it was almost like I had never left. But there were some major changes. On offense, Dick Hoak was now the backfield coach (since 1972), and Noll had recently decided to become his own quarterback coach. Lionel Taylor was still the receivers coach. Bud Carson was now the defensive coordinator and secondary coach. Woody Widenhofer was linebackers coach, George Perles was defensive line coach, Paul Uram was special teams coach and Lou Riecke was still the weight coach.

I knew Lionel from my prior stint with the Steelers and Dick also as a former Penn State player when I coached there. But I knew the defensive coaches only vaguely. Chuck Noll had hired George in 1972 and Woody in 1973 directly from college, without any experience in the pros, just like me in 1971. I think that is an incisive bit of insight into how Chuck was able to build a Super Bowl contender so quickly—with fresh blood from coaches as well as players from the draft. Bud had been an assistant at North Carolina (his alma mater) and South Carolina, and a head coach at Georgia Tech. Woody had been at Minnesota, Eastern Michigan and Michigan State and George had been an assistant for 15 years at his alma mater, Michigan State, sandwiched between three years as a high school coach. They would become well known in the NFL as the Steelers would win Super Bowl after Super Bowl in the 1970s with that great "Steel Curtain" defense. In fact, it was George who inserted Ernie Holmes into the starting defensive front four after I left.

Bud and Lionel became two of my closest friends and we later coached together at Los Angeles and Cleveland. In fact, we were together with the Rams in '79 when the Steelers beat us to win their fourth Super Bowl of the 1970s, and I'll get into that later.

Hired As Offensive Line Coach – My two years at Colorado had been quite an experience, as you will read about in Chapter 12. I had left for a week near the end of the 1973 spring practice for reasons I'll go into later. 1973 was one of the tougher years of my professional career. We lost the last four games of the season to end up with a 5-6 record. As a result, Eddie Crowder resigned as head coach, but retained the athletic director's job and went looking for a new head football coach. All of his assistant coaches were compensated to go to the American Football Coaches Association convention in late January to look for jobs. I asked and got permission instead to go to the Senior Bowl, which is like a professional football coaches' convention.

Now, during the previous spring of '73, when I had quit at Colorado for a week before the spring game, I had called Lionel Taylor, the Pittsburgh Steelers receivers coach, and told him that I had resigned. Later, he called me back and said that he had told Chuck Noll what I had done. Lionel said Chuck told him, "Tell Rad to hold on for a year." I said, "What does that mean?" Lionel said, "All I know is, he said to hold on for a year. How do I know what it means?"

Nine months later, in January of 1974, I called Lionel to find out where he and the Steelers staff were staying at the Senior Bowl in Mobile, Alabama. When I checked into the motel, neither Lionel nor any of the Steelers coaches were around. I asked where I could eat and then walked 10 blocks to a diner. Coming out of the diner an hour later, I spotted Lionel walking toward me. Man, was he happy to see me. After the motel people had told him I had walked to the diner, he went looking for me. After he had walked a while, he said he realized that he was a black man walking alone on a dark night in a white neighborhood in Mobile. He said he was just happy to see a friend of his. We both laughed because it seemed funny at the time, knowing it would be the same thing for me if our situation was reversed, a white man walking in a black neighborhood, which is a sad commentary on our times, then and now.

When I saw Chuck Noll the next day, he told me that he'd released his offensive line coach, Bob Fry. I had no idea that Bob was gone. I knew Bob very well from having coached with him for the Steelers in 1971. Chuck then asked me if I would like to be the offensive line coach for the Pittsburgh Steelers. I was surprised at his offer because I had been a defensive coach for the past 15 years. I had never thought of being an offensive line coach. However, when I was the linebacker coach at Penn State, I was also the assistant offensive line coach—without that title—during the era of one platoon football in the late 1950s and early 60s. I thought about Noll's offer for approximately 30 seconds and said, "Sure, why not," and accepted the offensive line position.

Down at the Senior Bowl, word got around fast that I was to be the new Steelers offensive line coach. A day or two later, I was riding the escalator down from the mezzanine to the lobby in the main hotel in Mobile. I spotted John Madden, the Oakland Raiders head coach, sitting in a lounge chair near the bottom of the escalator. John and I are the same age. I hadn't ever met him, but he knew who I was. We had both been linebacker coaches the previous decade. Madden saw me as I'm riding down toward him, and yelled, "Hey Rad, I hear you are the new offensive line coach of the Steelers. That was a dumb move. You should have stayed at linebackers coach. All you are gonna hear is, 'the offensive line isn't pass blocking, the offensive line isn't coming off the ball.' The offensive line coach ends up getting blamed for everything. You'll find out." Well, in my case, it took a while for John Madden's prediction to come true. We won two Super Bowls in my first two years as an offensive line coach, but believe me, John eventually was right.

Building A Champion – When the Rooney family hired Chuck without any prior head coaching experience they knew he had a sharp football mind. Chuck had spent eight years as an assistant with the San Diego Chargers and Baltimore Colts, and he knew how significant a staff can be in the development and performance of a team. Some head coaches never truly learn that, and it's one reason so many of them fail. A successful NFL team back then, before free agency, depended on their scouting system and the annual draft. Pittsburgh's scouting department, led by Art Rooney Jr. and Dick Haley, with Bill Nunn, Tim Rooney and Bob Schmitz, was exceptional, but few outsiders realized it at the time. The scouts also accepted the input of Noll's assistants, which is not always the case on other teams, and I know from firsthand experience. I'll go into more details about the Steelers scouting shortly, but through a couple of deft drafts and the shaping of the offensive and defensive lineups, the Steelers had almost all the right players in place when I rejoined the team as offensive line coach just before the Senior Bowl in January of 1974.

Three months later, we had what is now touted as the greatest Steelers draft of all time with wide receiver Lynn Swann as No. 1, linebacker Jack Lambert at No. 2, wide receiver John Stallworth and cornerback Jimmy Allen both chosen at No. 4. and center Mike Webster at No. 5. (We had traded No. 3 to Oakland.) Four of those five picks are now in the Pro Football Hall of Fame, along with five other players from that '74 team—Bradshaw, Greene, Jack Ham, Franco Harris, and Mel Blount. By the time we won our first Super Bowl the next January, we had just six players on the roster who had come to the Steelers from other teams—center Ray "Ranger" Mansfield, place-kicker Roy Gerela, punter Bobby Walden, and running backs Frenchy Fuqua, Preston Pearson and Reggie "Boobie" Harrison—but I'm getting ahead of my story.

1974 Hall Of Fame Draft – Once I was hired, Chuck immediately got me involved in scouting the Senior Bowl practices. One of the players that I knew a lot about was Mike Webster, a center from Wisconsin. When I was at Colorado, we played Wisconsin the second game of the 1973 season. I had seen a lot of film of him as a junior plus the first two games of his senior year, including a game against my Colorado defense. I already knew he was the best college center in the country.

A couple of our Steelers defensive coaches, defensive line coach George Perles and linebacker coach Woody Widenhofer, knew Webster's offensive line coach at Wisconsin, Charlie McBride. They knew a lot about Mike from Charlie. Mike was

Scouting Department (left to right) – Bill Nunn, Dick Haley, Tim Rooney, Art Rooney Jr.

very impressive in the Senior Bowl practices. Then, in the Senior Bowl game, Mike dominated the middle linebacker who became the fourth overall pick in the entire draft by the Chicago Bears—Tennessee State's Waymond Bryant. Bryant was out of the league five years later, and I still wonder what the Bears scouts had been drinking when they were watching the Senior Bowl film that year. After Mike's performance in the Senior Bowl, Noll thought Mike was a No. 1 draft pick. But the scouting department—Art Rooney Jr., Dick Haley, Bill Nunn, Tim Rooney, and Bob Schmitz —said that because of his small size—about 6-foot-2, 218-pounds—some teams had him listed as simply a good free agent. They insisted we shouldn't take him No. 1 and could get him later in the draft.

Besides Mike, the other most impressive player at the Senior Bowl was Lynn Swann, a wide receiver out of Southern Cal. He was head and shoulders above the other receivers at the bowl practices. All the other Steelers coaches raved about Swann, too, especially Lionel Taylor, our receivers coach. Lynn was listed 10th on our receiver list because his timed speed in the 40-yard dash was 4.7. Nobody drafts a 4.7, wide receiver No. 1, no matter how talented the receiver is. Finally, shortly before the draft, the decision was made to have Lynn Swann retimed. The Steelers were part of a scouting combine with several other teams named BLESTO, and a BLESTO scout retimed Lynn just for the Steelers. His new times were 4.5 in two separate 40-yard sprints. Based on this information, we jumped Lynn's name from 10th to first on our receiver list and put him near the top of our master list of the best athletes.

Jack Lambert

When the commissioner announced it was time for the Steelers first pick, there seemed to be unanimous agreement when the Steelers picked Lynn Swann as our No. 1 draft choice. The second round pick was much more uncertain. The Steelers staff was trying to decide between two linebackers. One was a fast 4.6 linebacker from UCLA named Cal Peterson. The other linebacker was a taller, thin, good all-around athlete from Kent State who ran a 4.8. His name was Jack Lambert. Finally, after much deliberation, linebacker coach Woody Widenhofer picked Lambert for the Steelers second round draft choice. He thought Lambert was the tougher player, who would be a bigger help on special teams while he was learning to be an outside linebacker. Dallas drafted Peterson in the third round and he had a spotty seven-year NFL career with three teams.

The Steelers did not have a third round pick but we had two selections in the fourth and we talked about Mike Webster and a virtually unknown receiver named John

Stallworth who was still available. I first heard about Stallworth when Lionel came into the offensive coaches' office a week or so before draft day and said, "Rad, come with me. You've got to see this kid." I said, "Who?" He said, "This player is from this small school called Alabama A&M." So I went across the hallway into a meeting room and watched film with Lionel of this player he was raving about. The player was tall, skinny, fast, coordinated, and seemed to have great hands. He looked phenomenal. The only drawback was that this was not major college football. You knew he had to look impressive for the receivers coach to run across the hallway and make a new offensive line coach come and look at him. Well, the Steelers also ranked him as a No. 1 pick in ability, but the scouting department said there was a good chance that he would be available in a later round because he wasn't playing for a major college. There was some discussion about Webster, but it was decided that because of his small size Mike had a better chance of being available later. Stallworth was still around when we picked him in the fourth round, and the No. 82 choice overall.

When it was time for the Steelers second fourth-round choice, Jimmy Allen, a 6-foot-2, 4.5 or 4.6 cornerback from UCLA, was available and we picked him. I knew Jimmy from Pierce Junior College because I had tried very hard to recruit him for Colorado. Again, the scouts said that Mike Webster had a better chance of being available for the next pick than Jimmy. Webster was still available and became the Steelers fifth-round draft pick, and the 125th choice overall. Two centers were selected ahead of him, Mark Markovich, from my alma mater at Penn State, as the 43rd overall pick in the second round and Scott Anderson of Missouri as the 77th overall selection in the third round. Both were out of football within five years.

The scouts had been right in saying they thought Webster would still be there. All five of the Steelers first five draft picks in 1974 made the team and had great careers. Who could have predicted that four of the first five Steelers picks in the 1974 draft would later be selected for the NFL Hall of Fame? As the *Sporting News* reported in 2010, that 1974 draft is still the only one in which four Hall of Fame players were drafted by one NFL team in single year.

EDITOR'S NOTE: The Steelers also struck gold in the 1974 free agent market. Five free agents made the 1974 roster: Reggie Garrett, Marv Kellum, Reggie Harrison, Randy Grossman and Donnie Shell. All contributed to the Steelers greatness especially Donnie Shell who made five Pro Bowls as a safety and was the best special teams player I had ever seen in my 50 years of coaching.

Donnie Shell

May Be Better Than Swann –

In the spring of 1974, the Steelers held a four-day mini-camp for the 1974 rookie draft picks and free agents. After the first day's practice, I was curious about the ability of our No. 1 draft choice, Lynn Swann. I asked receivers coach Lionel Taylor what he thought about Swann now that he had worked with him in practice. Lionel raved about Swann, about how he excelled catching the ball, running routes, having a burst of speed after the catch, having great jumping ability, learning quickly, etc.

Swann and Stallworth

Finally, after ten minutes of Lionel extolling Lynn's good points, I said, "Okay, that's great. Now tell me about Stallworth (who was our No. 4 pick)?" Lionel replied, "Maybe better than Swann!" I said, "You're kidding!" He said, "Nope, but that's all I'm going to say about Stallworth." And that was all he did tell me. Who was the better prospect seemed to be debatable.

Lynn Swann played nine years, had four Super Bowl wins and got into the Pro Football Hall of Fame as soon as he was eligible, five years after he retired. John Stallworth played five more years than Swann—14 years total—and also had four Super Bowl wins and then joined Lynn in the Hall of Fame as soon as he was eligible, five years after he retired. Who was the better prospect may be still debatable.

Offensive Line

Research, Blocking Changes And Bending The Rules –

As soon as the 1974 draft was over, I started to research offensive line play. I spent the spring and summer intensely studying offensive line play, watching hours upon hours of film, talking to dozens of offensive linemen and coaches and reading as much as I could about offensive line tactics and techniques.

First, I watched Steelers film from the previous three seasons. Next, I asked the Steelers coaches who they thought were the eight best offensive linemen in the National Football League, and I studied film of each. Then, I spent a couple of days visiting the San Francisco 49ers and Los Angeles Rams to get a good feel for what they were teaching their offensive linemen. The Rams Head Coach

Lockout Protection Technique

Chuck Knox was an old friend and I knew 49er offensive line coach Dick Stanfel from my brief time as a player with the Washington Redskins in 1957. After having done this research, I felt more confident in the changes I was to make in the Steelers pass and run blocking. One of the things I did was bend the rules a bit.

My experience as the Steelers defensive line coach gave me an unusual insight into trench warfare between the offensive and defensive lines. Although there were rules against holding, they were bent in favor of the defensive linemen who could grab an offensive lineman's jersey and shoulder pads and pull them to get around the blocker. So, I had to come up with something to counter the defensive linemen's advantage. I decided that the only way an offensive lineman could pass block a defensive lineman without holding was for an offensive lineman to make contact first with the heels of his hands and his elbows very slightly bent before contact and his arms extended fully upon contact. Contact should be made as high as possible on the defensive man's shoulder (not to the face) to stop him and push him back.

When I told my wife Nancy I was teaching my offensive linemen a new pass blocking technique where they extended their arms to make the first contact on the defensive lineman, she asked, if I was breaking the rules. At the time, a blocker could shove or push a defender but had to keep his hands cupped or closed and was not allowed to fully extend his arms straight out with elbows locked. I said, "Maybe, I'm breaking the rules, but what I am teaching is the only way to stop a defensive lineman's pass rush without holding. The rules also say that holding's against the rules, and I'm not going to teach holding. Rather than breaking the rules, I believe I'm simply bending the rules."

I also decided to teach drive run blocking, that is, moving a defender backwards in the desired direction, the same way I had taught it at Joe Paterno's football camp for underclass high school players in the mid-1960s. I designed a small 16" x 24" x 2" thick foam, vinyl covered shield that had the handles in the back, close enough to hold with one hand. The defender held the two handles of the shield in one hand and put the opposite shoulder and forearm behind the shield with the opposite foot forward—same foot, same shoulder rule—in a staggered stance. This was the strongest way to hold the shield. The offensive linemen then drove this human shield 10 yards in the desired direction. The basic rule was "10 yards back or on his back." On the follow through immediately after impact, I allowed the offensive linemen to push inside on the frame of the defender (but not on the shield) to the full extension of the arms while arching his back and accelerating his feet with maximum power. So in both pass and run blocking we were going to push and not pull all the way to full extension.

On pass protection, my purpose was to have the pass blocker make contact first, keeping the defender at arm's length at all times, stopping them with the heels of our hands on the pass rusher's shoulder pads, keeping arm length separation between the blocker and the rusher. No one had ever pass blocked that way before. Four years later the NFL revised the rules to accommodate the above blocking changes and a few years after that the colleges and high schools did the same.

Then, just before and during our 1974 preseason games I came up with a couple of ideas that would prevent the defender from grabbing a blocker's jersey—tight, taped jerseys that were ungrabbable.

Tailored Taped Jerseys A Crutch – I had heard of a few former professional offensive linemen in the past, like John Wilbur of the Dallas Cowboys, who had worn jerseys a few sizes too small so that the jersey would be harder for the defensive lineman to grab. I felt that this type of extra small jersey would restrict the arm movement of the offensive lineman and be uncomfortable. I wanted my offensive linemen to have skin tight jerseys but still be comfortable with full range of motion with their arms.

Two weeks before the first 1974 preseason game against New Orleans, I told our equipment man, Tony Parisi that I would like to have the offensive linemen game jerseys tailored skintight so that a defensive lineman could not grab the offensive man's jersey. Tony enlisted his mother-in-law to be our tailor. Tony did all the

Equipmant Manager Tony Parise (right)

measuring and fitting and his mother-in-law did all the sewing. The advantage of having Tony's mother-in-law rather than a commercial tailor was that we could keep refitting and re-sewing until the jersey fit was perfect.

The tailoring worked out great. We won all six preseason games and had great pass protection. However, a defensive lineman like Joe Greene, who had big strong hands could still grab a jersey at times, no matter how tight the fit. My wife Nancy and I had just had a porch converted into a family room in which we had used some two-way carpet tape. I got the idea that if I covered the shoulder pads with two-way carpet tape, then put the jersey on, that the tape would keep the jersey from sliding and the jersey would be impossible to grab.

On Monday before our first regular season game with the Baltimore Colts, my wife went out and bought a big roll of two-way carpet tape, and I brought home Bruce Van Dyke's tailored jersey. We had just traded Bruce to Green Bay and his jersey was close to my size, the smallest tailored offensive lineman's jersey. I taped the shoulder pads, put the pads on, and then asked Nancy and our daughter Lisa to help me pull the jersey on. I ended up feeling all stiff with my arms sticking out like Frankenstein. Nancy and Lisa tugged and pulled until they could pull no more. I still was stiff as a board. My tape experiment was a failure.

I told them to help me get the pad and jersey off. We took the entire pad off with the jersey still on the pad. I walked around the house for an hour trying to figure out why it didn't work. The jersey was tailored so that it fit me. The tape was only a glue. It should work but it didn't. Finally, after an hour, I started picking at the jersey on the pad, pulling on the wrinkles, smoothing the jersey out until I had the jersey perfectly smooth over the entire shoulder pad. Then I asked Nancy and Lisa to help me, and this time I put the shoulder pad on with the jersey already attached. Viola! A miracle! The jersey and pad fit perfectly. I could move my arms easily. I asked Nancy and Lisa to try to grab me. They couldn't. The taped jersey worked perfectly if I put the jersey on the taped shoulder pads before the player put the pad on. I could hardly wait to show the coaches and players my new invention.

The next morning, I told the Steelers assistant coaches about my jersey taping idea. The coaches were not at all enamored with the idea. One of them said that he didn't like the idea giving the players a crutch. I replied that none of the assistants had ever played offensive line. If they had, I told them, they would realize that an offensive lineman will take any crutch you could possibly give him. I then walked into my offensive line meeting at 10:00 a.m. I explained my two-way tape idea and showed them my taped jersey on my shoulder pad and they spontaneously started cheering and rushed at me and each wanted to be the first to try on the taped jersey. Not one seemed to be worried about being given a crutch. My taped, tailored jerseys were like a Christmas present from Santa Claus.

Pregame Ritual – Starting with the first 1974 league game against the Baltimore Colts, all the Steelers offensive linemen would immediately leave after the pregame meal for the stadium for both home and away games. They were always the first players in the locker room on game day, and the reason was that they wanted to freshly tape their shoulder pads and get their jersey adjusted on the pad perfectly so that nothing could be grabbed.

There was somewhat of an art to taping the pads, especially in covering the hole in the back of each shoulder pad. Then after the taping was done, they would lay the jersey inside out on the back of the pad. They would pull the pad through the jersey, and because of the stickiness of the tape, this not an easy chore. Mike Webster became an expert at pulling the pad through and a lot of the players had him do this for them. Then they would pick at the jersey until it was perfectly smooth all over. After that, they would put the pad on with the jersey attached. Next, they would have another player try to grab them. If any part of the jersey could be grabbed, they would take the padded jersey off and try to correct it. For most games I would try to grab them myself. If I got any cloth, I would make the player take the jersey pad back off and correct it. I also used this taping time to go over any assignments or reminders I wanted to impart. This entire process always took a couple hours or more. Every game at home or away for the next four years that I was their line coach, the Steelers offensive line did this pregame ritual.

With their tailored, taped and tight jerseys and extended arms blocking techniques, the Steelers offensive line of mid and late 1970 became one of the all-time best in the NFL. Some teams eventually noted what we were doing, a few followed our lead, and by 1978 the NFL finally changed the rules to make everything we were doing legal.

The Seven Dwarfs – When I became the offensive line coach for the Steelers, I had a couple of preconceived notions about who I was going to start. These notions were derived from my year as Steelers defensive line coach in 1971. First of all, I was certain Jon Kolb would start somewhere—left tackle, left guard or center—simply based on his athletic ability, speed (4.7), and strength (500 pound bench). The other player I was certain to start was Gerry Mullins. I told Gerry both before and after camp that he would be the starting right guard or right tackle. I just couldn't say which one it would be. I just wasn't sure at all how any of the other players would pan out.

The Seven Dwarfs (left to right) – Gordon Gravelle (71), Gerry Mullins (72), Mike Webster (52), Ray Mansfield (56), Sam Davis (57), Jim Clack (50), Jon Kolb (55)

They were mostly all veterans. Kolb had been the Steelers third round draft choice in 1969 out of Oklahoma State, and a starter at left tackle since 1971. Mullins was a No. 4 pick from USC in '71 and began getting some starts at tackle as a rookie but was primarily a backup at tackle and guard in '73. Ray Mansfield was the "old man" of the group. Ray had been originally drafted as a defensive tackle by Philadelphia at No. 2 in 1963 from the University of Washington. The Steelers picked him up in '64 and switched him to center in '66 where he became the long-time starter. When Jim Clack was signed as a free agent from Wake Forest in 1971 after he had played a season in the Continental League, he and Mansfield began sharing the center position.

Another free agent, and one of the best in Steelers history, was Sam Davis, who had played for little known Allen University in Georgia. The Steelers signed him in 1967 and he was a standout on the special teams until becoming the starting left guard in '70. Gordon Gravelle was Pittsburgh's No. 2 draft choice from BYU in 1972 and started some games at tackle but an injury had kept him on the sidelines for much of 1973. That left Mike Webster, whom we drafted in the fifth round a couple months before, as our best rookie lineman. Rookies Dave Reavis (tackle) and Rick Druschel (guard) made the team as backups, making a total of nine offensive linemen.

When the preseason was over, I knew I had seven players who would be first class starters in the National Football League. Rather than try to pick five starters from seven, I decided to play all seven. I told the players that we had seven starters.

Every one of the seven would play at least half of the game or more, and the two that didn't start the game would definitely be in the game in the fourth quarter, where close games were decided. Four of the seven would play one position only—Kolb at left tackle, Davis at left guard, Mansfield at center, and Gravelle at right tackle. Three of the seven would play two positions—Mullins at right guard or at right tackle, Clack either right or left guard, and Webster at center or either guard. Except for injuries to Sam Davis and Mike Webster in the second half of the 1974 season, this seven starter offensive line system remained in place through both the 1974 and 1975 Super Bowl seasons.

Now, not only was an offensive line with seven starters unique in the NFL, but it also was abnormal because it averaged about 20 to 30 pounds a man lighter and was smaller than the offensive lines in the rest of the league. Here's how they lined up: Mansfield – 6-foot-3, 250 pounds; Webster – 6-foot-2, 240 pounds; Davis – 6-foot-1, 240 pounds; Clack – 6-foot-3, 240 pounds; Kolb – 6-foot-2, 262 pounds; Mullins – 6-foot-3, 240 pounds; and Gravelle – 6-foot-5, 250 pounds. They all bought into what I was doing and really bonded as a unit and began calling themselves "the Seven Dwarfs," which seemed perfectly appropriate. As one Steelers official later told Pro Magazine years later, "...what (Radakovich) accomplished was to take a group of marginal players and make them one of the best offensive lines in the NFL." I appreciate the compliment, but like the original Seven Dwarfs, these guys worked very hard to accomplish what they did. And I certainly wasn't Snow White. Those Seven Dwarfs were a great bunch to coach, but they did have their quirks. I want to tell you about a couple of them.

Please Don't Trade Jon Kolb – Chuck Noll called me into his office in the spring of 1974, about two months after I had returned to the Steelers. He told me that Jon Kolb, the starting left offensive tackle for the past four years, was having marital problems, which apparently had caused him to lose weight. He now weighed about 230, whereas his playing weight was normally in the low 260's. Chuck informed me that he was going to trade him for his own good. Chuck told me that he traded a very good player a year or two earlier because of a similar situation. Well, I panicked. I told Chuck he couldn't trade my most talented offensive lineman who was a great person before I even had a chance to coach him. I told him I had a better idea: "Let's help Jon get rid of his problems but please don't trade Jon Kolb."

Dan and Jon Kolb

I said I had two cousins, Bob Garshak, and Ray Radakovich, who were expert divorce lawyers who could handle the case. Chuck agreed. We had a meeting with Jon in Chuck's office. We told Jon our feelings and Jon agreed that he should get a divorce as soon as possible. But he turned down our offer of my cousins as lawyers. Jon said he had a lawyer who could handle it. The lawyer did get John the divorce and custody of his son. Noll and I also had a meeting with some of the unmarried players on the team. We told the players to take Jon out with them so that he could meet other women. We had found out in our meeting with Jon that he had never dated anyone other than his wife before he got married. Jon was out with the players one night at the Anthony House in Upper St. Clair near Pittsburgh and met Debbie, who he eventually married. That's how I saved my best offensive lineman from being traded, and when Jon reported to camp a few months later, he was back up to 262 pounds.

Kolb Does The Opposite – I have to tell you one more story about Jon Kolb. Shortly after the vets reported to camp at the end of the players strike on August 14, I told Jon that he would be a great pass blocker if he did exactly the opposite of what he had been doing for the past five years. Jon was surprised and asked what I was talking about. Here's what I told him:

First of all, when the quarterback gives the starting count, I don't want you to pull your left hand like you are starting a lawn mower. I want you to do the opposite. Push off your left hand, don't pull. Second, instead of stepping up with your outside back left foot from your staggered left foot back stance, I want you to do the opposite. Simply slide back and bring your right foot back like a basketball or tennis player. Third, instead of winding up with your arms and punching the pass rusher in the ribs, while being bent over with your head down, I want you to do the opposite. Simply get your head up and back, stand up tall with legs slightly bent, bring your hands up directly without a windup and extend your hands and arms and hit the defender as high as possible in the top of the shoulder pads—but not in the face—with the heels of your hands, not the fists. Fourth, don't wait for the pass rusher to make contact, like you've been doing. I want you to do the opposite. You, the blocker, should make contact first.

Jon immediately wanted to try my suggestions out. After about 15 minutes trying out these new opposite ideas against a couple of volunteer pass rushers, it was obvious both to me and Chuck Noll, who was also watching, that Kolb was on his way to becoming the best pass blocker in the National Football League for the next six years. From what I know, Jon is the only offensive left tackle in NFL history to start four Super Bowl games and win them all without giving up a sack in any of them.

Don't Ever Do That To Me Again – Around the third week of the strike, I started to get concerned about one of my veteran linemen, Gordon Gravelle. Noll had stated that Gordon was going into his third year and that if Gordon didn't show that he was going to be a starter that Noll was going to cut him. I hadn't had a chance to coach Gordon, and I didn't know how long the strike was going to last. I decided that for both Gordon's benefit and my own that he had better come to camp. My problem was that I was not allowed to call him. Our owner, Dan Rooney, had given the coaches explicit instructions that no coach was allowed to call a player during the strike to convince him to come to camp. So I had my wife Nancy call Gordon.

Through Nancy, Gordon realized how serious I thought his situation was. He immediately came to camp. After Gordon showed up, I called Jack Ham, and told him what Nancy had done, and asked him to call Nancy. Well, Jack called Nancy, said he heard what she had done, and that he was reporting her to the head of NFL Players Union, Steve Garvey. Jack told Nancy she was in big trouble and then he hung up. Well, Nancy got all shook up until Jack and I told her we were just fooling. Her words were "don't ever do that to me again." Gordon Gravelle became the starting right tackle for our first two Super Bowl seasons.

Dan, Mike Webster and Gordon Gravelle (left to right)

This is another example of "Radgate" in action. I derived this from President Nixon's Watergate. Radgate was something I intentionally and secretly did for the benefit of the team that I was normally not allowed to do.

First Super Bowl Season

High School Drills – In the spring and early summer of 1974, there were no minicamps for the Steelers veterans. We had a one-week minicamp solely for the new draft picks, rookie free agents and veteran free agents. With this being the year of the players' strike, the bulk of the Steelers veterans—25 players—did not report for camp until August 14, five weeks and two preseason games after camp had started. I essentially coached the rookie linemen and tight ends in all my new blocking changes and drills for six weeks, counting one week of minicamp, before the veterans showed up.

Besides teaching the full extension of the arms in both pass and run blocking and driving man-held shields ten yards back or on its back, I taught quick hands and lateral movement the same as I had done when coaching linebackers. We did waves, mirror dodges, and mirror cross field—which were all originally linebacker drills I had created as the first linebacker coach at Penn State in the early 1960s—and everything was to be done with no wasted motion—no windups, and etc.

When the vets finally reported six weeks later, they had to work their tails off to catch up to, and hopefully, pass the rookies. Having scored 76 points in our first two preseason games without the vets probably provided some incentive. Three of the starters from the 1973 team never did catch up by the end of camp, resulting in the retirement of the right tackle Glen Ray Hines, the trading of the right guard Bruce Van Dyke and the moving of tight end John McMakin from first to third team, where he was eventually released at the end of the season. Three rookie linemen—Mike Webster, David Reavis, and Rich Druschel—and one new rookie tight end, Randy Grossman, survived the final cut and made the team. A newspaper article appeared shortly after our first league game with Baltimore where my players said they were doing college drills. But I told them they were high school drills and the only other football team doing these drills was Upper St. Clair High School in suburban Pittsburgh because I had given them to the head coach, Joe Moore, who was one of my best friends. More than 20 years later those mirror dodge drills would become part of Joe's age discrimination law suit against Notre Dame but you can read about that in Chapter Seven.

But myths sometimes die hard. In a 1999 book published by NFL Properties, *The NFL Century: The Complete Story of the National Football League*, a writer claimed I didn't invent the drills but had taken the drills from a local high school—which just goes to show that sometimes even writers get the facts wrong.

A Lesson In Poise – During a very hot and humid day around the fourth week of '74 preseason camp at St. Vincent College, a two-minute drill was being held near the end of practice. Mike Webster, the rookie center, was in a panic state trying to get everyone in the huddle quickly. He was screaming and getting very upset that some players were dragging their feet. Coach Noll blew the whistle and called the team together. He said he knew it was hot and knew that Mike was having trouble getting the huddle formed quickly enough, but said he needed to tell a story. He said that once there was a bunch of bulls grazing in the middle of a big field. One of the young bulls spied a bunch of good-looking, chunky female cows down along the fence and yelled, "Hey you guys, look at all those good-looking cows down by the fence. Let's run down and ride one of them!" The old bull in the bunch yelled out, "Hold on, young fella, I've got a better idea. Let's walk down and ride'em all!" And that was Chuck Noll's lesson in poise.

10 Worst Minutes Of My Life – At the end of my offensive line meeting held on the Monday before our last 1974 preseason game with Dallas, I asked Jim Clack, one of our three centers, to stay afterward. I told him I had to talk to him, but first I had to go to the copy room to run something off. I was gone about 10 minutes. When I got back I told Jim that I was setting my lineup for this last preseason game the way it would probably be for

Jim Clack

the season. I said he no longer was going to alternate with Mansfield and Webster at center because I wanted him to permanently play right or left guard for the rest of the season. I said Webster and Mansfield could handle the center positions and I needed him at guard. Jim breathed a big sigh of relief. He knew we would only keep two centers and because I wanted to meet with him alone three days before our final preseason game, he was sure he was going to be cut. He told me that the 10 minutes that I was gone, were "the worst 10 minutes of my life." I wonder if he remembered those 10 minutes after becoming the starting left guard in Super Bowls IX and X.

Play Until You're 40 – When I returned to the Steelers that year, Lionel Taylor, and I decided that he would teach the tight ends receiver skills and I would teach the tight ends blocking skills. Lionel also mentioned that I should take a close look at Larry Brown, who was going into his fourth year at tight end. Larry was a rookie when I was the Steelers defensive line coach in 1971, but he had not been the starting tight end in his three years. Well, 15 minutes into the first practice on the first day the vets reported, I realized Larry had awesome blocking talent. I told Larry after that first 15 minutes that he was on the first team and that's where he stayed for the next 11 years, both at tight end and tackle. Lionel was happy after all his hinting around for me to take a close look at Larry but it didn't end there.

Larry Brown (87) going to block Mike Curtis of the Baltimore Colts.

After the last 1974 preseason game with Dallas, I'm sitting at home watching Sam Nover's sports show on WPXI-TV and his guest is Larry Brown. And Larry's telling Sam that this is his last year playing for the Steelers. He says he's not sure how much he'll play this year, and he says he's not certain the coaches think he has much ability. After this season, Larry tells Nover, he was planning to go to dental school.

I was shocked by Larry's comments, and the next morning, I told Lionel what Larry had said on Nover's show. We both immediately went to see Larry and told him that he was going to play until he was 40 years old. We told him that after 10 years at tight end, when his 4.6 40 speed slowed to 4.9, we would move him to offensive tackle and he would play another 10 years. Larry said he didn't know the Steelers coaches felt that way.

Larry didn't quite make it to 40. He ended up playing 14 years—three more years at tight end and the last eight years at right tackle—including four Super Bowls and was 36 years old when he retired. In 2008, Larry was selected by Pittsburgh fans to the Steelers All-Time team as one of six offensive linemen that also included Mike Webster and Jon Kolb.

A lot of books have been written about that 1974 season when the Steelers, who had been down for so long, shocked pro football by winning their first Super Bowl. It was fun being part of it all and like everyone associated with the team I have a couple of special memories of the season.

Spaz Tells Bres – The first offensive line coach to visit me during our 1974 preseason at the Steelers camp in Latrobe, near Pittsburgh, and inquire about the new techniques that I was teaching the Steeler offensive linemen was a former Penn State player, Frank "Spaz" Spaziani. At the time Spaz was a co-offensive line coach with Tom Bresnahan at the Naval Academy where my Penn State coaching colleague George Welsh was now the head coach.

Spaz liked what I was doing and went back to Navy and told Bresnahan. Tom then came to visit me after the next couple of seasons to talk about offensive line play. Tom soon became the offensive line coach for the New York Giants, and then the Buffalo Bills when they were in four consecutive Super Bowls (after the 1990-93 seasons), which is one of the greatest achievements in winning consistency in NFL history. I've told this story because I'm very proud of the small part I played in Tom's success.

Incidentally, my coaching colleague later in Denver, Nick Nicolau, was the backfield coach for those Buffalo Bills during two of their four Super Bowl runs. Spaz was the head football coach at Boston College from 2009-2012.

Lionel's Receivers Manual – In the spring of 1974, my friend Joe Moore at Upper St. Clair High School asked me if I could get Steelers receiver coach Lionel Taylor to talk to his high school players about receiving skills. When Lionel played in the NFL, he led the league in pass receptions for five years. At the time, only Don Hutson had done better with eight seasons. Well, for about two hours, Lionel talked and demonstrated, and then had some of the players try his techniques. While driving back from the school, Lionel told me that he thought that was a great bunch of young kids, but he didn't see much ability there. He said that Upper St. Clair probably would not win a game in the fall. I said, "No, no, Lionel, you're wrong. What you showed them, Coach Moore will have them practice on their own at least an hour a day until the season starts. They'll probably go undefeated."

About two weeks later, I laid on Lionel's desk a manual with everything Lionel had said to the players at Upper St. Clair, perfectly organized into different parts with appropriate titles for each part and so on. Lionel had never put his thoughts about receiving on paper, and now it was done for him. Lionel hadn't known it, but Joe Moore had recorded Lionel's every word while he was talking and demonstrating, plus he had a couple of people taking notes the entire time. The result was a well-organized receivers manual that Lionel could now use to teach from. Lionel was ecstatic. And I should have bet Lionel on my prediction about Upper St. Clair's season. They not only went undefeated in 1974 but also in 1975.

Saga Of Henry Davis – When I went to the Steelers in 1971 as defensive line coach, Henry Davis was the starting left outside linebacker. Henry got hurt in the second preseason game. Jack Ham replaced him for the third preseason game, intercepted three passes in the game, became the starter at outside left linebacker, and Henry was relegated to special teams

In the 11th game of the season against Denver, the Denver special teams captain, Ken Criter, jumped off sides on a punt rush and knocked Henry backwards. As Henry was falling, he threw a quick 6-inch punch as a reaction. It was a bare-knuckle blow through the bars of Ken Criter's face mask—catching him flush in the face, knocking him out cold, breaking his nose and closing his right eye. Criter was still unconscious when they carried him off the field on a stretcher. The referee threw Henry out of the game and Criter went on a stretcher to Divine Providence Hospital. Criter didn't play the rest of the season but came back the next year and played for three more years. The rest of that next week I kept asking my players what we learned in the Denver game. The correct answer was, "Don't mess with Henry Davis."

For the next two years, 1972 and 1973, Henry was the starting middle linebacker and played very well. In the third preseason game in 1974, Henry got a concussion and rookie Jack Lambert moved from backup outside linebacker to starting middle linebacker for the fifth preseason game. The concussion ended poor Henry's career. Henry played six years in the league, first with the New York Giants and then four years with the Steelers. Each time that Henry got hurt in 1971 and 1974 he was replaced by a future Hall of Famer, Jack Ham ('71) and Jack Lambert ('74). When you think about that, that's not a bad NFL legacy to leave behind.

Strike During Training Camp – We were eagerly looking towards the start of training camp in July when everything went haywire with the players strike. I'm not going to get into the particulars of the strike. The NFL Players Association had been overhauled after the NFL-AFL merger in 1970, and by the spring of '74, the union was negotiating a new contract with the owners. The union was seeking limited free agency and guaranteed salaries among other things and the owners wouldn't budge. So, the players walked out on July 1, and all the teams then hustled to get whatever players they could into camp—the rookies, those veterans who had decided not to strike and the opportunistic free agents looking for their shot in the NFL. Our six-game exhibition season was set to start on August 3, and the all the NFL owners were determined to play those preseason games, with or without the regular players.

Yet, our team was unsettled because of our quarterback controversy and the after affects of the first NFL players' union strike, which had started at the beginning of preseason training camp in early July and had not ended until just before the second game of our six-game preseason schedule. The veterans reported to camp the Monday before the third preseason game.

We felt early in '74 that we were on the verge of taking a team to the Super Bowl. Since Chuck Noll had become the head coach in 1969, the Steelers had gone from a 1-13 record his first year to consecutive playoff seasons in '72 and '73, when they won the AFC Central Division but lost in the playoffs. I was the defensive coordinator at the University of Colorado the day Terry Bradshaw threw the tipped pass that Franco Harris caught that became known as "The Immaculate Reception." My wife Nancy and I were in an airplane flying to the Gator Bowl with Colorado and listening to the game on the radio. We could not believe it when Franco caught the ball caroming off Oakland's Jack Tatum and ran for a touchdown on the last play of the game to beat the Raiders in the 1972 playoffs.

A lot of pro football fans seem to think the Steelers won it all that year because of Franco's "Immaculate Reception," but that just shows you how bad memories are sometimes. The great undefeated Miami Dolphins team of 1972 beat the Steelers, 21-17, in the conference championship game. And in '73 the Steelers lost the first game of the playoffs to the Raiders, 33-14, when the Dolphins won their second Super Bowl.

However, despite Bradshaw's famous pass to Harris, two years later there was a controversy brewing over Terry being the starting quarterback. And I soon found myself in the middle of it.

Lynn Swann (88), Gordon Gravelle (71), Dan, Gerry Mullins (72).

CHAPTER THREE –
Bumpy Road To The Super Bowl

The Quarterback Controversy – Terry Bradshaw was in his second year in the league and his first full year as the Steelers starter, when I was the Steelers defensive line coach in 1971, and after watching him up close that season, I thought he was going to be a great quarterback. He was a high energy guy with a cannon for an arm similar to a rookie quarterback I was with 12 years later named John Elway.

Terry had some problems in 1973 mostly because of a dislocated shoulder in the fifth game of the season. The Steelers had won their first four games rather handily that year, losing 19-7 to the Bengals at Cincinnati and then beat the Jets. But in the rematch with the Bengals, Terry dislocated his shoulder in the second quarter, and his backup, Terry Hanratty, who was an All-American at Notre Dame and drafted the year before Bradshaw, came on to help win the game. A week later against Washington, Hanratty injured his ribs in the second quarter, and the team's third string quarterback, Joe Gilliam, who had hardly played since being drafted in 1972, brought the Steelers from behind to get the victory.

Terry Bradshaw, Chuck Noll, Joe Gilliam

That probably was the start of the controversy that haunted us into the middle of the 1974 season. As it turned out in 1973, with Bradshaw out and Hanratty hobbled by his broken ribs and a sprained wrist, the offense sputtered, and the Steelers almost missed the playoffs. Bradshaw returned for the last two games to help win the division title, but his shoulder was still bothering him and the Raiders won the first playoff game, 33-14.

Crossing The Picket Line – There were no spring mini-camps back in those days, but each year before the Steelers veterans reported for preseason training in July, we'd have a one-week minicamp solely for the new draft picks, rookie free agents and veteran free agents. This time in 1974 those few days with the rookies and free agents lasted more than a month as the veterans, with few exceptions, went on strike. As the strike continued, some of the veterans began trickling into their NFL training camps. One of those players was quarterback Joe Gilliam.

After about the third week of camp, Gilliam crossed the picket line on the Monday before the Steelers first preseason game at New Orleans. Naturally, Gilliam, who was our only veteran quarterback in camp, was our starting quarterback and he played very well. With just rookies and twelve experienced players, we beat the Saints, 26-7, and Joe threw a 14-yard touchdown pass to rookie John Stallworth. Seeing this, Terry Bradshaw reported two days later and started the next Monday night preseason game against the Bears, which we won 50-21. Terry played very well, but Joe Gilliam was even better. He took over for Terry in the second quarter with the Steelers leading 10-7 and proceeded to throw three touchdown passes, including one for 67 yards to Stallworth.

Two days later, the rest of the veterans reported to camp as the players association decided to end the strike and take their complaints to federal court. With the veterans back, the intensity inside the training camps increased and produced some friction between the strikers and the others, but that went away as we played out the rest of our exhibition season. And Gilliam continued to play extremely well.

In the next game against the Eagles, Gilliam led his third 80-yard drive of the night as Roy Gerela kicked a 19-yard field goal to win, 33-30. Then as the starter against the Giants, Gilliam was so impressive in passing for 225 yards and a touchdown in a 17-7 victory that *The New York Times* reporter covering the game, Neil Amdur, wrote: "...he showed the poise that has often been missing in Pittsburgh's two other quarterbacks, Terry Bradshaw and Terry Hanratty." Gilliam started our final exhibition game at Dallas and on the fifth play of the game threw a 56-yard touchdown pass to Ron Shanklin, then hit Stallworth for a 31-yard TD with 29 seconds left in the second quarter, before giving way to Bradshaw and Hanratty in the second half. We won, 41-15, to become the first Steelers team to go undefeated in the preseason, and Joe Gilliam had been the man most often at the controls. (Back then quarterbacks called their own plays.) Chuck Noll decided to start the regular season with Gilliam at quarterback. Nobody, not even Bradshaw, voiced objection.

Jefferson Street Joe – So, here was an 11th round draft choice from little, obscure Tennessee State—Gilliam—beating out the first overall NFL draft pick of 1970—Bradshaw—who had led the Steelers to two AFC Central titles, and the Steelers No. 2 choice of 1969—Hanratty—who had once led the most famous college team in the country, Notre Dame, to a national championship. Joe was talented and flashy. And perhaps, just as significant, he was black. In a racially diverse city like Pittsburgh that was unique in 1974, just six years removed from one of the most devastating civil uprisings in the city's history in the aftermath of the tragic Martin Luther King assassination.

Gilliam was "Jefferson Street Joe," nicknamed for the street that runs past Tennessee State in Nashville, and the toast of Pittsburgh. Even *The New York Times* took notice, when Dave Anderson devoted a full column to Gilliam, entitled "The Black Quarterback in the NFL," pointing out that Joe was just the second black player ever to start an NFL season at quarterback. James Harris started as a rookie in Buffalo in 1969, was cut three years later and in 1974 was a backup with the Los Angeles Rams. Anderson also cited Marlon Briscoe who had success at Denver in 1968, and then was "strangely" cut the next year in training camp and was now an outstanding wide receiver with Miami.

"If he retains his role," Anderson wrote in September of 1974, "Joe Gilliam, will be the N.F.L.'s most significant player this season."

Noting the injuries to Bradshaw and Hanratty that gave Gilliam his chance in '73, Anderson added perceptively, "They're both healthy now, but Bradshaw, perhaps too golden and too Louisiana for the steel-mill clientele is unpopular, and Hanratty is brittle, and Gilliam has arrived....With either Gilliam or Bradshaw or Hanratty, Pittsburgh should qualify for the A.F. C. playoffs."

Despite some early game jitters in the first quarter when he was booed by those always passionate Steelers fans, Joe looked sharp as we shut down the Baltimore Colts in our 1974 season opener at Three Rivers on September 16. He completed 17-of-31 passes for 257 yards, including two touchdowns of 54 and 4 yards as we beat the Colts 30-0.

It was too good to be true.

Despite this impressive first win, we began to have some problems with Gilliam as our starting quarterback. After shutting out the Colts in our opener, we went out to Denver to play the Broncos. Maybe we just didn't adjust quickly enough to the altitude but the Broncos jumped off to a 21-7 lead in the first quarter before Gilliam brought us back. We were leading 35-28 with about eight minutes left and were on the Denver 20-yard line when Gilliam did something very peculiar and radical. Remember quarterbacks called their own plays and Joe proceeded to throw the ball six straight times (there were penalties on two of the plays and he was sacked once). Denver's Tom Jackson intercepted the sixth pass Joe threw, and five plays later Denver quarterback Steve Ramsey threw a 23-yard touchdown to Otis Armstrong tying the game with 7:08 left. We took the kickoff and drove down to Denver's 7-yard line where Roy Gerela missed a field goal on the last play of regulation time.

Neither team scored in overtime, and the final score was 35-35. Gilliam completed 31-of-50 passes for 348 yards, one touchdown and two interceptions, and in the process set a new team record in pass attempts. Chuck Noll told the media after the game that "Gilliam was outstanding." John Ralston, Denver's head coach, said that Gilliam "had possibly the finest performance I have ever seen by a quarterback."

But in my mind Joe had definitely blown the game by not running the ball inside the 20-yard line when we were leading 35-28, and for the first time since preseason started, I got upset with Joe Gilliam at quarterback. It wouldn't be the last.

The next week Joe played poorly and we lost to Oakland 17-0 at Three Rivers. The defeat wasn't all Joe's fault, but he completed just 8 of 31 passes for 106 yards, threw two interceptions and had the disgruntled Steelers fans chanting, "We want Bradshaw" throughout the game. But Bradshaw continued to stay mostly on the sidelines. Noll tweaked our running game and the Steelers beat Houston,13-7, and Kansas City, 34-21, on the road and then defeated our biggest rival, the Cleveland Browns, at home 20-16. Gilliam put up big numbers against the Oilers and Chiefs but passed for just one touchdown. He hit on just 5 of 18 passes for 78 yards without any touchdowns against the Browns, but, most importantly, he did not run the ball in a number of obvious situations, and I had enough. I felt I had an outstanding offensive line to go with our great defense and Joe Gilliam was letting it go to waste.

With Bradshaw, I thought we had a better chance to be in the Super Bowl. We already had a great defense and all the offense needed was a quarterback who could pass, call plays, think on his feet, be a leader, control the ball and—most importantly—audible to running plays when necessary. I really believed Terry was that quarterback and I was going to keep telling Chuck Noll that no matter what. I've always been outspoken when I see things I don't like, and I still am. In fact, as you will read later, this natural tendency probably cost me a job or three. But, as I'll tell you in Chapter Seven, it also helped me become known as the Father of Linebacker U at Penn State.

Bradshaw Becomes The Starter Again – Since I had previously coached the Steelers defensive line in '71, Chuck Noll knew me pretty well by '74, so I'm sure he wasn't surprised when I told him on the Monday after our Browns game that I thought he should start Bradshaw. For three nights I met with Chuck after our work was done trying to get him to bench Gilliam and to give Bradshaw a chance to start. I told him it was not unanimous but almost all the coaches thought that Bradshaw should be given the opportunity to start. I told Chuck our pass blocking and run blocking was better now than it ever had been when Bradshaw was playing the previous years. I said Joe, not Terry had been the one to benefit from it. Of course, I realized this since I was the new offensive line coach. The only negative that I remember Chuck saying about Bradshaw was that Terry was afraid to throw the ball to the post pattern over the middle. Chuck was also the quarterback coach as well as the head coach, but I never did and still don't understand the meaning of that comment.

Dan, Chuck Noll, Terry Bradshaw

There was also a ton of speculation in the newspapers and on the radio about benching Gilliam. I don't know for certain if my nightly meetings with Coach Noll had any effect on his decision, but on Thursday of that week he announced that Terry Bradshaw would be the starting quarterback in our seventh league game versus the Atlanta Falcons. After Thursday's practice, I was walking out of my office when I ran into Joe Gilliam, who was going down the hallway to leave the building. He shouted, "Hey Rad, you weren't part of the lynch mob, were you?" I said "Joey, not only was I part of it, I led it." He said, "Oh, no!"

I told Joe, "I've got to drop these papers off at the copy room. I'll be right back. I want to talk to you about why." I walked down the hallway to the copy room, walked back two minutes later but Joe was gone. I ran outside to catch him but he was nowhere in sight. I never did have a talk with Joe about why.

Joe Gilliam Fades Away – That was the beginning of the end for Joe Gilliam as a Steeler. He hardly played the rest of the season, appearing in four more games in a mop-up role, and in just another four games in the 1975 Super Bowl season. He was placed on waivers after that season, and then after a brief tryout with the New Orleans Saints was out of the NFL forever. It's pretty well known what happened next. Tragically, Joe turned to drugs when he left football and fought heroin, cocaine and alcohol addiction for nearly the rest of his life, spending several years on the street, including a couple of years living in a cardboard box under a bridge. And then, in the late 1990s he got his life together, overcame his addictions and began running a football camp near his home in Tennessee, among other things. But on Christmas Day of 2000, four days short of his 50 birthday, he died of a heart attack. It was sad, truly sad, because Joe had great talent. He just didn't know how to use it properly.

"Earth to Rad!...Earth to Rad!...Earth Calling Rad" – Quarterback Terry Bradshaw was on the sideline telephone and wanted to talk to me in the Press Box at Three Rivers Stadium. It was late October of 1974, three days before Halloween, and the Pittsburgh Steelers were playing the Atlanta Falcons.

Atlanta was the seventh game of the regular season and we had won three straight after starting the year by beating Baltimore, 30-0, tying with Denver, 35-35—in what was the first overtime game in the NFL after the new rule for using overtime in regular season games was adopted that year—and losing to Oakland, 17-0. The loss to the Raiders at home had been ugly and frustrating. But then Chuck changed our pass-oriented offense to stress our running game, and with defense as our backbone we beat Houston, 13-7, and Kansas City, 34-24, on the road and Cleveland, 20-16, at Three Rivers.

It's unusual for an offensive line coach to be in the press box, but I had spent most of my previous linebacker coaching years in the press box. After our first five preseason games in '74 I thought I'd do a better job up there rather than on the field. Noll gave his okay and I moved upstairs starting with the last exhibition game and was there for half the season

I was on the players' phone alongside Dick Hoak, our backfield coach, who had another phone that was connected to Noll on the sideline. Well, all the quarterbacks sure got a kick out of calling me from down below. I don't remember who started it but whenever either of them—Bradshaw, Gilliam or Hanratty—wanted to talk to me or Dick, they would say "Earth to Rad! Earth calling Rad!" before they stated what they wanted, obviously referring to my "out of the world" mental persona.

In A Football Haze – Now, this wasn't the first time, the expression was used. When I was the defensive coordinator at the University of Colorado, my head coach Eddie Crowder started saying something like that during a squad meeting one day. I guess I was concentrating on something else—out of the world, so to speak—and Eddie wanted me to say something at the end of the meeting. According to a newspaper article by Bob Hurt, Eddie tried to get my attention by first using my name. Here's how Hurt described it:

"'Coach Radakovich,' (Crowder) said. The aide didn't hear him. 'Hey, Rad,' said Crowder. No answer. 'Rad,' yelled Crowder, but the assistant's eyes still were focused on infinity. In desperation, Crowder sing-songed 'Earth calling Rad. Earth calling Rad. Come in please.' Now, when players want to talk to the defensive coach, they say, 'Mars calling Rad.' Radakovich doesn't hear them anyway. His mind is engrossed with football. 'Rad has the faculty to close everything else out of his mind,' explained Crowder. 'He wanders around in a football haze.'"

I know Crowder meant that as a compliment, and I guess I do have a "football haze." I can just focus intently on something and block everything else out, like in the wrong house incident. That's probably what happened when Bradshaw and the other quarterbacks started calling, "Earth to Rad." Frankly, I thought it was pretty funny too, and I went along, often replying something like, "Rad to Earth. Rad to Earth. Go ahead Bradshaw."

Marching To A Different Drummer – Terry Bradshaw had a difficult time sitting on the bench, and before and after the Colts game he asked publicly to be traded. As he told the media: "I feel I'm good enough to start for some team in the NFL. So, if I'm not going to be able to start here, I wish they would trade me to a team that needs me."

Actually, the Pittsburgh Steelers was the team that needed him and that would soon become apparent.

Terry's biggest obstacle was not really Joe Gilliam but himself, and it had nothing do with his physical ability as a quarterback. He was tough, had a strong arm and could heave the ball a mile or throw pinpoint passes. But it was his mentality and intelligence that was constantly being questioned, and for a quarterback that is pure poison. Perhaps it was best summed up in what is now a famous comment made four years later on the eve of the Steelers game against Dallas in Super Bowl XIII when that blowhard Cowboys linebacker, Thomas "Hollywood" Henderson, mocked Terry with his snide remark that "He couldn't spell 'Cat' if you spotted him the 'c' and the 'a'."

Dan talks to Terry Bradshaw (12)

The ridicule Terry encountered because of the perception that he was dumb has been well publicized over the years, but nowadays even Terry makes jokes about it in his public appearances, especially on the Fox NFL football shows where his popularity has skyrocketed. But as he once told *Sports Illustrated* magazine 30 years ago, "I could get a doctorate in chemical engineering and they'd call me dumb."

From my perspective, the derision towards Terry all stems from the fact that he is different—a free-spirit, off-beat, a little eccentric and very much a country boy. I can relate to that because that's what people have been saying about me for about 60 years. They say I "march to a different drummer" and they're right. I've even heard people say, "Rad has a screw loose somewhere." I have an MBA and went to law school so the screw can't be too loose.

I admit I'm different but aren't we all? Most people just can't get used to someone not being like them. That's Terry Bradshaw and that's me. Back in college in the mid 1950s I didn't wear socks half the time and wore a t-shirt a lot and had a scruffy beard. Sounds a lot like many college kids today, right? But back then students dressed more conventional. I was like a hippie ten years before the Hippie Generation. My Penn State coach Rip Engle was so disturbed he sent me to a psychiatrist. Thirty years later, when I was the offensive line coach for the Denver Broncos, I had to see another "shrink" (psychologist) or the head coach, Dan Reeves was going to fire me.

I'll tell more about those visits with the shrinks later, but by the time I returned to the Steelers in '74 I had what I would call a "well-deserved" reputation for being a little different, flakey and spacey. Most of the Steelers players had seen this for themselves when I coached the defensive line in '71, and Dick Hoak, Jack Ham and Franco Harris probably passed around stories about me coaching at Penn State.

I even started telling stories about myself, like the time I walked into the wrong house in Cincinnati in the spring of '71 when I was the defensive coordinator at the University of Cincinnati and going to law school at night.

Wrong House – It was about 5:30 p.m. on a Friday afternoon and I was driving home in the off season from the university. As I turned my car into our driveway in the Pleasant Run subdivision, I noticed a large white van and some bicycles parked in the driveway. I surmised my wife Nancy must have company. I parked and walked through the garage, through the family room, into the kitchen where I put my law books on top of the refrigerator, and went and sat at the kitchen table with my back to the wall.

I looked up and saw a boy and a girl about 11 or 12 years old standing in front of the table with plates and kitchen utensils in their hands. They probably were setting the table. I looked to the right and saw a woman in her mid-30s dressed in a house coat or robe, in her bare feet with her hands on her hips staring at me. I looked to the left through the family room and saw a man standing in front of the fireplace in Levi's, bare feet and an undershirt like Marlon Brando wore in the movie, *Streetcar Named Desire*, with his elbow resting on the fireplace mantel. I must have walked by him when I came into the house.

I said, "What the hell is going on here? Where's Nancy?" Nobody said anything. I looked around some more, and then it registered. I said, "I must be in the wrong house." The lady in the house coat with her hands on her hips said, "Yes, you are!" I said, "Sorry," and got up from the table, grabbed my law books off the top of the refrigerator and walked back out through the family room. As I passed the man in the undershirt with his elbow resting on the fireplace, I said, "See ya," but he didn't say a word. I went out through the garage, got in my car and drove three blocks to my house.

I told my wife what happened and asked her to go see those people and explain that I accidentally, somehow, had gone into their house by mistake. I said I didn't know how that woman was going to explain me to her husband. Nancy said she had no idea how to explain what I did and refused to go. Anyway, I asked some neighbors about the guy who lived there and they told me he was always yelling at kids for running on his lawn, so I never did go back and apologize. To this day, I have no idea why I wound up in someone else's house that afternoon. Maybe I just had so much on my mind and was concentrating on law studies and coaching assignments. I have to admit it makes me seem like a wacko, and I know Terry Bradshaw's never done anything like that.

Back On The Sideline – About the eighth league game of the season, Hoak and I asked Noll if I could go back down to the sideline and put Chuck's phone on. That would then free Chuck to talk to anyone on the sideline without worrying about the phone, and Hoak and I could now communicate easier with the players. Now, with me on the sidelines, most of the time when Hoak or I wanted to tell the quarterback something, I'd tell Chuck first and he'd usually say, "Go tell Bradshaw" or "Go tell Gilliam," and I would go over and talk to the quarterbacks. This worked out great, plus the quarterbacks no longer had the fun of calling "Earth to Rad, Earth calling Rad."

Now, Terry wasn't an instant success after he replaced Gilliam in '74. He was erratic as the Steelers beat Atlanta and Philadelphia and lost to Cincinnati, throwing just one touchdown pass and three interceptions in those games. Chuck started Hanratty the next week at Cleveland and we won despite Hanratty and Gilliam combining for just three completions in 19 attempts for 81 yards, one TD and three interceptions. Bradshaw seethed on the bench but Chuck went back to him the next game against the Saints and Terry had his best game of the year up to that time, throwing for three touchdowns and running for another. But he was down again the following week in a big game with Houston at home and we lost 13-10 and the defense was about ready to take all three quarterbacks on a long, long ride like the Mafia was known to do.

But some light seemed to go on in Terry's head, and he played well as our running game and defense overcame the New England Patriots in the next to last game of the regular season, 21-17, to give us the AFC Central Division title. Terry got better and better as we beat Buffalo and Oakland in the playoffs and then won the Super Bowl against the Vikings, 16-6. Of course, Terry went on to be one of the greatest quarterbacks in pro football history.

I know some other people may take credit for helping turn around Bradshaw's NFL career, and maybe they deserve it. What I did in pleading for Noll to make Terry the starter for that Atlanta game may have helped, too. But, frankly, I would not have gone to Chuck if Joe Gilliam had been using better judgment in controlling the ball, and who knows how everything would have turned out.

I haven't seen Terry in years, but it wouldn't surprise me when I do see him that when greeting me he will shout out, "Earth to Rad! Earth calling Rad!" And we'll both laugh with the memory of that first Super Bowl season.

First Playoff Game—Dec. 22, 1974 – Three days before Christmas, we played the O.J. Simpson-led Buffalo Bills at Three Rivers Stadium in Pittsburgh. The big assignment for the Steelers defense was, of course, to stop O.J., who had broken Jim Brown's single season NFL rushing record the year before and had run over 1,000 yards (1,125) for the current 1974 season. Not only did the Steelers defense hold O.J. to 49 yards and Buffalo's total rushing game to 100 yards, but the Steelers offense also set an NFL all-time playoff record of 29 first downs. After being behind 7-3 at the end of the first quarter, the Steelers exploded for 26 points in the second quarter to practically ice the game by halftime with a 29-7 lead. O.J. caught a 3-yard touchdown pass in the third quarter to cut the lead to 29-14. A field goal by Roy Gerela in the fourth ended the scoring. Final score: Steelers 32, Bills 14, with the Steelers completely dominating the total yardage statistics, 438 to 264. Next stop, California and the Oakland Raiders.

Fashion Show Christmas Present – Two days after our Buffalo playoff win, I left the Steelers football offices located in Three Rivers Stadium to do some last-minute Christmas Eve shopping just across the Allegheny River in the downtown Pittsburgh business district. My plan was to go to some exclusive ladies clothing stores, see what was on sale Christmas Eve and get my wife a Christmas present for much less than it would normally cost. Well, when I was looking over the merchandise on sale at the Sax Fifth Avenue store, I happened to spot a dress on sale that Nancy had worn—and had loved—at the "Pittsburgh Steelers—Sax Fifth Avenue Fashion Show" held on a runway some 30 yards in length in the grand ballroom of the Pittsburgh Hilton Hotel nearly two months before, on Nov. 3. The sales slip on the dress said 75 percent off. I couldn't believe my good luck. What a great Christmas present! I bought the $400 dress my wife had worn in the fashion show for $100. I felt like we had won another playoff game. I definitely knew that I was going to be a hero when my wife opened her present Christmas morning.

Nancy (Dan's wife)

Daughter Lori (right)

Daughter Leslie

A year later, after we had won both Super Bowls IX and X, Nancy and I were invited to join the Penn State football staff at its annual three-day winter get together at the Allenberry Playhouse near Harrisburg that was owned by alumnus and former Penn State football manager John Heinz. Nancy wore that fashion show Sax Fifth Avenue dress the first evening. After admiring the Sax Fifth Avenue dress, the wife of one of the Penn State coaches told Nancy, "If Rad was still a college coach, you wouldn't be able to afford dresses like the one you're wearing." Nancy and I both got kick out of that comment. We never mentioned that I had bought the dress on a 75 percent off Christmas Eve sale.

"Steelers Fever," Joey Diven And Billy Conn – Shortly after leaving that Sax Fifth Avenue store in downtown Pittsburgh with my wife's Christmas present in a box under my arm, I heard someone shouting, "Hey Rad, wait up!" I turned around, and walking down the sidewalk were two big professional fighters from Pittsburgh, Billy Conn and his pal Joey Diven. Billy had been the Light Heavyweight Boxing Champion of the World back in 1939 and 1940 and had fought Joe Louis for the Heavyweight title in 1941 and 1946. Both Billy and Joey were close friends of The Chief, Art Rooney Sr., and I had first met each of them in The Chief's office earlier in the year. After exchanging greetings, they invited me to join them in a bar-restaurant nearby and tell them all about the Steelers team. Like almost everyone else in the city, they were infected with "Steelers Fever."

I told them I would love to talk to them about the Steelers but that I was doing some last-minute Christmas shopping and we'd have to do it another time. Well, they whispered something to each other, and then each of them grabbed me under an armpit, lifted me off the ground and carried me down the street into a bar-restaurant. They carried me through the door and onto a stool at the bar and said, "Now, tell us about the Steelers!"

Well, I did what any normal Steelers coach would do caught up in that situation. For the next 45 minutes I told them anything they wanted to know about the Steelers and answered all their Steelers questions to the best of my ability. They were wired up, excited and had a very bad case of "Steelers Fever!" Finally, they let me go. Was I frightened at all when they both picked me up off the ground? Not really, but maybe just a little bit. It certainly was a unique Christmas Eve experience.

Ten years later, there was an article about Billy Conn in the June 17, 1985 edition of *Sports Illustrated* entitled "The Boxer and The Blonde." The famous writer, Frank DeFord, called Joey Diven "the World's Greatest Street Fighter." I've often wondered if Joey and Billy ever fought each other, and, if they did, what was the outcome?

Art Thoms Lines Up In Steelers Backfield – At the beginning of the week before the 1974 AFC championship playoff game with the Oakland Raiders, my lawyer cousin Ray Radakovich said, "Rad, the Steelers can't beat the Raiders because Art Thoms always lines up in the Steelers backfield." Art Thoms was a Raiders defensive tackle who had played well in previous games against the Steelers. Earlier that season the Raiders had beaten us 17-0 and the previous year they had defeated the Steelers in a playoff game, 33-13.

Now, in those games, Thoms usually lined up in or slanted to the gap on either side of the center. One of the plays we had been practicing was a tackle trap on one of the defensive fronts that Oakland used on short yardage situations. This is a play where the offensive tackle pulls and blocks Art Thoms. A few hours before we left for California on Friday, I convinced Coach Noll that the tackle trap would be a good play for Bradshaw to audible to against all the various Oakland defensive fronts. The audible was "Brown 92" or "Brown. 93." Before I went to the airport, I drove to my cousins' law office, which was next to the county jail. He wasn't there but I left a diagram of a tackle trap on his desk with the statement, "We are going to beat the Raiders by letting Art Thoms line up in the Steelers backfield."

Saturday at the hotel in California, I held a two-hour walk-through of the tackle trap with my offensive linemen against all the various Oakland defensive fronts. I told my offensive linemen that if we audibled "Brown 92 or 93" 10 times that we would gain 100 yards on the play. During the game, Bradshaw audibled "Brown 92 or 93" eight times for a total of 88 yards and two touchdowns of 8 and 21 yards. Both touchdowns were "Brown 93" with Steelers right tackle Gordon Gravelle trapping Art Thoms each time. On the second touchdown run—a "Brown 93"—Art was seen in the game film pounding his fist on the ground after Franco ran by him.

The next day, *Pittsburgh Press* writer Phil Musick wrote about what we did:

"The Steelers controlled the ball on the ground—Harris getting 111 yards, Rocky Bleier a career high 98—and when the crunch was at hand, they trapped Thoms. 'We saw something on the films from the way Thoms played,' explained veteran center Ray Mansfield. Figuring Thoms could be trapped, offensive line coach Dan Radakovich huddled his troops for a half-hour Saturday afternoon (day before the game). 'Rad took us into that room and we went over every conceivable angle of the tackle-trap. We didn't call it in the huddle. Terry called it from the line.'"

So, there's no doubt in my mind that we helped win the game by letting Art Thoms line up in the Steelers backfield.

Cousin Raymond Calls Howard Cosell – My cousin Raymond, who watched the Steelers-Raiders 1974 playoff game on television, was so excited about the Steelers victory and the way we won it with a tackle trap—just like I had diagramed it on his desk—that he called Howard Cosell in New York right after the game. Raymond had never met Cosell, but I guess Howard just liked talking to anyone who called him. Anyhow, as a result of his conversation with Cosell, Howard made the following commentary on his nationwide ABC radio program the next morning:

[COSELL TRANSCRIPT - Monday December 30, 1974]

Hello everyone, this is Howard Cosell "Speaking of Sports"...

Looking back upon yesterday's stunning victory by the Pittsburgh Steelers over the Oakland Raiders, one can find, perhaps, an unsung hero in the form of an assistant coach on the Steelers, a man named Dan Radakovich. This is a fellow who for 17 years was an assistant coach at Penn State. He was the man who turned out all those great linebackers who now seem to inhabit the

National Football League—linebackers led by Number 59, Jack Ham, who had such a marvelous season for the Steelers. He went on a couple of years back, a few years back, to take over as an assistant coach at Pittsburgh for the Steelers, and he had a hand in forging that defensive line that is now the best in all of football, a line of Greenwood, and Greene, and Holmes and White. And THEN, he moved over to coach the offensive line, the offensive line that blew the Oakland Raiders defensive line right out of the ball park yesterday. So, while everyone is talking about the Jack Ham's of the world, and about Terry Bradshaw, and about Lynn Swann, and all the other great players who made Pittsburgh's victory possible yesterday, it might be well to take note of a fellow named Dan Radakovich, an assistant coach. I'll be back in 60 seconds....

After reading Howard's commentary years later, I realize I should have hired my cousin Raymond as my agent. He might have made Bad Rad rich and famous.

Forgotten Great Catch – An incorrect call by an official has always determined the outcome of some games. However, as a coach, you just have to live with it because sometimes the call goes against you and sometimes it doesn't. One of the greatest catches in Steelers history was botched by an official, but it is hardly remembered by anyone because it not only didn't count but it also didn't affect the outcome of the game—which was one of the most significant in Steelers history, too.

The setting was the Oakland-Pittsburgh AFC Championship game in Oakland on December 29, 1974. In the second quarter Terry Bradshaw threw an 8-yard pass to John Stallworth, which Stallworth snagged with only his left hand. Both of Stallworth's feet were a yard inside the sideline in the end zone and five yards from the end line, and he didn't juggle the ball. He was clearly in bounds when his feet hit the ground, but it was ruled no good because the official thought Stallworth was over the sideline and out of the end zone. This was years before the NFL implemented television replay rules. So, even though a television replay showed Stallworth had scored a touchdown, it didn't count.

Stallworth told me that years later he met the official who apologized for blowing the call. If there had been instant replay that catch may have gone down as one of the greatest receptions in Steelers history. Hardly anyone remembers it because the Steelers ended up winning the game, 24-13. I call it the most forgotten great catch in Steelers history because it was made in the game that determined who went to Super Bowl IX. We still ended up going to Super Bowl IX and beat the Vikings 16-6, and Stallworth still ended up in the Pro Football Hall of Fame. And nowadays Stallworth is a part owner of the Steelers.

Biggest Thrill Of All – Our game against the Raiders for the AFC Championship and a trip to the Super Bowl was one of the most unusual games I have ever seen. At halftime the score was tied, 3-3, and as I was walking alongside defensive coordinator Bud Carson to the locker room, I said, "Bud, this is a weird game. From the sidelines, all I saw the first half were Steelers jerseys. When we had the ball, our Steelers offensive lineman drove the Raiders defensive linemen backwards. When the Raiders had the ball, our Steelers defensive lineman drove the Raiders offensive linemen backwards. We completely dominated the Raiders physically the first half, and the score is tied at 3-3."

Although we were dominating physically, we had two problems. Our offense wasn't scoring many points and the defense was having a problem covering Raiders wide receiver Cliff Branch, who eventually caught nine passes for 186 yards. In the third quarter, Cliff caught a touchdown pass to put the Raiders ahead, 10-3, causing Bud Carson to bench Mel Blount, which upset Mel a lot. At the end of three quarters, we had controlled the ball twice as long as the Raiders, 29 minutes to 16 minutes, and we were still behind, 10-3. Our domination on both sides of the ball eventually took its toll, and we won 24-13, and went to the Super Bowl. Winning this game to go to the Super Bowl is the best feeling and the biggest thrill of all. I know it may sound a little odd, but just knowing that my team was going to be playing in the Super Bowl was a bigger thrill to me than winning the Super Bowl.

Ball Control And Defense – What I remembered most about those 1974 playoffs was that we dominated all three games with ball control and great defense. We had rushing yards of 235 against Buffalo, 224 against Oakland, and 249 against Minnesota, while the rushing yards against our defense was 100 yards by Buffalo, 28 yards by Oakland, and 17 yards by Minnesota. Times of possession were heavily in the Steelers favor. In all these games, Bradshaw audibled over 90% of the running plays. Our defense played strictly the stunt 4-3 in all three playoff games. Previously, it had just been one of many fronts. Thanks to ball control and defense, the Pittsburgh Steelers won the AFC championship and then the Super Bowl.

Bad Rad vs. Jimmy Brown – As we started to prepare for the Super Bowl at Tulane Stadium in New Orleans, Chuck Noll and our Steelers staff decided to treat the two weeks of practice before the game just like preseason camp. We were in full pads for six days, three days each week, and did all our one-on-one pass rush and one-on-one run blocking drills live and full speed. The Minnesota Vikings had an altogether different approach to the game, which involved giving their players some extra time off. The day before the Super Bowl game, I had a last meeting scheduled with my offensive line to go over our plays for the Vikings. I decided that we had seen enough of the Vikings. I told the players that we were going to have one last look at the Vikings. But instead of film of the Vikings, I showed them a 1956 black and white film of Penn State against Syracuse when I played against the great Jim Brown, and I had been in on a lot of tackles stopping Brown. At first the players didn't realize what they were seeing. Then, after a few plays one of the players yelled out, "That's not the Vikings." Then Mike Webster yells out, "That's Rad at middle linebacker." So we watched "Bad Rad versus Jim Brown," movies at the last offensive line meeting the day before Super Bowl IX. I don't know if what the Seven Dwarfs saw that day helped them against the Vikings great front four of Carl Eller, Alan Page, Jim Marshall and Doug Sutherland, but I know watching me try to tackle Jim Brown helped them to relax and relieve a lot of tension—and maybe even laugh a little. I know they got a big kick out of my claim that I put Jim Brown on his back with "very little help." In the film on that particular play, the "very little help" was shown to be four or five teammates participating in the tackle.

Super Bowl IX Eve – I had the evening free the night before Super Bowl IX. All football commitments—practice, meetings, etc.—were finished. My wife and I decided to spend the evening visiting Bourbon Street in the French Quarter. The streets of the French Quarter were packed with a sea of people and 90 percent of them were Steelers fans. It was a giant wave of black and gold with only a tiny sprinkling of Minnesota Viking purple and white. A gigantic Steelers party was going on. Nancy and I didn't want to drink any alcohol the night before the Super Bowl, so we stopped at a small shop that served hot chocolate. We spent the evening walking the streets, watching the Steelers fans party and peeking into the bars, shops and strip shows while sipping our hot chocolate. It was a pleasant and enjoyable evening in that so-called "Den of Iniquity"—the French Quarter—on Super Bowl Eve.

Super Bowl IX Pregame Tension – After the pregame warm-ups on the field, the teams returned to the locker rooms and had their last minute instructions from the coaches. Then as we waited for the time to leave for the field for the stadium announcer's introductions, the locker room got deathly quiet. After a few minutes, the atmosphere in the room seemed to be quite tense, when all of a sudden defensive safety Glen Edwards yelled: "What's going on here? Why is it so quiet? This isn't the Steelers. We have always been loose before a game. This isn't us!"

That broke the tension and everyone started to chat and talk and everything seemed normal again like it had been all season. In fact, when we lined up in the tunnel leading from the locker room to the stadium entrance to be introduced there was a lot of laughing and kidding around. Before the introductions, I waited with Head Coach Chuck Noll at the tunnel entrance. As we were standing there, I spotted a sign high up in the stands of Tulane Stadium and said to Chuck, "Look Chuck. That sign up there at the top of the stadium is from my hometown." The sign read: "Kennywood's Horseshoe Bar says 'Go Steelers!'" Some of my neighborhood friends had made it to New Orleans.

The Surprise Kickoff – The first half of the Super Bowl reminded me of the first half of our previous playoff game two weeks earlier against the Oakland Raiders, when we were tied 3-3 at halftime. In that game, as in this one, we had completely controlled the line of scrimmage on offense and defense. When I looked out on the field during the first half of the Super Bowl, all I saw were black and gold jerseys pushing the Vikings backwards. Yet, the score at halftime was Steelers 2, Vikings 0. Our defense had shut out the Vikings' offense and our offensive line was constantly opening holes in the Vikings front four to allow Franco Harris and Rocky Bleier to go rushing through. However, we had trouble scoring, and our only points came when Vikings quarterback Fran Tarkenton botched a pitchout deep in his own territory and had to fall on the ball in his own end zone. Our defensive end Dwight White, who had been in the hospital until that morning with the flu or pneumonia, touched him down for a 2-point safety. Despite our domination on both sides of the ball, we only led by two points at the half.

At the start of the second half, our kicker, Roy Gerela, flubbed the kickoff when his left plant foot slipped and his right foot hardly touched the ball and the ball bounced like an onside kick when it really was unintentional. Minnesota's Bill Brown fumbled the ball and Pittsburgh's Marv Kellum recovered at the Vikings 30-yard line. Four plays later, Franco scored from the 9-yard line on a fake trap sweep around the left side, following right guard Gerry Mullins, who cut down linebacker Wally Hilgenberg with a great block that allowed Franco to go into the end zone standing up. Gerela's extra point put the Steelers ahead 9-0 with $13^{1}/_{2}$ minutes left in the third quarter. I am sure everyone in Tulane Stadium, especially those guys in the press box, were probably talking about the great and gutty call by Coach Noll to surprise the Vikings with that onside kick to start the second half. They learned later what actually happened.

The only time the Vikings got close to the Steelers goal line in the second half was when Steelers safety Mike Wagner was called for pass interference at our 5-yard line. On the very next play, Minnesota's star running back, Chuck Foreman, fumbled; Pittsburgh's defensive tackle Joe Greene recovered and ended the Vikings scoring threat. However, four plays later we had to punt. Linebacker Matt Blair blocked Bobby Walden's punt attempt and Minnesota's Terry Brown fell on the ball for a Vikings touchdown. Fred Cox missed the extra point, and the Steelers lead was cut to 9-6 with 10:33 left in the game.

The Steelers proceeded to make a 66-yard drive, highlighted by a 30-yard pass from Terry Bradshaw to tight end Larry Brown. On third down from the 4-yard line, Bradshaw sprinted to his right and threw to Brown for a touchdown, and after Gerela's extra point we led 16-6 with 3:31 remaining on the clock. Soon after the ensuing kickoff, Mike Wagner intercepted a Tarkenton pass which basically finished the Vikings. The final score was 16-6, and for the first time in NFL history, the Pittsburgh Steelers were the champions and owners of the Lombardi Trophy as winners of Super Bowl IX.

The final statistics reveal the total domination of the Steelers. We outgained Minnesota in total yardage (333 to 119), rushing yardage (249-17) and first downs (17-9). Our star running back, Franco Harris, set a Super Bowl rushing record of 158 yards while the Vikings' star running back, Chuck Foreman, had only 18 yards rushing.

I also want to mention a couple of our unsung heroes in Super Bowl IX:
– Defensive end Dwight White was in the hospital with the flu or pneumonia until a few hours before the opening kickoff. Dwight not only played well but scored the safety by touching Tarkenton in the end zone in the first quarter;
– Backup middle linebacker Ed Bradley played the entire second half after replacing our great linebacker Jack Lambert, who was injured, and Ed played an exceptional game;
– Backup outside linebacker Loren Toews who replaced another of our great linebackers, Andy Russell, in the second half when Andy went out with an injury, and Loren also played very well.

Finally, when reflecting back on the Super Bowl I always think about the Lombardi Trophy, and there's a personal reason. Maybe you didn't know that just the names of the winning head coach and all of his assistants are engraved on the trophy. Yes, Bad Rad's name is there, not only for Super Bowl IX but also the next season for Super Bowl X.

The Radakovich Family at the 1974 Steelers Christmas Party.

CHAPTER FOUR – Bad Rad Day

After we returned home from Super Bowl IX, I introduced three of our Seven Dwarfs to "Bad Rad Day." "Bad Rad Day" was an annual event created in 1960 by one of my closest friends, Joe Moore, who in the early 1970s was one of the most successful coaches in high school football. You're going to read a lot more about Joe because of all that happened between us. As I look back on my career, there was no one outside of my wife who had as much influence on me or whom I trusted more. It all started when we met at Penn State, and I don't think it was coincidental that we really became close friends at about the time that the roots of "Linebacker U" were planted, so that's why I want to tell you a little about him.

In 1951, Joe had been a highly recruited, outstanding halfback at Pittsburgh's Schenley High School. But after one year on the freshman team at Tennessee, Joe transferred to Penn State. A year later Joe joined the Army, and two years later he was discharged and returned to Penn State. We became friends when we roomed together at the Phi Delta Theta fraternity where the football players stayed in the preseason of my senior year, 1956. We were a lot alike. Joe was a few years older than me but a little crazy like me, and had once been temporarily suspended from the team for punching a teammate. Joe was a reserve halfback in '56, and in our third game of the season against Holy Cross, he hurt his back so severely he could no longer play football. So, Joe used up his athletic eligibility in the spring of 1958 by playing varsity baseball, and then was asked to coach the freshmen backs in the fall of '58. At the same time, I became a graduate assistant and coached the line on the freshman team for the second straight year.

As Joe was about to graduate in May of 1959, I saw a posting in the football office for a head coaching job at Richfield Springs High School near Cooperstown, New York. I told Joe, and he got the job. Nearly 40 years later, Joe would be known as one of the greatest offensive line coaches in college football and the plaintiff in a prominent age-discrimination law suit involving Notre Dame and its then head coach Bob Davies.

Anyhow, in his first year at Richfield Springs Joe only won one game. So in the spring of his second year, Joe had me visit and give an inspirational talk to his high school players. My inspirational talk was about how to block, play off blocks and other aspects of playing football. Of course, besides talking I also demonstrated how to play. Joe called it "Bad Rad Day," and after Joe went 8-1 and won the league championship in 1960, he made "Bad Rad Day" an annual spring ritual wherever he was coaching.

In 1972, Joe became the head coach at Upper St. Clair High School in suburban Pittsburgh and he turned the program into a powerhouse. The same year that the Steelers won Super Bowl IX in 1974, Joe's team at Upper St. Clair went undefeated and was WPIAL co-champions. So, in the spring of 1975, Joe and I decided to do something different on our annual "Bad Rad Day." We decided to have Joe's eight best high school players compete against three Steeler offensive line starters in some off-season drills in the Upper St. Clair gym. I brought three Super Bowl starters: left tackle Jon Kolb, left guard Jim Clack and right tackle Gordon Gravelle. The Steeler players had no idea that they were going to participate in drills against the Upper St. Clair high school players. I had simply asked them if they would come and talk to the high school players about run and pass blocking and to be dressed in shorts and sneakers so that they could demonstrate.

It all started off innocently enough. First, we had Jon Kolb demonstrate the mirror dodge drill against Pat McGarvey, a high school linebacker who was Joe Moore's quickest player. Two cones were put seven yards apart on a straight line. Kolb was to be the dodger and would try to score on McGarvey, the mirror defender, by juking or dodging him in trying to get across the line between the two cones. The drill ran for 15 to 20 seconds. Well, Kolb could not score against McGarvey in two separate 20 second tries.

Then, we put Kolb as the mirror defender and had Pat Coleman, Joe's second quickest player, as the dodger who would try to score against Kolb. Well, Kolb wasn't about to let this high school kid score, especially since Kolb couldn't score on McGarvey. Anytime Coleman got close, Kolb jolted him backwards with both arms. Coleman couldn't score in his two separate 20 second tries. Joe Moore said that the next day Coleman kept pulling his shirt up and was proudly showing all the other kids in school his black and blue bruises all over his chest and arms that Kolb had given him.

Both Clack and Gravelle each went against two fresh high school players in the mirror dodge drill, and they figured it would be a snap. The Steeler players had done the mirror dodge drill for the first time the previous fall. What they did not know was that the Upper St. Clair players had been doing the mirror dodge drill for three years all year long. Joe Moore used to say that his players needed 500 hours of mirror dodge in order to graduate. These were the same drills Notre Dame coach Bob Davies would later claim were abusive when he didn't rehire Joe as offensive line coach after succeeding Lou Holtz at the end of the 1996 season, as you will read in Chapter Seven.

Besides the mirror drill, Joe and I had three other drills in which we rotated the eight high school players against the three Steelers. In addition to Joe, me and the players, we had two distinguished spectators sitting in the stands in the gym—my wife Nancy and Joe's wife Fran. When Nancy and Fran heard what Joe and I were doing, they both said they had to see it.

Joe and I even had to break up a fight that started between Joe's biggest player, Kurt Brechbill, and starting Steelers right offensive tackle Gordon Gravelle. After about 1$^{1}/_{2}$ hours of this competition between three NFL players and eight high school players, Joe and I declared the competition a draw. We said the real winners would be which team had the better season in 1975. The Steelers won the Super Bowl again, but Upper St. Clair went undefeated again for the second year in a row, and again were WPIAL co-champions. So in the end, the two-time Super Bowl Champion Pittsburgh Steelers versus Upper St. Clair High School on "Bad Rad Day" was a draw. Imagine that!

During the season, my wife and I attended an Upper St. Clair game against Trinity High School along with Jon Kolb and Jim Clack. After the game, I took Kolb and Clack into the Upper St. Clair locker room. Upon entering the locker room, one of the Upper St. Clair players spotted us and yelled, "Kolb and Clack are here." The entire team jumped up and stood and cheered continuously for about five minutes. They just wouldn't stop. When they finally finished, Joe Moore said, "How did we do, Rad?" I said, "Awesome, these two guys are offensive lineman. Probably never again will they walk into a room unannounced, be recognized, and get a spontaneous five-minute standing ovation."

Incidentally, my son Danny, who was an assistant manager on the Upper St. Clair's 1974 undefeated team, was the head football manager for Upper St. Clair's undefeated 1975 team. The 1975 Upper St. Clair players have had a lot of fun telling new friends over the years how their high school team held the Pittsburgh Steelers to a tie.

Football—Not Olympics—Gymnastics – Around the beginning of February, 1975, and after a weeklong Steelers coaching staff and wives vacation on Walkers Cay Island in the Bahamas (a bonus vacation by the Steelers for winning Super Bowl IX), I decided to take advantage of the special talents of our Special Teams Coach, Paul Uram. Besides being a quarterback in college, and a former high school football coach, Paul had also been a gymnastics coach at Butler High School where he had coached a couple of gymnasts who went on to become All-American gymnasts at Michigan State and other schools. In addition to being a gymnastics coach, he was also a national gymnastics judge at Penn State, Eastern and national gymnastic meets. Paul was inducted into the Western Pennsylvania Hall of Fame for gymnastics before he ever became a coach for the Steelers. With Paul's help, I decided to have my offensive linemen learn gymnastic skills in the off-season in order to gain better balance and control of their bodies. I was on the gymnastics team for three years at Homeville Junior High in West Mifflin Borough and felt that it helped me in playing football. I had installed new blocking techniques a year earlier of locking out the arms to full extension on pass blocking that required a coordination and skill not much different than a gymnast locking his arms out on the floor as he begins a hand spring and body

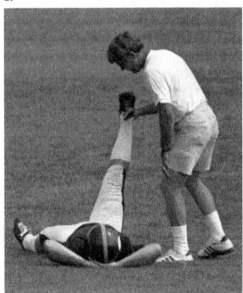

Paul Uram, Flexibility and Special Teams Coach

flip. All of my offensive linemen lived in or nearby Pittsburgh and had no trouble attending the three gymnastic workouts a week (Monday, Wednesday and Friday) for two hours each.

Paul taught them front hand springs, head springs, cartwheels, front and back no hand flips off a spring board, diving forward rolls, walking on their hands and five second—absolutely still—hand stands. Of course, Paul taught them how to spot each other and we had gymnastic belts and plenty of mats to avoid injuries.

Both Paul and I felt that the linemen benefited a lot from the gymnastics program. It surely didn't hurt as we won our second consecutive Super Bowl the next season. However, the offensive line players had so many off season commitments after winning the second Super Bowl in a row that it became impossible to schedule another off-season gymnastics program. It was a one-shot affair, but thanks to Paul it was a unique and beneficial experience for both my offensive linemen and myself. (No, we did not have anybody good enough to qualify for the Olympics.)

A Special Note: Paul Uram and I attended a Steelers reunion at a Steelers game in the fall of 2009. As we sat next to each other, I asked him how it felt to have his name on all four of the Lombardi Super Bowl trophies displayed on a table on the far side of the room. He had no idea what I was talking about. I said, "Come with me," and grabbed his hand and led him to the table on which the four Super Bowl Lombardi trophies (Super Bowls IX, X, XIII and XIV) were displayed. I showed him his name, Paul Uram, on all four trophies and astonished him. He hadn't known that the names of the winning Super Bowl coach and his assistants are on the Lombardi trophies (no players, no others). Paul's name had been on those trophies for approximately 35 years and neither he nor his family knew it.

Unusual Coaching Experience

Bud Carson's Chauffeur – After all we went through in my first year in Pittsburgh as the defensive line coach in 1971 and then as the offensive line coach on the Steelers first Super Bowl Champions in 1974, the next three years seemed to go rather quickly. But I want to tell you some of the things that I remember best about that period of my life.

Bud Carson was hired by Chuck Noll in 1972 as secondary coach, and then during that season made him defensive coordinator. But it wasn't until I returned to the Steelers in '74 that Bud and I became good friends. Later, as our friendship deepened, we would coach together in Los Angeles, New York and Cleveland. Bud had

Bud Carson

been an assistant at his alma mater, North Carolina, in 1957, and then went to South Carolina for one year in 1965 before becoming an assistant at Georgia Tech. The next year, Bud succeeded the great Bobby Dodd as head coach, and five years later Chuck Noll hired him to the coach the Steelers secondary.

Bud was now the defensive coordinator-secondary coach, and it was under Bud, defensive line coach George Perles and linebacker coach Woody Widenhofer that The Steel Curtain fully developed from my original linemen that first earned that famous nickname and now included the great linebackers and secondary. Bud was an excellent defensive coach but he had a major flaw. He had a physical disorder formally known as narcolepsy—a sudden and uncontrollable impulse to fall into a deep sleep. He took medicine for it and it was rarely noticeable, but, occasionally, it got him into some unusual situations

Bud and I rode together many times to our preseason camp at St. Vincent's College in Latrobe, about 70 minutes from our homes in Upper St. Clair as well as to the airport during the season for away games. Bud did drive, but when we rode together, I always did the driving. I used to tell Bud's wife, Linda, that the Steelers were paying me more to chauffeur the defensive coordinator and make sure he arrived safely for the game than for coaching the offensive line.

Bad Rad's Chauffeur – One Saturday morning in late July or early August of 1975 we had an intrasquad scrimmage at St. Vincent that lasted from about 10:15 a.m. to 11:45 a.m. As soon as the scrimmage was over, Bud and I walked directly to my car still in our coaching gear. We were making a quick getaway for home, and I asked Bud if he would mind driving. I said I was tired and didn't feel like driving. Bud said he had 10 hours sleep the night before, felt great and would not mind driving at all. Bud started the car and we headed down Route 30 towards Greensburg. I was in the passenger seat and closed my eyes to take a nap. After about three or four minutes with my eyes closed, I heard and felt the car go bump, bump, bump, bump! I opened my eyes and looked at Bud driving. He was fast asleep at the wheel, and we were on the berm of the highway. I grabbed the steering wheel and at the same time screamed, "Bud, wake up! Stop the car! Hit the brake!" Bud woke up startled and hit the brakes and we stopped. I said, "That's it. I'm driving." I got behind the wheel and Bud went in the passenger seat. I started the car and went down Route 30 towards Greensburg. Bud and I talked for a few moments, and a couple of minutes later I looked over at him and he was fast asleep. He slept the entire trip, until I pulled up in front of his house in Upper St. Clair an hour and 15 minutes later. Never again did I let him drive when we rode together, even if he had 10 hours sleep the night before.

Bud's Dealer Car – Now, it's a common practice for auto dealers to provide the coaches and others with cars to drive in exchange for some reciprocal benefit like season tickets. Well, about nine months after the incident driving back from training camp, the Steelers' coaching staff drove their year-old dealer cars to turn into the dealer at Three Rivers Stadium and get new dealer cars that same day. At about 4 p.m., Bud Carson left the office and got in his new dealer car and drove home to

Upper St. Clair. About 15 minutes later Woody, George and I walked out of the Steelers' office in Three Rivers Stadium and got in our brand-new dealer cars and followed each other home to Upper St. Clair. Woody was in the lead car. We each drove our new cars on Route 22-30 West, then onto Route 79 South when all of the sudden, Woody put his left arm out the window, slowed down, pointed at a car and pulled left off the highway onto a grass median strip. George and I followed in our cars. Bud Carson's new dealer car was parked in the median strip and Bud was fast asleep at the wheel. Evidently, he had gotten sleepy and had pulled left off the highway, instead of right. We woke him up and escorted him home.

Sleep Walking Bud – One of the Steelers coaches who roomed with Bud on away games either in 1972 or 1973 told me another sleeping story about Bud. Bud's roommate heard Bud get up in the middle of the night and go to the bathroom. When Bud came out of the bathroom he stopped at the foot of his bed, or what he thought was the foot of the bed, and he did a dive into bed. But being half asleep, he miscalculated and dove between the beds and landed on the floor between the beds. Of course, that made both Bud and his roommate wide-awake. Bud got bruised but did not get hurt seriously in his misdirected dive. Looking back, it's amazing to me that Bud survived his narcolepsy illness without ever seriously hurting himself.

Bud Carson and Jack Lambert (58)

Lying To A Friend – I learned a valuable lesson during training camp in '75 that might have cost me a friendship and probably much more. The Steelers' third round pick in the 1975 draft was a 6-foot-2, 215- or 220-pound skinny tight end from Maryland named Walter White, who could run like a deer. He had great hands and quickness. He couldn't block but had strong legs, and I thought he could become a good blocker. I knew Walter from when I was at Colorado University, two years earlier. We had tried to recruit Walter from the junior college that he attended but we lost out to Maryland. I was Walter's blocking coach on the Steelers and Lionel Taylor was his receiving coach. A week before the final cut, we had a staff meeting on personnel, and decided to definitely keep Walter. Lionel and I both liked him and we were both happy about the decision. The day of the final cut, I walked into the office and found out that we were cutting Walter White in the final cut. I couldn't believe it. I argued that we should keep Walter, but the decision had been made to keep three players at another position rather than at tight end.

Walter went on the waiver wire, and I received a call from a close friend, Steve Ortmayer, a Kansas City Chiefs coach who had coached with me at Colorado

University in 1972 and 1973. Ort said he was calling to find out if Walter White was worth picking up off of waivers. There was no way I wanted to lose Walter. I thought if Walter cleared waivers and nobody claimed him I could continue to argue about keeping him. So, when Steve called, I told him that Walter was awful, that he couldn't play in the NFL and so on. He thanked me, and later told me that he told his people at Kansas City that they could forget about picking up Walter because I said he wasn't good enough.

After I hung up the phone with Steve, I saw Lionel Taylor and told him what I had told Ort. Lionel said, "Rad, you're crazy. What do you think everybody in that scouting room did when they found out Walter White was put on waivers? They all ran to their phones, called their friends in the league and told them to pick up Walter. You better call your friend back." So I got Ort on the phone and said, "Steve, I lied to you. I'm sorry I did. Walter is a great prospect and I thought if he cleared waivers I could still argue to keep him. I realize now that there's no way he'll clear waivers. You better pick him up." He went back, told his people I had lied to him and why, and Kansas City picked up Walter. Walter White played the next four years at Kansas City, 1975-78, caught 160 passes for 2,382 yards for an average of 15 yards per catch. A knee injury at the end of the 1978 season ended his career.

Twenty years later Ort would get me back into the NFL in 1995 with the St. Louis Rams after I had been away for nearly four years helping build a football program from scratch at a small college in suburban Pittsburgh. More about all that later in this book.

Heard Footsteps – Along the way in my coaching career, I learned that a football coach should never question a player's courage. I found out in law school in 1970 that just going out for football displays a lot of courage in the eyes of the public. A coach who publicly—or privately, if proven—questions a player's courage puts himself in jeopardy for a defamation of character lawsuit. Well, an incident during the 1975 season was almost disastrous for me.

After a Sunday game, the Steelers players would have Monday off. They'd report at 10 a.m. Tuesday morning to review the game film from the past Sunday with the coaches and then have a light workout on their own before going home. During my film meeting with the offensive linemen and tight ends, I would give the players grading sheets. As they watched the game film, they could read the comments I had written about their personal performances on each and every play.

Immediately after this particular game film meeting—and I simply can't remember which game—I returned to my office, sat at my desk, looked up, and Larry Brown, our 6-foot-5, 240-pound tight end, was standing in front of my desk. He had followed me from the meeting. I said, "Larry, what do you want?" He said, "You are questioning my courage." I said, "Larry, what are you talking about?" He said, "On page four on the grading sheet, the 25th play, which was a pass, you put, 'Dropped pass. Heard footsteps.' You're questioning my courage." I said, "Larry, right now, I'm real busy. I've got something very important I've got to do for Coach Noll. Why don't you go do your workout and come back to see me before you go home. I just don't have time to talk to you right now."

Well, Larry left to go work out. As soon as he left, I got out the original grading sheets again and looked at play 25. Sure enough, I had put "Dropped pass. Heard footsteps" in Larry's box. This is a common expression in football that coaches use when a player drops a pass when he doesn't look the ball into his hands. But it also implies that he dropped the ball because he was looking at the defender because he was afraid of getting hit. I immediately changed the second part of the comment either by erasure or whiteout. The comment now read, "Dropped pass. Took eyes off the ball." I ran with this corrected page four grading sheet down to the copy machine—it was a mimeograph in those days—and made 13 new copies of the page four sheet. I went into the locker room and took the grading sheets out of the locker of the eight offensive linemen and the two tight ends, including Larry's. The players were all out on the field working out on their own and many just played touch football during this time. I also went to the desks of Chuck Noll and Lionel Taylor and got their copies of the grade sheets. I replaced page four on all these grading sheets by using the staple remover and stapler. I then took the grading sheets and put them back in the lockers and on the desks where I originally found them.

When Larry came back to see me after his workout, he told me again that I had written, "Dropped Pass. Heard footsteps on play 25 on his grading sheet" and that he was upset that I was questioning his courage. I immediately turned to page four of my grading sheets, showed him play 25 that said "Dropped Pass. Took eyes off the ball" and said I didn't know what he was talking about. Then I took him to Noll's and Taylor's desks and showed him play 25. Next I took him into the locker room and showed him his own grading sheet, which of course I also had changed. Next I grabbed tight end Randy Grossman's grading sheets from Randy's locker. Then I showed him some of the linemen's sheets. Play 25 on all of them said, "Dropped Pass. Took eyes off the ball." I finally said, "Larry, it's obvious you are mistaken. Now I've got to get ready for our staff meeting on this week's game plan." And I left him. He never mentioned the "heard footsteps" incident again; and I never again used that expression when grading a player.

Larry is currently the owner of a number of Applebee restaurant franchises in the Pittsburgh area. He never knew how I had corrected his grading sheet until I showed him this story in January of 2010. He reciprocated by giving me a $140 voucher to take my wife to dinner at one of his Applebee restaurants, which I did shortly thereafter. Not a bad thank you after all those years.

Weight Coach Solves Pass Blocking Problem – In the preseason of 1975, my offensive linemen were consistently getting their hands too wide on pass protection. They were dedicated weight lifters in the off season, and I blamed the frequent use of the bench press with the wide arm grip as the culprit. I decided that I needed something in the weight room that was similar to the full-arm extension pass blocking technique that I was teaching. I ran to Steelers Weight Coach Lou Riecke and told him of my problem. I told him that I wanted something in the weight room that made them think about pass protection, something that they could press at near full-extension with their hands close together. Lou thought for a moment and said, "Rad, we need to do an incline bench press." An incline bench has a slanted back so that when you sit on it you can lean back and push the weight bar up at near full arm extension three to six inches, the same as you would do to stop a pass rusher when locking out your arms and hands on his shoulders.

Well, we got an incline bench and from then on our pass blocking technique as a group improved and, we went on to win our second consecutive Super Bowl. Our weight coach, Lou Riecke, had come through in the clutch.

Incidentally, Lou Riecke was an LSU graduate who ran the 100-yard dash for the LSU track team in the early 1940s. His teammate in running the 100-yard dash was the famous Hall of Fame running back of the Philadelphia Eagles, Steve Van Buren. Lou also was an Olympic weight lifter and inventor of a weight machine called the "Riecke Machine."

Lou Riecke, Weight Coach

Early Bumpy Road – In the 1975 preseason, we were fortunate not to have any player holdouts for larger contracts, which usually happen after a team wins a Super Bowl. Holdouts are a main reason why it is so hard to repeat immediately the next year. However, we did have some bumps in the road early in our quest to repeat as Super Bowl champions. We struggled during the preseason, winning just three of our seven preseason games, and one was in the College All-Star game in a game that was called after three quarters because of severe weather in Chicago. Our final preseason game against Dallas produced another concern. In our final preseason of 1974, we had dominated the Cowboys, 41-15, but this time we were miserable on offense and defense and Dallas beat us, 17-16. The Steeler coaches, players and our fans were very leery about the ability of our team going into the season opener at San Diego.

Lynn Swann, Dan, Chuck Noll and Dick Hoak

Well, much to our pleasant surprise, we beat the Chargers easily, 37-0. *Pittsburgh Post-Gazette* writer Ted Colton correctly summed up the game by writing, "Like a jig saw puzzle, all the Steeler pieces, which seemed out of place during the exhibitions, fell together with the regular season opener!"

Our team confidence soared—probably to overconfidence—and we felt that in our next game we were going to annihilate the O.J. Simpson-led Buffalo Bills, just like we had in the first playoff game the year before, 38-14. We were in for a rude awakening. The Bills crushed us, 30-21, and O.J., whom we had held to 49 yards rushing the previous season, ran all over us for one of his finest days as a pro, gaining 227 yards. I can still see him running around our defensive left side, supposedly our best side, and going by me and Coach Noll—so close to the sideline that we could have reached out and touched him—on his way to an 88-yard touchdown.

Looking back, maybe that defeat was a blessing. We regrouped, improved, and won our next three games against Cleveland, Denver and Chicago, scoring 96 against our opponents' total of 18. We continued our winning streak through 11 games, making us undefeated in the AFC's Central Division with the best won-loss record (12-1) in the entire NFL with one game remaining against the Los Angeles Rams who had an 11-2 record. At that point in the season, we had wrapped up the home field advantage for the playoffs, and had nothing to gain by beating the Rams.

So, the coaching staff approached the game as we would a final preseason game. We wanted to win the game as a matter of pride, but to avoid injuries a much as possible, we did not want to play our starters more than half the game, which was enough to keep them in playing condition for the playoffs. I remember using our second year center (and future Hall of Famer) Mike Webster at left offensive tackle so that starting left tackle Jon Kolb would not have to play more than two quarters. Mike had never played at offensive tackle before, and he played well except for giving up a sack when Rams defensive end Fred Dryer beat him on an outside rush. I apologized to Mike after the game for putting him into a situation that he had never practiced before, but Mike just laughed. He was a guy who would do anything to help the team. We lost a close game, 10-3, and finished tied with LA for the best record in the NFL. No one had been seriously injured, and we were now ready for the first playoff game in Pittsburgh against the Baltimore Colts. But before I tell you about the playoff games and the Super Bowl, I need to tell you about the biggest game of our regular season against the Houston Oilers.

Curley Who? — The most memorable and biggest game of the 1975 Super Bowl season was our 10th game against the Houston Oilers in the Astrodome. We were 8-1 at the time and Houston was 7-2 under new head coach Bum Phillips. We had just beaten Houston 24-17 in a close game two weeks earlier and had lost to them, 13-10, near the end of the 1974 season. They had become a formidable opponent since they had acquired nose tackle Curley Culp from Kansas City in the middle of the 1974 season.

Curley had been to a couple of Pro Bowls since he began playing for the Chiefs in 1968, but they thought Curley was losing it and traded him to the Oilers. Bum Phillips rejuvenated him in Bum's new 3-4 defense and Curley was having his best year. By the end of the season he would be All-Pro again and named the NFL

Defensive Player of the Year by the *Newspaper Enterprise Association*, and then would make the Pro Bowl three more years before finally retiring in 1981.

Anyhow, Curley was the 1967 NCAA heavyweight wrestling champion from Arizona State, who was like a block of granite playing nose tackle over the center in Bum's defense. Curley also was quick as a cat, which was probably a result of his wrestling experience. Ray Mansfield, our experienced starting center, had problems blocking Curley the previous two times we had played Houston, the last time only two weeks earlier. I decided that instead of starting Ray at center and alternating him with Mike Webster (Ray would play the first and third quarter and Mike would play the second and fourth quarters) that I would play Webster the entire game since he seemed to play better against Curley than Ray.

Jim Clack

I called Ray into my office on Tuesday before the game and informed him of my intentions. He went berserk. He yelled, hollered and cried. He told me that he could block Curley, that I couldn't bench him and so on. I basically just sat there and listened to him because my mind was already made up. Finally after about 15 minutes of Ray talking and yelling and promising, I gave in. He had worn me down. I told him he was getting one more chance to start but he better block Curley. Otherwise, I said, Webster would be our full-time starting center, at least when we played against Curley. We also changed the blocking on our lead play and a couple of other plays because of Curley, primarily by having the guard and center stay on the double team on Curley all the way. Normally, one of them would come off on a linebacker after the initial double-team contact on the nose tackle.

We played the game in front of one of the largest crowds in Astrodome history up to that time, 49,947. The first half was one of the hardest hitting and loudest hitting games I have ever

Ray Mansfield

witnessed. We broke a tight game wide open in the third quarter. Franco Harris made two big runs on our lead C play where the play side guard and center double-team the nose tackle (Curley) all the way and the far guard pulls around the double-team for the linebacker playing over him that's reacting to the play. Rocky Bleier, our play side back went straight up to block the play side linebacker. Franco followed Rocky, then cut behind the pulling guard's block on the far linebacker and went down the far side line. Those two runs broke the game wide open.

On one of these lead runs by Franco, Ray Mansfield and Jim Clack blew Curley out, whereas Curley was lying on his back on their shoulders with his legs in air. Curley was at least four feet off the ground. Mansfield and Clack had driven underneath him and had driven him back and up into the air. When I saw this on our close-up line game film, I told both Mansfield and Clack that I would have the film clip of the block blown up and given to them as a present. I'm sorry to say that I never did get around to fulfilling that promise. After the end of the third quarter and Franco's two big runs, we were leading 32-9. I looked around and the stands were empty. I remember saying to linebacker Andy Russell on the sidelines, "Look. Andy, only your relatives are left in the stands."

Rocky Bleier

After the game, I remember Bum Phillips telling the reporters that Franco had broken the game wide open with a couple of lucky cuts back away from the intended hole. He didn't realize that because of Curley, that was how we designed the play and Franco had run it twice to perfection. While Bum was talking to the media, I went to a pay phone in the stadium and called my wife. When Nancy answered the phone, and before I could say a word, she said, "Curley who?" I laughed and replied "That's right, Curley who?"

The Play That Never Fails – I've got one more Curley Culp story that I've got to tell about the great Houston nose tackle. Early in the 1974 season, the Steelers offensive coaches came up with a short yardage and goal line play that had a tight flanker (or wing) go in motion and trap the defensive lineman aligned in either the far guard-center gap or aligned head-on the center. Then, the ball carrier would run through the hole created by the flanker trap. This play had succeeded every time we had called it over the past two years (more than 20 times), resulting in either a first down or a touchdown. It was so successful that we started to refer to the flanker trap as "the play that never fails." This flanker position was usually filled by one of our tight ends, most often by Randy Grossman.

Well, one Friday in 1975, as we were about to leave the practice field about two days before our Sunday game with the Oilers in late November, I yelled at Grossman, "Hey Randy, why don't we practice a couple of shots of you on the dummy on the foam mats

Randy Grossman

to make sure you hit Curley Culp low on the flanker trap play. Hitting him high could be disastrous." Randy replied, "Rad, I've got your message. I know I've got to hit him low. I don't need to practice it. I'm all set."

So, during the game, the flanker trap is called near the goal line and Grossman starts in motion to trap Curley, who's aligned on the center. Shortly after the ball is snapped, he hit Curley high at his shoulder pads and Curley knocks Randy backwards, sending him flying into the ball carrier who falls down for a 2-yard loss. Ouch! The play that never fails had just failed. Of course, this proved once again that there is no such thing as a play that never fails nor a player who doesn't need to practice his blocking skills. Right, Randy?

Randy blamed the failure of the play on the quarterback, Terry Bradshaw. He said that Bradshaw didn't give the start count correctly. Randy said he was almost past Curley when the ball was snapped, and, thus, not giving him a chance to get low on Curley. Sure, Randy. Whatever!

Andy's Fumble Recovery –

Our playoff game with Baltimore on December 27 in the rather mild 32 degree but slightly windy weather of Three Rivers Stadium was close for three quarters as we exchanged the lead twice until the Steelers led 14-10 at the end of three quarters. We pulled away in the fourth quarter, starting with a two-yard touchdown run by Bradshaw. Then, linebackers Jack Ham and Andy Russell combined to

Andy Russell, Donnie Shell

execute the most spectacular play of the game. Baltimore was driving for a touchdown when Ham and Russell took off on a double blitz. Ham got to quarterback Bert Jones first and sacked him, causing a fumble. Russell picked up the ball at the Steelers 7-yard-line and ran 93 yards for the final game-clinching touchdown. We had physically dominated a good opponent, outrushing them 211 yards to 82 and won, 28-10.

Icy, Snow Swept, Windy Playoff Game – The weather for the Baltimore game, with a wind chill of 22 degrees, was like a game in Miami compared to our game the following week against Oakland for the AFC championship and a trip to another Super Bowl. It was freezing cold, with winds of 18-20 miles an hour that made the 18 degree temperature feel like two degrees. With terrible weather conditions like that, the game was a defensive struggle for three quarters and we led 3-0 on a 36-yard field goal by Roy Gerela. Suddenly, 52 seconds into the final quarter, the game turned into an offensive shootout.

First, Jack Lambert recovered his second fumble of the game deep in Oakland's territory, and on the second play Franco Harris raced 25 yards for a touchdown to make it 10-0. Then Raiders Quarterback Ken "Snake" Stabler ended a 60-yard drive with a 14-yard pass to Mike Siani for a touchdown. We had to give up the ball, but minutes later Lambert recovered another fumble when L.C. Greenwood hit running back Marv Hubbard. That enabled us to go ahead 16-7 when John Stallworth made a leaping catch in the end zone of Terry Bradshaw's pass, but Gerela missed the extra point. We got the ball back again and seemed to have the game wrapped up when Bradshaw picked up a first down just after the two-minute warning. But then Harris fumbled and the Raiders drove to a third-and-two at the Steeler 24-yard line with 17 seconds remaining in the game from where old George Blanda, who was 48-years-old at the time, kicked a 41-yard field goal to cut our lead to 16-10. We blew the onside kick and Hubbard recovered to give Oakland the ball on its own 45-yard line with just seven seconds left. Stabler evaded our strong rush and threw a long 37-yard pass to Cliff Branch who was tackled by Mel Blount and a couple of other guys at the 15-yard line before he could get out of bounds. The clock ran out and we won, 16-10.

Hallelujah! We were leaving the freezing weather for sunny Florida and Super Bowl X against the Dallas Cowboys.

CHAPTER FIVE –
The Pass That Could Have Changed History

***Newsday* Scouting Report** – I have often been asked about the 1975 team and why it was so good. Of course, we coaches are biased. If you want an objective opinion of what makes a team so good, you should ask opposing players. And that's what *Newsday*, the Long Island, NY, newspaper did for its Super Bowl game day edition on Jan. 18, 1976, asking All-Pro Cleveland defensive tackle Jerry Sherk to comment on our offense and All-Pro Houston quarterback Dan Pastoroini to write about our defense; then make a prediction about the game. I think what they wrote was an accurate critique of our team. Here is their scouting report.

Steelers Offense by Cleveland All-Pro Defensive Tackle Jerry Sherk – *I think the one phase of the Steelers that everybody overlooks is the offensive line. To me, those guys are the unsung heroes of the Steelers. The big thing is each man in the line can play so many different positions. For instance [right guard] Gerry Mullins has also played right tackle, tight end and flanker. Against us they used him on a flanker trap. Yeah, they put him in motion. I charged and he trapped me from the flanker position. That's 245 pounds of flanker with a running start.*

What I'm getting at is they just move guys around freely and it doesn't hurt them. Like Jim Clack and Sam Davis can alternate a half each at left guard. Then two centers, Ray Mansfield and Mike Webster, alternate, and Mullins will go out, too, for Clack, with Davis in his spot. I don't know of any other team with the depth that can do that.

So what happens? Because of their depth, they're fresh and can come at you hard all the time. They like to pick a player who comes off the line quick, like me, and trap the guy, too. Like most teams won't trap you if you're on the center nose, but their center will let you go, take three or four steps and a tackle comes down and traps you all the way from his position.

With that line they can consistently establish the run. And Franco Harris is a game breaker. They test you up the middle right off. He (Harris) runs up the middle and bounces out. He always does. Everybody closes in to stop the three or four yard play and he bounces out. They can do it because of their strong line. They really don't get too far from the conservative type of ball. Franco gives them the big play. He might get two yards or 40 yards any time he carries the ball.

There's been a great deal of improvement in that line over the past three years. Clack, Mullins and Mansfield are something, and their tackles, Jon Kolb and Gordon Gravelle, are so strong and quick. And they have a difficult pass-blocking technique down to a science. They extend their arms almost straight out. It would be illegal if there wasn't a bend in their arms...anyway, what it does is shock you at the line of scrimmage. The first time I played them I felt like a ping pong ball. They bounced me back and forth from center to guard. They're good at it.

I'd have to go with Pittsburgh. Basically because I can see their strength and I don't see weaknesses. They're strong in every position.

[Special Note: Jerry Sherk made the Pro Bowl four straight years (1974-77) and in 1976 was voted the NFL's Defensive MVP by the Newspaper Enterprise Association.]

Steelers Defense by Houston All Pro Quarterback Dan Pastorini – *Undoubtedly, Pittsburgh has the best defense I've had the misfortune to play against. Their down linemen are the best in our conference. The key is the amount of pressure the front four puts on the passer, and the activity of the front four and the linebackers in working together. You can't find a better trio of linebackers than Jack Ham, Jack Lambert and Andy Russell. Their secondary does nothing fancy as coverage goes, no false looks or anything like that. They just work with all their linebackers, playing them off in a basic four-three defense.*

As a quarterback, you look at their defensive alignment and see nothing unusual. Their cornerbacks, Mel Blount on the right side and J.T. Thomas on the left, play a deep zone against the pass, which is tough to throw long against. But those guys take a gamble now and then for the interception (Blount led the league with 11 during the regular season) because they've got help from their safeties, Mike Wagner and Glen Edwards in what we call a double zone. What makes it all work is that big rush from the front four that puts extreme pressure on the quarterback and the tight coverage from the linebackers on backs and your tight end looking for the short completion. The thing is that overall, they never blow an assignment.

I know Dallas will use a shotgun and a lot of people are sold on the shotgun because it has done so well for them (the Cowboys). I'm not sure if it will be that effective against Pittsburgh because of their personnel. We used the shotgun against Pittsburgh but to no great effect.

I think the Steelers Front Four (Dwight White, Ernie Holmes, L.C. Greenwood and Joe Greene) will come after Staubach with more pressure than he's ever faced before. I don't think Pittsburgh will blitz against it (the shotgun) so much. The front four will probably run a lot of stunts, crossing each other in the pass rush, which is what they're so good at. They make so few mistakes, and do it so well that they force you to do things you don't normally do, and this screws up your timing.

I'm not much of a scrambling type quarterback, so their pass rush put a lot of pressure on me. Staubach, he's a good scrambler, so they'll have to control him. I'm sure he'll be running because he doesn't want to get into a second and fifteen or a second and 20 situation. That's the way the Steelers defense plays it. They get a sack and put you in a hole, and then you're forced to get out of it and you make a mistake.

I have to go with Pittsburgh. Their offenses are comparable, okay...it's going to be an offensive battle, and the Steelers defense is much stronger. Yes, I have to go with the Steelers by 10 points.

[Special Note: Dan Pastorini's team had a 10-4 record in 1975 with all its losses to playoff teams, two to the Steelers and two to the Bengals. Two of their wins were against playoff teams, the Dolphins and Raiders. Dan was a quarterback in the Pro Bowl for the AFC, which was played after the Super Bowl.]

Who's Percy Howard? – Anyone who watched Super Bowl X in person or on television remembers how exciting it was, right down to last play of the game when Glen Edwards intercepted a pass by Roger Staubach in the end zone. What most people don't remember is the play just before that one, a play that could have changed history, not only for the Steelers and Cowboys but for two specific individuals—Lynn Swann and Percy Howard. The game probably made Swann a Hall of Famer. He was the MVP of the game, making two of his famous acrobatic catches in the first half and then catching the game-winning touchdown on a 59-yard bomb from Terry Bradshaw late in the fourth quarter.

Who's Percy Howard? That's what I'm about to tell you.

The Steelers had not played Dallas in a regular season game since 1972, when the Cowboys won, 17-13. Our coaching staff was somewhat familiar with their 1975 team because we had played them in the last preseason games of 1974 and 1975. We beat the Cowboys 41-15 in 1974 and they won 17-16 in 1975. Neither team would go into the game over confident.

One of our main concerns going into the Super Bowl was the physical condition of Lynn Swann. Just two weeks before in the AFC championship game with Oakland, Swann had suffered a severe concussion after a clothesline hit by Raiders cornerback George Atkinson. It seemed to be up in the air whether Lynn would play much in the Super Bowl, and he hardly practiced in the two weeks leading up to the game. That would have been a major problem because just about everyone, including the Cowboys, thought we couldn't win without passing. There was a lot of trash talk in the days before the game, and a lot of it was aimed at Swann from the Cowboys six-year veteran safety Cliff Harris. I guess he was trying to intimidate Swann, who was just in his second season of pro ball and had not been a factor in our Super Bowl victory over the Vikings the previous year.

There was a unique fact about this Super Bowl, but we didn't realize it at the time. They were filming a new movie called *Black Sunday* about a terrorist attack on the Super Bowl using the famous Goodyear Blimp. The next time you watch that movie on television, look closely at who was playing—the Black and Gold Steelers. Frankly, the only thing I remember is seeing one of the stars in the movie, Robert Shaw, along the sidelines. But I've never paid much attention to who's on the sidelines anyway. However, whenever I see that Goodyear Blimp on TV now I think about Super Bowl X.

The start of the game surprised all of us. We kicked off and Cowboys linebacker Hollywood Henderson took a lateral from Preston Pearson on a reverse, running from right to left and ran up his left sideline with only Steelers kicker Roy Gerela between him and our goal line. Roy threw a body block, knocking Hollywood out of bounds at the Steelers 44-yard line and cracking one of Roy's ribs at the same time. The cracked rib definitely affected Roy's kicking the rest of the game. On the first play L.C. Greenwood sacked Staubach, forcing a fumble but Dallas recovered the ball. The game was less than a minute old and we already had two exciting plays. There was a lot more to come.

We held the Cowboys and they had to punt, but after we picked up a first down we also had to punt and our punter, Bobby Walden fumbled the snap. Dallas took over at the Steelers 28-yard line, and on the next play Staubach threw a 28-yard touchdown pass to wide receiver Drew Pearson. With just $4\frac{1}{2}$ minutes played, we were behind, 7-0.

As is typical of the Steelers, we ran the ball four straight times, and that may have given the Cowboys the idea we were going to be very conservative on offense. On the fifth play, Bradshaw called for pass to Swann down the right sideline. Swann streaked down the right side, just inches from the sideline marker with cornerback Mark Washington matching him stride for stride. Bradshaw's throw was a little overthrown but Swann, now a step behind Washington and magically keeping both feet in bounds, leaped high in the air over Washington's left shoulder and with his outstretched arms and hands he caught the ball and got both feet down inside the side line before being hit hard out of bounds by Cliff Harris. It was a spectacular 32-yard completion. Later, on a third-and-one at the 7-yard line, Bradshaw surprised Dallas from our tight running formation with a play we call flanker trap pass and hit tight end Randy Grossman in the end zone.

Swann's reception setting up the touchdown would be the first of many now famous acrobatic receptions by Swann in his Hall of Fame career, but the one most fans remember came just before the half. After Grossman's TD and Gerela's extra point with four minutes left in the quarter, the Cowboys went ahead 15 seconds into the second period on a 36-yard field goal by Tony Frisch. Then the game settled into a defensive struggle. But with about three minutes left in the first half, the Cowboys had us pinned down near our end zone, facing a third-and-six at the Steelers 10-yard line. If they could force a punt here, they could possibly take a six or 10 point lead into the halftime intermission.

Now, you have to remember that the Steelers quarterbacks called their own plays, unlike Staubach and the Cowboys who took their marching orders from Dallas' head coach, Tom Landry. On a video tape replay, you can see Bradshaw looking over the defense. Dallas looked like it was going to send eight or nine guys and Bradshaw seems to call an audible. The Cowboys stormed across the scrimmage line but our offensive line and backs beat them back as Bradshaw dropped back to the goal line in a protective pocket and threw the ball to Swann streaking down the right hash mark lines.

This time, Swann appeared to be beating cornerback Mark Washington as the ball sailed towards Swann at the 50-yard line, slightly underthrown. Washington closed quickly and tipped the ball to Swann's left. Swann leaped towards the ball over the back of Washington, and as both men were falling to the ground, Swann stretched his body and his arms as far as he could, and with his knees in Washington's chest Swann grabbed the ball to his own chest and went tumbling to the Cowboys 48-yard line.

Swann's circus catch didn't lead to a score—Gerela shanked a field goal try to the left—but it enabled us to run out the first half clock. However, this is the reception that put Swann on the cover of *Sports Illustrated* the next week and is one of the most memorable in football history because it has been replayed over and over for the last four decades on television, and nowadays through the internet on YouTube.

We seemed to dominate the game into the fourth quarter but we couldn't get over the goal line. When Roy shanked another field goal to the left in the third quarter from 33 yards, Cliff Harris mockingly patted Gerela on his helmet. That upset Steelers linebacker Jack Lambert who threw Harris to the ground. The referee had not seen Harris' taunting but almost threw Lambert out of the game. Both teams were really wound up now.

Early in the fourth quarter came the play that Dallas' head coach, Tom Landry called "the turning point of the game." We had the Cowboys in a fourth-and-13 at their 16-yard line and we made them think we had a 10-man rush on, but we actually didn't and Dallas didn't adjust. Our fullback, Reggie "Booby" Harrison, blocked Mitch Hoopes' punt, and the ball careened off Reggie's facemask and out of the end zone for a safety, making the score 10-9, in favor of Dallas.

After missing those two field goals, Gerela had donned a corset to protect his ribs and that helped him regain his scoring touch. The Cowboys kicked off to us following the safety, and we drove to their 20-yard line from where Gerela kicked a 36-yard line drive to put us ahead for the first time, 12-10. There was less than nine minutes left in the game. The Steelers defense continued to make plays and a short time later safety Mike Wagner intercepted a Staubach pass and returned it 19 yards to the Dallas 7-yard line. But we couldn't score a touchdown and ended up with Gerela kicking an 18-yard field goal for a 15-10 lead.

We stopped the Cowboys again, and with 3:02 left, we had the ball at the Steelers 36-yard line with a third down and four. I'm sure everyone thought we would go for a first down on a run by Franco Harris or a short pass to Swann or John Stallworth. But in the huddle Bradshaw called for a 69 Maximum Flanker Post—a long pass down the middle to Swann. However, the Cowboys also guessed Bradshaw would do something like that, and they called for an all-out blitz by linebacker J.D. Lewis and safety Cliff Harris from Bradshaw's blindside.

Bradshaw sidestepped Lewis, but a fraction of second after throwing the ball he was belted by defensive tackle Larry Cole. The ball must have traveled 70 yards in the air but it was picture perfect. Swann ran down the middle of the field, again beating defender Mark Washington, caught the ball inches in front of Washington at the 5-yard line and ran into the end zone standing up. Bradshaw never saw the touchdown. He was helped off the field by teammates and was out for the rest of the game. This time Gerela's extra point attempt hit the cross-bar—the corset wasn't perfect—and we now led, 21-10.

But Dallas was far from done. Staubach took them quickly downfield, going 80 yards on five plays with Roger throwing a 34-yard bullet pass to Percy Howard in the left corner of the end zone, just as our defender Mel Blount fell down when they both crossed the end zone a second before Howard caught the ball. Now, maybe you're asking me if I'm sure it was Percy Howard and not Drew Pearson? Yes, it was Percy Howard, the Cowboys third wide receiver. Tony Frisch's extra point made it 21-17 but neither Staubach nor Howard was done.

There was 1:48 left in the game and everyone knew Dallas would try an onside kick. Some of us were thinking about the Cowboys game against Minnesota in their first playoff game, when Staubach threw a bomb to Drew Pearson in the last minute to upset the Vikings, 17-14. Gerry Mullins recovered the onside kick at the Dallas 42-yard line. Terry Hanratty, who had played briefly in one game all season, replaced Bradshaw at quarterback. The Steelers gained only one yard in three running plays as Dallas used its timeouts, and with 1:28 to play, we had a fourth-and-9 at the Dallas 41-yard line. Hanratty went to the sideline to confer with Chuck Noll and it was decided to run the ball rather than risk a possible mishap on a punt. A mishandled punt snap early in the game had led to the Cowboys first touchdown.

Rocky Bleier gained just two yards, and Dallas took over at their 39 with 1:22 remaining and no time outs. In three pass plays, the Cowboys reached the Steelers 38-yard line. On the fourth play, Staubach threw a long pass into right side of the end zone towards—you guessed it—Percy Howard. Howard leaped for the ball at the same time as two Steelers defenders—J.T. Thomas and Glen Edwards. The ball, untouched by any Steelers, bounced off the top Howard's helmet and fell to the ground. Years later, Howard told the NFL network, "If I had jumped maybe just a split second later I would have gotten that pass."

Pass from Staubach untouched by any player bounces off the top of Percy Howard's helmet with 3 seconds remaining in the game.

There were now three seconds left. Staubach had one last throw into the end zone, and he launched the ball towards Drew Pearson. But strong safety Mike Wagner batted the ball into the air and weak safety Glen Edwards intercepted it as time ran out, and the Steelers won Super Bowl X.

The Steelers defense sacked Staubach seven times, which was then a Super Bowl record, and forced him to scramble on numerous occasions. We pressured him into an uncharacteristic three interceptions, and allowed the Cowboys just 108 yards rushing. Swann caught four passes for 161 yards, also a Super Bowl record then, and had fully recovered from that concussion two weeks earlier.

Think about how lucky the Steelers were and how different it would have been if Percy Howard had caught that last pass? In my opinion, Howard not catching this ball was the luckiest play in Steelers history. Howard would have been the Super Bowl hero, perhaps the MVP instead of Swann. Maybe, there would have been no Steelers dynasty. The psychology of the two teams would have changed, and perhaps the Cowboys would have won Super Bowl XIII two years later instead of the Steelers.

Then there was the decision by Chuck Noll not to punt that led to the Staubach pass that bounced off Howard's helmet. That could have been one of the most criticized coaching decisions of all time if Howard had actually caught that ball to win the game. I was near Chuck when he told Hanratty not to punt but I didn't hear him. When I saw the team was not going into punt formation, I started to run out onto the field, but Chuck grabbed me, pulled me back, and said, "We're not going to punt. We're running the ball." I thought he was crazy, but, luckily, it all worked out.

As for Percy Howard, that touchdown pass he caught was the only reception he ever had in the NFL. Howard was really a freak, one of those track stars or basketball players Dallas tried to turn into wide receivers. The most famous was Olympian Bob Hayes who became an All-Pro receiver. Howard had played basketball but not football at little Austin-Peay in Clarksville, TN. He was 6-foot-4, 210 pounds with good reflexes and Dallas timed him at 4.4 in the 40-yard dash. The Cowboys super scout, Gil Brandt, thought he might be a good receiver and kick returner.

Dallas signed him as a free agent in 1975 and he made the team as a backup receiver behind Drew Pearson and Golden Richards. But the only playing time he had in the regular season was on special teams, and in eight games his only statistics were a total of two kickoff returns for 51 yards. It's doubtful Percy would have played in the Super Bowl if Richards had not been hurt earlier in the game in a couple of skirmishes with Mel Blount. A few months after the Super Bowl, Howard was out of the NFL forever.

I have to tell you even I had forgotten about Percy Howard. And I didn't realize that next to last pass to him had bounced off his helmet until I went to the library recently and looked at a video tape of the game. If you check the newspapers back then, the sportswriters thought the ball bounced off Howard's shoulder.

A couple months after seeing that video of the untouched ball bouncing off the top of Howard's helmet, I ran into Gil Brandt at the 2011 NFL Scouting Combine in Indianapolis. I mentioned Percy and those two passes at the end of the game and we laughed about it. Gil agreed with me that the pass Howard missed really could have changed history. Gil also said they thought Percy had a chance to be a great player, but in a preseason game the next year he suffered a devastating knee injury returning a kick and his career was over.

The NFL network brought Howard back into the limelight in March of 2008 as part of its series entitled "Top Ten One Shot Wonders." He was No. 6, behind such more familiar names as one-time Steeler quarterback Tommy Maddox and two Cowboys, quarterback Clint Longley and defensive back Larry Brown. The NFL Network showed replays of both passes thrown to Howard by Staubach, and a had a short interview with Howard, who succinctly summed up the pass that could have changed a lot of lives: "Every time I see Roger he says, 'Bird,' they called me Bird back then, 'if you would have caught that one you would have gone down in (history).'"

Halftime Of Super Bowl X – We were trailing 10-7 at halftime and I knew Chuck would have some encouraging words for the players, but I never heard them. During the first quarter of Super Bowl X against the Cowboys, I saw right offensive tackle Gorden Gravelle get grabbed and thrown aside on a pass rush by Dallas left defensive end Ed "Too Tall" Jones. In the second quarter I saw Too Tall do it again. When Gordon came off the field, I checked his jersey and sure enough I could grab some cloth when he simulated a pass block. At halftime, Gordon and I went into the empty shower room in the locker room to re-tape his shoulder pads with carpet two-way tape in order to make his tailored jersey ungrabbable. When I was done, Gordon put on the shoulder pads with the jersey attached and I tried to grab him different ways. I couldn't get any cloth so he seemed to be okay. By this time, halftime was over. Gordon stuffed Too Tall Jones the second half and didn't get beat once nor get his jersey grabbed. We won 21-17. Gordon and I never did find out what head coach, Chuck Noll said at halftime of Super Bowl X.

Nancy's Forever Ring – Super Bowl rings are one of the most cherished possessions in all of football. You can coach or play in the NFL for years and never earn one. Some people keep their rings in a safe deposit box and others have sold theirs because they needed the money. I have three of them but two of mine are a little different than anyone else's, and for a reason I'm quite proud about.

During the Steelers 1975 preseason camp in Latrobe, I wore my Super Bowl IX one carat diamond ring to practice a few times. One day after I had walked off the practice field, showered and had dinner I looked at my right hand and my Super Bowl ring was missing. I realized the ring must have slipped off my hand during the afternoon's practice. I ran out to the field and looked around quickly and couldn't find it. I went to my half hour coaches' meeting at 7 o'clock and then to my offensive line meeting at 7:30. After an hour, I adjourned the offensive line meeting and recruited about 8 to 10 people with flashlights to help me look for my ring. One person later said I had over half the camp looking for the ring but that wasn't true. After about 15 minutes of shining flashlights in my practice areas on the field, one person spotted a gleaming object with his flashlight. Lo and behold, the gleaming object was my Super Bowl IX ring.

When the Steelers coaches and players received our second ring for Super Bowl X, and knowing myself, I decided that since there was a good chance of me losing one or both of the Super Bowl rings in the future, that I should use the diamonds in the ring to make an engagement ring for my wife, Nancy. When I asked her to marry me 19 years earlier, I couldn't afford an engagement ring.

I went to Star Jewelry on the fourth floor of the Clark Building on Liberty Avenue in downtown Pittsburgh and asked the jeweler and his lady assistant if they could take the three diamonds out of the two Super Bowl rings, replace the diamonds with the best zircons (imitation diamonds), and make my wife an engagement ring with the three real diamonds. I asked them the cost, and the jeweler said they could do it all for about 50 or 55 dollars.

I said, "I'm not sure you understand. I want the best zircons for the Super Bowl rings and the best gold ring prongs with the three diamonds showing." He said, "I do understand. That's all it would cost. But I must warn you. I've been in this business a long time, and when a woman gets an engagement ring she wants it to look like an engagement ring." I said, "Will it look nice?" He said, "With the three diamonds it will be beautiful but it will be different. I replied, "This woman has been waiting 19 years for this ring. I'm sure that she wants it a little different." His lady assistant laughed at my comment. The jeweler said he would work on the ring over the weekend and I should call him around 4 p.m. on Sunday and he would let me know how he was doing on the ring.

On Sunday I was out driving with my wife in the car when I remembered to call the jeweler. I asked my wife the time. She said it was about 4:15. I told her I had to find a pay phone and make a call. She said, "Who are you calling?" I said, "I can't tell you." I found a pay phone and called the jeweler. He told me that the rings were done and I could pick them up the next day; cost 55 dollars. When I returned to the car my wife asked who I had called. I again told her I couldn't tell her. We rode in silence the rest of the way home.

The next day, I picked up the rings after I left the Steelers office, and on the way home I stopped at the home of my friend Joe Moore in Upper St. Clair. I told Joe I had to figure out how to get Nancy dressed up to give her the new diamond ring. I wasn't going to wait for an anniversary. I wanted to give it now. So, we decided that when I got home I would tell Nancy that Joe had an important announcement to make and that he and his wife, Fran, and Nancy and me should get all dressed up and go to the LeMont Restaurant where Joe would make his announcement and we would all celebrate. The LeMont was one of Pittsburgh's best restaurants, located at the top of Mount Washington with a great view of the city. I told Joe he couldn't tell Fran about the ring because I knew Nancy would call Fran immediately. So, Joe told Fran to tell Nancy that Joe hadn't told her either what the surprise was.

I went home and told Nancy to get all decked out because we were going to LeMont's for dinner to celebrate Joe's secret announcement. Nancy said, "You guys are crazy! Nobody goes out on Monday night. I'm calling Fran!" Fran told Nancy she was getting dressed up and that all Joe had told her was that he had a surprise for her. So, Nancy put on one of her nicest dresses. Now I had to figure how to give her the ring before we got to Joe's house.

So, I went out to my car and put the box with the ring underneath a handkerchief in the center of the front seat. This was before bucket seats. When we got in the car to drive to Joe and Fran's home, Nancy was sitting against the passenger door with her elbow sticking out the window. Now I had to get her to sit closer to me so that she would sit on the handkerchief with the box holding the ring underneath. I said, "Why are you sitting over there? Before we were married, you use to sit right next to me." She said, "What are you talking about?" I repeated what I had said. She said, "You're goofy." I said, "No, I'm not. This car is not going to start until you sit close by me like you used to before we were married." She said, "You're serious, aren't you?" I replied, "Damn right I'm serious." She said, "All right. I'll sit next to you," and she moved over and sat right on the handkerchief. I started the car and we immediately drove to Joe's house, which was about 15 minutes away.

"What's this" Nancy said as she felt underneath her butt and discovered the ring box. I didn't say anything and kept driving. She unwrapped the small package that the box was in and opened the box just about the time I was pulling into the Moore's driveway. As she looked at the ring with the three diamonds—a half carat on each side and a full carat in the center—it dawned on her what I had done. "You took the diamonds out of your Super Bowl rings and made me a ring," she said. "Yep," I stuttered. She asked if Fran knew. I said, "She knows I have a surprise but doesn't know what it is." Nancy opened the car door and ran into Joe and Fran's home yelling, "Fran. Fran. Rad got me a ring!"

Well, we went to The LeMont, and then stopped at about four other bar-restaurants where Nancy could show off her three-diamond engagement ring, saying to the bartenders, "Look what my husband got me. Isn't he nice?"

Although I didn't mention Nancy's new ring to anybody at the Steelers office, word eventually got around. A couple of assistant coaches cornered me in the office kitchen and complained about what I had done. "How could you do such a thing? Now, our wives will expect us to do the same with our Super Bowl rings." I replied, "To have that ring done and the diamonds in the Super Bowl rings replaced with zircons cost me a grand total of 55 dollars. If I can be a hero in my house for 55 dollars, I don't give a damn about what your wives think!"

Five or ten years later, the jewelry business featured a new three diamond engagement ring for ladies that they called "The Forever Ring," with the three diamonds representing today, tomorrow and forever. When my wife saw that she said, "Look Rad, your idea for my ring was years ahead of its time."

How about that?

More Unusual Coaching Experiences

Not Entirely A Bed Of Roses – Coaching the offensive line in Super Bowl seasons of 1974 and 1975, was not always a smooth operation. I remember our starting right guard Gerry Mullins walking off the field on me at least twice. He basically said that he wasn't going to do what I wanted him to do and left the field.

Both times I didn't say anything, ignored him in my evening meeting, and went out the next day and coached him like nothing had happened. Another time, I had center Mike Webster repeat a drill that I felt needed corrected. The second time Mike did the drill he used less effort. I told him to do it again and he used even less effort the third time. Well, Mike was one of the greatest hustlers and hardest workers that has ever existed on a football field. When Mike loafed on me, I knew I had lost the players. I said, "I'm not coaching you guys anymore," and walked away and did not coach them for the rest of practice. The next day, I never mentioned the incident and coached as if it had never happened.

There was another occasion during the practice week for the first playoff game against Baltimore in 1975 when the offensive linemen were goofing off in a group drill we were doing against our defensive lineman. I got upset and said, "I'm not going to coach you guys anymore. I'm out of here!" I then walked over to the receiver and secondary 7-on-7 pass drill. Defensive line coach George Perles and center Ray Mansfield tried to convince me to return. I told George that he could coach the offensive linemen if he wanted to but that I wasn't going to. Finally, Chuck Noll came over and said, "Rad, don't you realize that we have a playoff game Sunday?" I said, "That's why I'm upset. My players don't realize how important Sunday's game is. That's why I'm not coaching them," and I didn't for the rest of practice. The next day, I never mentioned the incident and coached the players as if nothing had happened.

Another time in a meeting with the offensive line and tight ends, we were watching film of practice and I was upset at what I was seeing on the screen. Tight end Randy Grossman asked me if I would run that play over again that we had just watched. I took the 400-foot reel of film off the Kodak projector to where Randy was sitting, put my ball point pen in the center hole of the reel and let all 400 feet of the film unravel from the reel onto his lap. The bundle of film almost completely covered him and as I was letting the film unravel I said, "Here Randy, you can have all the practice film to run back all you want. I can't stand to look at any more of it. I'm out of here," and I left the meeting. When we met again, I never mentioned the incident. Okay, there was a little of Bad Rad's motivational style going on in this one, but as I said, coaching the offensive line was fun in those Super Bowl years, but not entirely a bed of roses.

Joe Had To Go – After the fanfare died down from winning Super Bowl X, the Steelers organization got back to football business. It was a foregone conclusion that Joe Gilliam would be traded. He had been late at least 30 times for quarterback meetings during the 1975 season and I'm not exaggerating. Chuck Noll was the quarterbacks coach as well as the head coach. It got so bad during the playoffs that Noll demoted Joe to third quarterback for the two weeks of Super Bowl practice in Miami. When the rumor was heavy that Joe was going to be traded, two of our best defensive players, Jack Ham and Mike Wagner (both white), came in my office and said they needed to have a private conversation with me. They wanted to know if I could meet them shortly in a restaurant in Market Square. I said I would and I did.

Ham and Wagner told me that they wanted to win a third Super Bowl, that Bradshaw got hurt at times, and that Joe Gilliam with his super ability was still our best bet as a backup. They said that they knew Joey was a screw up, but said to fine him $150,000 or more, but to keep him somehow. I told them that I would deliver their thoughts to Coach Noll. The next day I went into Noll's office and told him what they had told me. Chuck said it didn't matter what those two thought. Joe Gilliam had to go. He said a group of black players had come to him and told him that they wanted Joe out of here. They said Joe was an embarrassment to them and if Joe wasn't traded or released, that they would not play for the Pittsburgh Steelers. I then asked Chuck for the specific names of the black players who felt this way. Chuck told me and it sounded like a majority vote of our black players. Definitely Joe had to go. A week later, Joe Gilliam was gone, released and picked up by New Orleans. I was ignorant of Joe's drug abuse at the time, but I suspect that our players were not.

Good Idea Down The Drain – Shortly after Gilliam was released in January I went to Noll with what I thought was a great idea to replace Joe. I said, "Chuck, there's a quarterback named Joe Theismann who's playing third string for the Washington Redskins who I think would be the perfect guy to replace Joe Gilliam." Then I explained why to Chuck.

When I was at Penn State back in 1967 we tried to recruit Joe Theismann. He was a 6-foot, 165-pound quarterback from South River High School in New Brunswick, NJ, who we thought was a great prospect. J.T. White, our defensive ends coach, was recruiting him, and went to see him play in a basketball game. J.T.'s report was that Theismann was the quickest player he had ever seen on a basketball court. Now, J.T. had attended Ohio State in the 1940s and then transferred to Michigan and had played basketball as well as football in college, so his opinion was highly regarded. J.T. said, "He's not the best basketball player I've ever seen, but he sure is the quickest. You should see him on defense." Well, as everyone knows, we didn't get Theismann. He went to Notre Dame, was an All-American and was drafted in 1971 by the Miami Dolphins in the fourth round. But he didn't sign with Miami. He went to Canada where he was very good for three years. Then in 1974 he signed with the Redskins where he played behind Sonny Jurgensen and Billy Kilmer in 1974 and Kilmer and Randy Johnson in 1975. He got to throw 11 passes in 1974 and 22 passes in 1975. In fact, they had him returning punts in 1974. (He returned 15 punts for 154 yards.)

I said to Chuck, "Theismann's got a strong arm, and with his quickness he would be able to run those sprint outs and quarterback bootleg passes and runs that you like. He'd be great on the lateral option play you like. (We had a play called "Fake 32 Lateral Left to the Fullback" that was really a dive option play.) I know this is a guy that you'd love and he's sitting on the bench in Washington. If I were you, I'd do everything in my power to get him." Chuck replied, "We'll do it. We'll get him."

Well, a week or two went by when Chuck called me into his office and said, "We can't get your guy Joe Theismann." I replied, "Why not?" Chuck said, "He's making more than twice as much as Bradshaw!" I said, "No, you're kidding." Chuck said, "It's true. In his basic contract he makes more than twice as much as Terry. It's impossible to get him here." I thought, "Wow, another good idea down the drain."

Now, at the time of our conversation Terry Bradshaw had been the winning quarterback of two straight Super Bowls. Before that, he had been the No. 1 pick of the entire 1970 draft. Theismann had been a fourth round pick in 1974, played three years in Canada and had sat on the bench for two years with the Redskins, completing just 19 of 33 passes. It's still difficult to believe Theismann was making all that money just to run back punts.

Of course, we know Bradshaw and Theismann went on to have great NFL careers. Terry played for 14 years and Joe for 12 after first playing for three years in the Canadian Football League.

My Biggest Draft Mistake – The NFL draft can be a difficult process because of all the varied opinions that go into the evaluation of the players. Sometimes, you get lucky, like the Steelers famous draft of 1974. But we make mistakes, too, and I made a doozy in 1976. When getting ready for the draft, I had watched films of offensive tackle Jackie Slater from Jackson State. He looked like a good player on film. Bill Nunn, our scout who was in charge of black colleges, set up a workout with Slater for me. Right before I was ready to leave for Mississippi for Slater's workout, Noll asked me to go somewhere with him. I can't remember to where or why. I told Chuck that I couldn't go with him because I had to go to Mississippi to work out Slater. Chuck told me to forget about the workout. He said he had watched films of Slater and that he couldn't pass block. So I told Nunn to cancel the workout and I went with Chuck.

During the draft, we had two great first and second round picks in tight end Ben Cunningham from Clemson and center Ray Pinney from Washington. In the third round, the Steelers' organization gave me the choice of picking Jackie Slater or Ron Coder, a defensive tackle from Penn State, who was projected to be an offensive lineman. I debated through the entire time allotted before the pick, and finally picked Coder. Our first preseason game in August was against the college all-stars in Chicago in what would be the last of the great annual games that matched the winning NFL or Super Bowl team against college players who had just graduated. Ray Pinney was a center for the all-stars, and I asked him who he thought was the best college all-star offensive lineman. Ray replied, "Without a doubt, the best all-star offensive lineman is Jackie Slater." I knew right then that I had blown a draft pick. If I had worked out Slater as Bill Nunn had originally wanted me to do, I easily would have picked him in the third round of the draft.

Three years later I got to coach Slater with the Los Angeles Rams, saw his ability, and knew that's what would have happened. Coder ended up a good football player. We traded him to Seattle after his rookie preseason camp, and he was a starter for four years in the NFL and then two years in the World Football League. Jackie Slater, however, became the first NFL offensive linemen to play 20 years and was inducted into in the Pro Football Hall of Fame in 2001. In his acceptance speech at the Canton ceremonies, Jackie thanked several people for helping his career, including me and his other prime coach with the Rams, Hudson Houck, saying we were "the best line coaches that a guy could have." Not working out Slater in the spring of '76 and thereby not selecting him was definitely my biggest draft mistake.

Blocking Defensive Coordinators – During the fall of 1976, the University of Pittsburgh won the national championship and their star running back Tony Dorsett won the Heisman Trophy. Pitt's coach was Johnny Majors, who almost won the Heisman when he played at Tennessee in the 1950s. So after Pitt won the national title, Tennessee turned around and hired Johnny to resurrect his alma mater's floundering football program. To replace Majors, Pitt hired Jackie Sherrill who had been head coach at Washington State for just that '76 season after serving as a Majors' assistant at Pitt from 1973-75. And that's how "Bad Rad Days" at Upper St. Clair High School ended when Sherrill then hired my friend Joe Moore as Pitt's backfield coach.

Sherrill also grabbed Jimmy Johnson from Jimmy's alma mater, Arkansas, where Jimmy had been the defensive coordinator and made him his number one assistant and Pitt's defensive coordinator. One day in early August of 1977, Joe Moore and Jimmy visited our Pittsburgh Steelers preseason camp at Latrobe, accompanied by a wealthy Pitt alumni booster. After watching both morning and afternoon practices and having dinner at St. Vincent College, the four of us went to a local bar to have a few drinks. As we were talking, our conversation turned to a discussion about the full extension of the arms on pass protection that I had started three years earlier. Now, Jimmy had been an All-American nose guard at Arkansas when they played the Arkansas 5-2 monster defense—called a 3-4 in this day and age—and he wanted to know more about my arms maneuver. So I said that I would show him how the arms were used by demonstrating against him there in the bar.

The bar wasn't crowded and there was a large clear space where I could demonstrate. I told him to try to rush the passer and I would attempt to stop him. Well, he tried time after time to rush the passer and he couldn't get off the line of scrimmage because of my blocking. Finally, after about 10 tries, he started to try to knock my arms down or away, which was a smart move. But I simply slid my hands back on him quickly so he still couldn't pass rush very effectively. I'm at least six inches taller than Jimmy and I have a much longer reach then he has. So, I did have an unfair advantage on him. Plus, he had never seen the use of the arms the way that I had used them.

Joe Moore and the rich Pitt booster were having a great time laughing as Jimmy was trying to get off of the line of scrimmage. I told him afterward that when he started to knock the arms away that he was getting the gist of how to beat that type of pass protection. When I had my meeting with the Steelers offensive linemen the next day, I told them what had occurred with Pitt's defensive coordinator and me. I finished my story by saying, "If our offensive line can stuff the opposing team's defensive lineman like I stuff defensive coordinators, we will have a great offensive line."

This wasn't the last time I would use a bar as a football practice field and the next time I did it in Los Angeles, I took on one of Hollywood's most famous actors, but that, again, is another story.

Of course, Jimmy Johnson went on to become a successful head coach at Oklahoma State, then won a national championship as the head coach at Miami University of Florida before leading the Dallas Cowboys to their back to back Super Bowl championships in 1992 and 1993. One more thing, in 1980 when Jimmy got his first head coaching job at Oklahoma State, one of the first moves he made was send his new offensive line coach, Tony Wise, and his receivers coach, Butch Davis, to visit me that spring at the Los Angeles Rams for our six day minicamp. Naturally, we went out to have a drink at a bar but we left the hand to hand combat back on the field.

He's Going To Be A Great Player – I have to tell you a little more about Ray Pinney. When we chose Ray I considered him to be the best center in college football. I had thought the same about Mike Webster two years earlier. Besides center, I was trying to teach Ray both the guard and tackle positions. One day early in the regular season, Ray was having trouble pass blocking a defender, using a club pass rush technique. I had Ray stay after practice. I also asked John Banaszak, a backup defensive end, to stay and help me work with Ray on Ray's pass blocking. John was our most recent acquisition on the defensive line, having made the team as a free agent from Eastern Michigan. That, of course, made him my prime candidate anytime I needed a live blocking dummy.

I asked Banny to pass rush Ray Pinney using the club technique. Banny rushed Ray five times and beat Ray using the club technique all five times. We took a break, and I then had Banny rush Ray five more times. Again Ray got beat all five times. George Perles, our defensive line coach, was watching this pass rushing drill because he wanted to see how his defensive lineman would do against my rookie. Well, I continued this drill and Pinney finally blocked Banny. We had stayed out after practice for over an hour. When Ray finally had some success, we stopped and went inside to the locker room.

A short time later, as I'm walking past the scouts' office, scouts Dick Haley and Tim Rooney came running out and wanted to know what was wrong with Pinney. I said, "What are you talking about?" They said that Perles had told them that John Banaszak had just beaten Ray Pinney in a pass rush drill a bunch of times. I said, "That's right. Banny did beat him a number of times, but you should have been there. Every time Ray got beat, he jumped up and said let's go again. We stayed out there for over an hour after practice, because Ray wouldn't quit. He's going to be a great player." And he was.

Three years later, Ray Pinney was a starting right tackle in Super Bowl XIII, which the Steelers won, 35-31. In that same Super Bowl XIII against the Dallas Cowboys, John Banaszak was a defensive starter. Not bad for a couple of young guys who participated that day in one of Bad Rad's blocking drills.

End Of The Seven Dwarf's – After the two consecutive Super Bowl seasons of 1974 and 1975, some changes occurred in 1976 which brought an end to the offensive linemen referring to themselves the "Seven Dwarfs." First and foremost was the placing of Mike Webster as the full-time starter—playing the entire game rather than just a half—and making 14-year veteran Ray Mansfield Mike's backup for Ray's last year before his retirement. Starting right tackle Gordon Gravelle hurt his back lifting patio blocks at his house in preseason and couldn't play at the beginning of the regular season.

We also lost backup left offensive tackle Dave Reavis to Tampa Bay in the 1976 expansion draft and acquired center Ray Pinney of the University of Washington as our top pick in the second round of the regular 1976 draft.

10 Game Winning Streak – No team has ever won three Super Bowls in a row and only seven teams—Green Bay, Miami, San Francisco, Dallas, Denver, New England and the Steelers (twice)—have two back to back. What happened in 1976 gave me a pretty good insight as to why. You not only need talent and the right attitude but you also need luck.

We started out the season with a horrible 1-4 record. There seemed to be a lot of fallout from our two consecutive Super Bowl victories. Some of the players went to too many banquets, gave too many speeches, played too much golf, etc. in the off-season.

With a 1-4 record, we sure hadn't played like two-time Super Bowl champs. Our defense had given up an average of 332 yards and 22 points per game in those first five games. This was not the way we had normally played defense the previous two years. Three of those four losses were by three points or less.

Then, starting with the sixth league game against Cincinnati, a wondrous victory parade of 10 straight wins began, nine league games and one playoff game. Our defense improved dramatically, giving up an average of 186 1/2 total yards and 5 1/2 points per game in the 10-game win streak that included five games without giving up a point (five shutouts). Our offense averaged 232 1/2 rushing yards and 27 1/2 points per game in the streak. It was a great example of ball control and great defense. Another amazing fact was that rookie Mike Kruczek of Boston College, our other second round draft choice that spring, was the starting quarterback in six of the 10 wins because Terry Bradshaw had been hurt in our first Cleveland game. Five minutes after beating Baltimore, 40-14, in our first playoff game, a small private airplane crashed into the upper tier of the Baltimore's Municipal Stadium. Thank goodness the game was a blow out and the stands were empty. Nobody, not even the pilot, got hurt. We didn't know it then but the plane crash was probably a hint that our 10-game winning streak was over. But that's another story.

Take A Miracle To Win – When the dust cleared from our victory over the Colts, we had only one healthy running back, Reggie Harrison, to play in the AFC championship game at Oakland, which determined who would represent the AFC in Super Bowl XI. Our doctors said Franco Harris and Rocky Bleier—both of whom had run for more than 1,000 yards in the regular season—as well as Frenchy Fuqua weren't healthy enough to play in the game. Reggie was a third year pro and a very good back who had gained over 100 yards in some of the games during the past three years when Franco couldn't play because of injury.

In our offensive staff game plan meetings on the Tuesday before the game, we had one of two choices to make: either simply put a wide receiver—Swann,

Stallworth or Frank Lewis—at the half back position, teach them the plays and run our regular offense with a few adjustments, or we could go to a two tight ends, one back offense with different variations of the one back formations. The three offensive assistants, including me, simply wanted to put a wide receiver in the backfield, teach him the plays, and run our normal offense. Chuck Noll was fascinated with the prospect of putting in one back, two tight ends formation with different substitution groups. Chuck was the head coach and determined to do the one back offense, and that's what we did. We evidently didn't keep it a secret from our opponent because an Oakland player later told one of our players that they practiced against a one back, two tight end formation in all three of their main practice days before the game. I also had seen the one back formation hinted at in the *Pittsburgh Post-Gazette* on Thursday morning before the game in an article entitled, "Trainer's Room A Busy Scene," by Vito Stellino:

The Steelers walking wounded were walking a bit better yesterday. But that's about all they were doing.

The Steelers began their regular drills in freezing weather for the annual Oakland war Sunday, but three of their running backs—Franco Harris, Rocky Bleier and Frenchy Fuqua—were back in the training room getting treatment.

Bleier was soaking his foot in ice and Harris was getting treatment on his ribs while Fuqua got treatment on his calf muscle...

In an unusual move, Noll walked over to reporters on the sidelines at practice yesterday and said they couldn't write about what moves he was making if they wanted to watch (practice)...

Basically, Noll has two choices. He can switch a player to a running back slot or he can go with a three-receiver offense.

Obviously, Chuck Noll was naïve in thinking he could tell the sports reporters what they couldn't write about. Also obvious was that anyone reading the article would surmise that the Steelers, with only Reggie Harrison healthy as a running back, were going to use mainly one back formations in the upcoming AFC championship game. With local sports reporting like this, Al Davis had little need for the spies that he was frequently supposed to be using.

So we not only had new formations, but our opponent knew about them before we played them. During the first half of the game our players made many substitution errors going in and out of the game. Some of the terminology was confusing, like "double tight" or "wing right tight" and so on. The score at halftime was 17-7 in Oakland's favor. Our entire time in the locker room at halftime was spent with Chuck Noll going over the proper substitution for each formation group. I stood there watching this halftime meeting on substitution and thought, "instead of going over how to beat the other team, when to audible and what to call and stuff like we normally do at halftime, we were all simply trying to learn how to get the proper players into the game in their proper groups." I had a helpless feeling, and I knew then that it would take a miracle for us to win this game. No miracle occurred. Oakland won 24-7 and went to the Super Bowl.

I still have a newspaper clipping of an Associated Press story on the game with the headline, "Raiders Oust the Crippled Steelers," but what really was frustrating were the comments by their coach, John Madden. He said Franco and Rocky wouldn't have made any difference. "You put the men you have out there for 60 minutes and you play the game," Madden said. He was right about playing the game, alright, but as Chuck told the reporters, "It's tough to come into the biggest game with your hands tied behind your back, with two of your biggest weapons out." It's also tough when the other team already knows your game plan.

I'm Not Playing Right Tackle – Now, offensive linemen are a different breed than defensive linemen. They don't' get the publicity their defensive peers do unless, of course, they make a big mistake, like allowing a sack, and when that happens you never know how they'll react. When Cleveland beat us for our fourth loss in the fifth game of the 1976 season, Cleveland's defensive end Joe "Turkey" Jones beat our right offensive tackle Gerry "Moon" Mullins—who was still bothered by a groin injury—on a pass rush early in the fourth quarter. Turkey pushed quarterback Terry Bradshaw back a few yards and then picked Terry up and speared him head first into the ground. Turkey was penalized 15 yards for unnecessary roughness, but Terry was carried off the field in a stretcher and missed a couple of games, giving Mike Kruczek his big break. Obviously, this play got an enormous amount of publicity, and Cleveland won the game, 18-16.

Gerry "Moon" Mullins

Mullins normally played right offensive guard and had started both of our Super Bowls at right guard. Moon was playing right tackle because Gordon Gravelle, who normally played there, had hurt his back in the preseason moving patio blocks for his wife, Molly, and hadn't been able to play. After the game, Moon informed me that he wasn't playing tackle anymore. He said he was playing guard, period! At the time we were 1-4 with our next game against bitter rival Cincinnati. I needed Moon to play right tackle. I told him that he was playing right tackle against Cincinnati. He again refused. I then told him that we were not in pretty California where he grew up. This was Pittsburgh, a steelworker's town. I said that Gerry "Moon" Mullins would be announced as the starting right tackle on the loudspeaker before the game. If he didn't run out, nobody else would. Then we would get penalized for delay of game. When everybody would want to know why, I would tell them that Gerry Mullins doesn't want to play right tackle for the Steelers. I said after the game he'd be lucky to make it to his car without getting stoned to death with beer cans and bottles. He still said he didn't care. He wasn't going to play right tackle. Well, before the game, the starting Steelers offensive team was announced, and when they called the name Gerry "Moon" Mullins as the starting right tackle out trotted Moon. He played right tackle that day; we won 23-6, and started on that 10-game winning streak. Moon never mentioned not playing right tackle again.

When the Steelers went on to win Super Bowls in 1978 and 1979, Moon was again the starter at right guard. He's the only guard in the history of the NFL to start four super Bowls and have his team win all four of them.

Agent Orange – While writing the previous story about Gerry Mullins I am reminded of his agent, Howard Slusher, who I met at the Steelers' office in 1974 when Howard was not only Gerry's agent but also the agent for the 1974 Steeler first round draft pick, wide receiver, Lynn Swann. Howard had an undergraduate degree in psychology from Ohio State and a law degree from the University of Southern California. Howard got his start as a football agent in 1968 when he was an associate professor of sports psychology at USC and represented one of his students, Jim Ferguson, a USC linebacker who was drafted in the 17th round by the New Orleans Saints. Starting in the football agency business with Ferguson, Mullins, Swann, Sam "The Bam" Cunningham and other USC football players, Slusher's agency business grew until he was representing a number of well-known sports stars like San Diego Chargers' QB Dan Fouts, Baltimore defensive end John Dutton, and basketball clients Seattle Sonics' Gus Williams and Phoenix Suns' Paul Westphal.

As Howard's agent reputation grew, there was a rumor at the Steelers after we won Super Bowls IX and X that Howard was going to negotiate a contract for all of my seven-dwarf offensive line players as a group. That never came off but Howard did represent three of my starting Steelers offensive linemen: guards Gerry Mullins and Jim Clack and tackle Gordon Gravelle, plus a few other Steelers players. Never to my recollection did the Steelers front office have a problem negotiating with Howard the four years that I was there (1974-7). Six years later when I was with the Denver Broncos, future Hall of Fame cornerback Mike Haynes of the New England Patriots, who was represented by Slusher, became available for a trade in November of 1983. Our defensive coordinator Joe Collier desperately wanted the Broncos to trade for Haynes. Joe considered Mike to be one of the best cornerbacks in the NFL. The Bronco's front office told Joe that they wouldn't consider trading for Haynes because they did not want to deal with his agent, Howard Slusher. This greatly upset Collier, who thought the Broncos should try to get Mike Haynes no matter who his agent was.

Well, in November of 1983, the Oakland Raiders, who were in our division, made a trade with New England for Haynes. At the time, the Raiders had the same win-loss ratio as the Broncos, 6 wins, 3 losses. After obtaining Mike, the Raiders won six of their seven final games to wind up at 12-4 while the Broncos won three of their final seven for a record of 9-7—and one of these losses was a close 22-20 one to the Raiders. However, both teams made the playoffs with the Broncos losing the first wild card playoff game to Seattle while the Raiders defeated Pittsburgh, Seattle and the Washington Redskins to win Super Bowl XVIII.

In a recap of the Super Bowl XVIII game where the Raiders beat the Redskins, writer Bob Carroll in the book *Total Football—The Official Encyclopedia of the NFL* makes the following statement about Super Bowl XVIII: "Marcus Allen was named the game's 'most valuable player'—Raider's cornerbacks Mike Haynes and Lester Hayes also deserve special mention for holding the Redskins' vaunted receivers Art Monk and Charlie Brown to a mere four catches combined—none in the first half [the Raiders led 23-3 at halftime] when the game was decided."

I often wonder what would have happened if Joe Collier had gotten his way and the Broncos instead of the Raiders had traded for Mike Haynes in November of 1983. Fourteen years after that trade Haynes was voted into the National Football Hall of Fame and his presenter was his agent, Howard Slusher.

Recently, I came across a copy of *People Magazine* dated December 9, 1985, with an article on Howard Slusher by writer Jack Friedman entitled "Howard Slusher, Sports' Least Secret Agent, strikes fear and loathing in the hearts of team owners." The article had some rather interesting quotes from a few NFL general managers and team owners:

—" *'Howard Slusher's not an agent, he's a terrorist,' snorted New York Giants General Manager George Young at a recent NFL meeting."*

—*"Cleveland Browns owner Art Modell...once called Howard 'the number one thorn' in pro football's side. Modell vowed never to draft one of Slusher's clients, simply to avoid the anguish of dealing with him."*

—" *'He's always looking to exert the most possible leverage,' says Dan Rooney, president of the Pittsburgh Steelers. In particular, says Rooney, Slusher is a master of managing news to turn up the pressure."*

—" *'Howard's tough but fair,' says (Denver's) Pat Bowlen. 'He's the best in the business...What makes a Slusher holdout so aggravating is that he only represents the better players—the type that are very close to an owner's heart. The type, in other words, that wins championships.'"* [Bowlen took over from Edgar Kaiser, Jr. the year after I was hired.]

Friedman wrote that Slusher is known as the "king of the holdout," adding, "So poisonous is his reputation among some of America's wealthiest sports-franchise holders that the unyielding L.A. attorney is almost better known by his pseudonym, Agent Orange [because of his reddish-orange hair]. Slusher has become famous—in some circles, infamous—for having his player-clients hold out and keep holding out until they are offered the serious-money contracts they seek."

I haven't seen Howard for years but I knew he had worked for Nike. Then in January of 2012, my wife Nancy and I attended Joe Paterno's funeral at Penn State.

Afterward we were at a reception for funeral guests at the Centre Hills Country Club. Shortly after we arrived, Nancy said she had seen Nike CEO Phil Knight sitting at a nearby table with Sue Paterno. I walked over to the table, said "Hi" to Sue and introduced myself to Phil. I asked Phil if he knew Howard Slusher. Phil replied that not only did he know him but he was "one of the most despicable persons that he had ever known." I then replied, "Sounds like a friend of yours." Phil laughed and said, "He's my best friend. How do you know him?" I told him that early in Howard's career as a pro football agent he had represented some of my Steelers offensive linemen, and when we played the Los Angeles Rams in the last game of the 1975 NFL regular season, Howard had all the Steelers coaches, trainers, equipment men and front office personnel at a dinner reception at his house in Palos Verdes. In those days Howard seemed to have a negotiating relationship with the Steelers that was nothing like his later reputation in the NFL as "Agent Orange, King of the Holdouts." Maybe one reason the Steelers won four Super Bowls in six years was because the Rooneys knew how to deal with Agent Orange Howard Slusher.

Late Surge Saves The Season – After the 1976 season, Tom Moore replaced Lionel Taylor as our receivers coach (Lionel went to the L.A. Rams). We started the 1977 NFL season without two of the original Seven Dwarfs who were our offensive line starters for the 1974 and 1975 Super Bowl seasons. Gone were 14-year veteran center Ray Mansfield, who retired after the 1976 season, and 7-year veteran right offensive tackle Gordon Gravelle, who was traded in the 1977 preseason to the New York Giants for a No. 2 draft choice. Tight end Larry Brown was now the starting right tackle. Because of an injury to Jon Kolb, second year player Ray Pinney started the season at left tackle. New backup additions to the offensive line were center Ted Peterson of Eastern Illinois, our fourth round draft pick in 1977, and offensive guard Steve Courson from South Carolina, whom we drafted in the fifth round after Peterson.

The 1977 season started off well with the Steelers shutting out San Francisco, 27-0, on opening day at Three Rivers Stadium. The highlight of the game was the Steelers' use of a college straight option running play seldom seen in professional football. We ran it a number of times with great success. Another factor was the performance of first time starter Pinney at left offensive tackle in place the injured Kolb. Ray was so impressive that our players awarded him the game ball afterwards for his play against the 49ers' All-Pro defensive end Cedrick Hardman.

The play of our offense plus the shutout of the 49ers by our defense may have made us overconfident or complacent because we proceeded to win only three of our next seven games for a 4-4 record going into the last six games of the season. We had lost that eighth game to Denver, 21-7, and at that point we sure did not look like a playoff team.

But we had a late surge with four straight wins, and with an 8-4 record we were back in contention with two games remaining in December. We lost to Cincinnati, 17-0, in our 13th game, and that left us with only a slight, mathematical chance to make the playoffs and a chance to save our season.

I Beg Your Pardon — So, in the last week of the 1977 season, the Steelers had to beat the San Diego Chargers and the Cincinnati Bengals had to lose to the Houston Oilers in order for the Steelers to win the Central Division title and make the playoffs. The Cincinnati game started slightly before the Steelers game. During our game, after every series of play, our players who were coming off the field would ask, "What's the score?" inquiring about the Cincinnati game, which we were listening to on a radio on the bench. Finally, near the end of the third quarter of our game, we found out that Cincinnati had lost. Now, we knew if we won, we would definitely make the playoffs. The intensity of our players definitely picked up. After one of our defensive series in the fourth quarter our starting right defensive end, Dwight White, ran up to me and yelled, "Rad, get Loren Toews out of the game. Get him out!" Loren was our right outside linebacker. I said, "Dwight, what's wrong?" Dwight said, "I'll tell you what's wrong. Do you know what Loren said to me? I'm in my stance waiting for a defensive charge call. If Loren says 'Ram' I go in. If he says 'Lion' I go out, if he says 'two gap' I play straight. I say, 'Loren what's the call?' He doesn't answer. I scream, 'What's the call? What's the call?' He says, 'I beg your pardon.' Can you believe that? 'I beg your pardon.' Rad, get him out of there." Dwight was truly frustrated. I told him to talk to Loren himself and get their calls straightened out. We ended up squeaking by San Diego 10-9 to win the division and make the playoffs.

Last Game With The Steelers — But our season came to an end in a 34-21 loss to Denver in the first playoff game. The game was highlighted by a big fight between both teams on the last play of the first half with the score tied 14-14. The fight started between Steelers defensive left tackle Joe Green and Broncos offensive right guard Paul Howard. I tried to break up the fight and got carted off the field by a bunch of the Broncos players, but luckily no one hit me. As reporter Vito Stellino wrote in the *Pittsburgh Post-Gazette* the day after Christmas:

The Steelers impaled themselves on their own mistakes in a 34-21 Christmas Eve loss to the Denver Broncos...Although Tom Jackson's two interceptions in the fourth period finally turned the game, the Steelers really lost it in the first half on two mistakes: a blocked punt and Franco Harris' fumble. That gave Denver two touchdowns...

The incredible thing is that the Steelers had a 183-44 edge in yardage at halftime and yet the score was tied 14-14. If the Steelers hadn't given away two scores, there would have been no fourth period interceptions because the Steelers would have been protecting the lead.

But as [TV broadcaster] Don Meredith likes to say, "if ifs and buts were candy and nuts, we'd all have a Merry Christmas." The Steelers woke up to find coal in their stockings.

And that's how my last game with the Steelers ended.

CHAPTER SIX – The Roots of Linebacker U

About the time that I was coaching the Pittsburgh Steelers offensive line, Penn State became known as "Linebacker U." I'm not sure when I first heard the nickname, and from what I've been told no one has been able to confirm when the term was first used. But the name evolved over several years starting in the early 1960s because of all the outstanding linebackers that had been coming out of Penn State and going on to play professional football.

Half dozen players in particular helped establish Penn State's early reputation and a couple of them didn't even play linebacker in college. One of them was Dave Robinson, an All-American end at State in 1962 who became a three-time All-Pro linebacker for the Green Bay Packers' NFL and Super Bowl championship teams in the 1960s. Robinson also was a pretty good receiver and blocker on offense but he was an outstanding defensive end, and in 1961 Robby and the other starting Penn State end, Bob Mitinger, were arguably the two best defensive ends in the country. A defensive end position in Penn State's 5-2 defense was very similar to the outside linebacker position in the pro 3-4 defense. That was Mitinger's senior year when he also became a first team All-American and then went on to play linebacker for the San Diego Chargers.

Two contemporaries of theirs on that '61 team were Ralph Baker and Bill Saul. In 1960, Baker was a freshman nose guard on defense and a center on offense and moved to defensive end as a sophomore. We switched him to center-linebacker in 1962, and he later spent 11 years with the New York Jets as a starting linebacker, including the Jets' Super Bowl champs of 1968 that upset the Baltimore Colts in one of the most historic games of all time. Saul was a center-linebacker on Penn State's second unit, known as the red team, and because of the limited substitution rules at the time this unit played as much as the blue team which started the games. Bill was the second round draft choice of the Baltimore Colts in '62 and eventually played eight years as a linebacker in NFL.

As Robinson, Mitinger, Baker and Bill Saul were making names for themselves as linebackers in the pros, four linebackers at Penn State—Dennis Onkotz, Jack Ham, Pete Johnson and Jim Kates—were helping make Penn State one of the elite teams in college football. From the second game of the 1967 season until the second game of 1970, Penn State went undefeated in 33 straight games, won two Orange Bowl games, and finished second twice in the national rankings.

To give you an example of how good of a linebacker Onkotz was, in 1968 and 1969 Onkotz and a linebacker from Tennessee, Steve Kiner, were the only two players in Division I college football to be consensus All-Americans both years—and that's documented by the official NCAA record book. Ham was one year behind Onkotz and overshadowed by him, but Ham also became a consensus All-American in his senior year of 1970. Both Onkotz and Ham are in the College Football Hall of Fame, as is Dave Robinson.

Several outstanding linebackers followed this initial group throughout the 1970s. They included All-Americans like Charlie Zapiec in 1971, John Skourpan in 1972, Ed O'Neil in 1973, Greg Buttle in 1975 and Kurt Allerman in 1976, as well as Lance Mehl in 1979, who wasn't an All-American but should have been. Most of them had pretty good careers in the NFL. Then there were a couple of defensive linemen from that era who, like Robinson and Mitinger, played linebacker in the pros. One was John Ebersole, who was an outstanding defensive end on those great teams of '68 and '69 and wound up as a starting linebacker with the New York Jets for several years. Another was Jim Laslavic, who also never made All-America, but after playing linebacker as a senior in 1972, had a 10-year career with Detroit, San Diego and Green Bay. Perhaps the best known of the linemen turned linebacker in the pros is Matt Millen, who played linebacker in his first year at Penn State. Millen was a linebacker on four winning Super Bowl teams, and then became even better known as a broadcaster and general manager of the Detroit Lions.

Pat Livingston, the sports editor of the *Pittsburgh Press*, took notice of all our Penn State linebackers in a column headlined, "Does Green-Thumbed Paterno Grow Linebackers On Trees?" published on December 8, 1974. Here is part of what he wrote:

"They're calling Mt. Nittany an incubator of linebackers, just as another central Pennsylvania institution, Hanover Farms, is an incubator of horse flesh...The Lions have turned out All-Americans in each of the last six years, and list 10 linebacker grads on National Football League rosters at the present time."

That's how the name Linebacker U came about, and I should know. I coached that first wave of linebackers from Saul and Baker to Ham and Onkotz and then taught my successor as Penn State's linebacker coach how to coach the rest of them. That's why I'm now considered "the Father of Linebacker U."

Frankly, I'd never thought of myself as "the Father of Linebacker U," until a few years ago when my co-author of this book, Lou Prato, and a couple of other sportswriters began mentioning me in their stories about Penn State linebackers. Because my successor had been the linebackers coach for so long—from 1970 to 1999—most everyone in the media, and the fans, believed he was the coach who started it all. I never gave it a thought because I was too busy with my own coaching career. I'm happy to have started this "Linebacker U" tradition, so I want to tell you how it all began.

Kennywood Childhood – I grew up in a small community approximately eight miles southeast of Pittsburgh, along the Monongahela River, called Kennywood. Kennywood was part of West Mifflin Borough and was next to Kennywood Park, which, at the time, was the largest privately-owned amusement park in the world. Kennywood is one of the oldest amusement parks in the country, beginning in 1898 as a trolley park, and is still going strong. In 1987 it was declared a National Historic Landmark and now bills itself as "America's Finest Traditional Amusement Park," with 31 major rides including five roller coasters and three water rides.

Our three bedroom house was situated on the corner of Shadynook Avenue and Valeview Drive. The end of Shadynook connected with a dirt and gravel road that led into the back entrance of Kennywood Park, which was about 300 yards from our house. In fact, Kennywood's current giant roller coaster goes over the end of our street.

We lived so close to the park that we could hear the music being piped over the park's loudspeaker. For at least 10 years, Kennywood Park's closing song at 11:00 p.m. would put me to sleep. The opening lyrics are the title of the song and it goes like this: "For all we know, we may never meet again..."

One of the main attractions at the park when I was growing up was a show featuring circus acts around the lagoon in the heart of the park. Every day at 4 p.m. and 8 p.m. crowds would gather around the lagoon and watch world famous performers like the clown Emmett Kelly and the Flying Wallenda's high-wire and trapeze act or others such as The Great Zacchini family that was shot from a cannon, the Chinese Acrobats, Seldon "The Stratosphere Man" and the guy who did those one fingered handstands. A lot of the performers and the people who ran the rides in the park were from Florida and they rented rooms in the community. The Wallendas, the Zacchini family and others stayed in our house or my grandparents' house next door or with other close neighbors. Some of them used to practice their acts in our back yard. Emmett Kelly, Barnum and Bailey's most famous circus clown, was at Kennywood for six weeks every summer while the circus was retooling in Florida for the next season. He rented a room three houses away, and he had a miniature circus clown's bicycle that he let me ride every so often

I remember the day the Zacchini girl got shot out of the cannon and broke her arm during the 8 p.m. act when she landed in the net on the Kennywood island stage. Her sister, who had two kids and hadn't done the act in eight years, flew in the next morning and got shot out of the cannon at the 4 p.m. act. They were professionals and they weren't going to miss a performance. Both sisters roomed in our house while Mr. Zacchini was staying next door at my grandparents' house. I asked the older sister how she could be shot out of the cannon when she hadn't done the act in eight years. She said simply, "It's what we do. It's what our dad taught us from the time we were little children."

I have been thinking about the Zacchini's most of my life. I cannot imagine me or anyone in my family being shot out of a cannon. People may think I'm crazy but I'm not that nuts. Then, I recently ran across a book published in 2006 entitled "The Book of Useless Information." This item caught my attention: "Approximately sixty circus performers have been shot from cannons. At last report, thirty-one of them have been killed." Based on additional research, I discovered that 35 or more Zacchini family members were shot from cannons and none of them were killed. Hmm. Maybe I should have tried it. It might have made me a better linebacker.

I didn't realize it at the time but looking back, I believe the code of loyalty, dedication and professionalism practiced by those circus performers found their way into my psyche and helped shape my character. I know that watching them perform was one reason I was on the gymnastics team at Homeville Junior High School.

The fact that so many people who worked at Kennywood Park also lived in the community made it easy to get free tickets. Another benefit for us was the Kennywood Park Athletic Field where they held track meets and special picnic events. We played baseball on the field when it wasn't being used for a Kennywood Park event. On occasion, a Kennywood cop would come by and kick us off but not very often.

One of the common picnic events back then was the egg throw or toss contest. In an egg toss, two partners get five yards apart and throw an egg to one another. If either partner breaks an egg their team is eliminated. After each successful catch, the partners each back up a step. This continues until there is just one set of partners with an unbroken egg. Winning partners may end up 40 yards apart at the end of the contest. My cousin Garsh and I used to enter these egg throwing events frequently even though we weren't associated with the picnic being held that day. We almost always won first prize. (It's a skill!)

As I remember it, I thought I had a great childhood. Like a lot of kids growing up in an ethnic neighborhood in Western Pennsylvania in the late 1940s and early 1950s when the steel mills were thriving, we were always playing sports. We played touch football, basketball and baseball in season and roamed the woods around Kennywood. We had a natural shower in the Kennywood woods from an 8-foot water fall formed in a creek. We had a cave with a natural spring in the cliffs overlooking the Monongahela River. In the late spring, summer and early fall, we had Kennywood Park to loaf in or play around in.

There was a basketball hoop outside our house at the corner of the two streets that my brother and I and our friends put up about the time I was in the 5th grade and he was a senior in high school. The hoop was a magnet for all the kids in the neighborhood. At any one time we would have six or seven basketballs in our garage, because our friends would simply leave their basketballs there when they went home.

Both my parents worked while raising me and my brother Lou, who's seven years older than me. My dad, Mike, worked in the steel mill. At the same time my parents ran a monument and tombstone business named the Kenmore Granite Co. that my mother, Bridget, was in charge of.

Lou and I used to make spending money for a number of years by going to the local cemeteries during the week before Memorial Day offering to clean tombstones. We used hydrochloric acid in a glass bottle and charged $3.00 for normal dirty ones and hydrofluoric acid in a wax bottle and charged $5.00 for the very old and real dirty ones. One time, my brother spilled three drops of hydrofluoric acid onto his leather work shoes and the acid burned three holes through his shoes, socks and blistered his feet. Dangerous stuff.

Put Back In 2nd Grade & Johnny Sanders – I'll never forget a couple of things that happened to me in the third grade that made an impression on me the rest of my life. Near the end of the first half of that year, we were getting ready to take mid-year exams the next day and the teacher had a bunch of us at the blackboards that went all around the room on three sides. The lady principal came in the room and was checking our work on the blackboards, when she looked at my blackboard work, and said, "What kind of writing is that?" I looked at her and said, "What's the matter? Can't you read? It's American." She said, "You come with me!" And she grabbed my arm, pulled me out of the room, up the stairs to the second story, opened a classroom door and said, "You belong here." Then she told the second grade teacher, "This is a new student for you." And she left. The second grade teacher gave me a desk in the front row. They were having a reading session and she asked me to read. I read a book aloud and when I was finished she said, "Why are you here?" I said that I really didn't know, but I told her of the incident. At the time, I was one of five persons who were on the third grade honor roll. Anyway, when I got home, I told my mother and she went to the school and got me back in the third grade the next day. I don't know if it was what I said or the tone of my voice, but from that moment on I watched what I said around my teachers. This was probably the first of many times that I heard the expression, "He has a bad attitude."

Now, let me tell you about a friend in my third grade class named Johnny Sanders. Johnny was a black kid and we didn't have many black kids in our class. He was No. 1 on that third grade honor roll, and he was smart, articulate and personable; a brilliant kid. After the third grade I went to school in a different district and I didn't see Johnny Sanders again until the 10th grade when my cousin Garsh and I saw him at Duquesne High School. We were amazed. Johnny was almost illiterate. He was in shop, the vocational curriculum. He spoke very poorly and was hard to understand. In the six years between third and 10th grade, he turned into an altogether different human being. We've all read a lot about how important the pre-school and the first three years of schooling and environment are but Johnny Sanders shows that the age of 9 through 14 are very important also. I found out years later that Johnny Sanders died a wino at age 30. As I look back, I believe my initial friendship with Johnny and what happened to him in high school helped form my views about race. That's why I paid special attention to the backgrounds of my black players and one reason I related so well with them. Subconsciously, I've probably had Johnny Sanders on my mind all my life.

1st Athletic Experience – When I was about 10 years old, I had my first memorable athletic experience on Thanksgiving Day. The guys in the big kids' gang that included my older brother Lou played a Thanksgiving Day football game at the Kennywood Athletic Field that we called the Turkey Bowl. The Top of the Hill guys played the Bottom of the Hill guys. We lived in the Bottom of the Hill. These were high school guys or a few years older. The Bottom of the Hill had only 10 players. So my brother offered my services as the best player from the little kids' gang. I made a tackle early in the game and the guy I tackled told my brother if I wasn't careful I would get hurt. My brother told him, "Worry about yourself. My brother can take care of himself." Our Bottom of the Hill team won the game.

When I was in the seventh grade I made my first official organized team. I went out for the junior high varsity basketball team and I was one of only two seventh graders to make the team. That was also the year my dad quit the steel mill, sold the monument and tombstone business and bought The 5th Avenue Hotel in Glassport, which was a combination beer garden and hotel. The hotel is still a local landmark, but after three years my parents sold the bar-hotel and started an appliance business in Duquesne. After three years in the appliance business, my dad went back to the mill.

My Piano Stories – Starting in the 4th grade, I took piano lessons. My older brother Lou had begged for a piano, took lessons for six months and then quit. My parents said they paid good money for the piano and they picked me to play it. I wanted to play drums, but, of course, that wasn't going to happen. Anyway, I took lessons from Mrs. Goldberg at $2.50 for a half hour each week for 4½ years. I didn't mind it for four years except when my mother made me leave the basketball game outside in the street to come in the house and practice "Yankee Doodle Dandy." My sixth grade teacher found out I took piano lessons and recruited me to play for the grade school assembly—grades one through six at Homeville Elementary. I was not going to play "Clair de Lune" or "Chopsticks" before my buddies, so I picked out a song that I thought would get their attention. It went like this: "To the jungle far away. Bang! Bang! Bang! I am going for a stay. Bang! Bang! Bang! I'll see the cannibals. Bang! Bang! Bang! And all the animals. Bang! Bang! Bang!" And so on. The whole school went wild, cheering and screaming. My buddies loved it. And I was never asked to play in school again.

In the summer between eighth and ninth grades, I organized a baseball team that played in the Morning Glory League for ages 11 to 13 at West Field in Munhall. West Field was a historic field because it was the home field of the famous Homestead Grays baseball team of the National Negro League. Some of the games were Saturday morning which interfered with my piano lessons which were also on Saturday mornings. So I cut a number of lessons that summer and didn't practice the piano very much. At the end of the summer I was set to play at the annual recital where parents and relatives are invited and everybody gets all dressed up, and I was practicing with my teacher, Mrs. Goldberg, when she said, "Mr. Radakovich, could you please stop for a moment." I reached out, stopped the metronome and said, "Okay." She said, "Would you please do me a favor?" I said, "Sure. What's the favor?" She said, "Please don't' tell anybody I'm your teacher!" Needless to say, after I told my parents about that, my piano lessons ended. Years later, when I was coaching and would get very upset with a player, I would tell them my piano story. And they usually would say, "Okay coach, I get your meaning. Don't tell anybody you're my coach." Then I would say, "I didn't say that. You did. But if you like I'll tell you my piano story again."

My parents told me that someday I would regret giving up the piano. I said, "No way." Years later, when I was a senior in high school, another senior who was a piano student for Mrs. Goldberg at the same time I was but not as advanced as I was at that time, gave a magnificent piano concert at the school, and I thought, "If I wouldn't have quit, I could have been that good." I've regretted quitting ever since.

First Recruiting Experience – My first recruiting experience occurred in that Morning Glory Baseball League in that same summer between eighth and ninth grades. We were in a playoff game and I was playing second base and the opponent on first tried to steal second. I took the throw from the catcher, blocked the bag and laid the base runner out. The head of the league who was umpiring was Nick Klisky, the head football coach at Munhall High School. He came running out to second base to see how bad the base runner was hurt and he turned to me and says, "Son, you'll never play baseball for me, but I'd love to have you on my football team. How about coming to Munhall when you graduate from junior high school next year?" I tried to transfer from Duquesne to Munhall High School the middle of my sophomore year but my dad wouldn't sign the transfer papers.

Football—A Man's Game – To fully understand how I became a linebacker guru, I need to tell you about my playing days in high school and at Penn State. I didn't start out wanting to be a linebacker as many kids do today. Like a lot of kids growing up I played pickup football games with my buddies, but I really liked basketball better. I didn't really get interested in football until my cousin Garsh and I went from Homeville Junior High to Duquesne High School in the 10th grade, and we decided to go out for the football team as ends.

After a week's practice, we were both still substitutes for the sixth team and only because there weren't enough players for the seventh team. At the end of the first week, on a Saturday afternoon, there was to be a two to three hour scrimmage to determine who goes to football camp for two weeks in Ligonier, which was 40 miles away. Seventy kids were trying out for the team but only 44 would be going to camp after the Saturday morning practice. Garsh and I went home for lunch and decided we weren't getting a chance because we had come from West Mifflin Borough, a different school district that did not have a high school, and nobody knew us. So, we decided to quit. I told my mother and she said, "I thought my son wanted to be a man." I said, "What's that supposed to mean?" She said, "I always thought that football was a man's game. Does my son want to be a man or not?" I said, "Okay, I'll give it one more shot and go to this afternoon's practice, but I'm telling you they're not giving me a chance."

So, I went to practice but my cousin Garsh didn't. I watched the scrimmage for a couple of hours when the coach, John Donelli, said, "Go in at end," I went in at left end. They ran a sweep my way and I tackled the ball carrier for a 7-yard loss. Coach Donelli blew the whistle and said, "That's it. Scrimmage is over. The kid that made that last tackle goes to camp." So I got in the scrimmage for just one play and got to go to camp for two weeks in Ligonier. I've sometimes wonder how my life might have been different if I had quit after one week like my cousin.

Camp Wintergreen – Anyone who went through a preseason high school football camp back then knows what happens. There was an unusual, and painfully uncomfortable, initiation ritual the first night of camp for first year players. We stayed in open-air screened cabins that surrounded a big grass courtyard bordering a creek which was dammed up for swimming and bathing. You had to go through the woods to the football fields, which were really just wild grass fields with the weeds cut low. Around midnight on the first night at camp, after the coaches who stayed in the nearby house were in bed, a group of upper classmen went to the cabins of the first year players with bottles of Sloan's Liniment and Wintergreen. They rubbed this liniment and wintergreen oil into the testicles of each of the first year campers. I remember one of our black rookie players standing on a camper bed with a knife drawn saying, "Nobody's going to wintergreen me," and one of the wintergreen upper classman saying, "Get Will." Will was one of the upper class black players. Will walked into the cabin and saw the rookie player standing on the bed with the knife. He picked up the end of the bed with the player still on it and threw it against the wall. "Wintergreen him," he said and they did.

Two years later, in my senior year, Coach Donelli said he would take anyone to camp who gave total effort regardless of size and ability. So he took two physically immature sophomores who weighed less than 120 pounds to camp to prove a point. Well, on the first night of camp, the coaches heard screaming in the middle of the night and they came out into the great grass courtyard and found these two small sophomores tied to the flagpole and in shock from the wintergreen. They rushed them to the hospital where they were treated for shock and sent home. That ended the wintergreen initiation at Duquesne High School's preseason camp. My former players in college and the pros may find this surprising because they think I'm a little wild, but I never had anything to do with the wintergreening. That wasn't my style and I thought it was disgusting. In fact, I was the captain of the football team when that last incident happened, and I was glad Coach Donelli ended it.

Anyhow, when I got back from football camp my sophomore year, I wrote a poem about camp and the initiation which my buddy Eddie Menzie read in English class. I forgot most of it, but I do remember a few lines. It started, "We got on the bus, all 44. The sophomores were last through the door…" Then later it went, "Oh my gosh, alas, alack! The pain, the burn is coming back." That last part was referring to that wintergreen initiation. I can still feel the burning.

Dan (first from left) sitting on bench during a 1950 Duquesne High School game.

Make Him The Snapper – The second or third day of that first summer camp in my sophomore year turned out to be one of the most significant days of my life, but I sure didn't realize it back then. After the first or second day of camp, the second team center, "Weedi" Flowers, left because he was playing behind Ed Kleist, who eventually went to Penn State on a scholarship. The coaches brought Weedi back and made him a starting tackle, which moved a sophomore, John "Yunno" Durik to second team center. Now, there was no third team center, whose main job was to snap the ball to the quarterback during ball handling or pass skeleton drills. Essentially, the third team center simply snapped all day while everybody else practiced. So Coach Donelli yelled out, "Where's that last kid that we brought to camp." Remember, I was playing end at the time. "Make him the snapper," Donelli yelled. And that's how I became a center-linebacker because centers played linebacker on defense. Looking back, I sure owe old Weedi a big favor. Somehow, End U or Defensive End U just doesn't sound right.

I guess being a linebacker was really my calling but at the time I just did not know it. During one of the scrimmages in the second week of camp, I was playing linebacker and made a lot of tackles. Coach Donelli stopped the scrimmage and said he wished he had more players like this little kid that was making all the tackles. I was just 5-foot-11, 135-pounds at the time and would play for the junior varsity that year, but Coach Donelli obviously liked my spunk because I dressed for the varsity games.

I became a starting linebacker in 1951, my junior year, and it was a pivotal year for me. I now realized I loved to play linebacker because it all came natural to me. I'll never forget an incident in the '51 preseason camp when about five of the starting seniors cornered me after one of the scrimmages and wanted to know who was giving me the signals—letting me know what play was coming. They said I couldn't make all the tackles I was making unless somebody was signaling the direction of the play to me. I yelled back at them, "Just because you guys signal to each other and to your buddies doesn't mean that I get signals." I knew that they gave signals to Vincy, one of their buddies who was trying to be a starter. I took it as a great compliment and was pretty damn proud of it, too.

Then, at the end of junior year camp, Coach Donelli told me I better start making good grades because I was going to get a football scholarship in two years if my grades were good enough. I really hadn't given much thought to college, but that's when I realized I could have fun and go to college, too. So, I started to try and do well in school. As a result, even though my grades were poor or average in the 9th and 10th grades, they were good enough my junior and senior years to be admitted to any Ivy League school or military academy.

"Cookie" Becomes "Bad Rad"

Poor Coopuss – That was also the year I got a new nickname. Since I was a baby, I had been called "Cookie," and I'll bet if some of my former players had known about the nickname and what it really meant I'd have never heard the end of it.

One day when I was in high school, I walked into the kitchen and said to my mom, "Hey mom, how did I get the nickname Cookie?" She was at the stove making dinner. She said, "You don't want to know." I said, "Mom, it's my name. How did I get it?" She said, "I'm not telling you." I said, "Mom, it's my name. You've got to tell me." She said, "Do you really want to know?" I said, "Yes, I really want to know." She said, "All right, I'll tell you.

"When you were a baby," she said, "I used to get together with my married lady friends and their kids or babies. (My dad was Serbian and my mother was Polish.) My married Serbian lady friends used to rock you and say, 'Poor Coopuss! Poor Coopuss!' and my married American lady friends would say, 'What are they saying? What's this Coopuss?' I wasn't about to tell them what it meant, so I said, 'Oh, that's just Serbian for cookie.' So, my American lady friends would rock you and say, 'Poor Cookie. Poor Cookie' But when the Serbian ladies rocked you saying 'Poor Coopuss' what they were really saying was 'Poor Cabbage Head. Poor Cabbage Head.' Coopuss is cabbage in Serbian."

New Nickname – So my nickname was really Cabbage Head but I sure didn't want that to get around. Some of my friends had begun calling me "Rad" because it was short for my last name but I was still known best as "Cookie." That all changed in my junior year. I was the starting linebacker in our first game against Brownsville, which we won, 29-0. After the game a lot of players and fans went to the Duke Restaurant, a local hangout about four blocks from the football stadium that had music and dancing in the back part. I was standing outside the restaurant with some of the other players, and along comes Frank Pacacha, a former basketball player for us who was at that time a freshman on Duquesne University's basketball team. Frank yelled, "Did you see Rad make all those tackles tonight? Rad is Bad! Rad is Bad! Bad Rad!" In the slang of the 1950s, bad sometimes meant good. Anyway, my friends started to call me "Bad Rad," and before long everyone else did, too. Of course, even today some people think the nickname refers to me being a little nasty or disobedient, which is far from the truth, although I have caused a little "trouble" for others now and then, as you will read. In any case, it sure beats being called "Cabbage Head" all my life.

Recruiting Was An Experience – I was the captain of both my football and basketball teams my senior year, and after the football season, I was recruited by a number of colleges. I visited four schools—Boston University, the Naval Academy, Pitt and Penn State—but had several others interested in me. Recruiting is a lot different today but I had a couple of weird experiences.

Harvard – One day a recruiting representative from Harvard stopped by the high school and got some of the teachers all excited. They called me into the principal's office and had a meeting about me going to Harvard. They explained that they never had a student from Duquesne High School go to Harvard and what a big deal it would be for me if I went there. When they were done talking, I finally told them that there was no way I was going to go to that sissy school. Well, the principal, Ray Henry, got so upset with "my attitude," as he called it, that he expelled me. My mother had to come to the school the next day to get me back in.

Ivy – Another recruiter from an Ivy League school—and I can't remember the school—invited me to dinner at the William Penn Hotel in downtown Pittsburgh. That's where I first met Joe Walton, who was from Beaver Falls, which was several miles the other side of Pittsburgh from my home. Joe's dad, who was a well known football coach, was there, and if I remember right, I talked a little. Joe hardly said a word but his dad dominated the conversation. I sure didn't know then that one day Joe would be my boss at the New York Jets and Robert Morris College. Oh, Joe can't remember the name of the Ivy League school either, but he went to Pitt where he became an All-American end.

Indiana – I had scheduled a visit to Indiana where Gene Gedman from my high school was a star player. Gene later was captain of the 1956 world champion Detroit Lions. When Indiana found out I weighed just 165 pounds, they asked me to return the plane tickets they had sent me, but told me if I had gained 30 pounds by August to call immediately. I returned the plane tickets.

Boston U – I had to visit Boston University because the head coach was my high school coach's brother, Aldo "Buff" Donelli. Their main recruiting pitch was that there was a 10 to 1 ratio of college girls to college guys in the city of Boston because of all the girls' schools and the fact that Harry "The Golden Greek" Agganis had just finished playing quarterback for them. Anyone under 60 may not remember Agganis, but he had been an outstanding player and the No. 1 draft choice of the Cleveland Browns in his junior year. But he wanted to play baseball, and a few months after my visit Agganis was playing first base for the Boston Red Sox. Tragically, he died of a pulmonary embolism in 1955. However, I didn't want to go to Boston U simply because I wanted a better brand of football.

Navy – I had a very poor experience at the Naval Academy. I visited Navy with Bill Freshwater, a center from Munhall, and we stayed two nights in the Boathouse there. The second night, the coaches woke us up at 3 a.m. in the morning to listen to a recruiting talk from the head coach, Eddie Erdelatz. Erdelatz had supposedly just returned from one trip and was taking another immediately. I was half asleep and have no idea what he said. One of the junior midshipmen we knew in high school stopped by to talk to us and he was bald. When we had last seen him he'd had a lot of hair. That shook us up, plus the fact that they had 12 formations a day. (A formation occurs when a group of midshipmen stand in line for attention for a few minutes or longer.) At the beginning of the trip back home, we made the mistake of telling the man who drove us to Annapolis that we didn't want to go there. He had a midshipman son who was killed in Korea and he yelled at us. It was an unpleasant return trip.

But it didn't end there. Because of my trip to Navy, I had to miss a basketball game. I had asked my head basketball coach, Bill Lemmer, if it was okay since we could not win the section of our conference. We were in third place and we were playing Baldwin, a team that we had beaten by 30 points the first time we played them. He said, "Okay." Well, we lost to Baldwin in a close game. When I got back from Annapolis, Ray Henry, the principal, who was a former basketball coach, chewed me out, screaming that I had let the team down and so on. The first time we had played Baldwin I had scored 27 points. I told him that Coach Lemmer had given me permission to miss the game but that didn't faze him. He expelled me again for whatever reason, and, once again, my mother had to come to school the next day to get me back in. See why my nickname, Bad Rad, fits so well.

Pitt – But nothing was weirder than my visit to Pitt. That was one place I really didn't want to visit. I wanted to go away to school and had absolutely no interest in going to the local Skyscraper University. We all called it "Skyscraper U" because of the Cathedral of Learning, the main building for all the classes, is a big tall building. That didn't seem like a college to me. But their coaches and scouts kept calling me and I kept saying I wasn't interested. Finally, one of them asked if I had seen the Nationality Rooms at the Cathedral of Learning. I said, "What are the Nationality Rooms?" He said, "What nationality are you?" I said, "My dad is Serbian and my mother is Polish." He said, "We have a Yugoslavian Room for Serbians and also a Polish Room. They are all about these nationalities. They are very interesting." I said, "Yeah, I'd like to see them."

So I reported that Saturday to the Pitt Field house at 8:30 a.m. Pitt had about 40 recruits there. They told all of us to go down below into the locker room, report to the equipment room, get a pair of socks and a jock strap, take off all our clothes, put on the socks and jock strap and get in line to the training room. Well, I did that, and was at the very back of the line with Junior Shoaf, a 6-foot-5, 280-pound nose tackle from Brownsville that I had played against, and Bert Cecconi, a quarterback who was the younger brother of Bimbo Cecconi a former great Pitt player and later a Pitt football coach. Inside the training room the seven Pitt football coaches were seated against one wall with the head coach, Red Dawson, seated in the middle. The doctors were giving each player a brief physical and the trainers were measuring different parts of the body and calling out the measurements. Junior Shoaf was announced at "6-foot-5, 280-pounds." I stepped on the scale after him. They announced, "Dan Radakovich of Duquesne, 6-foot-2, 169-pounds, 12-inch biceps, etc." Red Dawson, yelled out, "Hey Radakovich, do you play basketball at Duquesne?" I said, "Yes sir. I'm captain of the team." He then said, "You guys must have a hell of a fast break!" And everyone laughed, me included. I was so naïve I didn't realize until later he was being sarcastic.

After the physical was over, they told everyone to get dressed and wait outside the building. I was outside talking to two linemen from McKeesport I had played against, Nino Scorsi, who was 6-foot-5, 250-pounds, and Vince Scorsone, who was 6-foot-1, 225-pounds, when Capt. Tom Hamilton, the Pitt Athletic Director, walked up to our group. He introduced himself, and then said, "Radakovich, does the streetcar go anywhere near where you live?" I said, "Yes, sir, the 68 goes right past my house." He then said, "Here's a dollar for transportation home." Then he turned and put one arm around Nino and one around Vince and said, "Nino, Vince, let's go to lunch," and walked away and left me standing there holding the dollar. Needless to say, I've never forgotten that, but it really didn't affect me because I wasn't going to Pitt anyway. By the way, I still haven't seen the Nationality Rooms 59 years later, but since I live only 20 miles from the Pitt campus, I intend to do so one day to finally see what I missed.

Penn State – Penn State was by far the best place I could go. Two players from my high school were already there, Peter Schoderbek and Ed Kliest, and they liked it a lot. My neighbor across the street, Pete Hornfeck, the chief engineer for the new Greater Pittsburgh Airport being built at that time, also went to Penn State and loved it. Frank Patrick, the backfield and secondary coach, recruited me and it was one of the easiest decisions my life.

Duquesne Serbs – Now, I have to tell you another recruiting story. This one had nothing to do with football, but it tells you a lot about my ethnic heritage and the old cliché about this being a small world. It occurred after my senior basketball season in 1952-53, and I was recruited to play for the Duquesne Serbs amateur basketball team, which was going to play in the national Serbian Federation (SNF) Basketball Tournament in Milwaukee. That year, the Duquesne Serbs were National AAU champs, National Slav champs, and National Croatian champs. In previous years, they had been runners-up seven times in the National Serb tournament, but had never won it. The saying was "always a bridesmaid, never a bride."

After winning three or four games, the Duquesne Serbs were again in the finals for the eighth time against the Aliquippa Serbs who were loaded with talent. Aliquippa had two college All-Americans—Al Greco from the University of Maryland and Mickey Zernich from Pitt—plus George Mikan's back-up center for the world champion Minnesota Lakers. The Aliquippa coach was Press Maravich, the father of future basketball great Pistol Pete Maravich, who became an All-American at LSU and an All-Pro in the NBA. This was to be the second time I had played against a Press Maravich coached team. After my junior basketball season, we had played a scrimmage game against Monessen High School, which was Press' high school team. What I most remember after that game was this little kid, Pete, in the passenger side of his dad's car with the window open, dribbling the ball outside the car. He was still dribbling when his dad started the car and started to pull out of the parking lot. There was a clue right there on how great that kid was going to be.

Anyway, we won the final game against Press Maravich's Aliquippa team and were Serbian National Champs for the first time. That began a celebration like I've never seen before. People back in the hotel were dancing in the lobby, in the halls, and on the elevators. Serbian bands called Tamburitzans were everywhere playing and singing, each player in the band getting $20 apiece just for playing a certain song. Steve Borovich, a Canadian hotel owner and a former great Duquesne Serbian basketball player who was in his 40s but dressed for our games, jumped up on the bar of the Milwaukee Serbian Club and ordered 15 fifths of whiskey to be placed on the bar, and shouted, "free drinks for everyone." The Serbs sure did know how to celebrate and that's one reason I've always been happy to be a Serb.

Bad Rad Needs To See A Psychiatrist

Captain Of The Freshman Team – I don't remember much about my freshman year in 1953, except I had a lot of fun like most freshman, and I adjusted quite easily to the classroom. I do remember I was captain of the freshman football team. My line coach was a graduate assistant named Joe Yukica, who played on Rip Engle's first Penn State team in 1950 and later became the head football coach at Boston College and Dartmouth. I used to tell him I was the first player he ever coached.

We played the Navy freshmen in a unique football game at Annapolis because there was a foot of snow on the ground and they didn't shovel it off. There were gutters shoveled around the perimeter of the field, on the goal lines, and on both 40-yard lines, but the snow on the playing field was a foot high. My roommate, Ray Alberigi, scored on a 65-yard punt return, which has to go down in the record books as the slowest punt return in the history of football. He had to keep raising his feet above a foot of snow as he ran. We won 25-0. The captain and center for the Navy was Bob McElwee who later became a long-time referee in the NFL. When he was officiating one of my NFL games one year, he told me that he had pictures taken of the deep snow on the playing field that day and would send me some copies. But he never did.

Dan's Freshman Roommate, Ray Alberigi

Pretty Freshman Girl – Now, here's one of those Bad Rad stories for you, and you might not believe it but it's true. During fall camp of my sophomore year, in early September of 1954, I was walking with Don "Beetle" Bailey from old Beaver Field after practice to the Phil Delta Theta fraternity house, about a block away, where the football team was staying during the preseason practices. Beetle was a senior and our starting quarterback, but he was a little "off the wall" like me. As we passed in front of Rec Hall, Beetle said, "Hey Rad, the freshmen are in. Let's go to the Waring Hall snack bar and bug the freshmen girls." I said, "Good idea," and we crossed the street and went into Waring Hall.

In the snack bar, we saw three freshmen football players, Emil "Babe" Caprara, Jack Farls and Ron Markiewicz, talking to a group of girls at a table sitting with their backs against the wall. I said hi to the guys and sat down next to one of the guys. I saw this good looking freshman girl sitting opposite me. I nudged the guy, pointed at the girl and said, "Hey, does she lay down?" which was a saying we used suggesting sexual promiscuity. The girl immediately stood up, pointed at me and said, "You are the most ignorant person I have ever met," and proceeded to walk right out of the snack bar. Two years, four months, and many apologies later I married the girl, and in 2012 Nancy and I celebrated 55 married years together. Babe Caprara was the best man at my wedding and Jack Farls hitchhiked 300 miles (from Freedom to Easton, Pa.) to be there. Bad Rad, indeed! This truly was a case of love at first slight.

The Slide Block – At least a week or more before my first varsity game in 1954 against Illinois in our season opener at Champaign, Don Balthaser—our captain, starting center and linebacker—got hurt. So, Frank Reich (who had alternated with Balthaser the year before) and I began alternating at center. Both the first and second teams alternated in those days of one platoon substitution rules. A few days before the game, my head coach, Rip Engle, saved me from getting decked by my offensive line coach, Sever "Tor" Toretti. Rip had the offensive team line up against the Illinois defense and he asked each player his assignment on a trap play. When Rip got to me at the center position, he said, "When the linebacker gets up in the pulling guard's face, we are going to use the 'slide block.' Now Danny, what do you do on the slide block?" I just looked at Rip because I didn't know what he was talking about.

"A slide block?" I said. "Yes," said Rip. "What do you do on a slide block?" Coach Toretti called me "Bones" because I was so skinny and he chimed in. "Bones," he said, "tell the Great White Father what you do on a slide block." I said, "Well, on a slide block, you…you…you…slide!" Tor pulled back his right arm to slug me while yelling, "You smart ass." Rip quickly grabbed his arm to stop him from hitting me, saying, "It's okay Tor, it's okay!" Then Rip explained to me that the slide block was when the center blocked back on a linebacker in the pulling guard hole instead of staying with the double team on the nose tackle. I found out afterwards that Coach Toretti had told the other centers, Balthaser and Reich, about the slide block when I wasn't there. Tor was quite happy when I then did it in practice.

Just before we got on the train for Illinois, Coach Engle told me that because of my inexperience Frank Reich was going to start the game at center-linebacker but that I would play a lot. In those days of one platoon football, the second unit played almost one-half the game. I sat on the train with Jack Sherry, who played defensive end on my side in our defense, and on the way to Champaign we went over all the defensive calls, etc. Well, we won a close game, 14-12, in one of Penn State's all time upsets, and Reich was probably the only player in America that weekend who played all 60 minutes of the game. Because of that he made Unsung Hero of the Week in one of the newspapers, and I didn't get to play one down. Maybe the incident with the slide block was responsible for me not playing.

Balthaser recovered from his injury, and that ended my chances of playing much my sophomore year. But I became a pal of our quarterback, Beetle Bailey, and he was a character. Some of our teammates thought we were a lot alike in that regard. We had a lot of laughs together, and I'll never forget what happened at Pittsburgh's Schenley Hotel when we played Pitt in our final game of the 1954 season.

Beetle Goes To Church – The Schenley Hotel was where Penn State always stayed Friday and Saturday for the Pitt games because it was just a block or so from the Pitt campus. Now, there were a lot of college hangouts in that Oakland section of Pittsburgh and a couple of the players would sneak out after curfew, and one of them was Beetle, who was from Pittsburgh.

Well, on the morning of the game, at about 5:30 or 6 a.m., Beetle was walking through the deserted lobby, after having been out all night, when a man sitting in a chair reading the newspaper dropped the paper and ran up to Beetle. It was Head Coach Rip Engle. Rip was an early to bed, early to rise type of guy. "Don, Don," he said. "What's wrong? What are you doing up at this hour?" Beetle replied, "Coach, I'm so worried about the game that I got up and went to church." Rip said, "Oh, Don, that's wonderful. But go on up and get some rest and get off your feet."

Old Beetle scored our final points on a 3-yard quarterback sneak and we won 13-0. I even played some in the fourth quarter. We were all really happy, especially our seniors, shutting out our biggest rival, Pitt, for the third straight year—17-0, 17-0, and 13-0. You can imagine the party we had back at the hotel celebrating.

Knocking On The Door Of Room 319 – Late that night, I'm partying in the hotel and in walks Beetle. "Rad," he says, "I just saw Billy (Kane) with a girl and he went in Room 319." I said, "You did?" and he said, "Yep. He had this chick and they went in Room 319." So, Jerry Bruce, the freshmen coach's son, and I went looking for Billy, who was a good friend and a sophomore halfback. We get to Room 319 and I pounded on the door, yelling "Open up. I know you're in there with a girl, Billy. Open Up." And I kept yelling and pounding. The door opens and I go running in the room and stop at the foot of the bed.

Sitting up in the bed in a night gown and her hair in curlers was Sunny Engle, the head coach's wife. I turned and saw Rip holding the door and I yelled "Sorry, wrong room," and tried to run past him into the hallway. He grabbed me by the arm and there was no way I could get loose. Rip was strong. He said, "Danny, I want you to promise me something." I said, "Sure, coach, anything, anything." He said, "I want you to go find Billy and put him to bed and then promise me you'll go right to bed. Promise?" I said, "I promise. I promise." "Okay," he said, and let me go. I went down the hallway cursing Beetle for having set me up with that phony story and wondering what happened to Jerry Bruce. I'm yelling softly, "Jerry where are you?"

Then a closet door opens where the hotel kept the mops, buckets and brooms. Jerry had seen Rip when he first opened the door and had run and hid in the mop closet.

For years later, Beetle was laughing about how he set me up to go storming into the head coach's bedroom in the middle of the night. Beetle passed away in the spring of 2010. Beetle was a good football player. He played quarterback in the famous East-West Shrine game in San Francisco after the 1954 season and was named the Most Valuable Player. More importantly, he is truly one of the great characters in the history of Penn State football.

Intramural Boxing Tournament And The Ali Shuffle – When you are a linebacker you have to like to hit people and be willing to get hit yourself. That's why many linebackers are the toughest and nastiest guys on the team. Think Dick Butkus of the Bears or Jack Lambert of the Steelers. One of Penn State's all-time tough guys was Chuck Drazenovich, who I would meet a couple of years later at the Washington Redskins camp. Chuck had won the NCAA heavyweight boxing championship in 1950, but Penn State had dropped boxing as a varsity sport when I was a freshman after the '54 spring season. That made the annual Intramural Boxing Tournament in winter of my sophomore year a very popular attraction

After the 1954 football season, in the middle of November and soon after Penn State had dropped boxing as a varsity sport, I was talking about boxing with one of those guys from the disbanded boxing team, Eddie Yarosz. Eddie was a fellow sophomore who was still on a full athletic boxing scholarship but without a sport. He was a former undefeated Golden Gloves champion for two or three years. And his dad, Teddy Yarosz, had been the world middleweight champion while his uncle, Tommy Yarosz, fought as a middleweight and light heavyweight. Tommy lost just eight fights and was never champion himself, though he lost to Bobo Olson, Jake LaMotta and Randy Turpin. Eddie told me that if I entered the Intramural Boxing Tournament at Penn State that he would train me. Why not? I was a pretty tough guy at linebacker, right? So, I signed up for the Heavyweight Division. I was 6-foot-2 and weighed 175-pounds.

As soon as we started boxing training, I asked Eddie to show me how to hit the speed bag like all the boxing pros did. He said, "We're not going to waste time hitting the speed bag. You're not going to be a professional fighter." He said, "I'm going to teach you only two things and you'll win all your fights easily. I'm going to teach you how to throw a left jab and a right cross. Period!" I said, "How about a hook?" Eddie said, "No way. Just the left jab and the right cross. You send the left jab straight out and snap the fist inward so that the knuckles are up and you send the right cross straight out and snap the fist inward so that the knuckles are up. That's it. You don't do anything else." Well, that's all I did and I won my first two fights easily, all by unanimous decisions. But I really didn't think I was strong enough to knock any one out.

The third and final fight for the heavyweight championship was to be against another football player, Willard "Bull" Smith, a 5-foot-11, 230-pound nose tackle, who was a freshman. Lenny Moore, our outstanding halfback who was later elected to the Pro Football Hall of Fame, was Bull's boxing trainer. Lenny used to see me in the Waring Hall snack bar where I first met my future wife and tell me that he was teaching Bull all kinds of combination punches and that Bull was going to destroy me. I'd tell Eddie Yarosz about these conversations and he'd just laugh. Finally, Eddie said, "If you want to work on something special, we'll work on your opening." I said, "My opening? What's that?" He said, "We'll work on how you start the fight."

So we did. He said, "When the bell rings to start the fight, you will stick your left fist straight out like Frankenstein as you go toward Bull. When you get to him, throw a right cross with all your might and you might knock him out." Now this sounded crazy to me but Eddie seemed to be no dummy. Besides being a boxer, he was a math major which meant he took harder math courses than the engineers. So, we worked on the opening.

There must have been five or six thousand spectators in Rec Hall for the Intramural Boxing finals. When the bell sounded for the start of my fight against Bull, I did exactly as planned. I ran across the ring toward Bull with my left sticking straight out and then hit him with all my might with a right cross. I caught him flush on the face and he spun around into the ropes. I guess I wasn't strong enough to knock him out. Anyway, I peppered him for two rounds. I think I got tired of hitting him because I could hardly raise my arms for the third round. Also, I think Bull finally realized I wasn't strong enough to really hurt him. So with Lenny continually yelling at him, Bull came out for the third round, swinging big roundhouse haymakers. I kept ducking and he kept missing and I could hear the spectators screaming at each miss. He never did touch me and I won a unanimous decision, the heavyweight title, and made a vow that I would never box again. Maybe those 16 ounce gloves had something to do with it. But I was exhausted and could hardly lift my hands afterwards. But I sure gained greater respect for that former great Penn State and Washington Redskin linebacker in the 1940s and '50s, Chuck Drazenovich, and other fighters, particularly for those who go 15 rounds in championship fights.

One final note about boxing. About 10 years later in the mid '60s, *Sports Illustrated* had a diagram of the Ali Shuffle on the cover. That was one of the footwork techniques of the great heavyweight boxing champion Mohammed Ali. I looked at that diagram and realized the Ali Shuffle was simply the way a good athlete moves in most other sports. In fact, I was teaching the same movements to my linebackers and had called it the "Rad Shuffle." So, after I saw that cover, I went into my linebacker meeting and told my linebackers I had used the shuffle in the ring in 1954. Adapting one of Ali's trademark saying, I said to the linebackers "Float like a butterfly. Sting like a bee. Mohammed Ali stole the shuffle from me!"

Bad Rad Sees A Psychiatrist – In the spring of my sophomore year, Rip Engle called me into his office. I had been complaining about the lousy food in the dormitory cafeteria. I also complained about not playing enough my sophomore season. Then, of course, I had busted into Rip's hotel room in the middle of the night after the Pitt game. He and the other coaches were bothered by how I dressed. Half the time I didn't wear socks and usually I wore a gray t-shirt and jeans rather than a nice shirt with buttons or a sweater and trousers, which was the style of most college guys back then. I also was growing a beard to celebrate Penn State's 100-

year Centennial as a college, which was going on all that year, and my hair wasn't always combed. I guess I looked like a hippie, but this was 10 years before people who dressed like me were called hippies. Anyhow, Rip asked me if he could schedule an appointment for me with the school psychiatrist. I said, "Sure, why not?"

When I sat down with the psychiatrist, his first questions were about whether or not I like girls. After about three of these types of questions I got up and said, "I'm out of here," and walked out. Rip never asked me about my psychiatric interview, but I'm sure he found out. My mother solved the lousy food problem by buying me a revolving five dollar meal ticket at the Penn State Diner. I shaved the beard after the centennial celebration was over, and I even began wearing a nice shirt and trousers—once in a while.

Bad Rad Is Ubiquitous – My first start came in my junior year in the third game of 1955 against the University of Virginia at Richmond, when senior center-linebacker, Captain Frank Reich, was injured. We won, 26-7, and, I had a good game, intercepting a pass, blocking a punt and making a bunch of tackles. I remember a sportswriter for the Richmond paper wrote in his column that "Dan Radakovich was a ubiquitous party from Penn State." I didn't know what he meant. I got back to school and looked up ubiquitous in the dictionary. It means "a person who seems to be everywhere at once." Wow! That's probably the best compliment any Penn State linebacker has ever had. For the past 30 years I've been asking the various great Penn State linebackers—like Jack Ham, Shane Conlan, Greg Buttle, Dennis Onkotz, Ralph Baker, Matt Millen, Lance Mehl, John Skorupan, etc.—who was the greatest Penn State linebacker. Most of them just laugh at me but some of them start rattling off names, sometimes including themselves. But I always tell them and everybody else that as the official "ubiquitous" linebacker I rest my case. The other former Penn State linebackers can continue to argue who was the second best or second greatest Penn State linebacker.

One more thing. Shane Conlan, who had an outstanding career at Penn State and the Los Angeles Rams, recently reminded me of how we originally met on the first day of the Los Angeles Rams minicamp in the spring of 1995. I was the new Rams offensive line coach under new head coach Rich Brooks, and the players had just come out to the field. Shane said he was lying on the ground during pre-practice stretching exercises when he felt a shoe nudge him in the ribs. He looked up and he said the first words I ever said to him were, "who is the greatest linebacker Penn State ever had?" He said he replied "I don't know," and then I answered "You're looking at him."

And now you are reading about him.

Chasing Oscar – Coming back to Penn State on the train after the Virginia game was an experience I'll never forget because I almost punched the lights out of our equipment manager, Oscar Buchenhorst. I was lying on the top bunk of the double bunk bed in the stateroom watching a card game being played below me. The door opens up and Oscar sticks his head in and starts screaming my name and yelling that I was "lower than a snake in the grass," whatever that means, and a bunch of other stuff. I had no idea what he was screaming about, so I jumped off the bunk and went after him as he took off. I chased him through four railroad cars trying to catch him. He was screaming as he was running, yelling, "Either Radakovich goes or I go and I've been here 23 years." It was just like you see in the movies. After running through four railroad cars, some players stopped me and made me go back to the card game. I guess I'm lucky I didn't catch him because I might have hurt him bad. Anyway, things calmed down and I went to bed in the Pullman car.

About two or three in the morning, Coach Toretti shakes my bunk and says that the Great White Father wanted to see me. That's what Tor always called Rip Engle because of Rip's full mane of white hair. So I follow Tor in my

Junior Bad Rad

pajamas to a railroad car stateroom in the middle of the night and all the coaches are there. They all start yelling at me about my incident with Oscar and I start yelling back until they realized I had no idea what Oscar was screaming about. They started to worry that I was going to quit the team, but I told them I would never do that. Well, we finally found out what had made Oscar so mad at me. After the game, the team went back to the hotel in Richmond because the train didn't leave until later that night. Oscar was in charge of checking that all the players got onto the train. Paul North, a tight end, was late getting to the train and Oscar started to yell at him. Paul told Oscar that the only reason he was late was that he had to go back to the hotel to make sure that Bad Rad didn't miss the train. Actually, I had been one of the first one's on the train. But Oscar got upset with me because of Paul's story. I never talked to Oscar again. Would you?

Sleeping Beauty – Three weeks later, I was kicked off the team temporarily in what I'd like to call a "Bad Rad Moment." On the day before the Penn game in Philadelphia, I stopped in one of the player's rooms over the noon hour and fell asleep on his roommate's bed while he took a nap on his own bed. I don't even remember who it was, but he got up and without waking me, went to the short practice we had before we took the train to Philadelphia. I awoke about 4:45. Practice was from 4-to-5. I ran up to Beaver Field, which was about 300 yards away, and told Rip that I had slept in. Rip said that because of the sleeping incident and what had probably happened with Oscar earlier that I was off the team. So, I went to Philadelphia on my own to see the game and sat with the Penn State students in the grandstands. That actually was a lot of fun, but I hated not being down on the field.

On Monday I went out for practice as if I were still on the team. Rip spotted me and blew the whistle, called the whole team together and said that Danny wanted to address the squad. I know he wanted me to apologize like Jesse Arnelle apologized two years before for punching Pete Schoderbek during a practice scrimmage. Jesse was a really serious guy and was Penn State's first black all-university student president that year. That had been a real tear jerker. Well, I started to apologize and spouted stuff like all the other linebackers and centers were better than me anyway, and some other stuff I don't remember, but as I continued talking in my own inimitable way, everybody started to giggle and laugh—even the assistant coaches. But when I was done, Rip said that it was great that I apologized and let me back on the team. Bad Rad made it through another escapade.

Bad Rad vs. Jimmy Brown – That following Saturday was my most memorable game as a player for Penn State, partly because I had something to do with the outcome. College football historians regard this as one of the greatest Penn State games ever. It was against Syracuse and Jimmy Brown at Beaver Field. We won the game 21-20, but it was really a battle between two of the greatest football players who ever played the game—Jim Brown and Lenny Moore. Brown had 159 yards rushing, another 95 yards on kickoff returns and scored all of Syracuse's

Rip Engle, Frank Patrick and Dan — Photo of Mural in Beaver Stadium of 1955 Syracuse Game.

points. Lenny had 146 yards rushing and a touchdown, and they both made great plays on defense, with Lenny stopping Brown from scoring a touchdown on the second-half kickoff with an ankle tackle at midfield. Twice we had to come from behind and finally won it late in the fourth quarter with an end zone interception by quarterback Milt Plum, who had thrown to Billy Kane for one touchdown and scored another on a 3-yard run. Despite the eventual historical significance of the game, the result was not that significant except to help us avoid a losing season. We finished 5-4 and Syracuse was 5-3.

When I was coaching later and told my players about the game and how I had been instrumental in stopping Jimmy Brown, they often didn't believe me. I guess I couldn't blame them, when you figure that he had 159 yards rushing. If you ever get to Beaver Stadium, go to the first level near the tunnel where team enters the field from the locker room. You'll see a giant mural painted on the wall that shows Rip Engle and our backfield coach Frank Patrick sending me into that game. Here's basically what happened.

Syracuse's basic offensive formation was an unbalanced line, Wing-T, two tight ends alignment. This put four linemen, including a tight end plus a close wing back, on the long side of the center and two linemen, including a tight end, on the other (short) side of the center. The halfback and fullback were split deep in the backfield and the quarterback was under center.

Jim Brown ran for a bunch of yards in the first half when the first unit was in the game. In those days of one platoon football, both the first and second units played in each of the four quarters. Syracuse's basic best play was double-teaming the outside linebacker with the tight end and wing back to the long unbalanced line side and going around end with the fullback and both pulling guards leading the way for Brown.

I saw this from the sideline. So, when I got in the game in the first half, I kept calling an adjustment in our 5-3 defense called "E-Go." This sent our defensive end to crash into those pulling guards and allowed me to slide quickly to the outside, causing the double team to miss me. I played the Syracuse fullback so that Brown had to run outside where Billy Kane, our cornerback, could tackle him from the outside in and I from inside out pursuit. We pinched him between us. The E-Go worked great when I was in there in the first half. At halftime Syracuse led, 14-7. In the first series of the second half, after Lenny had tackled Brown on the kickoff, Jimmy went wild again and Syracuse went ahead, 20-7. I was put back in with our first unit early in the second half, right after Syracuse scored and I played the rest of the game, and kept calling out the E-Go adjustments. We stopped Brown after that first touchdown of the second half, and Lenny had a great second half. We came from two touchdowns down to go ahead 21-20 and were on their 2-yard line going for another score when the game ended.

After the game the coaching staff gave special recognition to Lenny Moore for his great second half performance, to me for calling "E-Go" to stop Jimmy Brown and to sophomore end Jack Farls for blocking the extra point that was the difference in the game.

Summer School – That summer before my senior season in 1956, I went to summer school because I needed nine credits to be eligible for the fall. During the nine weeks of summer school I had coffee almost every day in the student union with the assistant coach at nearby Tyrone High School who was taking courses towards his Master's Degree. Neither of us could have dreamed at the time that my new friend, Chuck Knox, would one day be one of the best coaches in the NFL, from 1973-1994, as the head coach of the Los Angeles Rams (twice), Buffalo Bills and Seattle Seahawks. Chuck used to yell at me about how could I smoke cigarettes and play football, and I would yell back that I was the best player Penn State had, and the smoking didn't matter. Of course, it did, but a lot of us didn't think so back then. Chuck and I became good friends. In later years when I was the linebacker coach at Penn State, I got him involved in an argument on pass blocking with our line coach at the time, Joe McMullen. They had different footwork techniques for pass protection. Joe taught chopping your feet up and down while Chuck taught sliding your feet like a basketball player. Chuck tried to back out of the argument but I wouldn't let him. I yelled at him to stick up for what he believed. And when I became the offensive line coach in 1974 for the Pittsburgh Steelers, Chuck was the first coach I went to visit, and he was one of the reasons I was able to quickly learn what it would take to coach the offensive line in the NFL.

Now, going to summer school back then was not as easy to do as it is for players nowadays. Your scholarship did not pay anything for your summer, and since you had to pay for your own room, meals and tuition, you needed to find a job in State College or have a well-to-do grandmother. So, the first thing I did was get a room for the summer at the Kappa Delta Rho fraternity, which was basically empty for the summer except for a few guys going to summer school. I can't remember but it was either free or a minimal sum. For meals, I first got a job cleaning windows at the Nittany Lion Inn, right next to Beaver Field. If you cleaned windows for three hours you got a meal. I cleaned windows for six hours and then went down to eat my first of two meals that I had earned. Well, I found out that they had special food for the help that was totally different from what they served in the restaurant.

So after one lousy meal I quit cleaning windows at the Nittany Lion Inn and got a job in the kitchen of the popular Corner Room restaurant which was across the main gate of the campus. That job paid minimal wages for meals at their regular prices. I quickly discovered I had to work three hours to get enough for a meal, so after two days I quit there, too. For the first month of the summer, I basically ate one meal a day down the street at the Rathskeller, which was more of a bar than a restaurant and one of the few bars in State College at the time. Spider, the chef, had cube steak and French fries for 90 cents and another ten cents for a beer. And, no, I was not 21.

About the middle of summer school, someone told me that they needed waiters for a corporate business management group at the Delta Upsilon fraternity house. It would be for one month and my pay would be meals. I went there, worked about 30-40 minutes serving each meal and then ate. The food was fantastic. By the next week, there were about eight football players working there. I asked them why they were there. They said, "Rad, when you said the food was great, we had to come because normally you say everything is lousy."

A Historical Turning Point – Two games stood out for me my senior year: Ohio State and North Carolina State. None of us knew it then but what happened in Columbus on October 20, 1956, is now regarded as a major turning point in the history of Penn State football. Ohio State was undefeated at 3-0 and ranked No. 5 in the country, and we were just 2-1 and a three touchdown underdog. Penn State hadn't played Ohio State since 1912, when Ohio State, trailing 37-0 walked off the field at the beginning of the fourth quarter. That also was a historic game and left such a bad taste that it took more than 40 years for the bad blood to go away. One of their current star players was offensive guard-linebacker Jim Parker, who later had a Pro Football Hall of Fame career as an offensive tackle with the Baltimore Colts. He made some remarks the night before the game about how Ohio State was looking forward to the game "because we wanted to show an Eastern team what Big Ten football looks like."

Dan, Joe Paterno, Rip Engle, Jimmy O'Hora (front) returning from Ohio State Game.

Well, we took charge from the opening kickoff and not only shocked the Ohio State players but their record crowd of 82,500 plus inside the stadium and the regional television audience. We moved up and down the field and might have scored a couple of touchdowns if not for a couple of interceptions. But our defense and Milt Plum's punting kept them away from our goal line nearly the entire afternoon. We broke the scoreless tie midway through the fourth quarter after a booming 72-yard punt by Plum and our defense had forced them to punt from close to their own end zone. We went 45 yards for the touchdown and Plum kicked the extra point.

That woke them up because Coach Woody Hayes did something he rarely did—throw a couple of passes, but he had to pull off a couple of trick plays against our defense to do it. After taking the kickoff, their halfback completed two long passes of 33 and 42 yards on halfback option plays and their big sophomore running back, Don Clark, bulled over us from the 3-yard line for the touchdown with less than two minutes remaining. They were penalized for too many men on the field before kicking the extra point, and when they did try it, the ball was wide. We recovered the onside kick, ran out the clock, and carried Rip off on our shoulders.

Now, I don't really remember much about that fourth quarter, but I read about it later. I got knocked out early in the fourth quarter when I tackled Don Clark. He knocked me over backwards, kept pumping his legs, and his knees hit me in the face at least four or five times before he was down. Rip Engle later got a letter from a fan who said in 30 years of watching football he'd never seen a player get hit like Clark's knees hit my face. Rip said he replied by writing, "Did you see who made the tackle on the next play?" I happened to make the tackle on the next play. But, after that series I was on the bench, because that's when they found I was cuckoo.

So, we upset Ohio State, 7-6, and sure showed Jim Parker and his teammates what they could do with their Big Ten football. In a column the next week by Sports Editor Al Abrams in the *Pittsburgh Post-Gazette*, Abrams quoted one of the Buckeye assistant coaches, Ernie Godfrey, telling him "That Radakovich and [the other linebacker Sam] Valentine were really something. They and the others pushed us around all day. Our lads up front aren't small by any means as you can see by Parker over there but Penn State just plowed through or over them at will."

Abrams had talked to Godfrey while he and others were watching an Ohio State practice in Columbus. *"We saw a group of Ohio State freshmen bang into Parker shoulder-to-shoulder as part of the drills,"* Abrams wrote. *"Some 15 of them charged into Big Jim three times each without budging him an inch. When it was over, an Ohio State man remarked: 'That's the fellow Valentine and Radakovich worked over. They really gave him a lesson, pushing him all over the place.'"*

That game helped make Sam, who was our captain, Penn State's first first-team All-American since 1948.

Our biggest opponent, Pitt, also was aware of how Sam and I played, not only in that game but for the rest of the year. A few days before we played Pitt in our last game of the season, Pitt assistant Ernie Hefferle told a Pitt press luncheon: "I think you read Rip Engle's quote that Valentine is the best linebacker he's ever had, and you can't discount Radakovich. You'll see that No. 51 [my uniform number] all over the field."

Later, our assistant coaches said the Ohio State victory was the most important win in Penn State history because before that they were usually steered to the second line players by high school coaches but afterwards those same coaches would show them the best players they had.

Illegal Penalty For Legal Substitution – Our shocking upset over Ohio State stunned the football world. And after we beat West Virginia, 16-6, the next week at home we jumped up to No. 11 in the coaches' poll and No. 12 in the AP poll and now we had a shot at a postseason bowl game. There were just five bowl games back then—the Rose, Cotton, Sugar, Orange and Gator—but we blew our big chance at a bowl when we lost at Syracuse two weeks after beating Ohio State.

It actually was a very close game, 13-9, and we may have won if we hadn't been hosed by an official. Complaining about officiating has been part of football almost from the beginning but this really was a bad call. It was all over one of those quirky

115

substitution rules that were in college football at that time. We had lost three fumbles and thrown three interceptions but still had a chance with less than two minutes left and Syracuse about to punt from its 35-line. But when Rip sent in our starting quarterback, Milt Plum, Syracuse claimed he wasn't allowed in the game under the crazy substitution rules about a player re-entering a game in the same quarter. The officials agreed with Syracuse despite our protests and penalized us 15 yards.

Amazingly, we did get the ball back twice on Syracuse fumbles in the last minute or so but we threw another interception and then tried a desperation pass on the last play of the game. Our entire team was convinced we would have won if Milt had been in the game. Syracuse didn't lose another game and went to the Cotton Bowl. Films proved the officials were wrong about Plum's substitution but that didn't do us any good.

Playing Against Former Penn Staters – Our next to the last game of the season against North Carolina State at home was significant because their head coach, Earl Edwards, and their defensive coordinator, Al Michaels, had been long-time assistants at Penn State under Bob Higgins. And Bill Smaltz, their head freshman coach, was Penn State's quarterback in the early 1940s and one of the best in the country at the time. When Higgins retired after the 1948 season it was rumored that Earl Edwards would be the next head coach. That's who Bob Higgins had recommended. Well, Joe Bedenk, then the line coach and a one-time Penn State All-American in 1922, got the head job. Here's the unusual part. Bedenk was also the head baseball coach and he wanted to continue at that so he assigned Edwards to run spring practice in 1949 while Bedenk coached the baseball team. After spring practice, Edwards left to take a job as an assistant at Michigan State. After that one season Bedenk resigned as head football coach and Rip Engle was hired. Bedenk stayed on as Rip's line coach for a few years and continued as baseball coach until he retired. Al Michaels continued as Penn State's secondary coach until Earl Edwards got the head coaching job at North Carolina State in 1954, and then hired Al as defensive coordinator.

This background gave this game extra importance to Rip, Joe Paterno and the rest of the Penn State staff. Al Michaels, by the way, was considered by the Penn State coaching staff as one of the smartest coaches in football. Anyway, this was considered a critical game for Coach Engle's staff. The game was scoreless until we scored with three minutes left to go ahead, 7-0. They scored with one minute remaining to tie it up, 7-7. Then we scored with 15 seconds on the clock when Les Walters caught a pass at the 4-yard line and dragged a couple of tacklers into the end zone to win the game 14-7. The fans went wild and rushed onto the field. One guy got a hold of me around the 50-yard line and offered me a job with the FBI. He said they needed people like me. I think the guy was caught up in the moment because I never saw him again. But I can tell you the fans got carried away emotionally by a close victory, and not only fans, but players, too, especially one they called Bad Rad.

Getting Carried Away By A Victory – I don't know what possessed me, but as soon as I got dressed after the NC State game, I hustled out to Route 322, which is only a block from the stadium, and hitchhiked 200 miles in the rain to Easton. That's where the girl I first met in the in the Waring Hall Snack Bar lived. Her name was Nancy Fluck, and not long after she stormed out of the snack bar when I was a sophomore, I apologized profusely for my inappropriate behavior and months later we began dating. That night after our North Carolina State game Nancy and I were sitting at the kitchen table in her house after her parents went to bed and I asked her to marry me. It seems the FBI guy was not the only one carried away emotionally by the close victory. She said, "Yes."

The win over NC State gave us a 6-2 record with just one game left at Pittsburgh, but we knew going into that game we were just a long shot at a bowl game. Before we played them, Pitt had the same record as we did, 6-2, and the Cotton and Orange Bowls were still interested in them but not us. Pitt was a seven-point favorite, but the game ended in a 7-7 tie after we missed a short field goal from inside the 10-yard line near the end of the game. Despite the tie, Pitt went to the Gator Bowl.

As soon as the season was over I withdrew from school. I had a cut a lot of classes and hadn't studied much that fall. I was a business major and figured it would be smarter to pull out while I could before I flunked out. That way I'd have an easier chance getting back in to finish my degree.

Blue-Gray Game – I was invited to play in the Blue-Gray All-Star game in Montgomery, Alabama, and the Hula Bowl All-Star game in Hawaii. I accepted the Blue-Gray and turned down the Hula Bowl. To this day, I don't know why I did that. It was not a good decision for a couple of reasons. First, I found out later that everyone who went to the Hula Bowl loved it. And secondly, I never dreamed there would be so much racial tension surrounding the Blue-Gray game.

The Blue-Gray game was on Christmas Day, and I went to Montgomery about 1½ weeks before to practice. My maternal Aunt Josephine and Uncle Ed Darst were living in Montgomery. He was a Colonel in the Air Force and was going to the Air War College in Montgomery that year. My parents came and stayed at their place. So the game was like a family reunion for me. After I arrived I noticed a strange factor. There were no blacks on either team and never had been. I didn't really think or know much about segregation. I wasn't naïve. I had played with blacks since I was a kid and some of the best players at Penn State were blacks, like Lenny Moore, Rosey Grier and Jesse Arnelle. I never had any problems and always got along well with my black teammates. I was aware of racial prejudice, too. When I was a sophomore in 1954, we played against TCU at Fort Worth and it was the first time the city had allowed an integrated team with blacks to play a football game there. I remember our team had to stay at a big cattle ranch outside of town because no hotel would allow our black players to register.

But now I was seeing the effects of racial segregation up close. We were there about a year after the famous Rosa Parks bus incident when she refused to give up her seat and move to the back of the bus. We traveled to and from practice on a bus. Whenever our bus stopped at a stop light someone would yell, "Everybody alert for snipers. Get ready to duck. Etc." Wherever we went in town—to restaurants, movies, parking garage, hotel, shoeshine stands, and so forth—the black employees or workers would say, "I hope you Yankees beat those Rebels bad!" or "Beat the hell out of those Rebels!" or something similar. We won 14-0, and I remember Bear Bryant being on their staff. He was at Texas A&M then. Three years later in 1959, he would be the head coach at Alabama and I would be on the field as a Penn State assistant when Alabama played against a black player for the first time in the Liberty Bowl.

The Wedding — After I asked Nancy to marry me on November 17, I only saw her twice briefly before we got married January 26 in her hometown of Easton. She came to our final game in Pittsburgh and I flew back to Easton after the Blue-Gray game at the end of December. Her mother and my mother did all the arrangements. We had two receptions, one in Easton and one a week later in Pittsburgh. The reason we had the second one in Pittsburgh was that my mother said for 30 years she had been contributing her help free at the Serbian weddings in Duquesne, PA, and she wasn't going to be cheated out of her turn. Nancy and I both giggled during most of the wedding ceremony and the priest afterward wanted to know why we were laughing during such a serious ceremony. We told him it was just "nerves." It was probably because we couldn't believe it was happening. Bad Rad and the girl who had called him "the most ignorant person she had ever met" when they had first met in Waring Hall two years earlier were now husband and wife.

I'll tell you more about the honeymoon in Chapter 17, but five days after my wedding on Jan. 26, I was drafted No. 17 by the Philadelphia Eagles. Vince McNally, the general manager, for the Eagles flew into Pittsburgh. My wife and I met him at the airport. I signed a contract for $6,000 without a bonus and he flew away. There weren't any mini camps in those days, so I didn't have to report to the Eagles until July 5th. My wife and I stayed with my parents in Pittsburgh for the next six months. Nancy went to work for Koppers Co. and I had a number of odd jobs like working for a carpenter and including one selling the Colliers Encyclopedia. I can still remember the beginning of my sales pitch: "I'm not here to sell you anything. I'm here on a mission. Are there any children in the household?" And so on. One day my sales manager and I were thrown in jail for disturbing the peace because we were knocking on doors of homes where husbands worked the night shift in the mill, slept during the day and were awakened by us. That night in jail ended my career of selling encyclopedias, and helped me to realize how important it was for me to return to Penn State and finish my degree and get started on a career after football.

Little did I realize at the time that my lifetime career would be in football as an assistant coach in college and the NFL; that I'd become a coaching nomad that would take me all over the country and also to Europe; and, perhaps, most significantly, I would become known as the "Father of Linebacker U."

CHAPTER SEVEN -
The First Professor of Linebacker U

Rip Engle hired me on a whim to coach Penn State's linebackers as an undergraduate assistant coach during the team's spring practice period in 1958. But that wouldn't have happened if I didn't go back to Penn State to finish up my undergraduate business degree after being cut by the Philadelphia Eagles in the summer of 1957.

Drafted By The Eagles – Although I was one of the starting linebackers as well as the starting center for Penn State in 1956, I thought I might not have the size and weight—6-foot 2, 180 pounds—to play in the pros. The Steelers probably didn't think so either but their cross-state rival, the Philadelphia Eagles did because they drafted me in the 17th round—the 194th overall selection—of the 1957 draft. There were only 12 teams in the NFL back then but there were 30 rounds in the draft. One-hundred-forty-six players were taken after me, so you can see that the Eagles thought I was good enough to be drafted that high.

One of the players drafted after me in the 17th round was a quarterback from a small college in California, Jack Kemp. Of course, Kemp went on to be a star quarterback in the rival American Football League and helped organize the AFL and NFL Players Association before becoming a congressman and eventually the Republican candidate for Vice President in 1996. But in '57, the Detroit Lions cut Kemp after training camp and, ironically, he wound up as a reserve with the Steelers that season before they cut him too—as did three other teams before he became a star in the AFL, which goes to show how fickle it can be when you're just trying to make the roster of a pro football team. In Chapter 15 I'll give you and another example of the unpredictability of the draft that involved Jack's son, Jeff.

Now, the Eagles had drafted me as a linebacker and there were just seven linebackers taken ahead of me. And when I reported to the Eagles preseason camp at Hershey, just as I expected, I had a problem with my weight. I had gained 23 pounds from my last year at Penn State but at 203 pounds I was still 15-20 pounds lighter than the next lightest linebacker, Tom Scott. Tom was about 220-225 pounds, and a four-year starter at the left outside linebacker position in the Eagles defensive scheme.

The Eagles' great linebacker Chuck Bednarik, who had been All-NFL for the last six or seven years, was about 245 pounds. They gave me the locker right next to Bednarik's. I can still remember walking into the locker room on occasion when cornerback Tom Brookshire would come up to me and say, "Rad, don't talk to him today. He's in a bad mood." So that day I wouldn't talk to Bednarik. On days he wasn't in a bad mood, he was fun to talk to.

The Eagles had some outstanding rookies on that 1957 team—quarterback Sonny Jurgensen from Duke, halfback Tommy McDonald and safety Jimmy Harris of Oklahoma and fullback Clarence Peaks from Michigan State. McDonald went on to become a Hall of Fame receiver, but what really impressed me about him in the first scrimmage was the way he tackled on defense. He put a couple of running backs on their back in the first scrimmage. I could see why Oklahoma had such an outstanding team the previous three years. To this day, McDonald is the quickest guy to jump up after being tackled that I've ever seen. We had a couple of preseason scrimmages. I played both outside and middle linebacker, made a lot of tackles and intercepted a couple of passes in those scrimmages. As a result, I immediately became a starting linebacker.

Preseason Games – I started the first preseason game as a right outside linebacker against the Baltimore Colts. The other starting linebackers were Bednarik in the middle and Tom Scott at the other outside linebacker position. I don't remember anything about the game except we lost. The next game was against NFL champion Detroit Lions, and I started the game at middle linebacker and Bednarik was at outside linebacker with Scott. Well, I played middle linebacker for about a quarter or less. We had a big blitz where I blitzed the guard-tackle gap. Lou Creekmur, the Lions All-Pro tackle who was pass-blocking our defensive end, saw that I was free to reach quarterback Bobby Layne. As I was going past Creekmur, he reached out and punched me. It didn't hurt, but the referee saw it and penalized the Lions 15 yards. Bednarik asked me what the penalty was for, and I told him that Creekmur had punched me. Well, that started it. Bednarik started getting on Creekmur's case. "Creekmur you baby, why don't you pick on somebody your size?" he yelled. A few plays later, Bednarik and Creekmur got into a fight and both were kicked out of the game. We had no other outside linebackers to put into the game. I don't' remember why but they must have been hurt. So we played a double eagle defense, which had no middle linebacker, for the last three quarters of the game, and that meant I had to play right outside linebacker for the rest of the game. I never did get another chance to play middle linebacker. I'm still awed in looking back at Bednarik and Creekmur. This was just an exhibition game and they were screaming and fighting like it was the championship game. That's probably why both of them are in the Pro Football Hall of Fame.

My Last Game As A Player – I didn't start but I played a lot in the next game against the Green Bay Packers. I still don't remember much about the game, but Paul Hornung who had won the Heisman Trophy at Notre Dame, was a rookie quarterback for the Packers and I got to tackle him once on a Packers' sprint out play.

Then, wouldn't you know but our next game was against the Pittsburgh Steelers at home on Labor Day weekend, and I was the starter again against my old hometown team. Ever since that day, I've wondered how many players have found themselves in similar situations—playing against their favorite team as a kid or the team that cut them. You want to go all out to show them up for various reasons and earn their respect. What I didn't know then was that this was to be my final game as a professional football player.

This was also the first game for Buddy Parker as a head coach for the Steelers. He had been the head coach of the champion Detroit Lions the previous season but had suddenly resigned in the middle of the 1957 Lions training camp, saying he could no longer handle the players. The Steelers hired him two weeks later as their head coach, demoting Walt Kiesling. In order to get to know his team better, Buddy Parker coached our game from the press box.

In our Eagles team meeting before the game, cornerback Tom Brookshier expressed concern about covering Steelers wide receiver Jack "Goose" McClairen alone on a deep hook pattern. Goose was 6-foot-5 and Brookshire was a half foot shorter at 5-foot-11. Essentially, Tom was told not to worry about it. The first quarter was all Eagles. We scored 10 points and our defense didn't allow the Steelers past midfield. In the second quarter, the Steelers found a way to move the ball by completing four passes on the deep hook pattern to Goose McClairen for 51 yards—plus the Eagles were hit with three pass interference penalties on the same pattern. As Jack Sell of the *Pittsburgh Post-Gazette* wrote, "The Eagle defender [Brookshire] got disgusted covering him [McClairen] and resorted to holding and pushing (him), resulting in three costly pass interference penalties." Mainly because of the deep hook passes to McClairen in the second quarter, the Steelers led 14-10 at halftime.

During our halftime discussion, the Eagles coaches asked where I was on this deep hook pattern. I was doing my assignment, which was covering the Steelers rookie fullback, Lionel Reid, who was running in the flat. The Eagle defensive coach told me that we weren't sure how good the fullback was and didn't know whether he could even catch well. So, he told me to go and help the corner, Brookshire, on the hook pattern.

Well early in the third quarter, the Steelers ran that deep hook pattern play on first down, and their rookie fullback ran out into the flat. I ignored the fullback and went back to help the corner on McClairen. We both hit McClairen and he dropped the ball. Second down was a repeat. Brookshier and I hit him again and he dropped the ball. On third down the fullback went in the flat again. I ignored him for the third straight time and went back to help the corner. This time, Steelers quarterback Ted Marchibroda, threw the ball to the fullback, who was wide open and ran for about a 20-yard gain. On first down the Steelers ran the same play for the fourth straight time. The fullback went in the flat and I went back to help the cornerback as the coaches had told me to do. They threw the ball to the wide open fullback again and he ran down to the 1-yard line. On the next play there was a pile-up at the goal line, and I got hit in the back by—Guess who?—the 6-foot-5 wide receiver Goose McClairen, and they carried me off the field. Ironically, the play didn't count because there was a penalty for backfield in motion, and the Steelers never did score. So, on a non play, I ended up simply with bruised ribs, and the Steelers went on to win a close game, 17-12. It's not often a team runs the same play four times in a row. I believe it only occurred because Buddy Parker was in the press box and he could clearly see the coverage, and being the head coach he had the authority to call the same play repeatedly.

Getting Cut – Two days after the game, the Eagles made their final cut. Even though I was starting, I thought I might get cut because of what happened in my final series in the Steelers game. Well, I made the cut with one exhibition game left, and the Eagles gave us two days off to get ready for the season. I had dropped out of school at the end of the 1956 season because I had a cut a lot of classes and hadn't studied much and figured it would be smarter to pull out while I could before I flunked out. So, I used the two days to go back to Penn State to see about getting back into school to finish up my degree in business.

Since we had another preseason game left, I still wasn't certain I would make the roster. The second day I was back with the Eagles in Hershey, I was released. The Eagles had decided to bring quarterback coach Tommy Thompson and veteran defensive lineman Jim Weatherall out of retirement. Rookie Sonny Jorgensen had been starting at quarterback and the Eagles probably thought he needed more experience since Thompson had been the quarterback the year before. Anyway, the Eagles had to release two players to make room for the new players, and one was this skinny linebacker from Kennywood who had been hurt and carried off the field.

The Eagles head coach, Hughie Devore, told me he wanted to try and place me with another pro team but I said it was more important right now for me to try and get my undergraduate degree.

Coaching Freshman Football – I called Dean David McKinley, the Associate Dean of Penn State's College of Business Administration, and told him that I was coming back to school. At the time I needed a total of 48 required credits in business to graduate. Earlier, I had been in Physical Education for one year but didn't like it and most of those credits didn't count. School had already started and I found out later that Dean McKinley personally registered me with each of my professors—six required courses for a total of 18 credits. To help with our finances, my wife Nancy found a job with the Personnel Department of the University, which was a great boost.

My next move was to see Athletic Director Ernie McCoy about scholarship aid. I explained that I had played four years for Penn State but only received athletic aid for seven terms, instead of eight because I had withdrawn during the seventh term. Therefore, I figured that the athletic department owed me another term. Ernie said he agreed and would love to do it but he couldn't because I was now a professional since I had signed a contract with the Eagles. He said it was against NCAA rules to give aid to professionals, but he said he could pay me $250 if I coached the line of the freshman team. I said okay, and that's how I got started in coaching. College athletics, particularly football, gets a lot of heat for supposedly abusing the academic mission but not at Penn State, and because of our mutual academic priority I became a football coach.

Dick Hoak, Steelers Backfield Coach

That first freshman team that I coached had some notable players, starting with quarterback Dick Hoak. Dick would become the MVP of the 1960 Liberty Bowl victory over Oregon, and then go on to a 10-year career with Pittsburgh as a halfback before becoming a long-time assistant coach with the Steelers, and a good friend of mine.

Several others also played pro ball. Stew Barber, who was an end and tackle, played offensive left tackle for nine years with Buffalo, making the Pro Bowl five straight years, and then from 1979-83 was the Bills' general manager. Halfbacks Jim Kerr and Lew Luce spent a year or so with the Redskins and the unforgettable Don Jonas played briefly with the Eagles. Donnie is a character, I guess a little like me, who once lived for a time with Coach Rip Engle after getting into a little trouble off the field. Donnie played and coached semi-pro football for seven years, and then played quarterback and halfback for three teams in the Canadian Football League from 1970-74 and was the league's MVP with Winnipeg in 1971. Then in 1979 he volunteered to help start the football program at Central Florida University and coached the team for three years as CFU began its long road from Division II football to Division I. I used to see him almost every year at a golf tournament.

Two other players from that freshman team never played pro ball but they were really good players and leaders, Henry Opperman, who became captain of the 1960 Liberty Bowl team, and guard Bill Popp, who ended up being an excellent football coach at Albright in Reading, PA.

Perhaps the best player on the entire freshman team was Red Worrell, a highly touted fullback from suburban Pittsburgh. After that 1957 freshman season Red went home for Thanksgiving and was putting up a TV aerial on the roof of his parents' house, when he touched a high tension wire and was electrocuted. A few months later Penn State created a trophy in his honor that is still given to a player at the end of spring practice based on "exemplary conduct, loyalty, interest, attitude, and improvement"

Anyway, quarterbacks Hoak and Jonas led the freshman team to an unbeaten season with wins over West Virginia, Pitt and Navy. The Navy game was the most memorable one in the five years I would coach the freshmen. Navy had a freshman running back named Joe Bellino, who later would be everyone's All-American and win the Heisman Trophy in 1960. We knew about him from prep school, and Henry Opperman purposely kicked the opening kickoff away from him. However, the player receiving the ball threw a cross field lateral to Bellino, and he went about 85 yards for a touchdown. Navy somehow scored another touchdown quickly and had us down 14-0 in the first quarter. From then on, we dominated the game. Both our halfbacks Luce and Kerr had around 100 yards each and Red Worrell was unbelievable. He ran wild for 220 yards himself, and Hoak also had a bunch of yards running at quarterback. We had more than 500 yards rushing and won the game 28-14.

At the end of that fall term, my grades going into finals for my final six courses were four A's, one B and one F. I mention this because of an unusual incident that occurred. The F was the result of a grade of 45 on the midterm exam for an economics course because I had accidentally skipped one of the pages on the exam. Anyway, I was concentrating all my study efforts at the end of the term on economics, because I needed a B on the final just to pass the course with a D. Well, the word got out that Rad was studying economics hard and I was recruited to tutor the guys in the Alpha Epsilon Phi fraternity who were taking economics. There were a bunch of them since almost everyone in that fraternity majored in Business. Here I was with an all university average below a C at about a 1.93 and tutoring 15 to 20 guys in an economics course that I was currently flunking! Anyway, I passed economics, ended up with four B's, one C and one D (in economics), immediately began concentrating on my next semester and began thinking about a Master's Degree.

The Father Of Linebacker U

Becoming A Linebackers Coach – One day the following spring, when I was no longer involved with football, I was passing through the football office for some reason or another while the coaches were in a meeting. One of the coaches happened to see me and called me into their meeting. They were having a discussion on how linebackers should play and they asked my opinion—I guess because I had been a pretty good linebacker for Penn State from 1954-56. Well, I've never been shy about giving my opinion, so I described the different parts of linebacker play, and some of what I said disagreed with some of the things the others were saying.

Joe Paterno, who was then the quarterback coach, said, "If you're so smart, why don't you come out this spring and coach the linebackers?" I said "What will you give me?" Joe looked at Rip Engle and said, "Rip?" Rip thought for a moment and said, "I'll give you $100." I said, "Okay, I'll do it." And that was the beginning of how, years later, I became known as the Father of Linebacker U.

My first linebackers that spring were center Steve Garban and offensive guard Charlie Ruslavage, both of whom had been my backups at center-linebacker on the 1956 team. They were now the starters in 1958 and Steve would soon become the captain of the team. At the end of the 20 days of spring practice, both Steve and Charlie were looking good, and I was offered $2,600, technically as a graduate assistant, to coach the linebackers through the '58 season. The money would pay for my first year of graduate school in business, but I turned it down when the Washington Redskins called and I decided to give pro football another shot.

Redskins Preseason Camp – In early July, I flew out to the Redskins training camp at Occidental College, near Pasadena, California. The Redskins were training there because their first preseason game was against the Los Angeles Rams in the *Los Angeles Times* Charity game. The game always drew over 100,000 people and the proceeds from that game alone paid for the entire Redskins training camp. What I vividly remember most about the training camp was the awesome food and awful smog. The food was incredible, probably better than any training camp I've ever been in before or since. But the smog in the late afternoon was very bad, and during heavy traffic time, from 4 p.m. to 6 p.m., my eyes would burn and water because of all that smog. (Catalytic converters for cars had not been built yet.)

I also remember meeting two people that I would work with in the future as an assistant coach. First, there was Joe Walton, the starting tight end and the Redskins second round draft choice out of Pitt the year before, whom I hadn't talked to since that dinner with the Ivy League recruiter 5½ years earlier. I also met Laverne "Torgy" Torgeson, who was winding up his NFL playing career as a linebacker and would become one of the best known assistant coaches in the league. We would coach together with the Rams in 1979 and 1980.

Then there was Jim Hanifan, who had played two years in Canada and was a free agent receiver with the Redskins. Jim had a long career as a coach with the St. Louis Cardinals, first as a well known offensive line coach and then as the head coach. Years later, he reminded me that we were together at the Redskins. At first I couldn't remember until he said, "Life is just a bowl of cherries," and I said, "You're right." I used to sing that song all the time

I also have to tell you about two older, veteran players who impressed me. I couldn't get over how starting quarterback Eddie LeBaron handled the ball. They called him "Little Eddie LeBaron" because he was just 5-foot-7, but he handled the ball like a magician and was a pretty accurate passer despite his size. He had been the Redskins 10th round draft choice in 1952 out of the College of the Pacific, a small school near his home on the west coast, and when I saw him he already had played in two Pro Bowls and would play in two more before retiring with the expansion Dallas Cowboys after the 1963 season. After watching Eddie in training camp and then later on television I was convinced size doesn't matter in how good a player can be as long as he has ability and determination.

The other player who caught my eye was Gene Brito, a 6-foot, 220-pound defensive end who was as quick as a cat, and in awesome shape. I was surprised how he lapped everyone the first day in the 12-minute run at the end of practice. Gene also was a Californian who had played at Loyola Marymount. He wasn't drafted until the 17th round in 1951, but had been All-Pro the last three seasons and in '58 would play in his fifth Pro Bowl. In my entire career as an NFL assistant coach, I can remember only one other defensive lineman who was in as good physical condition as Brito. That was L.C. Greenwood, who also lapped the entire Steelers team in 1971 in the 12-minute run on the first day of practice.

Meeting Chuck Drazenovich – But the person I met in camp who had the biggest influence on me as a linebacker coach was a fellow Penn Stater, Chuck Drazenovich, who was in his 9th year as the Redskins starting linebacker. Penn State had great linebackers long before it became known as "Linebacker U' and Chuck was part of the lineage that stretched back to Penn State's first first-team All-American, William "Mother" Dunn in 1906. Leon Gajecki also was a first team All-American in 1940 but Chuck may have been Penn State's best linebacker of all-time—or, at least, until Onkotz and Ham came along—but he never made All-American. However, as I wrote in the last chapter, he was the NCAA heavyweight boxing champion in 1950 and one of the stars of Penn State's great undefeated football team of 1947 that finished fourth in the country. Most Penn Staters don't even realize that the 1947 team played the greatest statistical defensive game in NCAA Division I history when they held Syracuse to a minus 47 yards total offense in 1947 with a 47-0 victory. It's still in the record books.

On the first day of practice, the Redskins linebacker coach, Joe "Terrible Terry" Tereshinski, was discussing how the outside linebackers should play when heads up on the tight end. He wanted me in a staggered stance with my inside foot way up in front of the outside foot and bent over the front knee. I didn't want to do it that way and called over to Chuck Drazenovich, who was lined up at middle linebacker, and said, "Chuck, how would you play this?"

Chuck came over, lined head up on the tight end in a parallel stance with his feet equally apart, his knees slightly bent, and bent over from the waist arms hanging down naturally. On the snap count, the tight end tried to release to one side. Chuck moved laterally, like any good basketball, tennis, racquetball or handball player, brought his hands up quickly on the tight end's upper chest and shoulders and stuffed the tight end on the line of scrimmage. Tereshinski, the linebacker coach, immediately said, "That's okay for him, but not for you." I replied, "I want to do it exactly like he did it." And that's the way I did it and then taught it all the time that I coached linebackers.

In 2002, on the 70th anniversary of the Redskins, Chuck Drazenovich and Gene Brito were two of 67 players and three coaches selected as the 70 Greatest Redskins of all time.

Redskins Drills – We practiced three days before we had our first scrimmage and some of the drills we did were a little strange, and, frankly, a little dumb. They had a tackling dummy on a pulley with a weight on the other end. If you hit the dummy with your shoulder, wrapped your arms around it and drove your feet—like a good tackler would—well, after you drove it back a foot or two, the dummy would fly off your shoulder, and almost flip you on your back, and the coach would say "No good." But if you hit the dummy with your shoulder, wrapped your arms around it and fell to the ground with your feet stopped, the coach would say "Good tackle."

They also had a blocking dummy with a cable running down through the center of the dummy. The cable was attached to a board overhead and to the ground below so that the dummy could spin on the cable. If you went at the dummy hard, hit it with your shoulder and drove your feet hard, you would knock the dummy back a couple of inches. Then it would spin and you would fly off the dummy, fall on your face, and the coach would say, "No good." But if you ran up to the dummy, put your face in the middle of it, stuck out your elbows and ran in place, the coach would say, "Good block."

In another drill, the coach would give the ball to a 300-pound lineman on one side of the seven man sled and put a linebacker on the other side of the sled. Then he'd tell both to run full speed around the sled and have the linebacker tackle the lineman. It was like a kamikaze drill—suicidal—and a good way for a lot of linebackers to get hurt.

From that time on, I have never conducted any drills that didn't make sense or that were harmful to my players. I can thank the Redskins for that—and for connecting me up with Chuck Drazenovich—but for little else.

Getting Injured – On the fourth day of training camp we had our first scrimmage. I was playing right outside linebacker and on about the fifth or sixth play there was a big pileup on a running play. The whistle blew, and I started to walk away from the pile when a 300-pound-plus lineman rolled off the pile onto the back of my legs. I felt the right knee pop out and go back in, and that ended my scrimmage. After a few days on crutches I simply stood or sat around for the next three or four weeks letting my knee heal. To have something to do, I used to put a football on top of a tall dummy and Rudy Bukich, the injured quarterback, who was nicknamed "Rifle", would throw a ball and try to knock the other football off.

My leg healed enough by the first preseason game in that 100,000 plus *Los Angeles Times* Charity sellout against the Rams that I could run straight ahead without pain. I dressed for the game but I didn't expect to play and didn't. I was released the next day just as I expected because I hadn't done anything to make the team. Looking back, I guess it was one of those so-called blessings in disguise because that led to how I became Penn State's first official full-time linebacker coach.

Graduate Assistant To Full-Time Linebackers Coach

Returning To Penn State – After being cut by the Redskins in early September of 1958, I immediately went back to Penn State. Preseason practice had just started a few days before and when I arrived the team was having lunch at the Phi Delta Theta fraternity house where they stayed until classes began. I walked up to the table where Rip Engle, the head coach, was sitting and said, "Rip, is that offer to attend graduate school and coach still open?" He said, "You've got it."

My basic duties were to coach the varsity linebackers in preseason and spring practice. But when the freshmen reported about a month after the varsity, I was assigned to coach the freshmen linemen and be an assistant to the long-time freshman head coach Earl "Pappy" Bruce. And that turned out to be one of the most prophetic junctures of my life because it was with the freshmen that fall where Joe Moore and I forged our deep, lifetime relationship that intertwined throughout our football careers. Joe was then the backfield coach of Penn State's freshman team and a senior finishing his undergraduate degree.

Even while coaching the freshmen, I continued to work with the varsity linebackers, but it was on the freshman team that I found my first linebackers with raw talent. Remember, players also had to play offense at that time and it was usually the center, fullback and one of the offensive guards who played linebacker on defense. An offensive end was an end on defense, too, but in the 5-2 defensive schemes of the era, the defensive ends were similar to outside linebackers.

Among the players on that 1958 freshmen team were center-linebacker Bill Saul and end Bob Mitinger, who, as I wrote earlier, were among the first wave of linebackers to make an impact in the pros. Another good one was center-linebacker Jay Huffman, who became a three-year starter in his sophomore year and was the Most Valuable Player in the first Liberty Bowl in 1959. Jay later played with the Quantico Marines.

That freshman team was loaded with other talent, too, including quarterback Galen Hall, who was the Most Valuable Player in 1961 Gator Bowl, and halfback Roger Kochman, a first team All-American in 1962. Here's an example of how much talent we had. In the NFL draft of 1959, when 360 players were selected, only one Penn Stater was taken, fullback-linebacker Maury Schleicher as the 50th overall choice. Four years later, when the draft was limited 280 players, seven Nittany Lions were picked, with Saul, Mitinger, Kochman and defensive tackle Chuck Sieminski among the first 47 selections.

Our freshmen played three games in 1958 and we easily won all of them. But the only thing I really remember from that season involved my friend Joe Moore. We were ahead of the Navy freshmen by about 25-0 when they finally completed their first pass in the third quarter for about a 10-yard gain, and Joe came running over to me yelling "Whose area is that? Who is supposed to be covering there?" I yelled back, "Joe, that's their first completion. Get the hell out of here and go worry about your backs!" We were two typical young coaches.

Joe was coaching in upstate New York when I coached the freshmen in 1959 but the player I remember most from that team was the end Dave Robinson, who became an All-Pro linebacker with the Packers. Dave had the talent to play any position on offense or defense. As I look back, I believe Dave was probably the best all-around football player I saw during my 17 years at Penn State.

I also had a pair of good, hustling, hard-nosed freshmen linebackers who I knew could become starters on the varsity, Joe Blasenstein and Bernie Sabol. When they moved up the next season Joe was an immediate starter at left guard. I have to tell you a couple stories about those kids.

We were getting on the bus to go to Annapolis for the Navy freshman game and Joe Blasenstein was refusing to get on. He didn't see me and kept saying he wasn't going to go to Annapolis without me because he thought something had happened to me. Well, I was just around the corner talking to someone and when he saw me show up, he got on the bus. I have to admit I was flattered by the loyalty he showed to me. So, now it's the opening kickoff of the game and Joe ran down and made the tackle but was knocked out cold. After the trainers revived him, he came running to me on the sideline, grabbed me by the collar and started to scream, "You told me that if I went full speed and tackled the ball carrier I wouldn't get hurt!" I yelled, "Joe, think about what you did? What did you do wrong?" He said, "What do you mean?" I said, "Think about it." He let me go and after a minute he said, "You're right. I had my head down. That's why I got hurt." I said, "You got it." Joe really took to my coaching and became a really good college linebacker.

Bernie was involved in an unusual incident one day while I was running an "apron drill." This is when a linebacker or any defensive player would align in a 4-foot square—we called it a box—and an offensive player would take a four or five yard run at the defensive player in the marked off square and try to knock or block him out of the square. Bernie was one of the blockers and got knocked out cold trying to block the defender out of the box. When this happened, I called for the trainer to take care of Bernie and moved the apron drill about 10 yards away and went on with the drill. Well, this old alumnus saw all this and reported me to Rip Engle. He said he had been watching Penn State football practices for 35 years and he had never seen anything near as brutal as the apron drill that I was running. Rip didn't say much but told me that in the future to make sure the hurt player was all right before continuing on with the drill. Heck, I knew Bernie was all right. Like Joe, he was an aggressive, tough kid who could take a hit and give one back, and if they can't do that they better not be playing linebacker.

The First Liberty Bowl – The varsity had an outstanding year in '59, the best since Rip had become the head coach in 1950, and near the end of the regular season had a shot at the national championship, but lost to Syracuse 20-18 when both teams were undefeated. Syracuse went on to win the national championship, and Penn State beat Alabama 7-0 in the first Liberty Bowl, when there were just seven post-season bowl games, and finished with a 9-2 record.

Besides coaching linebackers, I had to run the scout team's Alabama defense, which was the 6-2 scheme that Coach Bear Bryant and his assistants had come up with a year or two earlier. This was an innovation by the Alabama staff utilizing alignment numbers that are now used by every coach in America in teaching defensive and offensive assignments. This might be a little difficult for a non-football person to understand but it works this way:

Each of the two linebackers controlled his side—right or left—of the ball by yelling out numbers. "Twenty Seven" meant the defensive man over the offensive guard would line up head on the guard (a two

Jay Huffman

technique) and the defensive tackle (next wide man) would line up inside ½ of the tight end (a seven technique). "Thirty Five" meant the defensive linemen over the offensive guard would line up over his outside ½ (a 3 technique) and the defensive tackle would line up on the outside ½ of the offensive tackle (a five technique). This is just some trivia I thought might be interesting.

Anyway, as I mentioned, one of the linebackers I personally coached, Jay Huffman, won the Liberty Bowl's Most Valuable Player Award. I believe this had an important impact on my career, because shortly afterward, I was asked to become a regular linebacker full time assistant football coach at Penn State, starting January 1, 1960, with basically the same duties I had before, and a starting salary of $5,000 a year. I think that Jay making MVP clinched the job for me.

Beside my title of linebacker coach, my new academic title was assistant professor. Back then, Penn State coaches were considered faculty members in the College of Physical Education. Thus, we were given academic appointments. What we taught was football, although some of the coaches taught other courses in the department. The head coach was a full professor and the rest of us were assistant

1960 Penn State Football Coaching Staff
Front row (left to right): Jim O'Hora, Line Coach; Frank Patrick, Backfield Coach; Earl Bruce, Freshman Coach; Rip Engle, Head Coach
Back row (left to right): Sever Toretti, Line Coach; Joe Paterno, Backfield Coach; Dan Radakovich, Linebacker Coach; J.T. White, End Coach

professors. When Joe Paterno was named associate coach in 1965, he also earned an academic promotion as associate professor. I know this may all sound like blasphemy to many academics in other disciplines, but, frankly, this system enabled us to keep track of our players in the classroom because we were on the same level as their other professors.

My new assignment gave me enough money for my wife, 18-month old son, and me to leave our apartment on College Avenue. And with $1,500 borrowed from my parents for a down payment, we built a new house in Circleville, two miles from campus. A bunch of the freshman football players moved us into our new house in May 1960 before the school year ended, and I can vividly remember Andy Stynchula, our senior tackle, who was drafted in the third round by the Redskins, running the heavy wax machine over our brand-new hardwood floors.

In Bed With The Wrong Woman – Andy must have become more familiar with the house than me because a year or so later he and his wife Teresa visited with us on a Penn State game weekend. By then he was starting for the Washington Redskins, but they weren't playing that weekend. The four of us were in the kitchen talking on Friday night, when Teresa said she was tired and was going to bed. Nancy, Andy, and I continued to talk for a while until I said, "I'm going to leave you two. I've got a game tomorrow, and I've got to get some sleep." And I went to bed. I'm sound asleep when I feel somebody shaking me. I wake up and it's Andy. I looked up and see my wife standing by the door. I said, "What's wrong?" Andy said, "You're in bed with Teresa." I turned over to my right, and there's Teresa's head right next to mine. Thank goodness, both my wife and Andy were laughing. What happened was my wife had given Andy and Teresa the master bedroom. Either I didn't know that or had forgotten it, but when I went to bed I got undressed in the dark and got into bed and went to sleep without ever realizing there was a woman already in the bed. Word got around pretty quickly about me being in the bed with the wrong woman and no one was really surprised. They just figured it was another typical day—or night—in the life of crazy Bad Rad.

The Tavern And "The Hay's In The Barn Party" – In the fall of 1959, Rip Engle's football staff had a cocktail party for the coaches and their wives every Thursday evening from 6:30 to 7:30 during the season. Each week the party was held at the home of a different coach. There was a specific reason the parties were held on Thursday. During the season, the main practices days were Tuesday, Wednesday and Thursday. The end of practice on Thursday meant that the majority of the preparations for the coming game on Saturday were completed. We called our affair, "The Hay's in the Barn Party" because this was to be a time to relax and socialize with the wives. The coach and wife who held the party that particular week were responsible for making a dinner reservation for the group at 8 o'clock at a local restaurant of their choice. Some of the restaurants the group went to at the time were the upstairs dining room of the State College Hotel Corner Room in downtown

State College, the Boalsburg Steak House and the Red Horse Tavern in Pleasant Gap. After dinner, at approximately 10 o'clock, everyone went home. They never went to one of the town's most popular restaurants, The Tavern, because they felt it was really a gathering place for students.

My wife and I were not original members of the group when it started in 1959 because I was a graduate assistant coach at the time. After I was hired as a full staff member and linebacker coach in 1960, Nancy and I were invited to join the fall cocktail party and dinner. We went to seven parties before it as our turn to be the hosts. The seventh affair had a unique twist to it when it became Joe Paterno's turn to be the host because he was single at the time and lived with Jim and Bets O'Hora's family. (Jim was our defensive line coach.) So, Joe's cocktail party was held in his bedroom in O'Hora's home, and we squeezed 15 people into the bedroom for a one hour cocktail party. That was truly a unique experience.

The next Thursday Nancy I and I sponsored "The Hay's in the Barn Party" and we had to pick out a restaurant for dinner. The only negative concern we had was the expense of the dinner. We had been spending between $20 and $30 each week for dinner for the two of us. My salary was $5,000 a year, slightly less than $100 a week and we had just built a new house with $1,500 I had borrowed from my parents for the down payment. We had a $120 a month mortgage payment, plus a two-year-old son, so we were literally pinching pennies. With this in mind, we went down to the Tavern Restaurant, which is across the street from the Penn State campus and still quite popular today because of its atmosphere and dinner prices. At the time, spaghetti was the house specialty, and a plate of spaghetti cost only $1. That's one reason the students flocked to the place. We talked to the twins who managed The Tavern, Joe and Andy Besket, about seating 15 of us for dinner. The twins showed us a special room up a few steps off the main dining room that would be perfect for our group. We made the reservation for 8 o'clock that Thursday and informed the other coaches. A couple of the wives criticized our choice. They thought it would be a bad move to go to a place where the students might go. I informed them that we would be in a private room and not near students.

Well, we had the cocktail party at our new house and dinner at the Tavern and everyone loved it. The twins treated us like royalty. The food was excellent and, best of all, very inexpensive. I'll bet not one couple had a dinner tab of more than $10, and I believe Nancy and my bill was around $5. From that Thursday on, all the Thursday night dinners for the football staff's "The Hay's in the Barn Party" were held at the Tavern on into the 1990s. During those 30 plus years that I traveled from job to job around the country I always knew where I could find Joe Paterno on a Thursday night from 8 to 10 o'clock during the football season—at The Tavern.

Nancy and I are still amazed the tradition of those Thursday night dinners at The Tavern lasted as long as it did, and we are extremely proud of our part in starting it all.

Early Years Coaching Linebackers – Over the next few years, I began refining my linebacking techniques and drills. I was also learning a lot from the other assistant coaches. I was now on their level, an accepted and respected junior colleague and full-time assistant, but I was still their student in many ways and they continued to teach me a lot—not just about defense but much more about football—on the field and off it.

I was the first full-time assistant hired since J.T. White came as the end coach in 1954. Four of the assistants had been there even before Rip became the head coach in 1950—defensive line coach Jim O'Hora, offensive line coach "Tor" Toretti, backfield coach Frank Patrick, and freshman coach Earl Bruce. Rip had agreed to retain all of them when he was hired as long as he could bring one coach with him from Brown, where he had been the head coach from 1944-49. Two of Rip's assistants at Brown turned him down, but his star quarterback and safety, Joe Paterno, said he would help him for a year before going to law school. Of course, we all know how that turned out. There was a lot of experience and knowledge in that staff.

Like me, Jim and Tor had played for Penn State in the 1930s, and they had both been coaching at State since the late 1940s. Frank had been an All-American back at Pitt in the late '30s and then played a couple of years with the Chicago Cardinals before going into coaching. Earl had been a head coach for years at California State Teachers College (now California University of Pennsylvania), and before J.T. went into coaching he had the unique distinction of becoming the only man ever to play on the Rose Bowl teams of two different schools, Ohio State in 1942 and Michigan, his alma mater, in 1948.

Rip's first staff remained pretty much intact throughout my time at Penn State, and expanded after Paterno became the head coach in 1966. Rip was able to get the administration to create a new position as full-time recruiter in 1960 and Bob Newcombe was hired. When Bob left after the '62 season Tor replaced Bob. Tor was a "natural" because he was one heckuva recruiter. Another of Rip's players from Brown, Joe McMullen, replaced Tor. George Welsh, who had been an All-American quarterback at Navy, also was added to the staff the same year, primarily as the scout team coach but also to help coach defensive backs. Bob Phillips joined us as receivers coach and Welsh became the quarterback coach when Paterno moved up in '66 as our responsibilities were redefined. Just before my last year in 1969, McMullen left and two other former players from our teams in the mid '60s came aboard as assistant line coaches, Jim Weaver (centers and guards) and another assistant (tackles). Most of them were still coaching at Penn State long after I departed.

Now, I mention all this about the staff because without those other coaches, I don't think Linebacker U would have evolved the way it did. The linebackers who first established Penn State's reputation didn't have just one mentor but many. From the time they were recruited and became freshmen until they graduated and went into the pros they were taught and influenced by every coach on the staff, and those coaches deserve as much credit for creating Linebacker U as I do.

Getting An MBA – Frankly, when I officially joined that staff in January of 1960, it was business as usual, and I was still going to class trying to finish up my Master of Science Degree in the business curriculum. When the spring term was over I had completed all 24 of the course credits for the master's degree, but still needed to write a thesis for six credits to actually receive the degree, so I went to see my thesis advisor, Professor Max Richards. He gave me a list of over 30 books to read and told me to come back to him with an idea for a thesis, which he could approve. Needless to say, I put my writing of a thesis on hold.

Two years later, in the spring of '62 I was still reading when Professor Sam Wherry, the head of the Department of Insurance in the business school, told me the business school was putting in a Master of Business Administration curriculum identical to that of the Harvard Business School and that I could get an MBA without having to write a thesis. With the permission of Rip Engle, I went back to graduate school for another one year and a half of full-time study. And from the fall of 1962 until May of 1964 when I graduated in Penn State's first MBA class I was both a full-time football assistant coach and a full-time graduate student. So much for crazy Bad Rad, eh?

During the 10 years that I was Penn State's linebackers coach, there was a significant change in the rules that transformed college football forever. It occurred in early 1965 when the NCAA finally permitted unlimited substitution, thereby eliminating the need for players to play both offense and defense. Linebackers no longer had to be centers, guards or fullbacks but could concentrate on their specialty. For that reason alone, there have been more and more outstanding linebackers coming out of college and becoming stars in the pros.

Ralph Baker – But before that rule change, I had a couple of two-way players who I was certain were going to be big-time defensive specialists. One was Ralph Baker, who was on our freshman team in the fall of 1960. Ralph was a nose guard, meaning he played over the center. In the three freshman games we played, Ralph made more tackles in those games than any player that I had ever seen in my 55 years as a coach and player before or since—over 30 tackles in each of the three games. He had a knack of bringing his shoulder and forearm quickly into the center as the ball was snapped, keeping the center from getting to his body as he used his hands on the center's chest to quickly get off the center's block to either side and make the tackle. This skill was probably a big reason why he later became a great linebacker both for Penn State and then the Jets. Ralph moved to defensive end as a sophomore but he was a spot player. But in the spring of 1962, we switched him to linebacker. As the saying goes, Ralph took to linebacker like a duck takes to water. He simply had a knack on both runs and passes to make a lot of plays.

Ralph was one of the best linebackers I ever coached. Years later, I would help him become the linebackers coach of his NFL team, the New York Jets, and, subsequently, I would replace him in that same position. But that's another story.

Stuffing Glenn Ressler In One-On-One Drill – The fall of 1961 ended up being the last year I would have to coach the freshman linemen. We had two new graduate assistant coaches that fall who not only became successful coaches in college and the NFL but became involved in my life later on—Augie Tammariello and John Beake.

One of the last freshmen I coached became one of Penn State's greatest players of all time, but that seemed quite farfetched when we began practice. Glenn Ressler was a farm boy from a very rural part of north central Pennsylvania and he didn't know a lot about football, but we could see he had raw potential.

I started Glenn at middle linebacker in the first freshman game and he blitzed every play, even though no blitzes were called. But at 6-foot-2, 230 pounds he was very impressive physically. At one of the earliest freshman practices, I was demonstrating how to stop a blocker from a down lineman position. I had put on a helmet, shoulder pads and jersey. Then, I would go one-on-one against a freshman lineman and get my shoulder and forearm under his helmet, get my hands on his chest, drive my feet, and take the blocker backwards. I was only 25 years old at the time and had been demonstrating this way for the last four years and had always stuffed the freshmen lineman, even the great All-American Dave Robinson when he was a freshman.

Glenn Ressler

Anyway, this practice day I picked Glenn to be the blocker that I was going to demonstrate my defensive skills on. I told one of the graduate assistant coaches, Augie or John, to give Ressler the snap count. Well, when Glenn started at me, I got my shoulder and forearm under his helmet, got my hands in his chest, and stood him right up. Then he started to walk and he drove me five or six yards straight back. I yelled to the players and graduate assistant coaches, "What did I do wrong? I didn't drive my feet on contact. I didn't accelerate my feet." I then said, "Let's go again, Glenn. Everybody watch me accelerate my feet on contact and stuff him backwards." The second time Glenn started at me, I stood him up again and tried my damnedest to accelerate and drive my feet but when he started walking, he drove me back again five or six yards. We did it a third time with the same result. By this time the graduate assistant coaches were laughing at my predicament. Sometimes, no matter what, a mismatch stays a mismatch. We knew, or at least should have known, right then that Glenn Ressler would be a great player.

In his junior season, Glenn was switched to defensive nose guard and center, and became the dominating player on the team on both defense and offense. His blocking for fullback Tom Urbanik earned them a nickname that year as "Paul Bunyan and His Ox" after Glenn's play on offense and defense led Penn State to a stunning 27-0 upset over No. 1 Ohio State at Columbus in midseason. In his senior year he was an All-American and won the Maxwell Award as college football's best player, and then went on to start at offensive guard on the Baltimore Colts Super Bowl team of 1970. Not a bad career for a former Penn State freshman linebacker.

Augie Tammariello

Glenn is now in the College Football Hall of fame, and all I can say is that he is one linebacker that I'm glad we switched to defensive nose guard aligned on the center because he played that position better than anyone I've ever seen in my 50 years of coaching.

EDITOR'S NOTE: The two graduate assistant coaches helping me (and laughing) in the above drill with Glenn Ressler both had very distinguished football careers. Augie Tammariello became the offensive line coach for William and Mary and Colorado University; then the head football coach for the University of Louisiana – Lafayette Ragin' Cajuns for six years.

John Beake won a few championships as head coach of Nyack (New York) High School; then was the offensive backfield coach for the Kansas City Chiefs when they won Super Bowl IV. After stints in the Denver Broncos scouting department and front office, he was the general manager of the Denver Broncos during their four Super Bowl years (runners-up in back-to-back Super Bowls XXXII and XXXIII and winners in back-to-back Super Bowls XXXII and XXXIII). Following that, John was in charge of football operations for NFL-Europe.

John Beake

I'm proud to admit that I was Augie and John's football tutor for the one brief year at Penn State (1961-62) when they were both getting their master's degrees.

The Intensity Of Joe Blasenstein – Of all the players I coached at Penn State, there was no one like Joe Blasenstein. Joe didn't have the natural talent or super skills that would make him a great linebacker like Baker or Jack Ham, but no one had more heart, desire or intensity than Joe. Joe had entered Penn State in January of 1959 and that made him eligible to participate in 1959 in spring practice even though he was just a freshman.

After the first couple days of spring practice, the trainers called me aside and wanted to know why we recruited this kid. They said he had a soft body, wore thick glasses, wasn't fast, was only 6-foot, 200-pounds, etc. I said, he displayed a lot of energy and it was too soon to tell if he'd be any good. After a while, Blasenstein showed so much intensity that Rip Engle said that in his 30 some years of coaching, he had never had a player even one third as intense as the Blazer.

Even though Blasenstein was a starting freshman center—and a good one—Joe Paterno, who was in charge of quarterbacks, refused to let him be a center for the varsity. Paterno said there was no way he was going to let a player that intense snap the ball to his quarterback. So we switched Blasenstein to guard and he adapted so well he became a starter with another sophomore guard, Dave Robinson—yes the same Dave Robinson, who moved to end after seven games and became an All-American—and the Blazer started the rest of his career.

Anyway, Blasenstein did not believe in normal team drills or "Thud" as many teams call it. He would hit anybody who came near him and hit him at full speed. After awhile players came to accept that and either hit him full speed or they wouldn't touch him. The football team stayed at the Phi Delta fraternity in preseason and one day Joe got a phone call. I went to his room and he was asleep on a bunk bed. I gently shook him to tell him he had a phone call. He woke up by lunging out of bed, slamming me against the wall and beating on me. I kept yelling, "Joe wake up. It's me, Rad." I finally got his attention before I got hurt.

Then, in the spring of 1962, we excused some seniors from spring practice who had started the previous two years, like Robinson and Joe, so they could have a break from football but also so we could give more work to their backups. At the top of that senior list was the Blazer. Because he had enrolled early, Joe had already participated in three spring practices, and he also was a two-year starter. But Joe being Joe, he rebelled at the idea of missing spring practice. He just flat out refused to miss. I finally got through to him by telling him if he dressed for spring practice we would kick him off the football team permanently. In those days, spring practice was 20 practice days and was held on the golf course, starting at 3:30 p.m. Well, Joe went to the golf course at three o'clock, stood on the sideline at the 50-yard line of the main practice field until 5:30 on every one of those 20 practice days. Don't ask me to explain why, because I can't. Maybe "Tor" Toretti, our line coach said it best. "Danny," he told me one day, "We know there is a God in this world because he made Blasenstein blind, small, weak and slow. If God had made him normal, he would have destroyed everybody."

I have one more story about Joe that really tells you the type of person he was. This happened at Joe's last game, the 1962 Gator Bowl in Jacksonville against Florida. As I was walking into the Gator Bowl stadium before the game, an older alumnus, and I don't remember who it was, came up to me and handed me some coins. "Rad, here are three silver dollars for good luck." Well, I had no use for these silver dollars, so in my short pregame meeting with the linebackers—Ralph Baker, the Blazer, Joe Galardi and Bernie Sabol—I said, "I'll give these three silver dollars to the linebacker who plays the best game."

Well, the team really didn't play well and we lost, 17-7. I went into the locker room and said, "Joe Blasenstein played the best" and put the three silver dollars on the shelf in his locker. He grabbed the three silver dollars and threw them on the floor and said, "You don't have to pay me to play," and left with his towel to take a shower. I picked up the silver dollars and put them in the pocket of his pants hanging in his locker. About 20 minutes later, Sabol came over to me and said, "Coach Rad, Joe found the silver dollars in his pants and threw them on the floor again. Here they are." I said, "Keep them Bernie," and that was my last experience coaching Joe Blasenstein. I didn't see much of Joe after he left Penn State but he became a high school coach and once told me he disliked the violent drills used by his fellow high school coaches. I guess he tried to steer his intensity in a different direction.

Joe became a licensed pilot and was last reported to be flying medical doctors in a private charter airplane to different locations in Africa.

The Creation Of Mat Tackling & Mirror Dodge Drills – There was another linebacker I had during this time who never made it to the pros but was a good, solid college player. Bob Kane would have a big influence on my life on and off the field and today is one of my best friends. Bob is the brother of Billy Kane, a starting halfback and teammate of mine from 1954 through 1956. Billy was a little bit off the wall like me but his brother was much more serious about life. Bob also had a great love for football and was determined to play despite a serious childhood injury that fractured his skull and left leg and left him with a spine that was out of line. Despite this, Bob played fullback in high school, and then was recruited by me for Penn State in 1961 to try and follow the footsteps of his big brother.

During a half-speed pickup tackling drill midway through his sophomore season, Bob hurt his back and was told that he could never play football again. I was really upset and felt I had been the cause. Before the injury, Bob had been one of my best tacklers. It seemed like every other tackle that he made he would cause a fumble. He would hit them, accelerate his feet and drill the ball carrier right into the ground. After he got hurt, I never did the half-speed pickup tackling drill again. Instead, I invented a full speed "Mat Tackling" drill. This is where the ball carrier is holding a small protective shield and the tackler drills him back and down into the mat. It's more realistic, more like a game, and nobody's going to hurt their back. Anyway, when Bob was told he couldn't play football anymore, he became a student coach, helping with the freshman team in '63.

Over the summer of 1963, Bob had visited his sister, who was married to the swimming coach of the University of Maryland. Bob swam all summer and his back started to feel better. While coaching the freshmen team, he continued to swim at the Penn State pool. Right before spring practice in 1964 Bob made a deal with the team doctor and athletic director that he could practice and play as long as he was not involved in any contact drills except scrimmage and games. He could be in team or breakdown drills as long as they weren't live. This means that in any two-hour practice he would have nothing to do for anywhere from 15 minutes to one hour. I told him that he should use this free time to work on his biggest weakness, which was lateral movement.

So, for this purpose I invented another drill just for him that I called the "Mirror Dodge." A player aligns himself between two cones that are on a line at various distances—say, five, six, seven or eight yards apart—and tries to stay in front, or mirror, another player who is trying to get across the line and score by dodging or juking the mirror player. For this purpose, I assigned two different players each practice to take turns trying to dodge or juke him. Eventually, Bob got so good laterally that I incorporated the drill for all the linebackers and continued to use that and the "Matt Tackling" drills throughout my coaching career. Probably none of that would have happened if Bob had not got hurt in my half-speed tackling drill.

To the great surprise of a lot of people, including the doctor who said Bob would never play again, he became the starting middle linebacker in 1964, simply by being evaluated on scrimmage play. He had to have had the best practice deal of any player in history. Bob was the starter when we beat Ohio State 27-0 in 1964 in one of the greatest defensive games in Penn State history. He was still a starting linebacker when we opened the 1965 season against the eventual national champion Michigan State. I remember him making over 30 individual tackles and assists in the game. However, when my co-author Lou Prato and I recently reviewed the game film, we counted 29 tackles where Bob either made the tackle himself or assisted in making the tackle. But he also missed five tackles, including the first one when the Michigan State back went by him to score the Spartans first touchdown on a 35-yard run. Bob, if you're reading this, maybe with a little more practice in the mirror-dodge drill you might have made that tackle. Except when another injury took him out of the lineup, Bob was in the thick of the action the rest of the year. I can't remember any other of my linebackers overcoming the pain and challenges that Bob did just to get on the football field, and then being as successful as he was.

Mirror Dodge On Trial – Nearly 35 years later, the mirror dodge drill gained notoriety when then Notre Dame Head Coach Bob Davie claimed it was abusive in his testimony as a defendant in a law suit filed by my friend Joe Moore. In 1988 Coach Lou Holtz had hired Joe to be Notre Dame's offensive line coach, and in Joe's first year Notre Dame won a national championship and they haven't won another since. Joe was so good that when he was coaching the offensive line at Pitt in 1984 that *Sports Illustrated* called him "the best line coach in America" because he had produced such All-Americans and Hall of Famers such as Bill Fralic, Mark May, Russ Grimm and Jimbo Covert.

Bob Davie was another guy from the Pittsburgh area and for two years (1980-82) he and Joe were on the football staff at Pitt. Then, in 1994 Holtz hired Davie away from Texas A&M to be his defensive coordinator. When Holtz left Notre Dame after the 1996 season, Davie was selected his successor. Despite the fact that just about all of Joe's starting offensive linemen at Notre Dame had been drafted by the NFL, one of Davie's first moves was not to rehire Joe, saying he wanted a younger man. Joe, who was about 20 years older than Davie, who was then 42, filed an age discrimination law suit against Davie and Notre Dame, and the case went to trial in the summer of 1997. One of Joe's attorney's, Richard Lieberman, wrote a book about it all in 2001 entitled: *Personal Foul: Coach Joe Moore vs. the University of Notre Dame*.

At one point during the trial, Lieberman wrote, Davie and Notre Dame attempted to prove Joe was abusive to his players and Davie "passionately told the jury" that my mirror dodge drill was a perfect example: "The mirror-dodge (sic) drill he used in practice, which forced two players to move back and forth at full speed, mirroring each other for long periods of time, was, Davie said 'abusive to me and also to the players who saw it on defense.'"

Later in the trial, Joe's lead attorney, Mimi Moore (no relation to Joe) had Joe demonstrate the mirror dodge drills to the jury. "Standing in the middle of the courtroom with [law associate] Bill Wortel acting as an offensive lineman," Lieberman wrote, "Joe acted out the mirror-dodge (sic) drill while the jury watched intently. 'The name of it tells you what it is. It is the same as if you are looking in the mirror; you would hope your reflection would be directly in front of you. So we call it a mirror. Whatever he does,' Joe said as Bill shifted from side to side, 'I want to mirror him.' The two slid back and forth across the courtroom floor as Joe explained the procedure, saying the drill was harmless; he often used it with high school players. Typically two kids would practice the drill while the others watched, and then two more would follow. 'My theory of coaching is that football is a game of spurts and rests.'

"'Coach Moore, did Coach Holtz ever tell you not to use either of those two drills?' asked Mimi. 'No'" Joe replied.

It's evident to me that Bob Davie, though a defensive coach, did not realize that the mirror dodge drill was originally invented as a defensive drill to teach linebackers, secondary and defensive linemen better lateral movement and change of direction that you normally learn from playing tennis, handball, racquetball, badminton and man for man defense in basketball. As I wrote above, it was invented so that Bob Kane, a Penn State linebacker who was not allowed to participate in contact drills, could work on improving his lateral movement. Furthermore, each mirror drill lasted only 15 to 20 seconds. How could Davie possibly think the drill was abusive?

The mirror drill is basically a follow the leader drill involving change of direction and that's basically defensive football. Joe Moore used it because it's also a great drill for teaching lateral movement in pass protection. Never in my wildest dreams did I ever think that a drill I invented would be demonstrated in a court room to show it wasn't abusive.

Nor in my wildest dreams did I ever think I would go one-on-one in the mirror drill with the Scarecrow from the movie *The Wizard of Oz* with in the middle of a bar near Hollywood. You can read about that in Chapter 14.

CHAPTER EIGHT – Rip's Last Five Years

Many of the folks who knew me in high school and my undergraduate days at Penn State were shocked when they found out I had quit my coaching job at Penn State after the 1969 season because I wanted to go to law school. Because of how I dressed and acted sometimes, I don't think many of them realized I was smart enough to get through college let alone earn an MBA and study the law.

I started thinking about law school in the early 1960s when I became a full-time assistant. My cousin Bob Garshak was going to law school part time at Duquesne at the time and when my younger cousin Raymond Radakovich started going in the late '60s, I was determined to do it too. My cousins and I were good friends and I have to tell you a couple of football stories about them.

My Cousin Raymond – Raymond was 10 years younger than me but loved football, and when he was going to be a high school sophomore in the late summer of 1961 he told me he was going to try out as a lineman for the West Mifflin High football team. So, I invited him up to Penn State for a visit. He was about 6-foot, 180-pounds, and I figured I'd simply help him get started by teaching him how to stop an offensive lineman one-on-one and to come off the block to make the tackle. Each day we put on a helmet and shoulder pads, and I had him get his shoulder under my helmet, get his forearm and then arms and hands on my chest or shoulders and then come off my block to either side. After the third day of doing this, a big lump swelled up on the back of my neck from the Riddell helmet popping back against my neck resulting from Raymond's shoulder popping my face mask up and back. I solved the problem by wrapping a towel flattened out around my neck. I showed the equipment man and trainers my neck bump and told them to tell Riddell about it. They did, and the next year, Riddell helmets had a piece of rubber or foam attached to the back rim of the helmet. One of these days, I'd like to talk at someone at Riddell to see if I'm responsible for that attachment.

A couple of weeks later, I was back in Pittsburgh talking to cousin Bob Garashak, who had played basketball and football with me in high school. He had been watching Raymond in football practice. He said, "Rad, explain something to me. I'm watching our cousin Raymond go one-on-one against this big Flanigan kid. Flanigan goes to block our cousin. Raymond hits him, straightens him up and takes him backwards and the coaches are screaming, 'No, no, Radakovich. You're too high. You're standing up, get low.' Now it seems to me our cousin was doing a good job against Flanigan."

I said, "Yes, he was. He was doing exactly what I taught him." It goes to show how different coaches can have different conceptions of how to play. Two years later West Mifflin went undefeated, beat Butler high for the WPIAL championship, and my cousin Raymond made first-team all-state. He turned down my Penn State scholarship offer and went on scholarship to the University of Pittsburgh. But two years later, I was successful in recruiting his younger brother, Dave Radakovich, who played as a backup linebacker from 1967-69 when Penn State had those two great undefeated teams. Oh, and that Flanigan kid? Jim Flanigan also went to Pitt and was a pretty good linebacker. He was the No. 2 choice of the Packers in 1967 and played in the NFL for five years.

The Study Group With The Big Dumb Football Player – As for my MBA, when Professor Sam Wherry enabled me to switch from the Master's of Science program to the MBA in the fall of 1962, I already had 24 credits passed in graduate school. I was immediately scheduled into an advanced management case course taught by Max Richards, a Harvard graduate, who was in charge of the MBA program and by far the toughest professor in the entire business school. Professor Richards was also my thesis advisor in the school's Master of Science program. I had him for three courses in undergraduate and graduate school and had flunked one of them. So I knew how tough he was, and the word was out that he had flunked almost half of the previous class that had taken this case course. The student nickname for him was "Max the Ax." When the first written case assignment was given, I went home and worked on it two full days and one night, and didn't go to bed one night because I knew how tough he was. Well, when the graded case papers were handed back, I tied for the highest grade on the paper, a B plus, with Nick Fallieras, who had an undergraduate engineering degree, got an MBA, and later went to medical school and became a gynecologist. (Nick was a pretty smart cookie. As an undergraduate he also was the roommate of Penn State quarterback Pete Liske.)

As soon as the class was over, the five graduate assistants who were all on academic full scholarships for graduate school—Fallearis, Lew Wheeler, Alex Goldberg, Bob Vierick, and Wilmer Leinbech—cornered me and asked me if I would join them across the street in the student union for a cup of coffee, which I did. They told me that they had met after the first class and discussed who would pass and who would fail. Remember, I said almost half the previous class had failed, and one of them had said, "That big dumb football guy has no chance." They obviously didn't know that I had Max Richards for three previous classes. Now, because I had received the highest grade on the first case paper, they were begging me to join their study group. I remember one of the other graduate students walking by, and someone in our group said maybe they should try to get that guy to also join our group, and one of the others said, "No, he's not smart enough. He only had a 2.9 average as an undergraduate." I wasn't about to tell them that I only had a 2.1 average as an undergraduate. Anyway, I accepted their offer to join and spent the next year and a half in a study group with five of the smartest graduate students in the business school, and graduated in Penn State's first MBA class in May 1964. Being able to join that study group was one of the luckiest things to ever happen to "this big dumb football player."

Meeting Dave Joyner's Father – Instead of writing a thesis for the MBA degree, like that required for the business MS degree, we were required to write a paper that solved a current company problem. After calling a number of companies, Bob Joyner, the manager of Erie Technical Ceramics in State College, told me he needed an incremental cost analysis of two new products at various rates of production. One of these products was the "ultra sonic microphone," which could start a garage door opener up to 200 feet away. Sometime during the six months that it took me to complete this project Bob asked me if it were possible to get him a locker at Rec Hall on the Penn State campus. He said he had a chubby seventh-grade son named Dave, who read books all the time and didn't get any exercise, and Bob wanted to take him to a gymnasium. So, I got him one of our wire cage lockers in Rec Hall.

Dave Joyner

A number of times in the next year, I would be playing pickup basketball in Rec Hall and look up at the indoor track, which was at the top of the upper tier of the grandstands, and see Bob Joyner with a wrap around one knee jogging and limping around the track with his chubby 12-year-old kid trotting behind him. It had to be tough for Bob to run because he had suffered severe body and leg wounds at Corregidor in the latter part of World War II, and at the time was running on a leg with a fused ankle and a deep bone infection. Shortly after that, Bob got his son to go out for wrestling, which was the beginning of an impressive athletic career.

Dave was such a standout wrestler in high school, winning two state heavyweight championships, that Penn State offered him a full wrestling scholarship as well as a full football scholarship. He utilized the wrestling scholarship for three years and then used the football scholarship for his senior year. By the spring practice of 1969, in his freshman year, he had developed from a good high school player into a great college prospect; we had a problem of where to play him. As a sophomore, Dave was the third best defensive tackle behind Reid and Smear and the third best offensive tackle behind Vic Surma and Tom Jackson, all of whom were seniors. Finally, he was told to stay on offense. As a sophomore, he was a backup offensive tackle on our great undefeated 1969 team, and in his senior year of 1971 he was a co-captain and a consensus first team All-American. In wrestling, he won three eastern heavyweight titles and was a runner-up in the NCAA tournament. Oh, Dave also was an academic All-American and won an NCAA Post-Graduate scholarship which helped put him through medical school where he became an orthopedic surgeon, and eventually a trainer for the U.S. Olympic team.

Who would have ever thought he would one day be the acting athletic director of Penn State? He's come a long way athletically from when he was a chubby seventh grader that only read books, and it all started with that wire cage locker at Rec Hall.

Bowl Memories

I have a lot of memories of my early years coaching under Rip Engle and being part of his outstanding staff but there's not enough room in this book to tell you all of them. Let me share a few from on and off the field.

Liberty Bowls – I have to tell you a couple of things about the first Liberty Bowl in 1959 that I had not mentioned in Chapter Six. One occurred at the post-game party for both teams in Philadelphia's Warrick Hotel, called the Governor's Ball, where we accidentally stumbled upon a name for our third child. Nancy and I were walking up the stairs to the banquet ballroom when we heard an Alabama player calling his girlfriend, "Leslie, Honey, where are you? Leslie, where are you?" We remembered that seven years later when we were searching for a name for our middle daughter, Leslie.

This was our first bowl trip and even though the weather was freezing, the Liberty Bowl folks had a great entertainment show after the banquet. They were all young entertainers most people had never heard of at that time. The master of ceremonies was a Philadelphia guy named Ed McMahon and he had a buddy with him named Johnny Carson. Three years later, Carson was hosting the *Tonight Show* with McMahon as his sidekick. Another of the entertainers was Dick Van Dyke, who later became famous in the *Mary Poppins* movie and *The Dick Van Dyke Show* on television. Then there was a comedian, Jonathan Winters, who had just been released after spending six months in an insane asylum. My wife and I and my former teammate Jack Farls talked to Winters for a bit after the entertainment and he was truly nuts and very funny offstage as well as on.

We went back to the Liberty Bowl again in my first season as full-time assistant, and one of the things I remember about the 1960 varsity season was that the second team, known as the red team, consistently played better offense than the first, or blue, team. Keep in mind again that because of the substitution rules Rip played both the red and blue teams equally. Galen Hall, now a junior, who had thrown the touchdown pass off the fake field goal on the last play of the first half that beat Alabama in our first Liberty Bowl, 7-0, in 1959, became the quarterback for the blue team and senior Dick Hoak was quarterback for the red team. I wrote in the last chapter how Hoak had been the quarterback on our unbeaten freshman team in 1957, but had played halfback his sophomore and junior years.

We lost three of our first five games in 1960 by close scores and sometime around there, Hoak was offered the spot with the blue team but turned it down and said he'd still stick with the red team. We won three of the last four and then beat Oregon in the second Liberty Bowl, 41-12, and finished 16th in the polls. Hoak, the quarterback for the second team, was voted the Most Valuable Player of the game. I specifically remember Hoak running a play the staff came up with that we called the "dive keep," which was a quarterback option involving two running backs. A few years later, the University of Houston started using the same play, called it the "veer option" and made an entire offensive scheme based on that play.

1961 Gator Bowl – After two cold Liberty Bowls, we were happy to play the next bowl game in the south in 1961. Once again, we came back from a record of 4-3 to win our last three games, and two days after beating Pitt, 47-26, we were invited to the Gator Bowl in Jacksonville to play Georgia Tech. Pitt whined about us running up the score but we threw only two passes in the fourth quarter. Pitt's quarterback was a kid named Jim Traficant, who thirty or so years later would become an infamous congressman and spend several years in prison. So much for participating in sports keeping you out of trouble.

I'll never forget the hotel we stayed in. Jacksonville was still a segregated city and because we had a couple of black players we stayed 30 miles away in St. Augustine. It's a famous old hotel, the Ponce De Leon, which was built by Henry Flagler, who had every stone and all the materials imported from Europe. This was a very classy place, and at that time opened for just the months of January, February, March and April. It was a hotel that only the very wealthy stayed in, but they opened it a couple weeks early for us. The food was fantastic, and my wife ordered shrimp cocktails for breakfast, lunch and dinner. It was like living in the classiest castle you could imagine.

Galen Hall (25), Joe Blasenstein (62), Hatch Rosdahl (67)

Dick Anderson catches pass for 1st down in 1961 Gator Bowl

As for the game, it seemed like everyone in the south thought we weren't good enough to be playing Georgia Tech, who was No. 13 in the country with a 7-3 record and had only given up 4.4 points a game. My linebackers were seniors Jay Huffman and Bill Saul, juniors Joe Blasenstein and Joe Galardi and sophomore Bernie Sabol, and they were a very tough group. But our best defensive player was Dave Robinson and he would become the first black to play in a Gator Bowl game. Tech jumped out to a 9-0 lead and their fans were feeling pretty smug about it. But we went ahead 14-9 at the half, and then Robinson made the greatest play of the game early in the third quarter, leaping over blockers to sack the quarterback and force a fumble that Robby recovered. On our first play from their 35-yard line, quarterback Galen Hall called a play action pass, and I can still see Junior Powell being wide open, like by 30 yards, and scoring the touchdown. We won 30-15 and Galen was the MVP.

1962—Blue And White Wins Because Of Green – This could have been Rip's best ever season. In the preseason we were ranked third in the country by the AP, but when Army upset us 9-6 at West Point in our fourth game we fell to No. 14 and never recovered, even though we were undefeated the rest of the season.

One week before we played Army in 1962 was one of the most unusual games in my entire coaching career, because the third team, that we called the green team, was responsible for winning the game. Normally the blue team played the first half of each of the four quarters and the red team played the second half of each quarter. This game against Rice in Houston was probably the most humid game in football history. The humidity was 99%, but it didn't rain. The Rice coach, Jess Neely, said that in his 21 years at Rice as head coach, this was the first time on a dry night that he could hear the water squishing in the player's shoes as they ran by.

We were losing 7-6 at the half after we botched the extra point kick, and spent the last couple of minutes of the first half stopping them twice inside our 10-yard line.

Dave Robinson

At halftime, some players from both teams had to be carried into the locker rooms. I can remember walking alongside our Dave Robinson as he was being carried on a stretcher through the tunnel that led to the locker room in Rice Stadium. I had on a short sleeve shirt, and had spent the first half in the press box, and I was soaked as if I had been caught in a rainstorm. Because of the heat, we decided to start the second half with the green team, which was our third team. One look at Dave Robinson lying on the stretcher probably helped prompt that decision. Well, the green team completely dominated the dehydrated Rice first and second teams almost the entire third quarter until we put our starters back in. The blue and the red teams played the fourth quarter and we won 18-7. The decision to start the second half with the green team is without a doubt one of the smartest strategic moves in Penn State football history.

Back To St. Augustine With A Stop At The White House – Going into our last game against Pitt in 1962, we were being mentioned for several bowls, including two of the only four games then played on New Year's Day—which every player dreams about—the Orange and Cotton bowls. We beat Pitt, 16-0, to finish the season at 9-1, but as just the ninth ranked team in the final AP poll, then taken at the end of the regular season, our best offer was the Gator Bowl again. The seniors felt they had earned a New Year's Day game and deeply resented the snub by the college football world. With some pushing by the coaches, they reluctantly agreed to go back to the Gator Bowl if they could spend Christmas at home. And when a 6-4 Florida team was chosen as the opponent, their lukewarm enthusiasm for the game diminished even more. It all climaxed in a lackadaisical performance and a 17-7 loss. But the Gator Bowl trip wasn't a total disaster for me personally. We had chance to get together with President Kennedy, and then I met Rocky Marciano, and Al Davis.

We left two weeks before the game, practicing the first week at Annapolis and the second week again in St. Augustine. While we were in Annapolis, we all went to the White House in Washington and met President John F. Kennedy. Nowadays, many teams get invited to the White House, usually because they've won some national or world championship, but back then it was a rarity. I can't remember who arranged our visit, but I remember it was a cold day, and President Kennedy came out on the steps of the White House in just his suit coat and talked to the team. He seemed to know a lot about Rip Engle and Joe Paterno when they both were at Brown. The President couldn't believe that we had beaten Navy so badly that year. The score was 41-7. But then someone informed him that it was the first game of the year and Roger Staubach had not yet become the starting quarterback for Navy, which he did shortly after our game. The White House took a couple of photos of us when we presented President Kennedy with a Penn State football, but, unfortunately, I'm not in the picture. It was quite a shock to all of us when the President was assassinated less than a year after we were with him. He seemed so vibrant and full of life.

Rocky Marciano And Al Davis – Another time that same week, a couple of the coaches and I went to the Red Horse Tavern or Café one evening in Annapolis and ran into Rocky Marciano in the bar. When he was the undefeated heavyweight champion world in the 1950s he was hero to a lot of kids and guys of my generation. We talked to him for about an hour, and he was very personable. I was amazed at how big boned he was, with thick wrists and hands. He said he weighed about 185 pounds when he fought and he now weighed 245 pounds and still looked trim. People say it is a small world and it sure was that night.

During the practice week in Florida before the game, Al Davis stopped by for a visit. He had just become the head coach and general manager of the Oakland Raiders after two years as an assistant coach with the Los Angeles Chargers. I had heard of him a few years earlier, because he had coached Donnie Caum, one of our players, in an All-Star game and Donnie had liked him as a coach. Davis was at our practice to try to sign our two All-Americans, Dave Robinson and halfback Roger Kaufman, for the new American Football League. Al was a very talkative young coach at the time and I remember getting upset with him because he kept telling our players that we would crush Florida and would beat them by four or five touchdowns. I also remember Dave Robinson telling me that one reason he decided to play in the NFL was that Al Davis had told him he would have a much better chance of playing in the AFL than the NFL. That tells you that sometimes a person can talk too much, and as the years passed, Davis lived up to his controversial reputation.

Eliminating Starting Blocks – Once a season was over back then, many head coaches and assistants went to coaching clinics around the country to learn things from other coaches. In February of 1963 I was at the Coach of the Year clinic being held at the William Penn Hotel in Pittsburgh and I ran into another young assistant coach I knew who had an idea that he thought would revolutionize football. I was standing in the hotel lobby with another coaching friend, John Hyder, when this assistant backfield coach at William and Mary, Lou Holtz, came by. "Rad," Lou said, "I've discovered that my backs can start quicker from a two-point stance than from a three-point stance." I said, "Lou, you're kidding." He said, "No, I'm not. I did it all year and they started quicker from a two-point stance than from a three-point stance." I said, "Lou, you've just changed the entire track world. In fact, you've just gotten rid of starting blocks. They're not needed anymore. You had better notify our Olympic team." Lou left and John asked, "Who was that?" I replied, "Just another one of my enthusiastic young coaching friends. What Lou probably meant was that his backs could execute their assignments better from a two-point rather than a three-point stance, which is a valid statement not only for backs but for wide receivers. But if you took what he actually said to be literally true, he would indeed have changed the track world." It was a unique and short conversation. Of course, Lou had a lot more ideas that worked and he became one of the most successful head coaches in college football.

Deaf Player Hears "Go" – One of the most unusual plays I've ever seen occurred on the first play from the line of scrimmage in our first game of the 1963 season at Oregon. After we returned the opening kickoff and lined up for the first play our halfback, Gary Klingensmith, went in motion. Then, before the snap of the ball, he suddenly took off and ran through both lines and deep into the Oregon secondary before anybody else in the field had moved. Now, Klingensmith was apparently the first totally deaf person to start on a major college football team, and being deaf, Gary was supposed to start when he saw the center snap the football. Of course we were penalized for offside. When Gary came out of the game, Rip Engle slowly asked him, "Gary, why did you start before the ball was snapped?" Gary, who communicated by reading lips, said. "I thought I heard somebody yell 'GO,'" and he laughed. And so did Rip. After the game, our sports information director Jim Tarman asked Gary why he had gone offside. Gary said, "Well, everyone is always asking you about that deaf player, so I decided it was time to let them know." The kid had a great sense of humor

After four straight years of going to a postseason bowl game, we stayed home in 1963 after finishing with a 7-3 record. We were in the Top Ten briefly after our first three games before back-to-back losses to Army, 10-7, and Syracuse, 9-0, knocked us down. We were still being mentioned for the Cotton, Gator and Bluebonnet bowls when we travelled to Pittsburgh for our traditional last game of the season. Pitt had lost only to unbeaten Navy and it appeared that the winner of our game would be invited to one of the bowls. But everything went haywire for all of us that Friday when President Kennedy was assassinated, and all the college football games were postponed for one week. The next week Pitt beat us 22-21 on a fake punt by Pitt fullback Rick Leeson for a long gain that led to the winning touchdown. It was one of the best games of our series, and one of Penn State's most disappointing losses, but the bowls had already made their arrangements and neither one of us made it to a bowl game.

1963 Ohio State Game & Dick Butkus – In the fall of 1963 in Columbus, we were playing Ohio State in the eighth game of the season. We were 5-2. They were 5-1-1, ranked No. 10 by the AP and heavily favored. The stars in their backfield were halfback Paul Warfield, a future NFL and college Hall of Famer, and fullback Matt Snell, later a star for the New York Jets in Super Bowl III. At the pregame breakfast, Ralph Baker, our captain and linebacker, and later starting linebacker for the Super Bowl III champion New York Jets, was reading the sports page of the Columbus paper and said in a skeptic voice, "Hey Rad, is this Butkus guy from Illinois any good? The papers keep raving about him." I said, "I don't know, but we've got film of him. (Ohio State and Illinois had tied 20-20 in the third game of the season.) We just show you players the last three games, but we look at all the films we can get. We brought the Ohio State Illinois game on the trip. We've got three hours before we get on the bus to go to the stadium. Would you like to look at it?" He said "yes," so I told him to get all the other linebackers to meet me in my room to watch the film.

I remember not having a take-up reel and letting the film from the projector drop into a wastebasket. Well, I told them Butkus' number and let the film roll. I didn't make any comments and just replayed a play when requested. When the film was over, and I was rewinding it, I said to Ralph Baker, "Well, what did you think of Butkus?" He said, "He's the best player I have ever seen. He's unbelievable." Butkus had 19 individual tackles in that 20-20 tie with Illinois. Well, that afternoon Penn State beat Ohio State 10-7, and Ralph Baker had 15 individual tackles and 12 assists for a total of 27. The moral of this story is, if you want your players to play well, show them films of Dick Butkus the morning of the game.

Ralph Baker (left) with Rip Engle

After four straight years of going to a postseason bowl game, we stayed home in 1963 after finishing with a 7-3 record. We were in the Top Ten briefly after our first three games before back-to-back losses to Army, 10-7, and Syracuse, 9-0, knocked us down. We were still being mentioned for the Cotton, Gator and Bluebonnet bowls when we travelled to Pittsburgh for our traditional last game of the season. Pitt had lost only to unbeaten Navy and it appeared that the winner of our game would be invited to one of the bowls. But everything went haywire for all of us that Friday when President Kennedy was assassinated, and all the college football games were postponed for one week. The next week Pitt beat us 22-21 on a fake punt by Pitt fullback Rick Leeson for a long gain that led to the winning touchdown. It was one of the best games of our series, and one of Penn State's most disappointing losses, but the bowls had already made their arrangements and neither one of us made it to a bowl game.

Evolving Into A New Defensive Scheme

One Of Woody Hayes' Worst Defeats Of All Time – The 1964 season
seemed like a disaster from the start when we lost our first three games and four of the first five by relatively close scores. We had an extraordinary number of fumbles and turnovers, and our offense just couldn't seem to do anything right. But we won our next two games, and in the eighth game we played undefeated Ohio State in

Columbus. Just like all three of our previous games in Columbus, Ohio State was heavily favored and once again ranked high in the polls at No. 2. I can remember Joe Paterno and me inviting John Hyder, a former head coach of Bishop Guilfoyle High School in Altoona, to sit with us in the press box. Two of John's former players were starting for us—tight end Bill Huber and cornerback Mike Irwin. On the first play from scrimmage, Mike stepped in front of the Ohio State receiver and dropped an interception that would have been a sure touchdown. Woody, who hated to pass, tried to surprise us but before the game Paterno had predicted Ohio State's first play would be a pass, and we were ready.

That first play must have been an omen of things to come, because we went on to give Woody Hayes the third worst beating of his entire coaching career. The Penn State offense controlled the ball the entire game. We won 27-0 and Ohio State didn't get a first down until picking up its first one on a penalty late in the third quarter. When the first team defense left the field for good in the middle of the fourth quarter, they had only played 38 plays and had held Ohio State to a total offense of minus 30 some yards. Ohio State ended up getting another 30 yards against our backup players. My three linebackers that day were middle linebacker Bob Kane and John Runnells and Bud Yost on the outside. I don't believe I ever had three linebackers play better than they did that day. However, the biggest star of the game was nose guard Glenn Ressler, who consistently drove the Ohio State center into his own backfield. Glenn definitely played like an All-American that day.

The Last Player Bowl Vote – Our upset of Ohio State stunned the football world and most people couldn't believe it when they first heard the score. We won our next two games and won the Lambert Trophy as the best team in the East, but in a players-only meeting our players voted down an invitation to the Gator Bowl. The seniors had a bad experience in the '62 Gator Bowl, not only in losing but in the housing accommodations on an isolated military base in Annapolis, and they also felt they already accomplished a lot by turning around the season and winning the Lambert Trophy. Glenn Ressler, our best player, also didn't want to go for personal reasons and that was a big influence on the rest of the team. It was a big disappointment for me because assistant coaches and their wives love to go to bowl games.

I also was disappointed because I felt by the end of the season, this 1964 team may have been the best in the country as well as the best Penn State team I had seen in my then 12 years as a player and coach. Nearly 50 years later, I feel the same way. But what Ressler and the seniors did by their vote, did not go down well with the athletic administration, and that was the last time the Penn State football players were given the right to vote on whether or not to go to a bowl game. Thereafter, the coaching staff and administration made all the decisions about the bowl games. Players would still vote but only to decide which bowl the players preferred. Even then, they could be overruled, and five years later the new procedure may have cost Penn State a chance at the national championship.

Con Job – While recruiting in the winter after the 1964 season, I learned another valuable lesson that would stay with me the rest of my life. I found a kid who I thought would be a very good player. He was a 6-foot-4, 235-pound offensive and defensive tackle from western Pennsylvania, and I thought he was as tough as nails. But when Joe Paterno heard about it, he warned me about recruiting players from this high school. He used to recruit that area and he told me that there were some deceptive people in the past in that school system. Joe said that didn't mean that I didn't have a real good player there but to be careful and investigate everything that I can. Well, I went into the high school at the same time my friend Augie Tammariello was recruiting there for William and Mary. The school gave us the principal's office to talk to the player since the principal wasn't there. I had the player strip down to his shorts. Augie asked me what I was doing? What was I looking for? I told him that Paterno had told me to be very careful, and I really didn't know what I was looking for. The kid looked all right to me and I told him to put his clothes back on.

Well, I gave him a full scholarship, and on the first day of freshmen practice in shorts and a T-shirt, no pads or helmet, he dislocated his shoulder in a walk-through. Historically, Earl Bruce, the freshmen head coach, would have the freshmen walk-through two trap plays, "4A" and "85B," the first day of practice. The kid came up to me later as I was walking off the varsity practice field and he was all worried that he was going to lose his scholarship. I told him he would not lose his scholarship, but I had to know the truth. He told me he had had problems his entire senior year, and that in one game his left shoulder dislocated eight times and the right shoulder dislocated three times. He said that the principal, the coach, his father and the doctor told him not to say anything when he was being recruited. On his physical papers, which the high school team doctor signed, it said "slight separation," which is like saying he had a scratch in high school. He asked me to have Penn State fix his shoulders because he knew he could play. I told him to have his dad or his high school fix his shoulders. Anybody who could play a football game in which his shoulders dislocated 11 times was certainly tough enough to play, but we had already wasted enough money on him.

The kid ended up doing odd jobs around the football office like cutting out newspaper clippings for our head recruiter. I don't want to mention his name because he turned out to be a good guy. He got his degree and became a big supporter of the Penn State football team. So, I learned that even if you're warned of a con job, you can still get conned.

Pioneer Ranch – It was obvious that Joe Paterno was a pretty smart guy, and I want to tell you one thing about him that I don't believe anyone really knows until now. He's the man who started the summer training camps for high school and junior high school players that have become so popular around the nation in the last 40-50 years. It was way back in 1961 when Lou Hanna, the head coach of Cory High School, told Joe that he had a ninth grade son who was going to be his T-formation quarterback. Lou was a single-wing coach and knew nothing about the

T. Lou told Joe he would give him $100 if Joe would coach his kid for one week on how to be a T quarterback. Joe essentially said, "Lou, if you, as a coach, are willing to give me $100 to teach your kid, maybe a lot of parents would be willing to do that." And that's how those two started the first private football camp—then known as The Joe Paterno Quarterbacks, Receivers and Centers camp—at Pioneer Ranch in Cooks Forest, about 132 miles northwest of State College. The owner of the camp was Roy Van Horn, who became a rabid Penn State fan because of the camp.

I first went to coach at the camp for the first two sessions in June 1965. Each session lasted six days, and I picked a nice shady spot where I held my drills for the centers. On Friday of the second session, the 13th day, one of my legs swelled up so that it was fatter at the ankle than it was at the knee. When I woke up the next morning, the other leg swelled the same way, and I had two fat swollen lower legs. I thought I had ptomaine poisoning or something bad. The doctor in the Tyrone Hospital emergency room said that I had so many mosquito bites from the knee on down that the combined poison had caused the swelling, and that it would be gone in a day. It was, but it had sure given me a scare.

Evolving Into The Multiple Defense That Helped Change Penn State Defensive Football – A few years later, I was involved with Joe Paterno and the rest of our football staff in changing how our team played defense. Most fans watching football know very little about the fine points of the game itself. They watch the quarterback and the running backs and they may know what a blitz and a screen pass are but they have no idea what a "cover two" is even when they hear broadcasters talk about it. In reality, the offensive and defensive schemes and idiosyncrasies can be complicated unless you are really into it. So, I will try to simplify what I am about to tell you about a defensive alignment that I originally suggested in the spring of 1965 that Joe modified that changed our defense.

In the early 1960s, most teams used one of a variety of basic defenses. One was a 4-3-4 that used four down linemen, three linebackers and four defensive backs. Another basic defense was a 3-4-4 with three down linemen, four linebackers and four defensive backs. A third defense was a 5-3-3 that used five down linemen, three linebackers and three defensive backs. This 5-3-3 was our prime defense in 1964. We played this defense with a type of zone coverage called rotate, which we officially called State Rotate. In this defense, the two linemen on the outside were normally called ends but we called them "Heroes" because we played them like strong safeties. The outside linebackers were called "Lefty" and "Rocky." This was basically the defense we used to win our last five games in 1964, including our big upset over Ohio State, 27-0.

The problem with using this State Rotate defense in 1965 was the fact that our All-American nose guard, Glenn Ressler, was graduating and we had no one to replace him. I knew that Notre Dame had a very good defense in '64, playing a 4-4-3 defense that Notre Dame defensive coordinator John Ray had copied from Johns Hopkins, a small college in Baltimore.

So, in the offseason before spring practice in 1965, I played around with the notion of combining our 5-3 rotate defense with the Johnny Ray's 4-4. Simply, by having a player who could be a down lineman, or nose guard, in the 5-3 and a linebacker in the 4-4, we could play the 4-4 without changing pass assignments in rotate coverage. Notre Dame played their 4-4 with a type of man to man coverage. Under my suggested scheme, we could also easily shift to any basic defensive alignment in football, like the 4-3, 6-1, and 3-4, etc. By having a player play both as a down lineman and also be a linebacker (Jim Kates 1967-69), we could play a true completely multiple alignment defense with very little changes in coverage assignments, regardless of the coverage—man-to-man, zone or rotate zone.

I was excited about this multiple concept and the 4-4-3 rotate defense and presented it to the coaching staff in a meeting we had before '65 spring practice. The coaching staff also seemed enthused. Rip Engle told me to work out all the alignment adjustments and split rules that would have to be made against different formations, like a double wing or a wide slot to one side or three wide receivers to one side, etc. I worked on it an entire weekend and had 10 full pages written to present to the staff at the Monday meeting. As soon as the Monday meeting started,

Jim Kates down lineman and linebacker

Jim O'Hora and Joe Paterno presented a 6-2-3 defense that Nebraska played that Jim and Joe had studied over the weekend. It was decided that this was what we were going to play, and I asked what about the multiple 4-4-3 defense that I had presented. Rip glanced at the 10 pages I had given him and said, "Danny this has too many pages. We could never learn all this anyway."

Well, 1965 turned out to be Rip's last season as the head coach. For a couple of years he had talked about retiring when he was 60 years old and March 6, 1966 would be his 60th birthday. We thought we'd have a pretty good season, but we started out with three losses in our first four games just like in '64. This time there was no miracle ending and we finished with a 5-5 record.

UCLA's Helmet Telephone – Something happened in our 1965 game against UCLA at Beaver Stadium that tells you how far some coaches will go to win. It's an example of how a coach will distort the spirit of a rule for his own advantage and says a lot about his integrity because it is really cheating. UCLA had a new coach, Tommy Prothro, who had taken Oregon State to the Rose Bowl the previous season. UCLA was a pretty good team with an excellent sophomore quarterback, Gary

Beban, who would win the Heisman Trophy two years later. We both had lost to the same team, Michigan State, in our season opening game, and UCLA had a week off before playing us. (Michigan State would go on to share the national championship with Alabama that season.) As our UCLA game progressed, our offense struggled, giving up a 10 points on a pair of fumbles, and UCLA had a 24-7 lead late in the third quarter. That's when Rip Engle was approached by a man with a walkie-talkie that was used by the Beaver Stadium parking lots. Although the game was continuing on the field, the man asked Rip to listen to the walkie-talkie. Rip was surprised to hear a UCLA coach talking to Gary Beban, who was in the game.

It turned out that the walkie-talkie frequency used by Penn State's traffic and parking people was also being used by UCLA to call plays for their quarterback. An assistant coach in the press box would see what defenses we were running and then give the quarterback an audible to call. Once the play started, the assistant would even tell Beban when to run when his receivers were covered or which receivers to throw to. That was how Beban scored a touchdown on a six-yard rollout near the end of the first half.

But there wasn't much we could do because we didn't think there was a rule against it. After the game we learned there was an obscure NCAA rule that stated, "There shall be no direct communication from the sideline with players on the field," but it only brought a five-yard penalty. Anyhow, Rip gave the walkie-talkie to his friend who was Rip's guest on the sideline and the president of Corning Glass Co. Rip's friend listened to the UCLA coach the rest of the game. A few years later the NCAA barred the use of phones in helmets, and, of course, the NFL would one day allow receivers in quarterback helmets. Despite what I still believe was quite unethical by UCLA, we almost rallied to win the game, but fell two points short in the last minute, losing 24-22.

It was typical of Rip's class not to say anything about the walkie-talkie incident after the game, but sportswriters found out about it the next day. At first, Prothro denied knowing about their technological advantage but later admitted he approved of it. We never trusted UCLA or Prothro again. Two years later at our next home game with UCLA, I had to leave the press box to go down on the field to be an alternate defensive signal caller with defensive coach Jim O'Hora because we were afraid of UCLA stealing O'Hora's defensive signals. Some of the signals Jim sent in were phony while I was sending the real signals. We still lost again but it was close, 17-15, and the key play was a blocked punt UCLA recovered for a touchdown. UCLA was No. 3 in the country at the time, but that was the last game Penn State would lose for three years.

One more thing, the UCLA assistant coach calling the shots for Gary Beban in 1965 was a one-time Georgia Tech quarterback named Pepper Rodgers. In the 1969 Orange Bowl Rogers was the head coach at Kansas when Penn State came from behind in the last minute to win the game 15-14, and finish No. 2 in the nation. I guess the football Gods always get their revenge.

Rip's Last Year – That 1965 was a sentimental season for me because it was the last one with Rip Engle as my head coach. Rip was a great guy who was originally a mentor and became a good friend. I know he thought Bad Rad was a little crazy when I played for him, but after coaching for him Rip learned I was just different. Remember, Rip had kicked me off the team before the Penn game in 1955, let me back on the next week and eventually hired me five years later as a full time assistant coach.

I guess, as people have said all my life, I just marched to my own drummer. Without Rip, Joe Paterno and the other Penn State coaches, I never would have become the first professor of Linebacker" U and maybe there wouldn't even be a Linebacker U today—at least at Penn State. Thank you Rip, and God rest your soul.

Dick Anderson and Rip Engle

CHAPTER NINE - Joe Paterno Era Begins

New Head Coach – Right after the 1965 season I decided to leave Penn State and Joe Paterno tried to talk me out of it. Then one Friday in mid February, Joe saw me in the hallway near the football offices in Rec Hall and said, "Danny, are you still going to leave?" I said, "Joe, as soon as I can swing it. I'm out of here." He said, "Rip's retiring. It's going to be announced Sunday. I'm the new head coach." I said, "Congratulations." He said, "If I get you a $2,200 raise will you stay?" I said, "I'm here." I was making $7,800, and $2,200 would put me at it an even $10,000 a year. But wouldn't you know it; I almost got fired before I could earn a penny of that new money. On Monday, Joe had his first staff meeting at one o'clock, but I went to the student union building over the noon hour and forgot about the meeting. I walked into the football office at two o'clock and the meeting was just breaking up. Bad Rad moment. Of course, I apologized and caught some hell for missing Joe's first staff meeting, but I was grateful that he didn't throw me out of there on his first day as the head coach.

Fort Rad – While 1966 is known in Penn State football for being Joe Paterno's first year as the head coach, it also was the year I built "Fort Rad." As I have written, I have been pretty well known for my quirkiness, but when I started to do some landscaping at my house in 1966 I had no idea the project would become a lifetime symbol of my eccentric personality. It all started with my decision to fix up the front yard of my three-bedroom ranch house because of Paterno rehiring me for his new staff. I now felt my family would be at Penn State for a number of years in the near future, and the $2,200 raise enabled me to make some improvements on our home.

We lived a couple of miles west of the campus, along a country road in a small housing development of about 12 houses called Circleville. We had a short sloping driveway leading off the road to our integrated garage and I decided to build a retaining wall along the road in the front yard and up the driveway to the garage. There were a few stones piled up in the nearby farm fields that had been cleared, so I used those stones for my wall, stacking and cementing them into two 30-foot long, 10-foot high retaining walls. I was then going to get two or three truckloads of top soil to level off the front yard to the top of the retaining walls but I realized if I did that I would have a 10-foot drop off in my front yard that would be dangerous to my children. Now about this time in the late spring and early summer, some Penn State football players came by, saw what I was doing and started teasing me about "Fort Rad."

Well, as I worked throughout the summer, I knocked down the two walls to three feet high, and then terraced the yard by building four more 3-foot high, 30-foot long walls behind the original walls. Then I filled in the area behind the walls with top soil and my wife and my mother planted flowers, shrubs and pine trees. I guess that made the property even look more like a fort because the nickname stuck, and even today, players and others who were around the football program then still laughingly refer to my former house on Circleville Road as "Fort Rad."

Now, I didn't build the walls myself. Joe Paterno had kept all of Rip's staff and added Bob Phillips, who had been coaching Montour High School in suburban Pittsburgh, to fill the vacancy created by Joe's promotion to head coach. Bob spent his spring and summer helping me and even recruited some of his coaching friends to work with us. Later Bob ended up with back problems which he blamed on his work on my stone walls.

Anyway, if you are ever in the State College area, drive through Circleville and you can see for yourself those terraced stone walls in front of the house known forever in Penn State football as "Fort Rad."

Second Multiple Defense Presentation – Shortly after Bob Phillips had joined our staff we were having a staff meeting before spring practice, when I again brought up the multiple front defense that I had presented the year before. Once again, everyone seemed to like it, especially Joe. But once again, it got shot down. Jim O'Hora said we had to decide if we were going to be basically an odd defense— meaning a defensive lineman on the center—or an even defense—with no lineman on the center. I had no answer since I wanted to do both. Well, it was finally decided that we would play a basic 5-2 defense that's called a "34" defense nowadays. I had been voted down again. I was a little surprised because I thought Joe might be a little daring in his first year as the head coach but as the year evolved Paterno was pretty conservative. However, Joe did like a couple of my ideas.

Preseason Recruiting – A few years earlier I had suggested to Rip Engle and the staff that we should change the starting dates of our two-week preseason staff meetings from August 15 to August 1 and ending August 14. Since we started preseason practice September 1, I felt this would free us up for two weeks, starting August 15, to visit high school preseason football camps, which started August 15, and evaluate and recruit players. I believed if eight assistant coaches visited 10 schools each in this two week period, we'd reach 80 teams and over 100 prospects that could be evaluated, figuring at least one prospect per school. Well, Rip vacationed at Cape Cod until August 14 so that ended that idea. But as soon as Joe became head coach he implemented my proposal. I don't remember how many players we recruited, if any, from these efforts, but I do believe it helped us avoid a lot of mistakes. The success of Penn State's recruiting in Joe's first two years attests to this, when we recruited such future stars as Dennis Onkotz, Jim Kates, Pete Johnson and others.

Best Players Always As Linebackers – In Joe's first year as head coach in 1966, my starting linebackers in our 5-2 defense were not nearly the athletes in all-around athletic ability that I had in previous years—especially in 1964 when we had an outstanding defense with linebackers with great speed like John Runnels and Bud Yost. I can remember bugging Joe about this one day in '66 when I placed a newspaper clipping on his desk that stated something like, "The University of

Tennessee Volunteers always puts its best athlete (except for quarterback) at the middle linebacker position." I don't know what impression that made on Joe, if any, but I do know that he made a major statement to me concerning our defensive personnel late in our game with UCLA that season about everyone playing defense the next spring. (See Below) And what he said that day at UCLA definitely had a positive impact on the future ability of our linebackers and the evolution and history of Linebacker U.

Formation Change – Joe made another change from what Rip had done when he switched our offense from the Wing-T to the I-formation. He believed it was the best way to use the talents of our running backs and quarterback.

Joe Paterno's 1st Game As Head Coach – I doubt that Joe Paterno's first win in his first game as a head coach over Maryland, 15-7, on September 19, 1966 is celebrated every year in the Paterno household, but it is in mine. That's because my daughter Leslie was born on that day. Yes, the one named after that Alabama player's girlfriend at the 1959 Liberty Bowl. Also one of the players that I personally coached was Mike Reid. Mike was a sophomore linebacker playing in his first game. Freshmen were ineligible in those years but we put Mike on the first team the first day of spring practice of his freshman year because we obviously thought he was a great prospect. In all my 17 years at Penn State, Mike made the first-team sooner than any other player. Later, we switched him to defensive tackle and he won the Maxwell Award in 1969 as the nation's outstanding player and the Outland Award as the nation's outstanding lineman. Mike had an outstanding game against Maryland. Six of our points were the result of three safeties and Mike was responsible for the first two and almost the third one on the last play of the game. It was an indication of how good he was going to be in the future.

The next week we travelled to Michigan State to play the defending co-national champions and we were clobbered, 42-8, scoring our only touchdown late in the fourth quarter against their reserves. Then we came home and looked horrible in losing to Army, 11-0, as we gave up four fumbles and three interceptions in game that had been rated a toss-up.

Athletic Director's Threat To Fire Joe Paterno – I was leaving the press box after the Army game when Ernie McCoy, the athletic director, said loud and clear and probably for my benefit: "If we don't get rid of that I-formation by next week, we'll be having a new head coach." Well, I thought this might be serious and told George Welsh, the other young assistant on our coaching staff, and we both decided we'd better tell Joe. So we did. Joe said McCoy was right about the I-formation but he wasn't going to let McCoy think that he, McCoy, was running the team, so we were going to stay with the "I" for one more week before we got rid of it. Meanwhile, he went to see McCoy, and yelled at him about scaring his young coaches, and he got an apology from Dean McCoy.

But Joe changed his mind before we played Boston College at home and switched back to the Wing-T. He also switched quarterbacks, putting in junior Tom Sherman, who had been playing mostly as a defensive back. It worked as Sherman led us from a 15-8 halftime deficit to a 30-21 victory.

The Moment Joe Paterno Started To Become A Great Coach – However, the next week we got killed again at UCLA, 42-11, and they rubbed our noses into the ground by making a successful onside kick with just 38 seconds left in the game. I was standing on the sideline next to Joe about the time that happened when he turned to me and said, "Danny look at that scoreboard. Never again will you see that scoreboard act like a pinball machine against us. Next spring practice, everybody plays defense."

I was a little stunned. I wondered exactly what he was talking about. It all became clear after the 1967 season, and in retrospect, I believe this may have been the most momentous decision Joe ever made. This was the true birth of Linebacker U.

The following week we beat West Virginia, 38-6, but our up and down season continued to the end and we finished a mediocre 5-5. For the first two weeks of the next spring practice, everybody except starting quarterback Tom Sherman played defense. Defense became the cornerstone of Paterno's teams and our best athletes would play defense first unless they were absolutely vital to our offense. And for the next three years we were 30-2-1—and undefeated in the last two of those seasons—with a defense some consider to be one of the best to ever play in college football. That defense turned Penn State into one of the elite football powers in college football. And being the defensive linebacker coach wasn't bad for my career, either.

Do It Again – I have one other vivid memory of that 1966 team and it occurred during practice. We had been struggling all year on defense, but freshman halfback Charlie Pittman was playing on the scout team and frequently running through our first team defense for big gains. After every big gain, either I or one of the other defensive coaches would yell, "Run it again." When we ran it again, Charlie always would get stuffed at or behind the line of scrimmage. One day, after about the 10th time that we said run it again, six guys hit Charlie at the line of scrimmage. He came back to the huddle and said, "Man, that's the best 'second time around team' I've ever seen." In addition to helping our defense that year, I believe those drills helped Charlie become a great running back and Paterno's first All-American tailback in his senior season.

Defensive Spring Practice – When Joe told me late in the 1966 UCLA game that "next spring, everybody plays defense" he meant it, and it became a reality in the spring of 1967. We had 20 practice days in the spring, and for the first 10 practices, every player except the starting quarterback played defense for at least half of those 10 sessions. This required a fairly complex practice schedule to achieve. During the 1966 season, we assistant coaches had a meeting with Joe and requested that he make up the practice schedule by himself. These meetings to make up the schedule had involved the whole staff's participation and took up a lot of time. Lucky for us, by agreeing to do the practice schedules himself, Joe now had to get up at five in the morning to have the practice schedule done for our 9 a.m. meeting. It also meant no evening staff meetings after practice ever again for the assistant coaches. The only problem we had with the "everybody played defense" scheme was that our backup quarterback, sophomore Chuck Burkhart, looked like he was going to be a starting corner on defense. It took a lot of convincing by quarterback coach George Welsh and Paterno to talk Burkhart into giving up being a starting corner. That was one of the best moves Paterno ever made. When Chuck became the starting quarterback in 1968, he proceeded to win every game for the rest of his career, leading our great undefeated 1968 and 1969 teams

Going With Experience – At the end of spring practice in 1967 and during the first few weeks of fall practice, the coaching staff realized that a number of our young players were better athletes than our veterans. We discussed making a number of changes about who the starters should be, but although Joe agreed that the younger players were better, he did not want to lose his first game of the season because of inexperience and rookie mistakes. He even quoted another great coach George Allen, who was then head coach of the Los Angeles Rams, on the subject of "rookies." One of Allen's most famous quotes was, "For every first-year player you start, you lose a game." Another was, "Rookies have no place in the starting lineup of an NFL team."

We had installed a number of new defensive coverage's that fall. Joe had worked on designing those coverage's during the summer—cover 2 zone, cover 2 man, half coverage, 4 mini, etc. Joe had also decided to play the 4-4 alignment, similar to what Notre Dame did, with the cover 2 man coverage. We called this defense 6 short, and used it basically on a passing down. Otherwise, we were still basically a 5-2 monster, or rover, defense.

We lost the opening game to Navy, 23-22. Navy had about 550 yards in rushing, passing and return yardage in total offense, which was the most in the country that day. That meant, statistically, we had the worst defense in the country, but still only lost by one point. We made two basic changes for our next opponent, Miami. First, we went to the 4-4 with rotate coverage that we called 6 rotate, which was the same defense that I had suggested and the staff had rejected the previous two years, and adjusted all the other basic alignments by having a player who could play either a down linemen position or a linebacker position. For the next three years, this player was Jim Kates and in 1970 and 1971 it was Gary Gray. The second change was to play the young 10 or 11 sophomores—or "rookies"—who were better athletes than our veterans. Joe decided to do this gradually during the first quarter of the game, putting them in one or two at a time. It was a night game in the heat and dreaded humidity in Miami's Orange Bowl and Miami was an 11 point favorite. It also drizzled throughout the game but our kids didn't let any of the weather conditions bother them. A great 50-yard punt return by Bobby Campbell set up a touchdown reception by Ted Kwalick that gave us a 6-0 lead at half time and we dominated the second half, scoring after a 90-yard drive. Miami didn't score until we muffed a punt in the last 30 seconds of the game and we won, 17-8. We didn't know it at the time, but this game—and our revolutionary defense—started a new era of winning football at Penn State. Joe said later the victory saved his coaching career and he credited our great defense, Campbell's punt return and Kwalick's nine pass receptions with turning the season around.

Crowd Cheering A Loss – The next week at Beaver Stadium we played undefeated UCLA, which was averaging 37 points a game with Gary Beban still at quarterback. UCLA won, 17-15. They scored one touchdown off a blocked punt late in the third quarter and another in the fourth after recovering our fumble at our 29-yard line, and then recovered our onside kick with one minute left to seal the game. That's when a strange phenomenon occurred. At the time, we didn't dress at the stadium's small home team locker room and had to take a bus to our football facility a half mile away. As soon as our game was over, all 46,000 fans in Beaver Stadium stood and cheered and kept cheering for the 10 or 15 minutes it took for our players to get on the bus, and they were still cheering as the buses left the stadium. I've never seen anything like that before or since. That was on October 7, 1967. Penn State didn't lose another game until they lost to Colorado on September 26, 1970.

We finished the '67 regular season with an 8-2 record, and in the next chapter I'll tell you about the great North Carolina State game and what my linebackers did that gave us our first national exposure. We went to the Gator Bowl to play Florida State, and it was here that Joe really grabbed the headlines with another of his "momentous" decisions—one that backfired but brought him instant recognition as a daring young coach.

When In Doubt, Punt! – Florida State had won seven straight to wind up 7-2-1 and, as one of the highest scoring teams in the nation, averaging 36.2 points a game, they were favored by several points. But in the first half, our offense moved the ball well and the defense came up with interceptions that stopped one Florida State threat near the goal line and another setting up a touchdown for us late in the second quarter. That gave us a surprising 17-0 lead at halftime. Midway through the third quarter our defense made another tremendous goal line stand at the 3-yard line, but after three plays we had a fourth-and-six inches near our own 15 with 5:30 left in the quarter. Now came Joe's momentous decision. Instead of punting, we tried a quarterback sneak.

We didn't make it, and two plays later, Florida State receiver Ron Sellers caught a touchdown pass. They kicked off, we fumbled the ball and they recovered. On third down, a Florida State back swung out of the backfield on our right side. Our linebacker, Dennis Onkotz, had him on man for man coverage but saw the quarterback looking inside and jumped the curl. The quarterback passed to the linebacker's man swinging wide and he ran to the 1-yard line. They scored on a quarterback sneak. The score was now 17-14 and we're hanging on for our lives.

With 15 seconds left in the game, Florida State had the ball again on a fourth-and-four at our 9-yard line. Their head coach, Bill Peterson, who had played for a tie with Alabama earlier in the year, had been asked during the previous week if he would do the same thing if the situation occurred in the Gator Bowl. He had replied, "No way. The reason I did it against Alabama was that a conference championship was at stake." When he sent a kicker out to tie the game, his star receiver, Ron Sellers, was so upset that he would not leave the game. A bunch of their players had to drag him off the field. The kick was good and the game ended 17-17.

Coach Paterno got a ton of mail concerning his decision to go for it on fourth-and-one. Someone sent him the sign, "When in doubt, punt," which was displayed prominently on the secretary's desk for the next couple of years.

Scissors In The Glove Compartment – I'm not going to go into much detail about our undefeated '68 and '69 seasons because if I wrote about all of my memories in those two years I would need another book. But I do have to tell you about an unusual off-field incident early in the fall of '68 when Nancy was expecting our fourth child.

One day, a physical education professor named Benny Amato burst into our staff meeting in the football office all excited. Benny had just delivered his wife's baby in the back seat of his car that he had parked on the side of the road that led to the hospital in Bellefonte. Benny only had one good eye. The other is a glass eye. As he described it, "I'm holding the baby and I don't know what to do about the umbilical cord. So I bit it off and the blood squirts in my good eye and I can't see. I'm blind and I'm holding our newborn baby in the back seat of my car. I am in total panic." Well, somehow he got his vision back, the police came and escorted them to the hospital and everything was fine.

Now, with Nancy due to have our baby shortly, I had asked my next door neighbor Chuck Edmondson if he would take Nancy to the hospital if I was out of town scouting an opponent. Chuck had just taken his wife to the hospital to have their newborn child and he knew the Amato story. So, I told Chuck that if he had to pull over before he gets to the hospital, a pair of scissors will be in the glove compartment to cut the umbilical cord. Well, the baby came when I was out of town one week after Chuck's wife had delivered. Chuck got Nancy into my car, checked the glove compartment, saw the scissors there and drove in a panic straight to the hospital. When he went to check in my wife, the check in nurse said, "Weren't you just here last week?" Chuck replied "Yeah that was my wife. This is my neighbor," and that's when my youngest daughter Lori was born.

Multiple Defense—"Undefeated" – Our multiple defense that showed so much promise in 1967 really came alive in 1968 and I think we surprised everyone by going undefeated. This was the first year that we had practiced the multiple defense all spring and all preseason and we played exceptional defense all fall. We had only one close game in the regular season when our old nemesis, Army, almost upset us at Beaver Stadium, but Kwalick scored a touchdown by running back an onside kick late in the fourth quarter and we won, 28-24. That put us into the Orange Bowl, Penn State's first New Year's Day bowl game since the 1947 team played in the Cotton Bowl, and we were matched against the Big 8 champions from Kansas, coached by Pepper Rogers. Kansas had only lost once and was the highest scoring team in the nation, averaging 38 points per game, while our defense had given up just 10.6 points per game, so just about everyone predicted a close game. And it was.

Goal-Line Stand—12 Man Defense – For reasons I can't remember, I didn't play the normal starting right outside linebacker, Pete Johnson in the first half. I'm sure glad I played him in the second half. With 10 minutes left in the game, Kansas was leading 14-7 and had the ball fourth-and-one at our five-yard line. A field goal would make it 17-7, and probably ice the game. But they didn't kick! They lined up in a normal two-back formation, handed the ball to John Riggins, a future NFL Hall of Famer, going off their left side. Pete Johnson, our right outside linebacker, aligned in a down position on Kansas' left side tight end, took the tight end straight back, came off him and hit Riggins just below his midsection, taking him backwards and putting him on his back. I guess only Pepper Rogers knows why he didn't kick the field goal. He probably figured no one could stop Riggins for less than one yard. Well, Pepper figured wrong.

We took over the ball but had to punt, and for the next eight minutes neither team could move the ball much. With about two minutes remaining we had to punt, giving Kansas the ball at its own 38-yard line. All they had to do to win was pick up a first down but thanks to a couple of great plays for losses by Mike Reid, we forced Kansas to punt on a fourth-and-23 from their own 25-yard line. We put on a 10-man rush and Neal Smith partially blocked the punt and it went out of bounds at the 50. Chuck Burkhart hit Bob Campbell on a long pass route out of the backfield and down the left hash mark to the 3-yard line. Two plays gained little, and with 20 seconds left, we called a scissors run by Charlie Pittman up the middle. Before the center snap, Burkhart saw the middle was crowded with an extra linebacker and decided to fake the scissors to Pittman, keeping the ball and running around left end for the touchdown.

Chuck actually scored on a play that we've never run, a scissors keep. We went for two and threw an incomplete pass to the right side. I've heard that half the TV audience then turned off their TV sets, believing Kansas had won, 14-13. But Kansas was penalized for 12 men on the field. Bob Campbell then ran around left end to score the two extra points and we won, 15-14. Afterwards, the official told Joe Paterno said he spotted the 12 men right away. Later, the film showed that Kansas had had 12 men on the field for four straight plays. Burkhart had scored a touchdown on the scissors keep against 12 men, and it took the officials four plays to spot the 12th man. Paterno asked George Welsh and me why we didn't spot the 12th man from the press box. I said, "Hell Joe, we were too busy cheering."

Athletic Grievance Board – For years, some sportswriters and other folks with an agenda of their own have occasionally tried to drum up support for a union for college football players. Frankly, I think that would be a big mistake but this isn't the place to go into that debate. Ever since I began playing football in high school I've heard players complain about their coaches. It's just natural. Sometimes the complaints are legitimate but most of the time the players are just bitching for their own selfish reasons that usually conflicts with what the coaches believe is best for the team. Because I've always had empathy for the players and their complaints, especially on the college level, I almost got sucked into an inappropriate situation while we were having spring practice in 1969.

One day I received a phone call from my former economics 500 professor from the MBA program six years earlier, Dr. William Martin. He was in the process of trying to set up some sort of either college athletic player union or a sounding board or faculty grievance committee that the athletes could air their gripes against the coaches. I wasn't clear then, and I'm not clear now, exactly what it was about. It sure sounded fishy to me, but I agreed to talk to him. I told him 11 a.m. was the best time to meet and I promised him I would not tell anyone about our meetings.

We had at least three meetings in which he grilled me for information about the athletic department. Each time we met I had to leave a football staff meeting. I would tell Joe, "I've got an important meeting at 11 o'clock. I can't tell you what it's about or who it's with, but it's important. Can I go?" Joe would look at me kind of funny like and say, "Okay, sure go."

At the third meeting, the professor asked me if it would be better to talk to Joe Paterno or Gene Wettstone, our outstanding gymnastic coach, about his idea for this grievance committee—or whatever it was—for athletes. I had no idea what Wettstone thought and told the professor that Joe would be a great guy to talk to because he was acceptable to new ideas, etc. So I set up a meeting for Joe and Dr. Martin to have lunch together at the Nittany Lion Inn. When I saw Joe in the locker room before practice later that afternoon, he started to yell at me for having him talk to my professor. I said, "Hold on, he wanted to talk to you or Wettstone. This athletic grievance committee sounded scary and I thought it would be better if you knew about it." Anyway, Joe told me that he told Dr. Martin he would fight him every step of the way. I can just imagine what Joe actually said to him, but we never heard about that athletic grievance committee again.

4-Point Stance Versus 3-Point Stance – In the summer of '69 I was with a young guy who would one day become one of the famous line coaches in the NFL. I was in Pittsburgh coaching at a day camp for high school players in the Pittsburgh area and sitting in the camp's hospitality room listening to two of the camp coaches, Steve Petro an old-timer from Pitt, and Joe Bugel, a young coach from Western Kentucky. They were discussing an offensive guard's ability to pull from both a 4- and a 3-point stance. Joe's offensive linemen at Western Kentucky all played in a 4-point stance and he said that a guard could pull just as well from a 4-point stance as he could from a 3-point stance. Steve Petro said he couldn't. Joe said he could prove it because he had a highlight film of his season and the left guard could pull as well as anyone. Well, Joe turned the highlight film on and, sure enough, the left guard was an excellent player and an outstanding puller. When the film got to about the fourth or fifth game of the season, I said, "Both of you are crazy. The left guard is a great puller, but he's the only guy on the line in a 3-point stance." The film proved that this was the case for the entire season. Joe Bugel later became the offensive line coach for the famous Super Bowl Washington Redskins Hogs—who did not play from a four-point stance—and then a head coach for the Phoenix Cardinals and Oakland Raiders.

Bill Belichick – Coach Bill Belichick of the New England Patriots is a household name in the football world nowadays but when I met him more than forty years ago, I could never have imagined that he would become a famous pro football coach and one of his Patriot protégés, Bill O'Brien, would one day succeed Joe Paterno as the head coach of Penn State.

In late June or early July of 1969, George Welsh, who had been a great quarterback at the Naval Academy, asked me if I would coach for a week at the Naval Academy camp for underclass high school and junior high football players held at Messiah College near Harrisburg. The camp was run by Steve Belichick, who was Navy's chief football scout, and Jack Cloud, a linebacker coach at Navy. I coached the centers both for long snapping and for blocking. We coached the players, three times a day for five or six days. I had about 10 centers to coach. One of them was Steve's son, Bill, who wanted to learn how to long snap and block so that he could start for his high school team.

Bill wasn't very big, but he was the best player in the group skill wise. I can remember having him drive a defender who was holding a shield up a slight hill time after time. At that age, he was very personable, asked a lot of questions and did not have that "Doctor Death" personality he's now noted for. I enjoyed coaching him because he was very eager to learn. His dad became a good friend and I used see him every year at the American Football Coaches Association Convention. At the time I coached his son I had quit smoking for two years and was running six to 10 miles a day, so every time Steve would see me he would say "the runner." Someday, I intend to visit the football library that Steve and his son established at the Naval Academy. Bill ended up captain of his high school team, and, as we now know, went on to be an assistant coach with the Super Bowl Champion New York Giants and a future Hall of Fame head coach with all those Super Bowl teams in New England.

As to Bill O'Brien, I had a chance to meet him a few days after he was hired in January of 2012 and we had a brief conversation during which I mentioned my old connections with Bill Belichick. O'Brien seemed like a bright guy and from all I've heard he has a great football mind. It's tough succeeding a legend, as Alabama found out when Bear Bryant died. My old coach and friend, Joe Paterno, may have been the greatest college coach of all time. Joe and Bill O'Brien have a connection because they both played football at Brown University, so I guess that theory of "six degrees of separation" in life is proven again with me, Paterno, Belichick and O'Brien.

CHAPTER TEN –
The Phi Beta Kappas Of Linebacker U

In 1965, the NCAA finally changed the substitution rules and brought sanity back to the game by instituting unlimited substitution and eliminating all the quirky rules that drove coaches and players nuts. That meant players could be specialists in offense, defense and even special teams. Unlimited substitution was really not new. It had been part of football before 1953, but a lot of players were so good they played both ways, and some teams had so few players on their rosters that they had to play an entire game. In 1953, the rule makers decided to restrict the number of times players could go in and out a game. That meant players were forced to play both offense and defense. However, the NCAA tinkered with the rules just about every year and it became complicated and confusing to all of us. But in '65 unlimited substitution returned and it has never gone back. Since then, with very rare exceptions, the day of the great 60 minute players was over.

The new rules not only affected how we coached players but also the type of player we recruited. We have always been on the lookout for kids who were outstanding athletes, but now we began to focus on different skills and abilities because each position was different. Playing center on offense required one set of parameters and being a linebacker on defense had another. While we were scouring the high schools that fall looking for kids who fit our mold, there was a player on the freshman team who had the potential to be a big-time linebacker but was being used as a fullback.

Mike Reid, Lineman And Linebacker – Mike Reid had been a standout fullback and kicker at nearby Altoona High School, and with unlimited substitution now in place, that's where he started on the freshmen team. But at 6-foot-3, 235-pounds, Mike was quick, fast and agile and had a natural sense for going after the ball, just the type of linebacker I liked. When spring practice rolled around, I played him some at linebacker, but Joe Paterno, who was now our new head coach, moved him to middle guard, and he became an immediate starter. He proved why in our opening game against Maryland when he was credited in Penn State records with three safeties, including a blocked punt, as we won 15-7. I've been told no player in college football has ever made three safeties in one game, but there is no official NCAA record listed in that category. However, my co-author, Lou Prato, did some research on this, talking to the NCAA and even looking at the game film. From what he saw on the game film, he said Mike should not have been credited with

Mike Reid

the last safety when the quarterback threw away the ball from deep in the end zone because Mike was too far away from the quarterback. Two safeties, three safeties, Mike had a heckuva first game, and at the end of the year, Paterno called Mike "the best sophomore" lineman he had ever seen at Penn State.

Although Mike sometimes played at the linebacker position as well as starting at middle guard in 1966, I finally got my wish in the spring of 1967 when we moved Mike to left linebacker. But he tore a ligament in his knee wrestling Oklahoma's All-American nose guard Granville Liggins during a heavyweight bout at the NCAA wrestling tournament, and the knee was still bothering him all through our 1967 preseason practice. We opened the season at Navy, and Mike was in for just a couple of plays when he reinjured the knee and was out for the season. Incidentally, the wrestler who won that heavyweight NCAA championship in '67 was Curley Culp, who also played nose guard at Arizona State and later became an All-Pro for the Kansas City Chiefs and Houston Oilers.

Without football, Mike concentrated on his studies and his love for music, and I had a small role in all that. At the beginning of the spring 1967 term, Mike was enrolled in the business curriculum and was worried about some business accounting course. Being an MBA graduate and his coach, I was trying to help him with his schedule. Finally I said to him, "Mike, why don't you switch to the music curriculum?" He said, "Aw, Rad, I came to college to get an education. That's why I'm taking business." I said, "Mike besides sports, all you are interested in is music. You took piano lessons for 12 years. You have to figure out how to make a living in music. Think about it and call me back." Well, he thought about it and called me back and said he was going to switch to music. I remember telling him, "Mike, that's great. Remember to do anything you can to be in the good graces of those people in the music department. If they need a piano moved, offer to move it. They've probably never had a big football player in their curriculum before." Mike seemed happy with his decision because he was going to be working at and studying in something he was very interested in. I was even happier than Mike because I knew he was now definitely going to be academically eligible for his last two years of football.

Mike Reid Meeting Dave Joyner – I also want to tell you about something that happened off the field just after the 1966 season or early in 1967. I got a phone call from Bob Joyner, the manager of The Erie Technical Ceramics, which was the company that I did my MBA paper on. It was about his son, Dave, again. Bob said Dave, who was now State College High's heavyweight wrestler, did not have anyone to work out with. So, I asked Mike Reid, who also wrestled for Penn State, if he could work out with Dave and Mike said he'd love to because he also didn't have anyone near his size to work out with. Well, those two got together, and Mike won the Eastern College heavyweight wrestling championship in 1967 and Dave won the state high school heavyweight championship in both 1967 and 1968. They became fast friends and that deep friendship continues to this day.

Beethoven Versus Gershwin – Now, I have tell you about something that happened with Mike off the field later that shows the type of determination that was in his character and not just while playing football. During the 1969 season, I got on the bus for an away game and sat next to Mike. He was reading a book on Beethoven, and I asked him what he thought of Beethoven. He said he thought Beethoven was one of the greatest composers of all time. I said George Gershwin was better than Beethoven. I said Beethoven sounded too similar to the other classical composers like Bach, Brahms, Tchaikovsky, and Mozart, while Gershwin had created his own unique sound in "Rhapsody in Blue" and "American in Paris." A vigorous discussion about George Gershwin ensued that lasted at least an hour.

Mike Reid

Twelve years later, in the spring of 1981 at Penn State's first ever football reunion for all past players, Mike spotted my wife Nancy and me at the far end of the banquet hall. He ran across the hall to our table and yelled, "Rad, I did it! I did it!" I said, "I know! I saw a newspaper article that said you did it!" I hadn't seen Mike in 10 years and the article that I had seen about eight years previously was about the day Mike Reid performed Gershwin's "Rhapsody in Blue" on the piano with the Cincinnati Symphony Orchestra. He really had done it. Mike had come up with a great ending to our bus discussion.

EDITOR'S NOTE: Mike Reid won the Grammy Award for Best Country Song with "Stranger in My House." He also wrote "I Can't Make You Love Me" sung by Bonnie Raitt.

Reid And Smear Elected Co-Captains – By the start of spring practice in 1968, Mike's knee had healed. But in that year away from football he had found a new life in his music and extracurricular activities in the drama department, including a highly-acclaimed performance as Big Julie in the play, Guys and Dolls, and he went in to see Coach Paterno about giving up football. Joe was surprised, but being so quick on his feet Joe knew what he had to do. As Joe told us coaches later, he told Reid, "Gosh Mike, that's a shame because I just got done counting the votes and your teammates gave you the most votes for captain." Mike apparently said something like, "Oh really, isn't that something?" and decided to stay on the football team. Now, when the team voted for captain, only the head coach had counted the ballots. Joe had not revealed the vote count before he met with Mike, but after the meeting Joe named both Mike, a redshirt junior, and Steve Smear, a true junior, as captains for the defense and senior tackle John Kulka as captain for the offense. Of course, Reid and Smear were the captains of the defense again in '69 and we went undefeated both years. Who but Joe knew what the 1968 player vote for defensive captain really was? And I sure as heck was never going to ask him.

However, I never did get to use Mike at linebacker again. Joe moved him to defensive tackle that fall and for the next two years Reid and Smear were the best defensive tackle-tandem in college football. In his senior year, Mike won the Maxwell Award in 1969 as college football's best player and the Outland Award as the outstanding lineman. Years later he also was inducted into the College Football Hall of Fame, and Mike is now routinely selected to All-Century teams, including the prestigious 75-man squad chosen by *Sports Illustrated* in 1999. He also had an outstanding five-year NFL career, but quit at his prime to concentrate on his music career and has become famous as a country-music composer and singer. Mike never became a full-fledged part of our Linebacker U group. But Steve Smear did, even though he had to leave the country to do it. Steve was an outstanding linebacker in the Canadian Football League for six years, and now owns a prosperous insurance agency in Annapolis.

Mike Reid

Steve never received the accolades that Mike did, and that's too bad because he had nearly as much talent as Mike but was overshadowed by Mike in their two years as co-captains. Steve made a couple of second team All-American teams, but with so many other first team All-Americans on those '68 and '69 teams—like Onkotz, tight end Ted Kwalick, safety Neal Smith, tailback Charlie Pittman, and, especially, his fellow tackle, Reid—Steve couldn't muster enough votes. According to the NCAA record book, there's never been two defensive tackles from the same team who become consensus first team All-Americans in the same year. So, Steve was the odd man out.

My tie to Steve goes back to his high school playing days at Bishop McCort in Johnstown. Johnstown is about 80 miles from our campus, and I'd say the city is pretty divided between Penn State and Pitt fans. So, the high schools in that area were fertile ground for us, and I was one of the coaches responsible for keeping track of the best players for recruiting.

Recruiting Of Steve Smear And Jack Ham – After the 1964 season, which was Steve Smear's junior year, I was looking at film of the Westmont-Bishop McCort game with Westmont's assistant football coach, Paul Matsko. (Westmont and Bishop McCort High Schools were rivals in Johnstown.) We were specifically watching Westmont's senior offensive guard Gary Shaffer, and as I viewed the film, I happened to notice a player on the opposing team making a number of tackles. I asked Paul, "Who's that kid on the other team making all those tackles?" Paul replied, "Oh, that's Steve Smear. He's only a junior. Everybody in Johnstown knows him. When he was a little kid, he carried a ball, bat and glove with him everywhere. Besides, being good in football and baseball, he's a great basketball player." Well, I recruited Gary Shafer for Penn State but also identified Steve Smear as a top recruit for the next year.

Steve was a tight end in high school, but we felt he could be an outstanding linebacker. And through the fall of 1965 and early 1966, Steve was personally recruited by both our head recruiter, Tor Toretti, and by Joe Paterno, who had become the head coach in February of '66. Now, there was a teammate of Steve's at Bishop McCourt who had made absolutely no impression on me in '64. It was only in his senior year that he became a starter as a 6-foot-1, 165-pound guard and cornerback, and because I had already tabbed Smear as the only possible recruit at McCort when Steve was a junior, I didn't have to go to the high school in the fall of 1965. Well, the lightweight

Steve Smear

guard apparently didn't impress anyone in his senior year either. So, since no one was recruiting him, he and his family decided he should go to a military prep school to become a better player.

I first heard of Jack Ham in the early fall of 1966 when I stopped at Bishop McCort during their preseason practice. The head coach, Al Fletcher, told me about this former player named Jack Ham who was at Massanutten Military Academy, in Woodstock, Virginia. Coach Fletcher said Jack was 6-foot-2 and now weighed 185 pounds, could run fast, and could high jump well over 6 feet. The prep school was in George Welsh's recruiting area, so George got film of Ham, and after we both watched it, we still were not overly impressed, and were both undecided about whether he was scholarship material.

I saw Smear in the locker room in Rec Hall and questioned him about Ham. Smear told me Ham was one of his best friends and a very good athlete. Smear said Ham hadn't played basketball in high school but was a better basketball player than anyone on the Bishop McCort state catholic championship basketball team. McCort had beaten Schenley, the public school state champions, and had lost only to DeMatha Catholic of Maryland, which was generally accepted as the catholic national champions, by just 88-84. Smear had been the high scorer in the catholic state championship game and the Bishop McCort center was at Pitt on a full basketball scholarship. I said, "If Ham's better than anybody on your state championship team, why didn't he play on it?" Smear said, "Because he didn't think he was good enough! But I'm telling you he was better than any of us." I said, "Smear, you're full of it," and left.

Ham came up on a bus for a visit. I can't remember if we paid for bus fare, or whether we just said we'd meet with him if he ever came here. Smear seems to think it was for our Blue-White game. Anyway, I met Ham and Smear on a Saturday morning for brunch at the popular Corner Room restaurant on College Avenue and we talked. I don't remember much more about it, but Smear showed him the campus. I'm not sure he even met any other coaches on that visit.

About a month after the national letter of intent signing date, George Welsh received more film from the prep school. We watched it, and Ham is playing both offensive guard and corner in a two-deep defense. As an offensive guard, he couldn't have broken an egg. He just couldn't block anybody. But he was impressive on defense, as he ran in pursuit across the field. He didn't have the opportunity to make many plays, but he looked very, very good running. We still had one last scholarship left at the time. Well, George and I both decided that we were on a running kick since we were looking for speed, and Ham could at least run, so let's give him our last scholarship. We told Coach Paterno of our decision, and he said "fine." George called Ham and offered him a scholarship.

The next day George and I were sitting at our desks when Paterno walked in the room and said "Well, I've got a couple of real smart young coaches. You two have just given our last scholarship to a young man who was going to pay his own way to come here." One of us said, "What are you talking about?" Joe said, "I just got off the phone with Al Fletcher, the head coach at Bishop McCort. He told me that Ham and his dad had already decided that the dad was going to pay for Jack to go to Penn State."

And that's really how Jack Ham became a Nittany Lion. The story has often been told about Jack getting our last scholarship in 1966 almost as an afterthought and, as you have just read, it is true. No one could have envisioned back then that Jack would become one of Penn State's greatest players, perhaps our best linebacker ever, and then go on to have an All-Pro career with the Pittsburgh Steelers, and, subsequently, become the only Penn State player ever inducted into both the College and Pro Football Hall of Fames.

One more thing, Smear was right about his buddy. When Ham showed up on campus he was a better basketball player than anyone on McCort's state championship basketball team.

While Jack Ham was bulking up at the Massanutten Military Academy, Steve Smear was playing tight end for Penn State's freshman team. I wanted to get him on the varsity for my linebacking corps, but Joe Paterno felt we needed a defensive tackle more and switched him there before spring practice in '67. He was overwhelmed at first, but by the opening game of the '67 season at Navy, Steve was battling another sophomore, John Ebersole, for a starting defensive tackle position. When Ebersole was hurt in that game, Steve moved up for the Miami game the next week and started for the rest of his career. In 1970, the Baltimore Colts made him their fourth round draft choice, but Steve decided to play in the Canadian Football League. And that's where he finally became "a post-graduate of Linebacker U," playing six years at linebacker with Montreal, Saskatchewan and Toronto.

Another Future NFL Linebacker – Ebersole was another of those young defensive linemen who became a linebacker in the NFL. He was from Altoona High School, which was in my recruiting area, and who I had first seen as a junior in 1964 when he was a teammate of Mike Reid's. He was just as good a prospect as Mike, and had been selected a *Parade* magazine High School All-American. But he wanted to go to Kentucky with two or three other teammates from high school who we were not interested in. I told Toretti, who was in charge of recruiting, that I was going to lose him to Kentucky. Tor then visited Ebersole's grandmother and convinced her that John should go to Penn State. The grandmother then supposedly told John's mom that if John went to Kentucky instead of Penn State, that she and her son would be cut out of the will. So John ended up at Penn State. All I know is that when he signed a letter of intent, I was a happy coach.

In high school, John had played on the line, but with his size and weight—6-foot-4, 230-pounds—and quickness he could just as easily been a linebacker. However, he was a defensive lineman from day one and started that first game in his sophomore season, and then returned to continue starting after his injury. But in his junior season, Ebersole was primarily a back up to Reid and Smear, and, frankly he didn't practice very well. We talked and talked to him but nothing seemed to work.

Then in the spring of 1969, I was having John and Vic Surma run ten 100-yard sprints with a 30 second rest between each one. Surma was a letterman at offensive tackle that we were projecting as a starter and he was running simply to try to get in better condition. Ebersole was running as a penalty because we were continuing to be upset with the way he was playing in practice. They were to run each 100-yard sprint under 15 seconds or they would have to repeat that sprint.

A scout for the NFL Blesto combine named Mike "Moe" Scarry, who was from my hometown of Duquesne, was at practice that day and stayed out to help me time the sprints. Moe had been a defensive line coach with the Redskins and later would be the defensive line coach with the Super Bowl Dolphins. Anyhow, Surma ran all ten of his sprints under 15 seconds as he was supposed to, but Ebersole ran every one of his ten 100-yard sprints under 12 seconds. When they were done, I said to Moe, "Well Moe, what do you think about Ebersole running all ten sprints under 12 seconds?" He said, "I wouldn't have believed it if I didn't see it. I've never seen anything like that before." I said, "Neither have I." I went in, saw coach Paterno and said to him, "I don't know what Ebersole's

John Ebersole (89) and Gary Hull (80)

problem is, but it isn't conditioning. We don't have a player on this team in better shape than him." For whatever reason, from that day on John Ebersole practiced and played as well or better than anyone else on the team and had a great senior year. We moved him to defensive end where he started and played as a linebacker occasionally, depending on our defensive scheme and personnel in the game. In certain defenses, our defensive ends covered the flat area. Other times they covered the man out of the opponent's backfield just like a linebacker.

The Jets drafted John in the fourth round in 1970, moved him to linebacker and he played there for eight years, primarily as the starting middle linebacker—another post-graduate of Linebacker U.

Playing The Unbeaten Former Penn Staters – Now, it's well known that 1967 was the turning point in Joe Paterno's coaching career, but there was one specific game that season where my linebackers made the crucial plays in what is now recognized as the game that put Paterno into the national limelight. It's my belief that this also was the seminal game in the advent of Linebacker U.

It was the eighth game of the season and we had won four straight for a 5-2 record, which had surprised a lot of people because in Joe's first year as head coach we had finished with a mediocre 5-5. But we still had not made much of an impact and were nowhere to be seen in the weekly polls. However, we were now hosting the No. 3 team in the country, North Carolina State, which was unbeaten in eight games. Even if the poll voters hadn't noticed us, the odds-makers had because, surprisingly, Penn State was a two-point favorite. The game had an extra twist because NC State was coached by former Penn Staters—head coach Earl Edwards, defensive coordinator Al Michaels and freshman coach Bill Smaltz. We had played against our former Penn Staters once before, when I was a senior in 1956, and Milt Plum had thrown a 9-yard touchdown pass to Les Walters with 15 seconds left to win, 14-7. It was after that close and exciting game that I had asked my wife Nancy to marry me. This game proved to be just as close and exciting.

Three of our starting linebackers were sophomores: Denny Onkotz, Jim Kates and Pete Johnson. They were among the half dozen or so sophomores credited with turning around our season when Paterno had inserted them into the lineup early in the Miami game after our opening season loss to Navy.

Johnson, who had been a freshman running back like Onkotz, was the fastest of the three with a 4.5 40-yard dash time. Kates and Johnson were good, solid linebackers but Onkotz had superstar potential. They were all about 6-foot-2, but at 230 pounds, Jim was both a linebacker and a down lineman depending on which defensive front we were lined up in. Pete was awesome as an outside linebacker but had so much overall athletic talent that in his senior year we moved him to tight end to take Ted Kwalik's place. But Denny seemed to come up with more big plays than the other linebackers.

Denny had played quarterback and safety at Northampton High School, near Allentown. George Welsh had recruited him, and after he played halfback on the freshman team Paterno made him a linebacker. But as part of the scout team, Denny was often used as a linebacker, and we could see even then that he was better than some of the linebackers already playing for us in '66. He was such a natural runner and had such good hands that Joe also started using him as our prime punt return man. What's more, Denny was one of the most intelligent players on the squad, a biophysics major who had turned down Princeton to play at Penn State. He even went to class on Saturday mornings of our home games and everyone wondered how he could do that and still concentrate on the football game later that same day.

And, yes, Denny was in his early morning class before our game against NC State kicked off at 1 p.m. It was a sunny day but windy and there were scouts from the Sugar, Orange and Liberty Bowls among the standing room crowd of some 46,500. Okay, I didn't remember that but I looked it up. I did remember we scored early but had to look that up too. With just 3 ½ minutes gone in the first quarter, Ted Kwalick scored on an 18-yard touchdown pass from Tommy Sherman, and that was the first score NC State had given up in the first quarter all year, but it wasn't the last, and I do remember what happened next.

About three minutes later, NC State was driving at about our 40-yard line when Onkotz intercepted a pass and ran 67-yards untouched for a touchdown. That made it 13-0 when we missed the extra point but the game was just beginning. We almost scored three more times in the first half, but their defense stopped us once at the 5-yard line and again on an interception in the end zone, and we also missed a 33-yard field goal attempt. The second half was a defensive game but the momentum was shifting to NC State. They stopped our offense cold while they scored on field goals of 12 and 26 yards and almost had a touchdown but our safety Tim Montgomery took the ball away from their receiver in the end zone. Okay, I had to look that up, too, but what I remember most about the entire game was what happened with about five minutes left in the game.

NC State got the ball on their 32-yard line and drove all the way to our 1-yard line. They had fourth and one. About 40 seconds were left and they called time out. After the game, Joe told the media that he thought they would fake to their fullback Tony Barchuk, who already had rushed for nearly 100 yards, and go outside. But Jim O'Hora, who was in charge of our defense, thought they would go inside again and so did Tim Montgomery, who called the defensive signals on the field. So, Joe went with them. We later learned that NC State's coach Earl Edwards had first called for a pitchout—as Joe had originally figured—but his quarterback wanted to give the ball to the fullback up the middle. And that's what they did.

They ran a quick fullback counter play and our defensive left tackle Mike McBath burrowed underneath the offensive lineman and hit the ball carrier low, below the crotch and grabbing both legs, and my two linebackers, Onkotz and Kates hit him high, stopping him cold. We gave up a safety by running out of the end zone on the last play of the game to win 13-8. Later Joe would call that goal line play "one of the greatest plays in Penn State history." After the game, Onkotz and Kates were hailed as "heroes" but McBath was virtually ignored. The game had not been on television and the crowd only saw my linebackers hit their fullback, but no one saw McBath. And the play had happened so fast that the newspaper photos the next day clearly showed Denny and Jim making the tackle, but no Mike.

I went into detail on this because for the last 40 years Mike and I both believed that only he and I knew that he was the most important part of that great defensive play. We'd never seen it mentioned in any article about that game. Mike was an outstanding tackle who went on to play five years with the Buffalo Bills, and later became a leader in the NFL Players Association, as well as a stock broker. We'd see each other over the years and laugh about him being completely forgotten in one of Penn State's greatest plays. But in 2000, Mike told the story to my co-author Lou Prato, who was about to become the first director of the Penn State All-Sports Museum. Lou found a photo in the 1968 Penn State yearbook, the LaVie, that showed Mike making the tackle along with Denny and Jim, and that photo is now on display in a prominent section of the museum.

That goal line play along with that pass interception of a 67-yard touchdown also made Onkotz an All-American. The next week *Sports Illustrated* featured Onkotz in a long story about the game and the Associated Press chose him college football's "Lineman of the Week." A week later we accepted an invitation to the Gator Bowl, and shortly after Denny was named a second-team All-American. Of course, that was just the beginning for our team and Denny. As I mentioned, for the next two years we were undefeated and Denny was a consensus first team All-American both seasons. In 1995, he was inducted into the College Football Hall of Fame.

I wrote earlier that Denny might have even been a better linebacker than Jack Ham but he never had a chance to prove that in the pros. The Jets drafted him No. 3 and he was a backup along with his Penn State rookie teammate John Ebersole on a team that included Ralph Baker as a starting linebacker. But in the ninth game of the season at Los Angeles, Denny broke his leg so severely he was in a cast for five months. He sat out the next season and, as I wrote in Chapter One, was never the same.

In reflecting back, I believe it was Denny Onkotz who was the linchpin for what became Linebacker U. Denny was not only a great linebacker but his exceptional talent as a punt returner was unusual for a linebacker. Add that to the focus off the field on his colorful and scholarly academic endeavors—that also were highly-unusual for a football player at the time—and all that brought attention to Penn State as Linebacker U—an assembly line, if you will, for producing linebackers.

The media started looking at other Penn State linebackers and taking special notice of Dave Robinson, Ralph Baker, Bill Saul and others already in the pros. And those great plays against NC State is probably where it all began.

Playboy All-American – I have to tell you one more story about Onkotz and me. It was during spring practice in 1969. The NCAA only allowed 20 days of actual practice in the five weeks allocated for the spring. So, I was holding one two-hour meeting a week with my linebackers on Wednesdays from 7 to 9 p.m. for the entire five weeks. If a linebacker could not make the meeting, all he had to do was to see me on my own some time Thursday or Friday. We didn't even practice on Friday. If he didn't show, he had to run four laps, or two miles, around the three practice fields after Saturday's practice.

One Saturday, in about the middle of practice, linebacker Onkotz yelled to coach Paterno, "Coach, it's time." Joe said. "Okay Dennis, you can go." I said, "Dennis, where are you going?" He said, "I'm catching a plane to Chicago to go to the Playboy Club preseason All-American affair. Coach Paterno said it was okay for me to leave practice early." I said, "Dennis, you missed Wednesday's linebacker meeting and you didn't show up Thursday or Friday. You owe me four laps. He said, "But I've got to catch a plane to go to Chicago." I said, "You've got time to do the laps, get dressed, and still catch the plane to Chicago." He said, "You're not going to make me run four laps?" I said, "Yes, I am." He pointed his right arm and finger at me and shouted, "People like you are responsible for the sick society we have today!" I replied, "Dennis, I'm only 33 years old. It's not us people over 30 who are ruining the world. We haven't had our chance yet. It's those goofs over 40, 50, and 60 or worse screwing everything up. Now run the laps," and he did.

Dennis Onkotz

Jack Ham, Becomes "Fritz" – Now, at the start of spring practice in 1968, we moved Onkotz from inside linebacker to outside linebacker with freshman Jack Ham as his backup. On the third day of practice, we moved Onkotz back to inside linebacker and put Ham on the starting unit as an outside linebacker. This was a second-fastest promotion to first team in my 17 years at Penn State. Mike Reid had been put on first team the first day of his first spring practice in '66.

Ham was also the fastest man in a special timing drill we did, when, for the first time, we decided to film all our players in both the 10-yard and 40-yard sprints. This was done by the Penn State Physical Education and Research Department, which had some kind of a connection to the 1968 Olympics, which was being held that summer in the high altitude Mexican atmosphere. Of the more than 100 football players we filmed in two 10-yard sprints each, Ham had the fastest two times in both. That meant that of the over 200 times we filmed that day in the 10-yard sprint, Ham had the best two—faster than even high school sprinters like Paul Johnson, who had run the 100-yard dash under 10 seconds in high school. A 10-yard sprint is impossible to time by hand with a stopwatch because it occurs too fast. I thought, "Wow." That's all blocking punts requires—a fast 10-yard dash. So we got out the mats and

Jack Ham

had Ham practice blocking punts almost every day in the spring. He had a number of roughing the kicker penalties in our scrimmages. That fall he blocked three punts and one more in 1969 to set two Penn State records that he now shares with another All-American linebacker, Andre Collins, who blocked three in 1989 and one in 1986.

A year later at the 1969 spring practice, we made some more personnel shifts, and because of it we had to find a new nickname for Ham's position. First, we moved our starting right outside linebacker Pete Johnson to tight end where Ted Kwalick had been for three years. Then we moved starting cornerback Mike Smith into Pete's outside linebacker spot and inserted reserve defensive back George Landis into Mike's starting corner position. Because Mike was short, just 5-11, we wanted to have him play on the short side of the field, closer to the sideline, and we wanted Ham on the wide side or the two-receiver side if the ball was in the middle of the field.

Jack Ham (33)

Now, in the 5-3 or 4-4 defense, the outside linebacker was similar to the strong safety, and for years some people had called the strong safety position the "monster." But Rip wouldn't let us use the word "monster" because he refused to use any terms that he considered derogatory to the game of football. So he had come up with the nickname "Hero" for this strong safety instead of "monster." We decided to let Mike Smith keep the "Hero" name, but we needed a name that started with F for field or flanker for Ham's position. One of the coaches said, "How about Fritz DeFlores who owns Home Delivery Pizza?" That was a popular pizza restaurant where many of our players worked or loafed. So "Fritz" became the name of the outside linebacker, Ham, who lined up to the field [wide side] or to the flanker, and the nickname is still being used by Penn State today. In early 2010, I read an article where one of Penn State's star linebackers, Sean Lee, said "Fritz" was the current term for the weak side linebacker, which is just the opposite of the original meaning of "Fritz." Funny how things evolve over time.

Radgate – A couple of months later, at the beginning of the '69 preseason practice, Coach Paterno told me and the linebackers that we were going change our pass defense a bit. What we had been doing was run to our zone coverage area based on ball locations and formations and react off the pattern and the quarterback. I had even devised a drill for it called "Look-Search"—meaning look at the quarterback and search for the receiver. Now, Joe wanted the linebackers to run to spots on the field in our zone coverage, and when we got to the spot we were to react only to the quarterback.

I didn't think this was as good as what we had been doing, but I didn't feel this was the right time to argue with my head coach. Maybe that shows you how much I had matured over the years. But, then remember, I didn't have the nickname Bad Rad for nothing. So, I simply told my linebackers to start for the spot and then read the quarterback and pattern like we always did, and keep it to ourselves. In later years when I did anything secretive and kept it from the head coach, but for his benefit, I called it "Radgate," playing off the nickname from President Nixon's Watergate scandal in 1973.

Well, we went unbeaten in the 1969 regular season for the second straight year. How good our defense was is best exemplified by what Bob Anderson, Colorado's All-American quarterback candidate, said after our 27-3 victory over Colorado in the second game of the season: "I think this is the greatest defense I've ever played against." Anderson had rushed for a grand total of four yards, even though he was considered the best running quarterback in the nation. He also threw three interceptions and fumbled once. "The deployment of their linebackers bothered me," he said. "They always seemed to be right in the pass route...How do I like playing against Penn State? It's pretty discouraging."

At the end of the season we were matched up against a high-scoring Missouri team in the Orange Bowl. Missouri had an excellent passing attack and two of the fastest and quickest receivers in America in John Staggers and Mel Gray. At the first game plan meeting for Missouri with the defensive staff, Joe Paterno was looking at what Missouri does passing from its basic I slot formation and he said, "Gee, I wish we still played patterns. That would be perfect against this offense." I piped up, "We still do Joe. We've been playing patterns all year. We just start for a spot and adjust to the pattern." He didn't say anything for a couple of seconds, and then said "good" and that's how we set up the game plan for Missouri's patterns.

A couple days before the game we had some misfortune when George Landis, our left corner, hurt his knee. So, with Missouri's receivers being so fast, we told Landis to line up deep on everything unless he had flat coverage. Well, we won a close game 10-3 and scored all our points in the first quarter on a 29-yard field goal and a 28-yard touchdown pass from Chuck Burkhart to Lydell Mitchell. Almost the entire game was played in our territory, mostly due to our poor punt coverage. But our defense set an Orange Bowl record with seven interceptions and needed every one of them to win the game. Safety Neal Smith, Onkotz and Landis with his bad knee had two interceptions each, and defensive end Gary Hull had one interception. Mel Gray, who went on to become an NFL All-Pro, did not catch a pass. When the Missouri quarterback, Terry McMillan, was asked after the game, why he didn't throw the ball to Gray, he replied "I didn't see him the entire game." That was probably because we had our Fritz linebacker Jack Ham aligned in the slot on Mel Gray's side the entire game. The Fritz linebacker always lined up the flanker (slot side).

A few days later, Missouri Coach Dan Devine was quoted in a newspaper saying, "After looking at the film of the game, Penn State is by far the smartest defense I have ever seen. They made adjustments to our formations and plays that were better than I'd ever seen before, the best I've seen in twenty years of college football." I took special satisfaction in that.

One more thing about the Missouri game and George Landis. We wouldn't have even been playing in the game if Landis had not blocked two field goal attempts by Syracuse in the fifth game of our season to help us avoid a major upset. Partly due again to our poor punt coverage, Syracuse was deep in Penn State territory on four different occasions in the first half. Syracuse scored two touchdowns and twice had field goals blocked by Landis. Probably because of the blocked field goals, Syracuse passed up an opportunity for a third field goal try in the second half and went for it on fourth down and didn't make it. They were still leading 14-0 late in the third quarter when we came from behind, sparked by Onkotz who forced a fumble, and we won 15-14. No doubt, the two blocked field goals by George saved six points. With our great defense so loaded with All-Americans, George probably didn't get the credit for how well he played that season, particularly since he hadn't played much in previous years. So, after the Missouri game, I told George that the two consecutive blocked field goals in the Syracuse game and the two interceptions on basically only one good leg in the Missouri game, didn't make him an All-American but "ALL-WORLD," and you can't get any better than that. George may not have been part of Linebacker U back then but based on what he did in '69, I'll make him an honorary member.

Blowing The National Championship – The story of how we wound up playing Missouri in the Orange Bowl after the 1969 undefeated season has bothered me for 40 years. It was based on a lot of factors and has been immersed in controversy from the day it was announced. As I've already written, back in that era bowl games were set before the end of the regular season. In 1969, we still had games left with Pitt and North Carolina State when the bowls were making their deals on Sunday November 16. We were ranked No. 5 in the polls at the time, and the Orange Bowl invited us to play No. 6 Missouri, which had all but clinched the Big 8 Championship and an overwhelming favorite to beat a weak Kansas State team the following week. That would give them a 9-1 record, after a loss to Colorado in midseason. The Cotton Bowl wanted to match us with the winner of the Texas-Arkansas game on December 4, and both of those teams unbeaten and ranked above us at No. 2 and No. 4, respectively.

Ohio State was No. 1 and seemed to be a lock to repeat as national champions. At that time, a Big Ten rule prohibited a team to represent the conference in the Rose Bowl two years in a row and did not allow any Big Ten team to play in any other bowl game. Ohio State still had to play its biggest rival, Michigan, in its final regular-season game. All Ohio State had to do to win the championship was beat Michigan, and they seemed to be a shoo-in over a No. 13 Michigan team that had already lost twice, including a 40-7 defeat to Missouri. No. 3 USC, the likely Rose

Bowl host, still had a showdown game with its big rival No. 8 UCLA and both teams were unbeaten with one tie.

So on Sunday night, we had to take a vote to play either Texas or Arkansas in the Cotton Bowl or Missouri in the Orange Bowl. There were two trains of thought making the rounds among the players before the vote. One was that Ohio State was going to end up being No. 1 anyway and why should we play Texas in the crummy Cotton Bowl for No. 2, when we could be in classy, sunny Miami Beach. Plus, the administration had let it be known that Penn State would have a much bigger payday—about twice as much—if we play in the Orange Bowl, instead of the Cotton. The other train of thought, which I supported, was that Ohio State had a good chance to lose to bitter rival Michigan. If that happened, we'd be playing Texas or Arkansas for No. 1. Voting to play in the Cotton Bowl was our best chance to be No. 1.

Well, we had the vote in a secret ballot, and we were told that the majority of the team had voted to play Missouri in the Orange Bowl. I saw Joe Paterno in the football office the next day, and he yelled at me, "I know you're upset with the vote. But I think it's bad for the team that you're telling everybody that the linebackers voted to play in the Cotton Bowl." I yelled back, "The only person I told was my wife and, evidently, she told your wife and your wife told you. That's who everybody is." Then I left the office. Was I upset? Of course I was upset about blowing our best chance to be national champion.

Since then, Joe has occasionally been asked about the decision to go to the Orange Bowl. In his 1989 book, *Paterno: By the Book*, he wrote that before the vote he talked privately to three of our star black players, Charlie Pittman, Lydell Mitchell and Franco Harris. "This was at the peak of the new civil rights awareness," he wrote, "and I wanted to hear them out first about any choice among Southern cities... They didn't want to go to the Cotton Bowl. More specifically, they didn't want to go to Dallas, where (President) John F. Kennedy had been shot...The other players seemed sensitive to what their black teammates wanted, but if the majority wanted to go to Dallas, I believe Mitchell, Pittman and the others would have accepted that too....In a vote we took...almost everybody, it turned out for reasons I didn't expect, wanted the Orange Bowl."

Well, Michigan beat Ohio State, Texas beat Arkansas for the Southwest Conference championship and then beat Notre Dame in the Cotton Bowl and wound up No. 1. As soon as it was announced we were going to the Orange Bowl, many sportswriters immediately blasted us for ducking the Southwest Conference Champion, and that criticism only got worse after Texas won the national title. Some old-timers with long memories still criticize Penn State for that decision. And just writing about it all 40 years later gets me all upset again.

The Night Meeting – One last story about my last game coaching at Penn State in that 1970 Orange Bowl, but this one still makes me laugh when I think about it. We were staying in a great hotel in Miami Beach, and Joe evidently didn't think the coaches were taking the game serious enough. So on the night of the Governors

Ball, which we went to with our wives, he called a meeting of the coaching staff at 11 p.m. in his suite. We had not had a staff meeting at night after practice for three years—or ever since he personally made up the practice schedule. We left our wives and went to his suite all decked out in our suits and ties. It was some meeting. Every topic he brought up, either I or J.T. White, our crusty, old-time defensive end coach, disagreed with him, told him he was wrong, and so forth. Of course, we both had been drinking and were totally upset about the meeting. You could see the other coaches were enjoying J.T. and I arguing with Joe. Finally, after about a half hour, Paterno said, "Meeting over. I'll never do this again." I guess the moral of this story is "if you want to have a lousy meeting, schedule it at 11:00 p.m. at night after your coaches have been partying for three hours."

Coaching In Law School – Ever since I had received my MBA in '64, I had a desire to get a law degree. At the end of the 1965 season, I decided to leave Penn State, but I really can't remember why. It may have been something about the law degree or it might have been disappointment about the season. Our record was 5-5, and I had a long talk with Joe Paterno about leaving. I remember Joe saying, "We're going to look back someday on this conversation and realize what we are concerned about really wasn't very important and will laugh about it." Well, he was right. I stayed, and the reason why I wanted to leave has become so unimportant that I can't remember what it was about.

But after the 1969 season, I was determined to go to law school, so I needed to find a coaching job that allowed me to attend law school at the same time. I got a call one evening in early January of 1970 from Bob Kane, one of my former linebackers, who knew of my interest in becoming a lawyer and was currently attending Villanova Law School. He told me that the BLESTO football scouting combine was having its annual meetings before the NFL draft in Philadelphia. The BLESTO scouts visited football colleges all over the country, and Bob said that maybe somebody there might know of a school that would hire a coach and allow him to go to law school at the same time.

I immediately called Alex Bell, former Villanova head coach, and Moe Scarry, former Redskins assistant coach, two of the BLESTO scouts that I knew. They both said that they didn't know of anything I might be interested in at the moment, but they would keep alert for anything that might appeal to me in the future. The next morning in the football office, I asked George Welsh if the new head football coach at Temple, Wayne Hardin, would hire me. George knew Hardin from the Naval Academy. George said if he recommended me, the Temple guy would hire me as a coach in a minute, but that he would never go along with the idea of me going to law school at the same time. "Nobody will do that," George said. Just then, my telephone rang. The caller was Ray Callahan, the head football coach of the University of Cincinnati. He had received a call from Moe Scarry and said Moe had highly recommended me. Coach Callahan said he wanted to interview me as soon as possible about being his defense coordinator and also going to law school. His said his team had given up 656 points in 20 games the past two years, an average of 32.8

points per game, and he needed someone with new ideas. After I hung up the phone, I said, "George, I think I just found a job coaching football and going to law school."

Job Interview And Law School – I flew to Cincinnati the next day. Coach Callahan and I went alone into his office for my interview. After about a half hour of me at the blackboard explaining the new multiple defensive schemes we used at Penn State, he said to me, "Who came up with this stuff?" I said, "Well, I came up with the way we shift to the various fronts by having a linebacker also be a down linemen in certain fronts; Coach Paterno came up with the coverages and the way we play them; and the other defensive coaches—Jim O' Hora, Frank Patrick, and J.T. White—also contributed parts of it. It truly was a group effort." He said, "That's it! Interview is over. Let's go." I said, "Where are we going?" He said, "We're going downtown to the Chase Law School to get you admitted." I knew then that I had a football job that would allow me to go to law school at night.

Leaving Linebacker U – After I told Joe Paterno of my intention to be the defensive coordinator at Cincinnati and go to nearby Chase Law school, he made one last effort to keep me at Penn State. He said that Penn State was supposed to have a law school on campus in a few years, and if I stayed, I could go to law school on campus then. Well, it was 40 years later before Penn State finally has its campus law school as the first student entered it in fall of 2009. Once Joe realized that I was actually going to be gone, he asked me if I would convince our offensive tackle coach to take my job as the new linebacker coach.

He had never coached linebackers before, but we talked and he took the job. Before I left for Cincinnati, I tutored him for three weeks about linebacker play and our defensive scheme. In the past three years we hadn't had a defensive playbook, just notes that each coach had concerning his position plus a very brief diagram of defenses aligned on a basic two-back set that Coach Jim O'Hora always drew up. When I finished at the end of three weeks we had a notebook as fat as a New York City phone book. This was to be his football Bible for his first couple of years as linebacker coach. Bob Phillips, the receivers coach at the time, said he and Joe Paterno would get into a discussion or argument about some aspect of football and he would say, "Rad's book doesn't say that." I should have made a copy of that notebook. I could have turned it into a real book about coaching linebackers. I might have called it *How to Play Linebacker from High School to the Pros* by Bad Rad, the Father of Linebacker U.

Linebacker U Continues – Of course, Linebacker U didn't miss a beat. With so many seniors in '69, the 1970 season turned into a rebuilding year as the unbeaten streak came to an end at 33 games—which is still the school record—and they lost three games and didn't go to a post-season bowl. The next year, they were back in the hunt for the national championship until an upset at Tennessee, 31-11, in the last game of the regular season. But they redeemed themselves by dominating a highly regarded Texas team, 31-6, in the Cotton Bowl in a game Paterno said they had to win or else lose all that Penn State had accomplished from '68-'69. I mention this because that was the team where my influence on the linebackers began to fade. Gary Gray was the last Penn State linebacker left that I had personally coached.

One of the starting linebackers in that bowl game against Texas, Charlie Zapiec, had been a starting offensive guard on both our undefeated '68 and '69 teams. After our Orange Bowl win that 1969 season against Missouri, Charlie shocked me when he got on the team bus and begged me to play him at linebacker the next year, his senior season. Before I left Penn State to go to the University of Cincinnati, I told Joe Paterno about Zapiec's request. They moved Charlie to linebacker but Charlie was injured and didn't play. After sitting out a year with a medical red shirt, he became a first-team All-American linebacker in '71. I still can't believe a starting offensive guard on two undefeated teams would want to play a completely different defensive position in his senior year, but Charlie showed he had the talent and desire to be so successful. Although he was drafted fourth by Dallas, Charlie went to the CFL like Steve Smear and became an outstanding linebacker with Montreal and Ottawa from 1972-78. Twice he was on the CFL All-Star team and he played on two Montreal teams that won the Grey Cup, the CFL's version of the Super Bowl. Even though I didn't coach him, I am sure my "phone book" on linebacking was involved somehow.

Gary Gray had backed up Jim Kates as a sophomore in '69 and I felt Gary would be a good one. Gary became a two-year starter. John Skorupan had been a freshman my last year but by the time he graduated in 1973, he, too, was a first team All-American. Gray passed up pro ball but Skorupan played in the NFL from 1973-80 with Buffalo and the New York Giants.

Then there was one of the starting sophomore defensive backs on the '71 team. I don't mean John Cappelletti, who, yes, was a defensive starter and then moved to running back the next season and eventually became the only Penn State player to win the Heisman Trophy. His sophomore teammate was Ed O'Neil who was my last recruit, and I have to tell you that story.

In June of 1969, I was at Joe Paterno's summer camp for high school players at Pioneer Ranch in Cooks Forest, Pennsylvania, and we were in a full-court basketball game with the high school players at the camp. There was a loose ball and I went for it. One of the high school quarterbacks also went for it. He knocked me up against a tree, grabbed the ball, and went down the court with it. One of the other camp coaches ran over to see how badly I was hurt, and as he was helping me up, I said, "What do you think about that kid?" Instead of saying the kid was a dirty player or something like that, he said "I think he's a pretty good athlete." I said, "I think we ought to give him a scholarship." And that's how Ed O'Neil got the first scholarship for the 1970 freshman class at Penn State. Then, during the season, somebody in Ed's high school conference told us he wasn't very good. Now I'm thinking that we blew our first scholarship. Well, I left Penn State in January. Ed shows up at Penn State in September and he went on to make first-team All-American as a linebacker in 1973, and then played seven years with the Detroit Lions. The hunch I had when Ed knocked me into that tree really paid off.

Nothing Succeeds Like Success – In an article entitled "Getting Down To The Nittany Gritty" for *PRO Magazine* (the official magazine of the National Football League) dated November 12,1978, Glen Sheeley tries to explain the success of the Penn State linebackers in the NFL. Sheeley had seen it all first hand as a Penn State student for four years, and especially when he was sports editor of *The Daily Collegian* in his senior year of 1972-73. Here is Glen's story:

> It's no boast when Joe Paterno says, "By the time our linebackers leave here, there isn't anything they aren't doing right."
>
> To observers of NFL linebackers it must seem as if someone at Penn State has discovered the secret of cloning.
>
> This season, if all goes true to form, at least a dozen Penn State Alumni will be playing linebacker in Pro Football—Jack Ham (Pittsburgh), Ed O'Neil and Ron Crosby (Detroit), John Skorupan (Giants), Jim Laslavic (San Diego), Chris Devlin (Cincinnati), Kurt Allerman (St. Louis), Greg Buttle (New York Jets), Dave Graf (Cleveland) and new draftees Randy Sidler (Jets), Ron Hostetler (Los Angeles) and Tom DePaso (Cincinnati).
>
> Should you desire further proof of the popularity of the Penn State linebackers—or Nittany Lions that played standup defensive end in college and were drafted as linebackers—you can add former modern day NFL players Chuck Drazenovich, Dave Robinson, Ralph Baker, John Ebersole, Bruce Bannon, Tom Hull, and Dennis Onkotz. Another ex-Penn State linebacker, Charlie Zapiec, is considered one of the best defensive players in the Canadian Football League. [Editor's Note: Sheeley should have included Steve Smear, Penn State's co-captain of the great back-to-back undefeated teams of 1968-69, in his assessment because Smear also was an outstanding linebacker in CFL.]
>
> But if it isn't cloning, what is the formula?
>
> There are almost as many theories as there are Penn State linebackers, and any one of them might be considered part of the collective answer
>
> But the most accepted argument is that the Penn State linebacker has become a prized pro commodity because he experiences only a minimal transition from college to professional football.
>
> "The way we play our linebackers has a lot to do with their ability to go right into pro football," says Penn State coach Joe Paterno. "We ask them to play zone defense; we ask them to play man to man defense. We have a lot of complicated check-offs on the line of scrimmage that they have to make."
>
> And every pro coach will tell you that the rookie who spends his time performing by habit rather than having to think about what he must do, is the rookie least likely to get blocked out of a play or burned on a curl.
>
> Stated simply, the "split-six" or 4-4-3 defensive scheme devised by former Penn State linebacker coach Dan Radakovlch...features four linebackers, making them the defenses' pivotal defensive players With only three defensive backs behind them, the linebackers have more pass responsibility, and less chance of being surprised by the number of pass situations they see in the NFL.

Also, since the mid-1960s, Penn State has regularly placed its best athletes on defense. O'Neil was a high school quarterback. Mike Reid, perhaps the most splendid of the schools' defensive tackles, was a fullback. In the sophomore year before he began his charge for the Heisman Trophy, John Cappelletti played in Paterno's defensive backfield. Ham was a guard in high school. More specifically, the best of the defensive players were often at linebacker. Radakovich periodically bugged Paterno by putting a note on his desk: "I understand that Tennessee says it always puts its best athlete, with the exception of the quarterback, at middle linebacker..."

When studying the Penn State linebackers who have accomplished so much in the NFL, the logical player to examine is Ham, the Steelers All-Pro outside linebacker and the man who Paterno says "epitomizes what the Penn State linebacker is all about." Radakovich, who took a job with the Steelers as a defensive line coach in 1971, the year the Steelers drafted Ham, says with more than a touch of seriousness, "It wasn't just ironic, I wanted to follow Ham around a bit."

Woody Widenhofer, the Steelers current linebacker coach, came to Pittsburgh in 1973, Ham's third year as a pro. Widenhofer began his orientation by going back to 1971 game films. It quickly became clear to Widenhofer that Ham's only adjustment to the NFL had been getting used to cashing paychecks. In his first preseason game as a pro starter against Fran Tarkenton and the New York Giants, Ham intercepted three passes. "I couldn't wait to coach him after seeing that." says Widenhofer.

"I could tell by the films how quickly he had adapted. These days I've got to look very, very hard in the films to criticize Jack Ham...Because of his great athletic ability, he's always been a great ball-reactor. He's got great vision. The Penn State preparation was "ideal" Widenhofer says.

"By the time Penn Staters get here [NFL], I think they have a little bit of an edge over other people, especially in pass coverage," he explains. "Most of the colleges use a five-two defense, while we're basically a four-three. So, there's a big transition for most rookies. Penn State plays that split-six, which is like a four-four so those players have an advantage, they really do."

In addition to the basic Penn State assignments, which are similar to those in the pros, Paterno's team employed a "Cover Two" defense—which splits the field into halves for zone coverage – that only appeared in the NFL in recent years.

"We had that even before the pros thought of it," says Paterno. "We used that back in 1968 and I can remember a couple of pro coaches in those days coming up here and saying, "You couldn't use that in pro football—they'd eat it up."

Does Ham agree that his college training was the key to his immediate success in the pros? "The transition was easy," Ham says flatly.

"The four-four we played at Penn State was very similar to what we do in the pros for the outside line handoff. Most guys who come into professional football are physically able to play—they're strong and they can run—but they can't make a football team because of the mental part of it. We had that complicated defense at Penn State. Sure, there was different terminology being used in the pros, but, basically, I knew what had to be done and the philosophy of the zone defense, the way it should be and what the basic responsibilities of the outside linebacker were.

"I can't emphasize that enough. You see guys come to training camp looking like Charles Atlas, but they don't make the football team because of the errors they make out there. Joe's philosophy was that with the mental part of it you're going to win or lose football games. In the pros, I think it's even more so."

When Ham came to the Steelers' camp in 1971, Art Rooney Jr.'s only request was that Ham work on developing his upper body.

"I remember when he came up to my room the night before practice started," Rooney says. "He wasn't an impressive looking guy in his civilian clothes. The next day I found out he weighed only about 205 in his shorts. He had big-league legs, but his upper body was terrible."

In his eighth season, Ham now is listed at 225 pounds.

"I'll never forget my first preseason camp with the linebackers in 1974," Widenhofer recalls. "We have a coverage where our strong 'backer' [Ham] lines up over the tight end. He's got the flat responsibility.

"Now you've got to envision the flanker lining up maybe ten to twelve yards from the tight end sometimes. The quarterback takes a three-step drop and throws a quick-out to the flanker. Well, Terry Bradshaw took that three-step drop and turned and fired and Ham was about three feet in the air, went up in the line of fire and intercepted the pass. I couldn't believe it. All we ask is for the 'backer' to get into the throwing lane, react to the ball, and maybe get a piece of it. I always think about that particular play when I think of Jack Ham."

Four years of covering tight end Ted Kwalick in Penn State practices also helped Ham.

"When you're playing a lot of zone defense, your responsibility to the tight end is to never let him get an inside release on you," Ham says. "It penetrates your zone too quickly. But I practiced day in and day out on Kwalick at Penn State, not letting him get up the field deep in a hurry. First day in Steelers' camp, it was exactly the same thing."

It was the same as it was when Ham and Dennis Onkotz, an All-America linebacker who had boundless potential until he suffered a severely fractured leg with the New York Jets, teamed to help make Penn State the best defensive college team in the nation in 1968 and 1969.

To further indicate how smoothly Ham adapted to pro ball, he even withstood a rookie season under Chuck Noll, the Steelers' knowledgeable but stubborn head coach who was the team's linebacker tutor in 1971.

"It was incredible," Ham says. "I really thought Andy Russell [the Steelers' now retired veteran outside linebacker] and Noll were always getting into arguments over technique. Chuck would point out eighty-two fundamentals on how to do something and Andy would say, 'Chuck, that's fine, but it just doesn't work in a game.'"

Widenhofer still can't get over what Ham accomplished in the Steelers' AFC championship game at Oakland in 1974. Ham intercepted two Ken Stabler passes in the game, which lifted the Steelers to their first of two straight Super Bowl championships.

With the Steelers leading in the third quarter, Oakland was driving and looking for success with the pass since Pittsburgh had completely shut off the Raiders' running game.

"We have a coverage where Ham lines up on the strongside and they flood the weak zone," Widenhofer says. "Now, that's all the way on the other side of the field and Ham has to cover the fullback to the weakside. It's the type of coverage where you have to read very quickly and break like hell to get there.

"Well, they ran the halfback on a takeoff—they just ran Russell out of there. They put two wide receivers on the strongside and Jack Lambert went back and picked up the tight end hook. They ran the fullback in the weak flat, away from Ham, and Ham came across the formation, dived out, and intercepted the ball. I talked to Stabler after the game. He said he went to the fullback because he believed it couldn't be possible anybody else could be there. But Jack broke on the quarterback's eyes. It was a great, great play, one of the best I've ever seen."

Greg Buttle, in his third year with the New York Jets, should accompany Paterno on recruiting trips. He gushes about his Penn State experience.

"If you draft a Penn State linebacker, you're one step ahead of the game," Buttle says. "You get such a great coaching experience..."

Buttle claims linebackers who come from other schools are more "uncomfortable" when they enter the NFL.

"You have a lot of linebackers who come into the pros with no technique," Buttle says. "They may be tough, but they don't know the certain way to do something, like keeping your shoulders square to the line of scrimmage...It was a complicated system to learn, but once you understood what it was all about, it was easy. Everything else just fell into place."

Buttle says the pass coverage lessons were invaluable.

"In the pros, you're going to play the pass a lot of the time. The big thing is whether you can drop [back into a passing zone] as an outside linebacker, because it's such a big drop. But at Penn State the drop was the same thing. I played middle linebacker at Penn State and my drop there was as far as it is with the Jets as an outside linebacker."

Coupling such advantages with excellent lateral speed, a necessity at Penn State, Buttle was an immediate standout with the Jets.

"Some linebackers don't know the basic things when they get into the pros," Buttle says.

"And in the pros, it all happens so quickly, you get stuck and you stand there. The next thing you know, you're blocked. At Penn State, the biggest sin was staying blocked."

The rookies who are getting blocked, Buttle noted, are the ones who are eventually going to be wondering why their heads are ringing.

Even Detroit's O'Neil, who was drafted higher than any other Penn State linebacker (the eighth player chosen in 1973) but has developed slowly as a pro, can't fault the foundation.

"I would say the most important thing was the confidence built inside us as Penn State linebackers," says O'Neil, who, after playing behind former Penn State teammate Laslavic (now with San Diego), is expected to start in the Detroit middle this year. "At Penn State they worked really hard on the fact that the defense was built around the linebackers and that everything that happened, in one way or another, involved the linebackers."

Although people like Rooney still insist that "O'Neil was the best college linebacker in the country that year," O'Neil insists the problem has been one of attitude. "I didn't prepare myself mentally for a game that is a lot more demanding in the pros," he says.

Radakovich, the Penn State system's originator, has never accepted anything less than what he had in mind when he created the scheme. Radakovich has mellowed since the days when he would throw a pair of sunglasses to the field and shatter them, but he has maintained his strong opinions.

"Most people think linebackers are born," the 43-year-old Radakovich says, "but that's a bunch of garbage. They think they have a sixth sense, that they just know what plays are coming. What it is, is that they know how to use their eyes to gather information. The problem is, people ask them, 'How'd you get there?' and they say, 'Oh, I got the sixth sense.' That's nonsense."

Paterno took over as head coach in 1966 and Radakovich's defensive system was implemented in 1967. Radakovich says he learned from Penn State's 1964 season that the days when "we had very slow linebackers and probably the two poorest athletes on the team" were over.

"We went into the 1964 season with an excellent defense," he says. "We had beaten Ohio State twenty seven-zero and they had minus yardage when our first string came out. We played a five-three that year and Notre Dame had a four-four. By watching what they played, I realized we could play both and also play every other set in football. It was unique, as far as I know."

Radakovich spent an entire weekend drawing up his presentation, hopeful even though "it didn't' go over right away."

"You could switch to the different alignments and each had a different advantage to it without changes in the coverage. Like putting the middle linebacker down into the line or back off it. You could slide the whole line one way and all the linebackers the other. You'd have maximum flexibility with a minimum of assignment changes."

Radakovich had no doubt his players could handle the mental rigors.

The coaches knew the defensive plan would be useless if the players couldn't retain it.

"They have to be involved in the game, so they not only have to be good athletes, they also have to be smart kids," Paterno says, repeating the view of the Steelers' Rooney who says, "You know, I don't think I've ever seen a dumb kid come out of Penn State...Radakovich was extremely clever at emphasizing aspects that may have seemed unimportant to the player."

"I emphasized the simple things, like how to start laterally, not just slide," says Radakovich. "Or how you glanced ahead on pursuit instead of just looking at the ball. The Penn State linebackers knew how to use their eyes, swivel their head, glance for receivers coming into their zones. Most people, when they're teaching zone coverage, tell them to run back to an area and stare at the quarterback. But when you're playing zone and you're good, you have to know what people are in the area, even though you're playing zone. Like in basketball, you know where those guys are. You don't just slide with the ball."

Paterno obviously never felt Radakovich...[was] wasting time.

"The thing that has helped our linebackers the most is the job the coaches have done with them," says Paterno. "By the time they leave here, there isn't anything they aren't doing right."

All Paterno has to do is point to Ham as an example.

"Jack does everything that we're talking about," Paterno says. "Jack's smart, he's a great competitor and he's a quality person. He makes the big plays when you have to have them in the tough games. I think he would be a pretty good example of most of our kids. Some of them didn't have quite as much ability, but they did all those kinds of things for us."

Paterno had a logical explanation when he was asked about the ongoing linebacking phenomenon at Penn State.

"If a kid is a fine high school athlete and he has visions of being a top-notch linebacker," he says, "he knows that at Penn State he'll get the kind of training that will make it possible for him to be a pro.

"I think that once it started, then it became the old saying, 'Nothing succeeds like success!' "

Over the next three decades, Penn State produced such first team All-Americans as Greg Buttle, Kurt Allerman, Shane Conlan, Brandon Short, LaVar Arrington, and second team All-Americans like Lance Mehl and Scott Radecic. All of them made names for themselves in the NFL and several played with the New York Jets or New York Giants, and I even got to coach some of them in New York, too. I have a theory about that, too. I've been told that the nickname Linebacker U may have been the idea of Penn State's sports information director, John Morris, in the late 1970s. Unfortunately, John passed away a few years ago and no one at Penn State can confirm this. Frankly, I believe the name Linebacker U may have germinated in New York because of all those Penn State linebackers who had played there in the 1960s and 1970s. New York is the media capital of the world and the Penn State linebackers playing in New York made an impact, generating a lot of publicity. Maybe it was someone like the late sportscaster Howard Cosell who first uttered the words, Linebacker U, but there's no doubt in my mind that the national media based there helped make it happen.

There was a brief slump at Penn State at the end of 1999, but linebacker coach Ron Vanderlinden came along in 2001 and revived the "curriculum" with such recent Linebacker U graduates as Paul Posluszny, Dan Connor, Sean Lee, and Navarro Bowman. There undoubtedly will be more to come.

So, my nomadic journey in life began riding Emmett Kelly's clown bicycle around my neighborhood outside Kennywood Park, and after a successful 13 years of coaching linebackers at Penn State, I was now on my way to my first coaching experience outside of Happy Valley. Little did I know that I now had my own little one-ring circus that would take me all over the country and even to Europe over the next 40 years.

CHAPTER ELEVEN –
My Marco Polo Journey Begins

When I left Penn State in January of 1970 to go to the University of Cincinnati, I was 34 years old and I never envisioned I would spend the next 35 years in 17 different jobs from coast to coast and even Europe. A football coaching nomad. With all the travelling around from city to city that I did, you might think I was a clown for the Barnum and Bailey Circus. Or, with my off-beat personality, maybe I'd have been the guy shot out of the cannon or one of those high wire tightrope walkers. The truth is that Emmett Kelly, the Great Zacchinis and the Flying Wallendas probably rubbed off on me because, as I wrote earlier, they all lived with my family or our friends in my Pittsburgh neighborhood at one time or another. Little did I know I would never have another job longer than the one I had at Penn State.

Book Room Bedroom – I packed my tiny Renault with my clothes and bedding and drove 10 hours from State College to Cincinnati. In order to help me save money before my wife and I could find a house, the athletic department provided me a cot so that I could sleep in the book room in the corner of the athletic locker room, which was in the basement of the physical education building. This was a room where the books for the scholarship athletes were stored. Two of the room's walls were made of open wire fencing, and that meant anyone walking by could look into the room. About five feet above the cot was a big brass bell attached to the wall that automatically rang for the beginning and ending of a 50 minute class, starting at 6:00 a.m. and 6:50 a.m. and continuing the procedure throughout the day until 6:00 p.m. I had no need for an alarm clock that spring term. I wondered if that loud brass bell had anything to do with the fact that I now wear a hearing aid.

Benching A Two Year Starter – I was officially hired to replace the previous defensive coordinator, Sam Congie, and to coach the same position that he did—the defensive line. I got Jim Kelly, the former receivers' coach, to coach the defensive ends, which freed me up to simply coach the two defensive tackle positions in the 4-4-3 defense that was to be our basic alignment. After coaching the six or seven players at those two tackle positions for one week, I realized that only one, Bob Bell, could play. (After the season he was the No. 1 draft pick of the Detroit Lions and played eight years in the NFL.) One of the other players had been a starter the previous two seasons. When Coach Ray Callahan seemed skeptical about my negative judgment of this two-year starter, I had Callahan watch the two-year starter in a peel drill. That's when three blockers and a ball carrier align in a full I-formation opposite the defender. On the snap count, the blockers peel off in one direction and try to cut block the defender one right after another. On three separate attempts, the two-year starter never got past the first blocker. Each time he went down like he was cut with a scythe. Callahan immediately moved him to the offensive line, where he became a backup player.

Coaching Dilemma – After the first two weeks of spring practice, I realized I couldn't coach defensive tackles and still be an effective defensive coordinator. Coaching the defensive tackles did not allow me to be involved in any part of pass coverage, pass skeleton, pass drills, etc. I couldn't see enough of what was going on in practice. I told my wife about my dilemma. Nancy suggested that I try to make a deal with Dave Ritchie, the linebackers coach. So, I went over to Dave's house that night and proposed a deal. If I could coach just the outside linebackers, he could keep the two inside linebacker positions but also coach the defensive tackle positions. We would get rid of all the defensive tackles, except Bob Bell, and give them to the offense or demote them to the scout squad. We would replace the remaining starter and backup tackle positions with backup linebackers that Dave was already coaching. He went along with the deal and became a unique linebacker-defensive tackle coach, and by coaching outside linebackers, I was in an excellent location to be the defensive coordinator.

Dave Ritchie

Players Quitting—Good Or Bad – When spring practice was over, defensive end coach Jim Kelly informed the staff that we had a problem that the Cincinnati football team had never had before. Twelve full scholarship football players had quit the team during spring practice. I knew that we had probably increased the intensity in practice over what had occurred in previous years. We didn't berate, penalize, or try to run anyone off. We simply practiced hard. I asked what caliber of players was quitting—good, average, poor, etc? All 12 players that quit were poor players. I viewed this as a very healthy sign. The players that were quitting were the ones that had been just along for the ride.

Better Than Penn State – After our spring practice had finished, secondary coach David Dunkelberger, Kelly and I visited Penn State's spring practice for one week. We stayed at the Nittany Lion Inn, visited the football office, watched film, talked to the coaches, talked to some players like Jack Ham and went to the practices. We had an enjoyable week. On the drive back to Cincinnati, Jim Kelly says, "Rad, Dunk and I have been talking and we need to tell you something." I said, "What's that?" Jim said, "We think we are better than they are," meaning our Cincinnati defense was better at the end of spring practice than what we saw at Penn State. I said, "You're probably right." That was our first realization that we might have an exceptional defense in the fall. As for my old Penn State team, they lost three of their first five games—including a 41-13 defeat at Colorado that ended the school record undefeated streak at 31 games—but turned around and won five straight with a new quarterback and rejuvenated defense to finish 7-3 and 18th in the AP poll, and then voted to reject a Peach Bowl invitation.

Reporting Weight – Before our Cincinnati players left for the summer, we did something that was unique in my experience. We had a number of players that we felt were overweight. All the assistant coaches sat in chairs around the weight scale in the locker room. Each player on the team was weighed naked, and after a brief discussion among all the coaches, an agreed upon reporting weight was given to each player. If the player reported in the fall over the prescribed weight, he simply would not be allowed to practice, or be a member of the team until he made the weight. No other penalties or help would be given. If, for example, six weeks later, he made the weight, he could report for practice then. Defensive tackle Bob Bell, our pro prospect, weighed over 270, and I can remember calling him once a week the entire summer to see how he was progressing towards his reporting weight of 240. At the reporting date, he weighed in at 239½. Every player on the first two units made their reported weight. Our team of approximately 100 players had lost a total of over 500 pounds. Simply not allowing a player to participate if he didn't make the weight, proved to be a great motivator.

Deck Of Cards Playbook – During a linebacker meeting my last year at Penn State, I noticed Gary Hull, an outside linebacker, glancing at some index cards, and I inquired as to what that was about. He had put his assignment for each defense on a separate card and that was how he studied his assignments. I thought that was a great idea and put it to use when I went to Cincinnati. That first summer at Cincinnati, I drew up a master book of our multiple defensive scheme that was to be used by the defensive coaches only. For the players, I gave each of them a deck of approximately 50 3x5 inch index cards. Each card had a position assignment for a particular defense typed on one side and diagramed on the other side. A small silver ring held the deck of cards together. A player with a deck of 50 cards had the particular assignments for his position for 50 different defenses, which he could carry in his shirt or pants pocket. The deck of cards idea worked out better than any defensive playbook that I have ever been associated with. I only used it one other time, during my first year at Colorado in 1972, also with excellent results.

Legal Dribble – We started the 1970 season winning three of our first five games. The two losses were 7-3 to Tulsa in the opener and 6-3 to Tulane in the fourth game. With less than six minutes left in the Tulane game on a Saturday night, we were ahead 3-0 and had Tulane third-and-long deep in its own territory. The Tulane quarterback threw a complete pass for a first down. Cincinnati reporter Wally Forste wrote: "Tulane quarterback Mike Walke passed to end Jack LaBorde who dropped the ball but caught it on the bounce and ran another 11 yards to the Tulane 43. It was the first legal dribble we've seen in football." Everybody in the stadium saw the ball bounce except the officials. Three plays later, Tulane completed a long touchdown pass to win 6-3. This same Tulane team crushed the University of Colorado at the end of the season in the Liberty Bowl, 17-3.

That's Not Sal Casola – In the late spring of 1970, I received a phone call from a former Penn State teammate, Andy Moconyi, who was a high school football coach in Bethlehem, PA. Andy told me he had the best kicker in New Jersey and Pennsylvania, and wanted me to get him admitted. I got the kicker admitted to our junior college on campus, which was called University College. He would be ineligible the first year, but freshmen couldn't play the first year anyway, and could become eligible his sophomore year if he passed 24 credits with the 2.00 or better grade point average. I then forgot about him.

On Oct. 2, 1970 at about 6 p.m. on the Friday before our Saturday night Tulane game, I was sitting at my desk alone in the defensive football office when I heard a knock on the door. I opened the door and looked down at this little guy of about 5-foot-7, 150-pounds who was dressed in khaki fatigues. I asked who he was. He said he was Sal Casola, the kicker. I asked what kicker? He said Andy Moconyi's kicker. Then it registered. I wondered what Andy was thinking when he sent me this little kid as a kicker. I asked him when he would be ready to kick. He said, "Right now." So I took him down to the Physical Education locker room and got him some workout gear and a few footballs. Our other coaches and players were either in the football locker room or in the stadium getting ready for a brief night practice. Sal asked if he was going to kick in the stadium. I said, "Oh no, the team's going to be getting ready to practice. Let's go up to the intramural football field." There was no way I was going to let the other coaches and players see this kicking fiasco that was about to occur.

When we got to the intramural field, I told Sal to warm up on his own, gave him the footballs and tees and went and smoked a cigarette. After five or ten minutes, Sal said he was warmed up. I said, "Okay, Sal. Put the ball on the far 40-yard line and you can kick off to me." I stood on the 10-yard line, about 50 yards away. Well, Sal kicked the ball, and it kept rising as it went high over my head, high over the goal post and dropped down and hit the ground, 10 yards past the end line. Wow! That was an 80-yard kick in the air that was high enough to bring rain. I retrieved the ball, threw it back to Sal, stood at the 10-yard line again and told Sal to kick off again. Sal kicked off, and again the ball kept rising as it went high over my head, high over the goal post, and again dropped down and hit the ground 10 yards past the end line—another 80-yard whopper! I retrieved the ball, and yelled at Sal, "That's enough. Let's go." He said, "Coach, don't you want to see me kick field goals?" I said, "Oh yeah, Sal, but let's go over to the stadium." I had to let the other coaches and players see my new kicker. When we got to the stadium, I got a center and a holder and told Sal to kick field goals from the 40-yard line. He then kicked five straight 50-yard field goals that ended up high in the stands. Our players wanted to know if he could kick the next night against Tulane. Of course, he couldn't because he was a freshman who was ineligible.

I was gone for the three years that Sal kicked for Cincinnati. I was told that Sal once tried a 75-yard field goal in the game that was short because he kicked it too high. Sal didn't set any kicking records, but he did sign with the Buffalo Bills. Years later, in 1985 or '86, former Cincinnati Head Coach Ray Callahan and I were coaching with the New York Jets and were in Cincinnati to play the Bengals. So we decided to visit Jim Kelly, the former assistant with us at the University of Cincinnati. We asked what ever happened to Sal Casola, the kicker. Jim said Buffalo had drafted him in the 17th round of the 1974 draft. He said Buffalo was playing the Bengals the third preseason game of '74 in Cincinnati, and Kelly, who knew the Cincinnati coaches, had gone to the game. He said he was on the field talking before the game when he asked one of the visiting team coaches how Sal Casola was doing? The coach said Sal was doing well. Jim said he was Sal's coach and would like to see him. The visiting coach pointed to a player kicking field goals and said, "That's him over there." Jim looked and said, "That's not Sal Casola." The coach said, "Yes it is." Jim said, "I coached Sal Casola for four years and that's not Sal Casola."

It wasn't Sal Casola, Jim told us it was Sal Casola's brother, John! Sal supposedly had sent his brother in his place! Jim said Buffalo immediately cut Sal's brother. Now, that's the way Ray Callahan and I heard the story. But sometimes memory can play tricks on us. While researching for this book, my co-author, Lou Prato, found a story in *Sports Illustrated* about Sal's duplicity that tells it another way. This version was printed in the Scorecard section of the September 4, 1974 edition under the headline, "IDENTITY CRISIS."

Identity Crisis – *It was always touch and go, but for a while there it seemed possible that John Casola just might pull off one of the master switcheroos in sport. A month ago Buffalo waived its 17th-round draft choice, kicking specialist Sal Casola. Discouraged, Sal decided to quit pro football, which was all the encouragement brother John, who had done a little kicking himself several years ago at Marion Institute in Alabama, needed. When Kansas City Coach Hank Stram phoned Sal at the Casola home to offer him a trial, he reached John, instead, and John began the impersonation.*

Almost from the beginning, players suspected something fishy. For instance, Sal would fail to answer to his name. He finally explained that he was baptized John Salvatore Casola and that at home they called him John. Then there was the teammate who...had played against Sal in college. Casola could contribute nothing to the fellow's reminiscences of the game. A few of the curious lurked near the phone when he called home, but they were always stymied. Casola spoke in Italian.

The mask finally came off four weeks ago when Buffalo visited K.C. for an exhibition game. Casola warmed up as far away from the Bills as he decently could, but they saw him and wondered aloud. Said Buffalo Coach Lou Saban to Stram, "What have you been feeding Casola? He must have gained 30 pounds since he left our camp." Said Buffalo Kicker Boris Shlapak, "I don't know who that guy kicking there is, but it isn't Sal Casola."

Next day John confessed. After Stram cooled down, the coach said he wasn't mad a bit. "Actually I admire the man's determination. He came here because he seriously wanted a tryout with a pro club. He's got a strong leg, and in time could become a good kicker, but he'd have to work on his form."

After their interview Stram had a paycheck made out to John to take the place of several issued to Sal that John had feared cashing. Then two weeks ago, along with several other marginal players, John was waived by K.C, under the name of Sal Casola.

I have no idea why Sal sent his brother in his place. Either he was hurt or sick where he couldn't play or he simply didn't want to play professional football. But John must have been a pretty good kicker, too. Sal is still the best placekicker I've ever seen. I've never heard from or seen Sal Casola since 1970. I have tried to track him down to get the true story but I have no idea where he is today. I have presented two versions of Sal's story here—his former college coach, Jim Kelly's, and Sports Illustrated's version. Jim has passed away and I can't talk to him to verify his version. Personally, I believe Jim's version, but who am I to doubt *Sports Illustrated*.

My NCAA Record Throw – Cincinnati's sixth game of the year was against in-state rival Ohio University. Ohio had dominated Cincinnati the year before, 46-6. Obviously, it was a very big game for us. The cheerleaders held a special promotion that game to help boost attendance. Each fan was given a free kazoo upon entering the stadium and Izzy "Kazoo" Mills, the world's No. 1 kazoo player, was to perform at halftime. Now, in case anyone reading this never heard of Izzy or doesn't know what a kazzo is, it's a small instrument that produces music by humming. So, at the end of the first quarter when both teams change sides, the cheerleaders and Izzy Kazoo rushed onto the field, put a 5-foot tall microphone stand in the middle of the field on the 50-yard line and Izzy Kazoo started playing the song, "Mr. Touchdown USA" on the kazoo with the cheerleaders standing around him also playing kazoos. Both teams eventually got out of their huddles and lined up ready to play, but Izzy Kazoo and the cheerleaders kept playing their kazoos.

We were ahead at the time, 14-7, and I was afraid of a delay of game penalty on us as the home team. I yelled for someone to get Izzy and the cheerleaders off the field, but they kept playing and no one did anything. I took off running and got to the center of the field, grabbed the standing microphone with its 50-yard long extension cord and ran toward the sideline with this 5-foot microphone stand. When I got about eight yards from the 4-foot fence surrounding the field, I threw the microphone stand against the fence and it shattered into several pieces, almost like a grenade exploding. Well, the people in the stadium roared, and the roar lasted for at least a minute or two. We eventually won the game 29-21.

After the game, my wife said she had to tell me what happened in the stands when I threw the microphone. She said there was a lot of buzz in the stands with everyone commenting on what I did. My 7½ year old daughter, Lisa, started to cry, saying, "Why'd my daddy do that? Why'd my daddy do that?" and Mimi, her 12-year-old cousin sitting beside her, said, "Lisa, be quiet, and no one will know that's your daddy!" In writing about the incident the next day under the headline, "Kazzo Hums A Tune, But Fades Fast," one Cincinnati newspaper reported that I must have set the

NCAA record for a microphone throw, and another newspaper set the "record" at 19 feet, 8 inches. As a result of the incident, I got a bunch of letters from fans. One letter from the former retired radio broadcaster of the Cincinnati football team, Dick Bray, said that I had struck a great blow against the despicable unwashed generation. We were in the Vietnam and the hippie era, but I still don't see the logic of that statement. At the annual football banquet, the cheerleaders presented me with a gold microphone with these words engraved on the base: "NCAA RECORD MICROPHONE THROW – 19 ft, 8 inches" OCT 24, 1970.

Never Help A Friend – My past caught up to me in our ninth game of the 1970 season when we played Louisville. In the spring of 1969, my good friend John Hyder, who had been the coach at Bishop Guilfoyle High School in Altoona, called me at Penn State. John had recently been hired by Lee Corso, the new head coach at Louisville. John said Louisville desperately needed to recruit a quarterback, and did I know of anyone good enough for them to recruit? I gave him the name of a 6-foot-5 quarterback from West Mifflin, PA, named John Madeya. One and a half years later, I was at Cincinnati coaching against Louisville and the Louisville starting quarterback was the same John Madeya. Madeya threw two long touchdown passes and we lost a close game, 28-14. It just goes to show you what can happen when you help a friend.

Predictable Cradle Of Coaches – Cincinnati's 10th game in 1970 was against Miami of Ohio, whose record was 7-2 with both losses by one point to Toledo, 14-13, and Ohio U, 23-22. The school is known in the football world as "The Cradle of Coaches" because so many of its head coaches have gone on to national prominence at other colleges, such as Woody Hayes at Ohio State, Bo Schembechler at Michigan and Ara Parseghian at Notre Dame. In '70, the Miami defense was ranked No. 1 in a couple of categories, including total defense. They were also ranked No. 1 in punt coverage, having given up a total of three yards in punt returns in nine games—a phenomenal statistic. On offense, they had the best running back, Tim Fortney, and best pass receiver, Mike Palija, statistically in their history. They had beaten Cincinnati the previous year 38-0. However, they had a glaring weakness on both offense and on punt coverage. They were predictable!

On offense, they basically used only one formation: the I-slot, with a tight end on one side and two wide receivers on the other side. Essentially, they ran the ball to the tight end side and passed the ball to the slot side. We simply overloaded and played the run to the tight end side and put bump and run on their great wide receiver to the slot side the entire game with a deep safety behind on that side. We did this whether we were in a base defense or a blitz. We intercepted four balls that were thrown to Palija, who had bump and run coverage the entire game by cornerback Dave Gannelli. On punt coverage, their players ran very disciplined lanes. The outside three cover guys on each side would fan out and the rest of the players would run straight lanes straight down the field. There was a natural alley between the No. 3 cover guy, who fanned out, and No. 4, who ran straight on both sides. We decided to widen this alley on both sides and run a draw punt return instead of the more common picket fence up one of the sidelines. Our punt returner simply caught the punt and went straight up into one of the two natural alleys between the No. 3 and No 4 cover guys. The first return went for 50 yards and the returner Billy Hunter tripped over one of his own blockers. We had a total of almost 200 yards in punt returns that day, and the final score was Cincinnati 33, Miami 0.

I believe the moral of this story is if you want to keep the name like the Cradle of Coaches, you'd better quit being the "predictable" Cradle of Coaches. Ironically, the Miami head coach that day, Bill Mallory, would succeed Eddie Crowder as head coach of Colorado in 1974, just as I was leaving Colorado to go back to the Steelers.

No. 1 Draft Pick Bob Bell Versus No. 2 Draft Pick Jack Ham –

During the 1970 season, Bob Bell, our best defensive tackle and NFL prospect, and his position coach, Dave Ritchie, and I had an agreement that Bob could substitute himself freely in and out of the game. When he was in the game he had to go full speed until the ball touched the ground—no pacing oneself—and when he tired, we wanted him to take himself out of the game until he felt he could go full speed again. Bob did as we asked and had a great year on defense. At the end of the season he got invited to the East-West Shrine All-Star game. Dave and I had a meeting with Bob and told him we wanted him to do the same in the East-West practices as we had asked him to do in games. We told him to go full speed in every individual or team drill as much as reasonably possible. We told him that there would be a lot of pro scouts there and how you practice would impress them more than the actual game performance. Bob must have made a good impression because he was then picked No. 1 by Detroit in the NFL draft, supposedly to replace Alex Karras of NFL All-Pro fame.

Jack Ham

Shortly after that draft, I attended a banquet given in honor of Jack Ham in Johnstown. Of course, I had coached Jack in his first three years at Penn State and now he was a second round draft pick of the Pittsburgh Steelers. Jack had also played in the East-West game, and after the banquet, he asked me what the problem was with my defensive tackle Bob Bell. Jack said Bob ran around like a crazy man in the East-West practices, and Jack wondered who Bell thought he was trying to impress by being a dummy scrimmage star. I told Jack I couldn't believe he said that. I said Joe Paterno used to worry about practicing with no pads at the Orange Bowl because Jack Ham, who hustled like a madman, might get hurt. I said, "I told Bell to hustle like a crazy man in practice. You're a No. 2 draft pick, and he's a No. 1. You are twice the player he is, but he signed for twice the money you did, all because you didn't want to be a dummy scrimmage star."

Bell went on to an 8-year NFL career with Detroit (three years) and St. Louis (five years) while Ham played 12 years for Pittsburgh, has four Super Bowl rings and is in the Pro Football Hall of Fame.

Missed Seeing Super Bowl V – During the fall of 1970, football practice ended at approximately 6 p.m. every day. I would quickly shower and then drive a half hour to attend Chase Night Law School from 7 to 10 p.m. four nights a week, Monday through Thursday. On those nights, I usually got home around 11:00 p.m., at which time I would eat dinner that my wife had prepared for me. Since I had a job as a full-time defensive coordinator, I didn't have time to study. I simply made sure I had 100% attendance during the season. As soon as the season was over, with the last game on November 28, I had to cram as much studying in as I could in December because midyear exams were given early in January.

My wife and I took our four kids back to her parents' home in Easton for the two-week Christmas, New Year break, and I spent the entire two weeks in the Lafayette College library in Easton studying my law books. I had taken four law courses and my final exam was in contracts. Lo and behold, I slept through it. The exam started at 8 or 9 a.m. and I woke up about two hours later. I immediately called my contracts professor, and he told me he couldn't give it to me later because I might get the questions and so forth from another student. I begged and pleaded and offered to drive in and take it right away. Finally he relented and told me to come in the next day, which was Super Bowl V Sunday. While I took the contracts exam, my professor watched the Super Bowl on TV in his adjoining office. I missed seeing Super Bowl V, but I did pass the mid-year contracts exam with a C+. Four years later, I would get a close-up view of Super Bowl IX from the sideline.

Day Law School Rejection – One day in the spring of 1971, the Dean of the Cincinnati Law School, approached me about the possibility of transferring from Chase night law school to Cincinnati's day law school. This would be a big advantage for me because I would get my law degree in three years instead of the four years that night school required. Also, I wouldn't have night classes. He knew my grades were okay my first term at Chase and told me he thought it would be no problem for me to transfer. He just had to meet with his faculty to have it approved. The reason he approached me was because the university had put a freeze on salaries for a year and a half and I had been promised a big raise. We had improved the defense by 23 points a game over the previous two years and the administration was afraid that I was going to leave. Getting me in day school was a great way to make sure I would stay at Cincinnati for the next two seasons. The Dean told me to come over to the law school at 7 p.m. on a Friday—I had night classes at the Chase Law School the other days—and he would get me transferred to Cincinnati's day law school.

When I got to the University of Cincinnati law school building a few minutes before seven p.m., the dean of the law school was waiting for me outside the main entrance to the building. He said he had bad news for me. His faculty had turned down my request for the transfer from Chase to Cincinnati's law school. The reasons had nothing to do with my academic qualifications or grades at Chase. They were fine. The problem was political. The American Bar Association (ABA) had recently issued an edict that in order for a night law school to have ABA approval, it must be connected with a day law school. Since the Cincinnati Law School did not have a night law school, some politicians—some of whom were Chase night law school graduates—were pushing the Cincinnati Law School to accept Chase as its night school. The Cincinnati Law School faculty was totally against having Chase as its night school. Cincinnati Law School has never had a transfer student from Chase, and Chase had been in existence over 200 years. They said accepting me as a transfer student from Chase would be interpreted as a reason for accepting Chase as their night law school. That extinguished my last good reason for staying at the University of Cincinnati. After I left, Chase Law School became part of the University of Northern Kentucky, which is just across the Ohio River from Cincinnati.

Naturally, I was upset. I loved coaching at Cincinnati but without that raise I had been promised, or some help with law school tuition, I knew I would have a financial problem. Right before my law school finals on a Wednesday in the middle of May, I figured out our finances for the year up to that time—from May 1, 1970 to May 1, 1971. I had earned $14,700, and had spent $22,500. That was more than $7,000 than what I had earned and all I did was coach football and go to law school at night. My Penn State retirement of about $6,500, which I got for my 10 years as a full-time employee, was gone. My salary was still $14,700, I was still paying for my own law school tuition and books, and the university still had a freeze on salaries. I told my wife we couldn't afford to stay at Cincinnati. She agreed. I said "I wonder if the Steelers have hired anybody for the coach that died at San Diego State's spring practice six weeks ago?" Nancy said, "Why don't you call and find out."

I did. About eight days after my phone call, I was a member of the Pittsburgh Steelers coaching staff, and law school was put on the back burner. But that wouldn't be the last time I would be a coach at the University of Cincinnati. I was back less than two years later as the head coach—well, for a day or so.

CHAPTER TWELVE –
Rocky Mountain High and the Dawn Patrol

Just about everyone was surprised when I passed on Chuck Noll's offer after the 1971 season to be defensive coordinator and linebacker coach of the Pittsburgh Steelers. Chuck tried to keep me and I believe he assigned receivers coach Lionel Taylor to try to convince me to stay because Lionel was dogging me for two weeks. Lionel's main argument was that I should stay and try to help the Steelers win a title for Mr. Rooney, The Chief. This made me feel bad, but I still didn't change my mind.

Frankly, after that first year of coaching in pro football, I simply wasn't enamored with it. I also was disappointed the way the Steelers season had turned out as we gave up a lot of easy touchdowns and lost three of our last four games to wind up 6-8. Remember, too, this was when the Steelers were one of the biggest losers in pro football, and they had not had a winning season since 1963 when one of the best players was Dick Hoak, our versatile halfback and quarterback at Penn State.

I had spent 14 years coaching in college and I thought it was more challenging than the pros because you really had to build a new team from year to year. At that point, I figured college coaching would be my life and that I could be a head coach in a couple of years or so. I thought the Colorado job as defensive coordinator gave me that opportunity. I also liked the idea of trying to beat two of the best teams in college football, Oklahoma and Nebraska.

What I found at Colorado changed my entire perspective. Maybe I was spoiled by my experience at Penn State and Cincinnati. Boulder was certainly not State College, but I liked the community and it was a very friendly college town. In the early 70s, Boulder was the third most popular hippie community after Berkeley and San Francisco, but with my personality I felt quite comfortable there. It was what happened in the coaching area that was different—a radically dissimilar atmosphere from anything I had experienced at Penn State, Cincinnati or the Steelers. Maybe it was the air up there, the high altitude and sparse oxygen. Or maybe it was the wacky, free-wheeling hippie influence. I don't know. But it sure changed my outlook on my "chosen" profession.

I didn't know much about Colorado's head coach, Eddie Crowder, or the team, but I had a lot of respect for Colorado football because it played in the Big Eight, which most people thought was then the toughest overall conference in college football. At Penn State, we had played against the Big Eight champions in the 1969 and 1970 Orange Bowls—Kansas and Missouri—and they were both close games down to the end, but we won both.

Later I learned that Eddie had been a star quarterback at Oklahoma for the great Bud Wilkinson and then had coached under Wilkinson from 1956 to 1962 before taking over what had been a dormant Colorado program. Colorado was 2-8 his first year but by 1967 they were 8-2, finished in a second place tie for the Big Eight championship and beat Miami in the Bluebonnet Bowl to wind up 13th in the final polls. In my final year at Penn State in 1969, we played Colorado for the first time and won at Beaver Stadium, 27-3 as our defense forced seven turnovers. But, as I mentioned in the last chapter, the year I was at Cincinnati in 1970, Colorado stopped Penn State's 31-game undefeated streak in Boulder, 41-13. That season Colorado went on to lose to Tulane, 17-3, in the Liberty Bowl, the same Tulane team that was lucky to beat our Cincinnati team, 6-3, on a blown official's call late in the game.

Eddie had hired me to replace Jerry Claiborne, who had been there for just a year but had been the head coach at Virginia Tech from 1961 to 1970. Jerry left for the head coaching job at Maryland and that's how the defensive coordinator position opened up. The defensive coach for three years before Jerry was Don James who had become the head coach at Kent State and later would be the head coach at Washington. Eddie gave me full rein to make whatever changes I wanted to make.

The only coach I knew on the staff was offensive line coach Augie Tammariello, who as I wrote earlier, helped me get the job. The staff turned out to be unique because eight members ended up coaching many years in the NFL: me, Kay Dalton, Jim Mora, Steve Ortmayer, Steve Sidwell, Larry Kennan, Les Steckel and Carl Smith. Ortmayer later became director of football operations for two NFL teams, the Raiders and the Rams, and oversaw the transition of the Rams from Los Angeles to St. Louis in 1995. Meanwhile, Mora won two championships in the old USFL for the Philadelphia/Baltimore Stars, and then was the head coach of the Saints and Colts over a 15-year period. Steckel also was a head coach with the Vikings for a year while Augie went on to be the head coach for six years at the University of Louisiana at Lafayette. I don't know if you call that a high powered staff, but it certainly wasn't low powered

When You're Cool, The Sun Always Shines – From the beginning, the staff and players knew that I was not the conventional type of coach they were used to. In a book, *Football, CU Style*, author Fred Cassoti described me as "a quiet chain-smoking Slovak who isn't the type who impresses at first glance." Thanks a lot, Fred. But I just continued to do things my way as Bad Rad has always done and some of the things I did were unusual, I guess.

Two Colorado players, offensive tackle Greg Horton and defensive end Lenny Cuifo, used to remind me of the first time they met me, which was soon after I arrived in the winter of 1972. They said I was in the darkened film room watching film of Colorado's previous season when they turned the lights on. Greg and Lenny said they just wanted to meet the new defensive coach. After we talked for short while, one of them asked me, "Coach Rad, why do you watch film in the dark with your sunglasses on?" They said, I replied, "When you're cool, the sun always shines."

Now, what is strange about my reply is that 16 years later, I'm leafing through the *New York Times* when I spotted a story with a headline about a playwright who began his career by writing his first play while in Sing-Sing, the famous New York prison. This playwright, Miguel Pinero, who was raised on the lower East Side had written a couple of plays while in prison. One of them debuted on Broadway in 1976 and was titled *The Sun Always Shines for the Cool*. I couldn't believe my eyes. The convict had written a play that was titled with a saying almost the same as mine that I thought I had originated back in 1972. The only way I thought this was possible was that Colorado players Cuifo or Horton may have told the story of their meeting me around Boulder. As I said, Boulder was loaded with Hippies then and so was New York, particularly Greenwich Village and the lower East Side. I'm convinced my saying may have traveled the hippie pipeline between Boulder, San Francisco and New York City where this future convict heard it, liked it, and wrote a play with a similar title while in prison. Oh, I still watch game film with my sunglasses on but since we switched to video tape, the room doesn't have to be dark anymore.

Deck Of Cards Again – The coaches at Colorado in 1972 recruited right up to the first day of spring practice. My problem was that I had to insert a defensive scheme that was completely new to them without the benefit of pre-spring practice staff meetings. I was their third defensive coordinator in three years. I solved the problem by doing exactly what I had done two years earlier at Cincinnati. I put all the defensive assignments for all the defenses on a deck of approximately 50 3x5-inch cards. Each position—secondary, inside and outside linebackers, defensive tackles, and ends—had their own special deck of cards, which coaches and players could carry with them at all times in their shirt or pants pocket. Of course, neither the players nor any of the staff had ever seen this done. The deck of cards is a great way to learn assignments but I never used them again. It took a lot of time and effort to make up all those decks of cards, and I now wish I had been energetic enough to use them the remainder of my coaching career.

Hale Learns Golf – One day in the spring of 1972, after one of our Colorado University spring practices, I was getting dressed in the coaches' locker room in the Colorado Stadium team house when in walks professional golfer Hale Irwin looking for head coach Eddie Crowder. Hale played football at Colorado from 1964 to 1966 and in his junior and senior seasons he was an All-Big Eight defensive back and a football Academic All-American. He also was the 1967 NCAA individual golf champion, and after graduating he became a pro golfer in 1968. When I met him that day in 1972 he was starting his fifth year competing on the PGA Tour.

After an introduction and some brief conversation, I asked Hale how he was making out on the PGA Tour. Hale replied, "Rad, I've only won once in four years [at the Sea Pines Heritage Classic on Nov. 28, 1971]. I have a problem. I know I can hit the ball as well as anybody on the tour. I've got all the shots with the driver, woods and irons. But I have to learn how to win. I've got all the shots but I've got to figure how to win."

Hale's problem reminded me of a similar dilemma we have in football and probably most other competitive sports. Great technical skills are not enough to assure winning. Scouting and knowledge of the opponent is also very important. In golf, the competitive opponent is the golf course itself. I believe as Hale became more and more knowledgeable of the courses he was playing that he became better and better, figuring out how to win at least some of the time.

About eighteen months after our conversation, Hale earned his second PGA win, again at the Sea Pines Heritage Classic on Sept. 16, 1973. Nine months after that he got his third win and it was a big one, the 1974 U.S Open. Hale went on to have twenty PGA Tour wins and is one of only six golfers to have won three or more U.S. Opens in its 111-year history. He and Tiger Woods have won three while Jack Nicklaus, Ben Hogan, Bobby Jones and Willie Anderson have four. Hale won his in 1974, 1979 and 1990. His Open win in 1990 was one of the most exciting in that tournament's history. Hale came from four strokes behind at the beginning of the final round to make an improbable 45-foot birdie putt on the final 72nd hole to tie Mike Donald and Hale then won in a playoff.

Hale also won the prestigious Masters in 1974 and 1975 and played on five Ryder Cup teams in 1975, 1977, 1979, 1981 and 1991. While still active on the regular PGA Tour Hale was inducted into the World Golf Hall of Fame in 1992. In 1995, Hale switched to the Champions Tour, which is for seniors 50 and older, and in 2000 *Golf Digest* named him the 19th greatest golfer of all time. He is now the all-time leading winner in the history of the PGA Champions Tour with 45 victories compared to second place Lee Trevino with 29 wins.

Being an Academic All-American in football should have been an indication that Hale would eventually learn how to win on the PGA Tour. After all, this book is about football, not golf.

Offensive Coaches Catch Hell – The NCAA allowed 20 days of spring practice in 1972. After 16 practices, we had had three live scrimmages in which our defense played a basic 3-4 defense (called a 5-2 in college) with no stunts or blitzes because that is what head coach Eddie Crowder wanted and he was in charge of the offense. On the morning of the 17th day, I asked if we could just have one scrimmage where the defense could use all the fronts, coverage's, stunts and blitzes that we had been practicing on our own when we weren't in a team drill against the offense. I felt it was important to have film of one live scrimmage where we were playing the defensive scheme that we were going to use in the fall. Eddie agreed to have a two-hour scrimmage that afternoon to do what I wanted.

The first half hour of the scrimmage, the defense stopped a number of running plays for losses, made a few sacks, and caused a couple of fumbles. I thought that was to be expected because the offense had only practiced against a very vanilla 3-4 defense with no stunts or blitzes for 16 days. However, after one half hour Crowder blew the whistle, said practice was over and asked everybody to leave except the offensive coaches. I stayed on the field because I was curious as to what was happening. I was also upset because I felt I was being cheated out of an hour and a half of scrimmage film of my defenses. Crowder stood in the middle of the field at the 50-yard line with the offensive coaches circled around him and he proceeded to give them hell—a tongue-lashing for over one hour. He picked on each coach for at least 10 minutes of individual criticism, besides yelling at them as a group. I kept thinking he would be done in a minute or two, but he went on and on chewing them out. This incident was my first indication that coaching football at Colorado was going to be somewhat different than at the other places where I had been.

TV Show *Colorado Tomorrow* – Part of my deal to coach at Colorado in 1972 was to receive $6,000 for being co-host of a Friday evening TV show during the season from 6 to 7 p.m. called *Colorado Tomorrow*. An experienced TV person was also co-host, and a different Colorado football assistant was a guest each week with each receiving $1,000 for his appearance. The show was sponsored by Continental Airlines, whose creator and president was Bob Six, a big booster of the Colorado football team. We used to kiddingly call him "our owner." His wife, Audrey Meadows, had become famous as Jackie Gleason's wife Alice in the TV comedy *The Honeymooners*. I remember her as a very nice lady who wore a ton of Indian turquoise jewelry—necklaces, earrings, and bracelets—all at the same time. I had never worked on the air in television or radio and Audrey Meadows helped me out by coaching me on some pointers in running the show.

The basic format of the show was to talk briefly about the next day's opponent and then interview the guest assistant coach about his coaching position. We showed sound film (or video as it's now called) of the assistant coaching his players in practice drills. We also had a pre-recorded narration of him explaining the drills as the drills were shown. You could hear all the sounds from the practice field, like the impact of hits, coaches yelling, players groaning and moaning and that sort of stuff. I very much remembered the famous TV show, *The Violent World of Sam Huff*, where they had put a microphone in Sam's pads, and you could hear the impact sounds, moans, yells, whistles, etc. of the game. We taped the show each Wednesday evening, which was after Saturday's game plan had been completed for that week. I assume the show was fairly popular because I was told it had much higher ratings than the head coach's Sunday evening show. I definitely thought that the Friday 6 to 7 p.m. timeslot was ideal for the show.

But there is one thing that really irritated me on the show. My co-host, whose name I will not mention in this book because I don't even know if he is still living, kept asking me questions that you could only answer with a "yes" or "no." For example, he would say, "This team has a lot of speed. They have two guys as wide receivers who are 100 meter sprint champions and two guys in the backfield who can run just about as fast. They are fast, aren't they Coach Rad?" He should have been asking me questions such as, "What kind of receivers and running backs, does this team have?" That would have given me something to talk about. One day I told him to simply ask me questions that I could answer instead of questions that he'd already answered. He didn't change. My wife told me that I should be proud of the fact that I finished all the shows without decking him. I had always got along well with TV sportscasters and most of them were nice guys, but this one taught me there are also egomaniacs and jerks in that business as in any other.

1972—First Five Games – Our opening game in the fall of 1972 was in Boulder against the University of California, whose head coach Mike White would become a coaching colleague of mine six years later at the San Francisco 49ers. Jack Landon, son of Alf Landon, who ran for president of the United States as a Republican in 1936, was a pilot and a close friend and supporter of the Colorado football team. He flew five of our assistants, including me, in his six-seater small private airplane to Berkeley to scout Cal's spring practice game, which was open to the public. The flight was memorable as Landon flew us lower than commercial airlines through the Rocky Mountains going both to and from Berkeley. The views were awesome. We saw valleys, forests, mountains, etc. where no human has ever been. Many places could only be reached into and out of by helicopter.

Cal's spring game showcased a sophomore quarterback named Steve Bartkowski, who had a gun for an arm. I told our defensive players before our game with Cal that they would be telling their grandchildren that they played against Steve Bartkowski, and Steve went on to play 12 years in the NFL, primarily as the starter for Atlanta. We won 20-10 in a close game in which the defense played very well and even scored a touchdown on linebacker Ed Shoen's interception. Crowder congratulated me in the locker room and told the Boulder Daily Camera, "The defense really won the ball game for us. Our offense didn't look very good." We then won five of our first six games, with a 31-6 loss coming in our fourth game against Oklahoma State's wishbone offense with an unbalanced line. We were simply outplayed on both sides of the ball. I remember they made 13 out of 14 third-down situations. I made a note never to let that happen again

New And Different Experiences – There were some things I experienced during the 1972 season that were different than what I was used to. An example was the pregame meal. In my previous 19 years as a college and professional player and coach, our pregame meal had always been the same: steak, eggs, baked potato, green beans, toast with butter and honey, etc. At Colorado, the pregame meal was rock hard waffles and I don't even remember what else. What I did notice was half of the players didn't eat the supposedly scientific carbohydrate breakfast prescribed by the head trainer. I went back to my house before each home game and had my wife make me breakfast. I didn't know what the other coaches did and didn't ask.

Another thing that was different was the pregame tension. The night before every home game the players and coaches stayed in a hotel in Denver and went to a movie together in the early evening. Coming back from the movie before our first home game, some of the players were laughing about some things that happened in the movie. Coach Crowder overheard them and read them the riot act for not being serious about the game. One of our coaches was a former Colorado player who used to throw up before every game in the locker room bathroom. I was beginning to see why. I had a slightly unpleasant experience in the locker room after our sixth game with Iowa State, which we won 34-22. With the score 34-7 in the fourth quarter, I had put in the entire second defensive unit to play the rest of the game. I was feeling pretty good when I walked into the locker room because I thought the defensive first unit had played a great game. I had a locker next to Crowder, and he began yelling at me about how we stunk on defense and didn't reach any of our goals—one of which was to hold Iowa State's star running back Mike Strahan to less than 100 yards rushing. I yelled back that the running back had got his 100 plus yards in the fourth quarter against the second unit, and that Iowa State had scored its last 15 points against the second team defense. Iowa State had been 5-0 before our game and I told Eddie regardless of what he thought, I thought the defense played a great game against a previously undefeated team. Eddie didn't say anything back, but it was one of the few times I left the locker room feeling upset after what I thought was a great win. The tension was getting to me. By the way, the head coach of that Iowa State team was Johnny Majors, who four years later was the head football coach of the 1976 University of Pittsburgh national champions.

The Spy And The FBI – Now, here's one you're not going to believe. The biggest game of the year for Colorado in 1972 was the seventh game against Oklahoma in Boulder. Our record was 5-1, and we were coming off what I thought was a big win against previously undefeated Iowa State that made us No. 9 in the country. Oklahoma was No. 1 in both total offense (total yards gained) and total defense (least yards given up). They were unbeaten at 7-0 and were ranked No. 2 in the country behind Southern Cal in both the AP and UPI polls. The year before, they had beaten Colorado 45-17 and had gained over 600 yards rushing that day.

On Wednesday morning, October 18, 1972, during the week before the game, our offensive line coach Augie Tammariello walked into my office and said, "Rad, I've got a student in my office that I want you to listen to." I said, "What's this about?" He said, "You'll see." So we went to Augie's office, met the student, sat down, and listened to his story. He told us he had a roommate who was a first-year law student who had been a starting corner for Oklahoma's football team the previous year. He said the Oklahoma roommate had been bragging to him about sitting in the stands during Colorado's football practice Tuesday scouting our defenses, formations, and any other pertinent information he could gather about our team. Many teams, including us, had special defensive fronts designed just for Oklahoma's version of the wishbone formation. He was then forwarding his information by telephone to the Oklahoma coaching staff. The student said that he didn't think what his roommate was doing was right. We agreed that the roommate was wrong and that the student himself was right in telling us about the roommate. We asked him not to say anything to his roommate and that we would handle the situation ourselves. Augie and I immediately went to Coach Crowder and told him the spy story. Crowder then contacted a close friend of the football team who was a member of the FBI and lived in Boulder.

The FBI agent immediately came to the football office where he and Crowder made plans to catch the spy. Eddie had a team meeting right before practice that afternoon. He told the team about the spy and the plans to have the FBI catch the spy when he showed up in the stands to spy on practice. After each play at the beginning of practice, the players would look up into the stands as they were going back into the huddle and exclaim, "Is he here yet? Did he show up yet? Did they catch him yet?" Finally, after about 10 minutes of practice, the spy showed up and sat high in the stands. The FBI man let the spy take notes for about 15 minutes. Then he went over and told the young man that he was from the FBI and would the young man explain what he was doing. Well, the FBI badge frightened the spy so much that he immediately spilled the beans, telling about everything connected with the spying.

The spy said he had attended the Texas-Oklahoma game the week before. After the game, he had stopped by the Oklahoma locker room to congratulate the coaches and players on their victory. While he was there, a couple of the Oklahoma coaches cornered him and had asked him if he would help the team by scouting Colorado's practices during the week for them. We found out later from the Texas coaches that they had suspected Oklahoma had spied on them before their game, too. In their game with Oklahoma, Texas had lined up in a special formation to try a surprise quick kick when the Oklahoma players yelled, "Quick kick! Quick kick!" Oklahoma then blocked the quick kick, picked it up, and scored a touchdown. That incident convinced the Texas coaches Oklahoma had spied on their practices. So, Oklahoma spying on opponents was not an infrequent thing, but a well-kept secret. The student said the Oklahoma coaches told him how to do the spying and he agreed to do it.

Friday Night Defense – Now, as we prepared for the game, our defensive staff decided to simplify our players' assignments against the Oklahoma wishbone formation by playing only two fronts that we designed specifically for the wishbone. These two fronts were called 7 zone and Special Rotate. A 7 zone was an odd front with a man on the center and a special rotate was an even front with no man on the center. We also decided to flip-flop our defensive personnel according to the tight end side and the open side of the wishbone formation. One of the coaches asked me what we would do if Oklahoma broke the wishbone and lined up in a different formation. I said Oklahoma hadn't broken the wishbone formation in over four years. If they did break the bone, we would be ahead, and I would worry about it then. Period. When Friday's practice ended, I was concerned that we had practiced only one blitz called 7 smash super. I felt I needed another blitz. In those days, no one blitzed the wishbone, but I was determined to do so. Between the end of Friday's practice and the start of the defensive meeting Friday night, I devised a gut blitz—with two inside linebackers blitzing up the middle—from the special front alignment. I presented this blitz to the defense at Friday's night defensive meeting. Normally, Friday's supposed to be too late to put something new in. I told the players I was naming the new blitz "Special Cheat Super"—"special" because the front was designed "special" for the wishbone; "cheat" because when the FBI caught the former Oklahoma player spying on our practice Wednesday, we knew the Oklahoma coaches cheated; and "super" because the coverage was the same as in the blitz from the other front that was called "Seven Smash Super."

Anyhow, I remember that on the Friday before the game the Boulder and Denver newspapers reported on the spy story, and on Saturday we were a 17-point underdog. The largest crowd ever to see a sports event in the state, 52,022, turned out, and the crowd, who had read the story about the Oklahoma spy in the newspaper the previous evening, was cheering every warm-up exercise by the Colorado team as if a touchdown had been scored each time. It was the only time in my coaching career that I saw a crowd go nuts over pregame exercises. Coach Crowder met Oklahoma's head coach Chuck Fairbanks at the 50-yard line in the middle of the field before the game. Fairbanks extended his right hand to shake hands but Crowder stuffed both of his hands in his back pockets and refused to shake hands. Crowder started yelling at Fairbanks about the spy. Neither the crowd nor I could hear what he was saying, but you could tell by the body language that Crowder was giving Fairbanks hell, and the crowd was cheering like mad over it.

During the first half of the game, we played pretty well with our basic defenses of 7 zone and special rotate. However, we were behind 7-0 at halftime. I told the players and coaches we were going to let it all hang out the second half and blitz. In the second half, I alternated calling the two blitzes on first and second down. The first defensive series, I called 7 smash super on first down, and special cheat super on second down. The next defensive series, I called special cheat super on first down, and 7 smash super on second down. We dominated them so badly the first two downs, causing losses and fumbles, that every third down was long yardage and we played a 3-5-3 prevent on third down. Our offense was also playing well and scored three touchdowns to take a 20-7 lead at the end of the third quarter.

In the fourth quarter, Oklahoma broke the wishbone for the first time in four years. Their coaches were drawing up passing plays in the dirt on the sidelines. Ironically, one of their coaches was my friend Galen Hall, the star quarterback on Penn State's 1961 Gator Bowl team, who was now Oklahoma's offensive coordinator and quarterback coach. Colorado only had the 3-5-3 prevent defense to play against the normal non-wishbone formations. They finally scored with less than a minute to go to make the score 20-14. We recovered the onside kick and the game was over. I had called the defense I had put in Friday night twelve times for a total yardage gain of minus 14 yards. "Special Cheat Super" was certainly a special defense to stop the Oklahoma cheaters that was super. Not a bad performance for a Friday Night Defense.

I'm sure the emotion generated by the spy story had something to do with our victory. The win jumped us up to No. 7 in the AP poll, one slot ahead of Oklahoma, and into serious contention for the Big Eight Conference championship with Oklahoma and third-ranked Nebraska.

A couple more things.

The spy was Steve O'Shaughnessy, a former 1971 Oklahoma starting corner. He dropped out of Colorado Law School immediately after the spy incident, and I've often wondered if he ever became a lawyer.

Oklahoma didn't lose another game the rest of the regular season, beating Nebraska 33-10 in their showdown game for the Big Eight title, and then defeated my old Penn State team, 14-0, in the Sugar Bowl New Year's Eve. A few days later, Chuck Fairbanks resigned to become the head coach of the New England/Boston Patriots. A couple of months after that, the NCAA placed Oklahoma on probation and made them forfeit all their games that season because they had used two ineligible freshmen players. I guess the old saying is true. "Cheaters come to proof."

Unfortunately, we lost our next two games to Missouri and Nebraska but still finished in a third place tie in the conference, had an overall 8-3 record and were invited to play a 9-1 Auburn team in the Gator Bowl.

"Bad Rad" Coaches A "Bad Dude" – When I became defensive coordinator at Colorado University in 1972, I also became the defensive backs coach. I was extremely lucky to coach three very talented and experienced senior players as starters in our three-deep secondary defense, which was our base defense—a 4-4-3 with four linemen, four linebackers and three defensive backs. Lorne Richardson, a Canadian, was a starter at one cornerback, Cullen Bryant at the other cornerback and John "Bad Dude" Stearns was the starting safety. A year later, Lorne played in the Canadian Football League for Saskatchewan and was the Rookie of the Year of the CFL's Western Conference. That same year, Cullen, who was a consensus All-American for Colorado in 1972, was the second round pick of the Los Angeles Rams. The Rams made him a running back, and in 1979, he was the starting fullback in Super Bowl XIV. Lorne wound up playing four years with Saskatchewan and another with Toronto before leaving pro football and Cullen eventually played 11 years with the Rams and two with Seattle.

Last but not least, there was the leader of the defense, John "Bad Dude" Sterns. Bad Dude was an excellent tackler and hitter, and he got his nickname by the intensity and physical nature of his play. While the two cornerbacks, Loren and Cullen went on to play very well in pro football, Bad Dude made his mark in baseball. In his senior year of 1973, he led the college baseball nation in home runs—I believe he had 12—and was the No. 1 draft choice of the Philadelphia Phillies. As you have read, all three were extremely good athletes and played very well during the 1972 season, especially in the big win over previously unbeaten and No. 1 ranked Oklahoma.

In the summer of 1973, my wife and I went to see John Stearns play for his first minor league team in Reading, PA, managed by former Penn State great Cal Emery, who was the

Cullen Bryant

Lorne Richardson

John "Bad Dude" Stearns

MVP of the College World Series in 1957. I remember John telling me the big difference between playing baseball in Colorado and Pennsylvania was the humidity. He said most of those home runs he hit in Colorado would be long outs in Reading because the humidity holds the ball. Then, lo and behold, during the game, John hits a monstrous home run over the center field fence to help win the game. It was his second professional home run. He signed it, gave it to my wife and she still has it.

Shortly after that, John was traded to the New York Mets. Whenever the Mets came to Pittsburgh while I was with the Steelers from 1974-77, Nancy and I would go to Steeler owner Art Rooney's box in Three Rivers Stadium to watch John play. John was the starting catcher. Invariably, almost in every game we saw, John would win the game with a big hit—a double, triple or home run. We would seem to be his lucky charm.

John always wondered if he would have made it in pro football if he had tried that instead of baseball. I took him to the Steelers offices and showed him the scouting reports on him by the scouting combine and the Steeler scouts. Every scout had him rated as a third, fourth or fifth round draft pick and a sure shot to make an NFL club as a safety. This made John feel real good. Of course, if he wasn't rated high, I wouldn't have shown him the reports. John played the rest of his career with the Mets, and was selected to play in the All-Star game four times during a period when the Mets were not very good. After a series of injuries in the early 1980s, he retired at the end of 1984. But I remember a great play he made in 1978 that showed how tough he was. Pirates great Dave Parker, who had run over two other catchers the previous two weeks in trying to score at home plate, tried to run over John. Not only did Parker not score, but his jaw was broken in the collision with John. While John was unhurt, he proved once again that he really deserved the name John "Bad Dude" Sterns and that Bad Rad did coach a Bad Dude.

Radakovich Quits Undefeated – Three games before the end of the 1972 season my old coach at Cincinnati, Ray Callahan, resigned and when our regular season was over I decided to apply for the job. I had liked Cincinnati, both the school and the city, and I felt this would be the perfect place for my first job as a head coach. I called the athletic director George Smith and flew in for an interview on Friday, December 8, 1973. I had found out that Callahan had quit because he was afraid Cincinnati was going to de-emphasize football. There had been dwindling fan interest and a faction of professors had petitioned the president to drop varsity football. The president had ordered a study of the entire sports program, including intercollegiate and intramural sports, but when I met privately with him for a couple of hours he assured me that football would not be de-emphasized. I also was advised by George Smith that 95 grants-in-aid for football would be continued, but a university wide 10 percent cut in all department funds meant we would need to raise money to help take up the slack.

On the Monday after I returned home from my interview Smith called and I verbally accepted the head coaching position. Smith announced my hiring on Wednesday, October 13, saying he had 40 candidates for the position and I was the best of the seven men he had interviewed. I then flew back to Cincinnati Thursday evening to have a press conference and sign my three-year contract Friday morning. I had the press conference, and said I was leaving a great position in Colorado because of the challenge. "Call it a gut feeling I have," I told the media, "that Cincinnati can have a team that the city could be proud of." And I truly believed that.

But Cincinnati did not have the contract for me to sign. They said they would have one drawn up and mailed to me to sign in Colorado the next week. When I got back to Colorado, I received a lot of calls and a couple of telegrams and letters congratulating me, including a letter from a Cincinnati lawyer who wanted me to get involved with the Serbian community in the area. I also started putting together my staff, and one of the first people I called was my good friend Joe Moore at Upper St. Clair High School. I offered him a position as my top assistant and running backs coach. He accepted before we hung up the phone. Joe was the only new assistant I was going to hire. I intended to keep all of Ray Callahan's coaches that I had worked with in 1970 when I had coached at Cincinnati—Jim Kelly, Dave Ritchie, Dave Dunkelberger and Ron Blackledge.

Technically, I was still on the Colorado staff until after the bowl game and I wanted to help them get prepared for Auburn. So, I went to the football office Monday morning, and shortly after I arrived, Eddie Crowder called me into his office. He compared the head coaching job I was accepting at Cincinnati with the head coaching job that John Major's had just accepted at Pitt. Eddie reminded me of some of the things that I had told him about Cincinnati after my interview there— that some people in the administration wanted to drop football, that the budget for football was going to be reduced by $300,000, but for the first time at Cincinnati the head coach was going to be allowed to fund raise this amount or more and that I was going to have to hustle to raise money. He also reminded me that when I was previously at Cincinnati, I had to pay for my own tuition and books at Chase Law school and they had refused to let me transfer to their day law school, as well as placing a freeze on salaries with no raises

Now at Pitt, Crowder said, they were dropping their admission standards to the basic NCAA standard for eligibility and were increasing their number of football scholarships to the NCAA maximum allowed of 120. Pitt, like Penn State, historically gave a total of 60-80 scholarships. Eddie said Pitt was doing the right things to win and Cincinnati wasn't. Of course, Eddie was trying to convince me to continue as his defensive coordinator because our defense had really been the heart of our team. He was very convincing, and I eventually agreed with him. Then I called my wife to tell her of my decision to stay in Colorado. Nancy wasn't home and had gone out shopping. So I went ahead and called the Cincinnati athletic director and turned the head job down. If I had talked to Nancy first, I probably wouldn't have done it. She told me later she was really looking forward to my being the head coach at Cincinnati. That was one fateful shopping trip.

George Smith, the Cincinnati athletics director, wasn't happy and objected vehemently, saying it was wrong, threatening to sue and all sorts of things. Sure, he was also embarrassed and it didn't make him look good. But I hadn't signed a contract, and it was my life. I now had to tell my wife, the assistants at Cincinnati, and my good friend Joe Moore that I had turned the job down. Joe had already resigned at Upper St. Clair High School, so he had to ask for his job back, and thankfully for Joe and the school he got it. Two years later he went undefeated and did it the following year, too. I also had to tell Jim Mora, who was to take my job as defensive coordinator at Colorado that he wasn't going to be the coordinator. None of them were too happy and it sure wasn't easy.

I didn't say much about my reasons for rejecting Cincinnati. I simply said I was sorry to hurt Cincinnati and it was a tough decision that was personal and for family reasons. A newspaper in Colorado headlined my decision in red with the words, "Radakovich backs out of Cincinnati grid job." That hurt a little, but it was true. This was the first time I backed away from any challenge. But I loved the headline in the *Cincinnati Enquirer* sports section on December 20, 1972, stating "RADAKOVICH QUITS UNDEFEATED!

After I turned down the job, Cincinnati hired Tony Mason, an assistant coach at the University of Michigan. After his fourth year in 1976 when he had his best season record of 8-3, he left for the head coaching position at Arizona. Meanwhile, Johnny Majors awarded 83 new full scholarships his first year at Pitt in 1973, which had not had a winning season since 1963 and been 1-10 before Majors took over. Johnny had a 6-5-1 record in '73 and three years later Pitt won the national championship.

Always See An Opthamologist – Now that the Cincinnati folly was over, I knew I was going to be coaching at Colorado next season, and I needed to get my defense ready for Auburn in the Gator Bowl. Two days before the team flew to Florida, I was playing in a pickup basketball game in the gym. I caught the ball at the top of the key facing the basket. I faked right and went to drive left when the fingernail of the man guarding me accidentally scratched my right eyeball. I immediately went to our local doctor, a general practitioner. He told me I had a cornea abrasion and gave me some eye drop medicine for it. When we arrived in Florida, two days later I was still hurting. I went to see an ophthalmologist (who is an eye specialist), who told me, that if I continued to take the eye drop medicine that the Colorado doctor had given me, I would be blind in that eye within three days. He said that the eye was the fastest healing part of the human body. The problem in my case was in preventing the formation of scar tissue over the cornea abrasion. The ophthalmologist confined me to a darkened room for four days, along with a new type of eye drop medicine. I even had to have my meals brought into me. As a result, I missed almost the entire week of practice before the Gator Bowl game. At the end of the four days, my eye was completely healed. I had learned a valuable lesson: "When you have a problem with your eyes, always see an ophthalmologist." I also learned I wasn't as quick as I once was on the basketball floor.

Eddie Takes Control – We were a surprising 11-point favorite over Auburn, even though they had a 9-1 record and had upset the SEC champion Alabama, 17-15, while we were 8-3. That was probably because their starting quarterback had been injured and would not play. The game was mainly a defensive battle in which our four turnovers (two interceptions and two lost fumbles) essentially made the difference. Auburn led 17-0 before we scored with a field goal midway through the fourth quarter. An Auburn fake field goal pass for a touchdown against our 10-man rush made the final score 24-3.

There was a lot of criticism in the newspaper after the game. Jim Graham of the *Denver Post* wrote, "Somehow, somewhere, something was lost when this Colorado team was assembled this year. I'd say the team lacked 'Character.' You can't say this Colorado team choked because the defense played its heart out. However, as a squad this team has been guilty of lapses of mental concentration in several big games this year. I guess you'd have to admit the Buffaloes lacked dedication also. Some people call it pride."

Criticisms like this led some of our big boosters to tell Eddie Crowder that he had lost control of his football team. In the big banquet held one afternoon during the week before the bowl game, some of our senior football players had made a few hot shot, egotistical, smart aleck remarks about Auburn that reinforced the idea that Eddie had "lost control of the team."

Stung by this criticism, Eddie decided just before spring practice of 1973 started that he would show he was in total control of the team. He declared that the coaches would not have separate offense and defense meetings during spring practice, but we would meet always as a full staff. He also decided we would play a base 3-4 (Oklahoma) defense, with no stunts in the spring, and that we would discuss each position as a staff, whether it was on offense or defense, with Eddie in charge of the meeting. Well, we met every day that spring as a full staff from 8 a.m. to 3 p.m. I didn't have one defensive meeting with the defensive staff the entire spring.

A week before the spring game, Crowder had Steve Sidwell, the linebacker coach, in the front of the room and was demonstrating to Sidwell the linebacker stance that he wanted taught. Eddie was squatted down so low in his hands touched the ground. I yelled out from the back of the room, "You can't move laterally from that stance," and Eddie said, "Yes, I can," and started to spring left and right in what football coaches call a quarter eagle drill. I walked up to the front of the room after the meeting was over and told Crowder that he and I didn't agree on how football should be played. I said, "I quit," and went home. After being home about four days, a bunch of the assistant coaches came to my house and convinced me to return. They probably reminded me that I wouldn't get paid if I quit. I went to the office Friday morning as if nothing had ever happened and coached in the alumni game the next day, which we barely won as the old alumni outplayed us. Crowder and I never mentioned a word about my week's absence. I spent the rest of the spring meeting with the defensive coaches trying to recover from a wasted 20 days spring practice.

Recruiting The Selmons – We had two receiver coaches at Colorado for the 1972 season, Rick Duval and Larry Kennan. But after this season Rick left to become an administrator at Nebraska, and Larry was given the assignment of recruiting the Selmon brothers, Leroy and Lucius, from the state of Oklahoma. Their older brother, Dewey, had been the starting defensive nose tackle for the University of Oklahoma the previous two years and still had a year left. Larry did everything possible to recruit the Selmons. He even worked two days in the Selmon's family garden hoeing, weeding, etc. We all knew that Larry didn't have but one chance in a million of landing the two brothers. When the Selmons signed with Oklahoma, Larry was fired by Crowder. The Colorado coaching staff was all in shock, especially since Crowder hadn't even been around the weekend the Selmons visited. I wondered if Genghis Khan operated this way, and I knew 1973 was not going to be a good year for me or the Colorado football team. Leroy Selmon became an All-American, All-Pro and NFL Hall of Famer. As for Larry Kennan, he went on to become a major college offensive coordinator, a major college head coach, and a longtime NFL quarterback coach, and since 1999 has been the Executive Director of the NFL Coaches Association. Currently he is starting a new football program as head football coach at the University of the Incarnate Word in San Antonio, Texas.

Disloyal Or Disagreement – About a week before our 1973 fall practice started, Crowder stopped by my house, and informed me that he was dismissing Kay Dalton, our offensive coordinator and quarterback coach. When I asked why, Eddie told me that while being in charge of our players' summer workout program Kay had been disloyal in some manner, which didn't make sense. Eddie told me he was replacing Kay as quarterback coach with Mike Bynum, a young lawyer who worked for the university. Mike had been a defensive safety for Colorado as an undergraduate, and I thought he must've played quarterback in high school. He not only had not played quarterback in college, but he had never coached before. I told Eddie what he was doing was crazy. Eddie insisted that releasing Kay was necessary and that his decision was final. During the first week of preseason camp, some unbelievable changes occurred in our offense. Ken Johnson, the starting quarterback the previous two years, with 18 wins and six losses in 24 starts, was moved to fourth team. Joey Duenos, the backup for two years, was moved to third team, third stringer Clyde Crutchmer was moved to first team, and sophomore David Williams was put on second. We went from a drop back passer who could pass to a sprint passer who couldn't pass. Kay Dalton would have disagreed with Eddie, and probably did, on these quite drastic changes in the quarterback position. Thus, in Eddie's mind, disagreement became disloyalty. So, in 1973, the No. 1 and No. 2 quarterbacks from the 1971 and 1972, Ken Johnson and Joe Duenos, never did play when the game counted. Johnson later played one year in the NFL and then five years in the CFL and two years in the USFL. Kay Dalton went on to be an assistant for a couple of years in the NFL with the Buffalo Bills and later became an assistant and then head coach at the University of Northern Colorado.

Becoming A Receivers Coach – In the late spring of 1973, Les Steckel, one of our graduate assistant coaches in 1972, became our new receivers coach replacing Larry Kennan. Les had been a halfback in college, and shortly after he became the receivers coach, I called him into my office. I asked him how much he really knew about the receiver position. He modestly said, "Not much." I then asked him to tell me where they throw the ball more than any place else, in what league? He replied, "The National Football League." I asked him if it made sense to talk to someone in the NFL who knew a lot about receivers. He agreed. I told him I could get him an appointment to talk to a man who led the NFL in pass receiving five straight years, had his name painted on the inside of Denver's Mile High Stadium, and had coached with me at the Steelers in 1971—Lionel Taylor—but after that he should make appointments on his own with the best receivers coaches in the league. That summer, Les met with Lionel. Then on his own, he saw two of the other great pass receivers in pro football, Boyd Dowler and Raymond Berry, who were now coaches, as well as Pete McCully and other outstanding receiver coaches. I knew Les was starting on his path to becoming a great receivers coach, and he later coached in the NFL as a receivers coach, an offensive coordinator and a head coach.

Hope To Finish The Season – My most vivid memory of Colorado's 1973 season occurred in our game with Oklahoma. At the time we were 4-1 while Oklahoma, under new coach Barry Switzer, was undefeated with a tie in four games. Their last loss had been to us the previous season. I don't think they were spying on us anymore, but in the middle of the third quarter, Oklahoma was dominating the game. We were having a tough time stopping their fullback running the ball. At some moment, I noticed that our defensive linemen were aligned one yard off the ball. They were supposed to be squeezing the ball up tight on the line of scrimmage. No wonder the fullback was killing us. It was almost impossible to stop him for less than a 5-yard gain being off the ball as we were. The final score was 34-7 in Oklahoma's favor. After the game I asked the defensive coaches what the story was with the defensive linemen playing one yard off the ball. I was told that Head Coach Eddie Crowder had told the defensive line coach on Wednesday that he wanted the defensive linemen to align one yard off the ball versus Oklahoma. The line coach didn't tell me because he was worried about what my reaction would be. My reaction at that point, with five games left, was to just hope that I could finish the season. Because of the "dawn patrol" incident that happened, eight days later, I almost didn't.

Dawn Patrol – A week before the Nebraska game, at around 6:00 p.m. on Sunday evening, October 28, 1973, the Colorado defensive staff was meeting at a long conference table watching film of Nebraska. We had just beaten Missouri, 17-13, to give us a 5-2 record. There was a knock on the door, and one of the defensive coaches got up and answered it. At the door was Ralph Goldston, the offensive backfield coach. He said, "Rad, I've got to talk to you." I said, "Okay." So I got up and walked out into the hallway. I asked him what this was about? He said. "You've got 'Dawn Patrol.'" I said, "What?" He said that Crowder told him I was late for an

8 o'clock meeting last week, so I had to take Dawn Patrol tomorrow and run some defensive lineman who had broken some rule. Dawn Patrol was a method of punishing a player by having a coach waking the player up at 5 a.m. and making him run a couple of miles. Some football coaches use it as a standard punishment for everything. I yelled at Ralph, "Tell Eddie to shove Dawn Patrol up his ass!"

I then walked back into the meeting and sat down at the head of the conference table. One of the coaches then asked, "Rad, what was that about?" I said, "That was about freaking Dawn Patrol," and at the same time I picked the Kodak film projector up over my head and threw it down the length of the table. Part of it, the clicker replay unit and its cord, hit Carl Smith, one of our graduate assistant coaches. I said, "I'm out of here. I quit!" and walked out and drove home. At about 10 p.m., all the defensive coaches—Jim Mora, Steve Sidwell, and Steve Ortmayer—and both grad assistants, Carl Smith and Mike Messinger, came to my house and convinced me not to quit. I said, "Okay, but no way am I going to do Dawn Patrol." I found out later that in order to avoid any problems with Crowder, that linebacker coach Steve Sidwell had gotten up at 4:30 a.m. and had taken my infamous "Dawn Patrol."

The staff and the team were coming apart. The head coach who wanted to take full control of his team lost it. We were beaten by Nebraska, 28-6, and then lost our last three games to finish with a 5-6 record. Eddie saw the proverbial writing on the wall. He quit as the head coach, but stayed on as the athletic director. He told us he was going to hire a new coach who would be free to pick his own staff, so, unfortunately, we would have to find a new job. Hallelujah! I had been planning to get the hell away from this loony bin anyway.

I must have contracted the Rocky Mountain virus because 10 years later I would be back in Colorado, only this time for one season as a coach with the Denver Broncos. That year would be almost as bizarre as my two seasons up in Boulder because it was there that I met The Shrink.

So, I left Colorado after the 1973 season and was able to get back with the Pittsburgh Steelers in 1974. I now realized coaching in pro football had different challenges than the college game and could be even more fulfilling than working with the kids. As I wrote in Chapter Four although I was happy with the Steelers, particularly after they won their first two Super Bowls in 1974 and 1975, I was stuck as an offensive coach and I wanted to get back to defense. After four years with the Steelers, I guess the wanderlust from my childhood growing up around those famous circus performers also kicked in. Before the end of the 1977 season I knew I would look for another job elsewhere. A nomad again. The opportunity came in San Francisco in early January of 1978. It not only seemed like a good position but a great place to live, even with all those former hippies roaming around.

What I found at the San Francisco 49ers was even worse than my last year at Colorado. It was like a three-ring circus run by a general manager with gigantic ego and it didn't take me long to figure that out, but it cost me a bundle of money when I did.

John "Bad Dude" Stearns meets Bad Rad.

Rod Perry starting corner for Colorado in 1973. Later played for the LA Rams.

CHAPTER THIRTEEN -
From The Steelers To The Golden Gate

In early January of 1978 I got a call wondering if I'd be interested in a defensive coaching job for the 49ers. Although I really liked coaching for the Steelers in my hometown of Pittsburgh, I was intrigued for a couple of reasons.

First, I'd be coaching defense again. I always considered myself a defensive coach first—then and now. I enjoyed being an offensive line coach, but, originally, I only wanted to coach the offensive line for one year to try out some of my ideas. But since we immediately won a Super Bowl and then another, I was stuck as an offensive line coach. Secondly, nobody was offering me a head coaching job. If I was going to be an assistant, I might as well see the world.

The guy who called me was Les Steckel. Les had been a grad assistant in 1972 and the receivers coach in 1973 when I was at the University of Colorado. He had just been hired as the receivers coach for the San Francisco 49ers by Pete McCulley, the new head coach. I told him I'd be interested in talking, and after a bunch of phone calls I flew to the 49ers office in Redwood City, California

When I left Pittsburgh, we had over two feet of snow, which was one of the biggest snow falls in years. When I landed in San Francisco, the temperature was 68 degrees, and as I look back that weather probably was the main reason I accepted the 49ers offer to become their defensive coordinator-linebacker coach. I figured San Francisco was as good a place to go as anywhere. I thought I would love the area and I did.

What I didn't anticipate is my stay in San Francisco would be short. A year later the Pittsburgh Steelers, Bud Carson, Lionel Taylor and I would be back in the Super Bowl, but this time Bud, Lionel and I would be on the opposing sideline.

49ers Organization — The 49ers organization in 1978 was different from anything that I had previously experienced. Ed DeBartolo Jr. was an absentee owner. Joe Thomas was the general manager and he was in charge of everything. Thomas had become the general manager of the Baltimore Colts in 1972 after arranging for Robert Irsay to buy the Los Angeles Rams and then exchange the franchise with the Colts' owner Carroll Rosenblum, who moved to LA to take over the Rams. Thomas' tenure in Baltimore was quite controversial, and he went through five head coaches, including himself, before Irsay fired him and he was hired by DeBartolo. Pete McCulley was now his third head coach at the 49ers in less than two years and McCulley had been hired after the 49ers had lost their last three games in 1977 to finish 5-9. The previous year Thomas had fired Monte Clark after just one season, too, even though Clark's team was 8-6 and finished second in the Western Division.

Most of McCulley's nine assistants were also new, and eight of the nine—all of us except offensive line coach Mike White—were housed for the first four months at the Howard Johnson's Hotel about two miles from the football complex. Mike lived 30 miles away in Berkeley, so he went home every night. Each of us was supposed to be provided a car from a car dealer to drive, but we were only provided two cars, one for the head coach and one for all the assistants. We didn't get our dealer cars until the summer, six months after we were hired and well after our families arrived. That meant each evening we were basically stuck at the Howard Johnson's.

It was also unusual that the head coach and almost all the assistants wanted to stay on Eastern Standard Time instead of Pacific Coast Time. We'd leave the football office at 5 p.m. for the hotel, leave the hotel at 5:30 p.m., have dinner until 6:30 p.m. and drive back to the hotel. Everyone then went to their rooms by 7 p.m., and we hardly socialized. There was a big bar in the hotel. In the four months we stayed at the hotel, I was the only coach that ever went in it. And I went in it almost every night because I had no car and nothing else to do.

The responsibilities of the staff were definitely different from any other organization that I had been connected to. The football staff was only allowed to work on football and what happened on the playing field. The front office was responsible for the draft and trades. We were not even allowed to suggest a prospect or contribute to the draft in any way, nor could we suggest a trade. General Manager Joe Thomas ruled.

Another unusual thing was that only about 60 players were signed for camp. This was about 25 or 30 less than what the other teams were signing. Joe Thomas was making sure his rookie draft picks made the team. I felt sorry for the eight secondary players. Two or three were always hurt and the remaining five or six had to practice the entire time in the George Allen system, which our head coach, Pete McCulley, installed. We had longer seven on seven pass drills that any team in football. The secondary players had to loaf just to survive the practices. Pete also implemented a PTA weightlifting program. PTA stood for "pain, torture and agony." The PTA program was a bunch of exercises on different weight machines. The problem, in my mind, was that it wasn't very hard. I was 43 years old at the time. I could do it and I knew I couldn't play. I had never lifted a weight in my life. Another problem was that the players did the PTA program immediately before practice. We ended up with five times more hamstring injuries than anywhere I've ever been.

Our first preseason game was on a Saturday night against the Super Bowl champion Dallas Cowboys. We were to stay in a Dallas hotel on both Friday and Saturday nights. While I was sitting next to backfield coach Fred O'Connor on the Friday plane going to Dallas, the 49ers business manager came by and handed me my per diem meal money for the three day, two night trip. The players each got a per diem envelope containing $60, the amount designated by the players union. When I was with the Steelers, the coaches always got the same per diem as the players. Well, I opened my 49ers per diem envelope, and it contained eight dollars. I said to O'Connor, "Fred, if I didn't realize it before, I realize it now. I'm definitely not with the Pittsburgh Steelers anymore." Later in the year, when the 49ers were one 1-8, Pete McCulley and the secondary coach were fired. Fred O'Connor became the interim head coach, and for the last three road trips of the season, all the coaches then got the same per diem as the players.

Take This Job And Shove It – I was in the press box for that first Cowboys preseason game calling defensive signals down by telephone to secondary coach Jim Carr on the sideline, and Carr was then supposed to signal the defenses into our rookie middle linebacker Dan Bunz, who called them on the field. Like me, Carr was new to the staff, but he had spent nine years as a player in the NFL and 12 years as an assistant, and I guess he thought he knew more about defense than me. Some of the defenses I called in the first half were not signaled in, and almost none of the defenses I called during the second half were signaled in. The secondary coach was signaling in his own defenses. I realized I had a problem. We lost the game, 41-24.

I had a meeting with all the defensive coaches and told them that for the second preseason game against the Oakland Raiders that I would be on the field signaling the defenses in and the secondary coach would be up in the press box. One of the defensive coaches asked me if I had gone over this with the head coach. I said I hadn't and thought I could handle the situation myself. Earl Leggett, the defensive line coach, said he was going to go see the head coach about this and left the meeting. After a while, he came back and didn't say anything so I didn't believe he saw the head coach. We practiced all week with the assumption that I would be down on the field during the game calling signals. I had told the linebackers who would be the signal callers on the field that I would be giving them the defensive signals. In the locker room before the game, Pete McCulley, called me into his office and said, "I hear you are going to be on the field calling signals. I don't think we should be making any last minute changes." I said, "Pete, this isn't last minute. I've been going over the signals with the middle linebacker Dan Bunz all week. We're all set." I walked out and went out on the field for pregame warm-ups.

We played the Raiders on August 20th at Candlestick Park. I saw Raiders Head Coach John Madden with announcer Curt Gowdy, and went over and talked with them. A bumblebee got into the back of my shirt and Curt Gowdy pulled my shirt up and chased the bee away. After the pregame warm-up, we went back into the locker room. As I was reviewing the signals with Bunz, the secondary coach came over and said, "Coach McCulley wants to see you right away in his office." I walked into Pete's office and he said, "You're not going to be down on the field calling signals. We're not making any last minute changes." I said, "Pete I told you we'd been planning to do this all week." He said, "You're not going to be down on the field." I said, "Okay, I quit!" and walked out of his office, out of the locker room and into the stands.

I waited until both teams had left the locker rooms. Then I went back in the 49ers locker room, changed from my coaching gear into my regular clothes, and walked back out of the locker room. I went into the stands looking for my wife. I couldn't find her but ran into Art Rodich, the brother of my college roommate, Milo Rodich. I talked with Art for a while and then walked outside the stadium the second half and ran into a former Penn State teammate Maurice Schleicher, who had played four years in the NFL and AFL for the Raiders and later worked in their scouting department. He sat on his motorcycle and talked with me until the game was over. The 49ers lost, 31-14, and I was not surprised by the score. I found my wife after the game, told her what happened and we went home. The next day I bought a record of a popular song made famous by country singer Johnny Paycheck. I went home and played it over and over again for the next couple weeks. The song was "Take This Job and Shove It."

Sometime during the next weeks, United Airlines workers were threatening to strike at the San Francisco airport. My neighbor, Rich Johnson, fixed DC-10 doors for United and asked me if he could borrow my Johnny Paycheck record. "Take This Job and Shove It" became a United Airlines workers favorite song as it was played through their sound system, day after day during their strike negotiations.

Returning To The 49ers – The 49ers announced that I had resigned and McCulley appointed Carr the defensive coordinator, and another assistant, weight coach Floyd Reese, to coach linebackers. No reason was given for my resignation, but in an interview with Frank Blackman of the *San Francisco Examiner*, McCulley implied that I had asked to be on the sidelines during the games and but he wanted me in the press box, which was true. Blackman also wrote that my "low-key" and "intense" personality didn't fit with the "homogeneous (staff), characterized by high-spirited enthusiasm." What a crock that was.

When reporters called me, all I said was that it had been coming for a while, that I wasn't fired and that I had agreed with the 49ers not to comment. I did tell a friend from back in Pittsburgh, Norm Vargo, the sports editor of the *McKeesport Daily News*, that "it's the first time in my life I haven't been involved with football." I also told Norm that Thomas and McCully had called four times and tried to talk me out of quitting, but I said, "My mind was made up. Nothing they said to me would indicate that things might get better." And I kept my word. In fact, this is the first time I have told the complete story of what happened.

Johnny Paycheck may have made a great record but now that I had quit, his last name cut to the bone because I wasn't getting a paycheck now. I tried to get a job through the employment agencies, but when they found out what I did and my MBA education they were embarrassed about hiring me, especially part-time. My neighbor Rich also tried to get me a job cleaning out those United airplanes but that didn't work out either. It wasn't a pleasant time for me or my family.

I missed my paycheck and I also missed coaching, but I certainly didn't miss the 49ers or the games. The team was horrible from the start, losing their first four games, beating the equally horrible and winless Bengals and then losing four more by the end of October. A few hours after the eighth loss, 38-20, to the Redskins in Washington, I got a phone call from Joe Thomas requesting me to meet him at his home later that night at 9:00 p.m. When I arrived at the Thomas home about 8:45 p.m., Fred O'Connor, the 49ers backfield coach, arrived about the same time. Joe Thomas informed us that he had fired both Head Coach Pete McCully and Jim Carr.

Joe asked Fred to be the head coach and me to be the defensive coordinator and secondary coach for the rest of the season. The 49ers currently had a record of 1-8 and there were seven games left. We both accepted Joe's offer. I felt I had no choice because I was already out $11,000 for the three months that had passed since the day I had quit. I was hired at the same pay rate that I had before, but I got nothing for the time that I had been off.

The day I returned to the team, the 49ers players gave me a standing ovation. However, the losing continued. One month after the coaching change, the Steelers came to town for a Monday night game, and it turned out to be one of the most tragic days in the history of San Francisco. A week before, we lost in the closing seconds to a good Los Angeles Rams team at Candlestick, 31-28, but Nancy and I had spent Saturday night before that game visiting with my two old coaching pals at the Steelers, Bud Carson and Lionel Taylor. They also had left the Steelers and joined the Rams, with Bud coaching the secondary and Lionel the receivers. Naturally, we had talked a lot about our great years together in Pittsburgh.

The 49ers game against the Steelers was not on television because it had not been a sellout. But the city populace was in no mood to watch the game anyhow. Earlier in the day, Mayor George Moscone and Harvey Milk, the city's first openly gay supervisor (or councilman), were assassinated by another city employee named Dan White. The killings shocked the country, and I'm not sure the players felt like playing football. We lost, 24-7, to set a new club record by losing our eighth in a row, and it went to nine before we beat Tampa, 6-3, in our next-to-last game.

The final game at Detroit was really weird. We were losing 12-7 at halftime. In the second half, our defense held the Lions to a minus 38 yards total offense. Detroit still scored three more touchdowns by intercepting a pass, blocking a punt and picking up a fumble and returning all three turnovers for touchdowns, and we lost 33-14. Ed DeBartolo Jr., the absentee owner, was so upset by the craziness of the game that he came in the locker room after the game and gave a passionate speech to the team that he was going to make sure that the team was going to get better and become champions. Three years later, of course, the 49ers became Super Bowl champions under new coach Bill Walsh. Ed had made good on his promise that day in Detroit.

Ed DeBartolo Jr.

Unique Penn State Player – When I became the 49ers secondary coach in the middle of the 1978 season, the starting free safety, Chuck Crist, was a Penn Stater who had never played college football at Penn State. When he was in Salamanca High School in Salamanca, NY, he was a starting quarterback on the football team and a second team all-state basketball player. Penn State assistant coach J.T. White and Penn State head recruiter Tor Toretti offered Chuck a two-part athletic scholarship for basketball and football, which he accepted. When he got to Penn State, the football team coached by Joe Paterno wanted him to play defensive safety instead of quarterback. Chuck said that was not part of the deal and refused to report to the football team. So, he reported to the freshman basketball team coached by Freshman Coach Holmes Cathrall. The varsity coach was John Bach. Bach made Chuck a full time starter in his junior year and that season Chuck was voted the MVP by his teammates.

Chuck Crist

J.T. White had told the Dallas Cowboys about Chuck, and after his senior basketball season the Cowboys contacted him. When Bach heard about this he called Chuck into his office and asked if Chuck had an interest in playing professional football. Chuck said he did. Well, before coming to Penn State, Bach had been the head basketball coach at Fordham. His team manager at Fordham was the son of New York Giants owner Wellington Mara, John Mara. Bach called Wellington and told him about Chuck. Cluck flew to New York for a 30 minute tryout. Evidently he passed the tryout because he was invited to the Giants preseason camp by Jim Garrett, the defensive coordinator at the time. After four weeks of preseason camp trying out at safety, Chuck got discouraged and was considering leaving camp to take a teaching job in high school that he had been offered. New York assistant coach Emlen Tunnell, who had been a great defensive back for the Giants, told Chuck to stick it out because this was a once in a lifetime opportunity and that funny things happen in pro football. Then funny things did happen.

The Giants traded five-year veteran safety Scott Eaton to another team. Then the third play of the opening game of the regular season, eight-year veteran safety Spider Lockhart got hurt and Chuck became the starter for the next two weeks. He then played special teams and split time with safety

Chuck Crist

Richmond Flowers in 1973 and played a lot in 1974. In 1975, Chuck was cut the last week of training camp, sat home for five weeks and was picked up by the New Orleans Saints. He played for the Saints in 1975, 1976 and 1977, and in '77 was voted the MVP by his teammates. Just as the 1978 season started, Chuck was traded to the 49ers for linebacker Dick Vanderbundt. I wasn't with the 49ers when the trade was made. I was sitting at home, having quit my job as San Francisco's defensive coordinator and linebacker coach a few minutes before the second preseason season game, against the Oakland Raiders. I didn't meet Chuck until I returned to the 49ers as defensive coordinator and secondary coach before the tenth game of the season. As our starting safety, he intercepted six passes in the last seven games, and retired before the 1979 season. Not bad for a former Penn State basketball player who never played college football. Chuck Crist truly was a unique player from Penn State.

Talking With Bill Walsh – When the 1978 season was over, General Manager Joe Thomas and all the coaches were fired, and the coaches were told that the 49ers organization would pay their expenses to the Senior Bowl practice week to look for a job. I attended the Senior Bowl, and with the help of my old friends, Bud Carson and Lionel Taylor, set up an interview to be held a week later at the Los Angeles Rams coaching facility in Long Beach. When I returned to the 49ers offices in Redwood City to turn in my Senior Bowl expense account, I ran into the new head coach and general manager, Bill Walsh.

I knew Bill from my years at the University of Cincinnati and the Pittsburgh Steelers in 1970 and 1971 when he was an assistant with the Cincinnati Bengals. He asked me to meet with him in his office. He then proceeded to grill me on anything and everything about the San Francisco 49ers. Finally, he asked me about what I thought about his new job. I told him I thought he had the best job in the NFL. If I read the papers right, he had complete control of the draft, hiring, coaching and everything connected with winning. Ed DeBartolo Jr. would continue as an absentee owner but would give him full support. I told Bill that even Chuck Noll, who at that time had won three Super Bowls in five years, didn't have a job as good as Walsh's. Bill said that he tended to agree with me. He then asked me what my plans were. I told him I had an interview set up with the Rams and that I might be coaching against him in the same division. He wished me luck and then I left.

Bill Walsh

When I got home, I told my wife that I have probably passed up my best chance to be a trivia question at the Hall of Fame in Canton, Ohio. She said, "What are you talking about?" I told her about my meeting with Bill Walsh and told her I had the feeling that if I would've asked him for a coaching job with the 49ers that he may have given me one. Then a trivia question at the Hall of Fame will have been, "Which coach was hired three different times within one calendar year by an NFL team?" And the answer would have been "Dan Radakovich by the San Francisco 49ers in 1978." But I didn't ask.

Bill Walsh won two league games in 1979, four league games in 1980 and won the Super Bowl after the 1981 season. He really did have the best job in the National Football League. At the Rams, we beat the 49ers four games in a row in the next two years. We finally lost to them by a total of five points in both games in 1981, 17-20, and, 31-33. They won the Super Bowl that year and I and four other Ram assistant coaches got fired. I still wonder why I didn't ask Bill Walsh for a job that day. Maybe it just had something to do with my friends on the Rams coaching staff, or maybe because the Rams of the 1970s were big winners and had a better chance than the 49ers of getting to the Super Bowl, which we did after the 1979 season.

CHAPTER FOURTEEN - Hooray for Hollywood

From the time Carroll Rosenbloom switched franchises with Baltimore and took over the Los Angeles Rams in 1972, the Rams ruled the NFL's Western Division. After another losing season in 1972, Rosenbloom fired Tommy Prothro and gave my old friend Chuck Knox, a former assistant coach from Tyrone High School, his first NFL head coaching job. From 1973 through 1977, the Rams won the division, but couldn't get past the playoffs and three times lost in the NFC championship game. Knox's relationship with Rosenbloom deteriorated in those last couple of years, and shortly after the Rams lost its 1977 playoff game to Minnesota, Knox quit and signed a seven year contract with Buffalo.

Prior to Knox, the Rams had won two division titles under George Allen, but Allen had left Los Angeles in 1971 for those so-called greener pastures at the Washington Redskins, where he became renowned for winning with veteran players nicknamed "The Over-the-Hill Gang." However, those Redskins went to one Super Bowl and lost that one to the now-famous undefeated 1972 Miami Dolphins. But, as we all know, football coaching is like riding a carousel and roller coaster at the same time and so Rosenbloom decided to bring Allen back in February of 1978 to coach the Rams. Almost immediately, Allen clashed with Rams general manager Don Klosterman, and throughout training camp several players complained about Allen's hardnosed style. When the Rams lost their first two preseason games, Rosenbloom abruptly fired him and Rosenbloom and Klosterman promoted Knox's long-time defensive coach Ray Malavasi to head coach.

The Rams then won another division title under Malavasi but were beat up by Dallas in the conference championship, 28-0. Dallas proceeded to lose the Super Bowl to my old Steelers team, which I mention to show again how all this football stuff is just like those fun houses back at Kennywood Park and you never know what you're going to find around the next corner.

So, after the 1978 season, the Los Angeles Rams fired three coaches: the offensive line coach, the backfield coach and the quarterback coach, who was also the offensive coordinator, and then they hired only one new coach—me! Malavasi made Jack Faulkner, who was in personnel, the backfield coach and made himself the quarterback coach and offensive coordinator. Judging from the amount of salary money they saved by doing this, I should've asked for more money. I had actually replaced three people.

Lional Taylor, Ray Malavasi and Dan

227

Los Angeles Rams Interview – The Los Angeles Rams football offices in 1979 were located on the second floor of the clubhouse in the center of a public golf course in Long Beach. I interviewed there and was offered the offensive line job dependent upon salary negotiation by phone with Don Klosterman. I talked with him on the telephone in Lionel Taylor's office. My old friend Lionel was the Rams receivers coach. Don offered me $52,000, which was a nice raise over the $46,000 I had signed for at San Francisco. I knew that the Rams had offered the same job earlier to Jim Hanifan at $55,000, but he had turned them down and went to the San Diego Chargers. I told Don that I wanted $55,000. Lionel heard me and was afraid I might blow it. Don told me he would get back to me. He said he had to talk to Carroll Rosenbloom about my demand. In 1979, $55,000 was about the top salary for an assistant in NFL. Don called me back and said I would get the $55,000 per year for the next two years. I accepted. So, now I was back among friends with Lionel, Bud Carson, who was now the defensive coordinator, and Torgy Torgeson, the defensive line coach. And I was making money again and living in sunny, warm southern California. It wasn't Hollywood but close to it, as I was about to find out.

Carroll Rosenbloom's Funeral – A few weeks after my hiring in April of 1979, Rams owner Carroll Rosenbloom drowned while swimming in the ocean off a Florida beach. I never had a chance to meet or speak to him since he had given the final approval for my hiring by telephone. All the Rams coaches and their wives were invited to a celebration of life ceremony a week later, at the Rosenbloom estate in the exclusive Bel Air community. It was an eye-opening experience for my wife and me.

We left our car with valet parking at the front of the Rosenbloom mansion, were escorted through the bottom floor of the mansion, and out the back door to the estate grounds at the rear of the mansion. As we were leaving the mansion and entering the backyard part of the estate, I remarked to Nancy, "Well, babe, looks like we've hit the big time." Nancy said, "You don't even realize how big." I said, "What?" She said, "Look at that guy in a tuxedo over there in the weeds conducting that orchestra. That's Henry Mancini, the world-famous conductor." With all the chairs, tables, tents, and the big stage that had been set up on the gigantic lawns in the backyard, there wasn't room on the grass for the orchestra, so they had to set up in the weeds, to play the music.

Almost every owner and top administrator in the National Football League was there. I remember seeing Mr. Rooney—everyone in the Steelers organization past and present called owner Art Rooney Sr. "Mister"—and Ed Kiely from the Steelers, Joe Thomas and Ed DeBartolo from the 49ers, NFL commissioner Pete Rozelle, and many others from the NFL. There were also a number of Hollywood stars who had been friends with Carroll Rosenbloom. I saw Jimmy Stewart, Ricardo Montalban, Warren Beatty, Cary Grant, and Jonathan Winters. Cary Grant was 75 years old at the time. My wife Nancy and I decided that he was about the best looking 75-year-old that we had ever seen. There must've been at least 500 people at this affair in the spacious backyard of the Rosenbloom estate. We were told to treat the affair not as a funeral, but as a celebration of Carroll Rosenbloom's life. Rosenbloom is reported to have said that when he died he wanted to have a big happy party given in his honor. After waiting a couple of hours for Carroll's widow, Georgia to show, the entertainment for the party started.

A big stage had been erected on the lawn and rows of chairs had been placed in front of the stage. The Ram football coaches with their wives and the Hollywood stars and their wives were given seats in the front row. I remember Nancy and I were sitting two seats away from Jimmy Stewart and his wife. The master of ceremonies for the party was Jonathan Winters. I can still remember his opening remarks. He walked out on the stage, grabbed the standup microphone and yelled, "I loved Carroll Rosenbloom. I really loved Carroll Rosenbloom, and do you know why I loved Carroll Rosenbloom? I loved Carroll Rosenbloom because he was rich! Yes, because he was rich! Stay away from poor people, they'll tear you down." Well, the crowd went wild. Jimmy Stewart was laughing so hard, he almost fell out of his chair. I knew right then that this was going to be a different type of funeral or wake than I had ever been to. The entertainment for the next hour and a half consisted of many songs from Broadway shows like Fiddler on the Roof and other popular songs like "My Way," which must have been Carroll Rosenbloom's favorites.

After the entertainment was over, Nancy and I talked to Jonathan Winters. We reminded him that we had first seen him and talked with him 20 years earlier when he was one of the entertainers along with Johnny Carson and Dick Van Dyke at the Governors Ball after the first Liberty Bowl in Philadelphia in 1959. He remembered everything about that Liberty Bowl entertainment, including the fact that just before that entertainment he had spent six months in an insane asylum, and that the Liberty Bowl was his first entertainment gig afterwards. My wife then asked him to introduce us to his wife standing there. He denied that the woman was his wife while she extended her hand to show us the wedding ring. Just then, Carroll Rosenbloom's widow, Georgia, came by and Jonathan offered to take her back to her bedroom to console her. She told him she was too busy at the moment and had too many things to attend to. He then offered to come by at three in the morning to console her in her bedroom. Jonathan Winters was as nutty off the stage as he was on it. We later found out that Georgia Rosenbloom had inherited 70% ownership in the Los Angeles Rams. For the first time in history, a lady was the principle owner of an NFL football team.

The Scarecrow – At the start of the two-day 1979 NFL draft in the first week of May, the Los Angeles Rams organization gathered at their downtown business office on Pico Blvd. in Los Angeles. Between the two draft days, the coaches and scouts would usually stay overnight at the Century Plaza Hotel, which was close to the Rams business office on Pico Blvd. The first day of the draft would stop at 4 p.m., and near the end of our first day Bud Carson and I were sitting at one of the tables in the draft room when General Manager Don Klosterman came by and said, "Hey Steelers coaches, how about going out with me this evening? I can show you some of the town and also take you out to dinner." Since Bud and I had no previous plans except to go to the hotel, we quickly accepted Don's offer.

The first place Don took us to was the Bel Air Country Club, where he was a member. For those not familiar with Los Angeles, Bel Air is the exclusive residential area in Beverly Hills, which is adjacent to Hollywood. Many movie stars and celebrities belong to the Bel Air Country Club. Immediately after entering the club, Don took us to a private room where five or six men were playing cards. One of the card players was Jerry West, the general manager of the Los Angeles Lakers basketball team, and an NBA Hall of Famer. Don introduced Bud and me to Jerry, who talked to us for a minute or two before he resumed playing. We then proceeded into the main bar room, which was basically empty except for the bartender, and one or two members. We sat at a table and ordered some drinks.

Into the bar walked Ray Bolger, the famous actor-dancer who is best known for playing the Scarecrow in The *Wizard of Oz* movie. Don invited Ray Bolger to join us at the table and he was quite cordial and friendly. After a few minutes of general conversation, Bolger and I got into a discussion about dancing and football. I informed him that my brother Lou and my godfather's kids, George and Bernie Staisey, had taken dance lessons from Gene Kelly at the Gene Kelly Studio in Pittsburgh. My parents had taken me to the Kelly Studios, operated at that time by Gene Kelly's sister, to see if I wanted to take tap lessons, which I turned down (and which I now regret). Ray then proceeded to tell me that he was a better dancer than both Gene Kelly and Fred Astaire because he could do what they could do, which was tap dance and modern dance, but that he also could do ballet which they couldn't do. Later, when I told George Staisey, who was Kelly's best pupil in Pittsburgh and who starred in a Broadway musical called *Best Foot Forward* when he was 14 years old, what Ray Bolger had said, George said that's not true. Kelly could do ballet!

Anyway, I told Ray Bolger that I had a football drill called "Mirror Dodge" that I used that was similar to a dance routine. As I wrote earlier, two plastic cones are placed seven yards apart on a straight line. A defender stands between the cones a couple of inches in front of the line and tries to prevent a dodger from scoring—crossing the line between the cones. The defender does this by moving laterally to stay in front of the dodger and by sticking his arms out to keep the dodger at arm's length. The drill runs for approximately 15 seconds. As I demonstrated the drill on the table for Ray, I used two of the drink glasses for goals and the salt and pepper shakers for the defender and dodger. He got all excited and wanted to do the drill himself. He said the Bel Air Country Club bar room was basically empty except for our party and we could use two tables seven yards apart for goal markers. At the time, Ray Bolger was the president of the Bel Air Country Club, so we had no trouble using the tables as goals. Ray would be the dodger or jooker and I would be the defender who was to prevent him from scoring by crossing an imaginary line between the tables. The spectators were Bud Carson, Don Klosterman, the bartender and one or two other patrons in the bar.

We started the drill, and Ray started to run back and forth in front of me, gave me a quick juking move and was going to score. I stuck out both hands and arms extended and boom—he flew onto the top of the table being used as a goal marker.

I rushed to help him up and say I'm sorry, but Ray said he was fine and wanted to keep going. We started the drill again and after a couple of seconds, he gave me another quick move and was going to score again, and I popped him again with my hands and extended arms, and this time he flew over the table. At the time, I was 6-foot-2, 215 pounds, and Ray Bolger was about 6-foot-1 or 6-foot-2 and 125 or 130 pounds. He was a true featherweight. I helped him up again. I wanted to quit but he said, "No, this is fun," and we started the drill a third time.

Well, he moved back and forth, gave me another quick move, and it looked like he was going to score for sure this time. I reached out and knocked him over the tables again. I helped him up and he was laughing and still wanted to continue, but I said, "That's it, I'm quitting before someone gets hurt." Then I asked him how old he was and how he got so quick? He told me that he was 72 years old. Then he pulled up both of his pant legs and said, "Look at that," while pointing to two calf muscles that looked like softballs attached onto skinny sticks for legs. He said "I've been dancing since I was three years old." Well, I was 43 years old at the time and Ray Bolger was 72. With Don Klosterman and Bud Carson watching and laughing, I would have never lived it down if a 72-year-old had scored on me. When I went home the next evening after the second day of the draft, I said to my children at the dinner table, "Do you remember that scarecrow that's on The Wizard of Oz movie? Well, yesterday, your father whipped his butt in the Mirror Dodge drill!" Every time we see the movie on television, we laugh about the day their dad knocked Dorothy's Scarecrow on his butt.

Rams Minicamp And Tony Wise – In 1979, NFL teams normally only had one minicamp during the offseason. The Los Angeles Rams held a six-day, two-practices-a-day, helmets only (no other pads allowed) minicamp in the spring for the rookie draftees and free agents. The veterans participated the last three days of the six-day minicamp. Shortly before this minicamp, I received a call from my good friend Joe Moore, who was now the backfield coach at the University of Pittsburgh. He informed me that Tony Wise, a graduate student coach at Pitt, was going to be Jimmy Johnson's offensive line coach at Oklahoma State and would like to see me about offensive line play. I invited Tony to come to our six-day minicamp, which he attended with Butch Davis, who Johnson had just hired from a Tulsa high school to be his receivers coach.

The most important days of minicamp are the last three days when the vets are participating with the rookies in six practices. I had a lot of drills that the Rams veteran lineman had never done or seen before, so Tony got a good look at the players trying to do and learn these drills for the first time. I can remember Dennis Harrah and Rich Saul (whose brother, Bill, I had coached back at Penn State) trying to break each other's neck on a "grab the back of the head" drill. I had to coach them that if they grabbed the back of the head to let go. I didn't want any broken necks. In both practices on the vets first day, I had to correct veteran All-Pro center Rich Saul on something in every drill we did. The next day Rich did every drill perfectly from the start. I had never seen anyone improve so quickly. I accused him of going home and practicing all night. He denied this. I then told him he must have locked himself in the bedroom where his wife Eileen couldn't see him and practiced his moves in front of a mirror. Rich finally admitted that he had put a lot of thought into the drills that evening after the first day's practice. I can remember only one other time in my coaching career that a player improved in all the drills so quickly. Years later, in the spring of 1990 when I was with the Cleveland Browns, I worked out veteran center Mike Babb for the first time in the off-season. We had just traded with the New England Patriots to get him. I had to correct him in all the drills on a Thursday. We next met the following Monday and he did everything perfect, right from the start. Mike did admit that he had worked on the drills on his own over the weekend.

Rich Saul

When the six day Rams minicamp was over, Tony Wise went on to Oklahoma State as their offensive line coach. He had stood next to me during all 12 practices. Ten years later in 1989, when Jimmie Johnson was the new Dallas Cowboys coach and Tony was his offensive line coach, I read a football article where the reporter had asked Tony if he thought his college blocking schemes and techniques could work in professional football. Tony replied that he used the same blocking schemes and techniques that the Steelers used to win four Super Bowls in six years. And that he had gotten these schemes and techniques from Dan "Bad Rad" Radakovich, who was the Steelers line coach the first two Steeler Super Bowl years. Within three years, the Cowboys were in the playoffs and Super Bowl champions after the 1992, 1993, and 1995 seasons (Super Bowls XXVII, XXVIII, and XXX). Tony left the Dallas Cowboys after Super Bowl XXVII to coach for the Chicago Bears with their new head coach, Dave Wannstedt. In 2010 he was coaching the offensive line for Wannstedt at the University of Pittsburgh and retired after that season. Oh, and Butch Davis spent 15 years with Johnson before becoming the head coach at the University of Miami, then the Cleveland Browns and the University of North Carolina. He is now a defensive assistant with the Tampa Bay Buccaneers. That was one heckuva Rams minicamp.

Dennis Harrah

Bed Check On Fred Dryer – The Los Angeles Rams training camp in July was on the campus of Cal State Fullerton. Since three Rams coaches had been fired and I was the only new coach, I was assigned bed check for the first evening. The first practice was not until the following day. There had been a lot of publicity in the newspapers that day about the retirement of perennial All-Pro left guard Tom Mack. The papers were stating that Jackie Slater, who had been a backup player the previous three years, was slated to take his place. A few weeks earlier, when it looked like Mack was certain to retire, Ray Malavasi had told some reporters that if Mack retired, Jackie Slater would take his place. Upon learning of this, I immediately went to Malavasi and told him I was planning on Jackie Slater being the starting right tackle, not left guard. I said I was going to move the previous starting right tackle, John Williams, to guard. Ray replied that he had thought of replacing Tom Mack with Slater because Slater was such a good athlete. I agreed and said that's exactly why I'd rather he played tackle, and Ray said, "Okay."

Fred Dryer

Bed check was at 11:00 p.m., and my final bed check was at veteran defensive end Fred Dryer's room. Fred had been reading the papers. He said, "Rad, I see in the paper that you are going to play Jackie Slater in Tom Mack's left guard spot. Rad, I want to tell you that is a smart move. Yes sir, when Jackie Slater was at tackle, I ran over him, around him, under him—I simply destroyed him. Yes sir, Rad, you are one smart coach to put Jackie at guard." As I went to turn his light out, I said to Fred, "Fred, I got your message. I have to be the idiot of the world to play Jackie Slater at guard." Fred just laughed and I clicked off his light. Jackie Slater ended up playing 20 years at tackle— longer than any NFL lineman in history—and is in the NFL Hall of Fame. Fred Dryer in July 1979, knew what he was mocking me about. Fred was a real character. Once, Fred sponsored an ugly man contest at camp among the new players. He said first prize was a Robert Redford mask. I didn't attend, so I don't know who won.

Fred Dryer was damn fine defensive end in the NFL for 13 years before turning to acting. He became quite well known playing the lead in two TV series, *Hunter* and *Land's End*. When my middle daughter Leslie went into the entertainment business, she initially worked on both of Fred's shows. He never told her that her dad was an idiot for helping Jackie Slater become a Hall of Famer.

Rams Equipment Men – When the Rams went to training camp in 1979, I went to see head equipment man Don Hewitt and his son Todd at the beginning of camp. I wanted Don to do the same things that I had the Pittsburgh Steelers equipment man, Tony Parisi, do when I was the Steelers offensive line coach. I asked Hewitt to tailor the offensive linemen's jerseys until the jersey fit skintight over the shoulder pads. I wanted rolls of two-way carpet tape so the jerseys could be taped down tight to the shoulder pads. I wanted a special run blocking shield made (I needed about eight of those) and a special pass blocking shield made (I needed about four of those). Hewitt was a former successful high school coach who had a couple of undefeated seasons before he became the Rams equipment man. He took a lot of pride in his work, and the Rams organization considered him to be the best equipment man in the NFL.

Well, Don rebelled at my request. The Rams were a consistently successful team over the years and Don had never had to fill goofy and special requests like I was making. He probably thought, who did I think I was. A week or so went by, and I was not making much headway with Don. I got hold of his son, Todd, and started complaining. Todd promised me that he would convince his dad that I wasn't being a hotshot and that my requests would all be fulfilled. I know that Todd called Tony Parisi, the Steelers equipment man. Between Todd Hewitt and Tony Parisi, Don Hewitt finally became convinced that I was not some coach that thought he was hot stuff, and that my requests were important. So, Don fulfilled my request. Both Don and Todd became good friends of mine, and we had an excellent working relationship during my three years as a Rams coach.

The Party – Sometime during the early part of training camp in July or August of 1979, Georgia Rosenbloom Frontiere invited the Rams coaching staff and their wives plus the four team doctors and their wives to a private dinner party held in the rear grounds of the Rosenbloom mansion and estate in Bel Air. Also attending were general manager Don Klosterman, bandleader Ray Anthony with a lady friend, and Georgia's new husband, composer Dominic Frontiere, whom she married a couple of months after Carroll Rosenbloom's death. Dining tables and chairs were set out on a gigantic lawn and a wooden dance floor had been erected on the lawn with lights around it. Music was piped in. We ate, danced, talked, laughed and had a great time! What we didn't realize at the time was that Steve Rosenbloom, Georgia's stepson and president of the Los Angeles Rams football club, was not present and had not been invited. Neither had Steve's five vice presidents and their wives been invited. We found out later that having this great party and not inviting Steve and his vice presidents was Georgia's way of telling stepson Steve that she was taking charge of the club and that he was being booted out. In his will, Carroll Rosenbloom had named Steve president of the team but had left him just six percent of the franchise with each of the other four Rosenbloom children also getting six percent apiece. Georigia was given 70 percent. But since two of the five Rosenbloom children were hers, she really had control of 82 percent of the franchise, and she was going to use it.

A few weeks after the party, when it was official that Steve was leaving, there was a big article in the *Los Angeles Times* and three full pages were devoted to Steve Rosenbloom complaining about the party. That's when I found out how important the party was in playing a part in Steve's dismissal. The reason Don Klosterman was invited to the party and not Steve and his vice presidents became quite obvious. When Carroll Rosenbloom was alive, he was a very involved owner and participated in almost all administration decisions through Klosterman, his general manager. When Carroll died and Steve took over as president, Steve simply allowed Klosterman to keep his general manager's title but Steve promoted five of his own people to vice presidents, thus putting them all above Don and reporting directly to Steve. Thus, Klosterman became virtually just a figurehead as general manager. By inviting Don to the party and not Steve or the vice presidents, Georgia was showing the world and Steve that Klosterman would be back in charge of the Los Angeles Rams and reporting only to her. I learned that in the world of rich people and Hollywood, whether or not you were invited to a certain party seems to have a great deal of significance.

1979—The First Nine Games – You can divide the Rams 1979 season into two main parts in my mind. First, there were the first nine regular season games when the Rams were 4-5. Some of my offensive linemen were still struggling with the techniques I was teaching in those nine games plus I was still learning what we could and couldn't do. I can remember Dennis Harrah coming up to me during practice for our third or fourth league game and shouting, "Rad, I've got it! Rad, I've got it!" I said, "Dennis, what have you got?" He said, "You just stick them out! I've got it." He was referring to his arms on pass protection. We were into the season and the light bulbs were still lighting up. I also realized that we couldn't block some run plays as we had done at the Steelers or that they had previously done at the Rams. I decided to zone block almost all our runs. For some reason, we had a lot of injuries in the offensive line. After our fourth league game, our record was 2-2 and we had to play Doug Smith, the backup center at left guard and Dan Ryczek, our 6-foot-1, 220-pound punt snapper, at starting right guard for the next three games. We won the next two games against St. Louis, 21-0, and New Orleans, 35-13, with no problem, mainly because both teams played a 3-4 defense and the right guard was uncovered and basically double teamed almost every play with either center Rich Saul or right tackle Jackie Slater. Dan Ryczek was actually outstanding in both those games. Next, we played Dallas and got crucified 30-6. Dallas played a 4-3 defense with a down lineman on the right guard every down. Ryczek was caught in a physical mismatch.

During this time period, when I had Ryczek starting at the right guard position, I was having tryouts almost every day to pick up some linemen. I must've worked out 30 linemen in a three-week period. Finally, we signed Gordon Gravelle, my former starting right tackle in the Steelers first two Super Bowls, after the Giants had released him. We also signed Bill Bain, a former No. 2 draft pick of Green Bay, who had also played for Denver. Also, either after the Dallas or Giants game, I put rookie

Kent Hill, who had been practicing at tackle and had a slight knee injury, at the starting left guard slot. After nine games and a 4-5 record, we finally had a starting offensive line up of tackles Doug France and Jackie Slater, guards Kent Hill and Dennis Harrah, and center Rich Saul, and that was our lineup for our last 10 games through the Super Bowl.

Greatest Defensive Game In NFL History

Nolan Cromwell

— After we lost the ninth league game to the New York Giants, 20-14, at the Coliseum in late October for our third loss in a row and were 4-5 for the season, the outlook for the future looked pretty bleak. We had several key players injured, some out for the season, and we were struggling. Even our fans at the time didn't like us and booed us, even before games when they did show up. On Monday before our 10th game at Seattle, I asked Ray Malavasi if I could ride home with him after we finished the Seattle game plan, because I wanted to have a private conversation with him. My wife had driven me to work that day. So, we stopped at a bar on the way home. After we ordered a drink, I proceeded to talk. I said, "Ray, you're going to get fired. It's in all the papers, on radio and TV. We have a losing record, have lost the last three games, and all the sportswriters and announcers are saying you should be fired. If I was you and knew I was going to be fired, I'd want to go out fighting. I think you should make some changes." He asked me what I had in mind.

"First of all," I told him, "I think we should start practice at a set time. It's a bad way to start practice with half the team waiting around the practice field for the other half to get finished with their meeting. I don't like it and none of the other coaches like it either. And if I'm going to go down fighting, I'd want to have people who believe in Ray Malavasi the most to be along my side. You've got to change captains and make people like Larry Brooks and Rich Saul captains, players who will go to war for Ray Malavasi. Also, our running backs do not know what they are doing half the time. I want you to give me the running backs for their blocking assignments on both runs and passes, and give receivers coach Lionel Taylor the backs for their receiving and ball carrying assignments. I also want to go up to the press box and be on the phones to you

Jack Youngblood

and Lionel. We're getting no worthwhile information on defensive fronts and coverages. Half the time the coach on the offensive phone upstairs, Jack Faulkner, is suggesting plays Sid Gilman ran 20 years ago." Ray's reply was, "Yeah, I don't know what went wrong with him. He's getting senile." After I was through suggesting to Ray what I thought he should do, he and I discussed each particular point that I had brought up. Finally, he said that he would make all the changes I suggested the very first thing the next day. And he did!

Ray changed captains; he started practice at a set time; he had the offensive backs come to me for their blocking assignments and to Lionel for their receiving assignments; and he told the staff that I would be in the press box for the Seattle game on the offensive phone. Jack Faulkner, the offensive backfield coach, did not show up for the first hour of practice. He was seen going in to see the general manager. The changes appeared to have some effect because the practices that week seemed to be much crisper. The new captains were really into it.

Jack Reynolds

When I was in the locker room in Seattle getting dressed in my coaching gear about two hours before the game, I was told that Malavasi wanted to see me. I walked into Ray's office. Ray said, "Rad, you can't go up in the press box. It'll be embarrassing to Jack." I said, "Forget Jack, our jobs are on the line. I'm going to the press box." Ray said nothing to the contrary, so then I walked out. When it was time, I went to the press box and took charge of the offensive phone. Despite losing our starting quarterback, Pat Haden, late in the game, the Rams won that day, 24-0. Our defense set the all-time, statistical record for the best defensive game in the history of the NFL by holding the Seattle offense to one first down and a total yardage both running and passing of a minus 7 yards (minus 30 yards passing and plus 23 yards rushing), and it is still the all-time record in the history of the NFL. Our offense played a very important part in helping to set this defensive record by controlling the ball the entire game. We had 303 yards rushing and our quarterback Pat Haden was 17 for 21 in passing completions for 172 yards before he broke his pinky finger on his passing arm late in the first half when it got caught in an Astroturf seam.

Pat Haden

237

Winning this game made our record 5-5, and although we lost next week at Chicago, 27-26, the victory at Seattle was the key game in turning around our season and thrusting us toward the Super Bowl. After the game, I saw Jim Mora, who was Seattle's defensive line coach. I told Jim that one of our other coaches was waiting to see the Seattle offensive coordinator who was a friend of his. Jim told me to tell our coach not to wait. Jim said after he showered and dressed, and was leaving the locker room, the Seattle offensive coaches were still sitting on the benches in front of their lockers with their game gear on just staring straight ahead into their lockers. Jim didn't think the Seattle offensive coaches would be coming out for quite a while.

When I got home from Seattle I told my wife that something unusual almost happened before the game. I said, "Do you remember last year in San Francisco when I was upstairs in the press box and quit my job because the head coach wouldn't let me downstairs on the field?" She said, "I remember." I said, "Well, today before the game, Coach Malavasi told me that I couldn't go up stairs to the press box like I wanted to, and I almost quit my job, because now I was downstairs and wanted to go upstairs. I went upstairs anyway and avoided that decision to quit."

Incidentally, the quarterback for Seattle on that woeful day was Jim Zorn, who went on to be the head coach of the Washington Redskins in 2009 and 2010. The minus 30 yards passing that day in Seattle had to be the lowest point of his career.

Jackie Slater

Road To Super Bowl XIV – After the 26-27 loss in the next game at Chicago using rookie quarterback Jeff Rutledge, the Rams won four straight with our heretofore seldom-used backup quarterback Vince Ferragamo and a couple of appearances by veteran quarterback Bob Lee. Surprisingly, we actually clinched the NFC Western Division title with a 34-13 win at Atlanta before our last game at home against New Orleans. We lost to the Saints, 26-14, for a 9-7 record that was worse than all the nine other teams in the playoffs for both the NFC and AFC, including the four wildcards. I don't think most people gave us much of a chance to reach the Super Bowl. And after a bye week when the wild cards played, we traveled to Dallas as a 9½ point underdog in what sportswriters predicted would be a battle between our defense and the Cowboys potent offense quarterbacked by Roger Staubach and tailback Tony Dorsett. Our offense was supposedly the Rams weakness because of Ferragamo, a third year, fourth round draftee from Nebraska who had grown up in L.A.

Well, Ferragamo surprised everyone by throwing two first half touchdowns of 32 and 43 yards in the first half, but had two interceptions in the second half that helped Dallas take the lead early (12:56) in the fourth quarter. We lost a big opportunity later in the quarter when a pass interference penalty that would have given us the ball deep in the Cowboys territory was overruled by another official despite our protests. But then with 2:06 left in the game, Ferragamo hit Billy Waddy for a 50-yard TD that won the game, 21-19. Our defensive coordinator Bud Carson got a lot of ink out of this game for using seven defensive backs at once, several times during the game, against the Cowboys' shotgun offense. Bud called it his dollar defense—a nickel defense being one with five defensive backs, a dime with six defensive backs, and dollar meaning seven defensive backs. Dave Anderson of the *New York Times* wrote that Bud, "had upstaged Ray Malavasi, the head coach", but what it really did was show Ray's trust in us assistant coaches.

Vince Ferragamo

(Special Note: I remember asking Billy Waddy's agent, Steve Earhart, to give Billy a pep talk before the Dallas game. Steve was a former Colorado University Graduate Assistant Coach in Law School. Billy certainly responded by winning the game with his 50-yard touchdown catch and run.)

We were slightly favored by three points in the NFC championship game at Tampa Bay but the Buccaneers were the sentimental favorite because their popular, one-time University of Southern California coach, John McKay, who taken Tampa from a first year franchise team in 1976 to the brink of the Super Bowl in three years. The Bucs had the best defense, statistically, in the NFC: No. 1 in allowing the least rushing yards, the least passing yards, the least total yards, and also the least number of first downs. We totally dominated the game but could only score three field goals by Frank Corral to win 9-0. We rushed for 216 yards, outgained them in total yardage by almost 200 yards, controlled the ball for 21 minutes of the first half and only once allowed them to get within scoring distance.

After the game I remember a group of reporters surrounding Doug France, our left tackle, and asking him if he thought before the game that he could keep Tampa's best player, defensive end Leroy Selmon, away from the quarterback as well as he did. Leroy never got close to the quarterback all day. Doug's answer to the reporters was, "I've been telling you guys I'm the best left offensive tackle in the National Football League." When I heard the statement, I started to laugh. Leroy Selmon was so good coming out of college at Oklahoma that the Pittsburgh Steelers—who drafted last in the 1976 draft—considered giving up all their draft choices that year to Tampa for the No. 1 overall pick so that they could get Leroy. The Steelers had discussed it but it was never really taken seriously. In 1979, LeRoy Selmon was voted "Defensive Most Valuable Player in the NFL" by the Associated Press, Newspaper Enterprises, *Pro Football Weekly* and United Press.

Lee Roy was unlucky in two ways that day. First he was too good for me to ever think that one offensive player could consistently block him. Second, Tampa Bay played a 3-4 defense, with minimum blitzing, so that it was possible to double-team Leroy every pass play, either with an uncovered guard helping the left tackle or a back helping the left tackle. We doubled Leroy every pass play we called in the game, either with a back or guard. All Doug France had to do was set to Leroy's inside on every pass play. That's why both Doug and I were laughing when he was yelling, "I've been telling you reporters all along that I'm the best left tackle in the National Football League." I need to give a little advice right here: If you are a great defensive end coming out of college, don't go and play for a non-blitzing 3-4 defensive team, especially if you've made the mistake of being too good. Anyway, we won and had completed our miracle drive from Seattle in mid October and along the playoff road to Super Bowl XIV against the best team in the playoffs, my former team, the Pittsburgh Steelers.

Doug France

Family Ticket Deal – The best thing for me about coaching in Super Bowl XIV was that it was at the Rose Bowl in Pasadena and my children were all excited because they would be there to see it. At the time, Danny was 21, Lisa 17, Leslie 13 and Lori 11. They had our house in Huntington Beach plastered with signs and slogans about the game, and I made a deal with them concerning their tickets, which each had a face value of $30. Each of them would get a $30 50-yard line ticket worth $250-$350 in scalper prices. End zone tickets were $100-$150 in scalper prices. If they wish, I could sell each of their tickets for $250 apiece, give them the money, and let them stay home and watch the game on TV with $250 in each of their pockets; or I could sell each of their tickets for $250 apiece, buy $100 end zone tickets, and they could go to the game and sit in end zone seats with $150 in each of their pockets; or I could simply give each of them their 50-yard line seats and they could go to the game, sit on the 50-yard line, and enjoy the game, with no money in their pockets.

Guess which option they selected? Of course, the end zone tickets and $150 extra. The end zone tickets worked out great because they were right against the field where we held pregame warm-up drills. They got to talk to the players and coaches during the pregame drills and, actually, were much closer to the action than they otherwise would have been. Now, scalping tickets by coaches and players is common practice and not exactly illegal, unless you do it like our owner Georgia Rosenbloom's new husband at the time, Dominic Frontiere. We didn't know it then, but it was estimated later that Frontiere sold 16,000 tickets from the Rams allotment of 30,000 that he had obtained from his wife and had made a profit of about a half a million dollars. He never reported the income to the IRS, and in 1986 he was sent to prison for a year, placed on three years' probation and fined $15,000. Two years later they divorced. And I have to tell you a personal story about Dominic that still makes me laugh. Dominic was a former world champion accordion player, who at the time of his marriage to Georgia in 1979 was a music composer for a number of well-known John Wayne movies and television shows like Twelve O'Clock High and The Flying Nun. I found Dominic's company very enjoyable. I can still remember him telling me of his mother, who lived in New Jersey, getting off the plane at the Los Angeles airport with two gallon jugs of water. Dominic asked her, "Why the jugs of water mom?" His mother replied, "The last time I was here the sauce did not taste right. It must've been the water!"

Super Bowl XIV – My biggest thrill in football occurred when I was an offensive line coach for the Pittsburgh Steelers in 1974, when we beat the Oakland Raiders to qualify for Super Bowl IX. When I was the offensive line coach for the Rams in 1979, our win over Tampa Bay to qualify for Super Bowl XIV almost matched that feeling. To have a 4-5 record at midseason, and then to end up in the Super Bowl against my former team made the experience extra special for not only myself but also for two other former Steeler coaches—receivers coach Lionel Taylor and defensive coordinator Bud Carson. All three of us had coached on the Steelers first two Super Bowl teams, IX and X, five and four years earlier. This was not only a game of the Los Angeles Rams versus the Pittsburgh Steelers for us but also former Steeler coaches versus the current Steeler coaches. We all left the Steelers for personal reasons that had nothing to do with the other Steeler coaches, the players or the Steelers organization. We still loved the Steelers in one way, but we were now on the other side. We knew that the chief, Mr. Art Rooney, still considered us Steelers coaches and always would. Emotionally, I believe a person gets more wired up when competing against friends than enemies. Everyone seemed to think we could give the Rams some inside information on the Steelers because of our past, but as I told Ted Green of the *Los Angeles Times* before the game, "How much my information helps, who knows? The Steelers know us, too. They know the way we think, so it's still a guessing game."

Pittsburgh had won the Super Bowl the year before by beating Dallas, 35-31, and after back to back seasons of losing just six regular season games and sweeping the playoffs, plus three Super Bowl championships in five years, the pregame chatter was whether the Steelers were the best team in NFL history. The oddsmakers made them a 9 point favorite, the biggest spread since 1968 when Baltimore was an 18-point favorite over the Jets, and by game time, the number had moved up to 11.

The media said the Steelers had "no apparent weaknesses and many glaring strengths," but we were confident of victory. We had the third best defense in the NFC, first against the run, and I believed my starting offensive line of Doug France and Jackie Slater at tackle, Dennis Harrah and Kent Hill at guard and Rich Saul at center was the toughest in our conference, and maybe the league. These five starters plus back-up center Doug Smith were selected for a combined career grand total of 32 Pro Bowls.

You might find this difficult to believe, but I don't remember any of us ex-Pittsburgh coaches talking to any of the Steelers coaches or players before the game, off the field or on it. We were all business. Maybe Gordon Gravelle did. He had been one of my Seven Dwarfs with the Steelers on our two Super Bowl teams and we had picked him up from the Giants before the season to be a backup tackle. And perhaps our Rams secretary, Nancy Hatcher, also did. She was the Rams prime football secretary but before moving to California because of her husband's job, she had a similar job with the Steelers. I did do an interview for Myron Cope's popular call-in Pittsburgh radio show a couple of days before the game, but that was it.

The game was very hard-fought and for three quarters was very close. We were ahead 19-17 at the end of three quarters and then an unusual incident occurred. The entire Rams team sprinted almost full speed to change sides at the end of the third quarter. I've never seen that before or since, except on TV replays of that game. Early in the fourth quarter, the Steelers had the ball third-and-8 on their own 27-yard line when John Stallworth hauled in a long bomb 73-yard TD pass from Terry Bradshaw to put the Steelers ahead, 24-19. Then the Rams began a drive from their own 16-yard line to the Pittsburgh 32-yard line. But linebacker Jack Lambert picked off Ferragamo's pass to end the drive. In the closing minutes, Bradshaw used a long pass to Stallworth, and an interference call to give the Steelers their clinching touchdown to beat the point spread in a 31-19 triumph. It was an exciting game, but a tough loss for the Rams, and for me personally. Fred Dryer probably summed it best when he told the media in the locker room that, "We had them on the ropes."

No matter if you win or lose the Super Bowl game, there is always a team party after. Of course, when you lose it is pretty subdued. But we felt pretty good about ourselves. We came close to pulling off the biggest upset since Joe Namath led the Jets to that famous 16-7 win over the Colts in '68, and we did it with a patched up squad of committed veterans and a young reserve quarterback. My best memory about that party is when the Steelers young starting defensive end John Banaszak and his wife Mary came over to the hotel to visit us. Years later John and I would coach together at Robert Morris University.

A couple of days after the game, an article appeared in a Pittsburgh paper that one of the Steelers coaches, George Perles, said that I was stealing their signals the first half. I was on the phone in the press box, the entire game, and there's really no way to steal the signals up there when you are working in that hectic atmosphere. George knew I used to steal opponents signals once in a while when I was a Steelers coach on the sidelines. This taught me how easy it is for someone to take a scrap of information and make up a fictitious story based upon that information.

Bad Rad Disco – During the 1979 Rams season, in order to teach my offensive linemen their pass and run blocking skills, I used to imitate or mimic their poor blocking form by dancing with disco music playing. When I demonstrated what I thought was the proper form I'd yell "This is Bad Rad". Then I'd yell a player's name like Rich Saul, Dennis Harrah, Jackie Slater, etc. and I'd imitate what I thought was his poor blocking form. The players named this demonstration "The Bad Rad Disco!" I have no idea how much Bad Rad Disco helped to improve our blocking. But TV reporter (and former NFL player) Irv Cross found out about the Bad Rad Disco from the players and had his cameramen film it and put it on national TV a week before Super Bowl XIV. It's been over 30 years and I still haven't heard from one of the big TV shows like "Dancing With the Stars."

Mean Joe Greene And The Steelers Of The 1970s – With its victory in Super Bowl XIV, the Steelers became the first team in the NFL to win four Super Bowls and solidified their reputation as the "Team of the 1970s." That continues to be the Steelers lasting legacy, even though they now have won two more Super Bowls. After 1979, the team went into a slow decline from those Super Bowl heights as the players who made the team so great in the 1970s aged and retired. I have always looked back at my coaching days with the Steelers as, perhaps, the best time of my professional life. I felt I was an integral part in helping both the defensive and offensive lines develop into the great players that they became. Yet, a coach can get caught up in his own ego, thinking more of himself than his players did. Over the years, I've had a lot of players tell me while I was coaching them how important I was to them, but sometimes you wonder if they're just blowing smoke to stroke your ego.

Joe Greene and Jackie Slater after Super Bowl XIV, Hall of Famers Rad coached.

I have run into many of my Steelers players in the last 40 years but I have rarely asked them what they thought of my coaching. One day in the fall of 2010, I got together with Joe Greene, the Steelers great defensive tackle, the leader of that Steel Curtain defensive line that included L.C. Greenwood, Dwight White and Ernie Holmes. Many in the media believe Joe, whose popular nickname was Mean Joe, was the best defensive lineman in the entire history of the Steelers. Mean Joe played from 1969-81, became an assistant coach in 1987—-the year he was inducted into the Pro Football Hall of Fame. He coached with the Steelers, Miami Dolphins and Arizona before returning to the Steelers as a special personnel assistant in 2004. We met in August, 2010, at the Steelers preseason training camp at St. Vincent College in Latrobe. We sat on a bench outside the players' dormitory on a hill overlooking the practice field, and I pulled out my tape recorder and asked Joe to talk about our days together in the 1970s. Here's what he said:

"Having played and coached for 18 years, I know then the reason we won was we had good coaches. What you brought to us as a defensive line was very important to me, L.C., Dwight and Ernie; how we played all that time. Probably more important than what you brought to the defensive line was what you brought to the offense because up until then offensive linemen were just slugs. You put a work ethic in them in the style and technique work that the only other time I saw it was when you left and it was carried on by (your successor) Rollie (Dotsch).

"Those things were very important to the Pittsburgh Steelers, our coaching, and that in particular, because had the defensive line not got to the point where it did, it would have been very questionable whether we would have gotten to the Super Bowl. And I know if our offensive line hadn't got to that point where it got, we wouldn't have gotten there. No way! I mean how we played with Jim Clack playing center and guard weighing 250 pounds, playing a rookie, Mike Webster, at center and Sam Davis at guard. I don't know if Sam Davis would have played had you not been there. Even Gordon (Gravelle). You got him to play. No question about it. I know in my mind, that is what allowed us to get in a position to win. Otherwise, I don't think it would have happened. Very, very questionable whether those things would have happened. Really!"

I appreciated Joe's kind words. Hearing them now, sure helps me remember all the good things that happened with the Steelers.

The American Plan – The Los Angeles Rams coaching staff was told to take two weeks off after Super Bowl XIV. On the spur of the moment, my wife and I took a 10-day trip to Hawaii. We spent six nights in Oahu, staying in the same beach hotel as the pro football players that were participating in Pro Bowl practices at that time. I can still remember being with All-Pro NFC Center Rich Saul of the Rams and All-Pro AFC center Mike Webster of the Steelers on the beach and both of them demanding I tell them which one of them was the better center. Of course, I had coached both guys but I wasn't born yesterday, so, of course, I refused to answer their demand.

Nancy and I visited Maui for a couple of days, played golf, and then visited the island of Hawaii and stayed at the Mona Kea Hotel and Resort. This was a gorgeous resort built by the Rockefeller Foundation, on a volcano lava bed. The Mona Kea golf course bordered the ocean similar to Pebble Beach and was a beautiful layout After Nancy and I played golf, we went into the dining room for dinner and the prices on the menu were so expensive that we decided to forget about dinner. The rate we were paying for the room was by far the most expensive that we had ever experienced. The next morning, after we had checked out and paid for our expensive room, Nancy and I happened to see a sign in the hotel lobby advertising the American plan and the European plan. The sign said that dinner and breakfast was free under the American plan. When we had checked in the hotel the previous morning, we had signed up for the American plan but had hurried out to play golf and had never known about the free meals. After reading the lobby sign, Nancy and I went back to the hotel checkout desk explained what had happened and asked if we could get breakfast for free even though we had already checked out. The hotel desk clerk said, "Okay." Nancy and I went into the dining room, said we were on the American plan, and ordered the biggest and most expensive breakfast on the menu. That's how a couple of well educated but a little naive Americans learned about the American plan.

No Wasted Motion – Three weeks after the Super Bowl, just after I had returned from Hawaii in February of 1980, general manager Don Klosterman asked me if I could do him a personal favor. He wanted me to give a personal clinic to three offensive linemen from the University of Southern California as a favor to him. So, a few weeks before the 1980 NFL draft, I gave an all day clinic from 8 a.m. to about 5 p.m., with time off for lunch, to three Southern Cal senior offensive linemen. The three linemen were Brad Budde, who had won the 1979 Lombardi Award as the outstanding lineman in college football and whose his father Ed had played for the Kansas City Chiefs; Chris Foote, a big kid who had played at Fairview High School in Boulder, Colorado for my good friend Sam Pagano (father of current Indianapolis Colt Head Coach Chuck Pagano); and Anthony Munoz, a big kid of Mexican heritage, who had been hurt almost his entire last two years at Southern Cal. He had finally been healthy and played the entire Rose Bowl game a month and a half earlier. I methodically went over all the run and pass blocking skills and anything else about offensive blocking that I could think of during this approximately eight hour clinic. All three were drafted that year with Munoz and Budde going in the first round and Foote in the sixth. Cincinnati chose Munoz with the third overall choice (one of the highest picks ever for an offensive lineman) and Budde was taken eight players later by Kansas City. Budde played seven years with the Chiefs and Foote was with the Colts, Giants and Vikings for eight years, but Anthony Munoz played 13 years for the Bengals, and went to the Pro Bowl 11 consecutive times.

Special Note – Dick LeBeau, a former Cincinnati assistant in 1980 and currently the Pittsburgh Steelers defensive coordinator, recently told me that the Bengals head coach in 1980, Forest Gregg, personally attended Southern Cal's 1980 pro (workout) day. Dick said Gregg were so impressed with Anthony Munoz's workout that Forest had Anthony personally work out against him the next day. After putting Anthony through his paces and having him personally beat on and push Forest around in some blocking drills, Forest was bruised and convinced that Anthony had to become a Cincinnati Bengal. Dick said Forest personally made the decision to draft Anthony first with the third overall pick of the draft. Considering the fact that Anthony hardly played since his sophomore year, Forest Gregg's high pick of Anthony Munoz has to be considered one of the greatest judgment draft choices of all time.

Sixteen years later, in the fall of 1995, I was walking onto the football field in Green Bay as the offensive line coach of the St. Louis Rams for our first league game of the 1995 season, when I came upon St. Louis Rams offensive tackle Jackie Slater talking to radio football analyst Anthony Munoz. Jackie Slater was in his 20th year as a player and Munoz was doing the color for the radio broadcast of the game. We greeted each other, conversed a bit, and then Anthony said, "Hey Rad, do you remember that clinic that you gave years ago to Budde, Foote, and me?" I said, "Yeah, I remember." Anthony said, "That was a great session." I said, "That's nice of you to say." Then Anthony said, "I really mean it. That principle of no wasted motion was the greatest. When I took my kick step, I didn't kick up high like other guys. I slid my foot as close to the ground as possible and planted it is soon as possible. When I brought my hands up to pass block the defensive man, I didn't wind up and go from A to B to C but I came directly from point A in my stance to point B on the defender." I said "Anthony, you really do remember and after all this time. That was 16 years ago."

That tells you a lot about Anthony Munoz. He was elected to the Pro Football Hall of Fame in 1998 and is considered by some to be the best left tackle ever in the NFL. He definitely was one of the best. Of course, so was Jackie Slater, my big draft mistake of 1976, who played seven years longer than Anthony and was also inducted in the Hall of Fame, in 2001. I never had a chance to coach Anthony except that one day, but I sometimes wonder which one I would choose if it came down to blocking in a winner-take-all showdown.

Offensive Line Coach Joe Moore – One day in the winter of 1980, my friend Joe Moore, who was now the offensive backs coach at Pitt, was telling me that Pitt needed an offensive line coach again. They had three offensive line coaches in the past two years, and one had only lasted a couple weeks of spring practice. I said to Joe, "Why don't you take the offensive line job, yourself? You're always moaning about them anyway. I'll help you get started. Bring me in from California for a "Bad Rad Day" like we used to have once a year at all those high schools you coached. You already know most of what I do anyway."

Joe went to Jackie Sherrill, told him he wanted the offensive line job, got it, and I flew in from California a couple weeks before spring practice started at Pitt. I gave an all-day, inspirational talk to the Pitt offensive linemen in a locker room from 8:00 a.m. to about 3:00 p.m. I tried to inspire them by telling them how to play offensive line. Among others in attendance were Mark May, Emil Boures, Russ Grimm, Paul Dunn, and Rob Fayda. Jimbo Covert, who would play left tackle that year for Pitt, had not been moved from defense to offense yet, and so he wasn't there. After I was finished with my all-day talk, I told Joe that he also needed some good demonstrators to show these players how the blocking skills should be performed. We both concurred that we needed one person for the guards and centers and one for the tackles. We decided that I should ask Steelers center-guard Mike Webster and Steelers offensive tackle Jon Kolb. I knew they would probably be the best demonstrators of offensive lineman skills in the world. I called both Jon and Mike from California and asked them to visit Pitt's practice a few times. They said they would, and they did. I believe what we did may have helped Pitt have those great seasons that followed in 1980 and '81 and '82, and might even have assisted May and Grimm towards becoming All-Americans in 1980 and later NFL standouts.

Joe also needed an offensive line graduate assistant to help him. Joe had a kid who had played for him at Upper St. Clair High School and then had been an outstanding linebacker at the University of Connecticut and captain of Connecticut's 1976 team. For the last two years the kid had been the offensive coordinator and English Lit teacher at Worcester Academy, so Joe got Jackie Sherrill to hire Kirk Ferentz as his offensive line graduate assistant. Kirk Ferentz went on to become the offensive line coach at Iowa (with recommendations from Joe and me), and the Cleveland Browns, with a stop in between as the head coach at University of Maine for three years, and in 1999 became the head coach back at Iowa where he's been quite successful.

As for my old friend Joe, he immediately had great success as an offensive line coach. Pitt went 11-1 in each of his first two years and was ranked No. 2 in the country both years. Then, in Joe's first two years as offensive line coach at Notre Dame, in 1988 and 1989, their record was 12-0 and 12-1, respectively, and they were ranked No. 1 the first year and No. 2 in the second year. During a 16-year period, 1980-1995, Joe Moore probably produced three times as many NFL linemen as any other offensive line coach in the country. Many respected football people thought he was the best offensive line coach in the country, and Gil Brandt, the long-time director of player personnel for the Dallas Cowboys, stated publicly that Joe Moore was the best offensive line coach in the world. Joe passed away in 2003, but I'll bet there's not a day goes by that Kirk Ferentz doesn't think of him.

You've Got To Draft Grimm — When I returned to Los Angeles after my "Bad Rad Day" visit with the Pitt offensive linemen in the spring of 1980, I went to our Ram scouting department to find out the United scouting combine grades of Pitt's senior offensive linemen. There were two scouting combines operating in the NFL at the time and almost every NFL team belonged to one of them because it was expedient and saved money. The first such organization was BLESTO, which started in 1963 and was run out of Pittsburgh by former Steelers defensive back Jack Butler, who was inducted into the Pro Football Hall of Fame in 2012. BLESTO took its name from the first letters of the nickname of its five members—Bears, Lions, Eagles, Steelers and Oilers. The other group then was United. It started out known as CEPO in 1964, changed its name first to United and then in 1983 to National. BLESTO and National are still operating today, and almost all the current NFL teams but seven still belong to one of the two combines.

Anyhow, each organization graded player prospects differently. At BLESTO, the lower the grade numbers the better the player. For example, a 1.1 is a high or excellent draft prospect, a 1.5 is a middle round prospect, a 1.9 is a late round draft and a 2.5 would be a free agent type. At United, the higher the grade number, the better the prospect. Here's an example from the 1979 season when the two highest graded and best prospects were halfback Billy Simms, the Heisman Trophy winner from Oklahoma, and defensive lineman Bruce Clark of Penn State, the Lombardi Trophy winner n 1978. Both were given grades of 8.8. A 4 or 5 by United would be a middle round prospect and under a 3 would be a free agent.

Before the 1980 season started, Pitt offensive tackle Mark May had a grade in the 6-7 range, which meant he was considered a top pick. Russ Grimm, however, had a grade before the season of about 2.5, which is a projected free agent at best, and not draftable. This got me excited because after seeing Russ at the "Bad Rad Day" I did at Pitt, I thought he was another Mike Webster. In fact, they were almost identical in size except Grimm was an inch taller. I told the Rams scouting department that I wanted to draft him. I was told that the earliest I could draft an offensive lineman was with our fourth round pick. They were going to draft linebackers and defensive linemen before that.

During the 1980 season, I talked a couple of times with my close friend Joe Moore, Pitt's offensive line coach, and he told me that Grimm was playing great at center. Joe kept saying, "You've got to draft Grimm." I kept telling Joe to quit telling the pro scouts how good he was because I couldn't get him in the draft until the fourth round. Pitt had a great year, with an 11-1 record, and after the season was over I went to the scouting department and checked on Grimm's end of the season rating by the United combine. His rating had jumped from about a 2.5 to a 6.7, which now made him the highest rated center in the country. Later I found out that Washington Redskins offensive line coach Joe Bugel worked out both Mark May and Russ Grimm shortly after the season. He must have liked them because the Redskins drafted May No. 1 and Grimm in the third round, which killed my chances of drafting him in the fourth round and fulfilling Joe Moore's demand, "You've got to draft Grimm."

So, here is old Bad Rad, who coached Anthony Munoz for only one day in the winter of 1980 and Russ Grimm for only one day in the spring of 1980 and they both eventually wound up in the Pro Football Hall of Fame. That's why to this day I call both of them "Bad Rad's One Day Wonders."

Now, I'd also like to also list Mark May among my "One Day Wonders" but he was already pretty darn good, and I had known him since he was a Pitt freshman in 1977. That fall, Joe Moore told me Mark was not going home for Thanksgiving. I invited him to our house in Upper St. Clair for Thanksgiving dinner. With his great size and outgoing personality, Mark made a big hit with my kids. My four children still remember that Thanksgiving Day, especially when we are having dinner together on Thanksgiving.

John Frank Attends Rams Minicamp – In the spring of 1980, my cousin Ray Radakovich, who was partners in a law firm called Frank and Radakovich, called me and told me that his partner Alan Frank's son, John, was going to Ohio State on a full scholarship and was going to major in pre-med. Pre-med was not a problem for John because he was a straight A student. The problem was that John was recruited as a tight end by Ohio State and he couldn't block. Ray and Joe Moore, who had tried to recruit John for Pitt, had decided that John needed to see me to learn how to block. John's father was willing to pay his son's airplane fare and whatever other expenses were involved. My alma mater Penn State had also tried to recruit John.

The reason my cousin Ray, Joe Moore, and I were concerned about John, was that we had known John since he was a small boy. We had all gone to his bar mitzvah held at the LeMont, which has the best view of Pittsburgh from the top of Mount Washington than any other restaurant in town. John was a very good athlete, had played baseball and basketball with Joe Moore's son Johnny Moore since they were little. John Frank's father wanted John to play basketball but not football in high school. Alan had been captain of Carnegie Mellon's basketball team in college. The three of us, Ray, Joe and I, convinced Alan that John would just be another guy in college on the basketball floor, but that he could be a great tight end in football. So Alan finally let John go out for the football team in high school. John had great hands, and mainly what he did on the football field in high school was catch the ball. I told them to send John out to California for our week-long minicamp, which was coming up in early May. He could stay at my house.

John Frank

John went to the minicamp with me and I had him participate in all the meetings and drills exactly as if he were a new draft pick. My veteran players would coach him during the meetings. He caught passes and blocked and had a ball. He was very receptive to coaching. He loved it. Near the end of the very last practice he sprained his ankle while catching a pass thrown by our veteran quarterback Pat Haden. After practice, John was in the training room when a salesman was talking to our head trainer about a laser acupuncture machine (not Chinese needles) that was just out. The trainer said, "Try it on the high school kid's new ankle injury." The ankle was swelling up. The salesman and trainer then acupunctured John's swollen ankle. The next day, my wife, John, and I were being shown around Hollywood by Howie Leftkiewicz, a friend from Pittsburgh who worked in Hollywood. (Howie had been president of the Steelers Offensive Line Fan Club in the Super Bowl years of 1974 and 1975, and is currently president of the internet travel site, vegas.com, in Las Vegas.) As we are walking through Rodeo Drive, John, who had been limping since he hurt his ankle the day before, said, "Look, Rad. I can run. My ankle's better. I can run. The acupuncture worked." He showed us that the swelling was down, and that his ankle felt as good as new. John flew home the next day. A few weeks later, he played in the Big 33 All-Star game, which is the premier all-star football game in Pennsylvania. There was a quote in one of the papers by a major college coach (I can't remember who), which said, "I never saw a high school kid block as well as John Frank."

John went to Ohio State, was captain of the football team his senior year, and caught the winning pass at the end of the 1984 Fiesta Bowl game to beat Pitt, 28-24. I told Joe Moore, "See what happens when you help out a kid. He comes back to haunt you." When I was at the Minnesota Vikings before the 1984 NFL draft, head coach Les Steckel, who had been a receiver and tight ends coach, raved about the blocking ability of this tight end John Frank of Ohio State. He had no idea I knew John until I told him. John was drafted by the San Francisco 49ers in the second round in the 1984 NFL draft, played in two Super Bowls with the 49ers, and then voluntarily retired after Super Bowl XXIII, so that he could go to medical school and get started on a new career. He finished medical school and currently is an eye, ear, and nose specialist in New York City. Every once in awhile, there will be a clip on TV that shows John Frank of the 49ers on top of the Giants great linebacker, Lawrence Taylor, in a fight on the field. Someday I'll have to ask John what that was all about?

So, after one year with the Los Angeles Rams, life was pretty good again and things were looking up. But as I wrote earlier, my profession is a combination merry-go-round and roller coaster—and a three-ring circus, too. In the not too distant future I would find myself suddenly at the bottom—and I mean the bottom—with, literally, only a quarter left in my pocket, and wondering if I'd even get another ride on that roller coaster.

CHAPTER FIFTEEN – A Fork In The Road

We've all had bad dreams or nightmares and let me tell you about one. I've never felt so desperate or depressed. My family and I are living in a beautiful house with a pool in Huntingdon Beach, just south of Los Angeles, and I have this nice, comfortable job coaching for the Los Angeles Rams. Then, in what seems like a flash, I find myself anxiously trying to get home from a temporary job in a warehouse that I had taken just to make ends meet. But I'm 15 miles away sitting on a bench a couple of blocks from the Disneyland entrance and waiting nervously for a bus with no money to pay the bus fare. I'm sweating, distressed and disheartened and wondering what the hell has happened to me.

Only this wasn't a dream. It actually happened in March of 1982, and it was one of the lowest points of my life.

Nowhere in my wildest dreams did I think anything like this would happen, especially in the fall of 1980 when the Rams were coming off their first Super Bowl appearance. Here's how it all occurred. We didn't get back to the Super Bowl in '80 but we had a pretty good year and made the playoffs again as a wild card. We lost our first two regular-season games but lost just three more to finish with an 11-5 record. My two best memories of the season occurred off the field, and I guess they were typical of why they call me "Bad Rad." I entitle the first one "Cowboys and Indians."

Cowboys And Indians – It was a Thursday morning during the middle of the season and I was conducting a walk-through meeting on the practice field with my offensive linemen. We were walking through all of our assignments on our plays against the various defensive fronts and alignments that our Sunday opponent normally used. After about a half hour of the one hour scheduled walk through, I was so frustrated at the number of mistakes being made by my offensive linemen that I yelled, "That's the end of the walk-through. Let's go back to our meeting room."

When we got back to the meeting room, I asked them to give me the game plans that I had given them the day before to study. (An offensive lineman's game plan is a visual diagram of their assignments for each play against the various defensive alignments of the next opponent. It is actually a set of about 10 sheets of paper stapled together with four or five plays drawn on each sheet.) I then went outside the room and got a big hard plastic lid off of a large plastic garbage can that was just outside the door to the room. I placed the lid upside down on the floor in the front of the room and put all 11 of the paper game plans in the lid, around 100 sheets of 8 x11 inch sized paper. I then took a match

251

and lit the papers in the garbage can lid. Next I started to do an American Indian dance around the garbage can lid and began chanting "AY-YUH, AY-YUH, AY-YUH, AY-YUH, AY-YUH, AY-YUH, AY-YUH," just like I had seen Indians do in the movies and on television. My players started shouting, "Rad, what are you doing? What's going on?" I said, "I'm doing an Indian burial dance. You guys don't study your game plans. They're of no use. The same as being dead. So I'm burying them." And I continued to dance around the lid and to chant, "AY-YUH, AY-YUH, AY-YUH, AY-YUH, AY-YUH, etc."

They yelled, "You're going to burn the building down." I ignored their yells and continued to chant Indian style and dance around the lid. A couple of them ran next door to the locker room, got water in some containers, ran back in the meeting room and threw water on the game plan fire, putting it out. I then carried the partially-burned game plans out of the room on the garbage can lid, threw them in the big garbage can and put the lid on. When I went back into the meeting room, I told the offensive linemen that I had done the Indian burial dance of the game plan because I was upset with them. I said I had spent all that time on Tuesday drawing up the game plan and it was obvious during a walk-through that they hadn't looked at the game plan at all on Wednesday. And then I told them a story about the Cowboys and Indians.

"Years ago, a group of cowboys were camping next to a stream in the Black Hills of South Dakota. A couple of Indians were on the top of a hill and spotted these cowboys camping down in the valley. The one Indian said to the other Indian, 'Those Cowboys are in our territory. We can't have that. We've got to do something.' So the two Indians went around to the various tribes and gathered a war party of a few hundred Indians. They met on top of a hill overlooking the cowboys sitting around their campfire and the leader said, 'We'll teach those Cowboys not to come into our territory,' and they yelled, 'Geronimo! Charge!' and the Indians came down the hill with their hatchets, bow and arrows and spears, yelling and screaming, 'Death to the Cowboys.'

"The nine cowboys happily sitting around a campfire heard all this commotion and spied the Indians charging down the hill toward them. The Cowboys each ran to his horse, opened up the violin cases each horse was carrying, grabbed the Tommy Machine Gun inside each case, aimed at the Indians and, 'rat-tat-tat-tat-tat-tat-tat,' mowed down all those hundreds of Indians. Hatchets, spears, and bows and arrows were no match for those Tommy Gun's. The moral of the story is, "If you don't keep up with the times, you're going to fall behind and get clobbered just like the Indians. The second moral of the story is 'Don't mess with Cowboys from Chicago!'"

At the end of the story, offensive guard Dennis Harrah ran to the open door and slammed it shut. I said "Dennis, why did you slam the door shut?" Dennis said, "Coach Rad, if anybody comes by, and hears the way you talk, they'll call someone to take you away. I was doing you a favor."

Needless to say, I've told this story to players on other teams that I've coached in order to emphasize the importance of learning the technique skills that I was teaching.

Sleeping Beauty – Then there was day I was "Sleeping Beauty." It was the 14th game in our 1980 16-game schedule and we were in Buffalo to play the Bills.

We each had 9-4 records with a good chance to make the playoffs. Another incentive for both teams was that Chuck Knox, Buffalo's head coach, who had been the Rams head coach three years earlier, would be coaching against his former team for the first time since he had resigned after the 1977 season. So, this was the biggest game of the season for the players, coaches and the fans of both teams. After the team meeting the night before the game, I spent about an hour talking to Bud Carson's next-door neighbor from back in Pittsburgh, who had come to Buffalo for the game. I went to bed about 11:30 p.m. and had a wake-up call for 8:00 a.m.

The next morning I awoke and looked at my watch and panicked. It was 11:00 a.m. I called the hotel operator and asked why I didn't get my 8 o'clock wake-up call. She said she did ring me. Instead of the phone, they ring a bell above your bed. I asked her to ring the bell and she did. But the bell didn't ring. It shook a little but had no sound. The wake-up bell was broken. I dressed in a hurry, went to the front desk and found out the Rams team had left almost two hours before, which was what I expected. I asked if the hotel would use their passenger van to take me to the stadium. The hotel clerk said they couldn't use it for a special trip for one passenger. I told him about the wake-up bell being broken and threatened to sue the hotel if they didn't try to get me to the stadium before the game started at 1:00 p.m. He changed his tune and told the driver of the hotel van to drive me to the game.

About three miles from the stadium, we got caught in a horrendous traffic jam of cars going to the game, and we barely moved for an hour. I could see the stadium, but I couldn't get there. Finally we arrived, but since I didn't have a ticket, I had to talk my way in. A policeman took me inside by way of the Buffalo Bills football offices which were in the stadium. I went through the Bill's offices and got out on the field with about two minutes left in the first half. I told Ray Malavasi what happened and all he said was, "I was wondering where you were!" At halftime, my offensive linemen told me that they didn't tell anyone that I didn't show up for the pregame meal or the team buses because they were covering for me. They didn't want to get me in trouble. Well, the big game was close and we lost 7-10 in overtime. I have no idea if my missing the first half by being sleeping beauty had any effect on the final score, but I'd like to think it did.

Since I had to go through the Bills office and identify myself to get on the field, the entire NFL knew by the next day that I didn't show up for the game until halftime. But, theoretically, I really didn't sleep in because 11:00 a.m. in Buffalo is 8:00 a.m. in Los Angeles. We had just flown into Buffalo earlier that Saturday and my body evidently was still on west coast time. Anyhow, both teams ended up with 11-5 records and made the playoffs.

Ray Malavasi's New Contract – The following week was our biggest game of the season on Monday Night Football at home against the Dallas Cowboys. We completely outplayed the Cowboys and won, 38-14, in a game where one of the TV sportscasters said he had never seen a Dallas team dominated the way the Rams beat them that night. The next day was game plan day for the final league game at home versus Atlanta. After we finished with the game plan, I asked Ray Malavasi if he had signed his new contract. We all knew his contract was up at the end of the season. He said he hadn't. I told him, "Ray, you've got to sign a new contract this week, before we play Atlanta Sunday. We just beat the Dallas Cowboys 38-14 on Monday night TV. What are the chances of us doing that again? We've got no idea what will happen in the Atlanta game Sunday or the playoff game the week after that. You've got to sign now while you're hot." Ray agreed and said he would do his best to get a new contract signed before Sunday. The night before the home games, the Rams players and coaches stayed at the South Coast Plaza Hotel in Costa Mesa. Saturday night at the hotel, Ray came over to me and said, "Rad, I got it done. I signed my new contract." I replied, "Congratulations." We beat the Atlanta Falcons the next day 20-17 to end the season 11-5 and a wild-card playoff spot against Dallas seven days later. We played Dallas in the first playoff game the next week exactly 13 days from when we had beaten them 38-14. This time they crushed us, 34-13. I believe it was a good thing Malavasi had signed his new contract eight days earlier.

Can He Recruit? – Sometime in January of 1981, I received a phone call from my friend Joe Moore, who had just completed his first year as offensive line coach at the University of Pittsburgh. Pitt had a very successful 11-1 season and a No. 2 national ranking. Joe told me he had recommended his graduate offensive line assistant, Kirk Ferentz, to the University of Iowa head coach, Hayden Fry, for the offensive line coaching position at Iowa. Joe told me Hayden was a big Pittsburgh Steelers fan and had changed the uniform of the Iowa football team to look like an exact replica of the Pittsburgh Steelers uniform. Joe said he had told Hayden that I had tutored both Joe and Kirk and that they coached the Pitt offensive line the same as I had coached the Super Bowl Steelers offensive line in the mid-70s. Joe told me to expect a call about Kirk from Hayden.

When Hayden called, I told him all the standard good things one can say about a young coach like Kirk. I talked about how smart he was, how quick he learned, how he knew all the drills and techniques we used at the Steelers, and so on. Then Hayden said, "Can he recruit?" At that moment I was stumped. I knew Kirk had never recruited anyone. Since he'd finished playing linebacker for Connecticut, he'd had one year as a Connecticut student coach, two years as a prep school coach and one year as a Pitt graduate assistant coach. I didn't know what to say. Finally after a few moments of thinking I said, "Hey, I know for a fact that Kirk has never recruited anyone. He's never had the opportunity, but he does have a lot of people skills. He grew up in a wealthy neighborhood and was a good student at one of the best academic high schools in Pennsylvania and is a very confident and personable young man. When he walks in a prospect's house, the parents are going to say, 'That young man has a lot of class!' I think he'll be a great recruiter." Before Kirk went for his interview with Hayden, I told him how I had handled Hayden's recruiting question. Anyway, it didn't hurt because Kurt got the offensive line job at Iowa.

Iowa won the Big 10 in Kirk's first year as offensive line coach and went to the Rose Bowl. Since I was with the Los Angeles Rams then and nearby where the Iowa team was staying in California, I told Kirk I was going to come by and watch him coach his players in practice the week before the Rose Bowl game. Kirk called me back and told me that Hayden had closed all practices to everyone, even me. I told Kirk to ask Hayden again. Hayden still said, "No." Just writing about it 27 years later, I still get upset. What gratitude. Oh, Iowa got the crap beat out of them in the Rose Bowl by Washington, 28-0.

Of course, as we now know, Kirk Ferentz became an outstanding recruiter and assistant coach, and when Fry retired after the 2001 season, Kirk became Iowa's head coach. He is now one of the highest-paid college football coaches in the country as well the highest-paid state or public employee in Iowa.

Contract Trouble—On Strike – My first sign of problems with the Rams occurred in January of 1981 as my contract was expiring, and to this day I don't understand why things suddenly changed. I had been working on a two-year contract for $55,000 per year and the contract ended on January 31, 1981. Early in January, I went to see general manager Don Klosterman about signing a new contract. He told me to go talk to his assistant, Jack Faulkner. Jack had been the backfield coach in 1979 and had become an administrative assistant after that season. Jack and I really didn't get along and I refused to see him. Don said, ok, and said he'd give me a $2,000 raise if I signed right then. I said, "No way." He then said that he had bigger worries trying to get players signed and I left his office.

Don used the exact same ploy with defensive line coach Laverne Torgeson, who had been on a three-year contract. Torgy also refused to see the general manager's assistant, refused to accept a $2,000 raise and then took a job with the Washington Redskins for $70,000 a year, $15,000 more than his previous Rams salary. I told Malavasi what had happened and told him that I wasn't going to quit—you don't get paid if you quit—but I wasn't going to do any football work until I had a decent contract. So I went to the football office for the next four months, February through May, and drank coffee, read the paper and so forth, but refused to work on football. I was basically on strike, and I was obviously upset.

In my two years of coaching with the Rams, we had been to the Super Bowl in 1979 and in the playoffs in 1980. The offense in 1980 had led the entire NFL in rushing yardage—without a 1,000 yard rusher—and were second in the NFL in total offense. The Rams offensive line was considered by many as the best offensive line in the NFL. All of my five starting offensive linemen—Jackie Slater, Kent Hill, Dennis Harrah, Rich Saul and Doug France—signed new contracts after the 1980 season. They each received a $100,000 raise or more, and I had been offered a measly $2,000. Finally, late in May, Malavasi asked me what I was going to do? Was I going to start working on football or what? I told him the general manager had not talked to me and I had no idea why—and I still don't. Ray then asked me what it would take to get me to coach. I knew two of our coaches had received $10,000 raises last year after the Super Bowl. So I said, "A $10,000 raise." He left to see Klosterman, came back about five minutes later and said, "You've got it. Go sign the papers." And I did. I had always gotten along very well with Don Klosterman but we never talked about my contract again. And it still mystifies me why he treated Torgy and me the way he did.

Outside of the contract squabble, my most vivid memories of the 1981 season were once again off the field, and two of them happened during the fall training camp.

Congressman's Son – We were in a staff meeting discussing the first players who would be cut from camp the next day, and among the first players listed on our blackboard was a 6-foot, 200-pound rookie free agent quarterback from Dartmouth named Jeff Kemp. His dad, Jack Kemp, was a former star NFL quarterback, and, at the time, a U.S. Congressman. I couldn't believe it. But what I couldn't believe had absolutely nothing to do with Jeff Kemp being Jack Kemp's son. Our starting quarterback, Vince Ferragamo, had left the Rams for the Canadian League and Pat Haden, who had been the starter before his injury in the middle of the '79 season, was our only tested quarterback in camp. I believed Kemp was a great prospect and would be a good backup for us.

In my opinion, Jeff had by far the strongest arm and quickest release now in camp. He wasn't the best quarterback yet, but I thought he could be. He was a good athlete, intelligent, and had only one flaw – his height. At 6-foot, he was short for an NFL quarterback. Furthermore, on that first cut, we were keeping a young quarterback that we had cut the year before who did not have nearly the arm that Jeff had. I argued hard to keep Jeff and cut the other quarterback that we had cut the year before. Finally, I think I wore everybody down, and we cut the other quarterback and kept Jeff, at least until the second cut. After about another week's practice and before the second cut, quarterback coach Paul Lanham came to me and thanked me for convincing him not to release Jeff on the first cut. Jeff had convinced Paul by the second cut that Kemp would not only make the cut but was now certain to make the team. And that's how I helped Congressman and former NFL quarterback Jack Kemp's kid make a pro football team.

Jeff had a 10-year NFL career playing quarterback for five years with the Rams, one with San Francisco and four with Seattle. Years later, I told Raymond Berry, the former great Baltimore receiver, how Jeff had almost been released on the first cut. Raymond evidently told Jeff because shortly after that I received a thank you note from Jeff. It goes to show once again how one person can make a difference in the life of someone you hardly know.

Drew Hill's Takeoff Pattern – One also should be careful what they say because that can sometimes come back to haunt you, and I had a good lesson on that during the same preseason camp. I was reviewing a practice film with my offensive linemen, when we see on film our quarterback under throwing the Rams' fastest wide receiver, Drew Hill, on a takeoff pattern, which is a streak downfield where the receiver simply tries to outrun the defender on a long pass. Drew had to slow up and come back for the ball. I said, "Our quarterbacks should shorten their drop and throw the ball with all their might when they have Drew Hill on a takeoff pattern. I guarantee you I'll kiss everybody's bare butt in this room if any of our quarterbacks ever overthrow Drew Hill on a takeoff." After a minute or so about complaining about the under throws, I continued on with the offensive line meeting.

About one month later, as I am reviewing a practice film again with my players, going over their pass blocking techniques, a play occurred on the film where Drew Hill was overthrown on a deep pass. As I'm going over the blocking assignments and techniques on the play, all of a sudden the lights go on. Right guard Dennis Harrah and left tackle Doug France ran to the front of the room in front of the film screen, dropped their pants and undershorts and bent over with their bare butts sticking out toward me and the other players and yelled out, "Kiss it Rad, kiss it. Drew Hill was overthrown on a takeoff. Come on, kiss it." I yelled back, "That wasn't a takeoff; that was a deep post pattern." Dennis said, "Aw, come on Rad. We won't tell anybody. Just kiss it!" And I yell back, "No, no. It wasn't a takeoff pattern. It was the deep post. They're different patterns." But they really are not. Of course, there was no way I was going to kiss their bare butts, but it taught me to be careful of what I say to players because some things they don't forget.

Once the '81 season started, it seemed like déjà vu as we lost our first two games again; then we perked and won our next four and thought we were in pretty good shape. We then proceeded to lose eight of our final 10 games, including two very close games to the eventual Super Bowl champion San Francisco 49ers by a total of five points, 20-17 and 33-31, and to the Super Bowl runner up, Cincinnati Bengals, 24-10.

Howard Cosell And Joe Montana – The next to last regular season game in 1981 was another *Monday Night Football* game at home against Atlanta. Naturally, the popular ABC broadcast team of Frank Gifford, Don Meredith and Howard Cosell was in town. On the day of the game, I was walking through the lobby of the South Coast Plaza Hotel, where the Rams stayed the night before home games, and I saw Cosell sitting at a table. He saw me and waved to me to join him. I had gotten to know Howard from the previous games I was in that were broadcast on Monday Night Football. As I mentioned in Chapter 3, seven years earlier, Howard had devoted a few minutes of his radio program to a talk about me and my coaching the day after the Steelers beat the Raiders in 1974 to go to their first Super Bowl. I sat down at the table and we talked for a while. He asked me who I thought would win the Super Bowl this 1981 season, and I immediately told him I thought the 49ers would win it. Howard appeared shocked at the answer and he asked me why? I said that even when the 49ers only had won two games in 1979 and four games in 1980 the 49ers had a good offense. Now the 49ers had a great athlete at quarterback running the offense. This year, they finally had a good

Joe Montana

defense with four brand-new rookie secondary players, Ronnie Lott and company, plus a great linebacker group in Willie Harper, Dan Bunz and former Rams linebacker Jack "Hacksaw" Reynolds. I told Howard I had coached Harper and Bunz in '78, and I knew Hacksaw Reynolds from '79 and '80 with the Rams. I said they were now the best team in the NFL with a great coach in Bill Walsh, and Howard seemed impressed.

Then I told Howard my Joe Montana story. One day after Steelers practice in the fall of 1976, I was with my two cousin lawyers, Ray Radakovich and Bob Garshak, at my cousin Raymond's law office. One of them asked me, "What's wrong with Notre Dame, Rad? Why aren't they playing Joe Montana at quarterback?" I said, "Who's Joe Montana?" One of them replied, "Joe Montana? Who's Joe Montana? He's only the best athlete we've ever seen!" I said, "Where did you see, Joe Montana?" "At the round ball tournament," they yelled. "Wow," I said. From 1965 until 1992, the round ball basketball tournament, known officially as the Roundball Classic, had been played annually in the spring in Pittsburgh and was run by a guy named Sonny Vaccaro, who was a bit of a character. The best high school basketball players in the United States were invited to play the best basketball players in the state of Pennsylvania. Both my cousins had been starting athletes in college, Raymond for the Pitt football team and Bob for the Fresno State basketball team. Joe Montana was from Monongahela, which was not far from my hometown of Kennywood. For both cousins to say Joe Montana was the best athlete they ever saw at a basketball tournament that hosted the best high school basketball players in the country was a very strong statement. About a week later, Notre Dame was losing a game pretty badly, and they put Montana in the game. He brought them from behind to win the game and went on to lead Notre Dame to a national championship in 1977. "That's my Joe Montana story, Howard. That's why I'm picking the 49ers to win the Super Bowl!"

About that time, a man who I took to be a football fan came over to our table and asked Howard to autograph something. Howard gave the guy a hard time about interrupting our conversation, but finally submitted and gave the guy the autograph the man wanted. After the man left Howard turned to me and said, "God, I have such contempt for people." I said, "Yes, Howard, you really do." I thought Howard's comment was one of the most honest statements I had ever heard. He really did have contempt for people. Howard asked me how I was going to the game. I told him I was taking a team bus. He invited me to ride with him in his ABC network limousine. I accepted his offer and went to the game with him in the limousine. We beat Atlanta that night 21-16.

Six weeks later the 49ers actually did win the Super Bowl, beating Cincinnati, 26-21. The next time I saw Howard, he wanted some more predictions, but I didn't give him any. He still remains one of the most unusual and honest persons I have ever met, but he sure had an ego. One more thing, when I was hired by the Rams back in 1979, I told my "Joe Montana story" one day while we were having discussions about the draft. It made no impression, and that tells you a lot about the Rams' scouting organization at the time. The 49ers drafted Montana in the third round that year. Greatest third round pick they'll ever make.

Escaping The Guillotine (But For Only A Few Hours) – With six games left in the 1981 season and our record at 5-5, our head coach Ray Malavasi had decided the problem with the team was me and four other assistant coaches, and he decided he was going to fire us at the end of the year. But he didn't tell us. He

told some newspaper reporters, and in a bar, no less. Real classy, eh? We were flying back to Los Angeles from Cincinnati a couple of hours after we had just lost our sixth game, when one of the reporters told me and a couple of the other assistants we were going to get the axe after the season. The reporter said Malavasi had been drinking in the hotel bar with some reporters the night before the Cincinnati game and had told them that he was firing five assistant coaches and he named them, including me. His reasoning, supposedly, was that he had never had a chance to hire his own staff; that either previous head coach George Allen or owner Carroll Rosenbloom was responsible for hiring us. We were dumbfounded. Two years earlier, we had been 4-5 at midseason and had gone on to the Super Bowl. When Malavasi made those comments we were 5-5 and even with the loss to Cincinnati we still had a shot at the playoffs. When we assistants heard about what Malavasi said, we figured he had given up on the season—and he did, as we proceeded to lose five of those last six games. The atmosphere was sort of frigid the last six weeks of the season with five of the coaches knowing that the head coach had told the newspaper reporters that we would be fired.

American Express – Most of the practice time the week of the final game against the Redskins was taken up by the filming of an American Express commercial featuring Rams owner Georgia Rosenbloom Frontiere. I can remember running back Wendell Tyler being tackled at least 30 times in over an hour until they were satisfied with the scene. We lost that last game to the Redskins 30-7, and during the next year I saw Georgia's American Express commercial numerous times and it always reminded me of how bad things had gone my last year with the Rams.

After that last game against the Redskins on December 20, the coaches had a couple of weeks off before we reported back for work. On Monday, January 11, I reported for work around 8:30 a.m. and was told Malavasi wanted to see me. I went to his office and his secretary said he was in with another coach, and she would call me later if he still wanted to see me. Well, I never got called to see him that day, but the coach who was seeing him when I stopped by his office—Hewritt Dixon—got fired. Then another coach got called in and got fired. Then another coach and so on. When the head coach went home at five o'clock four assistant coaches had been fired—my good friends Bud Carson and Lionel Taylor as well as Frank Lauterbur and Hewritt Dixon. I went over to Mama Cosa's, a bar-restaurant a couple of blocks from the Rams offices, with a couple of the coaches who had been fired and they congratulated me on having escaped the guillotine.

The next morning when I got to the office about 8:00 a.m., I was told again that Malavasi wanted to see me. I figured I knew what was going to happen. I went in his office. He told me that he was making changes and that I was one of them. I said, "Fine, goodbye!" and walked out. I was in Malavasi's office less than three minutes. I found out later that I was supposed to be the first one fired the day before. But since I wasn't there when he called for me, he simply fired the other coaches, one at a time, and never got around to me. I don't know what took so long the day before with the other four coaches. I had only escaped the guillotine for a few hours.

Bill Walsh's Story – When I walked out of Ray's office, I bumped into Bill Walsh, the 49ers head coach. He and his team were at the Rams' practice facility to get ready for the Super Bowl, which was less than two weeks away. San Francisco was deluged with storms and they couldn't practice there. Bill said, "Rad, how are you doing?" I said, "Lousy, I just got fired, along with four other assistants." Bill said, "I can't believe that. We thought you were the best team we've played this year. (The 49ers had beaten us in two close games the past season, 20-17 and 33-31.) I can see you're upset. Come take a walk with me around your Rams facility. I want to see it plus I've got a story, I want to tell you."

We started walking around the circumference of the two practice football fields and he told me this story: "As you know, we only won two games my first year (1979) as 49ers head coach, four games my second year (1980), and started off this season losing two of our first three games this year. Before our fourth game, I get a call from a friend who works for the San Francisco paper. My friend tells me that on Monday after the New Orleans game, there will be a three full page exposé demanding that Bill Walsh be fired as the 49ers coach. Well, we beat New Orleans and my friend said they put off the three-page exposé until the next week. After we won three games in a row, my friend called me and said the newspaper had canceled the three-page exposé. We only lost one more game and now here I am playing in the Super Bowl after almost being fired after the fourth game of the season. So don't be discouraged."

Working In The Warehouse – I immediately started searching for a job in the NFL. My contract only ran until the end of the month. I had a big mortgage on my house in Huntington Beach and virtually no money in the bank. I also had to return my dealer car. (A dealer car is a car that the coach gets to use for a year for providing a car dealer with two season tickets.) I desperately needed to get another job quickly. Only three NFL teams changed head coaches at the end of the '81 season, and I began by contacting the new coaches: Mike Ditka at the Chicago Bears, Ron Meyer at the New England Patriots and Frank Kush at the Baltimore Colts. I knew all three, having had conversations with each of them in the past. But I couldn't land a spot with any of them because all three hired offensive line coaches that they had worked with previously.

Nearly two months had gone by and I was now getting concerned. I was just 46 years old, and so I decided that if I was going to be out of football for a year, I should get a job where I could learn something new. I interviewed with the manager of the nearest Paine Weber brokerage firm and the manager decided to hire me. I immediately made a telephone call to former Penn State defensive tackle Mike McBath, who, after five years playing for the Buffalo Bills, had become a very successful Paine Webber salesman in Florida. Mike told me to visit him and he would train me in how to make money in the brokerage business. Two days later, the California Paine Webber manager called me and told me that Paine Webber's main office had put a freeze on hiring and no new employees were to be hired for at least six months. I immediately called Mike and cancelled my visit with him. Now I got desperate.

It was the beginning of March. My last paycheck had been January 31. I had to get some money to make the mortgage payments on my house. So I called Jim Mora, who had just taken a job as the defensive coordinator of the Patriots, and had grown up in Southern California. Jim and I had coached together at Colorado in '72 and '73. I said to Jim, "You're a Southern California guy. Who do you know that might help me get a job in Southern California?" Jim said, "Rad, the only guy I know is my brother. He's in charge of about nine pharmaceutical drug warehouses for Bergen Brunswig Co. You don't want to work in a warehouse!" I said, "The hell I don't. I've got a mortgage to pay. I'll definitely work in a warehouse." Jim said, "Why, let me see what I can do," and hung up. About 20 minutes later Jim called me back. He said, "My brother said to report to this warehouse ready to work on Vermont Avenue in Anaheim at 6:00 a.m. Monday morning. The warehouse is located a couple of blocks away from the entrance to Disneyland. The personnel director will take care of you."

On Monday morning, my son Danny and I awoke at 4:30 a.m. Danny had to go with me because we were now down to one car and he had to bring the car home so my wife could have transportation. She also was working as a secretary at TRW, which was in another direction from Huntington Beach. Disneyland was about 15 miles from my house, but there were 44 red lights we had to go through. It took at least a half hour to drive there.

The personnel manager at the warehouse told me that he would start me off at $8.90 an hour, time and a half for overtime. Top pay in the warehouse was $9 an hour and that's what the guys who had been working there for 20 years got. Hours were 6:00 a.m. to 2:30 p.m., with a 15 minute break at 8:15 a.m. and a half hour break at 12 o'clock noon. I started out as an "order filler," which was 95% of the warehouse work force. An order filler would take a specific drugstore's order form, go to various product shelves throughout the warehouse and put each of the products ordered into a box or boxes for that particular drugstore. He would then set the box with the top open, and containing the order form, onto a giant conveyor belt that went around the warehouse in a big oval and finally past two persons called "packers" who were stationed on either side of the conveyor belt. Order fillers got bonuses based on the number of order lines they could fill in a week. Well, the fastest order filler in the warehouse was assigned to train me to be an order filler. After two days, he begged to be relieved of his training duties. He wasn't getting paid extra to train me and he wasn't filling enough order lines to earn extra bonus money.

Wrong Bus – Not long after I started working at the warehouse, I decided to take a bus home after work so my son wouldn't have to pick me up after work. I got on the bus, paid my $.75 fare, went one block, found out I was on the wrong bus and got off without getting a transfer pass. I then realized too late that I only had a quarter left in my pocket.

So, that's how in the middle of March, 1982, at three o'clock on a sunny 75° afternoon, I found myself sitting on a bench at the corner of Vermont and Anaheim Blvd. in Anaheim, California, and feeling overwhelmed and sweating profusely. I was dejected, distressed and desperate, and wondering what went wrong with my life? Just two years ago, I'd been a coach on the team that went to the Super Bowl. A year earlier, I'd been an offensive line coach on a team that ranked second in total offense in the entire NFL. Now, I had just finished working in a warehouse and didn't even have enough money in my pocket for bus fare to my home 15 miles away.

I can honestly say that was—and still is—one of the lowest points in my life. I sure to hell didn't feel like "Bad Rad!"

I took a few breaths, settled down and started thinking. And I thought about two of Joe Paterno's favorite sayings, "You either get better or you get worse; nothing stays the same," and "As you are going down, you've got to be thinking of getting up." So, after a few minutes on the bench, I decided to hitchhike home. It took me three hours. I told my wife what had happened. We immediately bought our next-door neighbor's 10-year-old Dodge Dart for $1,000, which was about all we had left in the bank thanks to our friends, Augie and Lou Tammariello, who a couple of weeks before had sent us $1,000 to help us out in our time of need. That money sure came in handy when we had to buy the neighbor's used car.

Singing Packer – After about two weeks as an order filler, a warehouse foreman, known as the "pusher," decided I might be better as a "packer." As an order filler, I had trouble keeping up with the men and women who were in their 20s to 40s and were quick as cats filling those order lines. One packer was stationed on each side near the end of the giant conveyor belt, which carried and transported the order-filled boxes. The packers checked each box to see that it was packed correctly. The packer then closed and sealed each box with a strip of paper tape. Each packer had a machine on his side of the conveyor belt which had four buttons on it for different lengths of paper tape. Depending on which button was pushed, the machine would spit out six-inch, or one, two or three-foot strips of paper tape. The packer would grab the tape strip with one hand, slap it on the box and send the box on its way to be delivered to the drugstore.

Well, being a packer put me right in my own element. Rather than just silently working most of the time like I had done and witnessed when I was filling orders, I got the other packer named Scotty to sing songs with me as we worked. I'd say, "How about 'You're A Grand Old Flag' Scotty? Do you know that one?" He'd say, "Yeah" and we'd sing, "It's a grand old flag, it's a high flying flag...," and so on. After a couple of days, the entire warehouse would join in singing. One of the warehouse favorites was "Matilda," made famous by Harry Belafonte, with the familiar lyrics, "Matilda, Matilda, Matilda, she'd take me money and run Venezuela," and so on. When there was a lull, with not too many boxes coming, one of the packers—always me—would go make boxes. I would open up the flattened cartons and staple the bottoms of the boxes on a staple machine that I worked with a foot pedal. Then I would put the box on a hook attached to a chain that moved along the top of the conveyor belt so that the order fillers never had to look for boxes. I used to pretend that I was Kareem Abdul-Jabbar of the Los Angeles Lakers, practicing my sky-hook as I sky-hooked a box onto the hook on this overhead moving chain. At the spot where the two packers worked was a red telephone, called the hotline. The hotline was only for emergency orders that had to be filled immediately by one of the packers.

Hot Line Rings – One morning in June, the hotline rang, I picked up the red phone and a voice went, "Rad, this is Tater" I almost dropped the phone. Tater was the nickname for Carl Smith who had been my graduate assistant coach at Colorado in 1972 and 1973. Carl was now the quarterback coach and offensive coordinator at North Carolina State University. I said, "Tater, I can't talk to you on this phone. This is the hotline. I can only take emergency drug orders on this phone." Tater said, "Your front office said it was okay to call you on this line. I told them it was important. Anyway, I called you because we need an offensive line coach. Would you be interested?" I said, "Sure would." He put NC State Head Coach Monte Kiffin on the phone and we talked for a minute or two. Later, during our lunch break, I was sitting at a table with five of my coworkers, all in their late 20s, and telling them about the telephone call I had received on the hotline from my friend Tater. I told them there was a job open as offensive line coach at North Carolina State, and that I had a good chance of getting it. One of the young guys who was the pusher piped up, "That's great. Rad. Would it be junior varsity or varsity?" I had to shake my head at that one. Anyway, I quit the warehouse at the end of June, spent a month at home and went to North Carolina State August 1 as offensive line coach.

Just to make a point, of all the jobs that I've had in my life, and I've had a bunch, I've never appreciated getting a job as much as I did the drug warehouse job. Nowadays, whenever I hear those songs, "You're A Grand Old Flag" and "Matilda" I have to smile at the memory of working with a great group of guys and gals during one of the worst periods of my life. As they say, "time heals all wounds."

Chuck Noll Calls – I had no intention of ever going back to coach on the college level. But I was very thankful for Monte's offer and I was determined to be an even better coach than I had been at Penn State, Cincinnati and Colorado. When I had accepted the North Carolina State job, I had told Monte Kiffin that if I got a head coaching position or if the Pittsburgh Steelers offered me a job, I was gone. I wanted to be honest and I figured the chances of either happening in the next year were practically nil.

About a week or two after I arrived at NC State in August, I received a telephone call one evening from Bill Nunn, an administrator and pro scout with the Steelers. Bill told me that I was going to receive a call the next day from Steelers Head Coach Chuck Noll. When I asked Bill, what the call was going to be about he just said, "You'll find out." The next morning I had my first meeting with the North Carolina State offensive linemen. This was the first time they learned that I was to be their coach, and I talked enthusiastically to them a little about offensive line play. That afternoon I received the expected telephone call from Chuck. He told me that Rollie Dotsch, the Steelers offensive line coach who had replaced me when I left the Steelers after the 1977 season, might leave. Chuck offered me Rollie's job as offensive line coach of the Steelers. I was shocked. A few months before I was working in a warehouse and couldn't afford bus fare. Now, I could get my old job back with the best organization in the NFL, and my friends.

And the money would enable me to move my family back to my hometown, too, something I couldn't afford to do yet on my NC State salary. North Carolina State paid $25,000 — $20,000 from the school and $5,000 that Monte Kiffin had borrowed from his mother. The Steelers job paid approximately $85,000, plus the chance to get playoff money and a Christmas bonus that the Rooney's always gave. The difference in money between the two jobs was more than $60,000. Plus I could go back to the Steelers for the third time in my career. The Rooney's were like family.

I wanted badly to accept Chuck's offer but I told him I couldn't. I felt guilty about the fact that just that morning I had told the North Carolina State offensive lineman that I was to be their coach. Sure, I had a perfect out because of what I had told Monte before taking the job. But I had just given my word to those kids about being their coach and they were all enthused. I felt the honorable thing to do was stay and coach them.

The next day I received a call from Rollie Dotsch, the coach who supposedly was leaving the Steelers. Rollie said, "What's the deal, Rad?" I said, "Rollie, what do you mean?" Rollie proceeded to tell me that he was offered the head coaching job with Birmingham in the new United States Football League (USFL) that was being formed to begin play in the spring of 1983. He told me Chuck had told him that he couldn't leave unless Chuck could hire me back. I told Rollie I wasn't going back to the Steelers. I then asked him if he took the new head coaching job, did he have to report right away. He said he didn't have to report until the middle of October, two months later. I then told him to tell Chuck that he would stay for two months and help train and counsel whoever Chuck hired as offensive line coach, which is what happened.

Two days after Rollie's call, Chuck called me again. He wanted to know about Ron Blackledge as an offensive line coach. Ron and I had coached together at the University of Cincinnati. When I coached the Steelers I had left tickets for a couple of games at the Will Call window for Ron and his son Todd. Little did I know at the time that Todd would lead my old college team, Penn State, to its first national championship in 1982, win the Davy O'Brien Award as the outstanding quarterback in the country and be the No. 1 draft choice of the Kansas City Chiefs. Anyhow, I recommended Ron and Chuck hired him. Rollie stayed for a while to help train Ron, and I stayed at North Carolina State, at least $60,000 poorer than I could have been.

I've thought about that situation many times since 1982 and how my life would have been different if I had accepted Chuck's offer. Just off the top, I know I probably would have coached in a few more Super Bowls. Perhaps, I also might have been offered a head coaching job in the NFL. It certainly would have been satisfying working for Chuck and the Rooneys, again, and living in Pittsburgh. It wasn't too long after that I realized if Chuck had offered me the job when Bill Nunn called the night before—before I had talked to the North Carolina State offensive linemen—I'm pretty sure I would've taken the job.

Was not going back to the Steelers the biggest mistake of my professional career? Absolutely, but I thought it was right thing to do at the time. Perhaps my decision can be summed up best by what the great Yogi Berra once said, "When you get to a fork in the road, take it."

Midseason Job Change – About a month into the North Carolina State season I realized what a horrendous mistake I had made. I didn't leave because of my loyalty to my new young offensive linemen but I soon found myself involved in a weird situation with my new head coach, Monte Kiffin.

North Carolina State got off to a fast start winning the first three games against Furman, 26-0, East Carolina, 32-26, and Wake Forest, 30-0. At this point I was feeling good about our offense. We were averaging 30 points per game. Then we played Maryland with Boomer Esiason at quarterback and lost, 23-6. Boomer was not the main problem, although he was very good. The main problem was Maryland played a wide tackle six (some call it a 6-2) defense and blitzed almost every down and stuffed us both on runs and passing. After the game, I inquired about our blitz control and found out we didn't have any. If I had known that, we could have just slid the line away from the tight end and have the tight end key the wide end or strong safety (whichever name you wanted to use). If he came, the tight end could block him. If he didn't, the tight end could release on his pattern. If we'd done this, we probably would have won 23-6. Anyway, a lesson learned.

Monday morning around 8 o'clock, Kiffin met with me in his office. He was very disappointed that our offense did not move the ball either running or passing against Maryland. He told me that he wanted to be the line coach. Now, Monte had coached defense all his life. I told him that I thought his idea was crazy. He didn't think so, and he wanted me to coach him every morning on offensive line play. Then in the early afternoon he would meet with the offensive linemen and coach them during practice. I asked him what I would do then? He said I could do some of his duties. I could go over and make sure Pete Carroll, the defensive coordinator, is doing things right. I said, "Oh no, I'm not going to tell Pete what to do when I'm not the head coach. That's not the way to win friends and influence people!" Monte was determined to coach the offensive line. So finally I said, "Okay, you're the head coach. I'll do what you want."

Now, I was a coach without a title and not much to do with the players. So, I gave myself a title, Football Advisor. Whenever someone asked me later what a football advisor was, I would give them an answer like I did in Denver to Tim Simmers of the *Rocky Mountain News* in a story he wrote about me in 1983: "When they asked me a football question, I answered it. If not, I said nothing."

For the rest of that season, I tutored Monte on the offensive line from 8 a.m. to 12 noon. He met with the offensive linemen from 1 p.m. to 3 p.m. every day and then coached the linemen from 4 p.m. to 6 p.m. every practice day. At noon every day I was basically done. In the afternoon, I drank coffee and conversed with the pro scouts—we had a few pro prospects on our team—and at practice, I would just walk around and observe.

Well, we won three of our last seven games to end up with a 6-5 record. One more win would have made us 7-4 and put us into a bowl. I wonder if we'd have gotten that one more win if Monte had not wanted to coach the offensive line. We'll never know.

Although I don't know for sure, I believe that the main reason Monte wanted to be the offensive line coach midseason was that he was bored being a head coach and becoming the offensive line coach was a chance to learn something new. Years later, when I read in the newspaper that Monte Kiffin was going to be offered the head coaching job for the San Francisco 49ers, I had a feeling that he would turn it down, which he did. A head coaching job didn't involve enough coaching for Monte.

Oh, yes that's Monte's son Lane, who once was an assistant for Pete Carroll at USC and then left Tennessee after just one season to succeed Pete at USC in 2010. When it comes to unpredictability, I guess the apple doesn't fall far from the tree.

EDITOR'S NOTE: In order to increase his football knowledge, a young Brad Seely turned down a $30,000 offensive line job at Lamar University in Texas to be my $5,000 graduate assistant at North Carolina State. He has since coached in four Patriots Super Bowls and is currently the 49ers special teams coordinator.

United States Football League – After the '82 season at North Carolina State, I applied for the head coaching job for the Philadelphia Stars of the newly formed United States Football League. George Perles, who I had coached with at the Pittsburgh Steelers, had originally taken the Stars job but had dropped out to become head coach of his alma mater Michigan State. So, I applied for the job and Carl Peterson, the general manager of the Stars interviewed me. During the interview with Carl and the owner, a real estate magnate named Myles Tanenbaum, I could tell that the owner was not at all interested in me. I knew that Carl and Jim Mora were friends. Jim and I had coached together at Colorado and Carl and Jim had coached together at UCLA. Jim was then the defensive coordinator for the New England Patriots. Remember, it was Jim, a year earlier, who got his brother to hire me for the warehouse job when times were tough.

So I called Jim to ask him to recommend me to Carl. When Jim called Carl on my behalf, Carl asked Jim to interview for the job. He did and got the job. Jim called me and felt bad about what happened but I told him I was glad he got the job. The only reason I called him to recommend me was because I didn't feel I had much of a chance after my interview with the owner. Jim then offered me a coordinator job on offense or defense, whichever I wanted. I thanked him, but I told him I felt sure I could get back in the NFL that year, which I did. As for Jim, he won a couple of USFL championships with the Stars, first in Philadelphia in 1984 and in 1985 when the franchise moved to Baltimore, and—ironically—two of his outstanding players were Penn Staters, quarterback Chuck Fusina, who finished second in the 1978 Heisman Trophy race, and receiver Scott Fitzkee. Jim went on to be the head coach for the New Orleans Saints (1986-96) and Indianapolis Colts (1998-2001). He currently is a football color announcer on TV.

While Jim was making a name for himself with the Stars, I was taking my circus on the road again and it eventually led to the Big Apple—New York City—where I had spent my honeymoon. There were no forks on that road but a couple of detours. And it was on one of those detours that I found myself sitting across from "The Shrink."

CHAPTER SIXTEEN - The Shrink

If I thought my experiences inside the coaching staffs at NC State, the Rams, the 49ers and Colorado were bizarre, they were minor compared to what I found at the Denver Broncos. As I wrote before about my time at the University of Colorado a decade earlier, maybe it's something in the air at that altitude, but this certainly was another Rocky Mountain High, or maybe I should say Low.

It actually started two years before, late in February of 1981, while I was still coaching for the Los Angeles Rams when my two-year contract had ended and I had not signed a new one. Around that time, Dan Reeves, who had been a player and an assistant coach for the Dallas Cowboys, was hired as Denver's head coach. I knew him vaguely, and so on March 1, I called him about the offensive line coach position. He told me that he would call me back about setting up an interview. When he called the next day, he told me that the conversation that we were about to have never took place. I asked him what he was talking about? He told me that the NFL owners had a rule among themselves that no NFL team could talk about a job with an assistant from another NFL team after March 1. Since it was now March 2, that ended that, and I eventually got my new contract from the Rams.

Denver Interview – Two years later, after my absurd experience at North Carolina State, I was job hunting again and heard that Jerry Frei, the offensive line coach for the Broncos, retired from coaching and became a Denver scout. I called Reeves in late December of 1982 and we set up an interview during Senior Bowl practice week in Mobile, Alabama in early January. Early on in my interview, Dan informed me that the offensive line job paid $50,000. I said, "No it doesn't. That's not good enough." He said that's what it paid and that all the other candidates who had been interviewed did not have a problem with it. I told him that I had made $65,000 a year with Los Angeles. I said, "There are 3,000 line coaches who would take the offensive line job for $50,000. Two or three of them are better than me. Try and find them!"

I got up and said I guess the interview is over and started to leave. Dan said the interview was not over and that he liked me better because I had my own mind. He said he thought the salary could be worked out. He just needed to get permission from the owner, Edgar Kaiser. The rest of the interview concerning the coaching went fine. At the end of the interview, Reeves said that my hiring wouldn't be finalized until I was interviewed by the Denver Bronco psychologist. I told him that I refused to be interviewed by a psychologist. He said that he didn't understand why not. Dan said they had done psychological interviewing in Dallas and never had a problem with it. None of the other candidates had a problem with it. Why was I different?

I told him that if he wanted to know what kind of coach or person that I was, then he should call players that I had coached or call coaches that I had worked with. But I refused to be evaluated for a football job by a non-football person. I then stood up to leave for the second time, thinking the interview was over. But Dan asked me if I would take the job if I didn't have to talk to the psychologist. I said I would. I found out later that I was the only coach on the Broncos who didn't have to talk to the team psychologist. His name was Kevin Somerville. I called him "The Shrink." Despite what Dan told me, the Shrink tried to interview me, but I told him I had it in my contract that I didn't have to talk to him. Later that season, the Shrink would save my job.

Like Father, Like Son – Shortly after my interview with Reeves at the Senior Bowl, I was offered and accepted the Bronco's offensive line job. I reported to the Broncos to sign my contract and to start working. After I signed the contract in Dan's office, Dan reached over and handed me a letter and said, "You might want to keep this in your personal files." I said, "What is it?" He said, "It's a letter from Dan Rooney, President of the Steelers, recommending you." Wow! I had never asked Dan Rooney, or anyone else for that matter, to recommend me to Denver.

> **DAN ROONEY**
>
> January 21, 1983
>
> Dear Dan,
>
> Would like to offer my recommendation of Alan Radakovich as a coach with you. Alan did a fine job with us in developing young people. I know you talked to some of our people about his coaching ability. He has a nice family. It was really too bad about Richie, we grew up together.
>
> /s/

Later I found out that Dan Rooney had walked into the Steelers kitchen one morning and overheard the Steelers assistant coaches mentioning that I had applied for the Denver opening as the offensive line coach. Dan Rooney sent this letter to Dan Reeves:

January 21, 1983

Dear Dan,

Would like to offer my recommendation of Dan Radakovich as a coach with you. Dan did a fine job with us in developing young people. I know you talked to some of our people about his coaching ability. He has a nice family. It was really too bad about Richie. We grew up together.

Dan

I know grown men shouldn't cry, but that letter actually brought a few tears in my eyes. It was something that would have been typical of The Chief, Art Rooney Sr. who was Dan's father and the founder of the Steelers. The old saying was certainly true: "Like Father, Like Son."

Special Note: Richie, the childhood friend that Dan Rooney referred to at the end of the letter, was Richie McCabe, who had recently passed away. Richie had been a Denver assistant coach and had played for the University of Pittsburgh, the Steelers and two other pro teams. I knew Richie and he was a highly energetic person who at the drop of a hat would coach veterans, rookies or kids in the playground, which was truly amazing. He was a good guy.

Claudie Minor Retires – Soon after reporting to the Broncos, I was told nine-year offensive left tackle Claudie Minor was retiring. Claudie was one of the most talented and best looking offensive line specimens that I had ever seen, and I wanted my shot at coaching him. So, I contacted him and scheduled a visit with him to try and convince him to play a tenth year. I even worked him out in a field close to where he lived, doing some of the drills and the techniques that I would be teaching. But at the end of my visit he told me he was still retiring. He had looked awfully good in the workout, which didn't make me feel any better. Claudie retiring meant that the Broncos would need a new starting offensive left tackle and would probably need to draft an offensive lineman or two in the upcoming 1983 NFL draft.

Trade For Elway – So, I became the Broncos' offensive line coach with a salary of $70,000 a year, which was a lot better than the $50,000 originally offered. Now, in January of 1983, the Broncos believed the team's most important need was at quarterback. Steve DeBerg was the only veteran returning, and there actually was

John Elway

room for two new quarterbacks. Our timing couldn't have been better. Nineteen eighty-three is now known famously as "The Year of the Quarterbacks" with such first rate prospects available for the NFL draft as Dan Marino of Pitt, Tony Eason of Illinois, Todd Blackledge of Penn State, Ken O'Brien of California, Jim Kelly of Miami, and John Elway of Stanford. The Broncos were selecting fourth in the draft, after Baltimore, Los Angeles and Seattle. Shortly before the draft meetings, the Broncos had a dinner for all the scouts and coaches at the Colorado Mining Company. Reed Johnson, the director of scouting, and Hein Poulus, the general manager, had a poll taken of the group concerning which quarterback to draft and what we would be willing to give to get him. The vote ended up unanimously to draft John Elway and be willing to give up Denver's two No. 1 picks in 1983 and 1984.

Quarterback Coach John Hadl did not want to draft anyone but Elway. Our receivers coach, Fran Polsfoot, had been the roommate of John Elway's dad, Jack, when both had been in college at Washington University. Owner Edgar Kaiser was a Stanford graduate. These five people—Hadl, Polsfoot, Elway's dad, Kaiser, and Dan Reeves—had John Elway convinced that Denver was the place for him. However, despite all the effort to trade up to be able to draft Elway, we couldn't do it. Elway was the first player drafted that year, by Baltimore, and when our turn came, we picked the No. 1 rated offensive lineman in the country, Chris Hinton, from Northwestern, which made me, as offensive line coach, very happy. I felt even happier when we picked another offensive lineman in the second round, Mark Cooper from Miami. Both players were immediately flown to Denver by the Broncos.

Edward Kaiser and Dan Reeves

Chris Hinton arrived first. I was to take him over to the Denver Wholesale Mart, where only store owners were allowed to shop, and get him some cowboy boots as a gift from the Broncos organization. We went to the Mart and Chris got three pairs of cowboy boots, with the most expensive pair being made of ostrich leather, which cost over $500. The total bill was more than $1,000. Hinton seemed delighted and excited to be a Denver Bronco. Meanwhile, John Elway flatly refused to play for Baltimore. He threatened to sit out the year and enter the draft again the next year. Less than a week after the draft, our owner Edward Kaiser came to see me and asked me if I would mind giving up Hinton to get Elway. I started to laugh because I knew he was just being nice. The entire organization had wanted Elway. I asked him what he was talking about. He said that he had been talking to Bob Irsay, the owner of the Colts, and that he thought he was going to be able to trade Hinton for Elway. I told him that although I really liked Hinton as a prospect, I would definitely agree with a Hinton for Elway trade—as if my opinion really mattered. In fact, I

Mark Cooper

told Kaiser that he could make our No. 2 pick, Mark Cooper, part of the deal, too. Edgar said that wouldn't be necessary; that he thought he could get it done with just Hinton for Elway, and that's what happened.

Chris Hinton was really upset with the trade because he really wanted to be a Bronco, but he went along with it. After the trade was finalized, Reeves asked me if I would call Chris and ask him to send the boots back. Since he wasn't going to be a Bronco, the front office would like to recover the amount of the boot bill. I told him there was no way I was going to call Hinton and ask him to send the boots back. I told him to call Hinton himself. Seven years later, when I was coaching in the Pro bowl in January 1990 after the 1989 season, Chris Hinton was one of our AFC Pro bowl players. I asked him if anyone had ever called him to send the boots back. He said someone from Denver actually did ask him to send the boots back. He said he told them to go to hell. He wasn't sending any boots back.

The Hinton for Elway trade story is one of the greatest coups by an owner in the history of the NFL. Hinton had a damn fine career, going to seven Pro Bowls and being named a first team All-Pro or All-Conference several times in an 11-year career. But Elway played 16 years with Denver, went on to the Pro Football Hall of Fame and is considered one of the greatest NFL quarterbacks ever. Oh, Elway's first start as a rookie was against the Pittsburgh Steelers in the opening league game of the 1983 season and it was not an auspicious start. John passed for minus one yard, but the Broncos beat the Steelers, 14-10, with a total of one yard passing due to Steve DeBerg's last-minute 2-yard touchdown pass to tight end Ron Egloff.

The Denver Offensive Line –
The offensive line I inherited in 1983 was a mixture with eight different levels of NFL experience and personalities. The most experienced player, 11-year veteran right guard Paul Howard, once tried to strangle me when I was with the Steelers when I broke up a fight between him and Steelers defensive tackle Joe Greene in

Paul Howard

Ken Lanier

the 1977 Pittsburgh-Denver playoff game. Next was starting nine-year veteran left guard Tom Glassic whose big hobby was playing miniature war games with lead soldiers, just like my son Danny. Alternating with Tom at left guard was fourth year veteran Keith Bishop, who, I was told, had once wrestled a bear and at one time threatened to quit football to become a sumo wrestler. (He would make the Pro Bowl in 1987 and 1988.) The center and leader of the linemen was seven-year veteran Bill Bryan. At left tackle was five-year veteran Dave Studdard and at right tackle was three-year man Ken Lanier. Backing up these six players, whom I considered starters, were rookie Mark Cooper at guard or tackle and second year Keith Uecker at tackle. They were the guys I had to protect a new franchise rookie quarterback from getting killed.

Dave Studdard

Keith Uecker

Bad Rad Isn't Bad, Just Different – During the Broncos preseason, the *Rocky Mountain News* published a story by T.J. Simmers on August 8, 1983 under this headline: "TASKMASTER – Radakovich building line with the work ethic." I believe this article, which quotes Head Coach Dan Reeves and some of my Denver offensive linemen, is a fairly accurate description of my coaching style throughout my career, as well as a look into my quirky personality. That's why I am printing part of it here.

GREELY – *Big body after big body is sent hurling through the air on Dan Radakovich's command.*

The bodies are sweating, huffing and puffing.

Radakovich is singing: "Anchors away, my boy, anchors away; set, hut, hut, hut. Do–dah, do–dah, do–dah. Go Army! beat Navy! Set, hut, hut, hut, hut. Go Navy, beat Army. Fuh-Fuh-Fa; way to go, guy."

Bad Rad ain't bad; he's just a horrible singer.

And different.

"He's definitely on a different drum sometimes," says Dan Reeves, the man who hired him to be his offensive line coach. "I talked to people around the country and they told me, you'll look over there and see him practicing and you'll wonder what the heck he is doing."

Bill Bryan

He has always been Bad Rad, a nickname he explains. "When I was a junior in high school I made a lot of tackles in my first game. We went to a pizza place after the game and this other guy, a basketball player, said 'Rad is bad.' I like it. Bad Rad. It rhymes."

But does it fit?

"He's not as bad as everyone makes him out to be," said center Bill Bryan, "but I admit I had my reservations in minicamp when other players were driving away in the snow and we [the offensive linemen] were still practicing."

Sunday, the quarterbacks, and running backs, and everyone else but the offensive linemen were back in their dorm rooms sleeping while the linemen were watching films of Friday night's game. The linemen still had to run a mile and a half and lift weights too.

"It's the toughest camp I've ever been in," says offensive lineman Tom Glassic.

And here comes an echo. "It's the toughest camp I've ever been in," says Bryan.

Rad works hard, concentrates so hard he walks by people without saying hello, "including me" says Nancy, his wife, and is well, strange, but delightful.

Listen: This is Rad talking.

"Confucius visits me on the mountain. 'What can I do with this guy?' says Rad. 'He's always winding up when he goes to block.'

"Confucius say: 'He who winds up is a toy.' 'That's it, Confucius,' says Rad. 'I don't want a toy playing for me.'"

There's more.

"If you are going to pass block like a revolving door, you ought to get a job in front of a department store."

And

"He who has tunnel vision should work underground."

"If you call him 'coach,'" says Keith Bishop, "he calls you 'player.'"

If you ask him questions in an interview, he is most gracious and most boring. He has an MBA in business from Penn State but is full of "I don't knows."

Keith Bishop and John Elway

Tell someone in the Bronco organization you are going to interview Bad Rad and they wish you "Good luck."

"He doesn't like small talk," says his wife.

Mention his name and the response is always the same: "He's different," and he says, "I'm not there when they are talking about me, so what does it matter? I don't care about my players understanding the man. I want them to understand what I am teaching."

In Bad Rad fashion, he delivers one of the most forgettable quotes: "Coaching is coaching."

On the field, the coach is just coaching. He has his players gasping in drills they do not like. "One player said, 'These are college drills,' " says Rad. "I said, 'you're wrong; they are high school drills.' "

He's a taskmaster on the field. "That was no good (Ken) Lanier," he says. "Do it again."

"No, no, Lanier. Do it again."

"This is fun," he says and he is looking at a very perturbed Ken Lanier.

"Then," says Bishop, "all of a sudden he will switch gears and be funny. The guy just cracks me up."

He will nag, though, and it never stops. "For me to coach, I have to criticize. But if I criticize loud, I have to praise loud, too."

That draws a chuckle from his charges. "We're still looking for the 'ata-boys,' " says Glassic.

One day during training camp, the tight ends were brought over to work with Rad. "You should have seen the look on their faces," says Bishop. "Fran Polsfoot (tight end coach) said later the tight ends were happy do to anything I asked as long as I didn't take them back to Rad," says Glassic.

Bad Rad's also unpredictable. Recently, he got up in a meeting and started dancing, showing his line the "Bad Rad Disco" which was made popular in Los Angeles with the Rams.

Dan Reeves and Tom Glassic

"He's a fundamentalist," says Reeves, "and I like that."

"The greatest coaching term in the world," says Rad, "is 'do it again.' "

"I don't make them good players; all I can do is point out their flaws. They do the rest."

T.J. Simmers wrote another article for the *Rocky Mountain News* that day about Tom Glassic that gives more insight into my coaching style. Here is a portion of that:

(Glassic) is now working for his fifth new offensive (line) coach... (Glassic) is a man of his own mind off the football field...He says what others would like to say and here is leadership in his way of doing business.

By his own remarks, he offers an example. He discusses his newest supervisor, Dan Radakovich. "Every coach you've ever had says, pretend you are hitting somebody even though there is nobody there. Keep moving those feet. Wind up and let it fly. Rad says, 'Don't hit anybody if no one is there. If no one is coming, don't move your feet. Why wind up when you can just raise your hands.' It all makes sense but how many coaches have ever made sense? Rad's using common sense, but coaches have not taught that before. So now we must revert back to logic."

As you can see, not everyone is happy with my style or my personality. But you can't please everybody. You have to coach your way and be yourself. Usually it works but sometimes it doesn't. That's not my problem. I certainly have not had any difficulty sleeping at nights. However, some people will never understand—including some of my head coaches.

The Shrink Appears – A strange situation occurred at the beginning of the 1983 the regular NFL season. During preseason camp and before the practices of each of our four preseason exhibition games, I had position meetings with the offensive linemen. Then on the Wednesday before the opening Sunday league game with the Steelers, the entire offense—players and coaches—met as a group with head coach Dan Reeves for the entire day before practice, 9 a.m. to 3 p.m. with a hour and a half break for lunch. The four assistant offensive coaches (Fran Polsfoot, Nick Nicolau, John Hadl and I) just sat there and listened all day until time for practice. Fran and Nick told me that once the season started in the previous two years, no offensive assistants had position meetings for the rest of those seasons. I then surmised that this must have been the way that Tom Landry ran the offense at Dallas. I was in total shock. In my previous 23 years as a full-time assistant coach with 7 teams, I had always had position meetings with the players I coached. The only total offense group meetings I had ever previously attended were assignment walk-throughs. I went into Reeves' office early the next morning and told him that I needed to have position meetings with the offensive linemen. He told me that he wanted to make sure everyone was on the same page at the beginning of the season and that I would get position meetings shortly.

Well, we won our first two games and lost the next two. Each week I went to see Reeves about having position meetings with my linemen and each week he put me off. Tuesday is game plan day, and on the Tuesday before our fifth game against Chicago, Dan had his weekly staff game plan meeting about the Bears in the projection room. The offensive coaches were sitting on one side of a long table facing the projection wall with the head coach in the center next to the projector. In attendance besides Reeves and me were Marvin Bass (quality control), John Hadl (quarterbacks), Nick Nicolau (running backs), and Fran Polsfoot (receivers). To start the meeting, Reeves asked each coach what his thoughts were about beating Chicago. "Rad," he said, "what do you think we need to do to beat the Bears?" I replied, "I have no idea of how to beat the Bears, and until I get meetings with my offensive linemen, I'm not going to have any ideas!"

It was very quiet in the meeting room. No one said anything for a minute or two. Then Reeves asked the other assistants about the Bears and the meeting went on while I sat there and listened but didn't otherwise participate. The next two days, I went to the all-day offensive group meetings and coached my players during practice. After practice on every Thursday during the season, the offensive assistant coaches would break down film for the next team we would play about 10 days later. As Hadl, Nicolau, Polsfoot, Bass, and I were watching the film, there was a knock on the projection room door. One of us yelled, "Come in."

Kevin Somerville (The Shrink)

The door opened up and the Broncos' business psychologist, Kevin Somerville, whom I always called "The Shrink," popped his head inside. He said, "Rad, I need to talk to you." I got up from the table, walked to the door and said, "Shrink, I've told you before, I don't talk to you," and I closed the door on him and walked back to the projection table. A minute or two went by, and then there was another knock on the door. One of the other coaches walked over and opened the door. It's the shrink again. He said "Rad, I've got to talk to you." I said, "Shrink, I don't have to talk to you; it's in my contract." He said, "You're going to get fired!" I replied "I'll be right with you" and walked out the door to talk to the shrink.

The shrink had a list of complaints about me that Dan Reeves had given him. First, and foremost, of course, was my refusal to participate in the game plan for Sunday's game against the Bears. Second, I hadn't done the statistics that quality control coach Marvin Bass wanted. For each game, Marvin had given me about 10 sheets of statistics that needed filled out. An example would be: "What did the 41 power run play average?" If I didn't have player meetings, there was no way I was going to fill out a bunch of worthless statistics. The shrink told me that sometimes you had to do the unimportant things to be able to do the important things. I said "No, I should have player meetings, regardless if I do dumb statistics."

The shrink said Reeves didn't like me wearing Bermuda shorts and flip-flops to the office, and how could I be a coach, if I did that? I said we were in an industrial area and there was no need to get dressed up. Besides, I said, Reeves wore those low-cut socks, with his sneakers. Another complaint was that I didn't talk to the head coach during the game; that I was non-communicative. I said I didn't talk to him because he was always looking at his play-calling sheet. I didn't think he wanted to be disturbed. Finally, the shrink said I had to apologize to Dan. "What are you talking about?" I replied. "He's the one not letting me have player meetings. He's the one at fault." The shrink said, "Were you or were you not wrong in not participating in the Chicago game plan?" I said, "I was wrong." He said, "I can help you get the player meeting, but first you have to apologize." I replied, "Okay, I'll apologize."

Early Friday evening, shortly after I arrived home from Friday's practice, I got a phone call from the shrink. He said, "I just got off the phone with Dan. He'll be home for another half hour before he goes out. Now's the perfect time to call him and apologize. Do it before he leaves his house." So, I called Dan, told him I was wrong and should have contributed to the Bears game plan. I said I was sorry but I was just so upset about not having position meetings with my players. I said I would like to talk to him again about that. He was very cordial and nice and said we could meet in his office after the brief Saturday morning practice. When we met the next day, I again apologized. He accepted it and then talked to me for the next hour about responsibility, and earning my stripes and gaining his confidence. I really didn't say much of anything, just listened. When he was done, I said, again, that I was sorry about not contributing to the game plan and went home.

In those days, we went home after the Saturday morning practice and later went to the airport to catch a 5:00 p.m. charter flight to Chicago. Shortly after I got home, the phone rang. My wife said "the shrink" was on the phone. The shrink told me he just got off the phone with Reeves. He heard that my meeting with Reeves went great. I said the meeting was awful; that I had listened to Reeves for almost an hour tell me that once I earned my stripes I'd start to get more meeting time. I said I felt like I was a first year graduate assistant coach. The shrink said, "Oh no!" I said, "Oh yeah!" The shrink then said, "Just make sure you talk to him during the game tomorrow and I'll see that you get your player meetings this week." I said, "Who are you kidding?" He said, "Just do it." I said, "Okay."

We played the Bears in Soldiers Field and got stomped, 31-14. During the game, I talked to Dan many times, saying things like "that was a lousy call" and "these refs are killing us," and other similar statements. That evening, after we had flown home from Chicago, the shrink called me on the phone. The shrink said, "That was wonderful today. I saw you talking to Dan a number of times during the game today." I said, "How can you say today was wonderful. We got crushed by the Bears 31-14." He said, "It doesn't matter. You talked to him during the game. You'll have your player meetings this week." I said, "You're nuts," and hung up the phone.

The next day, Monday morning, Reeves held his weekly 8 a.m. to 9 a.m. staff and organization meetings. At his staff meetings, everybody in the organization attended except the secretaries—all the coaches, scouts, trainers, etc. were there. At his meeting, Dan would talk about the game, what our problems were, what we needed to improve on, and so on. When this particular meeting was over and we were filing out of the room, Reeves said, "Rad, I need to talk to you for a minute." I walked over to the head table where he's sitting and he said, "The offensive linemen are so bad that I can't stand to talk to them anymore. You'll have to talk to the offensive line in meetings this week." I couldn't believe my ears. What a wonderful statement that was! Wednesday morning, about 15 minutes after the start of the offensive group meeting at 9 a.m., Dan said, "Offensive lineman, you're excused to go with Coach Rad now." When all the offensive linemen, about nine players, got in my meeting room, I closed the door and said, "I've got the offensive line meetings now, and we are going to forget all those rules that the Dallas Cowboys had and we're going to have just one rule in this room. We're simply going to try to figure out the best ways to beat the other teams and do that. Period!" They were all for that.

We beat the Oilers 26-14 the next Sunday in Houston, rushed for over 200 yards in the game, and had no sacks. I was feeling real good about the game, when Dan held the Monday morning 8 a.m. to 9 a.m. organization meeting. As I'm walking out of the room after the meeting ended, Reeves said to me, "Rad, the offensive linemen are still so bad, I can't stand to talk to them, and you'll have to take the offensive line meetings again this week." I was astonished. I had thought I had the offensive line meetings automatically for the rest of the year. But each Monday, after the organization meeting was over, he would call me over and say the same thing to me. He finally stopped doing it after we had won four games in a row. When Dan first gave me the offensive line meetings before that Houston game, he also gave the other offensive coaches one hour of position meeting time, which they never had during the previous two seasons.

On Thursday evenings, after the offensive assistants finished watching film of the future opponent 1½ weeks away, Nicolau, Hadl, and I always went to Via Villa, a bar-restaurant located across the parking lot from the football office. We'd have a couple of drinks and relaxed for an hour before we went home. One Thursday evening about a month after we started getting player position meetings, we were rewinding the film of the future opponent when Nicolau said, "Okay guys, we're finished. Now we can go over to the Via Villa." Hadl said, "Nick, I can't make it. I promised my wife I'd go shopping with her this evening. Nick said, "No John, you're coming. We won't be there that long." Hadl said, "Nick, I told you I'm going out with my wife." Nick replied, "Hadl, you've got to come. You've got to understand how the system works now. After we finish the film on Thursday, we go over to the Via Villa and have a couple of drinks with Rad. We tell Rad our problems, Rad tells the shrink, and things get better!" We laughed. Nick sure had it all figured out.

Nick Nicolau

Before continuing, I want to tell you about my old coaching friends. Hadl and Nicolau. John left the Broncos after the 1983 season to be the head coach for the Los Angeles Express of the World Football League, and he is currently the associate athletic director of his alma mater, the University of Kansas. Nick stayed with the Broncos through Super Bowls XXI and XXII. Later he was receivers coach for the Buffalo Bills in Super Bowls XXV and XXVI. He's now retired and living in Cape Cod.

Anyway, we won seven of the next 10 games after the shrink got involved and made the playoffs as a wildcard with a game to go. A couple of days before that last game at Kansas City, the owner had a Christmas party for the organization, which the coaching staff attended from 5 p.m. to 6 p.m. and then had to go back to the office. Later that evening, my wife Nancy was introduced to Kevin Somerville by John Beake, the team vice president. Kevin said to Nancy, "I know your husband hates me but I'm the guy that he calls "The Shrink." Nancy said, "Oh Kevin, Rad doesn't hate you. It's your profession he hates."

John Hadl and John Elway

Farewell Note To The Shrink – A few weeks later, after I had decided to leave the Broncos for the Minnesota Vikings, I asked John Beake if he could deliver a note from me to Kevin Somerville, the psychologist. I wrote:

"Dear Kevin. You know how I hated Marvin Bass' statistics but here are a few statistics that only you and I would be interested in:

- Before the Shrink: Denver Broncos 2 wins, 3 losses – offense averages 12 points per game.

- After the Shrink: Denver Broncos 7 wins 3 losses – offense averages 22 points per game and makes the NFL playoffs with 1 game remaining.

Sincerely, Dan Radakovich

P.S. I still hate your profession!

About five years after that I stopped by the shrink's business office in Denver and saw my note framed on Kevin's office wall. I was a little surprised, but gratified. So, as we were finishing up this book, my co-author, Lou Prato, and I wondered if the shrink still had that note. We tracked down Kevin and talked to him. He still had the note.

Shortly after his stint with the Broncos in 1983 Kevin left to become a principal in one company, Norwest Equity Partners, Ltd., and then in 2002 he also founded a second company called Successful Profiles, Inc. He works with chief executives and chairmen of boards to solve management organizational problems and travels 250,000 miles a year. I am telling you about his businesses since those Bronco years because of what he later told Lou.

"I haven't seen Rad since that day he showed up in my office. I had that note in my office for maybe 10 to 15 years. It was very, very funny. I would never throw something like that out. But I have made many moves over the years and its now in a box somewhere at home.

"When Rad called me he read this chapter to me and I was stunned. I remember everything in detail because that's my life, but I had no idea that he did. He got it all right.

"Rad is eccentric as hell. I never saw him without jeans and flip flops. He is such a completely independent, very self-confident human being. For the last 20 years I've worked with private equity companies who buy entrepreneurial or family-owned businesses. So the likes of Rad are pretty common to me, and I've had a life-long affection for them even if they tell me I'm full of crap. I just like those people. They're what America is all about. They're independent, self-confident, capable people. Unfortunately, they make terrible employees.

"The only way Rad gets away with being as eccentric as he is, he's completely competent. Most of the time people would describe him as a nut job, but he's completely competent."

Coming from you, Kevin, that is one of the best compliments I have ever received. However, as I wrote in that old note:

I still hate your profession!

CHAPTER SEVENTEEN -
From Siberia to Broadway

Joining The Minnesota Vikings — Our Denver Broncos season in 1983 ended in a thud as we were beaten by Kansas City, 48-17, and then lost the playoff game at Seattle, 31-7. A few weeks later, Reeves informed me that Les Steckel, my former coaching colleague at Colorado, had taken the head coaching job at Minnesota and had asked for permission to talk to me. Dan told me that he wanted me to stay with the Broncos, but that I had his permission to visit the Vikings and talk to Les about coaching there. Dan told me he realized there had been a few conflicts between us during the past season, but he said that was only because he had never known anyone like me before. I told him I really wasn't thinking of going to Minnesota, but since Les was a good friend of mine I should go visit the Vikings and talk to him. So, my wife and I visited the Vikings. Les informed us that if we joined the Vikings we could go on a week's vacation the following week with the Viking coaching staff in Jamaica. So, we joined the Vikings and went to Jamaica.

The Old, The New, The Unusual — The football staff that I joined at Minnesota was very different and unusual in makeup than any staff that I had ever been on. Six coaches were retained from the staff of the previous head coach, Bud Grant, and seven coaches, including me, were new. What was different was that there were 13 coaches—the largest staff I had ever been on. What was unusual were the relationships between the coaches from the previous staff. Les had previously been an excellent receivers assistant coach and had been promoted to head coach by general manager Mike Lynn over Les' good friend and Bud Grant's long-time offensive coordinator, Jerry Burns. Jerry had assumed that he would become the new head coach when Bud retired, but Jerry was staying on as offensive coordinator and quarterback coach, even though he had been passed over by the GM.

Another long-time Grant assistant, John Michaels, was moving to backfield coach to make room for me as offensive line coach, even though he had been Bud's offensive line coach for over 20 years. Linebacker coach Floyd Reese was moved to defensive coordinator. Previous defensive coordinator Bob Holloway was demoted to defensive quality control coach, whose primary duties were as a film scout for the defensive coaches. Reese, who had worked under Holloway for the past five years, was now Holloway's boss. Buster Ramsey, the long-time backfield coach for Grant, became a special assistant to the head coach to take care of odds and ends. This staff that was formed by Mike Lynn and Steckel was truly a blend of the old, the new, and the unusual.

Please Draft Ed West — The Vikings football organization was another one of those NFL teams that did not have the assistant coaches help with the players' draft. Only the head coach was allowed in the draft room with the scouts on draft day. The assistants were just in the office on draft day to help out if asked, and that's how I got involved in the 1984 draft. During the first round, the director in charge of scouting came out of the draft room and told me they were considering drafting Ed West, a 6-foot, 250-pound tight end from Auburn, and would like me to watch the Senior Bowl film of him and give the scouts my opinion.

I told linebacker coach Mike Sweatman that I was going to watch a film of a draft prospect for the scouts. Mike said he wasn't doing anything and would like to join me. He asked me who I was going to watch, and I told him I was going to watch a tight end from Auburn, Ed West. Mike said, "Heck, Rad, I don't have to watch him. When I was at Tennessee, we played Auburn every year. Ed West is a great player. I'm not gonna watch him." And he didn't, but I did. I watched Ed West and was very impressed. He was everything Mike Sweatman said he was. The other tight end in the Senior Bowl, Glenn Dennison of Miami, was drafted early in the second round by the Jets and Ed was as good as or better than Dennison. Ed's only detriment was a lack of height. He was only 6-foot-1, but he was an excellent blocker and had good hands. The Vikings needed a tight end, and I recommended Ed highly on what I had seen, and said we should draft him.

Well, the third, fourth and fifth rounds went by and we didn't draft him. I went into the draft room and told all the scouts that I guaranteed that West would make our team, and I would bet my house mortgage and everything I owned on it. Well, they went through 12 rounds and 17 tight ends and no one drafted him. I was assured that we would sign him as a free agent. The next thing I was told was that 18 clubs were trying to sign Ed West as a free agent, and that there was a bidding war between the NFL clubs to get him, and we didn't have the final bid. West signed with the Green Bay Packers and went on to have a solid 13-year career in the NFL, catching 230 passes and scoring 27 touchdowns. Six of the last seven Vikings' 1984 draft choices did not play a down in the NFL. The only one who did played in three games. Only the first three picks by the Vikings had decent careers, two for eight years and one for nine years.

I never met Ed West and he certainly doesn't know this story. It amazes me how emotionally involved a coach can get in such a short time about a player he'd never previously heard about, enough, I guess to remember the incident 29 years later. And I've sometimes wondered what would have happened to Ed if we had drafted him or signed him as a free agent.

Lawyer Tim Irwin – Let me tell you another story about how a coach can change a player's life, this time off the field. Sometime during the middle of the 1984 season I was sitting at a table with starting Vikings right offensive tackle Tim Irwin. Tim was in his fourth year after being a third round draft choice out of Tennessee in '81. I asked Tim what he did in the offseason and he proceeded to tell me about all the fun he had driving around a lake in his boat painted Vikings

Judge Tim Irwin

purple, and other things back home in Tennessee. I asked him if he had thought of working in the offseason and starting a career or going to graduate school or anything like that. I pointed to linebacker Fred McNeill and said, "Look at that guy. He's going to law school in the offseason and taking advantage of being a pro football player by preparing for a career." I told Tim how the former great defensive tackle for the Vikings, Alan Page, had become a lawyer, about my cousins Bob Garshak and Ray Radakovich being lawyers, about my former Penn State players Bob Kane and John Runnels who were now lawyers, and, finally, about my own experience of going to law school for one year at Chase University in Cincinnati while coaching at the University of Cincinnati. I told him that I thought he ought to go to law school in the offseason while he was playing professional football; and forget about driving around in the offseason in his purple Vikings boat. I never mentioned the law subject again the rest of the season.

Minnesota Vikings offensive right tackle Tim Irwin

Six or seven years later, I went to a Vikings preseason game in Cleveland, where I was living at the time, and stopped by to see the Vikings people I knew. When I saw Tim Irwin he started shouting, "Rad, I did it! I did it!" I said, "Did what, Tim?" I had no idea what he meant. He yelled, "I'm a lawyer, Rad. I took your advice and went to law school in the offseason. I passed the bar and I'm a lawyer now." I had no idea that he had even thought about going to law school after our conversation seven years earlier. Tim played 13 years with the Vikings and then a year with Miami and Tampa in 1994 before retiring. He had earned his law degree at Tennessee in 1990 and in 2000 opened his own law office in Knoxville, practicing criminal, personal injury, and sports law. Since 2005 he has been a Juvenile Court Judge in Knox County, Tennessee. Tim telling me back in the early 90s that he was a lawyer now was one of the most pleasant surprises of my life. What happened with Tim makes me realize that coaches or teachers do, on occasion, have a great influence on a player or student.

The Seabees – Not only was the coaching staff different at the Vikings, but the preseason camp also was different than the other camps that I had coached in. Les had organized an iron man contest to test the strength, endurance and conditioning of the players. The iron man contest was used as an incentive for the players to report in great shape. Les even had the Pepsi Cola Corporation sponsor the contest and provide prizes, programs, refreshments, etc., and the Vikings' fans were invited to attend. Players were given points on their performances on the various weightlifting tests and running events. The eventual winner and "Ironman" was tight end Steve Jordan. Les even had the Seabees, the construction battalion part of the U.S. Navy, design and construct an obstacle conditioning course on the property surrounding the Minnesota football complex. The players had to run this course after practice during training camp. Les had been an officer in the Marine Corps, and he still had friends with the Seabees, and they built the course for practically nothing.

My part of the obstacle course was that I was in charge of the runs (or climbs) up the hill. I stood on the top of the hill bordering the football field and waited for the group of players who had just finished another part of the obstacle course to gather at the bottom of the hill about 40 yards below me. I would then yell, "Charge!" and they would run the 40 yards up to the top of the hill. When the groups got to the top, I would send them to the right, along the top of the ridge, to Coach Jerry Burns' spot, which had a bunch of chin-up bars. I don't remember the other parts of the obstacle course except there was a part where the players ran through the woods for a long distance on a path constructed by the Seabees. I can remember telling my offensive linemen to stay behind veteran linebacker Brad Van Pelt, whom we had just signed, and to make sure he completed the course. I told them to carry him if they had to but not to let him quit. Anyway, Van Pelt completed the course, but the offensive linemen said they did have to help him along part of the way in the woods. I have never been in the military service of any kind, so this kind of training and conditioning was new, interesting and a bit different.

A Tough Season – The 1984 Minnesota season started off on a bad note, losing to San Diego, 42-13, in the home opener, and only got worse. We played nine consecutive very close games, winning three of the nine, with five of the six losses by an average of three points a game. After our 10th league game, a 27-24 win over Tampa Bay that made our record 3-7, the roof fell off. We were crushed in our last six games, losing all of them by an average of 27 points. In the last six games our defense gave up an average of 40 points a game while our offense averaged 13 points a game. It was a tough season with a tougher ending. The week after the last game, Les Steckel was fired. Bud Grant was reinstalled as the head coach, and I was looking for a job again. Just one year later, Les was in the Super Bowl as the quarterback coach of the New England Patriots, Bud resigned again and Jerry Burns became the head coach of the Vikings. So, here I was, getting back on the road wondering where the next fork would be.

Below Zero – As soon as the 1984 season was over, my wife and I moved out of our rented apartment and put all our furniture in storage. At the invitation of Chris Steckel, Les' wife, we moved into their house for the two weeks of Christmas and New Years vacation. They had left to visit family in California for those two weeks. We then moved into a brand new spacious and modern designed town house with cathedral ceilings, giant skylights, picture windows in the kitchen, etc. on a week by week rental deal that my wife had made with the owner. I borrowed six 3x6 feet rubber mats that were used for aerobic classes from the Vikings equipment man, Dennis Ryan. Doubled up, these mats were our beds for me, my wife and our 16-year-old daughter Lori, who was our only child still living at home. We borrowed two homemade milk can chairs from the Steckels to use at the kitchen counter, and a friend of my daughter's loaned us two outdoor webbed lawn chairs. We used one cardboard box for a coffee table and put a TV set on another cardboard box. That's how we lived for the next two months—in a big, beautiful, spacious, brand new house with no furniture. This was a long way from our home with a pool in Huntington Beach, but it was still "Home! Sweet Home!"

During this time, the ex-Minnesota coaches who were looking for jobs, like me, were allowed to use the Vikings' football offices to make phone calls. I was still going to the Vikings' offices every day. In the last two weeks of January, 1985, the temperature dropped to 25 degrees below zero, and the wind chill factor was 50 degrees below zero. I believe it was one of the coldest recorded two weeks in Minnesota history. I've never been to Siberia, but I'm certain we felt like it was Siberia. The radio and TV warned that any part of the body exposed outside would get frostbite within five minutes. In the morning, I would press the button to open the garage door, run to the car, start the car, and then run back inside. I would wait 15 minutes for the car to warm up—usually by having another cup of coffee—and then run out to the car and drive comfortably to the office. I did that routine for two weeks. Then, a month later I got a job coaching for the New York Jets.

I haven't written much about houses and apartments that my family and I lived in over the years. But I can tell you about that new experience of living in a house with no furniture. I would rather live in a classy house with no furniture than a junky house with a lot of furniture. Living in that classy house with no furniture was actually quite enjoyable. But, as Joe Paterno always said, it gets better or it gets worse and, from a housing stand point, I soon found that out in New York.

"New York, New York, It's a Wonderful Town"

Jets Linebackers Coach — When I started looking around for another coaching job, the one opening that appealed the most to me was with the New York Jets. Joe Walton, who I knew very slightly, became the head coach of the Jets in 1983, but after two successive 7-9 seasons the Jets released their defensive coordinator, secondary coach, and linebacker coach. My good friend Bud Carson had been the defensive coordinator at Kansas City since we left the Rams, but he wanted out of there. We decided we would both like to work together on defense for the Jets. So, he applied for the defensive coordinator-secondary

Joe Walton

job, and I applied for the linebacker job. As I wrote earlier, Joe and his father and I had dinner with an Ivy League recruiter in Pittsburgh 32 years before when we were in high school. Since then, I had simply said hi to him when I saw him. The Jets defensive line coach, Ray Callahan was the only defensive coach retained. I knew him well because I had been Ray's defensive coordinator when he was the head coach at the University of Cincinnati in 1970. Well, Joe hired both Bud and me even though he said he was advised by some people not to hire either one of us. I think we both had a reputation for being outspoken, and, as I found out, too many head coaches just want "yes" men on their staffs. I'm also sure that Ray Callahan had put in a good word for me. One of the conditions Joe gave us before we were hired was that we had to promise to play a 34 defense. Bud and I had no problem with keeping this promise, having coached a 34 defense in the past. But we also wanted to play some defense with four down linemen. So, we immediately came up with a 34 monster defense with the monster being the fourth down lineman.

Now I was back in my natural element, coaching linebackers. However, it was a strange circumstance because the coach who I was replacing was my close friend, Ralph Baker, a Penn Stater who was one of the best—if not the best—linebacker I had ever coached. Four years earlier, at the Senior bowl in January of 1980, I had sat at a bar in Mobile, Alabama with the then Jets head coach Walt Michaels. For at least an hour, I tried to convince Walt to hire Ralph Baker, who Walt had personally coached at the Jets in the late 1960s, as his linebacker coach. Walt's wife who was sitting at a table finally came up to the bar and yelled at me, "Why don't you quit begging my husband for a job and leave him alone?" I said, "Mrs. Michaels, I'm not begging for a job for myself. I'm trying to get your husband to hire a former player of his," and then I left the bar. Walt hired Ralph Baker as linebacker coach, and a year later, the Jets were in the playoffs for two straight years. Now, two years after that, the job that I had asked Walt to give Ralph was mine.

The Honeymoon – I had been to New York City many times to coach against the Giants or the Jets, but now I was going to live there, or at least in the suburbs. My wife and I laughed as we remembered when we were here together for the first time—on our honeymoon in 1957. We hadn't even planned a honeymoon but after our wedding reception in Easton we counted the gift money and found that we had almost $2,000 and decided we should go on a honeymoon. New York City seemed perfect for our budget. Neither of us had a car but we could take a train from Easton. Where in New York we wondered? "Let's go to Times Square and take it from there," we said to each other.

We arrived at Grand Central Station and took a cab to Times Square. As soon as we got in the cab, Nancy said, "Check the meter and watch where he drives. They'll take you for a joy ride and run up the bill." I said, "You've watched too many movies." We got out at Times Square, looked at the skyline and saw a tall building that looked like a hotel a couple of blocks away. We walked to the Claridge Hotel, which is no longer there. We got a room and after two days we decided to leave. They hadn't changed the towels, sheets, linen, etc. I was so upset that after I paid the bill I had forgotten to turn in the keys. I threw them in the street.

We caught a cab back to Grand Central Station and were going to go back to Easton. Before buying a ticket, we were looking at a bulletin board to maybe find another place to stay, when a little old black guy came up to us and asked if we were looking for a place to stay. We said yes and he showed us a pamphlet that had pictures of a very nice room and hotel at a reasonable price. We asked if it was far and he said "No, just a little ways." We said, "Okay." He looked like he was in his 70's or 80's, but he insisted on carrying both our suitcases. We followed him and thought we would never get there. We must have walked 20 blocks. We checked in at the desk and went to the elevator. We were a little apprehensive because it was a grain type of elevator with one of those  expanding open air doors. Two men got on the elevator wearing overalls. We were now wondering what we've got ourselves into. We got to our room and it was very big and nice. It had a bed in the center that you could walk all the way around. There were mirrors all around on the walls, but not on the ceiling.

I forgot to mention previously that on the day of our wedding, my wife informed me that our honeymoon fun would be delayed. But she wasn't about to postpone the wedding just because of that. I said, "It doesn't matter. Don't worry. No hurry." So instead of doing what married couples normally do on a honeymoon, we went to Times Square. We saw a book about sexual techniques on display in the window of a book store, bought the book, and spent the next few days reading it. I didn't know anymore than she did. I can still picture two approximately 12-year-old girls standing at the picture window of the book store, looking at the sex book on display and saying. "You go buy it." "No, you buy it." I don't know if they ever bought it because we went into the store, bought the book and left.

After about the fourth day of the honeymoon, I asked if we could do anything. "Is it time yet?" She said "No" and I said, "What am I supposed to do?" She said, "Take some laps around the bed." So I did. We did a lot of walking around the city. We kept looking for Central Park but never did find it. I remember we ordered spaghetti in this one restaurant and it came in a bright yellow sauce. That's when we discovered we were in an all-vegetarian restaurant. We had never been in or even heard of a vegetarian restaurant before. I know we sound like a couple of rubes from the sticks but we really had fun. On Friday, we took a train back to Easton, then drove to Pittsburgh for a second reception. In the meantime, I asked Nancy to have a talk with her mother about you know what. I assume she did because the wedding became official shortly after the second reception in Pittsburgh.

You have to admit that was a memorable honeymoon, and, now, here we were back in New York City again and looking for a house to live in. What we found was without a doubt the best residential area we ever lived in, before and since, and another memorable New York City experience.

Point Lookout A Unique Place – The Jets football complex was located on Hofstra University's campus on Long Island. My wife and I asked some of the people who worked for the Jets where they would recommend we live. They mentioned a number of areas, like Garden City, which was close by. We were told to definitely stay away from Point Lookout on Long Beach Island because that was where a lot of the Jets players lived during the fall football season. My wife, daughter Lori, and I were invited by new quarterback coach Zeke Bratkowski and Bud Carson, who were "batching" it until their wives arrived a month later, to temporarily live with them in a house they had rented in Point Lookout. After a few weeks of living in Point Lookout, but also looking in other areas, we realized why a lot of the Jets players lived in Point Lookout. The place was a hidden paradise. Nancy, Lori and I decided to find a house right there in Point Lookout and we did.

Point Lookout is a small, secluded beach town setting on the eastern edge of Long Beach Island. Immediately across the narrow strip of water connecting the ocean with the bay was well-known Jones Beach Island. The town of Point Lookout was a half-mile long, and a half-mile wide, with only one road in—the main street—and the same road out of town. Once inside the town, the Atlantic Ocean beach was on one side and the bay with the fishing boats was on the other side. Three streets ran parallel between Beach Street and Bay Street. Twelve streets intersected perpendicular to the streets. An exit road off of the Meadow Brook Parkway, just before the gates to Jones Beach Island, led over a drawbridge over the bay to get to the main road on Long Beach Island. Turn left and the entrance to Point Lookout was about one-quarter mile away.

During the three summer months of June, July, and August, houses in Point Lookout rented for $5,000, $6,000 or $7,000 a month, very expensive in those days. The other months of fall, winter and spring, a house would rent for $800 or $900 per month. No wonder a lot of Jets players lived there during the football season. We eventually rented a two story raised beach cabin house 1½ blocks from the beach and 2½ blocks the other way from the bay. We couldn't buy, because we were still trying to sell our house in Denver. We paid $1,500 a month, which was $600 or $700 more than the Jets players paid. But we had the house for the summer months also.

The decision to live in Point Lookout was one of the best decisions of our married life. We had four great years there. The half-mile long beach that was 1½ blocks away was for Point Lookout residents only. There was a small building on the beach where residents could store and check out their own personal beach chairs or other beach equipment. We had an outdoor shower attached to our house with a wooden privacy fence around it. We could get rid of our beach sand easily and never had to shower inside the house as long as the weather was warm enough. We hung a lot of our summer clothing out there. There was a ball field bordering the bay. I used to hit golf balls there with the high irons—eight and nine irons, and wedges. I did a lot of running on the beach when we lived there. I used to check the newspaper for information on the ocean tides. When the tide was in, the beach was too narrow, too steep, and the sand was too soft for running. When the tide was out, the beach was wide, much of it level, and the sand was firm—excellent for running. Sometimes I would run the beach at 1 a.m. or 2 a.m. for an hour or more if the tide was out, usually a five- or six-mile-run. I even quit smoking cigarettes my last two years in New York. Within a couple of blocks from our house, there was a coffee-breakfast-and-lunch place, a supermarket, a basketball gym connected to a fire house, three restaurant-bars and a travel bureau. While I was a runner on the beach, my wife rode a bicycle almost every day all over town. We loved the layout of the town. But the best part of the town was the young people and their parents that we got to know in our four years there.

My daughter Lori was a junior in Long Beach High School at the time. She and my wife attracted the young high school boys and girls—mostly boys—in Point Lookout like Pied Pipers. For the next four years, when the young folks weren't in school, at work, or playing sports, they were at my house every day. My wife loved their company. She laughed with them, fed them, gave them advice, etc. The youngsters were there so often I had to make some house rules. I had a lounge chair in the living room. I allowed them to sit in the lounge chair anytime they wanted unless I walked into the living room. Then, they had to jump out of the chair. When I came in the house, MTV had to be turned off or the TV switched to another channel. We got to be friends with most of the parents. One of the boy's parents was a prominent surgeon. Nancy was having some problems and the boy, Murdo Mackenzie, suggested that my wife see his father, Ranald Mackenzie. Nancy did and had a very successful surgery performed. This same doctor and his wife, Christine, gave us the free use of their apartment in Edinburgh, Scotland, for a week when we traveled to England in the spring of 1987. Because of the four years spent there was so enjoyable, Point Lookout is a place Nancy and I really miss.

Years later, Pittsburgh's pro scout Dick Haley left the Steelers and went to the New York Jets. I saw him and told him to live in Point Lookout. He went to Garden City. After a year in Garden City, Dick and his wife, Carolyn, moved to Point Lookout, lived there the next 10 years, and loved it—as I knew they would. Then there was Mike Sweatman, the New York Giants special teams coach, who I coached with at the Vikings. He lived in New Jersey and he would bring his two sons to our place on numerous occasions, park in our drive way, and go to our private Point Lookout beach. It was fantastic for all of us.

Crable's Corners – Soon after I was hired, I held a workout session a few days each week for the linebackers who stayed in New York in the offseason. Four of the guys I remember most who participated in these sessions were Lance Mehl, Greg Buttle, Kyle Clifton and John Woodring. Mehl and Buttle, a nine-year starter who would retire before the season opener, were graduates of Penn State's Linebacker U. After a couple of weeks, a linebacker with a knee brace showed up and participated in the drills I was coaching. After he made two very impressive pass interceptions in a look-search pass interception drill that we were doing (you look at the quarterback and search for the receiver), I yelled, "Who in the heck are you? Where did you come from? How could you learn this drill so quickly?" He told me his name was Bob Crable. He had played linebacker for Notre Dame in college. He was the New York Jets No. 1 draft choice in 1982. He'd played linebacker for the Jets in 1982 and 1983 but not in 1984. That's because he had ripped his knee during a Jets minicamp doing a drill that the Jet pro scouts always had prospects do when they were evaluating the prospect. The Jets had veterans do these pro scout drills once a year so that the new prospects' times in these drills could be compared to the veterans' times.

When Bob told me the story of how he had ripped his knee, it was a horror story, and should be a lesson for any scout or coach who gives such a drill even nowadays. It's called the "four corners" drill. Four cones are placed on the ground to form a square, each cone 10 yards apart (the circumference of the square is 40 yards). The player starts on the outside square at one cone. On the starting whistle, he runs forward straight ahead to the cone, then carioca's sideways, or laterally, to the next cone, runs backwards to the third cone, and then runs forward to the last cone, which is the finish line. The entire time the player has stayed outside the square formed by the cones. The drill is timed by the pro scouts with a stop watch. A player tries to complete the drill as fast as possible. A little less than a year earlier, Bob had ripped his knee in the third part of the drill when a player switched from the carioca to the backward run. His feet got tangled, one foot was behind the other when he fell and ripped his knee.

Bob Crable

The coaches or scouts handling Bob's drill must have been out of their minds. The carioca is probably the most used agility drill or warm-up drill in football, and also in other sports like Lacrosse. Many times, the first thing a player does when walking from the locker room to the field is the carioca as soon as he steps on the field. I mention this because my players and fellow coaches have heard me say many times, "If I ever get around to writing a book on football skills, the title of it will be, '*The Carioca is a Worthless Drill for All Competitive Sports!*'"

The carioca is a drill (or dance routine) where the player (or dancer) moves laterally (sideways) by placing the foot opposite of the direction he is moving in front of and then behind the other foot. If moving to his right, the player keeps placing his left foot in front of his right, then behind the right foot, then in front of the right, and so on. Every time the left foot goes behind the right foot when one player is moving to the right, the player is in danger of falling over and tripping. There is no competitive sport in the world where the far foot—the foot away from the direction in which a player is moving—goes underneath the foot in the direction that the player is moving laterally. This goes for football, basketball, tennis, racquetball, handball, badminton, etc. In all these sports, when moving in one direction laterally, the far foot always goes in front of the other foot. A scouting drill that involves a carioca is wrong. Bob Crable got hurt in a stupid drill.

I asked the Jets scouting department if they had abolished the "four corner" drill after Bob was hurt. They said, no, it was just a freak accident and they would continue to use the drill. I tried hard to have the Jets' veterans excused from the drill in mini-camp, but I was told they had to participate in it. I then said if they had to do the drill that I wanted to be in charge of running it.

Well, they did let me run the drill at the mini-camp for the next three years. Whenever a player group—like the linebackers group, secondary group, etc.—came to the "four corners drill," I would tell them that the drill's real name was "Crable's Corners" and tell them how Bob had hurt his knee doing it. I then told them that the most important thing was not the stop watch time but to avoid getting hurt like Crable did.

Crable's Corners, with its use of the timed carioca drill, is a prime example of many things done in the coaching field that haven't been given a lot of thought. The carioca has been taught by most coaches in football, but many have not taught their players how to run laterally and change direction laterally. Also, the fact that the Jets retained the "four corners" drill with the carioca part in it, even though a No. 1 draft pick ripped his knee, showed resistance to change a drill that had become traditional—even though I had given them all the good reasons to get rid of the carioca part of the drill.

Bob Crable became a starter as an outside linebacker by the middle of the 1985 season and started the next two seasons. He then reinjured his knee, sat out the 1988 season and he retired at the end of it. I've often wondered how good Bob might have been and how much longer he would have played if not for the stupid carioca in the Crable's Corners drill.

Jets Long-Snapping Coach – Oftentimes, coaches over coach, and I think a good coach is one who knows when to just keep his big mouth shut. I had another example of that with the Jets. Shortly after I was hired, special teams coach Larry Pasquale found out that I had been a long-snapper in college for punts, field goals and extra points and, that I had coached long-snapping in college and the pros. Larry immediately put me in charge of the teams long-snapping. At the first mini-camp, I introduced myself to Jets long-snapper Guy Bingham and told him that I was going to watch him snap for 10 punts and 10 field goals. After that, I told him I would try to correct any flaws or faults that I saw. Well, on the punt snaps, the ball went back 15 yards like a bullet always belt or chest high. On the field goal/extra point snaps, the ball went right between the numbers on the holder's chest with laces up every time. After I observed all this, I walked over to Bingham and said, "Guy, if I ever try to correct you in how to snap, tell me to go mind my own business." And that's how I coached the long-snapping for special teams coach Larry Pasquale for the four years that I was with the Jets. Later in a practice one day, Guy had a snap that was not his usual good snap. I walked over to him and started telling him what I thought he did wrong. I didn't get four words out of my mouth before he said, "Rad, go mind your own business. Don't tell me how to snap," and I just laughed as I walked away.

A New Defense – Putting in the new 34 defense that fall required three key players to learn more important roles, and two of those players were Penn Staters, Harry Hamilton and Lance Mehl. Hamilton, who was the safety, had to learn the new secondary calls as well as which linebacker was the fourth rusher in the 34 scheme so that he could keep his basic coverage calls synchronized with the rush. Mehl, an All-Pro outside linebacker, had to move to inside linebacker, be the defensive signal caller and, basically, run the defense on the field. Joe Klecko, our All-Pro defensive tackle, had to learn how to be a basic 34 nose tackle and a "cocked" nose tackle, meaning he had to be aligned on either side of the center.

Defensive line coach Ray Callahan and I made a special trip to Pittsburgh so we could learn how my old player, Jon Kolb, who was now the Steelers defensive line coach, taught Gary Dunn how to play a cocked nose tackle. Dunn was then the best cocked

Lance Mehl

nose tackle in the NFL. We also had to make sure we practiced and played our four down linemen defense, the 34 Monster, at least 25 percent of the time because we thought our four down linemen of Klecko, Mark Gastineau, Marty Lyons and Barry Bennett was one of the best four down linemen groups in the league. We also put in Buddy Ryan's 46 Bears defense, which had been instrumental in the Chicago Bears' success the previous two years and would help the Bears win the Super Bowl later that season. Our new Jets defense allowed 100 fewer points than the previous year.

Mehl and the down linemen were the keys because of their past experience as starters. Three-year back up Rusty Guilbeau and an 11-year journeyman linebacker we picked up from Kansas City, Charles Jackson, were new starters at outside linebackers, and Kyle Clifton was also a new starter at inside linebacker. They kept improving as the season went along and really helped make it all work. By midseason, Bob Crable took over one of the starting outside linebacker spots to make us even stronger on defense.

When the season was over, Mehl made the Pro Bowl as an inside linebacker. Lance was an excellent note-taker in our defensive meetings, very much like linebacker Jack "Hacksaw" Reynolds of the Rams and 49ers. I can remember telling the Jet linebackers how to play in a certain defense in a December meeting, when Lance raised his hand and interrupted me, saying, "Rad, back in October, my notes say that you told us a different way to play that defense." I realized he was right, so I said, "Lance, as you have pointed out, it's obvious in October I lied to you. This time I'm telling you the truth." What could I say? They laughed and, of course, never let me forget that I had changed my mind.

The 1985 Jets Season – Our brand-new Jets defense got off to a shaky start, when the Los Angeles Raiders scored 31 points in the first half of our league opener in the LA Coliseum. But we turned the game and the season all around in the second half. We shut out the Raiders in the second half, although we still lost the game, 31-0, and then beat Buffalo, 42-3, and Green Bay, 24-3. We did not give up a touchdown for 10 straight quarters. Then, we put together two five-game winning streaks before losing in the next to last regular season game to the eventual Super Bowl champion Chicago Bears in a close one, 19-6. We finished up with an 11-5 record after beating Cleveland 37-10 at home but lost a wild-card playoff game, 26-14, to the Patriots in Giants Stadium, as our four turnovers to their zero turnovers killed us.

Losing that game to the Bears was the toughest loss of the season. I thought quarterback Jim McMahon's ability to throw the ball accurately in the hurricane type winds that day was truly amazing. I also felt that Walter Payton's catch and 80-yard touchdown run was the result of an illegal pick by the Bears' wide receiver on Jets linebacker Lance Mehl who was covering Payton on the play. But it just goes to show how one official's call or non-call can change history.

Mark Gastineau And The Sports Cars — A couple of my most memorable experiences of the season occurred off the field. One involved Gastineau, the Jets' flamboyant defensive end, who drove me to all the Jets home games that were played in Giant Stadium in the New Jersey Meadowlands. In the preseason, Mark offered to take me to the hotel in Jersey that the Jets players and coaches stayed at the night before the game, and then from the hotel to the stadium the morning of the game. By going to the game with him, I could then ride back home after the game with my family. What made these trips such a memorable experience was that at each home game, Mark would be driving a different, very expensive sports car. The first home game, we rode in a Corvette; the next game, a Porsche; next game, a Ferrari; next a Maserati; and so on. I asked him how he got all these different expensive cars. He said that different dealers allowed him to use their sports cars for a week at a time. I knew Mark was one of the best-known New York Jets players, but I had no idea how he set up the deals for these cars. He even let my wife drive one for a weekend, a Nissan Z28. On an empty stretch of highway, she had it up to 120 miles an hour for a few seconds just to try it out. Anyway, I felt like a New York millionaire being chauffeured to the Jets games by the New York Jets All-Pro defensive end Mark Gastineau.

Mark Gastineau

Quick Hands — Nose tackle Joe Klecko had an outstanding 1985 season in our 34 defensive schemes. At the end of the year, he was voted All-Pro as a nose tackle and became the first player in NFL history to make All-Pro at three spots — defensive end (1981), defensive tackle (1983) and defensive nose tackle (1985). One of the reasons for Joe's success was the quickness of his hands moving from their position in his stance to their placement on the offensive lineman's chest or shoulder pads.

One morning during the middle of the season, I decided to have some fun with Joe. I said, "Joe, I've got to tell you what happened when I woke up today. Every morning for the last 30 years, I've stood in front of my full length mirror and said: 'Mirror mirror on the wall, who has the quickest hands of all?' And every time, the mirror has replied: 'Bad Rad, without a doubt, you do indeed have the quickest hands of all.' I would say: 'Thank you, mirror,' and go on my way. Well this morning when I said, 'Mirror, mirror on the wall, who has the quickest hands of all?' The mirror replied, 'Bad Rad, I must admit, Joe Klecko now has the quickest hands of all.' Well, I kicked that mirror and broke it into a thousand pieces. I had no use for a mirror that lies." Then I asked Joe, how he got those quick hands? Who had taught him? Joe replied that he had always had quick hands; that they were natural to him. I then told him that I had a 1977 close-up film of the Jets-Steelers game when he was a starting rookie tackle. The Steelers had won the game 23-20. I asked him if he would like to see it. He said he had a sack in that game and would love to see it. I invited him to come over to my house in Point Lookout where we both lived, and we would watch it together.

Joe Klecko

Joe showed up at my house at 8:00 p.m. with starting Jets linebacker Kyle Clifton. I turned the projector on and the three of us watched the film. Well, Joe is put flat on his back at least six times on running plays in the first half, and hardly gets off of the line of scrimmage on pass plays. The Steelers linemen, like future Hall of Fame center Mike Webster, are in their fourth year of having quick hands and extending their arms. Joe Klecko at this stage of his career as a rookie was not very good with his hands. The sack that he made was because of a busted assignment by a Steelers lineman. Nobody even tried to block him on that play as he rushed Terry Bradshaw and sacked him. I did not comment at all on Joe's play the first half. As soon as the first half was over, Joe said that he couldn't stay for the second half. He said that he had some business to attend to. So he and Kyle left. Kyle told me later that they went to Joe's bar-restaurant that Joe owned in a nearby town, and said Joe cursed me up and down the rest of the evening.

When Joe had told me that those quick hands of his were natural, I knew he wasn't quite telling the entire truth. I knew Dan Sekanovich and Ray Callahan, who were Klecko's defensive line coaches in his early NFL years, had worked on having quick hands. Joe Klecko's quickness with his hands was definitely a learned skill and not, to put it in his own words "natural," which is to his credit. He had worked hard to become an All-Pro defensive lineman.

Cool Proposal – One other thing I remember that year occurred after a game in December at Giants Stadium. My wife, daughter Leslie, and I were getting on an elevator going to a restaurant on an upper floor. Getting in the elevator at the same time was Ahmad Rashad, the former great NFL receiver who had become a well known TV sportscaster. I knew Ahmad from my one year coaching stint at the Vikings, plus having coached against him when he played at the University of Oregon. I introduced Ahmad to Nancy and Leslie and we all conversed a bit. I then told Ahmad that I had seen his proposal of marriage to Phyllis, who played the wife of Bill Cosby on Cosby's TV show, and thought that proposing to her on TV during the Thanksgiving Day game with Detroit was really cool. Ahmad then turned to my daughter and said, "Leslie, what was really cool about my TV marriage proposal was that she accepted. That was the cool part!" Little did we know that approximately 10 years later, Leslie would be producing a TV show in Las Vegas called *Caesar's Challenge*, that took place in the Caesar's Palace casino and hotel, and that she and her company would hire Ahmad Rashad as the host of the show.

As for my on field highlight of the 1985 season, it had to be the first Miami game at Giants Stadium in mid October. It was Joe Namath Night and the *Monday Night Football* crew was there to televise the game. The Dolphins also had won four straight and had scored no less than 24 points in 23 of their previous 24 games going back to their 1984 season opener. Their only stumble was a 38-16 loss to San Francisco in the Super Bowl. Even with that defeat, Dan Marino, a Pittsburgh area kid like Namath and me, had been sensational in his rookie year at quarterback. But beating Marino and Miami that Monday night, 23-7, by holding the high scoring Dolphins to their lowest point total in Marino's two-year career was an incredible achievement. And the biggest cheerleader on our sidelines was Namath, the greatest of all Jets quarterbacks, who was honored at halftime.

Dan Marino

So, despite our loss in the playoffs, we were all looking forward to the 1986 season. We believed that if everything went right we could make it to the Super Bowl. And it sure looked like we were headed that way when we set a team-record nine-game winning streak by late November. That's when Dan Marino got his revenge. But it would be my next NFL team that would kill us off in the playoffs and mark the beginning of the end of my idyllic life at Point Lookout.

CHAPTER EIGHTEEN -
From Times Square to The Dog Pound

As successful as Bud Carson and I were with the defense and especially with the improvement with our linebacking corps, Joe Walton believed I could be even more valuable to him and the Jets by shifting back to offense. Shortly after the Christmas and New Year vacation period, Joe asked me if I would be interested in being the offensive line coach. I told him no. I said I was satisfied coaching the linebackers. Besides, I thought our offensive line coach, Bill Austin, had done okay considering that both our starting offensive tackles had been holdouts and didn't report until one week before our first league game with Oakland. We had given up a team record 62 sacks but our veteran quarterback Kenny O'Brien did hold the ball too long at times. That night I told Bud, the defensive coordinator, about my brief talk with Walton and told Bud I was staying on defense. Bud said, "Good, I didn't want to lose you. Plus, you probably saved the offensive line coach's job."

A day or so later, Joe called me into his office, and again asked me to be the offensive line coach. Again, I said no. Then, he said what would it take money-wise for me to be the offensive line coach? I thought for a moment, and then said, "a $20,000 raise." (I was making $75,000 at the time). He said he didn't think he could do that. I said, "That's okay with me." A few days later, there was an announcement that offensive line coach Bill Austin was gone and that I was the new line coach. I went in to see Walton and he told me that I have a $15,000 raise. I said, "But Joe, I told you I wouldn't be the offensive line coach, unless I got a $20,000 raise." He told me that $15,000 was a good raise and that I should be satisfied with that. I thought about it, took the $15,000 raise and became the Jets offensive line coach.

When I told Bob Crable that I wasn't going to be his linebacker coach anymore, that I was going to coach the offensive line, he called me an asshole. I didn't realize he liked me that much. I then purchased a country song record entitled, "You Were Born To Be An Asshole," and presented it to him as a gift in the next day's meeting with the players. The entire room went wild when I played the record for him.

Players' Union Sues Jets – Soon after I became the offensive line coach, I was informed that the Jets were trying to trade our nine-year veteran, All-Pro offensive tackle Marvin Powell to another NFL team. I knew that Marvin had held out for more money the past preseason and had not reported for practice until the week before the first league game. I also knew that nine years earlier, in the winter of 1977, I had studied film of Marvin playing at the University of Southern California and had thought he was one of the best offensive tackle prospects ever to come out of college football. The Jets must have thought so, too, because they made him their No. 1 draft choice, and fourth overall that year.

I went to see Marvin and told him I would love to have my shot at coaching him. I begged him to call the head coach and tell him that he wanted to stay with the Jets and play for me. I even asked him to tell Walton and anybody else that he would be willing to do anything, even give up his role as union representative, in order to concentrate all his efforts on being a better player for the Jets. Well, he never did go and see Joe. The Jets traded him to Tampa Bay and we ended up getting sued by the players union on Marvin's behalf. In the lawsuit the Jets were accused of trading Marvin because he was a player's union representative. Well, a whole bunch of people in the Jets organization, including me, had to testify that he was not traded because he was a union representative, which was true. I had simply opened up a can of worms when I had suggested that Marvin tell Joe that he was willing to give up being a union rep to show how much he wanted to stay with the Jets. After a few days of testimony, the moderator (or judge) decided that being a union rep had nothing to do with Marvin being traded.

Of course, I was very sorry for the unnecessary trouble I had caused the Jets in having to defend against a lawsuit, but I still wish I would have had the chance to coach Marvin Powell. Marvin played two more years for the Tampa Bay Buccaneers and retired as an 11-year veteran.

No. 1 And No. 2 Draft Picks – The feeling within the Jets organization before the '86 NFL draft began was that we needed to select an offensive lineman some time during the draft, especially since we had just traded away our veteran offensive tackle Marvin Powell. Just like the staffs I had been on at the 49ers and Vikings, the assistant football coaches at the Jets in '86 had absolutely no say in the draft. The only one from the coaching staff allowed in the draft room was the head coach. The other people in the draft room were the pro scouts and the scouting director.

In the first round, we drafted an offensive tackle who had I had never heard of, and who I had no idea we were considering—Mike Haight of Iowa. I learned he was the Big Ten's offensive lineman of the year in 1985. As soon as I heard his name and school, I immediately called his offensive line coach, Kirk Ferentz, who was a close friend. Without telling Kirk about our draft pick, I asked him to tell me about Mike Haight. Kirk said, "Oh, he's a great kid." I said, "Where do you think he ought to go in the draft?" Kirk said, "Free agent. I think he'd make a good free agent." I said, "Well, your free agent is now our No. 1 draft pick."

In the second round of the draft, we took another offensive lineman who I had never heard of and didn't know we were considering named Doug Williams from Texas A&M. I also knew his line coach, Joe Avezzano, very well. I asked our director of scouting, Mike Hickey, about Williams. Mike said, "He's a big strong, good-looking guy [6-foot-5, 290-pounds], who doesn't play all that well, but I figured with your coaching, he could be a great player." I replied, "I don't want a guy who you think could be a great player with my coaching, I want a guy who can be a great player regardless of who's coaching him. I simply want the guy that everyone else wants."

Neither the No. 1 nor the No. 2 pick was good enough to be an NFL starter on a good team. We cut the No. 2 pick during training camp. His agent publicly criticized me in the papers for doing so. The Houston Oilers picked him up, tried to make a player out of him, couldn't and cut him two years later. We couldn't cut the No. 1 pick, so he was a reserve for my last three years at the Jets. He was a good kid; he worked hard and started several games for the Jets after I left; and retired after his seventh year in the league. Just as my friend Kirk Ferentz had said, he was a good kid and hard worker, who should have been a free agent.

If I would have known we were considering these two players as draft picks, all it would have taken was a phone call by me to each of their line coaches to have prevented wasting the No. 1 and No. 2 1986 Jets draft picks. For the price of two phone calls, we could have saved probably a combined one million dollars in bonus money that we gave those two kids to sign with us.

Left Tackle Right-Handed Stance – One of my most important problems to solve after the Jets had traded Marvin Powell to Tampa Bay was to find someone to play left tackle. The best and probably only solution was to try to make starting left guard Jim Sweeney the left offensive tackle. Jim had been both a guard and center in college for my buddy Joe Moore at Pitt and had been taken in the second round of the '84 draft. The Jets also used him a bit at center as well as guard, but he had never played tackle. After some convincing, Jim finally agreed to give left tackle a try but only if he could play from a right-handed stance. Now, in 1986 everyone who was a starting left tackle was in a left-handed stance. All the offensive line coaches in the NFL taught that. But I had known some very good left offensive tackles in the recent past, like Art Shell of the Raiders, who played left tackle very well from a right-handed stance. I knew if a player was a good enough athlete that it could be done. So I agreed to let Sweeney play left tackle in a right-handed stance, which he did for the next two years. As I remember, the only player Jim had a problem with that first year was defensive end Bruce Smith, the future Hall of Famer for the Buffalo Bills. But all offensive left tackles had a problem with Bruce Smith. Two years later, Jim Sweeney went back to his natural position of center-guard and ended up playing 16 years in the NFL; and one day, as you will learn, I would help him make an extra $600,000.

Jim Sweeney

Bad Rad Camp – My first request to Joe Walton after I became offensive line coach was to have a personal five-day mini-camp only for me and the Jets offensive linemen. Joe said okay, and I had the offensive linemen alone for five days from morning to night without any interference from anyone. The linemen who participated were centers Joe Fields and Craig Bingham, guards Dan Alexander and Ted Banker, tackle Reggie McElroy and brand new tackle Jim Sweeney. I think tackle Gordon King also may have been there. We talked football, watched football film, practiced football all day and also in the evenings. We ate lunch and dinner together. It was the only time in my coaching career I have ever had such a camp and I feel it was one of the best things I have ever done. The offensive line players even had "I survived Bad Rad's Camp" T-shirts made up.

Dan Alexander

At the end of the final day, I had an awards ceremony on the field, similar to the award ceremonies that are shown in old movies involving the French Foreign Legion soldiers getting the French Cross [Criox de Guerre] with the French National Anthem "La Marseillaise" being played. I had the players stand at attention, had the French National Anthem being sung on a tape player and had each player march up to get his award. I can't remember what I gave out as awards, but I can remember veteran guard Dan Alexander marching up, making two sharp military turns and standing at attention as I presented his award. I then kissed him on both cheeks and that broke everyone up. I mention this because I believe it was one of the reasons we got off to such a fast 10-1 start of the 1986 season and almost got on the cover of *Sports Illustrated*.

Sports Illustrated Cover—Almost

Before the '86 season started, we were optimistic about chances to get to the Super Bowl. We beat the Bills at Buffalo in our opener, 28-24, lost to New England, 20-6, at home then won our next nine games, setting a new team record. The Jets offense averaged almost 30 points (actually 29.7) per game in those 10 wins, and the ultra-critical New York media was raving about the offense and especially about the reorganized offensive line. After we beat Seattle, 38-7, making our record 8-1, *Sports Illustrated* interviewed the Jets offensive lineman and me for a possible article with our photo on the cover of the magazine. In the two weeks that followed the interviews and photo shoot, we beat Atlanta, 28-14, and Indianapolis, 31-16, to boost our record to 10-1. Our publicity department then received a phone call that the Jets offensive line, along with me, would be on the cover of *Sports Illustrated* following a victory in the next Jets game versus Miami. We had already beaten Miami in our third league game in the highest scoring overtime game by two teams in the NFL history, 55-48. Well, we went to Miami and got crushed, 45-3, and our appearance on the *Sports Illustrated* cover was canceled—and that's as close as I ever got to be on the cover of *Sports Illustrated*.

Ironically, the team that replaced us on the cover of *Sports Illustrated* that week was my alma mater, Penn State, with a photo of my former coaching peer, and former boss, Head Coach Joe Paterno, selected as the magazine's prestigious

Sportsman of the Year. A few weeks later, Joe's 1986 team upset the Miami Hurricanes to win Penn State's second national championship in what is still the most watched college football game in television history. So that just proves the famous *Sports Illustrated* Cover jinx is a myth. Unless, you think like Bad Rad and feel the *Sports Illustrated* football gods probably jinxed me and the Jets beforehand as a sacrifice in order to spare Paterno. Seems logical to me.

My wife Nancy and I still have copies of some of the pictures that *Sports Illustrated* took of us. We call them the "almost pictures" that almost made it in *Sports Illustrated*.

High And Low Season – That 55-48 overtime win over Miami to start the Jets on our nine-game winning streak was the highlight of the season. The victory was then the second-highest scoring game in NFL history with 103 total points. Naturally, the low point of the regular season was the 45-3 loss to the same Miami Dolphins that ended the winning streak and started the five-game losing streak that ended our regular season. Injuries to Joe Klecko, Lance Mehl, Mark Gastineau and several starters played a big part in losing those last five games but you can't make excuses. Every team has injuries. We still made the playoffs as a wildcard and defeated Kansas City in the first playoff game, 35-15, at home.

We were about a 7-point underdog in our second playoff game at Cleveland, which was red-hot with a six-game winning streak. But the game turned into a battle, and with about four minutes left we scored to go ahead 20-10. After the kickoff, our defense had the Browns in a second-and-24 at their own 18-yard line and forced their second-year quarterback, Bernie Kosar, to throw an incomplete pass. But the referee called a border-line roughing the passer penalty on Gastineau and that changed the tempo. We couldn't seem to stop them and Kosar led two scoring drives as the Browns tied the game with seven seconds left in regulation on a 22-yard field goal by 15-year veteran Mark Mosely. After what was a tiring and intense 17 minutes and two seconds of overtime, Mosely kicked a 27-yard field goal to give the Browns the win. At the time, this was the second longest overtime game in NFL history, didn't end until four hours and five minutes after the kickoff. Losing that game in double overtime after going ahead by 10 points with four minutes to go has to go down as one of the toughest Jets losses in its history. Cleveland's coach, Marty Schottenheimer, told reporters after the game that it was "one of the finest games in the history of this sport." Maybe it was but it certainly didn't feel like it back then. As Joe Walton told the same reporters, "It's a very empty feeling."

Two years later, Schottenheimer would leave the Browns; my friend, Bud Carson, the Jets' defensive coordinator, would succeed him; and I'd follow Bud to the Browns.

The Strike Of 1987 – When the 1987 season began, we once again felt we could be a serious contender for the Super Bowl. And the Jets got off to a great start by beating division rivals Buffalo, 31-28, and New England, 43-24. Then the 24-day player strike occurred. This strike was not as popular with many NFL players as the first one in 1982. The main issues were free agency and salaries but the union's rank-and-file were divided over the need to go on strike. Now, in 1982, NFL Commissioner Pete Rozelle cancelled the games until the strike ended. But this time, Rozelle and the owners had decided the NFL would continue with replacement players. So, Rozelle canceled the third league game while the staffs of the NFL teams scrambled to get replacement players for the fourth scheduled game, which for us was Dallas at home.

One of the prime replacement needs for the Jets was a good long-snapper for punts, field goals and extra points. I remembered that we had a great long-snapper at North Carolina State in 1982 who was on scholarship for long-snapping only. I couldn't remember his name so I called Carl "Tater" Smith, then the quarterback coach of the New Orleans Saints, who had been the offensive coordinator at NC State. Tater told me it was Martin Cornelson. I finally tracked Martin down. He was a broker on Wall Street and lived in New York City. We made a deal with Martin that was unique for professional football. Martin only had to show up on Saturdays to practice snapping and snap in the Sunday game.

As the strike went into its second week, a couple of veterans came into camp. Players did not get paid when on strike. If a player had $1 million contract, he was losing $62,500 a week being on strike. A player with a $500,000 contract lost $31,250 a week, one half of what the first player lost. Obviously, the highest-paid players were the ones most eager to report to camp. One day after the first week of the strike, I received a phone call in my Jets office from our All-Pro, Mark Gastineau, one of our highest paid players. Mark said, "Rad, I'm going to hire a helicopter and break the picket line by flying over the pickets and landing on the practice field. Isn't that a great idea?" I said, "Mark, this conversation has never taken place. I didn't hear what you said, and I'm not going to tell anybody," and I hung up.

Well, Mark decided to walk through the picket line, got into an argument with the players picketing, got in a fight with one of my offensive lineman, Guy Bingham, and got pelted with eggs by the pickets. Gastineau was not alone in crossing the picket line during the strike. Joe Klecko and a few others also crossed the picket line. Tight end Mickey Shuler, another of my fellow alums from Penn State, was a major voice in keeping players from crossing the line. The whole strike deal was a bit of a mess, and there were a lot of bad feelings among our players during and after the strike. Total solidarity, we did not have. Of the three games we played during the strike, we lost the first two to Dallas, 38-24, and Indianapolis, 6-0, and won the third strike game against Miami, 34-31 in overtime. After the Miami game, the union backed off some of its demands and settled the strike, and we went back to coaching our veteran players for our next game against the Washington Redskins. As for Martin Cornelson, the replacement long-snapper, he did a good job snapping in the three replacement games and became a minor celebrity—the only broker on Wall Street playing pro football on the weekends. A few years later, Martin was working for NFL products. It was a job he obtained through his connection with Jets equipment man Bill Hampton Jr., who had befriended him during his three-game stint during the strike.

After The Strike – That first post-strike game at Washington was a very important for both teams. The Redskins also had split their first two games before the strike but had won all three games with replacement players during the strike. Their record was 4-1 and we were 3-2. So, this game was the first in four weeks where all the veterans from both teams would be playing and we hoped that any animosity that had occurred between the players and management or among the players themselves was over. It seemed to be because our Redskins game was very close and was decided on the last play that the Jets had the ball.

As one might expect, it wasn't a very well played game, with a lot of penalties and mental lapses. And it got so bad that when we took the lead in the second half, the hometown Redskins fan started booing and chanting, "We want the scabs!" We blew a 16-7 lead in the second half and Washington kicked a 28-yard field goal with 54 seconds left in the game. We were able to get as far as the Washington 45-yard line after the kickoff but with 10 seconds remaining Pat Leahy's desperation 62-yard field goal attempt fell short and we lost, 16-17. Washington went on to win the Super Bowl and the rest of the season seemed anti-climatic for us. We won just three of our remaining nine games to end up with a 6-9 record. After our great start of winning our first two games against two division rivals, the strike was a distraction that hurt our team's performance. That seems to be as good an excuse as any other for a disappointing season.

The Vegetable – I have always kept myself in good shape by exercising, even with my smoking habit. Ever since my years at Penn State I had been playing racquetball. It was a ritual back then. The racquetball courts were right around the corner from the football coaches' offices in Rec Hall and just about all of us assistant coaches were on the court three or four times a week. Anyhow, the day after the last game of the Jets 1987 season, I played three games of doubles racquetball with three other coaches at the Jets complex. In the middle of the second game, I felt something pop in my lower back, but with only slight discomfort I finished playing all three games. After I showered, I went to the bank. Upon returning to my office, I was walking past the film video room when John Seider and Jim Pons, our video cameramen, saw me and both yelled, "What's wrong Rad? Are you okay? You're walking funny." I said, "I'm fine. Just a little stiff from playing racquetball." And I continued to walk down the hall toward my office, Before I reached my office about 20 feet later, I collapsed and fell to the floor.

Pons and Seider heard me fall, ran to my aid and got me to the training room. After a couple of hours in the training room, somebody took me home to Point Lookout. At home I stiffened up to where I could hardly even move, and I had a tough time rolling over in bed. I got to where I couldn't even walk to the bathroom. Three of my daughter's teenage friends would carry me into the bathroom. They did this at least three times that night. Finally, at four o'clock in the morning, I told my wife to call Jets head trainer Bob Reese. Bob sent Pepper Burruss, a young assistant trainer. When Pepper got to my house a half hour later, he said he stood at the foot of my bed and said, "Rad, how are you feeling?" Pepper said later that I replied, very slowly "I'm a vege-ta-ble!" Then Pepper called an ambulance, which took me to the hospital. They put me in traction for a week and released me. After that, Pepper had me do hamstring stretches in a heated pool for an hour twice a day for an entire month and then my back felt fine for at least a year. I was 52 years old at the time, and I never played racquetball again. As for Pepper, he has been the head trainer for the Green Bay Packers since 1993.

Pepper Burruss

Buddy Ryan Keeps His Job — The start of the Jets 1988 season was almost a mirror image of '86, but the team was much different. We lost 10 starters from the '87 team through injuries, trades or wavers and had 17 new players. I had to rebuild my offensive line with only two regulars back and our rookie No. 1 draft choice was making a lot of mistakes in the preseason and beyond. The best thing I did was move Jim Sweeny from his starting tackle position to his natural center position. New England beat us in the season opener, 28-3, but the next week we upset Cleveland, 23-3, and then won the next two against Houston and Detroit before tying with Kansas City, 17-17. But it went downhill from there. We finished at 8-7-1, which was a winning record, but not good enough for the playoffs. We lost three very close games to New England, 14-13, Buffalo, 9-6, and Kansas City, 38-34. We were close to being a playoff team, but football isn't horseshoes.

Our last game of the season against the New York Giants was a very important game, but not for us. We were mathematically out of the playoffs but not the Giants and their division rival, the Philadelphia Eagles. If the Giants could beat us, they would win their division and go to the playoffs. If the Giants lost and the Eagles lost their final game at Dallas, the Giants would still win their division and go to the playoffs. However, if the Giants lost to us and the Eagles beat Dallas, the Eagles would win the division, go to the playoffs and the Giants would stay home. The newspapers indicated that if the Eagles head coach Buddy Ryan didn't make the playoffs in this his third year, he would be fired. So, for Buddy to keep his job, the Eagles had to beat Dallas, which they did, 13-7, and the Jets had to beat the Giants, which is what happened, 27-21. The win over the Giants gave us a winning season and Buddy Ryan signed a new contract with the Eagles. And as it turned out, this was my last game as a New York Jets coach.

One And One-Half Days Of Royalty — After four years with the Jets, I guess my gypsy circus genes kicked in again when Bud Carson left the Jets to be the head coach at Cleveland and another old friend, Steve Ortmayer, became director of operations at the San Diego Chargers. During the last week of January, the Browns hired Carson to succeed Schottenheimer, and Bud said he wanted me to join him but we didn't talk about anything specific. Around the same time Ortmayer, who was on the Colorado University staff with me in the early '70s, was looking for new head coach at San Diego and was trying to lure Redskins quarterback coach Dan Henning. Henning had helped Washington win two Super Bowls and also had been the head coach in Atlanta for a couple of years in between. I was most interested in the San Diego Chargers. I had loved California when I lived there while coaching the 49ers and the Rams, and I'd always wanted to live in the San Diego area. I still had another year to go on my Jets contract, but I told Joe Walton I was interested in the Chargers and not the Browns. Joe told me he wanted me to stay with the Jets.

Before Henning was officially announced as the Chargers head coach, I flew to San Diego and met with him. During the interview Dan said he was interested in hiring me but he wasn't going to make a definite decision for a week or ten days because he had some other people lined up to interview. When I got back to the Jets after the Chargers' interview, Walton asked me what I was going to do. I said I wanted the Chargers job and I was going to wait and see if Henning was going to hire me. I said I had been with the Jets for four years, had been treated good and I liked it here, but that I didn't have a title or anything special that would help me get a head job in the future. So, I was going to try to go where the weather was great, San Diego. He said, "If you want a title, I'll give you a title. What title do you want?" I said, "Are you serious?" He said, "Yeah." Well, I knew receivers coach Rich Kotite had the offensive coordinator title. I couldn't ask for that. I also knew that Joe Bugle of the Redskins had an assistant head coach's title, so I said, "Assistant Head Coach." Joe said, "You've got it." So, I decided to stay with the Jets. I then called Bugle in Washington and asked him what the title of assistant head coach really meant. He told me it meant basically nothing except if the head coach gets sick and can't come to work—which is never going to happen—then you would be in charge. But, he said, the assistant head coach title gives him an advantage I don't have. I said, "What's that, Joe?" He said, "I get interviewed for head jobs and you don't."

Well, I went home that night and told my wife what had happened. She asked me what does the title mean? I told her what Joe Bugle had said and she said, "That's great. We're now like the King and Queen of England. You've got a title that means nothing. We're royalty now. We have to go out to dinner and celebrate" and we did. Two days later, Jets backfield assistant coach Bobby Hammond was waiting for me at the front door to the Jets office as I was arriving that morning for work. He told me Walton wanted to see me. Joe told me he had made a mistake. He said he couldn't give me the assistant head coach's title; that wouldn't be fair to offensive coordinator-receivers coach Rich Kotite. I said if that's the case then I was going to wait and see if Henning would hire me as his offensive line coach.

The next day, Walton called me into his office and said he couldn't wait around for Henning to make a decision. He said I would have to make a decision now whether or not I was staying with the Jets. I told him I was still going to wait on the Chargers decision. Joe said, "Then you're out of here." I replied, "Joe, even though you're kicking me out, I still like you," and I left. That's the story of my 1½ days as assistant head coach, a nothing title, which meant, in the words of my wife, that we had 1½ days of being "Royalty."

Joe Walton and I didn't talk again for five years, and when we did it was when he asked me to be an assistant coach for him again—only this time I would be his only assistant coach at this small college near the Greater Pittsburgh airport that didn't even have a football team yet. But I'll tell you more about that in the next chapter.

Back On Defense – The Jets didn't say they had fired me. They said it was resignation under "mutual agreement." Didn't matter. Even though Walton had bounced me, I was pretty confident I was not going to be out of job for long. I didn't contact Bud Carson, who was in the process of hiring assistants for his new staff, because I felt certain that I was going to get the Chargers offensive line job. But I didn't. About a week after I had left the Jets, Henning called and informed me that he was hiring a former coaching friend of his as offensive line coach, Larry Bechtel. Dan knew of my relationship with Bud and said he would call Bud on my behalf.

After I hung up the phone, my wife and I started to panic a little, wondering if Bud had filled his staff yet. If he had, I'd probably have to get another warehouse job like I did when I left the Rams seven years earlier. About an hour after I had talked with Henning, Bud called. He had talked with Henning, and he offered me the job as his defensive coordinator and linebacker coach. Bud had just rescued me from the unemployment ranks. (I was only unemployed one week.) Better yet, I was back on defense.

Also, I was coaching for a former rival team whose fans had made their one end zone section of the stadium famous by the name of The Dog Pound. In a previous year, I had gone into The Dog Pound during pregame warm-ups to stop a couple of dog pound fans from hitting my players with ice and snowballs, which they were throwing.

Anyway, I was excited to get back on defense because I had always considered myself a defensive coach. My first 17 years of coaching had been on defense. However, 12 of the past 14 years had been as an offensive line coach. It was definitely time to get back on defense.

Coaching Linebackers For A Former Rival – Now, we all know that Cleveland is a long way from San Diego and not just in mileage. Some of the city's critics sarcastically refer to it as "The Mistake on the Lake." But actually Cleveland is a good town, and very similar in character to my home area of Pittsburgh, which also gets a bad rap. Maybe that is why the Steelers and the Browns have always been bitter rivals. That now extends to the Steelers and the Baltimore Ravens since owner Art Modell transferred the original Browns franchise to Baltimore in 1996. And talk about irony. Instead of basking in the sun and warmth of San Diego as I had expected, I would find a permanent home in Cleveland for 10 years, even staying there long after I moved on to another coaching job.

Cleveland seemed to be a talented team, but they also seemed snake-bitten, having narrowly missed out twice on going to the Super Bowl with those famous late-game losses to Denver. I also liked the guy who was running the Browns' operation for Modell, Ernie Accorsi. Ernie and I knew each other at Penn State when he was part of the school's sports information team. Now he was the general manager of the Browns. This seemed to be a perfect situation for me with one of my best friends as the head coach, another of our mutual good friends and fellow coaches, Lionel Taylor, the tight ends coach, and another old friend as the GM.

Byner For Oliphant Trade – A few days after reporting to my new job as defensive coordinator-linebacker coach, the new football staff was informed by the Browns administration that five-year starting running back Earnest Byner was going to be traded. After hearing this, I went into the office shared by two assistant coaches who were also on the previous Cleveland Browns' staff—offensive coordinator and quarterback coach Marc Trestman and receivers coach Richard Mann. I asked them both how good Earnest Byner was. They told me Byner was a very good running back. In fact, they concurred that he was the best football player on the team. I then inquired about his attitude. Was he late for meetings? Did he not participate in the off-season program? And so on. Again, they both concurred in telling me that Byner had the best attitude on the team, was most conscientious and a pleasure to coach. They both also thought that he was one of the best running backs in the NFL. Then, I asked both of them why we were trading him. They said they didn't know why.

Ernie Accorsi

I quickly went to see Bud Carson and told him what Richard and Mark had told me. I told Bud that I didn't think we should trade Byner and Bud agreed. Bud went immediately to see Ernie Accorsi to tell him that he did not want Byner traded. About a half hour later, Bud returned and told me that Byner was being traded and that there was nothing that he could do about it. Bud said the decision to trade Byner had been made before Bud was hired and Byner was being traded regardless of what value he would bring. Evidently, he didn't bring a lot of value because Byner was finally traded for Mike Oliphant, a 5-foot-10, 180-pound running back, who had been a rookie with Washington. We had never heard of him and he sounded more like a wide receiver than a running back.

The entire coaching staff was skeptical of the trade for Oliphant. The rumor we heard at the time was that because Byner had fumbled in the a 1987 playoff loss at Denver and had incurred a crucial penalty in a 1988 playoff defeat against Houston, the owner, Art Modell, had said that Byner would never play another game for the Browns. Mike Oliphant played very little for the Browns, was injured a lot and was out of football in 1990. Earnest Byner went to the Redskins, immediately became their star running back, leading them to a playoff spot in 1990 and a Super Bowl win after the 1991 season. In 1990, he led the entire NFL in the number of rushes for the season, 297. He seems to have gone from the best player on the Cleveland Browns in the late '80s to the best player on the Washington Redskins in the early '90s. Based on hindsight, the trade of five-year Browns' proven veteran Earnest Byner for the Redskins' unproven rookie Mike Oliphant has to go down as one of the most non-beneficial trades in Cleveland Browns history.

A few years later, in the early 1990s, after I had left the Browns, I saw Browns owner Art Modell being interviewed on TV. During the interview, Modell stated that he had never interfered with the football operations of the Cleveland Browns. I know the Byner trade wasn't Ernie Accorsi's idea, so I guess some owners just have short memories. What's even more revealing is that in 1994, the Browns brought Byner back as a backup. He was still with them when Modell moved the team to Baltimore, and he started several games for the Ravens until his retirement at the end of the 1997 season at age 35; then Byner moved into the Ravens front office as Director of Player Development, and then running back coach before leaving the organization in 2004 to coach for the Redskins. I still wonder if Modell's guilt feeling about the Byner-Oliphant trade had anything to do with getting Byner back into his organization and giving Byner a job after his playing days were over.

Plan B – Nineteen eighty-nine was the first year of the new NFL Plan B rule which stated that an NFL club could protect just 25 players from free agency. Players not protected were free to negotiate for better contracts with other NFL teams. This rule had a tremendous effect on one part of the Browns' team—the defensive line. Three of Cleveland's defensive line starters were over 30, not protected by the Browns, and were free to negotiate with other teams—and they did. Tackle Bob Golic (31) signed with the Oakland Raiders, end Sam Clancy (31) signed with the Indianapolis Colts and end Carl "Big Daddy" Hairston (36) thought about retiring. New defensive line coach John Teerlinck tried hard to get Clancy to re-sign with the Browns but failed, but he did convince 13-year veteran Big Daddy Hairston to play another year. Our defensive staff worked closely with assistant general manager Mike Lombardi to find a couple of good defensive linemen. Finally, after a month of trying, we signed 11-year veteran Al "Bubba" Baker (32), Tom Gibson (25), Chris Pike (25), Robert Banks (25) and Andrew Stewart (23). These players along with one-year veteran Michael Dean Perry proved to be a very effective defensive line in 1989. We also picked up on Plan B offensive guard Ted Banker, who I had coached at the Jets, and he turned out to be our best performer on the offensive line in 1989.

Earnest Byner

Browns Defensive Staff – Bud Carson had been a defensive coordinator most of his career. Although he gave me the title of defensive coordinator, he called the defensive signals during the games. Deke Pollard was our defensive quality control coach. I was in charge of the defensive fronts and blitzes that we ran. Secondary coach Jed Hughes was in charge of any coverage adjustments made for various formations or motions, and defensive line coach John Teerlinck was in charge of all pass rush stunts that we used. I had known Jed for about 10 years, having met him when I was offensive line coach for the Rams. What I remembered most about him was when he was leaving the Vikings in 1984 to go to the Steelers, he asked me how much salary money he should ask for from the Steelers. I had never met or known of John before. We became good friends, and I believe the four of us—John, Jed, Deke and me—worked well together on defense in 1989.

What About Me? – During the late winter and early spring months of 1989, I brought in the linebackers who lived in the Cleveland area during the off-season for linebacker drill workouts three times a week at an indoor tennis facility. After the second or third day of these workouts, middle linebacker Mike Johnson said, "Coach, what about me? How come you keep telling the other guys what to do and how to play but not me?" I said, "Mike, I don't say anything to you because you do the drills better than anyone else." But he had a very good point. Obviously, one reason he was doing the drills better than the others was that he was paying more attention to my teaching. I should have been acknowledging that and commenting more on his performance. The better the athlete, the more he will benefit from coaching. It's better to coach and pay the most attention to the players who are going to be in the game. Mike reminded me of this with his, "What about me?" comment.

Mike Johnson

When the season was over, Mike told me that I had given him six tackles in a game in which he actually had eight tackles. He said he only cared about getting credit for one more tackle so that he could tie safety Thane Gash for the most tackles by a player for the 1989 season. I checked the game film in which I had awarded him six tackles. He had eight tackles. I had goofed. I called the publicity department and told them I had screwed up the tackle count for Mike Johnson in that game and that he had two more tackles than I had given him credit for. I was told it would be corrected, but it never was. Only Mike Johnson and I know for sure that Mike led the 1989 Browns in tackles by having one more than the safety. Such is life. One more thing; Mike made the Pro Bowl after that season.

Buy Or Build – Soon after I accepted the Browns job in late February, my wife came to Cleveland to look for a house to buy. After we had looked for a few days, I asked her, "Why don't we just find a lot where we want to live and build a new house?" She said, "If we could buy a house on the market, we could move in May. A new house wouldn't be ready until the middle of August at the earliest." I agreed, but said if we built a new house she could spend the summer with our kids in our current house in the beach town of Point Lookout on Long Island, NY. I could join her for my month's vacation in June but in July and August I would be at the preseason football camp with the Browns. I asked her if she would rather spend her summer in Cleveland or on the beach in Long Island. Plus she would have a brand newly built house to move into in Cleveland at the end of the summer. She spent the summer on the beach and we moved into a new house built in the Cleveland suburb of Strongsville, on August 18, 1989.

Returning To Pittsburgh – Cleveland's opening game in '89 was against the Steelers in Pittsburgh, and even remembering the game nowadays I still shake my head at what happened. It was unique in couple of ways. The Steelers hadn't beaten the Browns the last six times they had played—not since the Steelers had won a squeaker, 10-9, in 1985. The Steelers, who had dominated the Browns in the 1970s, were now being dominated by the Browns in the late 1980s. Five former Steelers coaches were now on the Browns coaching staff. Three of us—Bud Carson, Lionel Taylor and me—had been with the first two Steelers Super Bowl teams in the 1970s. Jed Hughes and Hal Hunter were Steelers coaches the previous year, in 1988. It was just natural that we were all fired up to play against our former team. What happened in the game was totally unexpected by both teams.

My Browns' linebackers scored three touchdowns themselves—two within three minutes late in the opening quarter. Outside linebacker Clay Matthews picked up a fumble by Steelers running back Tim Worley at the Pittsburgh 3-yard line and ran it into the end zone with about five minutes left in the quarter. Then, on the second play after the kickoff, Worley fumbled again and my other outside linebacker David Grayson recovered at the Steelers' 27-yard line, leading to a 27-yard field goal by Matt Bahr (another of those great Penn State players turned out by Joe Paterno). On the first play after that ensuing kickoff, Grayson stripped the ball away from Pittsburgh's Louie Lipps just as he was catching a pass from Bubby Brister and he went 28 yards for a touchdown. Bahr kicked the extra point and with 2:31 still remaining in the first period, we led, 17-0. We made it 30-0 by halftime and continued our blitzkrieg in the first 3½ minutes of the second half, when another Worley fumble set up one touchdown and Grayson scored another with a 14-yard return of an interception. I got Grayson on the bench phone early in the third quarter and told him, "David, you are leading the entire National Football League in scoring. Enjoy the moment because it will never happen again."

Our offense also played well that day. The final score was Browns 51, Steelers 0. It is still the worst defeat in Steelers history. The Steelers also were beaten badly by Cincinnati in their second game, 41-10. But after losing their first two games by a margin of 82 points, the Steelers recovered to beat us five weeks later, 17-7, make the playoffs, win their first playoff game and lose the second playoff game by only one point, 24-23, to Denver. The Steelers recovery in '89 from those first two horrendous losses ranks as one of the best comebacks in NFL history.

Division Winners – After that 51-0 blowout in our opening game, the Browns played sporadically the rest of the regular season, but were still able to win the AFC Central Division with a 9-6-1 record that was just ahead of the 9-7 Steelers. We lost five games to non-playoff teams but won five games against playoff teams, with two of those wins in the last two games of the season—Minnesota, 23-17, and Houston, 24-20. We played well most of the time on defense and some of the time on offense. What hurt us on offense was not having the two running backs from the three previous Browns seasons: Earnest Byner and Kevin Mack (who had been suspended by the NFL commissioner for the first 12 games because of a drug related incident). Getting Mack back really helped us win the last two regular season games to finish strong and win the division with a game remaining. That gave us the home field advantage in our first playoff game against the AFC's Eastern Division winners, the Buffalo Bills.

Late For The Plane – The day before our 14th game of the season at Indianapolis, I was late getting to the airport for the team charter. The airplane had already started to taxi out to the runway when I arrived. The attendants at the airport gate called the pilot of the plane and had him stop the airplane out on the runway. I was driven in an airport jeep out to the runway and climbed a set of stairs underneath the belly of the plane. The plane had been de-iced and I got a lot of the de-icing gook on my coat as I went up into the belly of the plane. Of course, as I was going down the aisle to my seat, all the players were cheering that I had made the plane. When I got to my seat, right behind head coach Bud Carson, and the cheering subsided, Bud turned around and said to me, "If we lose this game, it's your fault!" We lost the game, 17-13.

You Were At The Same Game – One of the perks that Bud Carson got as head coach of the Cleveland Browns was that his wife Linda could travel with him on the team plane to all of the away games. During the '89 season, Bud said, "Linda, I don't know if you should go to this next game. We lost the last game that you went on a trip with us." Linda replied "Bud, you were at that same game." Linda went on the trip.

The Interception And The Gloves – We had two weeks to prepare for our playoff game against the Bills on January 6, 1990. Buffalo's offense was very conservative during the regular season, featuring two running backs in the backfield and two tight ends. So we practiced stuffing the run for two weeks. The Bills surprised us by coming out in a one back, three receiver, one tight end formation for the first time that season and they played the whole game that way. Before the game we thought we had an exceptionally strong defense against the conventional two back formations. Evidently, the Bills coaching staff agreed with us and decided they would do better by opening up their formation. The game was a seesaw affair with both teams moving the ball well. They threw for 410 yards and rushed for 49, while we threw the ball for 251 and rushed for 90. The score went back and forth and came down to a final Bills offensive play in the final minute, on our 5-yard line with the score 34-30 our favor.

The No. 1 receiver for the Bills that day was their single running back, Thurman Thomas, who had 13 catches up until that final minute for 150 yards and two touchdowns. On defense, we played either a nickel with five defensive backs or a dime with six defensive backs for the entire game against their one back formation. Middle linebacker Clay Matthews had Thomas man for man on almost all of Thurman's 13 catches because we were playing 3 on 2 versus the 2 receivers on each side of the Buffalo formations. On the Bills' last play from the Browns 5-yard line, Bills quarterback Jim Kelly threw into the end zone to Thurman Thomas for what would have been his 14th and game-winning catch. But Matthews jumped in front of Thomas, made a great interception, and we won the game: Browns 34, Bills 30. Buffalo stayed with their new one back, three or four wide receiver offense for the next four years and went to four straight Super Bowls. Even though they lost to us, it's obvious they found out against us how they could move the ball.

Earlier that season, my wife Nancy and I were having dinner with Lionel Taylor and his wife Loren. Nancy asked Lionel if those gloves she saw the receivers wearing in the game were any good. Lionel replied that if he would have had those gloves when he played, that he would have set receiving records that would never be broken. Lionel had led the entire NFL in number or receptions for five seasons, which is still second behind only Don Hutson (eight seasons), in the history of the NFL. When Nancy heard what Lionel said, she turned to me and said, "You better make all the linebackers wear gloves!" In my next meeting with the linebackers, I told them what Lionel had said and what my wife had said. So they all got gloves to wear when we played the Bills. So, when Matthews grabbed that end zone interception, he was wearing the gloves. After the game, as Clay was walking out of the Browns locker room, he spied my wife and walked over to her and said, "It was the gloves, Nancy. The gloves won the game." Well, to this day Nancy tells the story of the gloves. I think she really believes that because of the gloves she helped beat the Buffalo Bills in the playoff game that day. Who's to say anything different?

Clay Matthews (before he wore the gloves)

Third Time's A Charm — After beating the Bills, the Browns traveled to Denver on January 14 to face their old playoff nemesis, the Broncos, for the AFC championship for the third time in four years. Denver had won the last two in close games decided in the last minute. During the current season the Browns had beaten Denver at home in fourth game of the year in a close game, 16-13. Denver was a 3½ point favorite but we were confident we could win this third chance to go to the Super Bowl.

Well, we were outgained by Denver in total yardage 497 to 256. We blitzed a lot and Denver burnt the blitzes with a number of big plays. The score at the end of three quarters was still close with the Denver leading, 24-21, going into the fourth quarter after we came from behind a 17-point deficit.

Then early in the last period, Denver's outstanding quarterback John Elway, who had been hot all afternoon, hit halfback Sammy Winder with a short pass against an all out Cleveland blitz that Sammy turned into a 39-yard touchdown run. Later in the quarter, a couple of Broncos field goals were added to make the final score: Broncos 37, Browns 21. The Broncos went to the Super Bowl for the third time in four years, although they lost to the 49ers. The saying "the third time's a charm" was certainly not true for the 1989 Cleveland Browns.

The Broncos lost all three shots at the Super Bowl after the '86, '87 and '89 seasons, and that's typical of life in football—Happy, one week, sad the next.

Back On Offense

Offensive Line Coach Again – The coaching staffs that lose the AFC and NFC championship games get to coach the NFC and AFC teams in the annual Pro Bowl played a week after the Super Bowl in Hawaii. My wife and I went to Hawaii for about 10 days where we had a chance to do some golfing while I coached the linebackers for the AFC team. We lost a close game to the NFC, and after the game, we flew back to Cleveland. My first day back at work Bud Carson called me into his office and said, "If you want me to stay as the head coach of the Cleveland Browns and if you want to continue coaching for the Browns, you will coach the offensive line for the Browns this next year." I said, "Bud, what are you talking about?" He told me that in the month since the Denver playoff game, the Browns administration had decided to make a number of changes in the organization. That shouldn't have been surprising. I remembered what had happened a year earlier when Bud had tried to keep the Browns from trading Earnest Byner to no avail. As for going back to offense, Bud knew that I preferred to coach on defense. That was the reason his opening statement to me was so strong.

Bud Carson

Bud said offensive coordinator and quarterback coach Marc Trestman would be released and a new offensive coordinator hired. He was also going to hire a new quarterback coach. Offensive line coach Hal Hunter would become the quality control coach for the defense unless I wanted him for an offensive line assistant. Secondary coach Jed Hughes also was being released and a replacement hired from outside. A new linebackers coach would be hired to take my place and the defensive quality control coach, Deke Pollard, also would be released.

To entice me to be the offensive line coach, I was given an assistant head coach's title and a raise. After Bud had told me of all the unexpected changes, it took me a while to decipher what had taken place. First, we had been historically one of the better Browns defenses statistically during the regular season. Three of the four defensive coaches (myself included) were gone from the defense. Defensive line coach John Teerlinck, secondary coach Jed Hughes, defensive quality control coach Deke Pollard and myself as linebacker coach and coordinator had worked well together. Jed and Deke being released really hurt. Of the four of us, Teerlinck was the only coach remaining on defense. On offense, I thought offensive coordinator-quarterback coach Marc Trestman had done a pretty good job considering he didn't have a bona fide NFL running back for most of the season, Remember, Earnest Byner had been traded and Kevin Mack was suspended for the first 12 games of the season. We had a great rookie scat back in Eric Metcalf, who should have been a wide receiver and later was for another team, the Houston Oilers. Then there was our starting quarterback, Kosar, who had been playing hurt throughout the season.

It was obvious that Bud or the administration didn't want to fire Hal Hunter, the offensive line coach, but they wanted me to coach the line instead. What a mess this was. I was especially upset about Jed Hughes being released. I finally decided that I had no choice and agreed to coach the offensive line. But I didn't want an assistant. I had never had one before and didn't want one now. As I should have realized, this was a big mistake—one that eventually helped cost me my job. So, Hal, the former offensive line coach, was relegated to quality control for the defense. I knew three of the new coaches Bud hired from our time with the New York Jets—linebackers coach Jim Vechiarella, quarterback coach Zeke Bratkowski and secondary coach Mike Faulkner. I didn't know the new offensive coordinator, Jim Shofner, who had played cornerback for the Browns from 1959-63 and then had returned to the Browns as an assistant offensive coach from 1978-80. Since 1981 he had been an assistant with Houston, Dallas and St. Louis.

When all the changes were made, we got ready for the season. With the new offensive coordinator coming in, Bud wanted me to change the terminology on offense from the previous year so he could understand it. So I changed all the offensive terminology. Now all the offensive players, plus the new coordinator, plus the assistants all had to learn a new terminology, plus a new offensive system because of a new coordinator. Looking back, I wonder how we could make all these changes and succeed. The answer is—we didn't.

A Forgettable Season – My primary mission was to develop a running game and protect an immobile quarterback, and I should have realized we were headed for a disaster when we had so many problems putting together an offensive line in the preseason. By the time of our season opener at home against the Steelers, all five starters from 1989 had either retired, were out with knee injuries or had changed position. We went through some 15 or 16 linemen, some of them free agents up from the developmental squad and only a couple who were experienced veterans or mid round draft choices, and here I was also trying to teach them a new system, too. It was not fun for any of us, and we altered the lineup throughout the preseason games just to find the right chemistry. We beat the Steelers, 13-3, but it was an ugly win, and Kosar, now in his sixth season, was sacked for a personal high of seven times in one game. But we lost our next two by relatively close scores, and when Schottenheimer's Kansas City Chiefs shut us out, 34-0, word leaked that Modell was on the verge of firing Bud. What's more, I was getting a lot of heat for our ineffective offensive line, and at least one know-it-all beat reporter from Columbus was blaming everything on Bud and his "staff filled with New York Jets cronies."

With three new starters in the offensive line, we beat our second biggest rival at Denver, 30-29, on a 30-yard field goal with five seconds to play. Our celebration didn't last long. We lost three more, and before our ninth game against the Bills in Buffalo Bud benched Kosar, who thus far in the season, had been sacked 23 times with eleven passes batted down at the line and 37 passes knocked down after his throws. We were creamed, 42-0, and Modell fired Bud. Offensive coordinator Jim Shofner took over for the remainder of the season, and we won just one more of the seven remaining games, and were blown out by the Steelers 35-0 in our next to last game at Pittsburgh.

As in most losing situations, everybody blames everybody else and the media goes off using a lot of undisclosed sources of quotes blaming one person or another. That happened frequently during the season, and that's why 1990 was really a forgettable season.

Early Retirement – When I left the Browns, I tried to find a coaching job in the NFL or a Division I college football team. I made hundreds of calls, but I couldn't even get one interview. I can remember asking Tim Rooney to call Tampa Bay for me because he knew the general manager. Tim had been in the Steelers scouting department when I coached there, and later with the Detroit Lions and New York Giants. Tim told me that the Tampa guy said, "Oh I remember him. He's the guy who marches to his own drummer." Tim said he told him, "Yeah that's right, and the players who follow him win!" I guess what players say doesn't really count with the brass unless it is negative. Evidently, Bad Rad had worn out his welcome in the NFL as well as the college campuses.

I had a year remaining on my Browns contract, so I didn't panic. But I didn't find a job in 1991 or 1992, and so at 57 years old I took my early NFL retirement in 1992 in an annuity form. The annuity was only about $30,000 a year but it was enough to pay the mortgage. My wife went to work for American Greeting Card Company, and we remained in our new house in Strongsville, Ohio. Our living room had a 20-foot ceiling. In between waiting for answers to my job hunting phone calls, I hit plastic golf balls against the 20-foot high living room wall with a Ben Hogan chipper club. I drove my wife nuts hitting the wall with those plastic golf balls. I even developed and patented a golf invention that I called the "swing sling" but that's another story. I ran in the woods behind our house for two hours almost every day with, my daughter Lori's black Lab dog, Yeager. That's basically describes what I did for 2½ years, and, believe me, it wasn't pleasant knowing I was unemployed and an untouchable, almost like I had leprosy.

Tim Rooney

Then one day, a former New York Jets coaching associate, Bobby Hammond, called me and told me that our former head coach, Joe Walton wanted me to call him. I didn't know it but my early retirement was about to end.

CHAPTER NINETEEN –
Small College Football

Married For Better Or Worse – Bobby Hammond called me three times over the course of a few days in July of 1993 to tell me that Walton wanted me to call him. I hadn't talked to Joe since he had bounced me from his office at the New York Jets 4½ years earlier. Knowing Joe, I knew he would never call me, so after Bobby's third call, I finally decided to call Joe. Joe told me he was glad that I called. He said he had taken a head coaching job to start a new football program at a small college in Pittsburgh named Robert Morris. He wanted me to be his defensive coordinator. I thanked him for the offer but told him I wasn't interested. I wished him good luck and hung up. Nancy asked, "Who was on the phone?" I said, "Joe Walton. He's taken a head coaching job at a small college in Pittsburgh and he wanted me to coach with him." My wife said, "What did you tell him?" I said that I told him that I wasn't interested in coaching small college football, plus the salary's not much. BAD RAD MOMENT! Nancy said, "Call him back. Call Joe Walton back and take that job." I said, "I told you the money stinks, plus I don't want to coach small college football." She yelled back, "Let me tell you something. I married you for better or worse, but not to hang around the house for two years. You're driving me crazy. Call Joe Walton back." So I did! And that's one of the reasons I've been married for more than 53 years. Sometimes I do listen to her.

So, off I went to Robert Morris. In a couple of years I would even be back in the NFL. And by the time I finally retired officially from coaching, Pittsburgh would be the center of my universe, just as it had been when I was growing up, and even Penn State would again be part of my orbit.

Right from the start I had reservations about the Robert Morris situation. Even before I accepted Joe Walton's offer I had told him on the telephone I was still skeptical about coaching at the school. But since I had promised Nancy I would talk to him, I told him I would visit the next day to check out the job and the college. Joe started to give me directions, but I interrupted him and said, "Joe, I know where Robert Morris is. It's right next to the county jail in downtown Pittsburgh." Joe said, "No, it's by the airport." I said, "Joe, I'm a Pittsburgher. Robert Morris College is by the jail." Finally, Joe convinced me that the Robert Morris building by the jail is only a small part of the college. I had flown out of the Greater Pittsburgh Airport over 50 times and never knew that Robert Morris College's main campus was close by.

Later I learned a little about Robert Morris and why it was starting a football team. The school started out in 1921 as the Pittsburgh School of Accountancy and became a junior college in 1962 when it began awarding two-year degrees. It was still located in a building virtually in the heart of downtown Pittsburgh. But that same year the school purchased 230 acres of farmland near the Greater Pittsburgh Airport in an area called Moon Township that had been owned by the famous Kaufmann's Department store family, which was the once the best department store in Pittsburgh. Seven years later, with the new campus fully operational, the school was officially named Robert Morris College with approval to grant bachelor degrees. Enrollment gradually increased, but a few years before Joe called me enrollment had trailed off and in 1992 was under 5,000 students.

So, the day after talking to Joe on the phone, I drove two hours from the Cleveland area where I lived to the Robert Morris campus, which is about 18 miles west of downtown Pittsburgh. The campus looked okay, like a typical small college campus. But I was shocked by what I found in the Sewall Center basketball arena where Joe said his office was. I walked across the basketball floor to a windowless hallway on the other side and on the right-hand side of that windowless hallway I found some windowless offices. The area resembled a dungeon—and still does. I spotted Joe Walton sitting at a desk in the first office to the right. We greeted each other, and then I asked, "Is this your office?" Joe said it was. I said, "I'm not living underground. I'm out of here," and walked quickly out of his office, down the hallway and started across the arena floor.

Joe caught up with me and said, "The office is only temporary. The president has promised me that we can search the entire campus and decide where we want our offices." Joe convinced me to stay and listen to him describe the football program he was hired to implement.

Joe said Robert Morris President Ed Nicholson made the decision to start a football team in order to help reverse the declining enrollment trend. When the school had a press conference a week earlier to announce the hiring of Joe, they did not even have a football on campus. A member of the athletic department had to go buy a football so that the press could take Joe's picture with a football. Everything concerning the football team had to be started from scratch. There were no locker rooms, practice fields, offices, or stadium in existence—or planned—for football. Joe said he had no idea who we would play because there was no game schedule. We would have to figure all that out as well as recruit players, coaches, equipment managers and trainers. One thing was for certain. For the first time since I began coaching at Penn State in the 1950s we had only one way to go and that was up.

Filling 550 Beds – Raising money was a priority, Joe told me. The team's main asset currently was a WATS line for the telephone on campus. We could make as many phone calls as we wanted anywhere in the United States, as long as we called from campus. After Joe and I visited for a while, the athletic publicity director, Marty Galosi, came by and took me for a brief tour of the campus. I can still remember standing on top of one of the high hills on campus with Marty saying, "See those dormitories down there. There are 550 empty beds in those dorms. That's why we're starting a football program. We've got to fill those beds." After I finished with Marty's tour, I asked Joe about the salary for the coaching job. He said the budget that Robert Morris had set up for the football program had designated $14,000 for a defensive coordinator. The school had also budgeted $25,000 for recruiting expenses. He said that the president had told him that he could take $16,000 from the recruiting budget to pay me a total of $30,000 a year. "Ouch," that hurt. My last salary with the Cleveland Browns was $165,000 a year. Finally I told Joe that under this set up, I didn't see how we could win a game. Joe disagreed. Buttering me up, he said, "You're wrong Rad. You'll come up with some crazy blitzes that the other team can't pick up and we'll win a few games the first year." I called Nancy and explained the Robert Morris situation. She said, "Take the job"—she had always liked Joe and Ginger Walton—and I did, which is another reason why I've been married 53 years. One year later, all 550 empty beds that Marty Galosi had mentioned were filled.

Great Deal On A Room – So, on August 1, 1993 I became the assistant head coach-defensive coordinator for Robert Morris College, and it would be more than a year before we would play our first game. Because of Nancy's job with the American Greetings Card Company, we couldn't move back to Pittsburgh. So, at 57 years old, I now had one of those modern-day "commuting marriages." I would commute from my house in Strongsville, Ohio, Monday morning and drive back home on Friday evenings—a one-way, two-hour, 128-mile drive.

I quickly needed a room to stay in near campus Monday through Thursday nights. I couldn't afford a motel every night and the school didn't provide a room, although they had 550 empty beds at the time. I called my coaching friend Joe Moore, who was now at Notre Dame. Joe put me in touch with a Pitt booster, Tom Nardozzi, and Tom sent me to a widowed Irishman named Tom Conway whose son was Moon High School's punter. The Irishman said I could stay in a room in his house and I asked him how much he wanted for rent. He said, "Whatever you can pay." I said, "$150 a month." He said, "Okay." What a great deal on a room. I stayed there until he sold the house and moved to Florida six months later.

But my "commuting marriage" was just beginning. I would do it for five years. And once we started playing games on Saturday's there would be times I would make the roundtrip within 36 hours. After I left the Irishman's house, I moved into a room for the next three years in my cousin Bob Garshak's house in West Mifflin that was about 30 miles and 45 minutes away from campus. The rent was another great deal—nothing. Then, I moved in with a friend, Lew Wheeler, who I had gone to graduate school with. We were both in Penn State's first MBA class which graduated in 1964. Lew was separated from his wife and living alone in this big house in Thornburg with a 30-foot living room ceiling whose 30-foot back wall was all window glass. The rent in this millionaire's house was also a great deal—nothing. I stayed for five years. If not for these great deals on a room, I would not have been able to afford to coach at Robert Morris. The deals saved me a lot of money and made it possible to commute from the Cleveland area all that time.

Now that I was at Robert Morris and thinking about the job of building a team from scratch, I became more enthused. I had never done anything like this before and neither had Joe. And here we were, two old pro coaches about to deal with youngsters who could have been our grandchildren.

Turning A Night Job Into A Day Job – After I had found a room to stay at near the campus Monday through Thursday nights, I walked into Joe Walton's office one morning and said, "Well, Joe, how do you like your night job?" Joe asked me what I was talking about. I said, "I'm talking about your night job. When you took this job, you took a night job. How do you like it?" He still didn't get what I was talking about, so I proceeded to explain: "The No. 1 priority of this football program is to recruit students who are football players. The more, the better. We don't have much money to recruit but we have a WATS telephone system. We can call students or players wherever and whenever, no limits. But they are in school until 3:00 or 3:30 [p.m.] every weekday. They don't get home until 4 o'clock and you can't call them after 10:00 p.m., and with basketball games many aren't home on Tuesday and Friday nights. Now, somebody has to make those calls to these high school prospects. Right now, there's only two people hired to make those calls from 4:00 to 10:00 p.m. every night. That's you and me."

Joe had never coached college football, whereas I had previously coached at three different colleges for a total of 17 years. I was bugging him about the night job because I was trying to make a point. I continued: "Do you want to make those phone calls every night until 10:00 p.m.?" Joe indicated he wasn't wild about making calls every night from 4:00 to 10:00 p.m. I said, "Well, I don't want to make them either. So, here's what I think we should do. We're allowed to hire seven assistant coaches (five part-time and two graduate assistants). Hire every one for phone calls. A part-time coach is going to earn $2,500 a year. Tell him he has to make phone calls at least one night a week from 4:00 to 10:00 p.m. for 25 weeks. That means we're paying him $100 a night for six hours of phone calls, or almost $17 an hour. (A graduate assistant, at that time, got a scholarship grant worth $9,000 a year.) Tell him he has to make phone calls at least three nights a week from 4:00 to 10:00 p.m. for 25 weeks. That means we're paying him $120 a night for six hours of phone calls, or $20 an hour. Tell both the part-time coaches and the graduate assistant coaches that they should pay us for teaching them how to coach. But we'll let that go. They will simply coach for nothing."

Joe agreed with my proposition and we hired every coach based on phone calls. We had turned a night job into a day job for both of us. After we hired all the coaches, the Robert Morris football office looked like a version of AT&T in the evenings with all the coaches making phone calls. Joe got to go home at 5:00, and I supervised and made some calls at night since I had a room nearby Monday through Thursday nights.

First Young Coach Hired – The first coach that Joe Walton hired after me in the fall of 1993 was a young graduate student already enrolled in Robert Morris. His name was Dave Harper. Dave did not play college football but he had been a scholarship basketball player at Wright State University outside of Dayton, Ohio. He did play quarterback in high school. Robert Morris' athletic director, Bob McBee, who had Dave in class, recommended him to us as a student who was volunteering his services for the football department for free. At first, both Joe and

I were leery because we thought he might be a spy for the athletics director. We knew politics was politics no matter what level we were coaching.

After a few weeks of Dave being around the football office, Joe and I both realized that Dave was no spy and had real talent for recruiting. Coach Walton offered him a two-year graduate assistant scholarship—we had two of them to give out—worth about $9,000 a year or $18,000 over two years. Dave immediately accepted the offer and the Robert Morris administration immediately rejected it. Since Dave was already a paid, enrolled student, the school would lose his tuition and fee money ($18,000 over two years). So we hired Dave as a part-time coach for $2,500 a year. The administration cost Dave $13,000 ($18,000 minus $5,000) over a two year period. But it allowed the football department graduate assistant scholarship to be given to someone else. Dave Harper coached our secondary for us and immediately became our best recruiter. When he got his Master's degree two years later, we hired Dave as the third full time member of the Robert Morris football staff. Dave recruited most of the starters on the Robert Morris football team the five years that he coached for us, plus at least one-half of the starters that won the national championship for us in the two years after Dave had left. The first young coach hired was probably the best coach hired. He was certainly the best young recruiter that I've ever been around.

As of 2010 Dave Harper was the Senior Associate Athletic Director/Director of External Relations at the University of Dayton, recruiting money instead of players. I wonder if that's as much fun. Probably pays better.

Prolific Phone Call – We didn't realize it at the time but Dave made one momentous phone call that led to the ultimate super success of our first season in the fall of 1994. Dave had sent out post cards to high school coaches in the Cincinnati, Ohio, area requesting names of prospective football players. A coach sent in a post card with the name of his all-state high school quarterback, Dante Payne. Dave Harper telephoned Dante's high school coach at the Cincinnati Academy of Physical Education, which was known as "CAPE." The coach said Dante was a very good player. The coach also mentioned a former player, Piante Crew, a defensive safety who was at Kemper Military Junior College, in Booneville, MO, near Columbia, who might be interested.

Dave contacted Piante and had Piante and Dante visit the Robert Morris campus together. While visiting, Piante told Dave that he had a buddy fullback at Kemper Military named Tim Hall who might be interested. Dave then asked Tim Hall to make a 19-hour bus ride to visit the campus and Tim did. Tim Hall liked Robert Morris and said he had a 6-foot-5 wide receiver friend, Robert Frazier, who also might be interested. Robert Frazier, whose home was in Florida, said he didn't have to visit Robert Morris. If it was good enough for Tim Hall, it was good enough for him.

Well, Dante Payne, the first player contacted, started at left corner for us and was possibly the best player on defense. Piante Crew, the second player contacted, was our starting strong safety and, arguably, the second best player on our defense. Tim Hall, the third player contacted, started at fullback, and eventually set two rushing records in what is now known as the NCAA Championship Subdivision (the old 1AA division) that were still the records in 2011. In our first season, he broke the record for yards per carry with 8.7 yards. In his two years, Tim also sent the division career record with an average of 7.4 yards per carry.

Robert Frazier, the 6-foot-5 receiver and the fourth player contacted, caught six touchdown passes in our first five games, and was by far our best receiver. A single phone call to a high school coach in Cincinnati had produced, arguably, the four best players on our team in its initial winning season. Without a doubt, that was the most prolific phone call in Robert Morris' 15-year football history.

John Jay—An Easy Decision – One of the first priorities for Joe Walton and me after I was hired was to look around the Robert Morris campus and decide where we wanted the football offices, locker room and practice field. We eventually decided to locate in and by the John Jay Building on the opposite end of the campus from the Sewall Center Basketball Arena. Inside the John Jay Building was an Olympic size swimming pool which we were told was rarely used. The pool could be filled in and used as a locker room. Also, inside the building was a basketball court which was the main gym when Robert Morris was a junior college, but was currently only used for intramurals. The home and visitors basketball locker rooms were being used as storage rooms. We could clear these out and convert them to two football offices for Joe and me. Outside the building and a short walk up a hill was a softball field and next to that an intramural field. We could use the intramural field as a practice field. Last, but not least, the John Jay location was about as far away as you could get from the athletics directors office. That made locating in the John Jay Building an easy decision.

Fired The Architect – While Coach Walton and I were contemplating how to proceed in making plans for the locker room and offices in the John Jay Building in the fall of 1993, we were told about a liquor store in Marietta, Ohio, that was converted into a very nice football locker room for the Marietta College football team. Joe and I and the architect that Robert Morris had hired to design our locker room and football offices made a special trip to see this unique locker room. We told the architect what we liked and didn't like about the Marietta locker room. We emphasized we wanted big open lockers and open space as much as possible. We did not want a cramped tight locker room like most high schools and junior high schools have.

A week after our trip, I'm walking to my car when the architect pulls up in his car and said, "Rad, I've got the locker room plans done. They look great. I've even got offices in there for you and Joe. I'm going to show the plans to Joe over the weekend." On Monday, I walked into Joe's office and said, "Hey Joe, I saw the architect Friday. He said he's got the locker room plans done and they looked great." Joe said, "They're awful. I saw them over the week end. The lockers are all bunched together tight in a small space, and he put two big rooms in the center of the space for offices for you and me. We didn't want offices there. We took him to Marietta with us and he didn't listen." I agreed, "He just didn't listen." So we fired him.

Completing The First Football Staff – Shortly after we hired Dave Harper as our first part-time coach, we hired four other part-time coaches: Receivers—Darnell Richardson; Quarterbacks—Tiger Walton, Jr.; Defensive Line—Jim Suley; and Offensive Line—Shelton Colbert. Two graduate assistant coaches were hired in the spring of 1994: Offensive Backs—Jason Lener; and Linebackers-Special Teams—Chris Brann. I remember a couple of incidents during this process of hiring our first staff. Graduate assistant Jason Lener was originally hired as the secondary coach. After Jason worked around the football office for two days, Walton noticed how smart he was. Joe then told me that he was going to have Jason coach the offensive backs instead of the secondary. Because Joe stole Jason from me, I now had to convince Dave Harper to be the secondary coach instead of the special teams coach and Chris Brann to be the special teams coach.

Our Mistake Becomes A Young Coach's Lucky Break – For the offensive line coaching position, the first person I called was "Tunch" Ilkin, who had just retired from the Steelers after a 13-year NFL career. I said, "Tunch, I'm offering you the Robert Morris offensive line coaching position. I can't offer you a salary but you can get your Master's degree in two years for free." Tunch laughed and said, thanks but no thanks. He now denies it, but I think he was still laughing when I hung up the phone. Then, Joe and I interviewed a young man just out of college who had been an offensive lineman for the University of Tulsa. His name was Lou Spanos. We decided not to hire Lou. So, Lou went out and interviewed with the Pittsburgh Steelers and got hired as the Steelers quality control coach for the defense. Lou was with the Steelers for 16 years and went to three Super Bowls, two of which the Steelers won. In 2010 he became the linebacker coach for the Washington Redskins and then the defensive coordinator for the UCLA Bruins in 2012. I've never said that we never made any mistakes at Robert Morris, but this mistake turned out to be a big break for Lou Spanos.

Corky Came Through In The Clutch – When Joe Walton and I decided that we definitely wanted the swimming pool in the John Jay Building to be converted into a football locker room, we told the administration that Corky Cost Construction Co. should be considered for the contract to do the job. I had known Corky from 40 years earlier when we had both played on the same team in a high school all-star game in August of 1953. Joe Walton and Corky had been football teammates at Pitt for four years (1953-57), and they were good friends. More importantly, Corky was a member of the Robert Morris Board of Trustees. A few days later, Joe and I moved into our new offices in the basketball gym in the John Jay Building where the original home and visitors basketball locker rooms were converted into our two offices.

After we were settled, we decided to take another look at the swimming pool in John Jay to see if we could come up with any more locker room ideas. When we walked into the swimming pool area, "lo and behold," Corky Cost was there with the Robert Morris President Edward Nicholson and other administrators talking about the locker room. Joe and I had no idea Corky was coming. After exchanging greetings, Joe, I and the president talked with Corky about the locker room project for the next hour or two. When Corky realized exactly what we wanted done and the amount of money the school had allocated for the project, he said we were about $200,000 short of what it would take to do the locker room the way it should be done. Finally, after some more conversation, Corky said, "Joe, I'll build you a locker room exactly as you want it. Whatever it costs over the amount the school has set aside, I'll cover. That will be my gift to you." Corky came through in the clutch! And that's how we got our new locker room built.

Our locker room and attached equipment room had a 30-foot ceiling with two giant skylights in each room—the original Olympic size swimming pool had four skylights—which made our new football locker room really unique. We found out that Corky's gift came to about $175,000. Joe and I often wondered what would have happened if we hadn't accidentally bumped into Corky and the president that day.

Joe Walton Celebrity Golf Tournament – As I mentioned earlier, raising money to help build and fund the football program was a big priority for us. Joe and I knew a lot of celebrities, so we decided that our best bet to raise money was to have a celebrity golf tournament, which we named the Joe Walton Celebrity Golf Tournament. In early January of 1994, we met with a college administrator to plan the golf tournament. We decided I would be in charge of recruiting the celebrities and Joe, with help from the college's public relations department, would be in charge of getting the sponsors. Then the administrator told us that the money earned from the golf tournament would have to go into a central college fund and be used to benefit different parts of the college as well as football. Upon hearing this, Joe and I both stood up and said, "We're out of here. We're not going to raise money for some other team or another part of the college when we desperately need money for football. If the other sports or other parts of the college need money, let them raise their own money." After we expressed our feelings and we were opening the door to leave, the administrator said to wait, that he had to call the president. Joe and I sat back down while he called and talked to President Nicholson. When he hung up the phone, he said, "The president said that the money raised by the Joe Walton Celebrity Golf Tournament will go in a separate fund to be used only by the football program. Joe and I stayed and helped the administrator finish the plans for the golf tournament. We felt like we had just won a big game. The golf tournament has averaged a net profit of over $50,000 per year for a total of over $1,000,000 for the past 19 years. Not bad for 19 days of work.

Equipment Man Quits – On the very hot day before our first practice in August, 1994, the first ever Robert Morris football players were issued their practice equipment in our new locker and equipment rooms. Our equipment man Al Giralico, who was in his 50s, was an equipment man for a number of years for an Arena League pro football team. He was recommended to us by Vito "Babe" Parilli, a former NFL quarterback and coach, who was good friends with Coach Walton and me.

At about 2:00 p.m., the equipment man came into Coach Walton's office and told Joe and me that he was quitting. He was all upset, sweating and crying that he can't take it. He said the job was too much for him, that he never realized the job was like this, and so on. He only had to equip about 30 players on the Arena team. We had 167 players to equip. He said he was going to die from exhaustion and heat stroke. Coach Walton told him to sit down, calm down and listen. Joe said, "Forget about quitting. No way are we going to let you quit. Quitting is not an option. You asked for this job and our good friend "Babe" Parilli recommended you. You are going to stay for the entire season."

Then both Joe and I told him what his problem was. He had to get a chair and an electric fan, sit down in the chair with the fan blowing on him—air conditioning had not yet been put in the locker room and equipment rooms—and delegate all the work to the four or five student managers that we had signed up. We told him to learn to delegate and supervise. He did as he was told and stayed for the season.

Student equipment manager Paul Gallagher did the equipment work so effortlessly that, on Joe Walton's recommendation, the president hired Paul as the college's first full time equipment man for all sports while at the same time attending classes. Four years later, Paul became an equipment man for the NFL Pittsburgh Steelers. He is currently working for a sporting goods company near Pittsburgh.

First Football Meeting – The first football meeting ever in Robert Morris' history took place in the auditorium in the library building the day before the first practice in August, 1994. At about 7:45 p.m., I was sitting on a wall in front of the library, along with a bunch of the players, waiting for the campus police to open the locked door to the building. While I am sitting there, a player nearby said to another player, "You won't believe what I saw in the locker room today. When we were trying on our equipment, I saw a player with four asses." He made a curving motion with his right hand and continued talking. "His butt curved here, then curved here, curved here a third time and then curved here. In fact, that's him sitting over there." He pointed to a young man sitting nearby who, we found out later, weighed almost 500 pounds. On that first Robert Morris team, we had eight or nine players who tried out who weighed over 350 pounds. One of them, who weighed 385 pounds, was our starting left tackle the entire year. When we timed our players in the 40-yard dash, I believe these overweight players set some NCAA records for slowness.

First Injury In History – Joe and I started out that first meeting by talking to the entire Robert Morris football team for one half hour. Then, Joe excused the defensive players and coaches to meet in another nearby building. When I got to the classroom and all the players had not yet arrived, I asked secondary coach Dave Harper if he knew where the restroom was. Dave told me to go straight down the hall to the end, turn right, go through two swinging double doors and then go down the steps to the basement floor to the restroom close by.

Well, I went down the hall, turned right, pushed through the double doors, walked to the steps and just as I reached the steps the lights went out and it became pitch black. I stepped into air and tumbled down the steps in pitch black darkness. At the bottom of the steps, I moaned and rolled over on the landing and tumbled down a second set of steps. I lay there, afraid to move and in the total darkness. As I'm moaning and groaning, I tried to feel if I could move different parts of my body. I'm really hurting but I seemed to be able to move everything. I crawled back up the steps, slowly feeling my way in the pitch blackness. When I pushed through the double doors, I saw a man standing in the hallway. He said, "Oh, I thought I heard something. That must have been you. After my class was over, I thought everyone had left the building, so I hit the main switch and turned off the lights."

The professor apologized for turning out the lights and I mumbled, "I almost broke my neck." When I got back to my defensive meeting in the classroom, I told the players what had happened to me. I was wearing a short sleeved shirt and Bermuda shorts, and after they finished laughing, I pointed to the bruises and scrapes on my arms and legs. Then I said, "I want you all to be witnesses to the first football injury in Robert Morris history."

No Football Scholarships – Robert Morris had been playing intercollegiate basketball since moving to the Moon Township campus and was classified as a NCAA Division 1-AA scholarship institution. But the football team was not going to give scholarships, so we were designated as a NCAA Division 1-AA non-scholarship team, which was the equivalent of a Division III non-scholarship team. So, Joe wanted to schedule a combination of 1-AA non-scholarship and Division III teams. President Nicholson had no intention back then of having a scholarship football team. As I mentioned above, his main purpose was to attract more students to the school and he believed a football team would help. In fact, when the president had introduced Joe and me to the faculty back at a Christmas luncheon in December of 1993 he said, "These are our two new admissions officers."

Now, some people might think it was a come down for me to be coaching kids rather than seasoned pros or mature college guys. Frankly, after all the experience I had, this was a new challenge. In coaching, the fundamentals and Xs and Os are basically the same. The prime difference is the widespread difference in player talent—size, speed, coordination, etc. But I can honestly say most of the time the youngsters were as receptive to coaching as the pros and sometimes more so because they weren't already hardened in their beliefs.

He Looked Pretty Good – During the preseason of 1994, Joe and I put the team through two scrimmages under game-type conditions. We were practicing a defense with multiple fronts, multiple coverages and plenty of blitzes, but during the scrimmages Joe would only allow the defense to play one front and one coverage—a base 4-3 front and a base 3-deep zone coverage. The second game type scrimmage took place on the Saturday a week before our first game against Waynesburg College. In both scrimmages, the defense crushed the offense. We had put most of the better athletes on defense and the offense couldn't block them.

Near the end of the second scrimmage, Joe told young backfield coach Jason Lenner to put in the new junior college fullback from Kansas City, who had just arrived three days before after an 18-hour bus ride. We didn't even remember the fullback's name. Jason said, "Coach Walton, he only practiced twice. He doesn't know any of the plays." Joe said, "Just tell him to run a belly right or a belly left and hand him the ball." The quarterback handed the ball to the fullback on a belly right and he ran for about 12 yards, running over three or four players. Next, he ran a belly left for 10 yards, running over four or five players. Another belly right and he ran for about 11 yards, again running over a number of players. After the third run, Coach Walton blew the whistle and said, "Scrimmage over."

As we were walking away from the field, Joe said, "Rad, we were awful on offense. We can't block anybody. We're going to get beat 100-0." I said, "Joe, I disagree with you. We're going to get beat 200-0. But it looks like we found ourselves a fullback on those last three scrimmage plays." Joe said," Yeah, he looked pretty good, didn't he?" We still couldn't remember his name. And that was the first time we saw Tim Hall run the way he would in setting those all-time NCAA Championship Division (old 1AA) rushing records I mentioned above.

First Game Plan Meeting – Six days before our opening game against Waynesburg Joe Walton and I were walking off the practice field after Monday's two-hour practice. Joe said, "Rad, we got that practice under our belt. Now, we can shower, have dinner, and then have a staff game plan meeting for Waynesburg." After we had showered and were getting dressed, Joe said, "Rad, where are all the coaches?" I said, "Joe, those three part-time coaches who don't live near campus have families that they went home to. The four other coaches are graduate students who have Monday class from 6:00 to 9:00 p.m." Joe said, "Where's my son Tiger?" I said, "Tiger's one of the graduate students that has class from 6:00 to 9:00 p.m. Right now, all four are in class." Joe said, "How are we going to have a game plan meeting?" I said, "Joe, I'm staying close by, so I'm going to eat dinner, then come back to the office and do the defensive game plan myself. You live 35 miles from here. You should go home, eat dinner and do your offensive game plan for Waynesburg yourself. Then, both of us will come into the office tomorrow and tell these young coaches what we're going to do against Waynesburg," And that's what we did. Joe never scheduled an evening meeting during the season for the next 15 years.

Jaywalking On The Los Angeles Freeway – During the second week of preseason practice, freshman quarterback Jake Newman, who had some sort of ailment or injury, finally dressed for practice. After two practices it became obvious that he had the best arm and would probably be the starting quarterback. Another freshman quarterback was Nate List, an option quarterback. Coach Walton and I thought he was too good of an athlete to play backup quarterback, so we moved Nate to defensive safety. After one day at safety—and he looked pretty good there—I decided that he might be a middle linebacker. He was just 6-foot-3,

180-pounds and our young coaches thought he would get killed trying to play middle linebacker. At the time, our middle linebacker was 6-foot, 240 pounds but he couldn't move quickly enough for me.

Nate was wondering if he could play middle linebacker. Kiddingly, I told him, "Nate, playing middle linebacker will be just like jaywalking on a Los Angeles Freeway."

Near the end of the first quarter of our Waynesburg game, when Nate came out

Dan and Nate List

of the game, I said, "Nate how is it going out there." Nate replied, "Rad, they're coming at me from every direction. It's just like being on a Los Angeles freeway."

Goal-Line Stand In First Game – I have a number of vivid memories of Robert Morris' first football game in the college's history versus Waynesburg College at their field on September 3, 1994. Waynesburg was about one hour away and on the morning of the game we went down there on two buses, one for the defense and another for the offense. During the bus ride, I held a defensive meeting going over assignments for the last time. I remember using a portable white grease board and a black marker to illustrate my diagrams. I also remember having no idea what would happen after the opening kickoff.

Surprisingly, at the end of the first quarter we were leading 14-0. Our 6-foot-5 wide receiver, Robert Frazier, had made a couple of sensational catches for 9- and 36-yard touchdown passes from quarterback Jake Newman.

Then halfway through the third quarter with Robert Morris still ahead, 14-7, Waynesburg had the ball on its own 27-yard line with third-and-21 to go. I called a 3-5-3 zone prevent defense, a very safe defense in this situation, or so I thought. The Waynesburg quarterback dropped back to pass. Their wide receiver on our right faked a quick four-yard out pattern and ran a streak down the sideline. Our right corner, whose assignment was the deep one-third zone on our right side, bit on the four-yard fake and was easily beaten deep by the Waynesburg wide receiver, who caught the pass and ran for a 73-yard touchdown. I couldn't believe it. Third and 21 and our corner who had the deep one-third zone bit on a four-yard out fake. How dumb could he be? They missed the extra point and that made the score 14-13 in our favor.

About a minute after the kickoff, our running back, Tim Hall, caught a short pass on a play we called "the lag draw trap pass" and ran for a 60-yard touchdown. The extra point gave us a 21-13 lead. Then about a minute into the fourth quarter, John

Mihalik, kicked a 40-yard field goal to make the score 24-13. Waynesburg scored again five minutes later on a 13-yard run by their star running back Fred Martinez to narrow the score to 24-19 but their run for two extra points failed.

When Waynesburg got the ball again, they moved down to a first-and-goal at our 6-yard line with 5:55 left in the game. Three straight runs got them about two yards. On fourth-and-4, they threw a quick slant to the wide receiver on our right and our right corner threw a body block on the wide receiver. The pass was incomplete but pass interference was called. It was now first down at our 1-yard line and we had to do it again. Three runs lost a total of three yards. They now had fourth-and-4 to go. They called time out. Defensive line coach Jim Suley, who signaled in the defenses that I call, told me to go out on the field and talk to the defense. I said, "I'm not allowed to go onto the field." He said, "Yes, you can. They've changed the rules." So I ran out on the field and had a meeting with my defensive players while the trainers were giving them little cups of water.

I told them Waynesburg was definitely going to pass. We could try to play a coverage defense or we could blitz and go after the quarterback. I asked what they'd like to do. Of course, they all said they wanted to go after the quarterback. I said, "Okay, I'm going to call the same blitz that I just called on the last play—'goal line lightning blast zero peel.' But this time I want the middle linebacker, Nate List, and the weak safety, Brian Dunn, to blitz the B gaps (guard-tackle) like you are supposed to do. The last play you both went in the A gaps (center-guard) where the defensive tackles go. Blitz the B gaps and get your hands up quick. You'll probably get in scot free. And, corners, watch the slant." (Everybody from our side was yelling, "Watch the slant.") That's what they had run when they got the pass interference call four plays earlier. Then I left the field.

Dan and Joe Walton

When the ball was snapped, both blitzers rushed the B gap. The middle linebacker and a defensive tackle came free. As he was being hit, the quarterback threw the ball quickly to his right to the wide receiver on our left on a quick slant pattern. Our left corner, Dante Payne, stepped in front of the slanting receiver and tried to intercept the ball, which bounced off his chest and fell to the ground incomplete. We had stopped Waynesburg on a goal-line stand that lasted eight plays. An eight-play goal-line stand in our first game ever! After we took over on the 4-yard line with four minutes left in the game, we moved and controlled the ball the rest of the game. The final score was Robert Morris 24, Waynesburg 19.

However, it might have been a different outcome if the officials had been paying more attention. When I went out on the field to talk to the defensive players during the time out before the eighth play of the goal-line stand, I was on the field illegally. Jim Suley was wrong when he said they had changed the rules in college to allow a coach on the field during a timeout. They had changed the rules in high school to allow this but not in college or professional football. If the official would have noticed and penalized me for being on the field illegally, Waynesburg would have had the ball on the 2-yard line, or half the distance to the goal, with first-and-goal. I had made a mistake and gotten away with it. This was my lucky day.

One more thing about that goal-line stand. On the fourth play of the goal-line stand, on fourth-and-4, Waynesburg's quarterback threw a quick slant to his left on our right corner and got a pass interference call and first-and-goal on the 1-yard line. On the eighth play of the goal-line stand, they threw a quick slant on our left cornerback, trying to outsmart us. However, our left corner was three times the player the right corner was. (Besides the interference call, the right corner was beaten on the 72-yard fake out and up streak for a touchdown.) Waynesburg may have outsmarted itself by trying to outsmart us. They threw that last slant right at our best defensive player. This definitely was my lucky day.

Monday Night TV – The second game of Robert Morris' inaugural 1994 season was similar to the first game because a last minute Robert Morris goal-line stand also played an important part in our victory. The game ended when time ran out with Monmouth College on the Robert Morris 1-yard line with the score Robert Morris 26, Monmouth 19.

The third and fourth games of the season were wins against Central Connecticut, 24-17, and Gannon, 28-0. Besides being a defensive shutout, the Gannon game was highlighted by running back Tim Hall gaining 208 yards rushing. His 95-yard touchdown run in the third quarter was shown on TV at halftime of the NFL's *Monday Night Football* game. What a boost for our brand new football team. We now had a record of 4-0 and had two weeks to get ready for the biggest game of the year—the Duquesne game.

Open Date Decision – The first team that head coach Joe Walton scheduled to play in our first year was the local Duquesne University Dukes. Duquesne is located in downtown Pittsburgh and was our natural rival. The football team was coached by two former Penn State players and teammates on Penn State's 1982 national champions, head coach Greg Gattuso and defensive coordinator Dave Opar. Joe and I immediately made what turned out to be a very smart decision. We didn't know if we would win a game that first year but we at least wanted to look as good as possible when we played Duquesne. We decided to have an open date the week before we played Duquesne so that we would have two weeks to prepare for the game instead of the normal one week. The extra week would give us a chance to put in new trick plays or new blitzes that they wouldn't have seen before. After we beat Gannon, 28-0, for our fourth straight win, that's exactly what we did. We used the extra week to put in a number of new wrinkles for Duquesne.

After the first week's practice, I went to New York City to attend my daughter Lisa's wedding to, coincidentally, a Duquesne University graduate, Peter Holsberg. She had specifically scheduled on the open date weekend because that was the only time I had free during the football season. Duquesne won its game on the open date weekend. So, both Robert Morris and Duquesne were undefeated going into their first cross-town rival game. Student interest on the Robert Morris campus was very high. The manager of the Robert Morris student book store, which sold Robert Morris labeled clothing and gear, told me he had sold at least 10 times the college labeled stuff the previous week than any other week in the school's existence.

Moon High School Stadium, where we played our home games, was packed with 8,016 fans. We dominated Duquesne. Besides moving the ball well and scoring on offense, we even scored a safety on defense. Our weak safety Brian Dunn had three interceptions in the game. The last time Duquesne had the ball in our territory, on about the 20-yard line, I called four straight blitzes and we sacked the quarterback four straight times for a total loss on that series of about 30 yards. We won, 28-6. Our open date decision had worked to perfection.

Coach Walton and I really looked at the Duquesne game as two old coaches from Pitt and Penn State versus two young coaches from Penn State. This time the old coaches won.

Flunking Football – Our undefeated streak ended in our sixth game against Wagner College. Our running back Tim Hall had another good game, but our defense was crushed by the Wagner running attack. Wagner narrowed the offensive line splits down to where my defensive stunts, loops, slants and blitzes had a tough time penetrating. Wagner rushed for 385 yards. I can remember talking to the starting defense on the sideline at the end of the first quarter when they were sitting on the bench. I yelled, "I know all of you came to Robert Morris for an education. Well, let me tell you something. You're all flunking football."

I was upset, but, physically, we just couldn't stand up to them. I watched a couple of our defensive linemen get driven back 15 yards off the line of scrimmage like they were on roller skates going backwards. The score was close for three quarters because we were moving the ball on offense. Wagner ended up winning, 38-21. The honeymoon was over. We had lost to a better team.

I haven't been able to verify this officially, but we were later told we were the first non-scholarship football team to win its first five games during its inaugural season, and Las Vegas, Nevada was the first scholarship college football team to win its first nine games in its inaugural season in 1974. Ironically, two of my coaching mates from the 1972 Colorado staff were coaches at Las Vegas—Steve Sidwell, the defensive coordinator, and Larry Kennan, the offensive coordinator.

Tim Hall

Winning Record – After the loss to Wagner, we tied St. Francis (of Loretto), 14-14, and beat Bethany, 38-14, and Mercyhurst (of Erie), 37-27, to end the first season of Robert Morris football with a surprising record of 7-1-1. The most notable factor in these games was the performance our running back Tim Hall versus Bethany and Mercyhurst. He rushed for 278 yards and 199 yards, respectively. For the season, he had a total of 1,336 yards in nine games and 154 attempts for an average of 8.7 yards a carry, which, as I have written, is the all-time NCAA record for the Championship Division. There is no doubt Tim was a major factor in our having a winning record in our inaugural season.

The sad thing is Tim was later killed in a bizarre drive-by shooting in his hometown of Kansas City. In 1996 he was drafted No. 6 by the Oakland Raiders and in 1997 he was the backup for the Raiders starting running back Napoleon Kaufman and punt returner Desmond Howard. The Raiders waived him just before the start of the 1998 season, and while he was back home in Kansas City, the Packers, Chiefs and Jaguars were talking to his agent, Ralph Cindrich, about signing him. Tim had grown up in a pretty tough neighborhood but had avoided getting involved with gangs and was making a good life for himself with his Robert Morris degree. So, he was staying at his mother's home waiting to hear from his agent when, on the last day of September, a lifelong friend asked him to go to the grocery store. At a stoplight two miles from his home, a half-truck pulled alongside the driver's side and someone fired a gun into the window. Tim's friend, the driver, ducked and the bullets hit Tim. He was killed almost instantly, the innocent victim of a gang shooting, just in the wrong place at the wrong time. I still can't help wondering what type of career Tim Hall would have had in the NFL and what his life would have been like after football. He was a good kid who deserved better.

Ortmayer Calls – I was quite pleased by what we did in our first Robert Morris football season. I had more fun than I thought I would and it felt great dealing with kids who were really listening and learning from what I was saying and teaching them. But in the latter part of January, 1995, I was in the Robert Morris football office when I received a phone call from a former University of Colorado coaching colleague—Steve Ortmayer. Steve had just accepted the job as the director of football operations at the Los Angeles Rams. Steve asked me if I would be interested in interviewing for the position of offensive line coach under new head football coach Rich Brooks. Bingo! After four years, I now had a chance to get back into the NFL. I said, "How soon do I have to be there?" Steve said, "There's a flight leaving the Pittsburgh airport in three hours." I said, "I'll be on it." (Robert Morris was only five miles from the airport.)

Now, here is another touch of irony that goes back to my Penn State heritage. Brooks had been hired after leading Oregon to the Pac 10 championship and playing Penn State in the 1995 Rose Bowl. The coach he succeeded with the Rams was my old friend from Pennsylvania, Chuck Knox, whom I had met when he was an assistant coach at Tyrone High School. Chuck had gone back to the Rams for a second run as head coach in 1992 but was fired after the '94 season.

After my two-day visit and interview with Coach Brooks, I was told that the final decision would be made within a week. Rather than go back East, I decided to visit and stay with my daughter Leslie while I was waiting. Leslie lived in Playa del Rey near the Los Angeles Airport. She worked on the Fred Dryer and Geoffrey Lewis TV show called *Lands End*, which was filming in Los Angeles. I can remember Mike Martz, who was already hired as the Rams receivers coach, driving me to Fred Dryer's office in LA where Leslie was. I asked Mike, who had sat in on my interview, what my chances were. Mike told me he thought I would get the job. Three days later, I received a call from the Rams. I got the job. After four years, I was back coaching again in the NFL.

What I didn't know is the Rams were about to move the franchise to St. Louis. Georgia Frontiere, the Rams owner, was working behind the scene to get league approval for the transfer to her hometown. In March, the league owners had overwhelmingly voted against her request but a month later the owners changed their minds in a 23-6-1 re-vote and we were on the way to St. Louis. I was very optimistic that this would eventually get me back to a Super Bowl, and even I was surprised when the Rams seemed headed that way early in the season.

Joe Walton wasn't surprised when I told him I was resigning Robert Morris to become the Rams' offensive line coach. I kidded him and told him I'd stay if he matched the Rams' offer—which was $95,000 more than the $30,000 I made with Robert Morris. Joe laughed and thanked me for helping to get the Robert Morris program started. So, Bad Rad's Nomadic Travelling Circus was on the road once more, setting up again in one of my favorite spots—Southern California. I guess it was fitting that my first stop back in California was stone's throw from Disneyland, near that bus stop and the worst day of my professional life.

Deke And I Are Roommates – Shortly after I was hired, I received a call from a former 1989 Cleveland Browns colleague, Deke Pollard. Deke congratulated me on my new job with the Rams. Deke was the defensive line coach at the time for Boston College. I told Deke the defensive line job at the Rams was still open. Deke made a couple of phone calls, got an interview and joined me about a week later as the Rams new defensive line coach. We then were roommates in a two bedroom apartment at the Marriott Residence Inn in Anaheim, a block away from the entrance to Disneyland. Since our wives were still back East, Deke and I hung around together for the next five months—until the Rams moved to St. Louis.

Bidding War Nets Sweeney $600,000 – The first order of business for the newly hired 1995 Los Angeles Rams coaching staff was the signing of free agents before the NFL draft in the early spring. Eleven-year NFL veteran offensive lineman Jim Sweeney, who I had coached in the late 1980s with the Jets, had recently been released by the Jets after 11 years. I wanted badly to sign Jim because I not only thought he could still play well, but he was versatile enough that he could play any of the offensive line positions—tackle, guard, or center. If he didn't become a starter—which I was sure he would be—he would be invaluable as a backup for any of those positions.

The Rams organization was pursuing some other opportunities at the time and put off making an offer until about a month later. When we finally made Jim an offer, the Seattle Seahawks got involved and offered Sweeney more. We got into a bidding war. Our last offer was about $800,000 a year. Sweeney signed with Seattle for just under a million dollars. When I next saw Jim, I asked him if the Rams had made him an offer of $400,000 right after he was released by the Jets, would he have taken it. Jim said he would have jumped at the offer and signed right away. I said, "If I didn't get involved you would have signed with Seattle for $400,000. By participating in a bidding war, I'm responsible for you making an extra $600,000. I think you owe me a cup of coffee plus a lunch or dinner. Jim said, "Okay." Seventeen years later, I'm still waiting but still hopeful of a free lunch.

Jim Sweeney started the entire 1995 season at center for Seattle. He then signed with the Pittsburgh Steelers in his hometown and was the primary offensive line backup for the next three years. He retired after the 1998 season, completing a 15-year NFL career.

Warren Sapp: Worth The Risk? – I've written before about the intrigue and closed door machinations that take place during the NFL draft, and the Rams selection of the No. 1 draft choice in 1995 was another prime example of that. Both the scouting department and the entire coaching staff were involved in the NFL draft in the Rams organization, similar to the Pittsburgh Steelers organization. On some teams, only the scouting department and the head coach were involved. The way the Rams were organized, there were a lot of people present in the draft room. The name on the top of the Rams draft list as the best player available in the 1995 draft was Warren Sapp, an All-American defensive lineman from the University of Miami in Florida. We were the sixth team to draft. Going into the first day of the draft, if Warren Sapp was still available, he would be our No. 1 draft pick.

However, before the draft began—either a couple of hours before or the day before—when everyone involved was in the draft room, Rams president John Shaw and director of football operations Steve Ortmayer informed us that Warren Sapp had flunked the NFL marijuana drug test that had been given at the scouting combine. This information made two inferences possible. One was that there now was a greater possibility that Warren Sapp would be available when our time to select our No. 1 pick became due. Second was the question, "If Warren Sapp was still available when our time to pick came due, and knowing that he had a positive marijuana test, do we still draft him No. 1? After explaining this situation, Ortmayer asked for a show of hands for who in the room still wanted to draft Sapp No. 1. Every hand in the room went up, including mine. Despite the Sapp positive marijuana test, every scout and coach thought that Sapp was so good a prospect that he was worth the risk.

Despite the unanimous vote for Sapp from the Rams scouts and coaches, the Rams did not select him No. 1. Evidently, the positive marijuana drug test made the Rams administration decide Warren Sapp was not worth the risk. Instead, the Rams picked Florida defensive end Kevin Carter.

Warren Sapp was drafted with the 13th pick of the draft by Tampa Bay as its No. 1 choice. The positive marijuana test cost him a lot of signing bonus money by being the 13th pick instead of the first or second. Both Kevin Carter and Warren Sapp eventually became immediate starters for their teams. Both eventually helped their teams win a Super Bowl. I've told this story to illustrate that the NFL draft is more than just an evaluation of player talent. Other factors often affect the decision on who to draft.

Preseason Camp In St. Louis – One of the big discussions concerning the Rams move to St. Louis was the location of the Rams preseason training camp. There was consensus of opinion among anyone who knew about the humidity and heat in the St. Louis area that St. Louis was not the place to have a preseason training camp. However, because of the perceived need to drum up Rams fan support in the St. Louis area, the decision was made to have training camp in the St. Louis area for the 1995 preseason only. So that year we trained at Maryville College in Chesterfield, near the Spirit of St. Louis Airport. In the following year, preseason camp would be held in a much more favorable location, about 150 miles north at Western Illinois University in Macomb, near Peoria.

Well, after almost a week of two-a-day camp, about 16 or 17 players were out with heat prostration. One player, tight end Troy Drayton—who was another Penn State alum—collapsed in the dining room during the evening meal and was rushed to the hospital. I already had left the dining hall, so I didn't see it happen. We were informed by the team doctor that if he had been alone in his room, he would have died. One of my offensive linemen who was in my meeting room that evening (I believe it was tackle Wayne Gandy) looked exhausted. I told him to forget about the meeting and go back to his room and lie down. He said the doctor had told him he had to stay around people so that if he passed out, help could be found quickly. If he collapsed alone in his room, he had been told he could die.

A player committee went to Head Coach Rich Brooks and beneficial changes were made in the training camp schedule. Everything turned out okay, but for a day or two, heat prostration and exhaustion was a real problem. Looking back with hindsight, the decision to have preseason football camp in St. Louis, even for one year only, was a mistake. I doubt if it made much difference in fan support. I guess the moral of this story is, "Don't mess with Mother Nature."

Where's Rad? – When the Rams 1995 preseason camp was over, I moved into a half of a twin house that my wife had found for me to rent in Soulard, the historical section of the city of St. Louis. Nancy then flew back East to our house in Strongsville, Ohio, and her job at the American Greeting Card Co. in Cleveland. I was only on a one-year contract and we decided to see how the season went before making a permanent move to St. Louis.

My first night alone, I slept in. When I didn't show up for the 8:00 a.m. staff meeting, all the coaches were asking each other, "Where's Rad?" No one in the Rams organization had my phone number or an address since I had just recently moved in and hadn't yet given the front office any information. Nobody knew where I lived. The Rams called Nancy in Strongsville and asked her for my phone number. She told them she didn't have my number because the phone company hadn't connected the phone yet. She gave them my new address in Soulard.

While sleeping in my bedroom on the second floor, I heard noises that woke me up. The noises were coming from the second floor porch just outside the bedroom windows. I got out of bed and went out on the second floor bedroom porch. I looked down and a bunch of young guys who worked in the Rams equipment room were throwing pebbles up on the porch and against the windows. They shouted that they had come to wake me up. I thanked them, told them that they could go, got dressed and drove to work. I got there a little before 10 a.m. and before my meeting with the offensive linemen. I really didn't miss anything but I had to put up with some of the coaches making fun by saying, "Where's Rad?" a number of times the next couple of days. I guess you might call that another Bad Rad moment.

Alternating Against Reggie White – I remember it was a very hot day when we played the Packers in that first game. The Packers had not lost a home league game in a couple of years. My immediate problem as the offensive line coach was figuring out how to handle All-Pro Packer defensive end Reggie White. I knew Reggie was too powerful for whoever I played at right offensive tackle, so I decided to alternate right tackles by series. I would play Darryl Ashmore at right tackle for three plays, then Clarence Jones for three plays, then Darryl again for three and so on. Reggie beat each of them a couple of times, but by the fourth quarter with the heat and a new fresh body on Reggie every three plays, Reggie was worn out and not a factor at all in the fourth quarter. We won a close game, 17-14, due to the heroics of Rams wide receiver Isaac Bruce. Isaac also was on special teams. At one point, he blocked a punt and on the very next play, he caught a deep 50-yard pass for a touchdown. I was proud of the part the alternating of the right tackles played on

Reggie White. Of course, the hot sun helped a bit, too. The two alternating tackles and the hot sun meant that Reggie actually was triple-teamed during the game. I guess that's what happens when a player is too good for his own good.

How Bad Rad Taught Reggie White "The Hump" – On December 29, 2004, Hall of Fame defensive lineman Reggie White passed away. News reports stated that Reggie was most famous for his pass rush technique that he called "The Hump." Former Steeler defensive lineman John "Banny" Banaszak was then coaching with me at Robert Morris, and I mentioned to Banny that The Hump was originally called "The Club," a technique that Chuck Noll had taught me in 1971 with the Steelers and I had taught it to All-Pro Joe Greene. Banny then informed me that Joe Green had taught him The Club in Banny's rookie year in 1975. When Banny was a player-coach for Carolina in the World Football League in 1983-84, he had taught The Club to Reggie White when Reggie was a rookie defensive lineman before he became a star with the Eagles. It seems that Reggie had become so good at "The Club" that he gave the club technique his own original name "The Hump." Wow! Forgetting about Chuck Noll and using deductive reasoning: Bad Rad to Joe Greene to John Banaszak to Reggie White meant that Bad Rad had taught Reggie "The Hump." No wonder Reggie White became a Hall of Famer!

John Banaszak

First St. Louis Rams Home Game – The second Rams game was the first home game in the new St. Louis Rams team's history. Players, coaches and all our new fans were wired up for this inaugural home game. The game had another special meaning for the director of Rams football operations, Steve Ortmayer and me. Jim Mora, the head coach of our opponent, the New Orleans Saints, was a former coaching colleague of Steve and me. We were all on the Colorado University coaching staff in 1972 and 1973 and were close friends. We won this first home game in St. Louis history by beating the Saints, 17-13. Steve and I waited outside the Saints locker room after the game to see Jim. After over an hour of waiting, Jim still hadn't come out of the locker room, so we left. Losing a game to two close friends must hurt more than we realized. The Saints beat us the second time we played them that season 19-10. Since we lost, Steve and I didn't wait for Jim outside the locker room after the game.

Good Beginning, Bad Ending – After beating Green Bay and New Orleans, the Rams won their third and fourth games against the Carolina Panthers, 31-10, and the Chicago Bears, 34-28. The new Ram fans in the St. Louis area were all excited about the undefeated Rams football team. We lost a close game to the Indianapolis Colts, 21-18, but recovered to win a tight match with the Atlanta Falcons, 21-19. The enthusiasm of the fans was at a fever pitch for their new football team with a 5-1 loss record and in first place in NFC Western division of the NFL. We were off to a good start and eagerly anticipating our next home game against long-time Ram rival San Francisco 49ers.

The 49ers came to St. Louis and crushed us, 44-10. Consecutive losses on the road to the Philadelphia Eagles, 20-9, and the New Orleans Saints, 19-10, burst our bubble. Three straight losses had given us a 5-4 record and we were now struggling to have a winning season. We recovered from the three straight losses by beating the Carolina Panthers, 28-17, at home. We still felt we were on a pace to qualify for the playoffs at the end of the season. However, two unexpected events occurred that hurt our chances. Starting veteran Rams quarterback Chris Miller suffered a career-ending injury and our defense collapsed and gave up almost 40 points a game in losing five of our last six games. Our last win was in our 13th game in New York against the Jets, 23-20. We lost the last three games of the season to Buffalo, 45-27, Washington, 35-23, and Miami, 45-27. Our final record was 7-9. We had a 5-1 record at the beginning of the season, and the exact opposite the last six games of the season with one win and five losses. The story of the 1995, St. Louis Rams inaugural season is simply "a good beginning and a bad ending."

After a two-week Christmas holiday, I was informed on my first day back in the Rams office that I was being let go. This didn't come as a surprise to me because when I was hired, I was told it might be only for a year. I also knew that disagreements in the middle of the season with the offensive coordinator probably sealed my fate. I wanted to run the ball more and he didn't and I had to go through receiver coach Mike Martz every time I wanted to run a new play, like a pitchout. When Nancy first met the offensive coordinator she said she knew we were not going to get along. I asked her how she knew and she said it was obvious because we were so different. She was right.

I paid the young guys who worked in the Rams equipment room to load the rented U-Haul van and I drove it back to Strongsville, Ohio. I knew that would probably be my last chance in the NFL. I had been trying for three years to get another NFL or college job when Joe Walton asked me to help him start the program at Robert Morris. After what happened in St. Louis, I figured my chances of getting back into the NFL now went from very slim to none.

I didn't give a thought about going back to Robert Morris either. When I left, Joe kept the same defense and hired one of Penn State's Linebacker U guys, Lance Mehl, who I had coached at linebacker in 1985 with the New York Jets when Joe was the head coach. Lance was from St. Clairsville, Ohio and succeeding me at Robert Morris enabled him to try his hand at coaching.

Back in Strongsville, I settled down for the winter and started to refurbish my golf clubs. A telephone call from Lance changed everything.

CHAPTER TWENTY –
The House That Bad Rad Built

About a month after I had left the St. Louis Rams, I received a call in February, 1996, from Lance Mehl who had taken my position as Robert Morris' defensive coordinator when I had left for the Rams. Lance told me that because of the 60 mile, one-way commute from his home in St. Clairsville, Ohio, to the college every day, he was seriously thinking of leaving the college. He said Joe Walton wanted to talk to me about returning to Robert Morris. I went to the college, visited with both Lance and Joe and made the decision to return to Robert Morris under my old title of assistant head coach-defensive coordinator.

I picked up where I left off at the end of the 1994 season without missing a beat. Although there were a few new players on the team, I was welcomed back by the defensive kids I had coached, and that was no reflection on Lance. Joe and Lance had another winning season in '95. Robert Morris finished 6-4 and again beat our cross-town rival, Duquesne, 38-20.

However, we still needed more talented players. And that spring we made a significant move to intensify our recruiting when Joe hired our former graduate student-part-time coach Dave Harper as a fulltime enrollment manager and director of recruiting. Dave was the best young recruiter that Joe Walton and I had ever known. His hiring full time was a terrific boost to our football program. What's also important is we now had three full time coaches—Joe, me and Dave.

Three Million To Seventeen Million – The Robert Morris administration was giving us more financial support but we still needed to keep raising money. Once again Joe put me in charge of recruiting celebrities for the annual Joe Walton Celebrity Golf Tournament on the third Monday in May. I was able to put myself into the tournament as the celebrity in a foursome that included Lou Astorino, who I had helped get admitted to Penn State's main campus 22 years before. I had seen Lou just twice since then, but what happened that day we played golf shows you how good deeds can pay off years later, and in ways you'd never think about. The ultimate beneficiary of this story was not Robert Morris, but Penn State and Joe Paterno.

This all began in January or February of 1964 when I received a phone call in the Penn State football office from Milan Carlo, editor of the *Srbobran*, the national Serbian newspaper that was produced on Pittsburgh's south side. I had met and knew Milan from the National Serbian Basketball Tournament that I had played in with the Duquesne Serbs basketball team. Milan was deaf and was talking to me through another person. Milan informed me that his nephew, Lou Astorino, had applied to Penn State in architecture, and had been accepted for one of Penn State's branch campuses but not for the main campus at University Park. Milan wanted to know if I could help get his nephew admitted to the main campus. He said his nephew had his heart set on going to Penn State. I told Milan to give me the young man's phone number and I would call him and find out the situation.

When I called young Lou, I found out his grades and College Board scores were easily good enough to be accepted at Penn State for architecture. I told him he had applied to the College of Science on campus, which was a mistake. At the time, we had about six or seven Penn State football players in engineering and one, Chris Weber, in architecture. All of them had started in the Division of Counseling. Back then, if you passed the engineering or architecture courses your freshman year with a 2.0 average or better, you were automatically transferred to the College of Science. I simply told Lou to re-apply to Penn State to take architecture through the Division of Counseling, which he did and got admitted to the main campus. When he came on campus to start his freshman year, he stopped in the football office to meet me and thank me.

The next time I saw Lou was 12 years later at a Hilton Hotel luncheon honoring the 1975 Super Bowl Steelers. One Steelers player or coach sat at a table with nine other fans. There were at least 50 of these fan-loaded tables. A guy sitting across from me at my table said, "Do you remember me?" I said, I think so. Aren't you the architect kid?" He said, "Yes, I'm Lou Astorino." I said, "How are you doing as an architect?" He replied, "I designed the Trimont!" I said, "Wow, that's great." The Trimont was Pittsburgh's latest modernistic condominium complex built sticking out from the top of Mount Washington overlooking the city of Pittsburgh. It's one of the greatest scenic views in the country. I said, "How's your uncle, Milan Carlo?" Lou said, "He wrote a book on Serbians in America. I'll send you it tomorrow," and he did.

I didn't see Lou again until that Joe Walton Celebrity Golf Tournament. On the first hole, I asked Lou who had designed the addition to the student union building at Penn State that I thought looked like a World War II German pillbox. Well, that got Lou started. On and off for the next 17 holes, he complained about all the additions and new buildings at Penn State and the fact that he had bid on a number of them and never came close to getting any architectural business there. Lou told me that the guy in charge of hiring architects at Penn State kept hiring his own buddies and not Penn Staters. Otherwise, Lou, his brother Dennis and I had a great day playing golf that Monday in May.

Two days later, on Wednesday, I received a call from Lou. He told me that he called to thank me for recommending him to Joe Paterno about renovating Penn State's locker room and office at their practice facility. Lou said Joe Paterno was sending a private plane Friday morning to fly Lou and his brother Dennis to Penn State. I said, "Lou, I don't know what you are talking about. I didn't recommend you to Joe Paterno." He said, "Joe just told me you did. I know you did." I replied, "You're crazy. I'm hanging up," and I did.

When I told my young coaches about Lou's crazy call, they reminded me that I did indeed recommend Lou to Joe Paterno. They said they heard it in the coaches' locker room at Penn State after practice the day that we all had visited Penn State's spring practice a month earlier. I didn't remember that at first but the comments by my young coaches spiked my memory. At that Penn State spring practice, Joe had told me he was going to remodel the locker rooms which were then in a building named the Nittany Football Center (now known as the East Area Locker Room) that also included a player's lounge, weight room, an auditorium for large group meetings and smaller meeting rooms. It was adjacent to the Greenberg Indoor Sports Complex where the coaches' offices and other meeting rooms were located. My coaches and I had told Joe about the recent renovation of the locker rooms at Pitt Stadium that Astorino had designed. Joe obviously had remembered our conversation and called Lou. I immediately called Lou's secretary, Susan, and told her to tell Lou that I did remember recommending Lou to Joe Paterno a month ago.

The following Monday, Lou called to tell me that he was going to draw up plans for a $3 Million renovation in the Nittany Football Center of Penn State's locker room, weight room, equipment room and player's lounge.

Lou also told me that Paterno's secretary had called him five times on Tuesday, the day after the golf tournament, but he refused to take the call because he thought his buddies were messing with him pretending to be Joe Paterno. When Lou got a call Wednesday from Joe Paterno, he told his secretary, "Give me the phone. I'm going to put a stop to this." When he got on the phone, it really was Joe Paterno.

On Tuesday, the day after the last call from Lou, my lawyer cousin, Ray Radakovich, called me and told me his son, Scott, was majoring in graphic arts and design at La Roche College and needed a summer internship at a company for class credit and wanted to know if I knew anyone who could help his son, who was deaf, find an internship. I told Raymond I thought I knew just the person. Lou Astorino's uncle was deaf. I also remembered Lou telling me that Lou did a one-year internship with an architectural firm between his junior and senior years at Penn State. Lou said the internship was the best thing he could have done at the time because he had a job with the internship firm already waiting for him when he graduated. I immediately called Lou, explained about Scott, and Lou asked me for Scott's home number so he could make contact with Scott. I said, "Lou, let me have Scott contact you." Lou said, "How can he? He's deaf." I said, "Lou, your uncle was deaf and he contacted me." Lou said, "Okay, have him contact my secretary, Susan."

I immediately called cousin Raymond back and told him to have Scott contact Lou's secretary, Susan Taslawski. Scott's mother, Susie, called Susan and set up an interview for Scott with Lou and his brother Dennis on Thursday. Scott passed the interview and got the summer internship on one condition. Dennis found out Scott played baseball. Scott had to play for Astorino's softball team, which he did.

A few weeks later, I received another call from Lou Astorino. Joe Paterno and his coaching staff liked the plans for the renovation of the Nittany Football Center so much that Joe decided to build a new facility from scratch which would not only house the practice locker room, weight room, training room and equipment room but also the coaches' offices, all meeting rooms and a bigger auditorium. Lou's $3 Million deal had just turned into a $17 Million deal and architect Lou Astorino finally got to design a building on the Penn State campus.

The $17 Million Penn State football facility is called the Mildred and Louis Lasch Building. Lou Lasch was a Philadelphia lawyer and a big booster of Penn State football. When I coached there in the 1960s, Lou Lasch and his wife, Mildred, used to party with the Penn State coaching staff and wives. Lou Astorino's firm also designed the University of Pittsburgh-Pittsburgh Steelers dual use building and practice facility in south side Pittsburgh and PNC Park in Pittsburgh, which is reputed to be the most beautiful baseball park in the country. Despite all these great sports facilities, Lou says his greatest creation is the only chapel that has been built in the Vatican in Rome in over 300 years, which is named the Chapel of the Holy Spirit. He is the only American architect to ever design a chapel in the Vatican.

Lou has received two awards as a Penn State Distinguished Alumnus, one from the University and the Alumni Association and another from the College of Architecture. He also was the commencement speaker at the 2010 Arts and Architecture graduation ceremonies.

I believe Lou still thinks I went home after the golf tournament and called Joe Paterno after he had complained about never having the chance to design a building at Penn State. My cousin's son, Scott Radakovich, became a graphic designer for the Lou Astorino Co. for 14 years. Scott now owns his own company, Radesign Creatives (www.radecreatives.com). And I never did find out who the architect was for Penn State that designed the World War II German pillbox addition to the Penn State Student Union.

Hank Fraley

Can My Buddy Come, Too?

— Shortly after my return to Robert Morris in March of 1996, our head recruiter, Dave Harper, was on the telephone trying to get a big offensive tackle named Jimmy Wingo to visit our campus. Jimmy asked Coach Harper, "Can my buddy come, too?" Dave said, "Who's your buddy?" Jimmy replied, "He's the tackle on the other side." Dave asked, "Is he any good?" Jimmy said, "Oh, he's real good and he's big, too. He's about 6-3, and weighs about 290, and a good athlete, plays basketball and baseball." Dave said, "Okay, he can come, too" At this point in time, Robert Morris was a non-scholarship school. We didn't have much to offer except the quality of the school itself, plus the chance to be coached and play for two former NFL coaches. Jimmy Wingo's buddy was named Hank Fraley, and they were from Gaithersburg High School in Gaithersburg, MD. Well, they visited our school together. During their visit, our other coaches had me demonstrate how we were going to teach run and pass blocking, which resulted in me pushing Hank Fraley around a bit. One reason I did this was because our other coaches told me that when I did this with a prospect we always got him. In this case it worked with Fraley but not Wingo. Jimmy Wingo's buddy Fraley came to Robert Morris but our original prospect didn't.

On the first day of 1996 fall practice, Robin Cole, our defensive line coach and former great Pittsburgh Steelers linebacker, ran over to me on the practice field and yelled, "Rad, you've got to see this fat kid. He's really something." I said, "Where is he?" Robin said, "He's over in my team drill," which was on another field. I walked over to the field where the team drill was going on, looked at the defensive linemen and said, "Which defensive lineman are you talking about?" Robin said, "Oh, no, he's not on defense. He's the fat kid on offense." He pointed to Hank Fraley and I watched Fraley in a dummy scrimmage for a few plays. Hank was highly energetic, hustled, looked athletic and was very impressive. He looked like he would be a great offensive lineman and Robin Cole was the first to spot it.

Well, Hank had an outstanding career, and in his senior year of 1999 we won the 1-AA mid-major national championship with him playing left tackle. During that year, Joe Walton kept yelling at me that we had to get Hank in the NFL. We knew that would be tough since we were a non-scholarship school. Because I had coached the offensive line in the NFL in the 1970s and 1980s, I knew a number of NFL offensive line coaches personally, So, I sent them all a highlight video of Hank's Robert Morris career and told them they should consider him. Well, none came to watch him work out, which let us know how much they thought of Robert Morris football.

I next called Chris LaSala in football operations at Pitt. I asked Chris if Hank Fraley could work out for the pro scouts at Pitt's pro day held at the Cost Center on the Pitt campus. Chris said that as soon as the Pitt pro day was over, he would announce that any pro scouts that wanted to stay could watch Hank Fraley of Robert Morris work out. That's what happened, and only one pro scout stayed for Hank's work out, Irv Eatman, an assistant offensive line coach of the Pittsburgh Steelers. Irv was impressed with Hank's work out and reported good things to the Steelers. Ken Stevenson, the head offensive line coach, then came to Robert Morris and interviewed Hank.

Hank was not drafted, but had five or six offers to sign as a free agent. I thought the videotape highlights I sent might have had something to do with that. Hank signed with the Steelers, probably because they had showed the most interest in him. I visited the Steelers at the beginning of their fall camp in Latrobe and then again on the final day. From what I saw, I thought Hank would easily make their squad, even more so when my old coaching partner and Penn State friend, backfield coach Dick Hoak, came up to me on the last day of camp and said, "Rad, your guy picks up stunts better than any rookie we've ever had." Wow. Coming from Dick really meant something to me. We did a two-on-two and three-on-three mirror dodge drill at Robert Morris that is great for teaching how to pick up stunts. Hank had done the drills for four years. Since no other Steelers rookies had ever had that experience, I felt that Hank should have picked up stunts better than any previous Steelers rookie. Hoak's comment also had given me even more confidence in my two-on-two and three-on-three mirror dodge drills. Some people now call those drills "Bumper Cars," which is a very appropriate name. I wish I had thought of it, but the name was coined by another NFL offensive line coach and a friend, John Matsko, who learned the drills from me.

Hank was still on the team when the Steelers started their preseason games. Now, in the preseason the Steelers had some injuries to their centers, most notably to their All-Pro center Dermonti Dawson. In the spring of 2000, I taught Hank how to be a center. I had him snapping the ball to the quarterback for at least an hour straight at three or four sessions in our auxiliary gym at Robert Morris. I felt that being able to play center would increase his chances of making an NFL team. Hank picked up playing center like a duck takes to water. When the Steelers preseason games started, Hank played center at least half of every game, and more than that in some. He probably played twice as much as any rookie ever had in preseason, plus, from what I saw, he played well.

At the final cut of the preseason, the Steelers decided to place Hank on the practice squad, believing he would clear waivers. Well, the other teams apparently had done their homework because I was told that 15 or 16 teams claimed him off the waiver wire. The Philadelphia Eagles had first pick and signed him. Earlier I had visited the Eagles, saw the offensive line coach, Juan Castillo, who is a friend, and talked with General Manager Tom Modrak, who was a former Pittsburgh Steelers scout. Tom and I discussed Hank and I assumed he was a lock to make the Steelers. Evidently, what Tom and I talked about concerning Hank didn't hurt him because the Eagles jumped at the chance to pick him up.

Hank was on the Eagles team for the entire 2000 season but never dressed for a game as the Eagles played their five starters all season. The next preseason, 2001, the Eagles' starting center, Bubba Miller, got hurt, and Fraley became the starter for five seasons, including four conference championship games and the 2005 Super Bowl. He was hurt midway through the 2006 season, lost his starting job and was traded to Cleveland where he started for three more years and then was traded to St. Louis in 2010. Not bad for a non-scholarship football player from Robert Morris. Robin Cole was sure right when he said, "Rad, you've go to see this fat kid." And thank goodness Jimmy Wingo asked Dave Harper, "Can my buddy come, too?"

One last note. When the Steelers put Hank on waivers, both Joe Walton and I were devastated. We were going to change our work schedule so that we could see Hank play on Sundays. We felt the Steelers had made a big mistake not putting him on the playing roster and we still do. Hank could have been their starting center for the next 10 years. Oh well, that's life.

Freudian Slip – When I look back at Robert Morris' 1996 season I still can't believe how well the team played in just our third year. Joe had beefed up the schedule each season and we added a couple of pretty good small college teams from other regions. We also were now in a league for the first time, the Northeast Conference (NEC). Our first game was at Mercyhurst College in Erie. The entire game was played in a heavy driving rain. I used a large golf umbrella on the sidelines the entire game to keep myself and my game plan dry as I used it while calling the defensive signals. I found out later from the Mercyhurst coaches and players that the use of the umbrella caused a lot of comment on their sidelines. It seems they had never before seen a coach with an umbrella on the sidelines. Neither had I in my entire career. We won the game in the driving rain 20-0 and my game plan remained dry the entire game.

We next played and beat Butler University of Indiana, 38-0, and then Towson State of Maryland, 7-0. Wow, three shutouts in a row. Besides talk about being undefeated at 3-0, there was a lot of buzz or talk about three straight shutouts by the defense and keeping the shutouts streak alive. Our fourth game was at Central Connecticut, which we won, 38-13, for our fourth straight win. As Joe Walton and I were getting undressed in the locker room, Joe said, "Well Rad, that was another good win, and I'm glad the other team finally scored. (Central Connecticut had scored their 13 points in the fourth quarter against our defensive backups.) I was getting sick and tired of hearing all the talk about the shutouts and of keeping the shutouts streak going." Oops! Did he not realize he was talking to the defensive coordinator? I believe the psychiatrist would call those shutout comments "a Freudian slip." Come to think of it, the "Freudian slip" about the shutouts may have been the biggest compliment I've ever received as a defensive coordinator. Our defense was playing so good that the head coach was irritated by all the talk about it.

The next week, we almost had another shutout. We were ahead of Gannon 40-0 when Gannon scored late in the fourth quarter to make the final score 40-7.

Not Outhit, But Outsmarted – When we played the University of Dayton for the first time in the sixth game of the season both teams were undefeated. Dayton was in the Pioneer Conference and Robert Morris was in the Northeast Conference, which was in its first year of existence. Both teams were unfamiliar with the caliber of play in each other's conference. The game was very hard-fought and hard-hitting. The scoring plays that won the game for Dayton were a speed option and a speed option reverse. On the speed option, our strong safety went for the quarterback instead of the pitch; and on the speed option reverse, our defensive end didn't look ahead of the ball on the fake of the option away from him and got fooled by the reverse. We didn't get outhit in the game, but on those two plays, we sure got outsmarted. Dayton broke our undefeated streak and won, 31-21.

After the Dayton loss, we beat Monmouth, 43-6, lost to Wagner, 35-38, and beat St. Francis, 16-15, to win the Northeast Conference and qualify for the postseason ECAC Bowl (Eastern Collegiate Athletic Confederation). We still had a regular season game left versus CW Post of Long Island, New York.

I Love This Defense – The last game of the 1996 regular season against C.W. Post was one of my most memorable games at Robert Morris. We were both non-scholarship teams that had already qualified for postseason bowl games. C.W. Post was a Division II non-scholarship team with an 8-1 record while we were an NCAA Division 1-AA non-scholarship team with a 7-2 record. They had a wide-open,

4-wide receiver offense with one back in the backfield and the quarterback under the center. They kept four wide receivers in the game always, even on the goal line. Their running attack was all zone runs, which meant no lineman pulled and no traps, and their passing attack was all drop back passes with no sprints or rollouts. They had very big offensive linemen, bigger than ours, and took big splits of three or four feet in their offensive line. They had a very productive and high scoring team, but big splits in the offensive line with no traps, counters, suckers, or any plays with linemen pulling. We decided to blitz or stunt on every play on defense so that we could penetrate those big splits. We also kept the weak safety free as a precaution on all the blitzes.

Right from the beginning of the game our defense penetrated those big splits and stuffed the C.W. Post offense. Near the end of the first quarter, we had stopped C.W. Post cold on its first four or five series with three downs and out. Our right outside linebacker, Fred Manalac, who was having a great game blitzing every down and sacking the quarterback or getting the running back for losses, came off the field screaming, "I love this defense! I love this defense! I love it! I love it!" Our defense stymied the C.W. Post offense the entire game and we won, 35-6. I'll always remember this game as one of the few times when I had a defensive game plan that almost worked to perfection, and the reaction of linebacker Fred Manalac running off the field yelling, "I love this defense! I love it! I love it!"

C.W. Post played two weeks later for the Division II non-scholarship National Championship and won, 28-6. Although we didn't play our cross-town rival Duquesne in the regular season, we met them in the ECAC Bowl, which pitted the MAC (Metro Atlantic Conference) champion against the NEC (Northeast Conference) champion. We won, 28-26, to finish the season at 8-2. We were both NEC and ECAC champions. Duquesne finished both the 1995 and 1996 seasons with 10-1 records. Robert Morris was the team that beat them both years.

Linebacker Fred Manalac was a Dean's List student who passed up his last year of eligibility the next year to go to medical school. Although in his words he yelled, "I love this defense," he must have loved wanting to go to medical school more. He is now a doctor. I used to tell Fred, "You're either the dumbest smart guy I ever met or the smartest dumb guy. I can't decide which." Eighteen years later, I still can't decide.

NFL Europe Draft – In January of 1997, I got a call from my former coaching colleague Lionel Taylor, who was now the head coach of the London Monarchs, an NFL Europe team. Lionel asked me to be his defensive coordinator with the Monarchs. Since NFL Europe played in the spring, the job was only for five months. I thought it would be great to coach in London in the spring and Robert Morris in the fall. The salary with the Monarchs was better then I received for a whole year at Robert Morris, $45,000 versus $31,000. Robert Morris President Ed Nicholson told me to take a leave of absence of five months and I accepted Lionel's offer. But I found out that I couldn't do that because the NCAA didn't allow any coaches to be working for a professional team. So I had to resign from Robert Morris with the full intention of being rehired again in the fall. My nomadic circus was on the road again and it was quite an experience.

The NFL Europe administration allotted a certain amount of money to each head coach of the six NFL Europe teams to get their staff together, to meet and look at film for three weeks and to have a player draft at the end of the three weeks. Lionel had our coaching staff stay in first class rooms in one of the new casino hotels in Laughlin, Nevada. The bedrooms and meeting rooms couldn't have been any better and the rates were about one fourth what it would have cost anywhere else. That gave us more of our per diem money to use for meals and the food in the casino restaurants was very good and dirt cheap. Our Monarchs coaching staff arrived in Laughlin, February 4 and had the draft approximately 2½ weeks later. Watching film of the player prospects and working on the NFL Europe draft in the Casino Hotel in Laughlin, Nevada, was one of the more pleasant experiences in my football coaching career.

Preseason NFL Europe – Preseason training camp for NFL Europe took place in Georgia, about 50 miles from Atlanta (I can't remember the name of the town or area.) All six teams trained near Atlanta. I can remember one of the other teams staying in the same housing complex that we were in. Denver quarterback John Elway's father, Jack, visited friends on the other team and I can remember visiting with him. We had a scrimmage with one of the other teams at the Atlanta Falcons complex. Two former head coaches that I worked with before, Dan Reeves and Rich Brooks, were now coaching with the Atlanta Falcons and came out of their offices to watch us practice. After about three weeks of practice in Georgia, we flew to London for the start of the NFL Europe season.

Move To London – After the London Monarchs team flew from Atlanta to London at the beginning of April 1997, the Monarchs coaching staff separated from the players and stayed in a recently built Marriott Hotel in Croydon, a town on the outskirts of London with a famous World War II airport. The Croydon Marriott Hotel was by far the classiest hotel in the Croydon area. The lobby had a full-time piano player at a baby grand piano every afternoon and evening. How much classier can you get? Lionel Taylor had pulled off another coup. We stayed there for the next three months—April, May and June.

Our practices and player meetings took place at the Crystal Palace athletic complex, which was a 45 minute drive away. The practice field with a track around it and covered bleacher seats was situated right next to the historic ruins of the Crystal Palace, a gigantic all glass building similar in size to one of our professional basketball arenas, which was built in the mid-1800s. The players were scheduled to lift weights and meet with the coaches in the mornings, practice in the afternoons and then have the evenings free. We played our home games in Stamford Bridge Stadium, home of the famous Chelsea Football Club, a professional English soccer team. One big difference between an American football stadium and a European football (soccer) stadium is the high chain-link fence with barbed wire on top that separates the fans in the stands from the playing field. This preventive measure against violence between the fans and the players and officials was tough to get used to. Also, at some games, police mounted on horses patrolled the circumference of the field. Six teams were in NFL Europe, and a 10-game regular season schedule was set up with each team playing each other twice. The team with the best record in the first half of the season (the first five games) would play the team with the best overall record for the entire season (all 10 games) for the NFL Europe World Cup Championship in the post season.

Inexperienced Coach – My main memory of the 1997 NFL Europe season with the Monarchs was my lack of experience in the league and my handling of the "National Rule," which stated that a national—defined as a British born player—had to play every other series of play in the game, or every other change of possession. We had three nationals on the London Monarchs. One was decent, but two couldn't have started on a poor American high school team. Well, in the second, third and fourth games—which we lost—our defense got burned a few times in each game because of the national who was playing at the time. It took me until the fifth game of the season to learn how to properly hide the national in our defense to avoid giving up easy scores. That was when I transformed from an inexperienced NFL Europe defensive coach to an experienced one.

Actually, the only thing I disliked about NFL Europe was the "National Rule." The rule was put in to help create an interest among the English population. Except for the nationals' immediate family, I don't believe it created any interest because the vast majority of the nationals couldn't play very well and that made NFL Europe football more inferior than it would have been. I believed then and I believe now that the National Rule was a big mistake, and I believe that's one of the prime reasons why NFL Europe eventually folded!

1997 NFL Europe Season – The 1997 NFL Europe season had two teams with 4-6 records—the London Monarchs and Franklin Galaxy—and three teams with 5-5 records—the Barcelona Dragons, Scottish Claymores and Amsterdam Admirals. Only the Rhein Fire, coached by fellow Penn Stater Galen Hall, had a winning record with 7 wins and 3 losses. That meant the Barcelona Dragons with a 4-1 record in the first five games played Rhein Fire in the NFL World Cup. Barcelona won 38-24.

Our last two losses were by four points to the Amsterdam Admirals, 9-13, and by three points to the Rhein Fire, 10-7. If we had won those two games we could have played in the World Cup. The 1997 NFL Europe was a very competitive six team league. And one of the standout players that year was Jon Kitna, the quarterback for the 1997 World Cup Champion Barcelona Dragons. He went on to have a 13-year NFL career playing for the Seattle Seahawks, Cincinnati Bengals, Detroit Lions and Dallas Cowboys.

No Double Dipping – My wife Nancy was able to make two airplane trips to London as part of my NFL Europe contract. She made one during the season for a week, and one for the last game of the season. After the last game we took a train underneath the English Channel to Paris for a few days. Then we took another train to Madrid, Spain, for two days, and then a train to the Mediterranean coast of Spain for two weeks before we flew back to the United States. We even let ourselves be bumped from a flight coming back and received a $1,000 voucher each for future flights. We were put on another flight one hour later. What a great vacation! I was ready to coach at Robert Morris in the fall and NFL Europe in the spring for the next 20 years.

The day after we returned home and two days before I was to report to Robert Morris at the beginning of July, I got a phone call from Lionel Taylor. Lionel told me that I couldn't go back to Robert Morris because the NFL Europe administration had just passed a rule for NFL Europe head coaches and offensive and defensive coordinators that stated "no double dipping," which meant I couldn't coach as a defensive coordinator in NFL Europe and still coach at Robert Morris. I told Lionel I had to go back to Robert Morris because Joe Walton wouldn't be able to find a defensive coordinator in July with preseason practice starting in August. I couldn't leave Joe in the lurch because he was counting on me.

That ended my intention of coaching in college here in the fall and in NFL Europe in the spring, all because someone had come up with a "no double dipping" rule. I thought "double dipping" would have been great because it would have allowed me to keep my hand in both college and pro football.

I knew I had just lost my last opportunity to ever get back in the NFL, and I decided I would spend my final years of coaching trying to help Joe Walton make Robert Morris one of the best football teams in the NCAA Division 1-AA.

Political Poll For ECAC Bowl – We had another good year in the fall of 1997 as we won seven games and lost three, but it could have been a great year. Those three losses were very close games, losing to Dayton, 16-13, Towson State, 33-30, and Mercyhurst, 17-10. We had one of those years where we had a good shot at going undefeated but couldn't quite do it. We ended up going undefeated in the Northeast Conference with a 4-0 record, thereby winning the conference title, and an opportunity to play in the ECAC Bowl again. But how we reached that championship game is an intriguing story with the type of backroom politics you'd find in Washington, DC.

It all started after our ninth game of the year, a win over St. Francis which gave us the NEC title with a game left on the regular season schedule against Gannon. The rules for determining the participating teams for the ECAC post season bowl game *did not* state that the winner of the MAC (the Metro Atlantic Conference) would play the winner of the NEC. The two participating teams were determined by a vote of a six-man committee made up of three representatives from each conference. This rule meant that it was possible for two teams from the same conference to play each other.

Well, on the Sunday after our ninth game, the committee took a preliminary vote. This was one week before the final vote, which was scheduled after the last game of the regular season. Georgetown of the MAC had an 8-1 record and Duquesne (MAC) and Robert Morris (NEC) had identical 6-3 records. Also, Duquesne had already lost to Georgetown, 20-0, earlier in the season. When the first vote was printed in the *Pittsburgh Post-Gazette* on Monday showing the preliminary standing for the ECAC Bowl, Georgetown was rated first with 30 points, Duquesne was rated second with 21 points, and Robert Morris was rated third with 19 points.

When the coaching staff at Robert Morris saw these totals, we wondered how our bitter rival Duquesne could be rated above us. We both had the same 6-3 record. Duquesne had already lost to Georgetown and we had beaten Duquesne the last three years. Coach Walton called a meeting of the Robert Morris staff to figure this out and we invited Dr. Chuck Zimmerman, head of our Math Department, to help us deal with this problem. Here is what happened:

Each committee member gave five points for first, four points for second, three points for third, two points for fourth and one point for fifth. Georgetown got five points from each committee member for a total of 30 points. The three NEC committee members gave Robert Morris four points each and Duquesne three points. If the three MAC members would have each given Duquesne four points and Robert Morris three points, Duquesne and Robert Morris would have been tied at 21 points each. But that's not what actually happened. Two MAC members rated Robert Morris third with three points each but one MAC rep rated us fifth with only one point! That's why we only had 19 points. We saw that the vote was truly a political poll.

So, if the MAC wanted to play politics, we'd do it, too. This is what we did. We called our three NEC representatives, explained what happened and told them what we wanted them to do if both Duquesne and Robert Morris won the next week and ended up with identical 7-3 records: vote us No. 1, Georgetown No. 2 and Duquesne No. 3. And that's what happened. Duquesne and Robert Morris both won their last games to end up with identical 7-3 records. When the final point total was publicized on Monday, Georgetown was still in first place with 27 points, Duquesne still had the same number of points as the week before with 21 points, but Robert Morris now had 22 points. That meant we would play Georgetown in the ECAC Bowl. Duquesne had just lost the Political Poll to play in the ECAC Bowl. Winning the Political Poll meant that we had beaten Duquesne four years in a row. We then defeated Georgetown, 35-13, to win the ECAC Bowl

Duquesne's head football coach, Greg Gattuso, complained in the newspaper that the spot in the bowl game should have been decided by a coin flip. He didn't mention the conniving that Duquesne had done in the Political Poll. However, if Duquesne had waited until the final vote to do the conniving, they would have won the Political Poll and we wouldn't have been able to do anything but complain about it.

Student Cameraman in Super Bowls XL and XLIII – In the spring of 1998, Rob Brakel, our student cameraman for Robert Morris football, asked me if I would call the Pittsburgh Steelers office and offer his services to work for free so he

could gain NFL experience as a cameraman. I called the head Steelers video director, Bob "Mac" McCartney, whom I knew from my five years with the Steelers in the '70s. I asked Mac if he could use any free camera help from our student cameraman. Mac said he had a minicamp coming up after the NFL draft and at the beginning of May. He said to tell the young man to stop by before then to see him.

Rob met Mac, worked the week of the minicamp and the week after. Rob then left after Mac told him he would contact him later. After six weeks went by Mac called Rob and offered him a full time hourly wage job which Rob did for three years.

Bob "Mac" McCartney

The Steelers then gave Rob a leave of absence to accept a cameraman job for the Berlin Thunder team in the 2000 NFL Europe Spring Season League. Rob's Berlin Thunder team won the league championship. When the season was over and Rob came back to Pittsburgh in July of 2000, the Steelers offered him a full time salaried job contract, which he accepted and did until the spring of 2007, when the long-time cameraman (Benny Greenberg, '82) of the Arizona Cardinals retired as the video director.

The new Arizona Head Football Coach, and former Steelers Offensive Coordinator, Ken Whisenhunt got the Cardinals to hire Rob Brakel, whom Ken knew from his time at the Steelers, as their Director of the Video Department and Head Cameraman. When the Steelers played the Cardinals in the 2009 Super Bowl XLIII, not only were two Cardinals assistant coaches, Mike Miller and Matt Raich, from Robert Morris, but also the Cardinals cameraman, Rob Brakel.

Rob likes to mention that he has a championship ring from every team that he's been a cameraman for: Robert Morris 1996 & 1997 NEC Champions, Berlin Thunder 2000 NFL Europe Champions, Steelers 2006 Super Bowl XL Champions, 2009 Cardinals NFC Champions (Super Bowl runner up).

A special note: Bob "Mac" McCartney is one of the two most experienced cameramen in the NFL. He is one of only five Steelers employees who has rings from all eight of the Steelers Super Bowl appearances—six Super Bowl winners and two AFC Championships (the Super Bowl runner up rings). Rob Brakel certainly learned his trade from the best!

In Super Bowl XLIII, the Steelers beat the Cardinals in a very close game, 27-23. Does that mean that the experienced McCartney is still a better cameraman than his young protégé Rob Brakel? I'm not going to answer that!

Losing Season But Competitive – Politics couldn't have helped the next year. We started the 1998 season off poorly, losing the first two games by 10 and nine points, respectively, to Buffalo State and Dayton. The remaining eight games were notable for two reasons. First, all four wins were by big margins. We beat Central Connecticut, Wagner, Sacred Heart and St. Francis by scores of 42-17, 42-17, 44-7, and 35-3, respectively. Second, all four remaining losses were by two points or less to Valparaiso, Monmouth, New Haven and Duquesne by scores of 19-17, 17-16, 26-24, and 24-22, respectively. Robert Morris football had its first losing season with a 4-6 record, but the above scores indicate we were still highly competitive and close to having a successful season.

A New Look In '99 – After our first losing season in 1998, we started off 1999 with another defeat. I found out in my NFL coaching career that losing can become contagious if you don't do something to stop it. Buffalo State had beaten us, 32-20, in Buffalo, and our defensive secondary was burnt a number of times and played poorly. So, I benched all four starters, and none of those benched started another game for the rest of the year. Besides a new secondary, I decided to switch to a 3-4 defense as our basic front and moved Brad Kirit, a two-year starter at defensive end, to nose tackle where he lined up on the center. I put in a bunch of blitzes and stunts from the 34 during practice and started the second game of the season against Dayton with this new format.

Well, we clobbered Dayton, 34-7, at home, and the four new players in the secondary and the new 3-4 defensive front seemed to work pretty well. We lost a tight away game at Valparaiso, 17-13, but then won our last seven games to finish with an 8-2 record and win the NEC conference championship. But best of all, Robert Morris was declared the NCAA's 1-AA Mid Major National Champions by Don Hansen's *National Weekly Football Gazette*. Changing the entire four players in the secondary and the defensive front to a 3-4 had given us a new look that resulted in a National Championship.

The four new starters in the secondary for the second game and the rest of the season were Nick Downes and Joe Austin at the corner positions and Raymond Thomas and Jason Hempstead at the safety positions. I've often wondered how, after both a spring and a preseason practice, I could have started the wrong players at all four secondary positions for the first game of the season. How dumb could I be? But then I corrected all four mistakes the next week. How smart was that!

Brad Kirit, our nose tackle in the 34 defense, was awesome, pushing every center we played backward from the line. Later, after his senior season, he lifted 225 pounds, 41 times for a pro scout. The record at the Indianapolis combine workouts was 43. When I heard what Brad had lifted, I yelled at him, "What's the deal. You told me you had beaten the combine record twice before lifting the 225 pounds, 45 times on one occasion and 50 times on another. Why didn't you break the combine record of 43 for the pro scout?" Brad replied, "He had me lift the 225 pounds after a two-hour workout."

As usual we had several players on that team who lived far from Pittsburgh. Their families rarely got to see them play but when they did the players, obviously, wanted to have a great game. That's what happened to our senior wide receiver J.T. Kirk when his family came from California to see him play for the first time at our home game against Wagner in early October. We were losing 23-16 with two seconds left on the clock, but quarterback Steve Tryon was able to get off one last pass. J.T. made a miracle catch in the end zone after time ran out to beat Wagner, 23-21. The Kirk family sure had a happy reunion that day. It sure made J.T.'s teammates and coaches happy too.

And here's another little touch of irony in '99 involving the Pittsburgh Steelers. Our linebacker coach during the season was Bob Babish. Bob was Steelers quarterback Terry Bradshaw's brother-in-law in 1972, and was one of the first guys to run on the field and mob Franco Harris after the immaculate reception that won the playoff game against the Oakland Raiders.

Last Piece Of The Puzzle – Now, we were looking forward to defending our 1999 national championship, and I only had one defensive starter who would not be returning from that team, outside linebacker Craig Herlan. Craig had used up only three of the normal four years of eligibility, but could not play the fourth because he was a non-qualifier when he was admitted to Robert Morris. According to NCAA rules at the time, a non-qualifier could not play his freshman year and only in three of the next four years regardless of how good his grades were, and Craig's grades were good. I agreed that a non-qualifier shouldn't play his freshman year, but to penalize him by not allowing him a fourth year of eligibility was not fair. For example, let's assume two players get admitted to the same school, take the same courses and neither play their freshman year. One is a qualifier and one is a non-qualifier. Assume they both play the same amount their next three seasons. Assume the qualifier has a 1.95 average and the non-qualifier has a 4.0 average in the same courses. The qualifier with the 1.95 average can play a fourth year but the non-qualifier with a 4.0 average can't. Now that's unfair.

Well, one day I was reading the sports page, and I read that Ohio State got its best basketball player, who was a non-qualifier, eligible for a fourth season because he took a test that said he could be eligible for the fourth season if he had a proven learning disability. I immediately got in touch with Craig and asked him if he had a learning disability. He said he did. He had papers since the third grade that proved he did. I checked with the NCAA and they said that he had to have had a test while he was in college to prove that he had the learning disability. Those tests he had before were not acceptable. All I had to do was get him tested.

I told our athletics director, Susan Hofacre, to look into it. She did and found out that it would cost $2,000 to have him tested. I couldn't believe it. I also knew that if you were going to pay a psychologist $2,000 to test for a disability, he sure as heck was going to say the person had one. Plus Craig already had a well documented one. I asked Susan to pay for Herlan's test. She could legally do so as athletics director, using our athletic funds, but she refused. Susan said if she paid for his test that every student would want a similar test paid for. What a load of crap that was. She later asked Matt Raich, our linebacker coach and recruiting director, "Was Rad really serious about getting that player tested?"

Well, I went to see Cassandra Oden, the lady who was in charge of students with learning disabilities at Robert Morris. Cassandra called around and found a psychologist who would do the test for $500. Now Matt and I had to convince Craig to pay $500 for the test. The school had just approved a "counter" program which meant we could give athletic aid to players who had need. (Rich kids couldn't get anything.) However, we could only give this aid to incoming freshmen and to no more than 10 players a year up to a limit of 30. At this time we had only given out four counters. Coach Walton said we could also give a counter to a player going into his fifth year. Herlan only had a $2,500 need, but we told him that if he paid the $500 for the test he would get $2,500 in scholarship aid from the school, which would give him a net of $2,000 to apply to his schooling. Finally he borrowed the $500, took the psychologist's test, had his learning disability verified and became eligible to play a fourth year. We now had the last piece of the puzzle in place. All 11 defensive starters from the 1999 National Championship team would be back for the 2000 season. Matt and I celebrated. We were looking forward to a great season—and it was.

Undefeated – With the entire defense (all 11 starters) from the 1999 season returning, the year 2000 was one of my most enjoyable years of coaching. We really didn't have any real weakness on defense. We expected to win and we did. There were a couple of tense moments in the season:
- Joe Austin's interception of a Dayton pass at the end of the game on our own 5-yard line to seal a 17-13 win;
- Beating Wagner, 38-31, in overtime;
- Playing Sacred Heart, when both of us were undefeated with seven wins but winning a tight game, 31-20.

It actually was a big year for both our offense and our defense. Our offense averaged 36½ points per game and our defense allowed an average of 14 points per game. We expected to go undefeated and we did. Our final record was 10-0. We won the NEC title again and repeated as the National 1-AA Mid Major Champions selected by Don Hansen's *National Weekly Football Gazette*. We also finished the season tied with Drake University for the longest current winning streak in the country at 17 wins in a row. And our 31-20 win at Sacred Heart was the only game they lost in two years. They went undefeated in 2001.

Iowa Visitor – Here's another example of how football coaching is really a very small fraternity. After our undefeated 2000 season, Iowa's head coach and my old friend Kirk Ferentz, sent his young linebacker coach, Bret Bielema, to see me for a few days about linebacker play. When I was coaching at a major college or in the NFL, I used to get frequent coaching visitors. However Bret was the first visiting coach I had from a major college in the seven years I'd been at Robert Morris. I think Kirk may have wanted to find out if I had any football secrets that I had not told him about before that resulted in our current 17-game winning streak. Anyhow, Bret had played nose guard for Kirk from 1989-92 and then became the Iowa linebackers' coach. He was a nice guy who really wanted to learn. We also had some fun off the field and spent a couple nights hitting some of my favorite haunts in Pittsburgh talking football. I made sure he had one of the famous Pittsburgh sandwiches from Primanti Brothers and a couple drinks in Station Square as well as at the 1902 Tavern in Market Square, which is owned by Jeff Joyce, a former quarterback coach and basketball coach at Upper St. Clair High School. Since 2006 Bret Bielema has been the head football coach of the Wisconsin University Badgers.

Bad Beginning, Good Ending – As Joe Paterno continues to say, you either get better or worse and in 20001 we finished 6-3. Yet, Joe Walton and I both considered it one of Robert Morris' best years. After losing the first three games of the season, we won our last six games, and averaged 40.5 points a game in those games. The story of the season was a bad beginning, but a very good ending.

After the season, the Pittsburgh Steelers Director of Football Operations Kevin Colbert, hired our linebacker coach and recruiting director, Matt Raich, to be a member of the Pittsburgh Steelers scouting department. Matt eventually worked his way back into coaching and is currently the linebacker coach for the Arizona Cardinals. To think that a small college that didn't even have a football team seven years ago was now a major pipeline to the NFL coaching ranks was phenomenal. I guess it's because Joe and I have such an extensive NFL background. But whatever the reason, it's something Robert Morris athletics is proud of.

Quitting Smoking – We won three of our first four games in the 2002 season, but then lost two games in a row in which we got shut out in both games. As Coach Walton and I were returning from the 29-0 loss at Wagner in the sixth game of the season, I felt a little strange shortly after we got off the airplane in the Pittsburgh airport. I told Joe to go on ahead because I had to go to the restroom. After I came out of the restroom, I felt a little woozy and breathless. I sat down for a few minutes until the feeling went away. Then I continued on my way to my car. In bed that night, I had to sit up on the edge of the bed to rest. Lying down made me breathless. I started to wonder if I should call 911 or just get dressed to go to the hospital emergency room. I had no pain. I just felt weird and was breathless. After about a half hour of feeling this way and debating in my mind what I should do, the feeling passed and I felt fine.

I felt good the next day, Sunday, and also Monday, but went to see my doctor, Alexander Cone, anyway. He told me to schedule a stress test at a local testing place. I went to the testing place and the receptionist there told me she could schedule me in four weeks. I told her I could be dead by then and started to walk out. "Hold on," she yelled, "the best I can do is next Monday." So I scheduled the test.

Seven days later I ran on the treadmill for the stress test, ate breakfast, came back, did the other required test and left with the promise that I would receive the results of the test in the mail in a few days. I left the testing facility feeling fine and drove my car into a parking lot around the corner to see my optometrist, Claudia House, a big Penn State football fan, about my eyeglasses. I rode an elevator up to her second floor office and talked with her about 15 minutes and left. I rode the elevator down one floor and walked out of the front door of the building and stopped. I had that weird feeling again. A little woozy and breathless, the same feeling I had a week earlier in the airport and again that night sitting on the edge of my bed. All I had just done was simply ride an elevator down one floor and walk a couple of steps to go outside the building. Again, I debated in my mind if I should wait until the feeling passed and go to work at the football office, or go back and see the doctor who had just given me the stress test. I decided to go back and see the doctor.

He was at lunch when I went back, so I sat in the waiting room for 45 minutes until he came back. The weird and breathless feelings were gone. That had lasted only a few minutes in the parking lot. When the doctor returned, I told him what had happened but that I felt fine now. He said, "By the way, you flunked your stress test. Sit in that chair, and don't move. I'm calling the ambulance for you. You're going to Sewickley Hospital." I said, "I don't need an ambulance. I feel fine. I'll drive myself to Sewickley Hospital." He said, "You're not getting out of that chair. It's not you I'm most worried about. It's me. I've done these stress tests for two years and you're the first patient who has returned, because he felt weird. If I let you go and you have a heart attack, stroke or anything else, I would be in a heap of trouble. You're not going anywhere until the ambulance attendants get here."

The ambulance attendants came, lifted me onto a stretcher and drove me in the ambulance to the Sewickley Hospital. All the coaches came and visited me in the hospital that night. I felt kind of guilty because I felt fine. Early the next morning, I was taken by ambulance to the Beaver Medical Center, wheeled into the operating room and given a catheterization of the upper body. The surgeon, Dr. Jasvinder Sandhu, found severe blockage in three main arteries coming from my heart and inserted three stents. When the operation was over, but while I was still lying on the operating table, Dr. Sandhu asked me if I smoked. I kind of hemmed and hawed, telling him I did off and on for 40 years, and that I only smoked once in a while now. He looked at me and said, "You've had your last cigarette." And that's the story of how I quit smoking.

Doctor Robert S. Nitzberg, my cardiologist, did not allow me to go to work or to the games for the next three weeks—which we lost. I returned for the last game of the season, which we also lost, 14-7, in overtime to St. Francis, in what may have been the muddiest game in the history of football. Our final record was 3-7. It was a tough year, but I did quit smoking.

Hindsight – My best memory of the 2003 Robert Morris football season is the performance of the fourth year senior third-string quarterback Rich Demaio in two of our games. We had won the first game of the year against Buffalo State, 33-23, but had lost the second to Monmouth, 17-10. When we played St. Peters in the third game of the season, we were behind at halftime, 24-10, so we decided to take a long shot and started our fourth year, third-string quarterback in the second half. Rich completed his first six passes and we came from 14 points behind to win, 31-24.

Rich continued to be our third-string quarterback and seldom played in our next six games. We lost our ninth game to Albany, 27-7, to bring our record to 6-3. Our last game of the season was against our cross-town rival Duquesne that we had not played in six years. We decided to start Demaio to jolt the team. This was Rich's first start in four years and was taking place in the last game of his college career. Well, Rich responded by completing 33 passes for 444 yards, both school records. Due to a couple of disastrous mistakes by our defense, we lost a close game to Duquesne, 33-28, to end the season at 6-4. Hindsight suggested that maybe we should have played Rich a lot sooner. Why isn't our foresight as good as our hindsight?

Rich Demaio became Robert Morris' graduate assistant quarterback coach for the next three seasons, coaching the quarterbacks he had played behind in his senior year. Isn't that an oddity? Rich became offensive coordinator and quarterbacks coach at Farleigh-Dickinson University and is currently coaching at Rhoads College in Memphis, Tennessee.

Two Hail Mary's – We weren't much better in 2004, winding up with a 6-5 record. But we beat Duquesne, 34-14, and a win over Duquesne is always the high point of our season. The low point was to eventual Mid-Major National Champions, Monmouth, in our third game. We were ahead, 27-22, and Monmouth had the ball on its own 20-yard line with eight seconds left on the clock. They threw a Hail Mary to the 50-yard line. Our right corner stepped in front of the receiver to intercept the ball. The ball bounced off our right corner's chest and directly to the receiver who was lying on the ground. There were two seconds left. And on the final play, Monmouth's quarterback threw another Hail Mary, this one deep into the end zone. Their tall receiver pushed our right corner in the back and tipped the ball. The receiver who had caught the previous tipped ball caught this one, too. Monmouth won, 29-27 on two Hail Mary's in the last eight seconds on two tipped balls to the same receiver. In all my years of coaching or as a spectator I had never seen two Hail Mary's in row like this in a game.

At the end of the season, Monmouth was declared 1-AA Mid Major National Champions by Don Hansen's National Weekly Football Gazette—thanks to two tipped Hail Mary's and an official who didn't call pushing the corner in the back for what should have been offensive pass interference.

Low Point At Robert Morris – The 2005 season was the worst in all my years at Robert Morris. It was a very tough year, winning only two games and losing eight, including a 23-12 loss to Duquesne in our season opener. My most vivid memory is the third game at Rowan. We were leading 28-0 at the end of three quarters. They scored four touchdowns in the fourth quarter on four long passing bombs to tie the game, and then beat us in overtime, 35-28. It was the lowest point of a season with a lot of low points. As you will read below, we got even with Rowan in the next year.

The House That Bad Rad Built – The 2005 season wasn't a total loss, however. In the first home game of the season, September 17, we played our first game in our new $10 million stadium, beating Butler 49-13. This was really a great small college stadium, with field turf and a seating capacity of 3,000 that could eventually be expanded to 10,000. Best of all, new offices for the football staff, the athletic administration and the coaches of our Olympic sports as well as a state of the art video facility were attached to the stadium. We also had two modern locker rooms, a training room, equipment room, weight room and press box. We had really come a long way from that day I walked into head coach Joe Walton's office in 1993. Robert Morris President Ed Nicholson decided the stadium should be named in honor of Joe. I kidded Joe and said there should be a big sign at the main entrance that said: "Joe Walton Stadium—The House That Bad Rad Built." Later in the season, after we lost a game Joe told me that they were going to change the name of that sign that I wanted to, "The House That Bad Rad Destroyed."

Getting Even With Rowan And No. 1 On Defense – Robert Morris' 2006 season of seven wins and four losses was one I really enjoyed and will always remember for a couple of reasons. It was my last season as defensive coordinator and we ended up leading the nation in Division 1AA (now known as the NCAA Championship Division) in four defensive categories: total defense, pass defense, pass defense efficiency and third down defense. We also got even with Rowan, the team that we led 28-0 going into the fourth quarter the year before that ended up beating us 35-28 in overtime. We held them to a minus 44 yards rushing and minus 19 yards of total offense to win 21-0 in one of the greatest statistical defensive wins in NCAA history. The other coaches on our defensive staff were Scott Benzel (secondary), Scott Farison (linebackers), John Banaszak (defensive line) and Mike Miller (assistant defensive line).

We played Sacred Heart in the last game of the season. When the score reached 41-0 in our favor at the end of the third quarter, I left the press box to go see my grandchildren in the stands. I had called my last defense for the Colonials.

Head Coach For A Day – I gave up being defensive coordinator and stayed one more year, 2007, as simply assistant head coach. The most notable occurrence for me that final season was that I was the interim head coach for the week of the Monmouth game when Joe Walton's wife, Ginger, passed away. We beat Monmouth, 20-17, on a last-minute field goal, after being behind 14-0 in the first quarter. That made my record 1-0 as a head coach. I figured it was time to retire. So I did.

Weekly Academic Check-In – Because of my 17 years of college coaching experience at five different universities, Joe Walton put me in charge of overseeing the academic performance of our football players starting in the fall of 1993.

I immediately set up a weekly check-in box system whereby a player would list on a card any grade on an exam, quiz, term paper, speech, etc. that he had received the past week and drop the card in the check-in box. In addition, at mid-term we sent each professor a card that he or she was asked to return only if the student-player had a current grade in his course below a C average.

Any player had to see me if he was having a problem such as low grades, lying about his grades, cutting a class three or more times, or not checking in academically. I would try to help him out in any way I could, such as arranging tutoring, telling him to buy a better alarm clock, or calling his parents if I thought it was necessary. Calling his parents was my secret weapon in my dealings with the players academically, and even just threatening to call the parents could make a big difference in his academic behavior.

I remember one example where Sam Dorsett, our star running back, was not checking in weekly and also had cut a class at least three times. When I telephoned his mother, she said she was taking a poker from the fireplace and catching the next plane to Pittsburgh, and when she saw him she was going to beat his butt with the poker. I told her, "No! No! It's not that serious. I just want you to call your son and encourage him to check in academically each week and to not cut any classes." During Sam's four years I called his mom two or three more times when I thought he might be slipping a bit academically. This former star player became a very good student who graduated, got a master's degree, and became the offensive backfield coach for Robert Morris. He is currently the running backs coach at St. Francis University in Loretto, PA.

Player Sam Dorsett   **Coach Sam Dorsett**

Breaking The Federal Privacy Act —
When the Robert Morris administration found out in 1994 that I was calling the parents of players concerning their grades, they sent a notice to Joe Walton stating that we could not tell the parents the grades without their son's written permission because we would be breaking a federal privacy law.

After Walton reprimanded me for breaking a federal law, I immediately telephoned my son Danny, who had done legal research for my lawyer cousins, Bob Garshak and Ray Radakovich. I told Danny to send me the part of the law—known as FERPA (Federal Educational Rights and Privacy Act)—that dealt with notification rights of parents for student grades.

I showed the law to Joe who immediately called the university administrator who was involved and read the pertinent part of the law I had been using. This states that "a school may disclose information from an 'eligible student's' education records to the parents of a student without the student's consent, if the student is dependent for income tax purposes." Joe told the administrator we were not breaking the law and we were going to continue informing parents of our players. At the time, all of our players were listed in the tax returns of their parents, which classified them as dependent students.

Shortly after, the administrator sent me a notice stating that although I could legally inform parents of "dependent" students their son's grades, I had to do it in person only because doing it over the telephone I wouldn't know who I was talking to. I called the administrator and said we were not idiots in the football office and that we had ways to make sure we knew who we were talking to on the telephone. I also told the administrator we only mentioned performance in class or grades when we felt it was necessary to help the player improve his grades. I said we also found out if we refused to inform any inquiring parent of their "dependent" son's grades we, indeed, would be guilty of breaking the federal privacy laws.

A side note. I wanted to include this little story to show I at least learned a little 30 years ago in my one year of night law school at Chase in Cincinnati.

Graduation Rate No. 1 – One more thing about academics. You can trace my deep interest in a player's academics back to Penn State. As I wrote earlier I hardly cared about academics as a player but that changed when I got married. And while I was working on my MBA in 1958, Rip Engle started an academic oversight program. Backfield Coach Frank Patrick was in charge, with all players checking in with Frank once a week. Rip also implemented a mandatory study hall at the library for all freshmen. Freshman coach Earl Bruce was in charge and all assistant coaches, including me as a graduate assistant, took turns as the study hall proctor for a week.

The study hall was Monday through Thursday, with hours of 8 to 10 p.m. during the season and 7 to 9 p.m. during the off season. We made sure the players sat apart from each other and didn't disturb anyone else in the library. After their freshmen year, the players were on their own, but we were not surprised when the upperclassmen also started going to the library to study because it was so quiet. I realized then that if you make academics a priority and monitor the players' progress they will take it all seriously too. We continued this academic oversight program throughout my entire time at Penn State, and so we assistants also spent a lot of time in the library, too. In fact, it was during one of the times that Joe Paterno was a weekly proctor that he met his future wife, Sue, who was in the library helping another student study.

I might add that from that small program started in 1958, the Penn State academic oversight program has grown into a full division within the athletic department involving all athletes, not just football. That's why Penn State has been one of the NCAA's perennial leaders in graduation rates since the NCAA started its own tracking in 2004. Anyhow, it was because of what happened at Penn State that led me to the monitoring program I set up at Robert Morris. And to prove how successful it was, I will quote from an Associated Press story of Oct. 3, 2007, that covered the NCAA's graduation rates for 318 Division I colleges and universities for athletes who enrolled from 1997-2000.

"There was...an improvement for football...from 65 percent to 67 percent in the NCAA calculations for the 119 teams in the new Bowl Subdivision, formerly Division I-A. The Championship Subdivision, formerly I-AA, increased its rate from 62 percent to 65 percent for its 117 teams.

"Only two schools had 100 percent graduation rates in football -- Boston University and Robert Morris. Boston's rating, however, was based only on players that enrolled in 1997 because the university dropped football after that season."

Wow! The NCAA declared us #1 in graduation rate. I wonder how much the weekly academic check-in and calling the parents played a part in this #1 accomplishment. It surely didn't hurt!

Saga Of Mike Miller – However, I can't look back at my career at Robert Morris without thinking about Mike Miller. There's an old saying about being in the right place at the right time and here is another great example of that.

Mike Miller had been a backup quarterback at Plum High School in suburban Pittsburgh. He attended Clarion University of Pennsylvania but did not play football in college. In Mike's first years out of college in 1994-95 he did an internship in the public-relations department of the Pittsburgh Steelers and then with the Indianapolis Colts when former Steelers offensive line coach Ron Blackledge was with the Colts. Mike had Blackledge call Joe Walton about a graduate assistant job in public relations. So, Blackledge called Walton and recommended Mike for a graduate assistantship but never mentioned public relations. Ron just assumed Joe Walton knew that's what it was about. Mike went to Robert Morris to interview with Joe for a graduate assistantship in public relations and in the spring of 1997 got hired as a graduate assistant to coach for the football team.

I wasn't around when Joe Walton hired Mike. I was in NFL Europe the spring of 1997. However, I believe Joe thought Mike's experience in public relations would be a great help in recruiting and for that reason hired him.

When the 1998 season ended, retired Pittsburgh Steelers Head Coach Chuck Noll wanted Joe Walton and me to be part of his coaching staff for a college all-star game to be played in Orlando, FL. The game was to be a match-up of players from Florida against players from the other 49 states that was called the American team. The two head coaches originally picked for the game were two retired Super Bowl winning coaches—Noll for the American team and former Miami Dolphins Head Coach Don Shula for Florida. Shula's former assistant coaches had some health problems, so Don resigned and former Cleveland Browns Head Coach Lindy Infante took his place with his former Cleveland staff.

On the second day of practice, at the start of the first warm-up drill called team starts, Chuck Noll and I were lined up alone, with no other defenders, opposite the offensive team. I was pretending to be a defensive end and Chuck was pretending to be a linebacker. On the snap of the ball on a drop back pass play, I started to rush and Chuck started to back pedal (breaking a basic Bad Rad coaching rule—linebackers should never, ever back pedal). I heard a "pop" like a cork popping from a champagne bottle. I looked back and Chuck was lying on the ground in pain. I ran over and asked what hurt. He said the back of his foot. He had snapped his Achilles tendon. He and his wife Mary Ann decided that he should be operated on by Steeler doctors. So, later that day they flew back to Pittsburgh.

Our coaching staff then had to decide how to proceed for the rest of the practices and the game without Noll. Besides being the head coach, Chuck was also the offensive backs coach for this game. Two of our Robert Morris graduate assistant coaches, Mike Miller (offensive backs) and Mauro Monz (quarterbacks), had driven to Florida on their own to attend the all-star game practices and volunteer their help when needed while visiting Disney World. Joe Walton, who was originally the offensive coordinator-quarterbacks coach for the game, now became the interim head coach. He made graduate assistant Mike Miller the offensive backs coach for the all-star practices and had graduate assistant Mauro Monz help him with the quarterbacks.

Chuck Noll's successor as the Steelers head coach, Bill Cowher, was watching the game on TV back in Pittsburgh when he heard the announcer explain about Chuck's injury and that Mike Miller was his replacement. Then the TV cameras showed a close-up of Mike talking to the running backs during the game. Mike knew Cowher slightly because Mike had done an internship in the Steelers' public relations department two years earlier. After the game, Cowher got Mike's cell phone number from the Steelers public relations department and called Mike in Florida and asked Mike to come see him at the Steelers office when he got back to Pittsburgh.

Mike went to see Cowher and had a conversation with him that resulted in Bill hiring Mike Miller as quality control coach for the Steelers' offensive team. When Noll snapped his Achilles tendon, his bad break turned out to be Mike Miller's big break.

After five years with the Steelers, Mike went to the Buffalo Bill's for two years as quality control and tight end coach. When the Bills head coach Mike Malarky resigned at the end of 2005, Mike Miller also was let go, and in the spring of 2006 Mike coached for the Berlin Thunder in NFL Europe. In order to keep busy after that season, Mike also accepted a part-time salary job at Robert Morris as assistant defensive line coach working with me and John Banaszak, and helping us lead the nation in four NCAA Championship [1AA] Division defensive categories.

After the 2006 season with us, he went to the Arizona Cardinals with new head coach Ken Whisenhunt, as quality control coach for the Cardinals. A few weeks after he joined Arizona, the new young receiver coach that Whisenhunt had just hired got in trouble with a prostitute and was fired. The receivers coaching job became open again and new candidates for it were being interviewed. Mike Miller said he knew more about the offense than the new candidates and asked to be interviewed for the receivers coaching job. Mike got his interview and got the job. He became the Arizona Cardinals receiver coach for the next two years. That made Mike the position coach for All-Pro receiver Larry Fitzgerald when the Cardinals played the Steelers in Super Bowl XLII. And one of the benefits of being Larry Fitzgerald's position coach is that Fitzgerald has paid for Mike and his girlfriend's trip to the Pro Bowl after the 2008 and 2009 seasons.

After the Super Bowl XLII, Mike was promoted to the title of passing coordinator for the Cardinals, and then in 2011 to offensive coordinator. To go from not playing college football to the Steelers and Colts PR departments to Robert Morris football staff to the Steelers and Bills, back to Robert Morris as defensive assistant, to the

Arizona Cardinals as receiver coach and passing coordinator to offensive coordinator has to be a "Ripley's Believe it or Not." And that is the saga of Mike Miller.

As for Mauro Monz, the graduate assistant coach who travelled to the all-star game after the 1998 Robert Morris season with Mike Miller, he was hired by Robert Morris to replace Dave Harper as our full time Director of Recruiting. After a later stint as the head coach at West Virginia State, Mauro became the receivers coach at the University of Akron, and currently is an offensive assistant coach at Youngstown State University.

Oh, and one more thing about that Florida all-star game. Our team and staff stayed at the Wilderness Lodge, a classy hotel in Disney World. We were accompanied the entire week by our wives and each coach was given a brand new van direct from the factory in Detroit to drive the entire week. This all-star game, sponsored by the Damp Rid Co., which produced laundry products, was one of the classiest events my wife and I ever attended, first class the entire week and another great vacation.

Retirement And Offense-Defense Camps – I must admit I have been having a lot of fun since my official retirement when I left Robert Morris at the end of the 2007 season. Like a lot of other so-called "senior citizens" I have spent a lot of time on the golf course and riding my electric pedal bicycle that I have nicknamed "bikeagra" because of the electric power boost to the pedals. Perhaps, best of all, I have seen more of my four children and six grandchildren. That has meant travelling coast to coast since my three daughters—Lisa, Leslie and Lori—live in New York, Oregon and Ohio, and Nancy, my son Dan Jr. and I live in Pittsburgh.

Of course, I could never leave football completely. So, I also have worked at various camps and coaching clinics during the spring and summer, including one of the best known national camps for underclass high school players known as "The Offense-Defense" Camps, which holds some 40 four-day training camps around the country. The staff is composed of college and former professional coaches with current NFL players invited to speak to the campers. Some of the past participants have become great players in college and the NFL, such as Ronnie Lott of the Super Bowl 49ers, and more recently Cam Newton, the 2010 Heisman Trophy winner from Auburn. Naturally, Penn State's senior camp is one of my favorite destinations. That always brings back memories because, as I wrote earlier, Joe Paterno had the first such private high school camp in the country. This also gives me the chance to be with some of the old Penn State coaches: Dick Anderson, Fran Ganter, Galen Hall, Jay Paterno, Bill Kenny, Ron Vanderlinden and Larry Johnson.

I especially have a good time coaching at all the offense-defense camps and clinics, and not just at Penn State. I get to see all those coaching friends, teammates and players that I have been involved with over the decades and we start reminiscing about the "old days." And you don't have to guess what we talk about because Bad Rad and his crazy stories and nomadic circus-like career are always brought up. They even tell me some I had forgotten. In fact, after hearing many of my cronies tell me that I should write a book, I did. And you just read it.

"Linebacker U"
Penn State's Greatest Linebackers

1. Bill Saul
2. Ralph Baker
3. Dennis Onkontz
4. Nittany Lion
5. Chuck Zapiec
6. Rich Milot
7. Jack Ham
8. Dan Radakovich
9. Dave Robinson
10. Don Graham
11. Shane Conlan
12. Jim Kates
13. Andre Collins
14. Doug Allen
15. Matt Millen
16. Lance Mehl
17. John Skorupan
18. Larry Kubin
19. Jim Laslavic
20. Chet Parlevecchio
21. Ed O'Neil
22. Opponent
23. Mark D'Onofrio
24. Greg Buttle
25. Walker Lee Ashley

INDEX

Abdul-Jabbar, Kareem 262
Abrams, Al 5, 115
Accorsi, Ernie 306-308
Agganis, Harry 101
Alberigi, Ray 104
Alexander, Dan 299-300
Ali, Mohammed 108
Allen, Chuck 9
Allen, George 7, 161, 220, 227, 259
Allen, Jimmy 23, 25
Allen, Marcus 88
Allerman, Kurt 92, 185, 190
Amato, Benny 163
Anderson, Bob 179
Anderson, Dave 40-41, 239
Anderson, Dick 145, 156, 363
Anderson, Scott 25
Anderson, Willie 204
Anthony, Ray 234
Armstrong, Otis 41
Arnelle, Jesse, ... 111, 117
Arrington, LaVar 190
Ashmore, Darryl 336
Astorino, Dennis 340-341
Astorino, Lou 339-342
Atkinson, George 71
Austin, Bill 297
Austin, Joe 352, 354
Austin, Ocie 15
Avezzano, Joe 298

Babb, Mike 232
Babish, Bob 353
Bach, Johan S. 169
Bach, John 224
Bahr, Matt 310
Bailey, Don 104-107
Bain, Bill 235
Baker, Al 308
Baker, Ralph 9, 91-92, 109, 134,
 137-138, 149-150, 176, 185, 286
Bakke, Eric . . . . Acknowledgements
Balthaser, Don 105-106
Banaszak, John 83, 242, 337, 358
Banaszak, Mary 242
Bankston, Warren 13-14
Banker, Ted 299, 308
Banks, Robert, ... 308
Barber, Stew 123
Barchuk, Tony 175
Barnum and Bailey 93, 191
Bartkowski, Steve 206
Beake, John 135-136, 279

Beatty, Warren 228
Beban, Gary 154-155, 162
Bechtel, Larry 306
Bedenk, Joe 116
Bednarik, Chuck 119-120
Beethoven 169
Belichick, Bill 166
Belichick, Steve 166
Bell, Alex 182
Bell, Bob 191-193, 198-199
Bellino, Joe 123
Belus, Bobbie Jo . . . . Acknowledgements
Bender, Tom 5
Bennett, Barry 293
Benzel, Scott 358
Berra, Yogi 264
Berry, Raymond 216, 256
Besket, Andy 132
Besket, Joe 132
Bielema, Bret 354-355
Bingham, Guy 292, 302
Bishop, Keith 272-274
Blackledge, Ron 212, 264, 361
Blackledge, Todd 264, 270
Blackman, Frank 222
Blair, Matt 53
Blanda, George 68
Blasenstein, Joe 128, 137-138, 145-146
Bleier, Rocky 12, 49, 53, 66, 74, 85-86
Blount, Mel 15-16, 23, 51, 68, 70, 74-75
Bolger, Ray 230-231
Borovich, Steve 104
Boures, Emil 247
Bowlen, Pat 88
Bowman, Navarro 190
Bradley, Ed 54
Bradshaw, Terry 10, 13, 23, 38-47, 49-51,
 53, 67-68, 71-74, 80-81,
 84, 86, 187, 242, 295, 353
Brahms 169
Brakel, Rob 350-351
Branch, Cliff 51, 68
Brando, Marlon 45
Brandt, Gil 75, 247
Bratkowski, Zeke 288, 314
Brann, Chris 323
Bray, Dick 197
Brechbill, Kurt 56
Bresnahan, Tom 36
Briscoe, Marlon 40
Brister, Bubby 310
Brito, Gene 125-126
Brooks, Larry 236

Brooks, Rich 109, 333, 336, 347
Brookshire, Tom. 119, 121
Brown, Bill. 53
Brown, Charlie. 88
Brown, Jim. .51-52, 111-112
Brown, Larry (24) Cowboys 76
Brown, Larry (87) Steelers 35, 53, 61, 62, 89
Brown, Terry 53
Brubacker, Ross 13
Bruce, Earl 127, 130, 133, 152, 360
Bruce, Isaac 336
Bruce, Jerry 106
Bryan, Bill 272-273
Bryant, Bear 117, 129, 166
Bryant, Cullen 210
Bryant, Waymond 24
Buchenhorst, Oscar 109-110
Budde, Brad 245-246
Budde, Ed 245
Bugel, Joe. 165-166, 248
Bukich, Rudy 127
Bunz, Dan 221, 257
Burkhart, Chuck. 161, 164, 179
Burns, Jerry 281, 284
Burruss, Pepper 303-304
Bush, George, W. 11
Butkus, Dick .5, 13, 149, 150
Butler, Jack. 248
Buttle, Greg 92, 109, 185, 188, 190, 290
Byner, Earnest 307-308, 311, 313-314
Bynum, Mike 215

Callahan, Ray 1, 182-183, 191, 195,
211-212, 286, 292, 295
Campbell, Bobby 162, 164
Cappelletti, John 184, 186
Caprara, Emil. 105
Carlo, Milan. 339-340
Carothers, Lynn . . . . Acknowledgements
Carr, Jim. 221-222
Carroll, Bob 88
Carroll, Pete 265-266
Carson, Johnny. 144, 229
Carson, Leon "Bud" 20-21, 51, 58-60, 219, 223,
225, 228-231, 239, 241, 253, 259, 285,
288, 297, 301, 304, 306-307, 309-311, 313
Carson, Linda. 59, 311
Carter, Kevin 335
Casola, John. 195
Casola, Sal 194-196
Cassoti, Fred 202
Castillo, Juan 344
Cathrall, Holmes 224
Caum, Donnie 148
Cecconi, Bert 102
Cecconi, Lou 102
Cindrich, Ralph 332
Clack, Jim 30-31, 34, 56-57, 65-66, 69, 87, 244

Claiborne, Jerry 202
Clark, Bruce. 248
Clark, Don 114
Clark, Monte 219
Clancy, Sam 308
Clifton, Kyle 290, 293, 295
Cloud, Jack. 166
Coder, Ron. 81
Colbert, Kevin 355
Colbert, Shelton 323
Cole, Larry. 73
Cole, Robin 343-344
Coleman, Pat 56
Collier, Joe. 87-88
Collins, Andre 178
Colton, Ted. 63
Cone, Alexander. 355
Congie, Sam. 191
Conlan, Shane 109, 190
Conn, Billy. 48
Connor, Dan. 190
Conway, Tom 319
Cook, Terri . . . . Forward
"Cookie" 100
Cooper, Mark 270-272
Coopus 100
Cope, Myron 242
Corral, Frank 239
Cornelson, Martin 302
Corso, Lee 197
Cosell, Howard 49-50, 190, 257-258
Cost, Corky 323-324
Covert, Jimbo. 139, 247
Courson, Steve. 89
Cowher, Bill. 362
Cox, Fred 53
Crable, Bob 290-291, 293, 297
Creekmur, Lou 120
Crew, Piante 321
Crist, Chuck 224-225
Criter, Ken 37
Crowder, Eddie 18, 21, 43-44, 198, 201, 202,
204, 206-209, 212, 214-217
Crutchmer, Clyde. 215
Cuifo, Lenny 202-203
Culp, Curly. 64-67, 168
Cunningham, Ben 81
Cunningham, Sam 87

Dalton, Kay 202, 215
Darst, Ed 117
Darst, Josephine. 117
Davis, Al 85, 148
Davis, Butch. 83, 231, 232
Davis, Henry 9, 37
Davis, Sam 30-31, 69, 244
Dawson, Dermonti 344
Dawson, Red 102

DeBartolo, Jr., Eddie 219, 223, 225, 228
DeBerg, Steve 269, 271
DeFlores, Fritz............................178
Deford, Frank.............................48
Demaio, Rich.........................356-357
Dennison, Glenn 282
Devine, Dan.............................180
Devore, Hugh............................122
Ditka, Mike.............................260
Diven, Joey.............................48
Dixon, Hewritt...........................259
Dodd, Bobby.............................59
Donald, Luke............................204
Donelli, Aldo "Buff" 101
Donelli, John 97-99
Dorsett, Sam............................359
Dorsett, Tony.........................82, 238
Dotsch, Rollie 244, 263-264
Dowler, Boyd............................216
Downes, Nick............................352
Drayton, Troy...........................335
Drazenovich, Chuck........ 107-108, 125-127, 185
Druschel, Rick.........................30, 34
Dryer, Fred.................. 64, 233, 242, 333
Dudley, Bill.............................1
Duenos, Joey............................215
Duffy, Mrs..............................2
Dunkelberger, Dave....................192, 212
Dunn, Brian.........................329, 331
Dunn, Gary.............................292
Dunn, Paul.............................247
Dunn, William...........................125
Durik, John..............................99
Dutton, John.............................87
Duval, Rick 215
Dyzak, Paul .... Acknowledgements

Eason, Tony............................270
Eatman, Irv.............................343
Eaton, Scott 224
Ebersole, John 9, 92,173-174, 176
Edmondson, Chuck 163
Edwards, Earl..................... 116, 174-175
Edwards, Glen 52, 70-71, 74
Egloff, Ron.............................271
Eller, Carl.............................7, 52
Elway, Jack 270, 347
Elway, John 39, 269-271, 273, 279, 313, 347
Emery, Cal.............................210
Engle, Charles "Rip" 45, 104-112, 114-116, 119,
          123-124, 127, 129-131, 133, 134,
          137, 144, 147, 149-150, 154-159, 360
Erdelatz, Eddie...........................101
Esiason, Boomer 265
Eury, Jennifer............... Acknowledgements

Fabus, Mike .... Acknowledgements
Fallieras, Nick..................... 142

Farison, Scott............................358
Farls, Jack 105, 112, 144
Faulkner, Jack 237, 255
Ferentz, Kirk 247, 254-255
Ferguson, Jim............................87
Fletcher, Al.......................... 171-172
Flowers, Richmond 225
Flowers, "Weedi"...........................99
Foote, Chris 245-246
Foreman, Chuck........................ 53-54
Forste, Wally 193
Fortney, Tim............................197
Fouts, Dan..............................87
Fraley, Hank........................ 342-344
France, Doug 236, 239, 240, 242, 255, 257
Frank, Alan.............................249
Frank, John........................ 249-250
Frankenstein.........................28, 108
Frazier, Robert 321-322, 328
Frei, Jerry.............................267
Freshwater, Bill 101
Freidman, Jack............................88
Frisch, Tony.........................72, 74
Frontiere, Dominic.....................234, 241
Frontiere, Georgia Rosenbloom........... 234-235
Fry, Bob.............................5, 22
Fry, Hayden 254-255
Fuqua, John "Frenchy" 23, 85
Fusina, Chuck 266

Gajecki, Leon 125
Galardi, Joe 138, 146
Gallagher, Paul..........................325
Galosi, Marty...........................318
Gandy, Wayne 335
Gannelli, Dave..........................197
Ganter, Fran............................363
Garban, Steve...........................124
Garret, Jim............................224
Garshak, Bob "Garsh" 32, 95, 97, 141, 258, 283
Garvey, Steve............................33
Gash, Thane............................309
Gastineau, Mark............... 293-294, 301-302
Gattuso, Greg.......................330, 350
Gedman, Gene...........................101
Gerela, Roy 12-13, 23, 40-41, 47, 53, 68, 72-73
Geronimo.............................252
Gershwin, George 169
Gibson, Tom............................308
Gifford, Frank 257
Gilliam, Joe 39-44, 46, 79-80
Gilman, Sid 237
Giralico, Al.............................324
Glassic, Tom....................... 272-274
Gleason, Jackie 205
Goldberg, Alex..........................142
Goldberg, Mrs............................96
Goldston, Ralph 216-217

Golic, Bob 308
Gordon, Joe .... Acknowledgements
Gowdy, Curt 221
Graham, Jim 214
Grant, Bud 281
Grant, Cary 228
Gray, Gary 18, 161, 184
Gray, Mel 179
Grayson, David 310
Gravelle Gordon 30-33, 56, 69, 76,
                             86-87, 89, 235, 242, 244
Gravelle, Molly 86
Greco, Al 103
Green, Ted 241
Greenberg, Benny 351
Greene, Joe 4, 6-8, 14, 16, 28, 50,
                             53, 70, 90, 243-244, 271
Greenwood, L.C. 4-8, 16, 50, 68, 70, 72, 244
Griese, Bob 14-15
Grier, Roosevelt "Rosey" 117
Grimm, Russ 247-248
Grossi, Tony .... Acknowledgements
Grossman, Randy 25, 62, 67, 72, 79
Guilbeau, Rusty 293

Hackett, Walt 2, 4
Haden, Pat 237, 250, 256
Hadl, John 270, 275-276, 278, 279
Haight, Mike 298
Hairston, Carl "Big Daddy" 308
Haley, Carolyn 289
Haley, Dick 18, 22-24, 83, 289
Hall, Galen 128, 144-146, 348, 363
Hall, Tim 321, 327-328, 330, 332
Ham, Jack   9-10, 45, 67-68, 70, 79-80, 91, 170-172,
                       177-179, 185-188, 190, 192, 198-199
Ham, Joanne .... Forward
Hamilton, Harry 292
Hamilton, Captain Tom 103
Hammond, Bobby 305, 316-317
Hampton, Bill, Jr. 302
Hanifan, Jim 125, 228
Hanna, Lou 152
Hanratty, Terry 39-40, 43
Hansen's, Don 352, 354, 357
Hardin, Wayne 182
Hardman, Cedric 89
Harper, Dave 320-321, 323
Harper, Willie 257
Harrah, Dennis 231-232, 242-243, 252, 257
Harris, Cliff 71-73
Harris, Franco 18-20, 23, 38, 49, 53-54,
                             66, 68-69, 73, 85-86, 90, 181
Harris, James 40
Harris, Jimmy 119
Harrison, Reggie "Booby" 25, 73
Hairston, Carl "Big Daddy" 308
Hatcher, Nancy 242

Hayes, Bob 75
Hayes, Lester 88
Hayes, Woody 114, 150-151
Haynes, Mike, 87-88
Heinz, John, 48
Henderson, Thomas "Hollywood" 44, 71-72
Henning, Dan 305-306
Henry, Ray 101-102
Hempstead, Jason 352
Herlan, Craig 353-354
Hewitt, Don 234
Hewitt, Todd 234
Higgins, Bob 116
Hilgenberg, Wally 53
Hill, Drew 256
Hines, Glen Ray 34
Hill, Kent 236, 242, 255
Hinton, Chris 270-271
Hinton, Chuck 4-5, 10
Hoak, Dick, ... 20-21, 45, 122-123, 144, 201, 343
Hofacre, Susan 353
Hogan, Ben 204
Holloway, Bob 281
Holmes, Ernie 4-6, 21, 70
Holsberg, Peter 331
Holsberg, Sarah .... Acknowledgements
Holtz, Lou 148
Hoopes, Mitch 73
Hornfeck, Pete 103
Hornung, Paul 120
Horton, Greg 202-203
Houck, Hudson 82
House, Claudia 355
Howard, Desmond 332
Howard, Paul 90, 271
Howard, Percy 71, 74-76
Hubbard, Marv 68
Huber, Bill 151
Huff, Sam 205
Huffman, Jay 128-130
Hughes, Ed 13
Hughes, Jed 308-310, 314
Hull, Gary 179, 193
Hunter, Billy 198
Hunter, Hal 310, 314
Hursen, Steve .... Acknowledgements
Hurt, Bob 43
Hustava, Mike .... Acknowledgements
Hutson, Don 36, 312
Hyder, John 148, 151, 197

Idler, Richard D. 5
Ilkin, Tunch 323
Infante, Lindy 361
Irsay, Robert 219, 270
Irwin, Hale 203-204
Irwin, Mike 151
Irwin, Tim 282-283

Jackson, Charles............................293
Jackson, Tom...............................41
Jackson, Tom (PSU).......................143
James, Don................................202
Johnson, Larry............................363
Johnson, Jimmy.................. 82-83, 231-232
Johnson, Ken..............................215
Johnson, Mike.............................309
Johnson, Paul..............................177
Johnson, Pete......................91, 164, 178
Johnson, Randy............................80
Johnson, Reed.............................270
Johnson, Rich..............................222
Jonas, Don.................................123
Jones, Bert.................................68
Jones, Bobby..............................204
Jones, Clarence...........................336
Jones, Ed "Too Tall".........................76
Jones, Joe "Turkey".........................86
Jordan, Steve..............................284
Joyce, Jeff.................................355
Joyner, Bob...........................142-143
Joyner, Dave..........................142-143
Jurgensen, Sonny...................80, 119, 122

Kaiser, Edgar................... 88, 267, 270-271
Kane, Bill.........................106, 112, 138
Kane, Bob............... 138-139, 151, 182, 283
Karras, Alex...............................198
Karwacki, Paul............... Acknowledgements
Kates, Jim.............. 91, 154, 161, 174-175, 184
Kaufman, Napoleon.......................332
Kaufman's Dept. Store family...............317
Kellum, Marv,..........................25, 53
Kelly, Emmett..................... 93, 190-191
Kelly, Gene................................230
Kelly, Jim (Buff. Bills)..................270, 312
Kelly, Jim (Univ. of Cinci.)...... 191-192, 195-196
Kemp, Jack............................119, 256
Kemp, Jeff............................119, 256
Kennan, Larry.....................202, 215, 331
Kennedy, John F..................147, 150, 181
Kenney, Bill...............................363
Kerr, Jim..................................123
Kiely, Ed 228
Kiesling, Walt..............................121
Kiffin, Lane...............................266
Kiffin, Monte.........................263-266
Kilmer, Billy...............................80
Kiner, Steve...............................91
King, Gordon..............................300
Kirk, J.T..............................352-353
Kirit, Brad................................352
Kitna, Jon.................................348
Klecko, Joe................. 292-295, 301-302
Kleist, Ed "Bozo"......................99, 103
Klingensmith, Gary........................149
Klisky, Nick................................97

Klosterman, Don.......... 227-231, 234-235, 255
Knox, Chuck 27, 113, 227, 253, 333
Kochman, Roger.......................128, 148
Kolb, Jon 30-32, 36, 56-57, 64, 69, 89, 247, 292
Kosar, Bernie......................301, 314-315
Kotite, Rich...............................305
Kronz, Fred.................................5
Kruczek, Mike..............................84
Kulka, John................................169
Kush, Frank................................260
Kwalik, Ted.......................162-163, 170

LaBorde, Jack 193
Lambert, Jack........... 23-24, 37, 68, 70, 73, 242
LaMotta, Jake..............................107
Landis, George........................ 178-180
Landon, Alf................................205
Landon, Jack 205
Landry, Tom........................ 72-73, 275
Lanham, Paul..............................256
Lanier, Ken........................... 271-272
LaSalla, Chris..............................343
Lasch, Lou................................341
Lasch, Mildred............................341
Lauterbur, Frank..........................259
Layne, Bobby..............................120
Leahy, Pat.................................303
LeBaron, Eddie 125
LeBeau, Dick..............................246
Lee, Sean..................................178
Leeson, Rick 150
Lefkowitz, Howie.........................250
Leggett, Earl...............................221
Leinbech, Wilmer,.........................142
Lemmer, Bill..............................102
Lener, Jason...............................323
Lewis, Frank................................85
Lewis, Geoffrey...........................333
Lewis, J.D..................................73
Liggins, Granville 168
Lipps, Louis...............................310
List, Nate............................ 327-329
Livingston, Pat........................ 13-16, 92
Lizanich, Andy............... Acknowledgements
Lockhart, Spider..........................224
Lombardi, Mike..........................308
Lombardi, Vince...................... Forward
Longley, Clint..............................76
Lott, Ronnie..........................257, 363
Luce, Lew.................................123
Lynn, Mike................................281
Lyons, Marty.............................293

Mack, Kevin..........................311, 314
Mack, Tom................................233
Mackenzie, Christine......................289
Mackenzie, Murdo.........................289
Mackenzie, Ranald........................289

Madden, John........................22, 221
Maddox, Tommy...........................76
Madeya, John............................197
Majors, John.................. 82, 207, 212-213
Malarky, Mike...........................362
Malavasi, Ray............... 227. 233, 236-239
Mallory, Bill............................198
Manalac, Fred...........................346
Mancini, Henry..........................228
Mann, Richard...........................307
Mansfield, Ray, ... 23, 30-31, 35, 65-66, 69, 83, 89
Mara, John..............................224
Mara, Wellington........................224
Maravich, Pete, ...103
Maravich, Press.........................103
Marciano, "Rocky".......................148
Markovich, Mark..........................25
Markiewicz, Ron.........................105
Marino, Dan........................270, 296
Marshall, Jim............................52
Martin, William.........................165
Martinez, Fred..........................329
Martz, Mike........................333, 338
Mason, Tony.............................213
Matsko, John............................344
Matsko, Paul........................170-171
Matthews, Clay..........................312
May, Mark..........................247-249
McBath, Mike................... 175-176, 260
McBee, Bob..............................320
McBride, Charley,........................23
McCartney, Bob "Mac"....................351
McCabe, Richie..........................269
McCoy, Ernie.......................122, 159
McCoy, Mike..............................10
McClaren, Jack "Goose".................. 121
McCully, Pete................... 219-222
McDonald, Tommy,................... 119-120
McElroy, Reggie.........................299
McElwee, Bob............................104
McGarvey, Pat............................56
McGee, Ben...............................4
McKay, John.............................239
McKinley, David.........................122
McMahon, Ed.............................144
McMahon, Jim............................293
McMakin, John............................34
McMillan, Terry.........................179
McMullen, Joe......................113, 133
McNally, Vince..........................118
McNeil, Fred............................283
Meadows, Audrey.........................205
Mehl, Lance.......... 290, 292-293, 301, 338-339
Menzie, Eddie............................98
Meredith, Don...........................257
Messinger, Mike.........................217
Meyer, Ron..............................260

Michaels, Al........................116, 174
Michaels, John..........................281
Michaels, Mrs. 'Walt"...................286
Michaels, Walt..........................286
Mikan, George...........................103
Mihalik, John..................... 328-329
Millen, Matt.............................92
Milk, Harvey............................223
Miller, Bubba...........................344
Miller, Chris...........................338
Miller, Mike.................... 358, 361-363
Mills, Izzy "Kazoo".....................196
Minor, Claudie..........................269
Mitchell, Lydell........................181
Mitinger, Bob.......................91, 128
Moconyi, Andy...........................194
Modell, Art.................... 306-308, 315
Moehler, Ron............... Acknowledgements
Modrak, Tom.............................344
Monk, Art................................88
Montalban, Ricardo......................228
Montana, Joe....................... 257-258
Montgomery, Tim.........................175
Monz, Mauro...................... 362-363
Moore, Fran....................... 56, 77-78
Moore, Joe........... 55-57, 77-78, 82, 127-128,
                       212-213, 246-250, 254, 319
Moore, Johnny...........................249
Moore, Lenny.................107-108, 111-112
Moore, Tom...............................89
Mora, Jim.............. 202, 213, 217, 238, 337
Morris, John............................190
Moseley, Mark...........................301
Mozart..................................169
Mullins, Gerry............. 30-31, 69, 78, 86-87
Munoz, Anthony..................... 245-246
Musick, Phil.............................49

Namath, Joe........................242, 296
Nardozzi, Tom...........................319
Neely, Jess.............................146
Newcombe, Bob...........................133
Newhouse, Robert.....................18, 19
Newton, Cam.............................363
Nicholson, Ed........ 318, 323, 324, 326, 346, 358,
Nicklaus, Jack..........................204
Nicolau, Nick................36, 275, 276, 278
Nitzberg, Robert........................356
Nix, Kent................................14
Nixon, President....................33, 179
Noll, Chuck 2-6, 8-10, 14-24, 31-32, 34,
                      38-43, 46, 49, 51-53, 58-59,
                      61-64, 74-76, 79-81, 85-86,
                      201, 225, 263, 337, 361-362
North, Paul.............................110
Nover, Sam...............................35
Nunn, Bill............ 18, 19, 22-24, 81, 263-264

O'Bradovich, Ed 14
O'Brien, Bill 166
O'Brien, Ken 270, 297
O'Connor, Fred 220, 222
Oden, Cassandra 354
O'Hora, Bets 132
O'Hora, Jim 130, 132, 154, 155,
158, 175, 183
Oliphant, Mike....................... 307, 308
Olsavsky, Jerry................ Acknowledgement
Olson, Bobo.............................. 107
O'Neil, Ed 92, 184-186, 188, 189
5, 9-10, 91-92, 109, 126, 158,
162, 170, 174-177, 179-180, 185, 187
Opar, Dave............................... 330
Opperman, Henry.......................... 123
Ortmayer, Steve 60, 202, 217, 304, 332, 335, 337
O'Shaughnessy, Steve 209

Pacacha, Frank............................ 100
Pagano, Sam.............................. 245
Page, Alan 7, 52, 283
Paige, Rod 11
Palija, Mike 197
Panella, Heather.............. Acknowledgements
Parilli, Vito.......................... 324-325
Parisi, Tony 28, 234
Parker, "Buddy"...................... 120-121
Parker, Dave............................. 211
Parker, Jim 114-115
Parks, Rosa............................... 117
Parseghian, Ara 197
Pasquale, Larry 292
Pastorini, Dan........................... 70-71
Paterno, Jay 363
Paterno, Joe 27, 88, 92, 114, 116, 124,
130-133, 137, 147, 151-154,
156-175, 177-179, 181-190,
199, 224, 262, 285, 300-301,
310, 339-342, 355, 360, 363
Paterno, Sue.............................. 89
Patrick, Frank..... 103, 111-112, 130, 133, 183, 360
Paycheck, Johnny......................... 222
Payne, Dante......................... 321, 329
Payton, Walter 293
Peaks, Clarence 119
Pearson, Drew 72, 74-75
Pearson, Preston...................... 23, 71
Perles, George 5-7, 20-21, 23, 60,
79, 83, 242, 266
Perry, Michael Dean....................... 308
Peterson, Bill............................ 163
Peterson, Cal............................. 24
Peterson, Carl............................ 266
Peterson, Ted 89
Petro, Steve 165
Phillips, Bob..................... 133, 158, 183
Phillips, "Bum" 64, 66

Pike, Chris 308
Pinero, Miguel 202
Pinney, Ray 81, 83-84, 89
Pittman, Charlie 160, 164, 170, 181
Plum, Milt 112, 114, 116, 174
Pollard, Deke 309, 314, 333, 334
Polsfoot, Fran..................... 270, 274-276
Pons, Jim 303
Posluszny, Paul 190
Poulus, Hein............................. 270
Powell, "Junior"......................... 146
Powell, Marvin........................ 297-299
Prato, Lou............ 92, 139, 167, 176, 195, 279
Prato, Carole .... Acknowledgements
Prothro, Tommy.................. 154-155, 227

Radakovich, Bridget (Mom) 94-97, 109, 117-118
Radakovich, Danny (Son) 57, 240, 261
Radakovich, Dave 141
Radakovich, Leslie (Daughter) 144, 159, 233,
240, 295, 333
Radakovich, Lisa (Daughter)..... 28, 196, 240, 331
Radakovich, Lori (Daughter)..... 163, 240, 288-289
Radakovich, Lou (Brother) 94-96
Radakovich, Mike (Dad) 94, 117
Radakovich, Mimi......................... 196
Radakovich, Nancy (Wife)........ throughout book
Radakovich, Raymond............ 32, 48-50, 141,
249, 258, 283, 341
Radakovich, Scott 341-342
Radakovich, Sue.......................... 341
Radecic, Scott 190
Raich, Matt......................... 353-355
Ralston, John 41
Rashad, Ahmad 295-296
Rashad, Phyllis.......................... 295
Ray, John 153
Reavis, Dave 30, 84
Redford, Robert 233
Reese, Bob............................... 303
Reese, Floyd......................... 222, 281
Reeves, Dan 267-272, 274-278, 281, 347
Reich, Frank......................... 105-106
Reid, Mike 159, 164, 167-170, 173
Ressler, Glenn 135-136, 151, 153
Reynolds, Jack "Hacksaw" 257, 293
Richards, Golden......................... 75
Richards, Max "The Axe" 134, 142
Richardson, Darnell...................... 323
Richardson, Lorne 210
Riecke, Lou 20-21, 62-63
Riggins, John............................ 164
Ritchie, Dave.................... 192, 198, 212
Robinson, Dave 91-92, 128, 137, 146, 148
Rodich, Art.............................. 221
Rodich, Milo............................. 221
Rodgers, "Pepper" 155, 164
Rooney, Art "The Chief" 1, 8, 19-20, 228, 269

Rooney, Art [Jr.] 5, 8, 18-19, 22-24
Rooney, Dan. 8, 19, 88, 268-269
Rooney, Tim. 23-24, 83, 315
Rosenbloom, Carroll 227-229, 234-235
Rosenbloom [Frontiere], Georgia 229, 234-235, 241, 333
Rosenbloom, Steve 234-235
Rozelle, Pete 228, 302
Runnells, John. 151
Russell, Andy...................... 9, 66-67, 70
Rutledge, Jeff. 238
Ryan, "Buddy"............................304
Ryan, Dennis 285
Ryczek, Dan. 235

Saban, Lou. 195
Sabol, Bernie 128-129
Sanders, Johnny......................... 94-95
Sandhu, [Dr.] Jasvinder 356
Sapp, Warren 334-335
Saul, Bill 91, 128, 146, 176, 231
Saul, Rich. 231-232, 235-236, 242-244, 255
Scarry, Mike "Moe"................... 173, 182
Schembechler, "Bo"........................197
Schleicher, Maurice 221
Schmitz, Bob 22, 24
Schottenheimer, Marty.....................301
Scorsi, Nico 103
Scorsone, Vince 103
Scott, Tom 119-120
Scotty "The Packer".......................262
Seely, Brad..............................266
Seider, John 303
Sekanovich, Dan 295
Seldon "The Stratosphere Man" 93
Sell, Jack 121
Sellers, Ron 162-163
Selmon, Dewey 215
Selmon, Leroy 215, 239-240
Selmon, Lucius 215
Shafer, Gary.............................170
Shaw, John..............................334
Shell, Art 299
Shell, Donnie 25
Sherk, Jerry 69-70
Sherman, Tom 160, 175
Sherrill, Jackie 82, 247
Sherry, Jack 105
Shipky, Jerry 1
Shoaf, "Junior".".........................102
Shoderbeck, Pete 103
Shoen, Ed...............................103
Shofner, Jim.......................... 314-315
Short, Brandon...........................190
Shula, Don 361
Shuler, Mickey...........................302
Siani, Mike...............................68
Sidwell, Steve 202, 214, 217
Sieminski, Chuck..........................128
Simmers, Tim "TJ" 265, 272, 274
Simpson, O. J. 47, 64
Sims, Billy..............................248
Sirkoch, John ....Acknowledgement
Six, Bob................................205
Skorupan, John........................92, 184
Slater, Jackie 81-82, 233, 238, 243
Slusher, Howard........................ 87-89
Smaltz, Bill 116, 174
Smear, Steve..................... 169-172, 185
Smith, Bruce 299
Smith, Carl........................202, 217
Smith, Doug........................235, 242
Smith, George 211, 213
Smith, Mike..............................178
Smith, Neal 164, 170, 179
Smith, Willard 107-108
Snell, Matt.............................149
Somerville, Kevin, "The Shrink"...... 268, 275-280
Spanos, Lou 323
Spaziani, Frank 36
Stabler, Ken "Snake".......................68
Staggers, John 179
Staisey, Bernie 230
Staisey, Dan 1
Staisey, George..........................230
Stallworth, John ... 23, 25-26, 40, 50-51, 68, 73, 242
Stanfel, Dick 27
Staubach, Roger............. 8, 70-76, 147, 238
Stearns, John "Bad Dude" 210-211, 218
Steckel, Chris.........................284-285
Steckel, Les 202, 216, 219, 281, 283-285
Stellino, Vito 85
Stevenson, Ken 343
Stewart, Andrew..........................308
Stewart, Jimmy 228-229
Strahan, Mike............................206
Stram, Hank........................ 195-196
Studdard, Dave...........................272
Stynchula, Andy..........................131
Styuchula, Theresa........................131
Suley, Jim 323, 329-330
Swan, Lynn 23-24, 26, 87
Sumner, Charlie........................ 2-3
Surma, Vic...............................173
Sutherland, Doug..........................52
Sweatman, Mike 282, 289
Sweeney, Jim.....................299, 304, 334
Switzer, Barry 216

Tammariello, Augie 18, 135-136, 152, 202, 207, 262
Tanenbaum, Myles.........................266
Tarkenton, Fran 8-9, 53
Tarman, Jim.............................149
Taslawski, Susan 341
Taylor, Lawrence 250

Taylor, Lionel 10, 17, 20, 25-26, 35-37,
60-62, 216, 219, 227-228, 236,
241, 259, 307, 312, 346-347, 349
Taylor, Loren 312
Tchaikovsky 169
Teerlinck, John 308
Tereshinski, Joe "Terrible Terry" 126
Theisman, Joe 80-81
Thomas, Joe 219-220, 222, 225, 228
Thomas, J.T. 70, 74
Thomas, Raymond "Smoke" 352
Thomas, Thurman 312
Thompson, Tommy 122
Thoms, Art 48-49
Thimons, Dennis 19-20
Tipe, Jim . . . . Acknowledgement
Toews, Loren 54, 90
Toretti, Sever "Tor" 105, 110, 137, 171, 173, 224
Torgeson, LaVerne "Torgy" 125, 228, 255
Traficant, Jim 145
Trestman, Mark 307, 314
Trevino, Lee 204
Tullio, Jim . . . . Acknowledgement
Tunnel, Emlen 224
Turpin, Randy 107
Tyler, Wendell 259

Uecker, Keith 272
Uram, Paul 20-21, 57-58
Urbanik, Tom 136

Vaccaro, Sonny 258
Van Buren, Steve 63
Vanderbundt, Dick 225
Van Dyke, Bruce 28, 34
Van Dyke, Dick 144, 229
Van Horn, Roy 153
Vanderlinden, Ron 190
Van Pelt, Brad 284
Vargo, Norm 222
Vechiarella, Jim 314
Vierick, Bob 142
Voss, Lloyd 4

Waddy, Billy 239
Wagner, Mike 53, 70, 73-74, 79-80
Walden, Bobby 23, 53, 72
Walke, Mike 193
Wallenda's, "Flying" 93, 191
Walter, Don . . . . Acknowledgement
Walters, Les 174
Walton, Ginger 319
Walton, Joe "Tiger" 323
Walton, Joe, Sr., (Joe's Dad) 101
Walton, Joe 101, 125, 285, 297, 299, 301,
305-306, 316-325, 327, 329-331,
333, 339-340, 345, 349-350,
354-355, 358-359, 361-362

Walsh, Bill 225-226, 260
Wannstedt, Dave 232
Warfield, Paul 14-16
Washington, Mark 72-73
Wayne, John 241
Weatherall, Jim 122
Weaver, Jim 133
Weber, Chris 340
Webster, Mike . . 23-25, 30-31, 69, 79, 244, 247, 295
Welsh, George 133, 159, 161, 164, 166, 171-172
West, Ed 281-282
West, Jerry, ... 230
Westphal, Paul 87
Wheeler, Lew 142, 319
Wherry, Sam 134, 142
Whisenhut, Ken 351, 362
White, Dan 223
White, Dwight 4, 6, 8, 10-12, 70, 90, 244
White, J. T. 224
White, Mike 205, 219
White, Reggie 336-337
White, Walter 60-61
Widenhofer, Robert "Woody" . . . 20-21, 23-24, 59-60
Wilbur, John 28
Williams David 21
Williams, Doug 298
Williams, Gus 87
Williams, John 233, 235
Winder, Sammy 313
Wingo, Jimmy 342-344
Winters, Jonathan 144, 228, 229
Wise, Tony 83, 231, 232
Whisenhunt, Ken 351, 362
Woodring, John 290
Woods, Tiger 204
Worrell, Red 123
Worley, Tim 310

Yarosz, Eddie 107, 108
Yarosz, Tommy 107
Yarosz, Teddy 107
Yost, Bud 151, 158
Young, George 88
Yukica, Joe 104

Zacchini, Family 93, 191
Zagaris, Don . . . . Acknowledgement
Zapiec, Charlie 92, 184
Zernich, Mickey 103
Zorn, Jim 238
Zimmerman, Chuck 350

Brown 93 (tackle trap): The play versus the Oakland Raiders that took the Steelers to Super Bowl IX

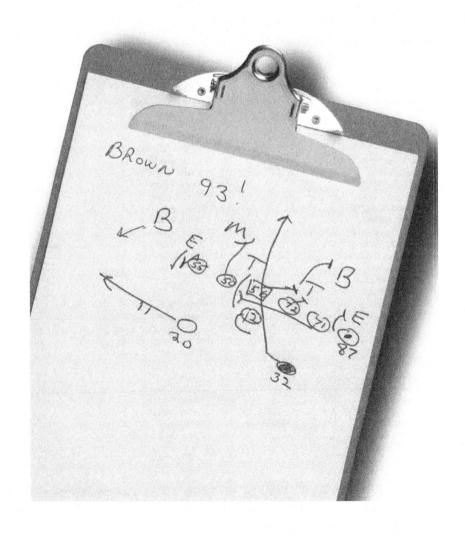

ACKNOWLEDGEMENTS

The first person I want to acknowledge is Coach Bud Grant, who is the first one that seriously told me I should write a book about my experiences in football. Bud had retired as head coach of the Minnesota Vikings after the 1983 season, and then came out of retirement in 1985 to take over the Vikings again after the Minnesota staff I was on in 1984 was let go. As I was packing up my material in the Vikings office, Bud approached me and asked what I was going to do next, look for another job in the NFL or what? As our conversation went on, Bud told me that I should write a book about my crazy profession and the nomadic life most of us football coaches live. I laughed at his suggestions and agreed I should, but I never gave it any serious thought until more than 20 years later.

Over the years I told stories of my football adventures and nomad life to many of my friends and also to my players on a rainy day when we couldn't practice. Some friends and players used to joke about me writing a book. But after Bud Grant, the next person who seriously talked to me about writing a book was Tony Grossi, Sports Editor of the *Cleveland Plain Dealer*. That was in 2007 when I was visiting the Cleveland Browns training camp to watch my former player at Robert Morris, Browns center Hank Fraley.

About a year later at a Penn State golf tournament, I was having a conversation with Lou Prato, a longtime friend from my Penn State coaching days who had helped develop the Penn State All-Sports Museum located in Beaver Stadium and was its first director from 2001-05. Lou has written several books about Penn State football and is now considered the unofficial Penn State sports historian. Lou had written a couple of magazine stories about me pointing out that I was Penn State's original linebacker coach and the true "Father of Linebacker U." I had never given that title much thought until Lou wrote about it. So, at the golf tournament, Lou said, "Rad, you should write a book about your college and pro football experiences." Wow! Lou was the second professional writer who had said that, and after thinking about it for a day, I told him I'd write a book if he would help me. He said he would. That's how the book came about.

Lou and I have spent years working on this book, but as Lou would acknowledge it has been mostly fun for both of us. Lou took the stories I wrote and transformed them into this book. We didn't always agree on what he wanted to do but Lou continued to tell me it was my book and I had the final decision. Through his diligence and research, he tried to make the book as accurate as possible. A few times Lou even spent hours in the Penn State library archives viewing old game film from my playing and coaching days just to insure my memories were correct.

We didn't just rely on my memory for this book. I had several boxes with scrapbooks and magazines that we were able to use to verify many facts. Lou found additional newspaper and magazine stories on the internet. Lou also used the internet to substantiate even such seemingly minor things like the years someone played in the NFL or the yardage made on a first down in a key play of a game. His research in that area led me to additional newspaper and magazines at a couple of Pittsburgh libraries and also inspired me to call my friends, former players and coaches to check out more facts. Heather Panella of the Moon Township Library was especially helpful. It's probable there are some errors in the book. We are not perfect, but we tried to be.

I know I have driven him crazy at times, and he's told me he now understands what my wife, Nancy, has been through for more than 50 years. He says Nancy's a saint, and he's not the first friend who has said that. I happen to think his wife, Carole, is a saint, too. She often had to put up with both of us when we had to work on the book at his home and that took a lot of patience.

Carole also helped us in the early stages of the book. When we started, Lou was busy finishing up one of his own books, "Game Changers: The Greatest Plays in Penn State Football History." So, it was Carole who took my original handwritten manuscript and typed it up for Lou to work on. Their offices in their home are back-to-back, and Lou said when he frequently heard Carole laughing at something she was reading while working on my manuscript, he knew I was on the right track with the book.

No one was more important to me in writing the book than my family—daughters Lisa, Leslie and Lori, and especially son Danny and my wife Nancy, a former executive secretary. Danny spent countless hours providing me with computer expertise for which I will always be grateful. My family encouraged me throughout this whole process, and I really don't think I could have completed it without them behind me all the way. It took a financial commitment from them as well as a spiritual one. I'm also what some people call "computer illiterate" and I can hardly type, too. So, it was my family who did it for me, using the computer for research and handling typing when I needed it.

Most all of the players I coached over the decades were special to me. One in particular has stood out and has become one of my best friends, Jack Ham. We have been through a lot together and I thank Jack for writing the foreword. Jack is like family to me and so is Bob Kane, the younger brother of my Penn State teammate, Billy. I first met Bob when he was 10 years old and I eventually recruited Bob in 1961 to play linebacker. Since then Bob has become like a brother and no one except the late Joe Moore has been closer to me outside my family. Bob probably heard most of the stories in this book more often than my wife and kids. And there are many players like Jack and Bob who either encouraged me to write this book or helped me in writing it. There are far too many to mention, but I am indebted to them, especially for helping me recall the details of stories in the book.

As for Joe Moore, from the time we coached the Penn State freshman team in 1958, Joe and I were as close as two friends could be and it stayed that way until his unfortunate death in 2003. I believe Joe is the greatest offensive line coach ever in college football and many others in our sport agree. As you will read, Joe was the central person in my life outside of my wife, and I am truly sorry Joe isn't here to read the book. RIP Joe.

I've served under 17 head coaches in my career and worked alongside hundreds of fellow assistants. I received help from many of them, too numerous to mention. They also were especially helpful in recalling the details of many stories in the book. But I would be remiss if I didn't mention six coaches: Joe Paterno, Chuck Noll, the late Bud Carson, Lionel Taylor, Ray Callahan and Joe Walton. They were all extremely important to me for different reasons. You'll learn why when you read this book but they truly were the backbone of my wandering career.

There are many other people who in one way or another helped me and Lou with the book and I know I would leave someone out if I tried to list all their names. You will read about some of them in the book. But here are a few special people I have to acknowledge:

My former coaching colleague Don Walter and my neighbor John Sirkoch were helpful in proofreading and making corrections in the manuscript.

The Pittsburgh Steelers organization, now headed by Art Rooney II, was most helpful in providing information and photographs for us, specifically Bob McCartney, Andy Lizanich, Mike Fabus, Mike Hustava, Dick Lebeau, Jerry Olsavsky, and retired Steelers employees Bill Nunn and Joe Gordon. Furthermore, I am truly grateful to the patriarch of the Steelers family, the late Art Rooney and his sons, Dan Rooney and Art Rooney Jr. There were dozens of others who have been part of the Steelers organization over the years who were helpful in many different ways, but again I know I would undoubtedly leave someone out if I tried to list all their names.

Jennifer Eury, the director of alumni relations for Penn State's Smeal College of Business, was helpful with our research. So were several people in the Paterno-Patee Library Sport Archives, especially archivist Paul Dyzak and Paul Karwacki.

Bobbie Jo Belus, the football coordinator at Robert Morris University, also helped with research, computer e-mail, the copying of documents and other material, and the search for photographs.

Dick Anderson, my best friend on the Penn State coaching staff over the last 25 years, who read parts of my manuscript as it was developing and helped gather several of the significant photographs that you will see throughout the book.

Ron Moehler, a high school friend of Jack Ham's and whose company designed the cover and format for the book, has been quite supportive with his advice. Lynne Carothers, Jim Tipe, Jim Tullio and Steve Hursen have also helped as we put the finishing touches on the final product.

I need to make a special note of thanks to the oldest of my six grandchildren, 13-year-old Sarah Holsberg, for coming up with the one word that best describes my family's travelling football life—Nomads—and that became part of the title of this book.

Finally, I regret that my former colleague, boss and good friend, Joe Paterno, passed away after this book was written and before it was published. I suspect he would have enjoyed reading it and the memories it ignited would have delighted him.

We all miss you Joe!

—Dan Radakovich, November 26, 2012

LOU PRATO is a veteran print and broadcast journalist who has covered Penn State football periodically since his undergraduate days at Penn State when Dan Radakovich was a player and then an assistant coach. He also is a lifelong Pittsburgh Steelers fan, dating from the late 1940s, and in the 1960s he wrote many stories about the Steelers, including the hiring of Coach Chuck Noll. Prato is the author of four books on Penn State football: *The Penn State Football Encyclopedia*, the definitive history of Nittany Lions' football; *What It Means to be A Nittany Lion* co-authored with Scott Brown; the *Penn State Football Vault;* and *Game Changers: The Greatest Plays in Penn State Football History*. Prato helped organize and start the Penn State All-Sports Museum and in 2001 he became the museum's first director, retiring from that position at the end of 2005. He is now regarded as Penn State's unofficial sports historian and is a contributing writer for two publications dedicated to Penn State football fans, *Blue White Illustrated* and *Fight On State* magazine. Lou and his wife Carole, who assisted Lou and Dan in writing this book, have been going to Penn State football games together since 1955, and Prato says Carole was a Penn State fan long before him.

Co-author Lou Prato and his wife Carol

CPSIA information can be obtained at www.ICGtesting.com
Printed in the USA
BVOW06*0129050316

439116BV00001B/1/P